Handbook of Adult Education

Handbook of Adult Education

Edited by

ROBERT M. SMITH
Associate Director
University Center for Adult Education
Wayne State University
University of Michigan

GEORGE F. AKER
Professor of Adult Education
Florida State University

J. R. KIDD
Professor of Adult Education
Ontario Institute for Studies
in Education

MACMILLAN PUBLISHING CO., INC.
New York

Collier Macmillan Publishers
London

Copyright © 1970 by Adult Education Association of the USA

Printed in the United States of America

All rights reserved. No part of this book may be reproduced or transmitted in any form or by any means, electronic or mechanical, including photocopying, recording, or by any information storage and retrieval system, without permission in writing from the Publisher.

Macmillan Publishing Co., Inc.
866 Third Avenue, New York, New York 10022
Collier-Macmillan Canada Ltd.

Library of Congress Catalog Card Number: 60–7359

printing number
4 5 6 7 8 9 10

Contributors

H. Mason Atwood
 Assistant Professor of Adult Education, Indiana University

Roger W. Axford
 Coordinator of Adult Education and Associate Professor, School of Human Resources and Development, College of Life Sciences and Agriculture and College of Education, University of Maine

Jane Berry
 Director, Continuing Education for Women, University of Missouri at Kansas City

Edgar J. Boone
 Professor and Head, Department of Adult Education; Assistant Director, North Carolina Agricultural Extension Service, North Carolina State University

Patrick G. Boyle
 Professor of Agricultural and Extension Education, College of

Agricultural and Life Sciences; Director, Staff Development, University Extension, University of Wisconsin

Edward W. Brice
President, Warner and Warner International Associates, Inc.

Nathan Brodsky
Deputy Assistant Secretary of Education, Department of Defense

Alexander N. Charters
Vice-President for Continuing Education, Syracuse University

Richard W. Cortwright
National Education Association

Roger DeCrow
Director, ERIC Clearinghouse on Adult Education

Eugene E. DuBois
Assistant Professor, School of Education, Boston University

Robert E. Finch
Director, Division of Continuing Education, Cincinnati Public Schools

George K. Gordon
Assistant Professor of Adult Education, Bureau of Studies in Adult Education, Indiana University

William S. Griffith
Associate Professor of Adult Education, University of Chicago

Ervin L. Harlacher
President, Brookdale Community College, Lincroft, New Jersey

Kenneth Haygood
Dean of Continuing Education, Cleveland State University

Andrew Hendrickson
Department of Adult Education, Florida State University

Norejane Hendrickson
Department of Adult Education, Florida State University

Joe R. Hoffer
Executive Secretary, National Conference on Social Welfare

Cyril O. Houle
Professor of Education, University of Chicago

Irwin R. Jahns
Assistant Professor of Adult Education, College of Education, Florida State University

Glenn Jensen
Professor of Adult Education, University of Wyoming

Eugene I. Johnson
Professor of Adult Education, University of Georgia

Malcolm S. Knowles
Professor, School of Education, Boston University

Contributors

Burton W. Kreitlow
    Professor of Adult Education, University of Wisconsin at Madison
A. A. Liveright
    Professor of Adult Education, Syracuse University
Jack London
    University of California at Berkeley
Rosalind K. Loring
    Head, Daytime Program and Special Projects, University Extension, University of California at Los Angeles
Paul A. Miller
    President, Rochester Institute of Technology, Rochester, New York
Margaret E. Monroe
    Director, Library School, University of Wisconsin
Leonard Nadler
    Associate Professor of Adult Education and Employee Development, George Washington University
John Ohliger
    Assistant Professor of Adult Education, Ohio State University
Hilton Power
    Regional Director, Foreign Policy Association
Lawrence Rogin
    Program Coordinator, The American University Labor Studies Center
Wayne L. Schroeder
    Professor of Adult Education, Florida State University
Paul H. Sheats
    Professor of Education, University of California at Los Angeles
Kenneth Stokes
    Pastor, United Church of Gainesville, Gainesville, Florida
Grant Venn
    Associate Commissioner for Adult, Vocational and Library Programs, United States Office of Education
Thurman J. White
    Vice-President, University of Oklahoma

Program Planning
What's new —
Family life educ.

Preface

The Adult Education Association of the USA last issued this Handbook in 1960. The two previous editions came a dozen years apart. The present Handbook may be the last one to appear at so long an interval and the last to appear in hard covers. The field of adult education is now changing so rapidly it may be necessary in the future to resort to a loose leaf format for the addition of supplementary information every two or three years.

In addition to bringing home the rapidity with which the field of adult education is changing, editing this Handbook leads to two observations. Perhaps most striking is the paucity of data concerning both the field as a whole and its various components. Several authors have ruefully confessed they had few reliable statistics upon which to base their chapters. Others offer mute testimony to the need for more information by their reliance on the two or three publications that speak quantitatively of such matters as clientele, subjects studied and institutional enrollments. Johnstone and Rivera's *Volunteers for Learning* (1962) seems to provide the greater share of the statistical information offered our readers. Hopefully, more sources of information will be available by the time the next Handbook is written.

Another impression concerns the persistence of the deep strains of idealism that first attracted so many adult educators to the field. Even with a considerable amount of sanguinity "edited out" the reader will encounter again and again in this book the same affirmation and sense of mission that pervades the works of leaders in generations gone by— people like Edward Lindeman, Morse Cartwright and Lymon Bryson. In an era not without turmoil, cynicism and slick professionalism, it is heartening to find so much unabashed idealism and such a consistent sense of social purpose. Despite its growing sophistication adult education appears to be just as much a social movement as ever.

Like its predecessors this Handbook is directed to several audiences —to any interested person seeking information about adult education; to the part-time worker, the paraprofessional or the volunteer leader; and to the professional worker, the scholar, and the graduate student in training. The varied chapters attempt to reflect the totality of the field. The reader will have to judge the extent to which so broad a compilation for so broad an audience has proved successful.

In selecting authors, the editors tried to achieve a judicious mixture of scholars and practitioners, of "old timers" and relative newcomers to the field. Geographical distribution was also taken into account; almost all regions of the nation are represented. The authors come from a wide variety of agencies and institutions. Some are administrators, some are teachers, and some are agency staff personnel. Some write from "inside" the field in which they are full-time specialists, while others from the "outside" write from the perspective the generalist can bring to such an assignment. Obviously, certain advantages and disadvantages accompany the selection of either type of writer.

Those who take an interest in such matters will notice that the organizational plan of the 1960 Handbook basically has been retained. This provides a degree of continuity. However, the major reason for staying with the previous plan was simply that no better rationale suggested itself, and we sought to avoid the pitfall of reorganizing just for the sake of reorganizing. Decisions about what *concerns* (Part I), what *institutions* (Part II) and what *program areas* (Part III) to include were made rather arbitrarily in the knowledge that the field has become so broad and so complex as to require a great deal of selectivity even in an encyclopedic work. The recommended readings accompanying each chapter are also highly selective and limited for the most part to readily available publications that have appeared since the last Handbook. (Incidentally,

Preface

despite the rapidity with which adult education is changing, there remains much useful information in the 1960 Handbook.)

A further word about the references. Each chapter is followed by a list of suggested readings which appear in alphabetical order by author. When an item in the reading list is cited in the text, in the manner of a footnote, it appears in brackets—e.g., [27] if the work alone is cited, or [27, p. 8] if work and page are cited, or [27;29] for two different works. It is worth noting that although the ERIC system ordering information does not accompany them, many of the references are available from ERIC, as described in Chapter 5.

The editors' method of proceeding was as follows: After receiving general guidelines from the Publications Committee of the AEA–USA, they developed a working outline. When the Publications Committee had approved the general plan, each editor assumed primary responsibility for one-third of the chapters. Robert Smith served as administrative editor.

The more than two years that this book was in preparation naturally saw many changes and new developments—some of which were difficult or impossible to incorporate into the text. Some organizations made name changes and others went out of existence. Some statistics became slightly obsolete. And the death of an author, A. A. Liveright, was a loss keenly felt by the field.

It goes without saying that many persons have to collaborate and work selflessly for a book of this size to come into being. The editors profoundly appreciate the generosity of the many who, alas, must go nameless. These authors have earned the grateful thanks of their colleagues in the field. They had to meet urgent deadlines and gather data at their own expense. Two specific acknowledgments should be made: Roger DeCrow was especially helpful in making available the resources of ERIC–AE, and a final word of appreciation goes to the Publications Committee under the outstanding leadership of its chairman Milton R. Stern.

The Editors
May, 1970

Contents

Prologue: The Handbooks in Perspective
    Malcolm S. Knowles AND *Eugene DuBois*
Introduction
    Paul H. Sheats

Part I   Forms, Function and Future
    1 The Social Setting for Adult Education
        Jack London 3
    2 Adult Education Defined and Described
        Wayne L. Schroeder 25
    3 The International Dimension
        A. A. Liveright AND *John Ohliger* 45
    4 Program Development and Evaluation
        Patrick G. Boyle AND *Irwin R. Jahns* 59

5 Information Resources and Services
    Roger DeCrow 75
6 Technology in Adult Education
    Eugene I. Johnson 91
7 The Educators of Adults
    Cyril O. Houle 109
8 Philosophical Considerations
    Thurman J. White 121
9 Research and Theory
    Burton W. Kreitlow 137
10 A Glance at the Future
    Paul A. Miller 151

Part II   Some Institutions and Organizations

11 Adult Education Institutions
    William S. Griffith 171
12 Colleges and Universities
    Kenneth Haygood 191
13 Community Colleges
    Ervin L. Harlacher 213
14 Public Schools
    Robert E. Finch 231
15 Public Libraries and Museums
    Margaret E. Monroe 245
16 The Cooperative Extension Service
    Edgar J. Boone 265
17 The Armed Forces
    Nathan Brodsky 283
18 Labor Unions
    Lawrence Rogin 301
19 Business and Industry
    Leonard Nadler 315
20 Health and Welfare Agencies
    Joe R. Hoffer 335
21 Religious Institutions
    Kenneth Stokes 353
22 Some Other Institutions
    H. Mason Atwood 371

Part III   Some Program Areas

23 Curriculum and Content
    Roger W. Axford 397

Contents

24 Adult Basic Education
    Richard Cortwright AND *Edward W. Brice* 407
25 Human Relations—Sensitivity Training
    George K. Gordon 425
26 Education for Family Life
    Norejane Hendrickson AND *Andrew Hendrickson* 439
27 Education for Social and Public Responsibility
    Hilton Power 457
28 Vocational–Technical Education
    Grant Venn 473
29 Continuing Education for the Professions
    Alexander N. Charters 487
30 Continuing Education for Women
    Jane Berry AND *Rosalind K. Loring* 499
31 Education for Self-Fulfillment
    Glenn Jensen 513

Appendix I   Directory of Participating Organizations of the Committee of Adult Education Organizations 527
Appendix II   General Information Sources in Adult Education 549
Appendix III   The Changing Focus: Contents of Past Handbooks 565
Index 579

Prologue:
The Handbooks in Perspective

Malcolm S. Knowles
Eugene E. DuBois

The first Handbook of Adult Education in the United States was published in 1934, eight years after the founding of the American Association for Adult Education. Subsequent editions appeared in 1936, 1948 and 1960. This 1970 Handbook is, therefore, the fifth in a series of works which, taken collectively, trace the evolution of the new field of adult education during most of the first half-century of its existence.

The central purpose of the Handbooks, as defined in the first edition, has been "to correlate in convenient reference form data relating to the many activities that have come to term themselves adult education enterprises." Each one presents a description of the field as perceived by its leaders at that time. But each one also reveals, often tangentially in the prefaces and topical essays, the leaders' concerns, fears, frustrations, and hopes in regard to the state of affairs both in society in general and in adult education in particular.

The Handbooks are, therefore, valid sources of data for answering the two questions with which this prologue is chiefly concerned:

Prologue

1. How was the field of adult education defined in its successive stages of development by the editors and authors of the Handbooks?
2. What have been the shifting concerns of adult educators as the field evolved?

Although adults had been engaging in continuing education in many forms for many years, there was apparently little awareness of a need for a comprehensive national organization to serve the total field of adult education before 1924. Credit for introducing the vision of a unified field of adult education belongs overwhelmingly to one man, Frederick Keppel (father of the recent U.S. Commissioner of Education, Francis Keppel). Shortly after he assumed the presidency of the Carnegie Corporation of New York in 1923, Keppel became disturbed by the paucity of information about adult education in this country and by the fact that though many national bodies dealt with different parts of the field, there was no agency that concerned itself with the problem of adult education as a whole.

Through Keppel's efforts the American Association for Adult Education (AAAE) was founded on March 26, 1926. Its primary purpose, as stated in its constitution, was "to provide for the gathering and dissemination of information concerning adult education aims and methods of work." The Association sponsored a variety of "Studies in Adult Education;" these studies, along with the quality of the articles appearing in its quarterly *Journal of Adult Education* and the informative annual reports of its first executive director, Morse A. Cartwright, established the Association as the information clearinghouse for a new field of social practice. By 1934 sufficient information had been accumulated to warrant bringing it together in convenient reference form, and so the idea of the first Handbook was conceived.

The 1934 Handbook

The intention of the editor of the first Handbook was to include both a directory of national organizations engaged in adult education and a listing of local adult education efforts of national importance. It is clear from an examination of the table of contents of this first Handbook (see Appendix III, page 567) that the map of the field as perceived in 1934 was somewhat like an early explorer's map of the Western Hemisphere. Perspectives were distorted, boundaries were confused, and elements were missing. Obviously, the editor and authors were in the process of discovering unexplored territory. The chapter topics included a random mixture of types of institutions, client populations, media and

Prologue

methods, and types of services. The institutional dimension of the field was described in terms of 16 types of agencies, with the notable omission of government agencies, health and welfare agencies (except for settlement houses), proprietary schools (except for correspondence schools) and voluntary organizations (except for men's and women's clubs).

The content dimension included only four distinct topic areas—the arts, music, political education and vocational education—a fact which made it clear that the curriculum of adult education could not be described in terms of the traditional subject-matter categories of youth education. Little attention was given to the methodological dimension of the field. Only courses, forums, reading, radio and visual education were treated explicitly. No mention was made of the new theories and practices in regard to program development that were being talked about in other publications at the time. And the list of national organizations in the field revealed the same difficulty in conceptualization that was encountered in describing the other dimensions: distinguishing between the major and the minor categories.

The chief concern reflected in the 1934 Handbook was the need for better public understanding of adult education as a field of social practice. Even though it explicitly stated that the unprecedented growth of the use of the term adult education had quite relieved the Association from the burden of propagandizing for the idea, the dominant spirit of the Handbook still was one of propagandizing for an understanding of the scope and significance of adult education.

A second concern was for the elimination of the profitmakers from the field. As stated in the Preface:

> In these years the difficult task has been to single out those enterprises free from the element of profit, of propaganda, or of other ulterior motive. The necessity of making such distinctions has become even more important during the last several years when, as was inevitably to be expected, charlatanism and profit-seeking have led traders in the market place to the belief that high financial returns could be realized from an unsuspecting adult public just becoming conscious of its educational opportunities as adults.

A third concern was the relative emphasis that should be placed on the vocational as compared with the cultural or avocational content of the field. The position chosen by the editors as the wisest for the Association was the middle ground.

The 1936 Handbook

The first Handbook enjoyed three printings, which assured the Association that the publication fulfilled a genuine need in the field of education and resulted in the decision to issue the Handbooks biennially. Accordingly, a second Handbook was published in 1936 in the same format and size as the first. This second edition contained the same basic shortcoming as the first: no real definition of the field.

However, a companion book also published in 1936 by the Association (ADULT EDUCATION IN ACTION, edited by Mary L. Ely) finally presented a conceptualization of the field and a format that became the prototype of subsequent Handbooks and gave shape and direction as well as adding stature and prestige to the field of adult education. The book consisted of condensed versions of 160 articles that had appeared in the Association's *Journal of Adult Education* since 1929. Among the authors of these articles were the intellectual giants of American society from 1925 to 1935. The contributors to the 1934 and 1936 Handbooks, on the other hand, were predominantly top practitioners in the field. Therefore, both books produced in 1936 must be considered in the historical context of the Handbooks.

Though it listed 28 more "National Organizations Having Adult Education Programs," bringing the total number to 189, the 1936 Handbook introduced no new concerns. In contrast, ADULT EDUCATION IN ACTION contained discussions of a philosophic, economic and esthetic nature. The tables of contents of both books (see Appendix III, pages 568 and 569–574) reveal how the field took shape from a rather formless potpourri.

The 1948 Handbook

The intention announced in the 1936 Handbook to publish a new edition every two years did not work out. The reason given in the Preface of the 1948 Handbook for the 12-year gap was the incidence of World War II, but the fact that the Carnegie Corporation discontinued its subsidy of the American Association for Adult Education in 1940 no doubt also had an influence.

The classification system for the adult education field developed in 1936 in ADULT EDUCATION IN ACTION clearly had an effect on the organization of the 1948 Handbook. Chapters were no longer presented in random order, but were grouped into categories and subcategories. However, the clear differentiation between agencies and content areas found in ADULT EDUCATION IN ACTION was not retained in the new Handbook. The frustration experienced by the leaders of the field in sorting out its elements and putting likes with likes is still evident after twenty-two years of trying. Morse A. Cartwright expressed the problem in the Preface to the 1948 Handbook in these words:

Prologue

This book attempts the impossible. In a country as large as the United States of America, where adult education appears in myriad forms and is presented through uncounted thousands of agencies large and small, it is quite outside human limitations to set forth an inclusive, detailed account of adult education activity.

By 1948 the previous preoccupations with "selling" the cause, eliminating the profit-makers, and resolving the conflict between proponents of vocational and proponents of cultural education had largely disappeared. The shape of the world following World War II induced a deeper level of concerns, expressed by Alain Locke, President of the Association, in the Foreword of the 1948 Handbook, as follows:

It is strange, or rather, sad to contemplate the extent to which we in America have tended to forget the social aim of adult education, or to subordinate it to opportunities for individual self-improvement. . . . The corporate age of adult education confronts us. Group education for social, intercultural, and international understanding looms up from the context of today's living to become the paramount problem and primary concern of the educator.

The 1960 Handbook

The years immediately surrounding the publication of the 1948 Handbook were times of ferment in the adult education field and of considerable change in the national organizational structure. The Carnegie Corporation grants for support of the AAAE were discontinued and Cartwright retired as its executive director. The Department of Adult Education of the National Education Association first made motions in the direction of converting itself from an organization oriented to public schools to one oriented to the total field, and thus threatened to supplant the AAAE as the field's coordinating structure. This direction was strongly opposed by the leadership of AAAE. In 1949 a joint committee of the two associations, after six years of prior study, recommended the two associations be dissolved and their memberships be brought together in a new unified organization. This action was taken, and the Adult Education Association of the USA (AEA) was founded in May 1951.

The leaders of the AEA were preoccupied for the next several years with the mechanics of building a new organizational structure, mapping strategies for serving the field, developing publications. They also had to deal with the forces bearing on the organization and with a new "angel," the Fund for Adult Education of the Ford Foundation. Although proposals were made for the publication of a new Handbook early in the life of the new organization, other priorities absorbed the energy of its leaders until the retirement of the AEA's first executive director in 1959 released his time for the compilation of the 1960 Handbook.

It is clear from a comparison of the Table of Contents of the 1960 Handbook with that of the 1948 Handbook (see pages 576–578) that during the intervening twelve years increasing attention was given to the understanding of the field in its historical, cultural and social context.

More rigorous criteria were applied for including agencies in the field as "adult education organizations," with the result that the number of institutions listed in the directory of organizations at the end of the book was reduced from 798 in the 1948 edition to 138 in the 1960 edition.

The basic typology for describing the field was retained, but by 1960 the distinction between institutional resources and program areas had become clearer. The confusion of elements within the categories that characterized the 1948 edition was lessened in the new Handbook. Obviously, the shape of the field was coming into focus.

One can perceive a shift from emphasis on rather basic practical concerns in 1948 (e.g., the motion picture, the discussion group, community organization for adult education) toward more theoretical and abstract concerns in 1960 (philosophy, learning theory, program development, public understanding). Perhaps this shift reflects a maturation of the field from being essentially a field of practice to being a field of study, theory, and practice—a hypothesis further supported by the greater emphasis in the 1960 edition on professional education, research, and a critique of the literature. As Benne and Powell pointed out in the 1960 edition, adult educators had been doing more "educating than philosophizing" in the past, and by 1960 the pendulum had started swinging in the other direction.

Interestingly, the 1960 Handbook was the first to devote a section to "The Future of Adult Education in America." It is as if until that time adult educators had been merely reactive—responding to pressures from the environment—and then suddenly began perceiving themselves as strategists for change. It didn't happen that suddenly, of course. In previous Handbooks concern for the future and strategy for influencing it were hidden in chapters dealing with other subjects.

History in the Handbooks

This brief analysis of the content of four previous Handbooks gives only one part of the evolution of the adult education movement in this country. But it does show adult education as a field of study and practice and of institutional arrangements in a process of identity-formation.

However, "the adult education field" is only an abstraction representing a complex mosaic of many elements—local, state and national insti-

Prologue

tutions and agencies; professional associations; constituencies; and program areas—that constitute the adult education movement. Constructing a comprehensive picture of the development of the movement as a whole would require a similar tracing of the evolutionary processes of each of the other elements in the movement.

The readers of the 1970 Handbook will have the opportunity to extend this analysis of "the field" ten years further. How differently is the field being defined in 1970 than in 1960? What shifts have occurred in the patterns of concern?

Introduction

Paul H. Sheats,
Professor of Education
The University of California
at Los Angeles

The 1970 Handbook accurately mirrors the diversity of the field and also echoes the confusion of tongues with which our leadership is afflicted. Some progress has been made during the last decade in providing a more adequate research base. Repeatedly, authors refer to what we have learned since the 1960 Handbook was published—and the prospects for the 1970's. This compulsion to face both ways, as the 1970 relief-map of the field is constructed reflects the impact of major social and economic changes upon adult education institutions, programs and *people* in our profession. The rate of change will accelerate even more rapidly in the decade ahead. This is perhaps the one thing we can all agree on. (Further, it may be the only thing we can predict with any degree of certainty!)

Rarely, if ever, has the author of the concluding and projective chapter in one decennial handbook had the opportunity to write the

Introduction for the succeeding handbook. To provide some polestars in navigating the seas of change, I shall use the same areas of concern employed in my final chapter of the 1960 Handbook to identify certain issues the 1970 contributors raise. Hopefully, this approach will provide both a bridge to the recent past and a platform from which to sight the next decade.

There is one disclaimer: I have not had access to final drafts of all the chapters. Therefore, the references to other chapters are illustrative rather than inclusive.

Aims and Objectives

Ten years ago we identified a continuum of objectives that should be the concern of adult education. The aims were polarized—from using adult education as an instrument of national policy to the meeting of individual needs. Today the controversy and the continuum remain, but the terminology has changed. We speak of community action and problem-solving vs. self-actualization.

The hoped-for role of adult education, as named in the foreword to the 1960 Handbook, was to usher in a new Golden Age comparable to that of Greece in the fifth century, B.C. That emphatically failed to materialize. Instead we reaped an age of revolt and fury characterized by confrontations, militancy, attacks on all segments of the establishment, alienation and withdrawal. The reactions of adult educators covered all points on the compass.

"Thank God—we haven't had any picket lines," said one adult education administrator recently. "It's only a question of time," said another. "This is a new ball game, and the score isn't even tied. Perhaps we need a new team that understands what the word *relevant* means."

Yet every professor of adult education knows his brighter graduate students are increasingly testing the curriculum for "relevance." Adult education has fared better than higher education in the 1960's revolution only because: (1) we lack the quaint notion of *in loco parentis;* (2) adult learners are nobody's captive audience; (3) adult educators, administrators and their clientele already are inside the establishment; and (4) although "inside" of it socially or institutionally, they also cope with the gritty, realistic world light-years removed from the pure academe. But can the profession continue to recruit men with "new eras in their brains?" I hope so.

It is fascinating to compare Robert Blakely's words in the 1960 Handbook with those of Edward Blakely. The former says our purpose is "the development of individuals who will fulfill themselves and freely serve the society which values individuals." Edward Blakely, in a state-

Introduction

ment from Western Community Action Training Inc. in San Francisco, says ". . . the current crisis in American education over whether students should determine what education is relevant and who should do the teaching has been resolved—by a bold new approach to *community* education." (Italics mine.) Perhaps those who believe in adult education for self-fulfillment and those who believe in adult education for maintaining or influencing the direction of social change can find common ground in the almost clinical description of the social setting in which we must operate in the 1970's. My view is that, unless adult education in the seventies gets closer to the "action," it will suffer dysfunction and the inevitable put-down by more socially relevant institutions. "The society capable of continuous renewal will be one that develops to the fullest its human resources, that removes obstacles to individual fulfillment, that emphasizes education, lifelong learning and self-discovery. In these matters our record is uneven—brilliant in some respects, shameful in others. And we are still far from having created, for either black or white, an educational system that produces self-discoverers and lifelong learners." (*Chronicle of Higher Education*, April 7, 1969.)

To complete this section on aims and objectives, I must expose the Achilles heel of adult education. We are essentially "establishment oriented." The life-pulse in the 1970's will come from those who are willing to break old molds and deal with the issues dividing us. If a mere 7 percent of our clientele is engaged in education for social and public responsibility we have a long way to go before we achieve action-oriented adult education. Perhaps we never shall and then the judgment remains for future generations: Did we exist only as the midwife to tradition? (There are, to be sure, worse roles, but it is important to ponder what our primary and secondary functions should be. Were we to reach consensus on these issues, we would be breaking all precedents in the field of adult education.)

Organization and Fiscal Support

The questions raised in the 1960 Handbook still haunt us although circumstances have changed considerably. New institutions, proliferations and mutations emerged. We have the ERIC Clearing House on Adult Education, the National Seminar on Adult Education Research, the growth of the community colleges, the expansion of company schools, to name only a few. It has not been all gain—termination of the Center for the Study of Liberal Education for Adults cost our field dearly although it is too soon to assess the full effects of this loss.

But the number of agencies that serve the educational needs of adults has not increased markedly. Current projections indicate that in

1974 we shall have for the first time more adults engaged in vocational and adult education than young people attending the formal system at all levels. Question: Can this demand be met without new agencies whose primary task is to provide adult education?

A related problem concerns the lack of trained manpower to do the job. The reluctance of the field to move toward a stronger emphasis on professionalism is pin-pointed in Part I. The dilemma is further complicated by the argument that there should be many ports of entry for those who choose a career in adult education. Supporters of this argument also point out that certification and licensing requirements could weaken the vitality which has characterized the field since its beginning. Our need for cooperative planning among adult education agencies at national, state, community and neighborhood levels has been exacerbated by the proliferation of programs in the 1960's. What, for example, should be the differentiated adult education functions of the public schools and the community service activities of the junior colleges, whose ranks have grown enormously in the last decade? How can we make it easier at the neighborhood level for the would-be learner to get information about opportunities already available?

Increased funding of adult education, especially by the federal government, has produced both intended and unintended results. Funding of adult basic education programs has led to the involvement of many state departments and local school systems which previously lacked staff resources in adult education. Title I of the Higher Education Act of 1965 similarly led to the involvement of colleges and universities which, up to that point, had shown little interest in continuing education. That programming has been skewed by these and other funding inducements seems undeniable. Moreover, it would also appear obvious that adult education programs are still inadequately financed in the public sector. The growth of company schools (with a projected increase from 7.2 million participants in 1965 to 17.5 million in 1974) suggests that business and industry consider adult education a sound investment.

One of the most important developments of the past decade is the size and strength of the corporate giants that have moved into the educational market place. (Their growing awareness that there *is* an adult education market may be construed by some as a belated status symbol—at least quantitatively, since it is the scent of sheer numbers that most attracts them.) Among the panoply of profit-making organizations engaged in manufacturing educational materials and equipment, managing adult education programs, conducting research and providing direct instruction to adults are Xerox, Time, General Electric, IBM, Raytheon, RCA, CBS, Minnesota Mining & Manufacturing, Litton, ITT, Lear Siegler, Westinghouse, Crowell-Collier-Macmillan, and others with the

Introduction

xxix

financial resources to make the total budget of the University of California seem small by comparison.

As Robert Pitchell has pointed out, the competition of corporations using contract funds may be a serious matter for the inadequately supported non-profit agency. He questions not only the ultimate cost to the taxpayer but also whether such an organization—the prime responsibility of which is to its stockholders and the profit it can make for them, and which, within that framework, controls the production of educational materials, research, evaluation, instruction and counseling—can act purely in the interest of education. ("Survey of the Current Situation in Higher Adult Education in the U.S.: Research, Problems and Issues," National University Extension Association.)

Programs and Methodology

There have been quantum leaps in programming theory and practice. That even more rapid progress will be made in the seventies is also clear. The communications explosion and the boom in education technology have placed new demands upon the adult education administrator and teacher: we may expect new opportunities for self-directed as well as group learning.

But again, there are problems. The new methodologies of the educational technologists are in many respects antithetical to the theories of adult learning espoused in the 1960 Handbook. The new emphasis on programmed learning, the specification of behavioral objectives, and the development of instructional sequences require the learner to follow docilely along the behavior-shaping track. Will this new pattern begin to supersede the reliance on teacher–student interaction and group discussion methods in the setting of learning goals? Is there perhaps an ethical issue involved we must soon resolve? (See John McDermott, "Knowledge is Power," *The Nation,* April 14, 1969.) It is most likely we are closer to brinkmanship in this regard than we realize. The heavier the investment in technological hardware, the stronger the economic pressures to amortize this investment in producing educational software—and, who shall act as gatekeeper vis-a-vis not only quality, but content? We hope this opens a new opportunity for graduates of doctoral programs in adult education.

Readers of the 1970 Handbook will have to cope with some new concepts and terms in research and evaluation and may need a course in professional upgrading themselves. The establishment of taxonomies in the cognitive, affective and psychomotor domains may very well aid the adult educator in selecting and organizing learning experiences, but there are other possibly important alternatives—for example, Robert

Gagne's Task Analysis approach (*The Conditions of Learning.* New York: Holt, Rinehart & Winston, 1966).

One of the bugaboos in adult education is the relative infrequency of program evaluation. It is encouraging to note in this Handbook that, in spite of inadequate funds and uneven competence in mastery of evaluation techniques, some progress is being made. But how one *measures* the degree of attainment of specified objectives is easier to grasp than the more complex process of judging the relative worth and appropriateness in terms of cost, feasibility and so on, of any given adult education enterprise. Thus, the Handbook can spur further study, analysis and discussion.

Concluding Observations

Carl Rogers has identified as man's greatest problem in the years ahead, not the hydrogen bomb, not the population explosion, but rather "the question of how much change the human being can accept, absorb and assimilate, and the rate at which he can take it." ("Interpersonal Relationships: USA 2000." *The Journal of Applied Behavioral Science,* Vol. 4, No. 3, 1968.) To learn to live with change, to influence change so that it becomes social progress, to humanize our institutions and our environment would appear to be high on the list of future priorities. As our society becomes increasingly (and frighteningly) more specialized, fragmented, depersonalized and alienated, this priority must be equated with survival needs as well as Maslow's clarion call for self-actualization needs. To the extent adult educators can utilize educational processes to resolve the problems that now block social advance and to maintain and restore the sense of human dignity and worth, will we live up to the high purposes that beckon us?

Introduction

financial resources to make the total budget of the University of California seem small by comparison.

As Robert Pitchell has pointed out, the competition of corporations using contract funds may be a serious matter for the inadequately supported non-profit agency. He questions not only the ultimate cost to the taxpayer but also whether such an organization—the prime responsibility of which is to its stockholders and the profit it can make for them, and which, within that framework, controls the production of educational materials, research, evaluation, instruction and counseling—can act purely in the interest of education. ("Survey of the Current Situation in Higher Adult Education in the U.S.: Research, Problems and Issues," National University Extension Association.)

Programs and Methodology

There have been quantum leaps in programming theory and practice. That even more rapid progress will be made in the seventies is also clear. The communications explosion and the boom in education technology have placed new demands upon the adult education administrator and teacher: we may expect new opportunities for self-directed as well as group learning.

But again, there are problems. The new methodologies of the educational technologists are in many respects antithetical to the theories of adult learning espoused in the 1960 Handbook. The new emphasis on programmed learning, the specification of behavioral objectives, and the development of instructional sequences require the learner to follow docilely along the behavior-shaping track. Will this new pattern begin to supersede the reliance on teacher–student interaction and group discussion methods in the setting of learning goals? Is there perhaps an ethical issue involved we must soon resolve? (See John McDermott, "Knowledge is Power," *The Nation*, April 14, 1969.) It is most likely we are closer to brinkmanship in this regard than we realize. The heavier the investment in technological hardware, the stronger the economic pressures to amortize this investment in producing educational software—and, who shall act as gatekeeper vis-a-vis not only quality, but content? We hope this opens a new opportunity for graduates of doctoral programs in adult education.

Readers of the 1970 Handbook will have to cope with some new concepts and terms in research and evaluation and may need a course in professional upgrading themselves. The establishment of taxonomies in the cognitive, affective and psychomotor domains may very well aid the adult educator in selecting and organizing learning experiences, but there are other possibly important alternatives—for example, Robert

Gagne's Task Analysis approach (*The Conditions of Learning.* New York: Holt, Rinehart & Winston, 1966).

One of the bugaboos in adult education is the relative infrequency of program evaluation. It is encouraging to note in this Handbook that, in spite of inadequate funds and uneven competence in mastery of evaluation techniques, some progress is being made. But how one *measures* the degree of attainment of specified objectives is easier to grasp than the more complex process of judging the relative worth and appropriateness in terms of cost, feasibility and so on, of any given adult education enterprise. Thus, the Handbook can spur further study, analysis and discussion.

Concluding Observations

Carl Rogers has identified as man's greatest problem in the years ahead, not the hydrogen bomb, not the population explosion, but rather "the question of how much change the human being can accept, absorb and assimilate, and the rate at which he can take it." ("Interpersonal Relationships: USA 2000." *The Journal of Applied Behavioral Science,* Vol. 4, No. 3, 1968.) To learn to live with change, to influence change so that it becomes social progress, to humanize our institutions and our environment would appear to be high on the list of future priorities. As our society becomes increasingly (and frighteningly) more specialized, fragmented, depersonalized and alienated, this priority must be equated with survival needs as well as Maslow's clarion call for self-actualization needs. To the extent adult educators can utilize educational processes to resolve the problems that now block social advance and to maintain and restore the sense of human dignity and worth, will we live up to the high purposes that beckon us?

Part I

Forms, Function and Future

Chapter 1

The Social Setting for Adult Education

JACK LONDON

Adult education has a particularly critical role to play in a rapidly changing society by providing information and knowledge that people need in order to cope with changing conditions. Consequently, adult educators must become familiar with the people they serve and with existing and emerging problems and issues—local, regional and national. Our method of presenting the social setting for adult education is to provide an analysis of (1) some of the demographic trends and changes that characterize our society and (2) some issues and problems that confront us as we struggle to strengthen and extend the vitality of our institutions or to change them in order to deal with the problems of the day. We shall also consider the role of education and adult education in helping people deal with the crucial issues of the times.

Any attempt to depict accurately the social setting within which adult education is carried out is limited by the lack of reliable data. While social scientists, the Bureau of Census, other governmental agencies and private organizations provide some useful quantitative and qualitative data, seldom do these data include the information or interpretation necessary to round out a meaningful picture of contemporary society [12; 13; 28]. Within these limitations we will seek to present some useful information for adult educators interested in understanding the social setting. We will examine selected indicators that characterize certain aspects of our country and a few of the most critical problems confronting the American people.

Population Characteristics

There are six basic characteristics of the U.S. population: heterogeneity, urbanization, mobility, marriage, mortality and education. Each of these contributes significantly to the social problems confronting the American public.

The first—and long recognized—characteristic of the U.S. population is the high degree of ethnic and racial heterogeneity as well as important regional differences. This is often typified by calling the United States a nation of nations. Successive deposits of population have created a multicultural and multiracial society in which nearly every nationality, race and creed in the world can be found.

The second characteristic is that the population of the United States is now largely urbanized and becoming increasingly so. From a nation characterized as predominantly agricultural with 95 percent of the populace rural, we have become a nation of urban dwellers with over 70 percent living in urban areas. The rapid growth of urbanization can be explained, in part, by the ratio of farmers to urban dwellers. Only when a society's agricultural surplus enables a farmer to feed many other people can a majority of the population afford to live in cities. One indicator of urbanization is reflected in the rapid change in the character of the labor force. In 1900, 37.5 percent of the labor force was in farming. In 1967 this figure dropped to 4.8 percent and is expected to decrease to 3.6 percent by 1975. Greater efficiency on the farm frees a growing number of the population to move to metropolitan areas to find jobs and make a life. This same urbanization trend is worldwide. For example, from 1900 to 1950, the population of the world increased by 49 percent while the urban population jumped about 235 percent.

The greatest increases of population have been occurring in metropolitan areas. While the central cities were sources of attraction during the period of much of our growth into an urban society, the recent and continuing trend is toward suburban living outside of the central core. The central cities have become the home of minorities, the aged, the disadvantaged, and other lower working class groups while white middle class and upper working class are migrating to the suburbs. Discrimination of varying intensity is a dominant factor in the much slower growth of racial minorities in suburban areas. In essence, most of the central cities have been declining in population as a consequence of the fairly rapid movement of the white population out of the core cities. It has been estimated that many of the largest cities will have the 50 percent and over concentrations of black residents in the next decade or two that some cities already approach.

What are the consequences of the existing patterns of urban growth for society? There may be a growth of separating subcultures on racial lines that will create tension, conflict and disruption arising from the frustration of, lack of opportunity for, and prejudice against racial groups. When members of a minority group experience rising expectations and a sense of their own dignity and self worth, frustration of these expectations will enhance these feelings [7; 9; 10; 11; 35].

Urbanism has consequences because it brings increased educational opportunities, increased use of mass media and higher rates of voting. Generalizations arising out of study of urbanization have led to the assertion that urbanism promotes greater tolerance and diversity; less religious observance; less stability; higher educational attainment; more mental illness, divorces, and suicides; higher crime rates (although crimes of violence appear to be proportionately more prevalent in rural areas); more rapid social change and greater freedom and anonymity. Yet, the whole concept of urban–rural differentiation is becoming suspect as the total society becomes urbanized in perspective and orientation.

The third population characteristic somewhat unique to the U.S. is its high rate of mobility. It is estimated that 20 percent of the people change communities each year, in addition to those who change residence within a given community. Men tend to be slightly more mobile than women and nonwhites more likely to move than whites. Peak mobility occurs in the age group 22 to 24 years, and thereafter the rate tends to decrease as age increases. Below age 35 married persons have higher mobility rates than single persons, but above age 35 married and single people have about the same mobility rates. While marriage, a job and a position in a community tend to stabilize people, job change, unemployment and marital status upset often serve to move one of the marriage partners out of the community. There are a number of implications resulting from urban mobility such as the impact of spatial dislocation upon behavior: in the most extreme form, mobility may result in erratic behavior and social disorganization; mobility weakens traditional forms of social control; it reduces the opportunity to develop community spirit; and it tends to accentuate the social problems that can be identified in cities. Mobility, on the other hand, may stimulate intellectual development and contribute to the rise of nonconformity, since different behavior norms are retained in the movement from one community to another. Under such conditions, norms lose their sanctions, and tolerance of nonconformity develops. Except for migratory workers, geographical mobility tends to be more common among the higher socioeconomic classes, who must be able to reestablish the same level of status held in the previous community of residence, make friends and establish roots.

Adult education can serve to facilitate the adjustment of mobile persons in their new community. Yet, the type of program activities developed by an adult educator will vary depending on the extent of mobility of the population in his community. By and large, adult education does not attract the newcomers to the community until after they have solved some of their more pressing problems. On the other hand, continuing education is becoming so important that even newcomers may utilize adult education programs to meet people and continue a program of study initiated elsewhere. It is conceivable that educational activities may be developed in the near future to help solve some of the problems of the more mobile person; and thus, the adult educator can play a role in assisting in the development of greater stability in community life.

The fourth characteristic is that the United States has a relatively high proportion of married persons. In 1900, 58 percent of males and 66.7 percent of females were married. These percentages jumped to 75.1 percent for males and 81 percent for females in 1960, and the trend continues upward. The character of the family and the role of its members have changed with the growth of urbanization as new functions have arisen and many traditional functions have been taken over by other institutions in the community. There are many ways in which an adult educator can help adults better understand their roles in their families through programs of parents education—e.g., parent nurseries, one indicator of change in the American family.

Related to marriage is the sex composition of the population. There are 96 males for every 100 females. In the ratio of men to women men predominate until age 25; thereafter there is a higher ratio of women. In 1966 there were only 77 males for every 100 females at age 65 and over; this ratio is expected to drop to 68 males in 1990. Since 1900, there has been a 50 percent increase in the proportion of maleless households because of the higher survival rate of females. The growth of population in the over 65 group, which increases at the rate of 1000/day, is largely due to women who have outlived their husbands—another kind of social problem facing society today.

The fifth characteristic of our nation is its low mortality rate. The U.S. death rate per 1000 population in 1965 was 9.4 as compared to an estimated world rate of 16, which demonstrates what the relatively high levels of medical care, sanitation and standard of living in the U.S. have accomplished in the sharp increase of life expectancy since 1900. Life expectancy at birth in 1900 was 47.3 years; in 1965, it was about 70 years, with 73.4 years for women and 66.6 years for men. The fact that people are living longer has many consequences for the total community.

The sixth characteristic to be noted is the high educational status of the population. At present the average American has completed about 12.3 years of schooling. Women continue to have a higher median educa-

The Social Setting for Adult Education

tional attainment than men for both whites and nonwhites. At the extremes, there are fewer women than men with less than eight years of schooling although more men complete four years of college or more. In educational attainment, the black adult male lags behind the white male by over three years, a statistic that has serious consequences for mobility opportunities within the society. Within each census of occupational groups, men of prime working ages tend to receive more annual income if they are high school graduates than if they are not. This finding can be utilized in the promotion of adult education for those without a high school diploma. Another important finding is that the number of college graduates in the population 25 years old and over is expected to rise from fewer than 10 million in 1968 to about 20 million by 1985. The educational attainment of our population is rising—a fact that can be of major importance in aiding the adult educator develop program ideas and activities for a population becoming more sensitive and receptive to the need for continuing education. An adult educator provides differentiated services to a community in accord with varying educational levels, and census tract data can pinpoint population characteristics in those segments of a community served by particular adult education facilities.

The Labor Force

The labor force continues to grow in accord with the rising population, the increase in productivity and the expansion of our gross national product [47]. Henry Wallace's goal of 60 million jobs, once a dream, became a reality, and we now approach an employed civilian labor force of 75 million. In 1890 the total labor force was slightly more than 22 million. In 1968 it was 81 million including the armed forces.

An important characteristic of the labor force has been the rapid growth of white collar jobs since 1900 (Table 1), which saw an enormous surge in the 1950's when the distribution of the labor force shifted so that a majority of jobs were white collar. And projected trends indicate a continued rise in these occupations [44] with increasing technology, automation, the growing bureaucracy in industry, business, and government, and the growth of professional occupations. Thus, the United States became the first industrial society whose labor force was not dominated by blue collar occupations. Furthermore, the long run trend in the reduction of farm workers continues largely as a result of the increasing development of mechanization and automation in agriculture and manufacturing, which has released an increasing segment of the labor force into service type occupations.

The greatest increases in the occupational groupings (from 1900 to

Table 1. *Percent Distribution of Major Occupational Groups by Sex in the United States, 1900–1975*

	1900	1920	1940	1950	1960	1967	1975
Male and Female							
White collar	17.6	24.9	31.1	37.5	43.1	46.0	48.5
Blue collar	35.8	40.2	39.8	39.1	36.3	36.7	34.0
Service	9.0	7.8	11.7	11.0	12.5	12.5	13.8
Farm	37.5	27.0	17.4	12.5	8.1	4.8	3.6
Male							
White collar	17.6	21.4	26.6	30.5	37.4	39.0	
Blue collar	37.6	44.5	45.6	48.4	46.6	47.8	
Service	3.1	3.7	6.1	6.2	6.5	7.0	
Farm	41.7	30.4	21.7	14.9	9.6	6.2	
Female							
White collar	17.8	38.8	44.9	52.5	55.3	58.4	
Blue collar	27.8	23.7	21.6	22.4	16.6	17.0	
Service	35.4	23.9	29.4	21.5	23.7	22.3	
Farm	18.9	13.5	4.0	3.7	4.4	2.3	

projections for 1975) have occurred in the professional and technical occupations. For example, in 1950 there were approximately 12,000 employed electrical and electronic technicians. By 1960 this group had expanded to more than 91,000—an increase of 679 percent. Aeronautical engineers increased their number by 142 percent in the same period. Overall, the professional, technical, and kindred workers increased their numbers by 47 percent in this 10 year period. After the professionals, the next largest increase was among clerical and associated groups, which grew by 34 percent. In contrast, farmers and farm foremen diminished their numbers about 40 percent while productivity in agriculture was increasing.

Women Workers

A significant and continuing trend has been the increasing number of women entering the labor force who are married and living with their husbands [27; 47; 48]. No longer can a woman assume that marriage becomes a way of leaving the world of work. Some women work for self-fulfillment, but evidence indicates that a growing number of women enter the labor force for economic reasons; and 58 percent of all women who had worked some time in 1964 were married. The notion that many women work to obtain money for luxuries is not true, although this reason

The Social Setting for Adult Education

obtains in some instances (particularly in upper middle class families). The main reason for continuing to work or returning to work appears to be the perceived need to maintain a standard of living desired by the family. In 1965 over four million mothers assisting in the support of their families had husbands who earned less than $5000 together with children under 18 years of age. Seven out of ten of the nonwhite wives not living on farms were at work. These data reflect economic necessity.

Changes in participation rates are resulting from the growing participation of women in the labor force. While there was a 7.7 percent increase in participation among males between 1950 and 1960, there was a 25.8 percent increase among females. The trend toward increasing numbers of females—single, married, widowed or divorced—will continue as projections indicate that the change between 1960 and 1970 will be 28 percent for females and 12.3 percent for males.

Many women who want to work in order to support themselves and their families or to supplement their husband's income are prevented from seeking employment because of a lack of adequate child-care facilities. To the extent that our communities provide more facilities for child-care, increasing numbers of women with small children will enter the labor force. If child-care facilities become more than simply baby sitting operations by providing educational programs for children and their parents, the growth of such resources may enrich existing programs of education for children and adults alike. While objections to women working are more likely to prevail in families with low educational attainment, these objections are likely to be reduced with the rise in the educational level in our society.

The growing importance of education and training is particularly significant for women. There is a continuing conviction in our society that education is not as important for women as for men. This view is not only held by men but also by a surprisingly high proportion of women. The emphasis on vocation, which characterizes American education (including adult education), engenders the idea that since the woman expects to marry and be supported by her husband, obtaining an education is less important for her. The increasing number of women entering the labor force, particularly after children are in school or after they have grown up and left home, negates this prevailing notion. While the typical woman may expect to marry, give birth to children, and accept the traditional role of wife and mother as her desired objective in adulthood, present day reality denies this assumption to an increasing extent as we noted previously. However, even when a woman holds the prevailing assumption that her proper role is that of wife and mother, continuing education should be important to her. The woman who keeps up with her husband intellectually and is excited enough about learning and education to communicate her feelings to her children is a much better wife, mother, homemaker, and citizen.

Growing Importance of Education

The role of education in our nation, and throughout the world, assumes greater and greater importance. Limited educational attainment restricts a nation's capacity to expand its productive efficiency. For the individual, limited education becomes a handicap in securing employment, assuming greater responsibility and advancing in status. More and more jobs are becoming technical—for which the educational prerequisites are rising. Formal educational institutions have become the selecting and certifying agency for manpower distribution within the society. The result is that the diploma or degree has become the price of admission for an increasing number of jobs.

Today, a dropout, who formerly could achieve some measure of success in the world of work, experiences increasing difficulty in even securing satisfactory employment. In practice, the dropout from school becomes a dropout from society unless he can secure some form of certification (often by returning to school or attending evening classes) that qualifies him to work.

Along with the growing importance of formal education, the need for continuing education has been accelerating. No longer can one "complete" his education. Yet, the rapid growth of educational opportunities outside of the formal system has been largely invisible and virtually unnoticed. Most of our attention has been devoted to school enrollments in the formal traditional educational institutions—elementary, secondary and beyond. A growing number of educators and training personnel should realize that many millions of adults are experiencing the need to seek education and training outside of the formal educational institutions. Recent studies have produced some rough data that illustrate the growing importance of vocational, technical and professional training to serve an increasingly larger segment of our adult population. Although the estimates and projections are tentative, they provide us with an emerging view of the increasingly important role of education and training on a continuing basis for an expanding segment of our labor force. The estimate that 17.5 million adults will be attending company schools for varying periods of time by 1974 (a jump from 7.2 million in 1965) suggests that to go to work will mean to be retrained on a continuing basis [8].

In a recent issue of *The Annals*, Wilbur J. Cohen [8] tabulates preliminary studies by Bertram M. Gross on existing patterns of adult edu-

The Social Setting for Adult Education

cation and vocational, technical and professional training, and projections for its changing character. (Since the data probably reflect some duplication of numbers and inadequate reporting, they emphasize the growing need to improve the reliability of data collection for formal and informal educational activities.) The data in Table 2 indicate a startling comparison between the number involved in the labor force, which is the central responsibility assigned to the adult years, and what Cohen defines as the learning force, whose potential clientele is the entire society. Combining the programs designed for adults, which would include vocational and adult education in the learning force, we find that by 1974 there will be more adults attending some type of training program than young people in the formal system. (It should perhaps be pointed out that the data presented in Table 2 do not appear to take into account the national survey of adult education conducted by Johnstone and Rivera.)

Table 2. *Learning[a] Force and Labor Force in the United States, 1940–1974*

	1940	1950	1960	1965	1970	1974
					PROJECTED	
Learning Force to Labor Force Ratio (percent)	84.2	82.9	101.9	127.0	141.7	159.4
Learning Force (millions)						
1. Formal school	29.9	31.5	46.0	55.4	63.0	68.4
2. Vocational, etc.	11.8	15.3	18.9	25.0	34.0	48.7
3. Adult Education	5.6	6.9	9.6	19.2	24.3	31.1
Total	47.3	53.7	74.5	99.6	121.3	148.2
Total Labor Force (millions)	56.2	64.8	73.1	78.4	85.6	93.0

[a] The composition of the learning force is as follows: (1) *Formal schooling:* preschool, elementary, secondary, and higher education. (2) *Vocational, etc.:* vocational, technical, and professional training outside the formal educational structure which includes professional and technical training, company schools, on-the-job training, correspondence schools, armed forces, and all other. (3) *Adult Education:* general, specialized, correspondence courses, all other.

In spite of the possible inaccuracies of data, the trend is clear and signifies the need to develop new conceptions about education and training at all levels serving a clientele of all ages. If we ever needed evidence that no one can complete his education in a complex industrial society, Table 2 presents the data. Adult educators, training specialists and educators from the formal educational establishment must begin to rethink the character of education and training with these facts in hand. The public, state legislatures and U.S. Congress must understand the new requirements for education and training demanded by an industrial society undergoing rapid change. If we are to secure adequate planning for the educational and training needs of our society, we must reexamine prevailing assumptions, existing structures, programming and curricula arrangements and the need to make education and training more relevant not only for vocational needs but for the human condition [6; 19; 25].

Problem Areas in American Society

Social Problems

The presence of continuous, rapidly accelerating change has given rise to various social problems which in turn cause conflict, confusion, confrontation and disunity [3; 4; 22; 26; 38; 39]. American society is increasingly characterized by a conflict in values sharply emphasized by a growing generation gap, a lack of integration among institutions and groups, the continuing failure of many institutions to deal with their problems and the existence of widespread social differences and levels of inequality—all of which reflect an array of social problems. The type of social problem that arises in society is determined by the character of industrialization and development within the society. For example, the transition from a preindustrial to an industrial stage of development presents physical survival as the dominant social problem. The existence of large pockets of poverty within this country indicates that segments of our population have not been fully integrated into the society. In particular, minorities and some working class people have not been integrated as first class citizens with equal opportunities to share in the benefits available to the affluent majority.

While there is no suitable criterion of social relevance that permits us to denote the pertinence and significance of a particular social problem, some problems can be identified as being more important and pressing for solution than others. Here, our personal standards of judgment enter into our selection and reflect our own bias and values. While the problems of race, the aged, poverty, youth, alienation, crime, mental illness, war and peace and the condition of our cities loom large within our society, other problems such as drug addiction, population crisis, suicide, family disorganization, alcoholism, pollution of the environment and the domination of the mass media by advertisers deserve serious attention. Most important, many of these problems are closely related and cannot be examined and treated in isolation. Limited space will permit only a few of these problems to be used as illustration. (A further treatment of some of the same issues is found in the chapter on education for public responsibility.)

The Social Setting for Adult Education

Adult education may have an important role to play by providing adults with information about existing social problems so that meaningful solutions can be worked out on local, regional and national levels. However, we must overcome a serious weakness in contemporary adult education programs that have been primarily concerned with non-controversial topics and vocational training at the expense of learning for better citizenship.

Minorities

One critical problem plaguing society is discrimination [18; 34; 35; 42; 50]. While more opportunities are being created for blacks and other minorities, the pace of improvement is far too slow. The nation still reflects a degree of racism that may be productive of even more severe conflicts and weaken the resolve and ability of the citizenry to deal with many other problems. Segments of the population do not share equally in existing opportunities proclaimed as being available to all. Examining certain selected measures of discrimination and inequality of opportunity, we find startling evidence—as revealed in Table 3—that efforts to eliminate discrimination and inequality have not advanced sufficiently to alleviate the growing tensions that engulf us [46].

The data speak for themselves. Negroes and other minorities are subject to many disadvantages which have their roots in discriminatory practices, inferior education and the particular occupational distribution that reflects inferior status and limited opportunity. Although progress is being made in the improvement of educational opportunities that may lead to better jobs, Negroes and other minorities are still heavily concentrated in the low paying, unskilled jobs. While only 10 percent of black women are in clerical jobs, 33 percent of the white women are so employed. Unemployment is another indicator of the inferior position of nonwhites with their rate being twice that reported for whites.

The ghetto, the deteriorating core of our cultural cities, and the continuing discrimination in housing in all sections of our country emphasize the severity of the problem of discrimination. The Report of the National Advisory Commission on Civil Disorders spells out the insidious character of white racism that infects our society. We need to recognize that the current black revolution may be one of the major forces for the greater humanization of our society and may induce more Americans to work together to eliminate the infection of discrimination and improve the condition of all people. As the Report found:

What white Americans have never fully understood—but what the negro can never forget—is that white society is deeply implicated in the ghetto.

Table 3. *Selected Measures of Discrimination and Inequality of Opportunity, 1965*

Selected Measures	White	Nonwhite
Income		
Median income of families	$6,858	$3,839
Households in poverty	17.1%	43.1%
Families with income of $10,000 or more	24.1%	8.3%
Education		
Median years of school completed, males 25 years of age and over	12.0 years	9.0 years
High school completed, persons 20–24 years of age	76.3%	50.2%
male	75.6%	51.3%
female	77.0%	49.4%
College graduates, 25 years of age and over	9.9%	5.5%
Labor Force Participation		
Male	78.6%	76.0%
Female	37.0%	46.1%
Employment (percent of total civilian employment)		
White collar occupations	47.5%	19.5%
Craftsmen–foremen occupations	13.5%	6.7%
Unemployment Rate (percent of civilian labor force)		
Adult males	2.9%	6.0%
Adult females	4.0%	7.4%
Teenagers	12.2%	25.3%

White institutions created it, white institutions maintain it, and white society condones it.

It is time now to turn with all the purpose at our command to the major unfinished business of this nation. It is time to adopt strategies for action that will produce quick and visible progress. . . .

Our recommendations embrace three basic principles:

> To mount programs on a scale equal to the dimension of the problem.
> To aim these programs for high impact in the immediate future in order to close the gap between promise and performance;
> To undertake new initiatives and experiments that can change the system of failure and frustration that now dominates the ghetto and weakens our society. [*31*, p. 2]

The Social Setting for Adult Education

Adult education can have a significant role to play in the attack upon racism and discrimination. If the education of the young is to be improved, we must secure greater involvement of the community. As we seek to improve the educational experiences and opportunities for children in the ghetto, and for suburban children, we must simultaneously involve their parents in continuing education.

But merely providing improved educational opportunities, however improvement is defined, is not sufficient to deal with the unequal distribution of life chances in our society. While education (and training) represents an important process through which minorities can advance upward in the world of work, discrimination and racism continue to loom large in limiting opportunities. For example, if a white person completes high school, his chances of being unemployed are cut in half while the graduation by a negro from high school has relatively less effect upon his ability to become and remain employed. Segmented or piecemeal attack upon the problem of discrimination is insufficient to influence the drastic changes that we must secure if this problem is to be reduced and eventually eliminated. A comprehensive effort supported by our government, our major institutions and the responsible leadership in our society must be combined to effect the necessary changes of experience, attitude, values and behavior.

The Aged

The aged experience a sharp reduction of income as they retire and live on pensions, social security and savings. A majority of household heads age 65 and older had less than $3,000 annual incomes in 1960, and there is no evidence that the economic condition of the aged has improved significantly since then. Apart from economic problems, which are even more severe for unattached individuals age 65 years and older, other problems loom large for older people in American society. For a male, being a non-worker and a limited breadwinner influences one's status, role in the family and feelings of self worth. Apart from being deprived of the companionship found in the work situation, the aged, with limited income and reduced mobility, find it necessary to reduce outside contacts and relationships. And the opportunity to find some new meaningful role and relevance as a person appears to diminish sharply with age and retirement.

While society expresses concern about improving their physical and material condition, the aged are seldom provided with the resources they need for relevance and a sense of worth. We tend to place them in "playpens" by providing recreation and similar endeavors while doing almost nothing to furnish them with the means to keep mentally alert.

We strip them of most of their meaningful roles on the assumption they are incapable of carrying them out effectively, with the rationalization that they deserve the right to rest and take it easy. Recreational activities are not sufficient to maintain mental abilities, contact with society, identity and sense of significance as a person. In consequence we can observe a growing alienation among the aged in our society [16; 23; 32; 33; 37].

It is unfortunate that adult education has not been more fully utilized to insure that the aged person's contact with other people is maintained. Most of the aged, and particularly those with low educational attainment, do not turn to education as a source of help. The common view that education is for the young inhibits many oldsters from utilizing it to participate in life as an exciting adventure. While the proof is clear that one is never too old to learn, there is widespread belief to the contrary by the aged, many professionals working with them, and the wider community; and this belief serves as a self-fulfilling prophecy. Continuing education can serve to expand horizons, develop understanding, assist in creating meaningful activities and bridge the gap between generations. Adult educators, if they believe the aged can learn, are in a unique position to organize learning experiences for them.

Poverty

The realization that there exist nationwide pockets of poverty has stimulated interest for their eradication. While there have been many proposals to help the poor, and a few have been put into effect, much of the effort has been less than successful. If it is maintained that those on welfare are lazy and programs are not devised to foster incentive and to retrain adults to reenter the world of work, our own inadequacies are revealed. A perspective which fails to see the poor as human beings but rather as inefficient machines is part of the problem. Dehumanized poverty programs have largely failed because the primary effect has been not to help the poor learn how to help themselves but to make them more dependent and keep them at the bottom of the industrial system. The theme of this brief section on poverty was spelled out in an article in which the authors state

a minimum approach by government in any society with significant inequalities must provide for rising minimum levels not only of incomes, assets, and basic services, but also of self-respect and opportunities for social mobility and participation in many forms of decision-making. [27]

Unless poverty programs strive to help the poor develop their own capacities and sense of relevance as human beings, we cannot expect much progress. We must involve the poor in decision-making affecting

The Social Setting for Adult Education

their lives. In large measure, the beneficiaries of poverty programs have been the professionals and government bureaucrats at all levels. As long as the primary focus of programs to alleviate poverty is upon manipulating the poor as objects, rather than upon their involvement, we can expect little genuine progress.

While economic, political, social and educational components must be developed in any program, all of these aspects must build upon the central notion of enlarging one's values and one's self concept and developing new motivations. For example, continuation of existing welfare systems will not produce resourceful and motivated individuals. In fact, the whole concept of welfare enhances dependency and debilitates one's sense of personal worth. Under most welfare programs, potentially employable welfare recipients are often faced with the prospect of taking home less earnings from a job than the minimum allowance provided them. An appropriate scheme of welfare must include adequate incentives and meaningful job opportunities. Finally, we should explore the possibility of providing all people with some form of guaranteed annual income that will make possible dignity and self respect.

Finally, there are many poor people who are so marginal that they do not qualify for welfare or any other form of assistance. They are the people who only have a minimal contact with society and are not visible enough to be counted. It is tragic that "the other America" can be neglected without guilt or a sense of shame. And most important, it is estimated that 15 million children live in poverty, which tends to transmit the culture of poverty across generations [14].

An important ingredient of any antipoverty program must be education if real change is to be achieved. The education and training needed to become employable must be supplemented by meaningful learning experiences that help the poor learn how to cope with the social forces that influence their lives.

The Paraprofessional Approach

An approach to the problem of poverty is to find additional ways of creating meaningful work for the economically disadvantaged segments of our population. One way to do this is to develop new positions that adults with limited education can fill immediately. The idea of a job as a career can provoke ambition, motivation, increased interest and greater self-fulfillment. Before discussing this approach, we will briefly examine the character of industrial change that suggests the importance of developing paraprofessional positions, particularly for the helping professions.

At the beginning of 1929, our labor force was primarily in the goods-producing sector of the economy. The goods-producing sector employed about a third more workers than the service-producing sector. In the early part of the 1950's, employment in the goods-producing and service-producing sectors was about equal. By 1967, as an indicator of the changes taking place, service and government employed 50 percent more man-hours than the goods-producing sector. Although employment in the service and government sectors has been increasing, the service share of the Gross National Product has remained fairly constant over the past twenty years because the service productivity has increased at a much slower pace than in the rest of the economy. For example, man-hours in farming are down 59 percent since 1947 but production has increased 42 percent. The rapid increase in employment in local government has been due to the increase of about three million teachers in the labor force since 1947, and the demand for teachers will likely increase as education becomes more and more important. Service-producing sectors of the economy now account for about 60 percent of employment, exactly the reverse of the situation in 1929, and the trend toward more service is increasing. A projection for 1975 indicates that the increase in the number of jobs in the service-producing sector will be about seven times as great as in the goods-producing sector. If these projections are accurate, the service sector will exceed the goods-producing areas of the economy by 80 percent by that time [49].

The projected increases in service (particularly in the helping professions—education, medicine, recreation and so on) suggest it will be difficult to provide the professionals needed to meet the demands of the economy. In addition, the decline in number of semi-skilled and unskilled jobs will lessen opportunities for people of limited educational attainment. Since the service professions will require many hundreds of thousands of additional personnel, one begins to grasp the tremendous potential for new kinds of careers. While college is a prerequisite for most human service fields, careers are emerging that allow a person with limited but specialized education to work under the supervision of professionals. Two options can be made available to these workers—to continue in the entry position or to obtain accreditation for promotion to full professional status. Thus, a worker can gain valuable experience while supplementing his on-the-job training with education toward professionalization. This type of career development can: (1) open up new opportunities for the disadvantaged who are now eligible only for jobs that are decreasing in number; (2) provide opportunities to achieve professional standing through a combination of work experience and education; and (3) fill the projected shortages in the human service fields [29; 30; 36].

Adult education can play a crucial role in new careers development.

It can provide a variety of program formats for sub-professionals who will need additional education to improve their skills and knowledge. It can help move upward those desiring eventual full professional status. As more people lose jobs in the goods-producing sector and in the mechanical service occupations, the demand for personnel in human service occupations will likely increase—a demand that will remain unfilled unless we devise programs of new careers for those who might otherwise become permanently unemployed. The main obstacle to the rapid growth of new careers thus far appears to have been the conservatism of many of those in the professional occupations.

Youth and Alienation

A major source of alienation has been the rapid social change of American society. The symptoms of alienation and powerlessness—distrust, anger, cynicism, a cult of the present and a need for immediate gratification—appear to be stimulated by our culture's impersonality, hypocrisy, emphasis upon efficiency and material consumption, rigidity of role definition and the vocational emphasis of formal education. Increasing numbers of youth are questioning the discrepancy between the adult generation's professed values and its conduct [1; 2; 17; 20; 21]. They are searching for a sense of identity and meaningfulness that eludes them. Adults are fond of remarking that the young will "mature" and grow up, with the expectation that they will join the middle class and become more conservative and "reasonable" as they enter adulthood; but events suggest that the "good old days" will not return. As our productive capacity rises and if the effect of technology upon the human condition results in growing alienation from one's self and one's values, the resulting social problems may well become more sensitive and inimical to the achievement of a sense of order and well being within the nation.

The growing unrest on college campuses (increasingly spilling over to the high school), teacher strikes, the use of drugs and the demonstrations against war and racism are indicators of a growing dissatisfaction with the quality and character of American institutions. The traditional purpose of education has been to assist the learner to acquire knowledge for the purpose of assimilating him into the ways of society. Students now seek to develop critical perspectives which will provide them with understanding and means of affecting the social, economic and political forces that mold their lives. They want guidance for their work and their relationships. With the continuing growth of a mass industrial society resulting in greater impersonality, youth are demanding more relevant education than merely training for the roles that they are expected to assume in the world of work. They are more critical of the adult generation and are demanding a greater voice in determining the conditions that influence them. While the primary focus of schooling continues to be the acquisition of knowledge, young people are demanding more active roles as participants in the educational process. Violence, repression, charges of a lack of discipline, and indifference to their demands will not satisfy the discontent and alienation among the young. The adult generation will have to listen and become more open to learning from the young if the existing conflict is not to be extended. No generation has a monopoly upon wisdom, and the young and the adults of all ages must find better ways of learning from each other.

Adult educators can play a vital role by offering their clientele programming that directs itself to the perspectives, outlooks, and ideas being expressed by the young. As adults unlearn ideas that are no longer relevant, they may become more sensitive and knowledgeable about youth and more willing to engage in a dialogue with them. To be sure, youth must listen to adults if genuine dialogue is to take place. However, the initiative lies with the adult generation.

Conclusions

In these times of crisis, adult education has a unique opportunity to provide learning experiences addressed to the crucial issues and problems confronting our people. Unless we look upon education as a process of helping people acquire the necessary skills to think clearly, critically and imaginatively, we are limiting students of all ages to becoming rote learners incapable of acting intelligently in a variety of situations. The highest purpose of education is not to train students for specific roles but to help them gain some understanding of the meaning of their lives and to become more sensitive to other people. Successful education occurs when we begin to understand the range and complexity of the relationships that affect us, and to be able to have sufficient self confidence in our own values to utilize them in our lives. To what extent is this model of education found in our adult education programs? In our judgment, this form of liberalizing education seldom is practiced because we favor the imitation of the traditional education fostered by the educational establishment. If adult education is going to be creative and meaningful, we must strive to find teachers who can make learning exciting. Hence, the role of the adult teacher is not only to convey significant material for study but to present it in a fashion that exhibits the joy of learning when it relates to one's life and experiences.

While the vocational and training function of adult education is both appropriate and necessary, we must offer learning that speaks directly to the human condition and helps students secure insight and understanding about conditions and circumstances that directly affect them. This may mean that more controversy will have to be introduced into the curriculum. Whether or not we can develop an effective democratic society will depend upon our success in finding ways of involving the majority of adults in educational experiences that foster a critical perspective, an openness to ideas, a willingness to tolerate differences of opinion and the desire to facilitate change as needed in our society.

References

1. Becker, Ernest. *Beyond Alienation.* New York: Braziller, 1967.
2. Becker, Ernest. *The Structure of Evil.* New York: Braziller, 1968.
3. Becker, Howard S., ed. *Social Problems: A Modern Approach.* New York: John Wiley & Sons, 1966.
4. Bredemeier, Harry C., and Toby, Jackson. *Social Problems in America: Costs and Casualties in an Acquisitive Society.* New York: John Wiley & Sons, 1960.
5. Burck, Gilbert. "The Still Bright Promise of Productivity." *Fortune* (October, 1968).
6. Clark, Harold F., and Sloan, Harold S. *Classrooms in the Factories.* Rutherford, N.J.: Fairleigh Dickinson University Press, 1958.
7. Cleaver, Eldridge. *Soul on Ice.* New York: McGraw-Hill, 1968.
8. Cohen, Wilbur J. "Education and Learning." *The Annals,* CCCLXXIII (September, 1967), pp. 79–101.
9. Conot, Robert. *Rivers of Blood, Years of Darkness.* New York: Bantam Books, 1967.
10. Gans, Herbert J. "The 'Equality' Revolution." *The New York Times Magazine* (November 3, 1968).
11. Grier, William H., and Cobbs, Price M. *Black Rage.* New York: Basic Books, 1968.
12. Gross, Bertram M., ed. *A Great Society?* New York: Basic Books, 1968.
13. Gross, Bertram M., and Springer, Michael. "New Goals for Social Information." *The Annals,* CCCLXXIII (September, 1967), pp. 208–218.
14. Harrington, Michael. "The Dynamics of Misery." Sidney Hillman Reprint Series No. 32. New York: The Sidney Hillman Foundation, 1968. (Adapted from Harrington, Michael. *Toward a Democratic Left.* New York: The Macmillan Company, 1968.)
15. Harrington, Michael. *The Other America: Poverty in the United States.* Baltimore, Md.: Penguin Books, 1963.
16. Henry, Jules. *Culture Against Man.* New York: Random House, 1963.
17. Hickerson, Nathaniel. *Education for Alienation.* Englewood Cliffs, N.J.: Prentice-Hall, 1966.
18. Jacobs, Paul. *Prelude to Riot: A View of Urban America from the Bottom.* New York: Random House, 1967.
19. Johnstone, John W. C., and Rivera, Ramon J. *Volunteers for Learning: A*

Study of the Educational Pursuits of American Adults. Chicago, Ill.: Aldine, 1965.
20. Keniston, Kenneth. *The Uncommitted.* New York: Dell, 1965.
21. Keniston, Kenneth. *Young Radicals.* New York: Harcourt, Brace & World, 1968.
22. Lindenfield, Frank, ed. *Radical Perspectives on Social Problems.* New York: The Macmillan Company, 1968.
23. Loether, Herman J. *Problems of Aging.* Belmont, Calif.: Dickenson, 1967.
24. London, Jack. "The Continuing Education of Women." *Adult Leadership,* XIV (April, 1966), pp. 326–328.
25. London, Jack; Weckert, Robert; and Hagstrom, Warren O. *Adult Education and Social Class.* Berkeley, Calif.: Survey Research Center, University of California, 1963.
26. Merton, Robert K., and Nisbet, Robert A., eds. *Contemporary Social Problems* (2nd ed.). New York: Harcourt, Brace & World, 1967.
27. Miller, S. M.; Rein, Martin; Roby, Pamela; and Gross, Bertram M. "Poverty, Inequality, and Conflict." *The Annals,* CCCLXXIII (September, 1967), p. 19.
28. Myrdal, Gunnar. "The Social Sciences and Their Impact on Society." In: *Social Theory and Social Invention.* Edited by Herman D. Stein. Cleveland, Ohio: The Press of Case Western Reserve University, 1968, pp. 145–163.
29. Pearl, Arthur. "New Careers: One Solution to Poverty." In: *Social Policies for America in the Seventies.* Edited by Robert Theobald. New York: Doubleday, 1968, pp. 77–104.
30. Pearl, Arthur, and Riessman, Frank. *New Careers for the Poor.* New York: The Free Press, 1965.
31. *Report of the National Advisory Committee on Civil Disorders.* (The Kerner Report.) New York: Bantam Books, 1968.
32. Riley, Matilda White; Foner, Anne; and others. *Aging and Society: An Inventory of Research Findings.* New York: Russell Sage Foundation, 1968.
33. Rosow, Irving. *Social Integration of the Aged.* New York: The Free Press, 1967.
34. Shibutani, Tamotsu, and Kwan, Kian M. *Ethnic Stratification: A Comparative Approach.* New York: The Macmillan Company, 1965.
35. Silberman, Charles E. *Crisis in Black and White.* New York: Random House, 1964.
36. Suhm, Lawrence L. "Cumulative Earned Leave." In: *Social Policies for America in the Seventies.* Edited by Robert Theobald. New York: Doubleday, 1968, pp. 105–132.
37. Tibbitts, Clark, ed. *Handbook of Social Gerontology.* Chicago, Ill.: University of Chicago Press, 1960.
38. Timms, Noel. *A Sociological Approach to Social Problems.* London: Routledge and Kegan Paul, 1968.
39. Truzzi, Marcello. *Sociology and Everyday Life.* Englewood Cliffs, N.J.: Prentice-Hall, 1968.

The Social Setting for Adult Education

40. U.S. Bureau of the Census. *Current Population Reports,* Series P-20, No. 169, "Educational Attainment." Washington, D.C.: Government Printing Office, 1968.
41. U.S. Bureau of Census. *Current Population Reports,* Series P-20, No. 171, "Mobility of the Population of the United States: March 1966 to March 1967." Washington, D.C.: Government Printing Office, 1968.
42. U.S. Bureau of the Census. *Current Population Reports,* Series P-23, BLS Report No. 347, "Recent Trends in Social and Economic Conditions of Negroes in the United States." Washington, D.C.: Government Printing Office, 1968.
43. U.S. Bureau of the Census. *Current Population Reports,* Series P-25, No. 388, "Summary of Demographic Projections." Washington, D.C.: Government Printing Office, 1968.
44. U.S. Bureau of the Census. *Occupational Trends in the United States: 1900 to 1950.* Bureau of the Census Working Paper No. 5. Washington, D.C.: Government Printing Office, 1958.
45. U.S. Bureau of the Census. *Pocket Data Book, USA, 1967.* Washington, D.C.: Government Printing Office, 1967.
46. U.S. Department of Health, Education and Welfare. *Health, Education, and Welfare Indicators.* Washington, D.C.: Government Printing Office, March, 1966
47. U.S. Department of Labor. *Manpower Report of the President Including a Report on Manpower Requirements, Resources, Utilization, and Training.* Transmitted to Congress, April, 1968. Washington, D.C.: Government Printing Office, 1968. (Also, earlier Manpower Reports of the President.)
48. U.S. Department of Labor, Women's Bureau. "Why Women Work." August, 1966 (WB 67-6).
49. Wolfbein, Seymour L. *Occupational Information.* New York: Random House, 1968.
50. Yinger, J. Milton. *A Minority Group in American Society.* New York: McGraw-Hill, 1965.

Chapter 2

Adult Education Defined and Described

WAYNE L. SCHROEDER

Physical and social phenomena exist independently of men's efforts to understand, define and describe them. The moon, as a physical reality, existed prior to man's recorded history; yet only recently has it been described with any degree of certainty. Similarly, education as a social reality has existed in its rudimentary form as long as man himself; but only recently has it been specifically defined and institutionalized. So has it been with adult education—perhaps the adult educator like the astronaut is now bringing to the object of his concern (adult education) the powers of observation and analysis required for accurate definition and description.

According to most authors, the evolutionary process of adult education has accelerated since World War I—especially since 1930. An understanding of this period of heightened activity requires at the same time some knowledge of the highlights in the history of adult education in the United States. The early history of this country is fraught with educational episodes which in retrospect may be labeled adult education. Yet these episodes were not, at the time they emerged, considered a part of any global social enterprise. Quite the contrary, they were largely isolated efforts of a few people (sometimes an individual) concerned with either their own intellectual growth or the "catch-up" educative needs of a specific segment of society. Some of these early flowering episodes of adult education, dependent as they were on the shallow root systems of narrowly defined need, soon withered and died; others, attaching themselves to the deeper root systems of established social institutions, continued to grow into the twentieth century and there fed upon conditions of expanding industrialism, incorporation, governmental support and professionalism.

During the seventeenth and eighteenth centuries, adult education taking its cues from society's concern for man's salvation, was largely identified with the task of teaching adults how to read so they could attain salvation through the Holy Scriptures. This period was one of amelioration wherein adult education episodes were largely imbued with the concept of charity [35]. Along with the charity schools of this period came Benjamin Franklin's junto—a collection of people who gathered weekly to discuss morals, politics and natural philosophy.

Between the Revolutionary and Civil Wars adult education was identified more strongly with the need for an enlightened citizenry in a democratic society—that is, with the need for man to be aware of and to understand his environment and to function as a responsible citizen [29]. This period ushered in such agencies as the American Lyceum, local institutes (Lowell Institute and Cooper Union), libraries, museums and adult evening schools.

Finally, the years between the Civil War and World War I were characterized by accelerating growth in form and substance. Some of the forms emerging during this period included correspondence schools, university extension (general and agricultural) systems, residential labor colleges, social service agencies and numerous voluntary associations. The substantive concerns of adult education under the forceful influence of intensified industrialization, immigration, emancipation and urbanization shifted from general knowledge and enlightenment to specific program areas such as vocational education, citizenship education, Americanization and public affairs. Among the diversified concerns of adult educators during this period, the one which gained most prominence was the Americanization of the foreign born—exemplified by the establishment of the Department of Immigrant Education of the National Education Association in 1920, which became the Department of Adult Education in 1924.

Adult education, even prior to World War I, was on the way to broadening its clientele and its substantive and institutional bases. But "the emphasis had been primarily remedial to make up those education deficiencies brought on by a lack of schooling [6, p. 1]." In 1919, however, a significant report was issued by the Adult Education Committee of the British Ministry of Reconstruction which marked the beginning of a new era in adult education in both Great Britain and the United States —an era characterized by a broader perspective and greater commitment. The essence of this report is revealed in the following paragraph:

Adult Education Defined and Described

The necessary conclusion is that adult education must not be regarded as a luxury for a few exceptional persons here and there nor as a thing which concerns only a short span of early manhood, but that adult education is a permanent national necessity, an inseparable aspect of citizenship, and therefore should be both universal and life long. [6, p. 1]

In his examination of what he called the modern era of adult education, Cotton identifies three periods of growth (or rationale as he puts them) which are of particular interest [6]. In the first period (1919–1929)—one of idealism—adult education was seen primarily as an instrument of social reform, social reconstruction and social progress. Numerous professional associations for adult educators began to emerge. Perhaps the most significant happening, in this regard, was the establishment of the American Association for Adult Education in 1926—marked by Knowles as that point in history when adult education became publicly defined as a discrete field of social practice [22].

The second period (1930–1946) of the modern era, in contrast, was a period during which attempts were made to adjust ideals to that which could be judged realistic. The writings of the professional adult educator began to appear with some frequency appealing for more specificity in definition and description. It was in the early 1930's that the first graduate program of adult education was established at Columbia University.

Finally, the period 1947–1964 was characterized by intensified movement toward greater professionalism and institutionalization. This period was further marked by an expansion of graduate programs of adult education, the establishment of the Commission of Professors of Adult Education, the beginning of a National Seminar for Adult Education Research and a proliferation of written materials concerned with definitions and delineation of adult education as a field of research, professional study and practice.

Since efforts to define adult education have roughly paralleled the growing professionalism which has occurred since 1930, the following exploration of the term *adult education* will draw only upon material of that period.

Approaches to a Definition

Since 1930 there has been an erratic though discernible trend toward greater precision in defining adult education. This might have been expected. If a profession is to emerge, a field of practice must develop clear career patterns, attain general recognition and acceptance by those who will be served, and identify a body of knowledge to profess —all three of which depend, in turn, on precision of definition.

Some definitions have been broad and inclusive while others have been narrow and exclusive; some have been descriptive while others have been analytical. This diversity has undoubtedly been due in part to the inherent diversity of what is being defined. As Ziegler puts it,

> one cannot speak of "adult education" as one can speak of the public elementary and high school programs, and expect a common understanding of what is meant by the term. For in addition to the range of activities which comprise adult education, this branch of education has been and continues to be conducted by a multitude of contrasting institutions and agencies each providing according to its own plan (or) method. [38, p. 130]

There has been confusion in the use of the terms *adult education* and *continuing education.* Some people use the terms synonymously; some draw sharp lines of distinction between them; and still others seem unable to decide. At the operational level, it has become common for adult educators who function within the context of colleges and universities to refer to their activity as *continuing education* while referring to all other educative activities designed for adults as *adult education.* At the philosophical level another distinction has appeared—that *continuing education* identifies an ideal; whereas, *adult education* identifies a deliberate means (along with elementary, secondary and higher education) to facilitate the realization of that ideal. Stated another way, continuing education is that idealistic and timeless conceptual thread that connects all deliberate efforts to help the human organism learn throughout life.

The issue concerning the inclusion or exclusion of "self-managed" learning is still unresolved. Some writers insist that there must be an organizational base and an educational agent involved in the educative activity if it is to be considered adult education. However, the amount of so-called self-education is rapidly increasing in American society. It would appear that a rational way out of this dilemma would be to utilize the process of education as the criterion rather than the existence of an organizational base or the presence of an external educative agent (for example, a process that includes a learner, resources for learning and a degree of system or organization in the activity).

Another problem arises out of confusion between adult education as a field of study or body of knowledge and adult education as a field of educational practice. Those engaged in adult education as a field of study are concerned with building a body of tested knowledge about the practice of adult education and with the diffusion of that knowledge among those who are, or who will soon be, practicing adult educators—those who plan, conduct and evaluate educational activities for adults. The distinction here might be analogous to that drawn between the body of

Adult Education Defined and Described

knowledge about how the game of football should be played and the actual playing of the game.

There is still no single definition universally accepted by adult educators nor is there a universally held public image of adult education. The adult educator and layman alike naturally tend to define adult education within the limits of their own immediate experience with it. Accordingly, adult education has erroneously been equated with the adult educational activities of the public schools, or with such specific program areas as remedial or vocational–technical education. The identification of adult education as remedial education, so prominent in the past, has to some extent been revived with the growth of adult basic education programs since passage of the Economic Opportunity Act of 1964.

In reviewing and analyzing some of the definitions offered for the field since 1930, a framework adapted from the work of Upton and Samson will be used [32].

Definition by Classification

A classification definition includes genus and species terms as well as statements that tend to differentiate the species from its genus. Writers who use this approach focus their attention on current activities. Some specify all *adult* learning activity as the genus and adult educational activity as the species, while others specify all *educational* (i.e., including elementary and secondary schooling) activity as the genus and adult education activity as the species. Both approaches involve at some point the differentiation of educational and non-educational as well as adult and non-adult.

Among those who consider adult learning activity as the universe or genus is Gale Jensen [18]. He identifies two species of adult learning activity. One species occurs in what is called a "natural societal setting" while the other occurs in the context of "learning organizations." Jensen points out that in the first instance learning is not a consciously directed affair; in the second instance it is, resulting as it does in ". . . controlled participation in a limited number of engineered activities devoid of many of the stimuli and complexities characteristic of everyday life [18, p. 107]." In a more general sense, Bryson also used this approach when he defined adult education as "all the activities with an educational purpose that are carried on by people, engaged in the ordinary business of life [5, p. 3]."

Those authors who have started with or emphasized in their classification the genus all educational activity are also numerous. One such author is Blakely, who states, "I would take the adjective off adult education and preserve the unqualified noun education for the process of deliberately educed growth regardless of the person." In this statement, he clearly identifies adult education as a species of the genus education. He then goes on to furnish a differentiation for the species: ". . . the mature person more consciously holds the objective and more consciously experiences and more deliberately directs the process [37, pp. 142–143]." It is important to note that Blakely's last statement was not derived from the concept "education," but rather from his understanding of the concept "adulthood."

Along similar lines, Reeves, Fansler and Houle suggest that adult education is ". . . any purposeful effort toward self-development carried on by an individual without direct legal compulsion and without such efforts becoming his major field of activity [29, p. 10]." Here, as in other definitions, the term purposeful helps identify adult education with the genus "education." Additionally, the phrases, "without legal compulsion" and "without such efforts becoming his major field of activity"—identified by numerous others as the voluntary and part-time nature of adult education—help differentiate the species from the genus. Sworder adds some aspects to his definition which were not explicit in the preceding definitions: the substance of the activity is related to the social roles of adults; the activity is variable in terms of the time span covered, the format used and the environment in which it is found; and the activity is "dynamic" in nature [37].

Definition by Structure Analysis

Through this type of definition, the functional parts of a structure are identified, described and related to form a Gestalt or functional unit. The parts commonly isolated—by such authors as Houle [16], Knowles [21], Venner and Booth [35]—are leadership, goals, content, processes, agencies, program areas, and clientele. Adapted to adult education, definition by structure analysis describes reasonably well efforts which have been made to devise typologies for the field.

To identify and order adult education has been no small task. The complexity of the agency and program dimensions alone are overwhelming. Consider, for instance, the statement by Ziegler, who suggests that adult education now includes:

The credit and non-credit or 'informal' courses at all institutions of higher education open to adults; programs of public schools, evening high schools and junior colleges; the secretarial and vocational work offered at commercial schools; the technical and management courses given by technical institutions

Adult Education Defined and Described

and professional graduate schools as well as by business, religious, fraternal, professional and public affairs organizations, associations and clubs; the religious education, public affairs forums, and creative arts courses to be found in many churches and synagogues; the lectures, films, discussion groups, art fairs and music festivals offered by public libraries, museums, and other civic institutions; the home demonstration and technical–agricultural work provided by the Cooperative Extension Service; the courses offered by government agencies and the armed forces to government employees (and others); the field of community development; education by television, the Commercial Correspondence schools and home-study departments of many universities; and finally, the enormous and increasing amount of independent self-study or self-education. [38, p. 131]

Organizational Leadership

There are three kinds of organizations which by various means furnish direction and leadership to the field. These are graduate programs of adult education (i.e., professional preparation for adult educators), governmental and philanthropic organizations and professional associations (agency and nonagency based).

Graduate Programs. Graduate programs in adult education, starting from a few scattered courses offered by a handful of universities in the 1930's, have grown into reasonable uniform curricula offered by 19 universities at the doctoral level and approximately 30 at the master's level. This growth has been facilitated by activities of the Commission of the Professors of Adult Education (of the Adult Education Association of the USA), established in 1957. Faculty members in graduate programs have been responsible for the professional training of an ever growing number of adult educators. More than 700 persons have now received doctorates in adult education. Substantially larger numbers have secured master's degrees or been served through single courses, workshops and institutes. Equally important have been the contributions of professor and student alike in building a body of knowledge about adult education.

Governmental Agencies. The second cluster of leadership organizations includes governmental (federal and state) agencies and private philanthropic groups, which through their funding policies and information dissemination procedures affect the directions taken by adult education. One of the more significant developments in adult education at the federal level occurred in 1965 with the establishment in the U.S. Office of Education of the Bureau of Adult and Vocational Education under which was placed a division of Adult Education Programs. This bureau and the units which preceded it have served the field in a number of important ways—by increasing public awareness of the need for lifelong learning; by drawing the practitioner's attention to outstanding programs and practices; by identifying trends and implications for adult educators; by encouraging public support for adult education; and by helping to clarify goals and policies of the field [26].

Another body which renders valuable leadership to at least a segment of the field is the National Advisory Council on Extension and Continuing Education established under Title I of the Higher Education Act of 1965. This group is charged with the responsibility of examining all Federal Extension and continuing education programs and reporting its recommendations for better coordination and planning to Congress.

In addition to the Bureau and Council, units at various levels of the federal government influence the field, primarily through funding of special adult education programs. Just how numerous such units are was revealed in a report published by the Adult Education Association of the USA in 1966 which reveals that nearly every major unit of the federal government holds promise of some kind of support for adult education [10].

At the state level, there is now at least one individual who has been given full-time responsibility for adult education in every state department of education in the United States and its territories. In addition, a number of states have established representative committees to help plan and coordinate the activities of various agencies in the state. More of this kind of activity may be expected as a result of a shift in federal funding policies—away from working through only a few institutions at the state or local level and toward working through a variety of agencies. It has been suggested that this shift ". . . calls upon the federal government to assume responsibility in assuring that its grants do not create imbalance and disharmony in the states [26, p. 45]."

Several private philanthropic agencies also have rendered important leadership to the field by supplying financial support for certain kinds of research and program activity. Three foundations appear to have had the greatest impact on adult education: Carnegie, W. K. Kellogg, and Ford, which together have contributed more than $76 million to the field—most to support innovation and research [9; 23].

Professional Associations. The third type of leadership organization is the professional association. The only comprehensive association for adult educators is the Adult Education Association of the USA. All others are either outgrowths of a special concern of a relatively small group of adult educators (exemplified by the Adult Education Research Conference and the Commission of Professors of Adult Education) or are agency based

Adult Education Defined and Described

(exemplified by the National Association for Public Continuing and Adult Education, the Association of University Evening Colleges and the National University Extension Association). In 1964, the Ad Hoc Committee of Adult Education Organizations (now the Coalition of Adult Education Organizations) was formed to provide liaison among the major professional associations and to focus efforts on tasks which are the common concern of all.

Goals

As we have seen, adult education in the United States developed somewhat chaotically in response to a great variety of special interests and needs rather than systematically in response to some overall plan and purpose. Professional workers have tried to establish direction—a set of goals. Some have proceeded inductively, some deductively. A. A. Liveright was one who did attempt to derive goals inductively. After studying the adult education activities of governmental and nongovernmental agencies he induced four major goals for the field: "occupational, vocational and/or professional competence; personal and family living competence; social and civic responsibility; and self-fulfillment [26, p. 4]."

The major issue which has plagued efforts to derive goals deductively has been "individual needs vs. societal needs." Some authors emphasize the individual, some the society. Those who emphasize individual needs as a basis for goal formulation usually justify their positions either by pointing out that such an emphasis is of the essence of democracy or that if the needs of the individual are satisfied, then the needs of society will also be satisfied, since society consists of and exists for individuals. Words and phrases commonly used by those who emphasize individual needs are: skills and knowledge necessary to make judgments about social change; self-actualization; self-fulfillment; liberal education; self-expression; realization of potential; creative arts and leisure education. Blakely offers an example of individualism in his statement, "I accept as the purpose of adult education the fostering of the growth of what is individual in each human being and the harmonizing of individuality with social unity, which unity should be based on a respect for individuality [37, p. 142]." Kallen suggests that basic to a philosophy of adult education is the premise that education of the adult is the recognition of his individuality, and that education should be the enabling, creating, and maturing of an on-going process of self-differentiation [20].

Those who emphasize social needs in their formulations do so with the conviction that people do not really exist apart from groups and society—that out of people's relationships come a vast array of needs on which adult education should focus. Common in these formulations are such words and phrases as social roles, developmental tasks, institutional need, adjustment to change, and transmission of the cultural heritage.

Finally, in searching for an all inclusive goal for adult education, Hallenbeck suggests that the goal of adult education should be "the mature personality"—further described as a person who is able to live creatively with the "persistent paradoxes of human existence; stability and flexibility, balance and activity, conviction and uncertainty, steadfastness and tolerance." Such a goal would serve the field by: specifying the ultimate objective in line with which immediate objectives could be defined; furnishing a basis for bringing together all the many parts of the adult education enterprise; removing the necessity for competition and clarifying the appropriateness of specialization [12].

Content

The content of adult education has neither horizontal nor vertical limits—that is, instances of adult education can be found that touch every body of knowledge known to man and that involve all levels of sophistication within each body of knowledge. Any content at any level which reflects the adult's interest and need to know appears to be the legitimate concern of adult educators. Some of the content is selected to achieve cognitive ends (facts, principles, cognitive skills, and so on); some to achieve affective ends (interest, attitudes, values); and some to achieve psychomotor ends (manipulative skills). It may be obvious by now that adult educators, when speaking of content, usually refer to problem areas or social roles rather than disciplines or bodies of tested knowledge.

In examining the subject matter of courses in which adults participated in 1961–1962, Johnstone and Rivera found the vocational area to be most prominent, with approximately one-third of all courses so labeled. Hobbies and recreation activities represented a fifth, and general education, religion, and home and family life each represented approximately one-eighth of the courses. Such subject matter areas as personal development, public and current affairs and agriculture each constituted 5 percent or less of the courses reported [19].

Processes

Some authors still speak of processes (sometimes methodology) as a single collectivity, but there appears to be increasing acceptance of the need to differentiate according to specific functions served. Coolie Verner has been the strongest proponent for such differentiation [33]. Verner and Booth identify three separate elements of process, each of which

Adult Education Defined and Described

describes a discrete function. First, "method" concerns the ways in which people are organized in order to conduct an educational activity: "A method establishes a relationship between the learner and the institution or agency through which the educational task is accomplished." Youth education has been dominated by the so-called class method (that is, a teacher and pupils in a classroom) while adult education, not being so institutionalized, finds itself using a rich array of methods (for example, travel, study groups and discussion groups). Verner and Booth suggest that "methods of adult education tend to fall into a classification scheme that is predetermined by the ways in which people are naturally organized in society." Accordingly, they posit the existence of individual methods (correspondence study, apprenticeship, internship and directed individual study); group methods (class, discussion groups, workshops, institutes, meetings and forums); and community methods (studies that lead to community action) [35, pp. 68–69].

While the findings of Johnstone and Rivera confirm that there is considerable methodological variation, they also suggest that the class still prevails as a method [19]. More than half (56 percent) of the courses in which adults participated employed the class method. Group discussion and lectures or talks were also represented, each being employed in about one-tenth of the courses. Next in order were correspondence study, private teachers and on-the-job training (approximately 8 percent for each). Educational television was employed in only 1½ percent of the courses reported; however, television is utilized in many educative activities other than those encompassed by the term "course."

The second major element is "technique"—or the way in which the instructional agent establishes a relationship between the learner and the learning task. Decisions about the use of techniques are based primarily on the nature of the learning task and the learner himself. Accordingly, three subcategories of technique have been isolated—information giving techniques (lecture, speech, debate, symposium, panel, forum, and so on); skill acquiring techniques (process demonstration, role playing, drill, buzz groups, seminar, case study, simulated performance and so on) and knowledge applying techniques (group discussion, buzz groups, and so on).

The third element is the "device"—that which serves "to extend the effectiveness of methods and techniques but cannot itself instruct." Devices are classified according to their nature and function: illustrative devices (result demonstration, films and so on); extension devices (radio, television and so on); environmental devices (arrangement of seats, room illumination, types of seats and so on) and manipulation devices (working models, simulations and so on) [33].

There are four more factors to consider in the structure of adult education: individual leadership; agency bases; program areas and the adult clientele.

Individual Leadership

Adult educators rarely enjoy the security of a clearly defined position in an accepted institution. The majority of adult education activities are under the supervision of those who do not have a career identification with the field. Each of these persons in his own way ultimately has an effect on the structure of the field.

The quantitative and qualitative aspects of individual leadership in adult education are clearly specified by Houle in the formulation of what he calls "the pyramid of leadership." At the base of the pyramid is found the largest group of leaders—volunteer leaders—distributed among thousands of agencies. At the intermediate level of the pyramid appears a somewhat smaller group of leaders for whom adult education is a part-time responsibility (staff members in public libraries; faculty members in schools, colleges and universities who teach both young people and adults; public health nurses; social workers). At the apex of the pyramid is the group of leaders who commit themselves to careers in adult education—sometimes called professional adult educators (directors of adult education in public schools, universities, colleges, libraries, museums, social settlements and prisons; professors of adult education; directors of adult education activities of voluntary organizations; directors of training in government, in industry and in labor unions; and staff of the Cooperative Extension Service).

Agencies

Adult Education is based in a multiplicity of institutions and agencies. Johnstone and Rivera identified eight kinds of institutions or agencies that conducted courses for adults [19]. Churches and synagogues and colleges and universities each sponsored 21 percent of the courses reported. Community organizations ranked third with 15 percent; followed by business and industry and elementary and secondary schools, each with 12 percent. Private schools and government sponsored 7 percent of the courses reported; the armed forces 4 percent. Further examination of these data reveals that only 40 percent of all the courses reported were sponsored by those institutions commonly identified with education (colleges and universities, elementary and secondary schools and private schools). The remaining 60 percent of the courses were sponsored by a variety of agencies whose primary function is not normally considered to be education.

Adult Education Defined and Described

Amid such diversity, the need for a typology is obvious. The one to be introduced has been adapted from the work of Houle [16], Knowles [21], and Verner [35].

Type I Agencies established to serve the educational needs of adults—adult education is a central function. The number of kinds of agencies in this category is not great, and they are generally concerned with the satisfaction of specific educational needs of special group of adults (rather than with the development of comprehensive programs to satisfy all the unfulfilled educational needs of all adults in a community). Two examples are proprietary schools and independent residential and nonresidential adult education centers. Proprietary schools, which according to Knowles enroll twice the number of adults as do the public schools, include business schools, correspondence schools and technical schools [21]. Independent residential and nonresidential centers, though not widely diffused in the United States, are more common than is usually recognized.

Type II Agencies established to serve the educational needs of youth which have assumed the added responsibility of at least partially serving the educational needs of adults—adult education is a secondary function. Included here are the public schools (adult evening or day programs), junior colleges (community service or adult education divisions) and colleges and universities (general extension divisions, evening colleges, residential centers and Cooperative Extension Service).

Type III Agencies established to serve both educational and non-educational needs of the community—adult education is an allied function employed to fulfill only some of the needs which agencies recognize as their responsibility. Libraries, museums and health and welfare agencies constitute examples of agencies which, though established to serve the more general needs of a community, become involved with adult education as one means of satisfying part of their total purpose.

Type IV Agencies established to serve the special interests (economic, ideological) of special groups—adult education is a subordinate function employed primarily to further the special interests of the agency itself. Generally agencies in this category (examples being business and industry, labor unions, government, churches and voluntary associations) are concerned with adult education to the extent that such education contributes to the effectiveness of the agency in fulfilling its primary purpose—governing, selling and spreading a doctrine. There are exceptions. The programs of some of the agencies included in this general category do reflect greater altruism than our introductory statement might imply. Some correctional institutions, for instance, are offering inmates an array of educative activity which would more commonly be expected of a vital evening division of a public school. And some businesses and industries are broadening their programs to include such areas as liberal education, recreational education, and the basic education of the unskilled and underemployed.

There are other differences to be noted and generalizations to be made with regard to the four types of adult education agencies:

1. Agencies of the first two types are accepted and recognized by the general public as adult education agencies; the latter two types may not be seen in the same light.
2. Under the strictest definition, agencies of the first type are the only genuine adult education agencies existing in the United States today.
3. While agencies of the first three types tend to be oriented to people, agencies of the latter type tend to be oriented to the organization.
4. None of the four types of agencies can be regarded as comprehensive in its adult education efforts.
5. Agencies of one type often relate to agencies of another type to achieve their general or specific educational objectives. Thus libraries (Type III) may furnish materials to be used in connection with an adult education course offered by the public schools (Type II).
6. A discernible portion of the adult education activities of Type II agencies might more appropriately be labeled youth education for adults.

Program Areas

Program, like most other components of the adult education structure, has an illusive character. The term has been variously used to refer to: (1) all the educative activities available to adults of a community (e.g., "Miami's adult education program"); (2) the total adult education effort of a given agency (e.g., the public school's evening program, the university's extension program); (3) activities designed for segments of the population (e.g., adult education programs for physicians); (4) social roles with which activities are related (e.g., home and family life education, citizenship); and (5) the nature of a specific activity (e.g., a course in remedial reading, or a lecture series on domestic issues).

The term *curriculum* is often used interchangeably with *program*. *Adult* educators are more inclined to use program, however. They desire to shake free from the restrictive and youth-oriented meanings which have attached themselves to the term curriculum.

Adult Clientele

The concept *adult*, in *adult education* has been defined in a number of ways. Verner cites three: by age, psychological maturity and social roles [34]. The term *psychological maturity* is functionally unmanageable and that of age tends to exclude groups of individuals who should be included. The result is that most administrators and researchers select criteria related to social roles. For example, two of the three criteria selected by Johnstone and Rivera are related to social roles (married or head of a household) and the other is related to age (21 years or older). Perhaps the most operational of all definitions (related to social roles) is this one: *An adult is anyone who has either discontinued or completed his formal education and is now trying to re-engage in the educational process.*

The question of who are the clients of adult education is summarily answered by Johnstone and Rivera. The authors found that:

The adult education participant is just as often a woman as a man, is typically under forty, has completed high school or more, enjoys an above average income, works full-time and most often in a white-collar occupation, is married and has children, lives in an urbanized area but more likely in a suburb than a large city, and is found in all parts of the country, but more frequently in the West than in other regions. [19, p. 8]

Definition by Operation Analysis

A third kind of analytical definition is called definition by operation analysis, which is appropriate "wherever words to be defined are the names of operations [32, p. 177]." Included in such definitions are the purpose of the operation and the functioning of the parts to achieve the purpose. Operation analysis seems to describe most closely the efforts of those who have referred to adult education as a process with a purpose and a system of elements or suboperations.

Verner, as he formulated his definitions of adult education, suggested that education is "the creation and maintenance of instructional situations that provide experiences in which both information and the control of the appropriate intellectual behavior are systematically and simultaneously acquired." Verner combines his insights into the concepts of "education" and "adulthood" to form this definition of adult education:

Adult education is a relationship between an educational agent and a learner in which the agent selects, arranges, and continuously directs a sequence of progressive tasks that provide systematic experience to achieve learning for those whose participation in such activities is subsidiary and supplemental to a primary productive role in society. [34, pp. 30–32]

It appears that Verner would assign most of the instructional decisions to what he calls the educational agent.

Essert was also moving in the direction of defining adult education by operation analysis when he stated:

Adult education is an experience of maturing, voluntarily selected by people whose major occupation is no longer that of going to school or college, in which these individuals or groups plan meaningful tasks and apply sustained inquiry to them. . . . the major portion of adult education in the nation is engaged in helping people meet their individual needs as they are interpreted by individuals themselves. [8, pp. 5, 8]

Essert strongly implies that when the process of education is adapted to the adult situation some significant changes take place in the operation of its parts—changes which would allow for considerable more involvement of the participant than that recognized by Verner.

Houle has offered still a third example of definition by operation analysis. He recognizes the situation in which an external agent makes most of the decisions and imposes the process of education as well as the situation in which the participants make many or all of the decisions that affect the structure and sequence of their learning experience. According to Houle adult education is the process by which men and women (alone or in groups) attempt to improve themselves by increasing their skills or knowledge, developing their insights or appreciations or changing their attitudes; or the process by which individuals or agencies attempt to change men and women in these ways.

Continued employment of this approach to definition would surely lead to research to determine how components of the instructional operation should be altered to fit the adult learning circumstance or circumstances. Moreover, the instructional operation, once set, could be used to weave diverse elements of the field together.

References

1. Bergevin, Paul. *A Philosophy for Adult Education.* New York: Seabury Press, 1967.
2. Blakely, Robert J. "What Is Adult Education?" *Handbook of Adult Education in the United States.* Edited by Malcolm S. Knowles. Chicago, Ill.: Adult Education Association of the USA, 1960.
3. Boyd, R. D. "Psychological Definition of Adult Education." *Adult Leadership,* XV (November, 1966), pp. 160–162.

Adult Education Defined and Described 41

4. Broudy, Harry S. *Aims in Adult Education: A Realist's View.* (Notes and Essays on Education for Adults. No. 28.) Chicago, Ill.: Center for the Study of Liberal Education for Adults, 1960.
5. Bryson, Lyman. *Adult Education.* New York: American Book Company, 1936.
6. Cotton, Webster E. *On Behalf of Adult Education: An Historic Examination of the Supporting Literature.* (Notes and Essays on Education for Adults. No. 56.) Boston, Mass.: Center for the Study of Liberal Education for Adults, 1968.
7. Dickerman, Watson. "What Is This 'Continuing Education'?" *Adult Education,* XV (Autumn, 1964), pp. 3–9.
8. Essert, Paul. *Creative Leadership of Adult Education.* Englewood Cliffs, N.J.: Prentice-Hall, 1951.
9. Essert, Paul. "Foundations and Adult Education." *Handbook of Adult Education in the United States.* Edited by Malcolm S. Knowles. Chicago, Ill.: Adult Education Association of the USA, 1960, pp. 230–237.
10. *Federal Support for Adult Education: A Directory of Programs and Services.* Washington, D.C.: The Adult Education Association of the USA, 1966.
11. Godbey, G. C. "After All, What Is Adult Education?" *Adult Leadership,* XV (November, 1966), p. 165.
12. Hallenbeck, Wilbur. *Some Philosophical Considerations With Reference to Adult Education.* n.d. (Mimeographed.)
13. Hallenbeck, Wilbur. "The Role of Adult Education in Society." *Adult Education: Outlines of an Emerging Field of University Study.* Edited by Gale Jensen, A. A. Liveright and Wilbur Hallenbeck. Washington, D.C.: Adult Education Association of the USA, 1964, pp. 5–25.
14. Hendrickson, Andrew. "Adult Education." *The Encyclopedia of Educational Research* (3d ed.). Edited by Chester W. Harris. New York: The Macmillan Company, 1960.
15. Houle, Cyril O. "The Education of Adult Educational Leaders." *Handbook of Adult Education in the United States.* Edited by Malcolm S. Knowles. Chicago, Ill.: Adult Education Association of the USA, 1960, pp. 117–128.
16. Houle, Cyril O. "The Emergence of Graduate Study in Adult Education." *Adult Education: Outlines of an Emerging Field of University Study.* Edited by Gale Jensen, A. A. Liveright and Wilbur Hallenbeck. Washington, D.C.: Adult Education Association of the USA, 1964, pp. 69–83.
17. Houle, Cyril O., and Buskey, John H. "The Doctorate in Adult Education, 1935–1965." *Adult Education,* XVI (Spring, 1966), pp. 131–168.
18. Jensen, Gale. "How Adult Education Borrows and Reformulates Knowledge of Other Disciplines." *Adult Education: Outlines of an Emerging Field of University Study.* Edited by Gale Jensen, A. A. Live-

right and Wilbur Hallenbeck. Washington, D.C.: Adult Education Association of the USA, 1964, pp. 105–111.
19. Johnstone, John W. C., and Rivera, Ramon J. *Volunteers for Learning: A Study of the Educational Pursuits of American Adults.* Chicago, Ill.: Aldine, 1965.
20. Kallen, Horace M. "On Liberating Adults: A Philosophy for Adult Education." *Adult Leadership,* XIII (October, 1964), pp. 98–100.
21. Knowles, Malcolm S. "The Field of Operations in Adult Education." *Adult Education: Outlines of an Emerging Field of University Study.* Edited by Gale Jensen, A. A. Liveright and Wilbur Hallenbeck. Washington, D.C.: Adult Education Association of the USA, 1964, pp. 41–67.
22. Knowles, Malcolm S. "What Do We Know About the Field of Adult Education?" *Adult Education,* XIV (Winter, 1964), pp. 67–79.
23. Knowles, Malcolm S. *The Adult Education Movement in the United States.* New York: Holt, Rinehart & Winston, 1962.
24. Kreitlow, Burton W. *Relating Adult Education to Other Disciplines.* Madison, Wis.: University of Wisconsin Press, 1964.
25. Lindeman, Edward C. *The Meaning of Adult Education.* Montreal, Canada: Harvest House, 1961.
26. Liveright, A. A. *A Study of Adult Education in the United States.* Boston, Mass.: Center for the Study of Liberal Education for Adults, 1968.
27. London, Jack, and Wenkert, Robert. *Some Reflections on Defining Adult Education.* Berkeley, Calif.: Survey Research Center, University of California, 1963. (Mimeographed.)
28. McMahon, Ernest E.; Coates, Robert H.; and Knox, Alan B. "Common Concerns: The Position of the Adult Education Association of the USA" *Adult Education,* XVIII (1968), pp. 197–213.
29. Ohliger, John. *Introduction to Adult Education: Syllabus for Education 672.* Columbus, Ohio: Ohio State University. (Mimeographed.)
30. Thomas, Alan. "Reflections on the Present State of Adult Education." *Adult Leadership,* XVI (May, 1967), pp. 17–18.
31. Tough, Allen. "The Assistance Obtained by Adult Self-Teachers." *Adult Education,* XVII (Autumn, 1966), pp. 30–33.
32. Upton, Albert, and Samson, Richard W. *Creative Analysis.* New York: E. P. Dutton, 1961.
33. Verner, Coolie. *Adult Education Theory and Method: A Conceptual Scheme for the Identification and Classification of Processes.* Chicago, Ill.: Adult Education Association of the USA, 1962.
34. Verner, Coolie. "Definition of Terms." *Adult Education: Outlines of an Emerging Field of University Study.* Edited by Gale Jensen, A. A. Liveright and Wilbur Hallenbeck. Washington, D.C.: Adult Education Association of the USA, 1964, pp. 27–39.
35. Verner, Coolie, and Booth, Alan. *Adult Education.* Washington, D.C.: The Center for Applied Research in Education, 1964.
36. Watson, Eugene R. "A New Identity Crisis in Adult Education?" *Adult Leadership,* XIV (June, 1965), p. 51.

37. "What Is Adult Education? Nine 'Working Definitions.'" *Adult Education*, V (Spring, 1955), pp. 131–145.
38. Ziegler, Jerome. "Continuing Education in the University." *The Contemporary University*. Edited by Robert S. Morrison. Boston, Mass.: Houghton Mifflin Co., 1966.

Chapter 3

The International Dimension

A. A. LIVERIGHT

JOHN OHLIGER

Until the last decade the field of adult education lagged behind other educational fields in the number of international exchanges of practitioners and professors, in participation in international organizations, and in international studies. Adult education may still be behind, but in the last ten years significant strides have been made. It would have been unlikely for a chapter with this title to have appeared in an earlier edition of this Handbook. Indeed, one important trend in adult education is its increasingly international character.

In these days of a nuclear threat of extinction and the rapidity of global communication and transportation it should be unnecessary to justify U.S. interest in the international dimension of adult education. The skeptic should examine two points: first, foreign involvement on the part of American adult educators may help promote the cause of international understanding, world peace and brotherhood. Perhaps with more knowledge of one another there will be less chance of misunderstandings that lead to conflict. Second, our own practices at home can be improved by making comparisons with programs in other countries, both developing countries and those with extensive educational traditions. John Lowe, the director of the Department of Adult Education and Extra-Mural Studies at the University of Edinburgh, has pointed out that "developing countries have shown they can make a significant reciprocal contribution. Faced with unprecedented problems they have resorted to original solutions. They are also uninhibited by some of the time-honored practices in developed countries which are no longer necessarily relevant to contemporary social needs [18]."

A. A. Liveright recently conducted a study of adult education for the U.S. Government. He made this recommendation, which is now being studied:

> Relevant experiences in other nations should be reviewed. Experiences in Israel in residential basic literacy education, Scandinavian experiences in meeting the educational needs of young adults, part-time college programs and correspondence, education experiences within the Soviet bloc—all may be relevant to adult education needs at home, particularly for the education of the disadvantaged. It is suggested that qualified researchers be called upon to submit relevant proposals to the U.S. Office of Education Bureau of Research and to the Cooperative Research Program for study grants. [15, p. 125]

And John Ohliger has written a monograph pointing out ways in which the U.S. could benefit from studying systematically the adult education activities of 30 other countries [19].

Two factors have inhibited the growth of international activities in American adult education: first, adult education has been slow to emerge as a legitimate area of university study and professional preparation. Thus many universities, the institutions often involved in international studies, have not focused on adult education, least of all, foreign adult education. Second, adult education has developed in such different ways and been defined so differently in various countries, it has been difficult to make useful comparisons. As Knowles has stated:

> In England and Sweden, for example, adult education evolved essentially as national movements for the education of workers. In Denmark a network of folk schools was created for the express purpose of refashioning a national culture. In most underdeveloped countries adult education has been used primarily as a means for eliminating illiteracy. In the Soviet Union adult education has served as an instrument of state policy directed at producing loyalty to the state and developing technical competencies required by national plans. . . . In the United States, on the other hand, the national adult education program has proliferated almost haphazardly in response to myriad individual needs and interests. [14, p. v]

Toward an Internationally Acceptable Definition of Adult Education

In the fall of 1967 F. W. Jessup and E. K. Townsend Coles, two officers of the Delegacy of Extra-Mural Studies at the University of Oxford, said flatly, "There is no internationally accepted definition of

The International Dimension

adult education [12, p. 9]." However, in the fall of 1968 John Lowe wrote that "the emergence of a world consensus about the aims of adult education is now evident [18]." Lowe may have been responding to the impact of an international conference that took place in the summer of 1966. At that time twenty-six adult educators from eight countries met in Exeter, New Hampshire, to explore comparative approaches to the field. After much discussion the participants agreed on the following as a potentially acceptable international definition of adult education:

Adult education is a process whereby persons who no longer attend school on a regular and full-time basis (unless full-time programs are especially designed for adults) undertake sequential and organized activities with the conscious intention of bringing about changes in information, knowledge, understanding, or skills, appreciation and attitudes; or for the purpose of identifying and solving personal or community problems. [17, p. 8]

The conference also agreed on this definition of an adult: "An adult is a person who no longer attends school as a primary or full-time activity and who is over twenty-one years of age."

At UNESCO and in many countries "adult education" is used as a generic term meaning "the education of men and women," and including any form of education. More and more the lower age boundary is not 21 but the age at which a person is no longer required legally to be in school.

Gaining currency internationally, mainly through the efforts of UNESCO, is a concept allied to adult education—that of *education permanente*, or "lifelong integrated education." In years past when adult educators spoke of "lifelong learning" some of them were referring to education during the adult years. Now educators of all types throughout the world are beginning to speak of lifelong integrated education or *education permanente* as a concept of a planned, integrated educational system, stretching from the home and nursery schools through elementary, secondary, post-secondary and higher education, and extending through all the adult years [7, p. 8].

At the 1965 meeting of UNESCO's International Committee for the Advancement of Adult Education the participants recommended that UNESCO endorse and promote this definition of *education permanente:*

The animating principle of the whole process of education, regarded as continuing throughout an individual's life from his earliest childhood to the end of his days, and therefore calling for integrated organization. The necessary integration should be achieved both vertically, throughout the duration of life, and horizontally to cover all the various aspects of the life of individuals and societies. [22, p. 8]

International Organizations and Conferences

Perhaps the most promising development in the international field is the growing number of organizations formed and conferences held. There have been three general world conferences of adult educators; a conference was sponsored in London in 1929 by the no longer existing World Association for Adult Education; UNESCO sponsored conferences in 1949 in Elsinore, Denmark, and in 1950 in Montreal, Canada. There have also been plans to hold conferences and form international organizations devoted to specific studies, particular functions, or in geographic regions.

Within UNESCO itself there has been since 1947 a department concerned with adult education. J. Roby Kidd, former chairman of UNESCO's Committee on Adult Education, comments that the UNESCO department "is limited in numbers of staff and some of the staff members are lacking in experience. Publishing has been infrequent, there has been little organized research, and the UNESCO journal on youth and adult education which was published for many years was discontinued in 1966. Despite the difficulties and limitations, UNESCO does provide a means by which communications at the official level can be conducted [20, p. 6]." It has been noted that the concept of *education permanente* has received worldwide attention through UNESCO. Outside of the activities of the department UNESCO has sponsored a number of international meetings of adult educators on such topics as education of women, the role of schools and universities, and the problem of leisure. The worldwide campaign to eliminate illiteracy has been planned and fostered by UNESCO.

Specialized Organizations

A number of specialized organizations have been formed. Kidd notes that:

The three international labor organizations each has an adult education program. One of them, the International Confederation of Free Trade Unions, sponsored a world conference on labor education and a labor film festival in Montreal in 1967. The International Workers' Education Association has been in existence since the thirties, holds annual seminars and conferences and publishes a journal. The International Cooperative Alliance has carried on an education program, and maintained relations around consumer education for at least two decades. [20]

Two functional organizations have been initiated to focus attention

The International Dimension

in schools and universities. The Adult Education Committee of the World Confederation of the Teaching Professions (WCOTP) was formed in 1959 at an international meeting in Washington, D.C. Robert Luke of the National Education Association's Division of Adult Education has been secretary and responsible for much of the effective work of the committee. It has met annually (usually in the city where WCOTP was meeting) since its inception, often assisting to sponsor a regional conference at the same time. And it has published material on such subjects as literacy, preparation of teachers, and *education permanente*.

In September, 1960, immediately after the UNESCO World Conference on Adult Education in Montreal, a group of 35 adult educators from universities in 14 countries met at the Sagamore Conference Center of Syracuse University and organized the International Congress of University Adult Education. From the beginning the Congress was provided with its secretary by the Center for the Study of Liberal Education for Adults. The Congress has sponsored one world and several international meetings of university adult educators, promoted the study of comparative adult education, and published a journal and occasional papers.

Regional Associations

The last decade has seen the blossoming of a number of regional associations of adult educators. Earliest to form, soon after the end of World War II, was the European Bureau of Adult Education which involves representatives from 12 Western European countries. Adult educators in Eastern Europe meet annually on a largely informal basis. In 1964 both the African Adult Education Association and the Asian South Pacific Bureau of Adult Education were established. Both groups publish journals. In 1966 a regional organization for adult educators was formed in Latin America. It is still in the embryo stage, but it is hoped that it will work with the new Inter-American Committee on Adult Education begun in the summer of 1968 at Mexico City. The Mexico meeting followed the international conference of 1967 in Montreal, which was well attended by representatives from the U.S., Canada and Mexico.

For many years the Adult Education Association of the USA has shown interest in international activity. Each national conference features an "international luncheon" with a renowned speaker. The 1968 conference considered a resolution to change the name of the organization to the Adult Education Association of America. The resolution was defeated on the grounds that this name might impinge on the activities of the Canadian Association for Adult Education. (A similar debate had gone on at the inaugural conference of AEA–USA in 1951.) The executive committee of the AEA was instructed to promote international interests in other ways. Some adult educators also take part in organizations such as the Society for International Development, based in Washington, D.C., which enrolls several thousand members, most of whom have worked abroad.

Foreign Travel by Adult Educators

A valuable side effect of international organizations and international conferences is that they provide opportunities for adult educators to learn about programs in other countries. During the past ten years there has been a marked increase in the number of United States adult educators visiting programs overseas either on sabbatical arrangements or on other kinds of briefer visits. UNESCO has published a guide for adult educators interested in studying abroad—many of them through the U.S. Agency for International Development. In reverse, the number of adult educators from overseas who visit adult education activities in the United States and Canada has risen significantly. Several university adult educators have had their visits to institutions in the United States arranged by the International Congress of University Adult Education during the last six to eight years—some with their expenses covered by grants from the Carnegie Corporation or the Ford Foundation. In addition persons active in public school adult education and labor education have also visited the United States.

Though the travel situation has improved it is still far from ideal for adult educators. The Institute of International Education reports there are now more international exchanges of personnel than ever before in history [27]. Yet one recent study indicates that adult educators traveling and working abroad comprise only about 5 percent of the exchanges [9]. During an extended international trip, A. A. Liveright found an additional problem. Although provisions for overseas study grants, Fulbrights, British Council Grants and similar arrangements have been useful in bringing some persons from Southeast Asia, India, Australia and New Zealand to North America and the United Kingdom, the influential educators, those in the best position to have a substantial continuing impact on the development of adult education in their home countries, haven't always been involved in such programs. There appears to be a definite need for more effective identification of people who can make a lasting contribution to such development and who will have the support of key persons in universities and government to develop long-term plans when they return. And the need also exists to make certain these people have the opportunity to observe programs in countries which have some experience directly relevant to the needs in their own country.

International Understanding

Even without foreign travel, adult educators can contribute to programs that promote international understanding. Jessup and Coles point out that though

little is known about the precise effect of educational efforts designed to promote . . . international and inter-racial understanding . . . in education, especially in these two areas, there must be an element of faith, of casting one's bread upon the waters; and, at least for the present, educators must accept that as part of their lot. [12]

According to Eugene Johnson, the United States voluntary associations (e.g., the YMCA and American Friends Service Committee) play a very important role in adult education for international understanding [13]. Johnson estimates that there are 400 non-governmental organizations conducting programs of education about various aspects of international affairs for American adults. (This number doesn't include the many groups whose primary mission is to lobby for or against particular legislative measures.) But despite the large number of groups in the field, Johnson concludes that comparatively few people are involved in the programs. He calls for voluntary organizations to work more closely with universities and to make use of the latest innovations in programming techniques.

Comparative Adult Education Courses

Another more specific and more focused way of promoting international understanding is through offering comparative adult education courses by those engaged in providing graduate professional training in adult education in the university. The last decade has seen the introduction of such courses into graduate programs. Here are some of the significant developments:

- Since 1965 the University of California at Los Angeles has been offering seminars in comparative adult education.
- Cornell University presents a graduate course in the international aspects of agricultural extension.
- There is a new graduate program in international adult education (formerly at Boston University) at Syracuse University.
- The Ohio State University offers a seminar in comparative adult education.
- During the summer of 1967 and again in 1968, John Lowe, professor at the University of Edinburgh, taught at the University of Michigan where he placed considerable emphasis on comparative

adult education. Much material on comparative studies is included in the regular program at Michigan.

Florida State University conducted a survey of training needs of adult educators in Central and South America and plans to establish an Inter-American training program within its Department of Adult Education.

The Department of Adult Education of the Ontario Institute for Studies in Education organized graduate courses in comparative adult education in 1967. The department publishes a quarterly journal of comparative studies [2]; it held an international seminar on methodology for comparative studies in 1968 [20].

Indiana University recently instituted a course in comparative adult education. Several faculty members there have had a long interest in the subject. Since 1961 the university's Bureau of Studies in Adult Education has been publishing a series of monographs on foreign adult education. Three have now appeared: Sweden, Liberia and Finland. Doctoral candidates in the Indiana program are encouraged to learn a Scandinavian language in order to facilitate their study of adult education in that part of the world.

In 1966 the International Congress of University Adult Education, in cooperation with the New England Center for Continuing Education and the Center for the Study of Liberal Education for Adults, arranged the First International Conference on Comparative Adult Education. Twenty-six persons attended: eight from overseas, five from Canada and thirteen from the USA. The report of the Conference was published as *The Exeter Papers* [17]. A second conference was held at Syracuse University before the 1969 Galaxy Conference of Adult Education Organizations in Washington, D.C.

Partly as a result of much of the above-mentioned effort at graduate schools and the experience of American educators abroad, the number of American doctoral dissertations concerning adult education in other countries has been steadily increasing. (So has the number of foreign students studying adult education in American universities.) The Commission of Professors of Adult Education (AEA) has a committee on comparative education to facilitate exchange of information relating to these kinds of activities.

International Adult Education

Generally, American foundations have supplied meager support for adult education programs overseas, but there are distinguished exceptions. The Carnegie Foundation awarded grants to support adult educa-

The International Dimension

tion in Kenya and the study of in-service training of teachers in Africa. Under Carnegie's Commonwealth program, adult educators from 20 countries have been brought to the United States. Other American interest has been concentrated on the sub-fields of literacy education, the Peace Corps, community development, management and labor education, correspondence instruction, religious education and health and nutrition.

Literacy Education. Probably the greatest concentration of international interest has been in this area. Since 1947, but particularly since 1960, UNESCO has mounted a worldwide campaign to eradicate illiteracy. The first global survey of a specific field of adult education was focused on literacy [5]. In 1966 the Committee on Adult Education of the World Confederation of Organizations of the Teaching Profession conducted an international workshop in Korea on "The Role of Teachers' Organization in Adult Literacy Education." Two private associations operated from the United States, World Literacy Incorporated and the programs associated with the Laubachs, have had a marked impact on literacy work in many parts of the world. Despite the attention paid to this field of work, however, it is interesting to note that at a UNESCO sponsored World Congress of Ministers of Education on the Eradication of Illiteracy in 1965 it was agreed that, "international cooperation and assistance have hitherto been far less generous in literacy teaching and adult education than in other fields of education [26, p. 33]."

Peace Corps. The Peace Corps has trained more persons for overseas work than any other civilian government agency. It has been found that the recipients of this training, mainly young people, are eminently suited to educating adults [21, p. viii]. This runs counter to the notion that only older people can educate adults. There is also the strong possibility that many of the concepts and approaches emerging from the Peace Corps experience overseas can be applied in the United States by adult educators working among the disadvantaged.

Community Development. The U.S. Agency for International Development (AID) has employed many adult educators to work as community developers in overseas technical assistance programs. Many of the lessons learned abroad are now being applied in the United States [23].

Management and Labor. Many universities are now offering special training programs for businessmen who plan to work overseas [8]. On the other hand, labor unions have concentrated less on training their professionals for overseas work and more on providing skill training for foreign labor leaders in the developing countries [29].

Other Forms of Education. Many churches are engaged in foreign mission work with a strong adult education component. The YMCA World Service, primarily with North American help, sends persons abroad to help start YMCAs and to do many forms of recreation, physical education, agricultural education, and community development. Through AID, the United States Department of Health, and private foundations, there have been substantial programs in health education in the greater share of the developing countries. The U.S. Department of Agriculture has sent hundreds of technicians abroad during the past thirty years to help train extension personnel and various other kinds of specialists.

Those who conduct education by correspondence have been meeting in an international association for more than a decade. American educators have contributed much to the exchange of information in this field. A notable example is Charles Wedemeyer at the University of Wisconsin who has trained educators from many countries in the organization and techniques of correspondence education [28].

Conclusions and Recommendations

Encouraging as are the various activities in international adult education, the increasing domestic interest about developments in adult education overseas, and the increasing exchange of persons from all around the world involved in adult education, there are a number of needs which are important to try to meet in the years just ahead.

At the present moment international activities in adult education are still at an early stage. They are not as well organized as they should be. Only meager funds are available for international exchange of information and people and for research. The following recommendations for improvement have been derived from a number of sources:

1. Through more effective financing and more active programs, there should be expansion of the two major associations concerned with international adult education: the International Congress of University Adult Education and the Adult Education Committee of the World Confederation of Organizations of the Teaching Profession. These two associations have the potential for improving and expanding their programs in the next decade. However, they will be unlikely to do so unless they have more financial support and a resultant increase in staff and funds for publications and the conducting of regional as well as world meetings.
2. There is a great need for more effective relationships between the increasing number of regional adult education organizations around the world. Many of these associations, handicapped

The International Dimension

though they are by inadequate resources, are serving well their own regions but none of them, as yet, is active in maintaining relations with other regional bodies.
3. Despite the fact that a number of national organizations are issuing worthwhile publications, little is done to insure that these publications reach the large international audience interested in them. Steps should be taken to provide for more effective distribution of these publications on a worldwide basis.
4. In addition to improving the distribution of national publications, there is an urgent need to more effectively distribute the international publications in adult education that already exist. Although the publication issued by the International Congress of University Adult Education [10] and the Adult Education Committee of the World Confederation of Organizations of the Teaching Profession are good beginnings, they are occasional and limited in scope.
5. Wider international participation in the increasingly effective national and regional adult education conferences should be provided for. Little effort is now made to let adult educators in various parts of the world know about annual conferences and international meetings of all kinds or to invite overseas adult educators to participate in regional and national conferences. Procedures should be developed to inform adult educators throughout the world of conferences they might be interested in attending.
6. There is need for securing greater participation of United States adult educators in overseas adult education conferences. In addition, funds should be made available to permit formal visits to overseas adult educators. With the decrease in grants from the Carnegie Corporation and the Ford Foundation, new sources of funds must be found.
7. An increasing number of overseas adult educators have had opportunities to carry on graduate studies in the United States and U.S. adult educators are beginning to find chances to carry on fellowship work as well as to serve as observers or visiting professors in overseas institutions. On the whole, however, these exchanges are rather limited and depend to a great extent on personal contacts. Such activities should be more adequately planned and greatly enlarged.
8. The ERIC research dissemination program now operating for the field of adult education at Syracuse University should be expanded so it can deal more effectively with international organizations, associations, and activities in adult education.

References

1. Caldwell, T. B. *French Universities and Adult Education.* Occasional Paper/1. Chicago, Ill., International Congress of University Adult Education, 1962.
2. *Convergence: An International Journal of Adult Education.* Ontario, Canada: The Ontario Institute for Studies in Education.
3. ERIC Clearinghouse on Adult Education. *Adult Education in Africa.* Current Information Series, No. 12. Syracuse, N.Y.: ERICAE, 1968.
4. ERIC Clearinghouse on Adult Education. *Adult Education in Asia, Australia and New Zealand.* Current Information Series, No. 13. Syracuse, N.Y.: ERICAE, 1968.
5. Hamori, Anne, and Dottrens, Robert. *Literacy and Education for Adults: Research in Comparative Education.* Paris: UNESCO, 1964.
6. Harrison, Roger, and Hopkins, Richard L. "The Design of Cross-Cultural Training." *The Journal of Applied Behavioral Science,* III (December, 1967), pp. 431–460.
7. Hely, A. S. M. "UNESCO and the Concept of 'Education permanente.'" *Indian Journal of Adult Education,* XXVIII (December, 1967).
8. Hitchen, David E. "International Business Education: The Executive's Viewpoint." *Training and Development Journal,* XXII (February, 1968).
9. Hyman, Herbert H., and others. *Inducing Social Change in Developing Countries.* New York: United Nations Research Institute for Social Development, 1967.
10. *International Congress of University Adult Education Journal.* Syracuse, N.Y.: ICUAE.
11. International Congress of University Adult Education. *Study Abroad for Adult Educators.* Paris: UNESCO/WS/0764.114 (IES), September 30, 1964.
12. Jessup, F. W., and Coles, E. K. Townsend. *International and Interracial Understanding: The Contribution of Adult Education.* London: National Institute of Adult Education, 1967.
13. Johnson, Eugene. *What Future for Voluntary Associations in International Education?* Washington, D.C.: Adult Education Association of the USA, 1967.
14. Knowles, Malcolm S., *The Adult Education Movement in the U.S.* New York: Holt, Rinehart & Winston, 1962.
15. Liveright, A. A. *A Study of Adult Education in the United States.* Brookline, Mass.: Center for the Study of Liberal Education for Adults, 1968.
16. Liveright, A. A., ed. *The Concept of Lifelong Integrated Learning "Education Permanente" and Some Implications for University Adult Education.* Occasional Paper/11. Brookline, Mass.: International Congress of University Adult Education, 1968. ·
17. Liveright, A. A., and Haygood, Noreen, eds. *The Exeter Papers: Report of*

First International Conference on the Comparative Study of Adult Education. Brookline, Mass.: Center for the Study of Liberal Education for Adults, 1968.
18. Lowe, John. "Recent International Trends in Adult Education." *Scottish Adult Education,* XLVIII (September, 1968).
19. Ohliger, John. *Listening Groups: Mass Media in Adult Education.* Brookline, Mass.: Center for the Study of Liberal Education for Adults, 1967.
20. Ontario Institute for Studies in Education. *Report of Seminar on Comparative Studies in Adult Education.* Toronto, Canada: OISE, 1968.
21. Pagano, Jules. *Education in the Peace Corps.* Brookline, Mass.: Center for the Study of Liberal Education for Adults, 1965.
22. *Report of the Third Session: International Committee for the Advancement of Adult Education.* Paris: UNESCO/ED/219 (February 23, 1966).
23. Shields, James J., Jr., *Education in Community Development.* New York: Frederick A. Praeger, 1967.
24. Ulich, Mary Ewen. *Patterns of Adult Education: A Comparative Study.* New York: Pageant Press, 1965.
25. UNESCO. *International Directories of Education: Adult Education.* Paris: UNESCO/ED.65/XV.4/AF (1966).
26. UNESCO. *Literacy as a Factor in Development.* Paris: UNESCO/CS/0765.27/EDA.8 (WS) (1965).
27. "U.S. Educational Exchange, 1966–67." *Bulletin, International Association of Universities,* XVI (August, 1968).
28. Wedemeyer, Charles A., ed. *The Brandenburg Memorial Essays on Correspondence Instruction.* Madison, Wis.: University Extension, University of Wisconsin, 1966.
29. Zack, Arnold. *Labor Training in Developing Countries.* New York: Frederick A. Praeger, 1964.

Chapter 4

Program Development and Evaluation

PATRICK G. BOYLE

IRWIN R. JAHNS

Two of the more perplexing words in the jargon of the adult educator are the terms program and evaluation. They are perplexing because they are used to communicate many divergent thoughts, ideas and practices. The variety of terms used—program, curriculum, curriculum development, programming, program implementation and program administration—offer ample evidence of the diversity and ambiguity involved. The task of this chapter, however, is not to explore the nuances of meaning attached to these words and conceptualizations; rather, its purpose is to identify and elaborate upon the core concepts that underlie the development and evaluation of educational programs in a variety of institutional and agency contexts and thus provide the practitioner the bases for a more systematic and orderly approach to his educational efforts.

The generalized notions that a person has of the concept, *program*, establish his basis for the identification and use of more specific concepts. In this chapter program is viewed as an all-inclusive term covering a variety of activities on the part of an educational institution or agency. Some of these activities are directed toward the gaining of more or less explicit educational ends, functions or "tasks-to-be-performed." Some are directed toward maintaining the viability of the agency or institution as a social entity.

Educational efforts can be directed toward target populations which are external to the agency, that is, those populations located outside the immediate organizational structure of the agency. These activities may be organized as a single activity such as a meeting or a lecture and may have little or no relationship to other educational offerings of the agency. On the other hand, they may be organized into more systematic, sequential, integrated units such as grade-level sequences and curricular or program units.

Other educational functions may be internally oriented and directed at diffusing information to persons who are integral members of the agency or organization. An example of this type of educational function would be the in-service training activities of an educational agency.

Maintenance activities, referred to above, would be less concerned with educational ends and more concerned with preserving the agency as a viable social unit in order to ensure its continuing capacity to fulfill its educational functions. Such activities are usually directed internally and often fall under the category of program administration. Examples include financing, provision of facilities and equipment, selection and allocation of supporting staff, reporting activities, and interunit coordination. Public relations efforts, even though of an educational nature, are usually intended to generate support for the agency. Consequently, they are illustrative of an administrative or maintenance function directed toward a population external to the agency.

Although maintenance functions play a central role in the operation of adult education institutions, they are important only insofar as they contribute to the development and implementation of the primary task—education. If they are perceived as being of primary concern in their own right, then, by contrast, educational ends become secondary and maintenance of jobs, for example, takes precedence over educational activities. Ideally, most activities and resources are directed toward the attainment of institutional ends or goals-to-be-attained rather than toward institutional maintenance, but this is not always the case.

Program development and evaluation, as the central concepts explored in this chapter, refer to the development of the plan for implementing and evaluating educational programs directed toward clientele outside of the agency and within the agency. Consequently, the concepts treated are basic to any educational program and vary only insofar as do the target populations, the subject matter and the available resources.

It is recognized that an effective program is the ultimate goal of the programming effort. Such a goal is more likely to be achieved where there has been some systematic, deliberate effort to develop a meaningful plan of action to be followed. Such a plan includes consideration of (1) the situation which is to be changed or improved; (2) educational needs of the target populations(s) translated into educational objectives; (3) learning experiences and plans for their implementation to achieve the desired objectives; and (4) the design for determining the accomplishments of the program and assessing its strengths and weaknesses. Thus, the content of this chapter is presented in terms of four basic concepts of curriculum or program development. The concepts include need, objective, learning experience and evaluation. Policies and procedures for the implementation of these concepts are not dealt with because of the variation among adult education agencies and institutions.

Need and Objective

Need is a complex concept, yet significant and far reaching in its implications for the adult educator. Researchers and writers have devised many different approaches to describing and defining the notion of need. Essentially they have reflected two different interpretations. The first interpretation is based upon the assumption of an inherent growth or need-fulfilling tendency in man. Maslow, for example, sets forth five sets of needs which are arranged in a hierarchy of "prepotency"; these, arrayed in order of their likely emergence, include physiological, safety, love, esteem and self-actualization needs [12]. Maslow theorizes that the emergence of one need usually rests on the prior satisfaction of another need which is more basic or prepotent. Thus the satisfaction of a given need sets up conditions in which higher level needs may emerge. Conversely, the deprivation of a more basic need results in activities which would result in the alleviation of that need before activities to satisfy higher level needs would again be performed. In such a system, man is seen as a perpetually wanting entity, fulfilling needs as they emerge.

A second interpretation of need is based upon the assumption of equilibrium as a natural state toward which man strives. Need is a condition that exists between what is and what should be, or between what is and that which is more desirable. Need is a key instigator of behavior in that it creates a state of disequilibrium. Man, then, is motivated to fulfill the need or find a substitute so that equilibrium between what is and what should be is restored. Thus, a need represents an imbalance, a lack of adjustment or a gap between a present situation or state of being and a new or changed set of conditions assumed to be more desirable. In this interpretation, a need always implies a gap.

This interpretation provides a framework which can be useful in the development of adult education programs. In utilizing this framework it is necessary to be able to compare what is (the present situation) with what should be—the more desirable condition. The result or product of this comparison will be the gap or the need. A need may be expressed in terms of the level of knowledge that one possesses, the present attitude one has, or the skills that one possesses. It may be interpreted in terms of desired economic, social or environmental changes or in terms of practices to be followed. For example, a broad economic need might be the desired adjustment in the level of annual income from $2000 to $4000. A broad social need might be the gap or imbalance in attitudes toward social justice.

The challenge, and more importantly, the responsibility of the adult educator is to have an adequate basis for determining what the present situation is and what it ideally might be. The adult educator must become aware of, and identify the changes that should take place in the learner in order to reach the objectives desired in the educational program. Tyler identified three sources of information that are helpful in the determination of need and in the development of educational objectives [15]. These are the potential learners themselves, contemporary society or the social and economic environment of the learner, and the subject matter area. It should be recognized that no single source of information is adequate to provide a basis for wise and comphehensive decisions about educational objectives. Each of the above mentioned sources has its own part to play in providing potential educational objectives. And, involving the potential learner himself often requires the adult educator to help the learner develop skill in recognizing his needs.

In using this framework, analysis and study of the potential learners and their environment can provide a basis for the determination of the present situation. The analysis of the potential learner can focus on present levels of knowledge, attitudes, skills, practices followed, or other indicators of behavior. A study of the environment or contemporary life of the learner can lead to the identification of crucial problems, issues or concerns to be resolved. Such a study might reveal poor housing conditions, low health standards, or inadequate recreational facilities. In any case, it is necessary to make a comparison of the situation as it is with what it should or, ideally, might be, in order to identify the gap or need which exists. This need can then be translated into educational objectives.

A continuous challenge for the adult educator is to have a realistic basis for determining what the situation might ideally become as a result of the implementation of an educational program. The adult educator, as a trained professional, can and should perform a major role in determining the ends or objectives that the program is to achieve. This can be done by utilizing such sources of information as research findings and opinions of scholars, needs and capacities of the potential learner, and the requirements and deficiencies that exist in social, economic and cultural aspects of the learner's immediate environment and in society in general. This approach implies that the educator must make some value judgments about "what should be," but these judgments, if based on the best available data, likely will be more realistic and meaningful than if

Program Development and Evaluation

based upon immediate pressures, subjective impressions or tradition. Thus, the adult educator should play an active role in developing programs that make a maximum contribution to the growth and development of the learner and to the society of which he is a part.

Levels of Objectives

A useful concept in program development is that of levels of objectives. The exact number of levels is relative. One can state objectives with degrees of specificity at several levels. The two extremes might range from a very broad statement, such as to improve society, to the other very specific extreme, such as to acquire skill in dancing the hula. Broad statements are useful in describing the objectives of the institution or agency. Intermediate level statements of objectives should indicate what the specific program or project is to accomplish. Such objectives may be stated in terms of economic or social ends to be achieved. An example would be the following, "Make the lakes in Paul Community free of pollution." At the more specific teaching level, statements of objectives should reflect the subject matter to be taught, to whom, and the behavioral changes sought. Some examples of specific teaching level objectives might be: adults developing skills in presiding over meetings; housewives understanding effective budgeting procedures; union members gaining a feeling of importance of equal opportunity for qualified job applicants.

The idea of levels of objectives provides a broad framework from which to view the cohesion and integration of the overall adult educational program. The specific educational objectives that a given course, unit, meeting or activity are designed to achieve should be identifiable with one or more of the general objectives for a program or project. A number of different meetings, courses, and other activities should all contribute to the objectives of a program or project. Thus the cumulative effect of the more specific objectives should describe the operationalization of broader goals or ends the agency seeks to achieve. In a like manner, broad objectives establish boundaries which help narrow and refine the specific educational responsibilities of the agency or institution.

The Behavioral Change to Be Attained

Three broad classifications of behavior have been identified by educational psychologists and taxonomies have been developed for each [1; 7; 14]. These classifications—consisting of the cognitive, affective, and psychomotor domains—are helpful to the adult educator in that they identify the three major foci of content in educational programs. The cognitive domain deals with those behaviors which are concerned with the recall or recognition of knowledge and the development of intellectual skills and abilities. The affective domain includes those behaviors which describe changes in interest, attitudes, and values and the development of appreciations and adequate adjustment. The third domain, the psychomotor, is concerned with the manipulative or motor-skill area of behavior.

The cognitive domain represents a hierarchy of complexity which starts with relatively simple behavioral tasks which require the learner to recognize or recall ideas, facts or phenomena and moves to more complex tasks which involve making value judgments and using standards as the basis for judgment. At the lowest level of intellectual functioning, some degree of understanding is required whereas each higher level requires more complex manipulation of cognitive content.

The same hierarchical arrangement has been established for the affective domain. At the lowest level of this domain, the learner is barely conscious of the existence of phenomena or stimuli. At succeedingly higher levels there is greater interaction between stimuli and learner until, at the highest level, various stimuli (experiences) are "internalized" and become the basis for guiding one's behavior.

The psychomotor domain includes a hierarchy from perception through the sense organs to complex overt action (like driving an auto) performed without hesitation.

These taxonomies should be useful to the adult educator for perspective on the emphasis to be given to certain behaviors in the educational program. They may suggest to him that more emphasis should be given to the application of knowledge and to the analysis of situations in which the knowledge is to be used. Such knowledge will also help the adult educator to state objectives more precisely so that it becomes easier to select and organize learning experiences and to evaluate.

The value judgments which all educators make about the objectives to be attained are basic in their overriding significance to the total scope of educational programs. Since objectives serve as the overall guide to the planned educational activity of the organization, these fundamental decisions must be made with care and precision. Three factors are important: first, if the program is to have maximum impact, educational objectives should be related to a clientele, that is, to a target population having similar problems and needs; second, a precise identification must be made of the behavioral changes which are needed or desired in the potential learners; and, third, the content areas which relate to the needs or problem areas of the clientele must be identified with accuracy. The content, of course, may be in terms of knowledge (concepts and principles), skills and/or values, or a combination of these. The quality of judgments made about these matters has lasting impact upon the overall effectiveness of the educational program; the preciseness with which objectives are determined often affects the degree to which programs are effective in bringing about desired behavioral change.

Learning Experiences

Having accomplished the crucial task of identifying the specific educational ends to be attained, the adult educator can concentrate on the concerns associated with their attainment. Emphasis on intended educational outcomes for a given target population with certain known attributes or needs focuses on the learner as the chief component of the educational effort. In analyzing the present competencies of the learner in relation to intended educational objectives, the educator considers those experiences that will result in maximum attainment of the desired behavior. Taken in this light, the educator is less a purveyor of information than a strategist who designs environments (situations, events, activities) in which learners are free to experience certain effects. It is the active interaction between the learner and the event—on a mental and/or physical level—which results in educational content being assimilated by the student. Thus, learning experiences are not what the instructor does; they are not what appears in an outline of a course; they are not the facilities, devices or techniques used. Learning experiences are what the learner actively interacts with, physically and/or mentally, as a result of his participation in the educational process. The educator's role is thus to help bring about an environment in which the desired reactions can, and will, be forthcoming from the student.

The environment in which the student learns is analogous to a manufacturing situation. The raw material is the learner prior to experiencing the educational process. The end product is the learner after exposure or processing. The nature of the educational process is such that the raw material is acted upon for the purpose of achieving the predetermined, desired end product. This end is some product which is marketable, or is otherwise in demand. Knowing the desired end, and the nature of the raw material, one can plan a series of events that will have high probability of yielding the desired end. As the desired end product changes, or as the raw materials change, the nature and/or number of events involved in the educational process may need to change. That is, the educator cannot expect to attain a new product with presently available raw materials by using the existing processing system. Likewise, to maintain a consistent product with varying raw materials requires an educational process that takes this inconsistency into account. Thus, the educational process can be considered as a number of variables that will change with the intended output and the known input.

It must be kept in mind, however, that the learner is an active participant in this process and is not a passive receptor of educational content. Constant focusing upon the learner in the educational process often helps to counteract the tendency of many educators to place emphasis on content, methods, hardware and the like as ends in themselves. More appropriately, educator behavior, instructional devices and methodologies are merely means to the desired end of behavior change on the part of the learner. The educator uses these means to create and limit an environment so the learner can pursue a limited number of clearly defined ends. The route(s) taken to attain these ends can vary for different learners depending upon such variables as personnel, facilities, materials, supplies and devices. These routes can be expressed in flow charts portraying the number of different learning experiences to be provided through various methods [4, 5].

Designing the Learning Experience

The design of specific, concrete learning experiences—events, activities, situations—takes its cue from the educational objectives to be attained. If the educator can specify the objectives of his educational program in behavioral terms which are consistent with the taxonomies of educational objectives mentioned in the preceding paragraphs, then the task of instructional design is clearly delimited. Competence in the use of the taxonomies should lead the educator to designing learning experiences that relate content to desired levels of cognitive, affective and psychomotor behavior. Practice in expected level of behavior with regard to specific content must be provided for in the program if such competence is to be gained by the learner.

Thus, if educational ends specify merely the memorization of specific facts—for whatever purpose this may be—then learning experiences must be designed and included to attain this end. If, however, the learner is to develop some competence in synthesizing diverse cognitive elements and applying them to particular situations, then the learning experience must include activities that allow the learner to practice this synthesis and application. To provide instruction at the lowest level of cognitive functioning—knowledge with its associated memorization and recall—and expect the student to be able to make the inferential leap to higher levels of cognitive functioning—such as synthesis and application of knowledge to concrete instances—is to do a disservice to the learner and to the educational profession. In addition, it reflects the low level of competence of the educator.

Similarly, the specification of behavioral ends in terms of the taxonomies helps in sequencing the events to be included in the educational program. In most cases, some degree of competence is required at the lower levels of cognitive, affective and psychomotor behavior before higher levels of achievement can be attained. This sequencing should reflect a more or less continual evolution of events which incorporates content necessary for higher levels of attainment. Tyler cites such sequencing, along with continuity (recurring reinforcement) and integration (interrelationship of content areas) as crucial considerations in the design of educational experiences [15]. The educational practitioner can take these design factors into account by the astute delineation of long range, intermediate and immediate educational objectives. These objectives should interrelate and reinforce each other in helping the learner move from his level of competence upon entry into the program to the desired level of competence upon termination of his participation in the program.

Instructional Behavior—A Confounding Factor

Even with the conscientious application of the taxonomies to the development of specific learning experiences, the desired results are often not attained. The administrator, the learner and the instructor are often perplexed by this. Unfortunately, many practices in the instructional setting are often less influenced by current developments in sociological and psychological research than they are influenced by less rational—although rationalized—sources. Wallen and Travers cite six sources from which teachers derive patterns of instructional behavior:

Teaching traditions wherein the teacher teaches as he himself has been taught.

Social learning in the teacher's background wherein the teacher consciously or unconsciously reinforces behaviors that are consistent with the middle class ideology he has (usually) learned.

Philosophical traditions which underlie the experiences the teacher has been exposed to in his prior learning—both academic and experiential.

Teacher's unique needs such as using authoritarian teacher-led approaches in order to express self-assertive tendencies.

School and community conditions that might dictate such factors as kind of discipline maintained, degree of formality and the like.

Scientific research from the various behavioral disciplines. [16]

Instructional methodologies based on scientific research and on philosophical traditions are among the least prevalent in the educational setting, even though most instructional personnel can readily cite the principles which have been espoused by both theory and research. This suggests that the prior educational experiences of the adult educator may not have been such to enable him to make higher level applications of the principles which were rotely learned in the classroom. Consequently, the only meaningful experiences guiding instructional behavior are often those which were more or less vicariously encountered in the educator's own formal education from nursery school through college. In addition, such factors as personality attributes of instructional staff and administrative edicts regarding classroom behavior may so inhibit the adult educator that no amount of innovation could counteract their negative influence.

The intent of adult educational programming is to have sufficient flexibility that the individual learner can attain the desired ends in the least time with the most efficiency. If instructional behavior is too inhibited, no amount of planning for individualized instruction, flexible time scheduling and the like will succeed. At no point is this more evident than in the often unintended effect educators have on the feelings the adult learner may have toward formalized education. Learning theory, developed through experimentation in the psychology laboratory, suggests that the conditions under which learning takes place, as well as the consequences of the learning, have an enormous influence on the future use of what is learned [9]. If either the conditions or the consequences of learning are physically or mentally uncomfortable, then the learned behavior will not likely be repeated or utilized. Conversely, comfortable conditions and consequences are more likely to evoke a given behavior. How often does the adult education classroom duplicate an elementary school setting which has a known consequence of failure for many? How often have inappropriate disciplinary tactics been used? There is nothing in "the book" that says learning cannot be fun. But what is needed is an educator who has learned that it can be fun, and who has learned how to make it fun, relevant and important for the learner.

Current Directions in Learning Experience Design

Before the advent of the printing press, the educator's job was to transmit accepted oral and written aspects of his culture to the learner. The introduction of the printing press and the consequent accessibility of printed matter to the aspiring student brought the learner more actively into the learning process in that he could pursue, independent of the teacher, those aspects of culture that were transmitted in written form. The educator was not replaced by this cultural innovation, but his role was changed. His role became more akin to programming materials to be used and arranging their sequence to achieve the desired ends. He was no longer the sole mediator between the learner and subject matter. The opportunities afforded the educator in broadening the scope and content of the subject matter to which the learner was exposed were vastly increased. His role expanded to include the selection of appropriate written materials to aid in the learning process; that is, he had additional tools to help him achieve desired educational ends.

The past two decades have witnessed a profound expansion in the vehicles and devices through which accepted—and less accepted—aspects of culture can be transmitted to the populace in general and to the adult student in particular. Rather than replacing the educator, these advances are exerting considerable influence on the nature of the tasks the educator performs. Such devices as teaching machines, programmed texts and videotape recorders have revolutionized the dissemination of knowledge. Regretfully, they have become the ends by which many persons are judging educational experiences. They have, however, enlarged the array of learning experiences that can be incorporated into the educational program. Used as means, rather than ends in themselves, these innovations can free the educator from his traditional role of information giving to that of designer of the learning environment. This requires that the educator have at his disposal a variety of supportive services, supplies and materials to be used as instructional resources. Technological innovations have the unique qualities of affording the learner an opportunity to proceed as fast or as slow as his unique requirements demand. They often afford immediate feedback of results attained, or, as in the case of the videotape recorder, provide feedback of a kind and quality not readily attainable from other means.

Other recent innovations, such as simulation and games, bring the learner into more active involvement in the discovery process and afford opportunities to test the reality and applicability of theories and concepts. Further, these innovations afford the learner opportunity to emotionally experience elements of reality within the protective confines of the instructional setting where a minimum of real world threat prevails. While traditional educational institutions have been slow in adapting to these innovations, numerous agencies, institutions, groups and individuals in public and in private enterprises have adopted them for use in intensive pre- and in-service training programs for adults.

Evaluation

A final consideration to take into account before an educational program can be implemented concerns the evaluation of the extent to which intended educational ends have been accomplished. Often evaluation plans are not considered prior to the implementation of the program. As a result, there are often inadequate bases from which to determine the success of the program. Many practitioners include judgments about any aspects of the educational program and environment in their evaluation efforts. Too often evaluative judgments tend to be made on the basis of information that is readily available rather than on the basis of information that would be most useful in assessing results. As an example, adult educators frequently make use of participants' feelings about the effectiveness of the program rather than any change in behavior.

Many educators state that education is the process of changing behavior patterns of people. They also agree that educational objectives (rather than instructional techniques to be implemented or content to be "covered") are the desirable and predetermined objectives they seek to attain. The purposes of objectives are to point out the end(s) toward which we are working and the direction in which we should work to achieve the desired ends. Program evaluation is the determination of the extent to which the desired objectives have been attained or the amount of movement that has been made in the desired direction.

This definition of program evaluation encompasses only a limited number of the evaluative judgments that can be made about the program. It is primarily concerned with assessing the ends which were attained and is not directly concerned with assessments about other aspects of the program such as the means used to attain objectives. Seen in this light, effective evaluation requires (1) clear, concise objectives or statements of intended educational ends to be attained; (2) bench mark or pre-program measures of the behavior(s) or behavioral patterns of the learner prior to his exposure to the educational program, and (3) measures of the behavior(s) or behavioral patterns of the learner after completion of the educational program. These requirements allow the educator to evaluate his program—that is, assess the extent to which the desired educational ends have been attained.

This type of evaluation is quite different from those assessments made regarding the means used to attain the desired ends. After the educator has determined the extent to which program objectives have been accomplished, it is quite reasonable to ask: "Why were these results attained? How can we attain better results next time?" Harris notes that appraisal can be made of four aspects of the educational program—plans and purposes, resources, processes and results or effects [6]. The first three—plans and purposes, resources, and processes—are identified as means to program results. It is examination of these aspects that can point out why certain results were attained. For example, the purposes or objectives may have been too vague, too ambiguous, too simple or too hard; the material and human resources may have been inadequate or the instructional processes inappropriate.

The Importance of Assessments

Both "means assessments" and "ends assessments" are carried out by a similar process. In its simplest form, these judgments involve a comparison of *what is* with *what should be*. It is a process of making a judgment about a situation which exists or which has existed as compared with some standard about the idealness of the situation. In program evaluation—that is, in assessing the educational objectives attained —the criteria or standards used in the judgmental process are found in the behavioral objectives formulated for the program. Consequently, evaluative measures should be consistent with the level of objectives formulated using the taxonomies of educational objectives. In assessing the adequacy of other aspects of the program—such as assessment of the means utilized—the criteria or standards used in forming judgments are not inherent in the program but reside in what experts define as attributes of good instructional programs. Examples might include the minimum lumination levels for adult classrooms or appropriate readability levels for textbooks. These criteria, or standards, established by experts—as a result of experience, research, and judgment—are important only to the extent they affect attainment of educational ends. Oftentimes, the practitioner will report educational effort (time and money used, materials distributed, instructional staff employed and so on), learning experiences provided (number of meetings held, type of text used), and participation (attendance or enrollment) as the bases on which the program is to be evaluated. These variables are important, but only to the extent they might explain the educational results attained on the part of the learner. It is essential to distinguish between means and ends if evaluative efforts are to be useful [*11*].

Both means and ends evaluative efforts vary in the extent to which they reflect the rigor and objectivity of scientific method. On the one hand they may reflect a rather casual approach to the observation of relevant variables, the specification of criteria and the forming of rational judgments. On the other hand, there may be a high degree of rigor, objectivity and rationality applied to the evaluative process. Obviously, the more "scientific" the approach, the more confidence that can be placed in the conclusions drawn. Ideally, evaluation efforts should be as "scientific" as limitations of time, cost and personnel will permit. If evaluation plans are begun early in the planning stages of the program, it is likely that better evaluation will result.

Adult educators evaluate for a variety of reasons. Foremost is the desire to have some basis upon which to improve their program. By assessing the influence of instructional strategies or materials used on educational outcomes, some more-or-less rational basis can be established from which to make program decisions. Some adult educators are concerned with evaluation only because they are required to report on their education accomplishments or because they must justify the continued existence of the program or agency. It would seem logical that observable behavioral changes in terms of knowledge, attitude or skill on the part of the learner (or behavioral products resulting from such change, such as jobs acquired, more income) would be the ideal basis for program improvement or reporting. Yet experience seems to indicate that the practitioner is more likely to report efforts expended or learning opportunities provided than educational attainment. And, unfortunately, where educational attainment is reported, there is the tendency to use standardized tests and the associated achievement scores, whether or not these data are related to the educational objectives of the program.

Why Evaluation Is Neglected

Many adult educators fail to evaluate their programs. Among the reasons that have been advanced are that they may have nothing to evaluate. In these instances, it is likely that no ends or objectives have been identified for the program other than to implement some technique, use some device, or cover some given area of subject matter. A second reason advanced is that the program objectives are often too intangible to evaluate. The stated objectives may be so broad that they are impossible to operationalize in behavioral terms, or they may be so vague that almost anything could be construed as relevant to their attainment.

A third reason that evaluation is neglected has to do with administrative lethargy. Evaluation—sound evaluation—takes work. Time and effort are required to adequately plan evaluation procedures early in the program and to implement such procedures whenever necessary. Frequently the educator—both the administrator and the instructor—feels that time is too valuable to "waste" on evaluation. Even where there is a desire on the part of the instructional staff to evaluate accomplishments, demands for the performance of other activities often take precedence over those directed toward evaluation.

Finally there is the possibility that a program will be criticized if people discover how negligible are the results. It would appear that this is exactly the intent of evaluation—to either improve programs or to weed out the less effective programs. Yet the educator may be so insecure that he does not want to know how well he is doing. Those educators who are genuinely concerned with quality can upgrade their efforts by recognizing that program evaluation is inextricably intertwined with the planning and implementation of the education program. A limited increase in attention to evaluation during the planning and implementation of the program will materially improve results.

References

1. Bloom, B. S.; Engelhart, M. D.; Furst, E. J.; Hill, W. H.; and Krathwohl, D. R. *Taxonomy of Educational Objectives. Handbook I: Cognitive Domain.* New York: David McKay, 1956.
2. Byrn, Darcie, ed. *Evaluation in Extension.* Topeka, Kans.: H. M. Ives and Sons, n.d.
3. Committee on Evaluation, AEA. *Program Evaluation in Adult Education.* Washington, D.C.: Adult Education Association of the USA, 1952.
4. Cook, Desmond L. *Program Evaluation and Review Technique: Applications in Education.* U.S. Department of Health, Education, and Welfare, Cooperative Research Monograph No. 17. Washington, D.C.: Government Printing Office, 1966.
5. Evarts, Harry F. *Introduction to Pert.* Boston, Mass.: Allyn and Bacon, 1964.
6. Harris, Chester W. "The Appraisal of a School: Problems for Study." *Journal of Educational Research,* XLI (November, 1947), pp. 172–182.
7. Krathwohl, D. R.; Bloom, B. S.; and Masia, B. B. *Taxonomy of Educational Objectives. Handbook II: Affective Domain.* New York: David McKay, 1964.
8. Krug, Edward A. *Curriculum Planning.* New York: Harper & Row, 1957.
9. Mager, Robert F. *Developing Attitude Toward Learning.* Palo Alto, Calif.: Fearon Publishers, 1968.
10. Mager, Robert F. *Preparing Instructional Objectives.* Palo Alto, Calif.: Fearon Publishers, 1962.
11. Matthews, Joseph L. "The Place of Evaluation in Extension." In: *Evaluation in Extension.* Edited by Darcie Byrn. Topeka, Kans.: H. M. Ives and Sons, n.d., pp. 10–12.
12. Maslow, Abraham H. *Motivation and Personality.* New York: Harper & Row, 1954.
13. Miller, Harry L., and McGuire, Christine H. *Evaluating Liberal Adult Education.* Chicago, Ill.: Center for the Study of Liberal Education for Adults, 1961.
14. Simpson, Elizabeth J. "The Classification of Educational Objectives: Psychomotor Domain." *Illinois Teacher of Home Economics,* X (Winter, 1966–1967).

15. Tyler, Ralph W. *Principles of Curriculum and Instruction: Syllabus for Education 360*. Chicago, Ill.: University of Chicago Press, 1950.
16. Wallen, N. W., and Travers, R. M. W. "Analysis and Investigation of Teaching Methods," *Handbook of Research on Teaching*. Edited by N. L. Gage. Chicago, Ill.: Rand McNally, 1963, pp. 448–505.

Chapter 5

Information Resources and Services

ROGER DE CROW

The nature of the adult education field—its size and diversity, its emergence as a professional and academic field, to name only three factors—sets the context in which publications and information services develop. From decades of experience and an ever-increasing amount of research, much more information is available on the education and training of adults than most people realize. Considerable material, unhappily, is lost since it comes from a disparate array of sources in a profusion of forms; much of it is "nearprint" which quickly is forgotten or consigned to a file cabinet. Other phases of education and, indeed, all the social sciences share this problem. Nevertheless, for adult education there exists substantial parts of a system of bibliographic organization which can be helpful when properly used, and improvement seems certain in the coming years.

The purpose here is to introduce some of the basic tools of information access and some of the new services which can help anyone concerned with the education and training of adults (see Appendix II). It is unlikely any significant problem in adult education can be solved solely by recourse to "the literature" since adult educators are concerned largely with practical application of knowledge and insight from an array of disciplines; on the other hand, there is hardly a situation for which substantial enlightenment or guidance does not exist somewhere in print, if we know how to find it. A secondary purpose here is to give a summary view of the nature and volume of adult education publication and the present state of information services in the field.

Volume and Nature of Adult Education Publication

Between April, 1967, and January, 1969, some 2900 documents entered the files of the ERIC Clearinghouse on Adult Education (ERIC/AE) at Syracuse University. From routine monitoring of this document flow and from analysis of a sample consisting of every tenth document in the files, the following impressions concerning the production of adult education literature were developed.

Diversity of Form

Neither books nor journals carry the main body of adult education information, since books and chapters from books constitute only 12 percent of the file; journal articles judged substantial enough for abstracting and indexing account for another 20 percent. Conference proceedings (6 percent) and speeches (2 percent) make a minor contribution. Reports, largely of research or data gathering investigations, practically none of them published, make up 26 percent of the collection. Miscellaneous documents in a wide variety of forms, judged important for some audience for some purpose, account for the remaining 34 percent. Roughly 39 percent of the documents are copyrighted and this, of course, includes most of the books and journal articles.

Sources

Universities (33 percent) and national associations, including many not primarily concerned with adult education (34 percent), are the chief producers, though commercial publishers (13 percent) and federal government agencies (14 percent) are also important sources. State departments of education are becoming increasingly active, accounting for about 4 percent of the ERIC/AE document flow.

Scattered Audience

Little adult education publication (perhaps 10 percent) is addressed to the profession in general. Overwhelmingly, authors write about a particular part of the field, and usually their close colleagues constitute the intended audience. Seldom, for example, does the university adult educator write anything intended for his public school counterpart;

practically never does the industrial trainer say anything in print to the rest of the field, though research in industrial and military training is of importance to all concerned with adult education.

There is some evidence supporting the impression that the "literature" consists largely of the university community talking to itself. About 36 percent of the sampled documents were primarily intended for this group. Public school adult educators (20 percent) and the trainers in business and industry (17 percent) appear to be target audiences for most of the rest of the documents. Considering the volume and importance of adult education in the following areas, the amount of literature produced seems remarkably small: cooperative extension (4 percent), religious organizations (4 percent), other voluntary organizations (7 percent), labor unions (2 percent), junior colleges (2 percent). In part, of course, the nature of the publications for workers in these areas—with their high proportions of voluntary and part-time workers and high turnover—makes them less suited to ERIC/AE selection policies. Despite the small proportion of total publication, there is nonetheless a substantial, useful and interesting body of information accumulating in each of these areas of adult education.

Subjects

The problem-oriented nature of much adult education work is clearly reflected in an impressionistic analysis of "what these documents are about." They deal in large part (about 40 percent) with a general problem area (e.g., adult basic education, management development) or (10 percent) the identifiable target audience with which the author is concerned (e.g., women, older citizens, professional groups). Methods and techniques of teaching adults (21 percent) and the administrative and organizational problems of sponsoring agencies (15 percent) are other areas of concentration. Learning-related characteristics of adults (4 percent) and a wide scattering of other subjects account for the rest. Again we should note that small proportions often represent large numbers of documents.

Style of Handling

About half of the documents ERIC/AE has collected apparently are based on some form of orderly investigation or research. These are: research reports using hard criteria for design and execution (17 percent); research reviews (6 percent); and studies involving systematic, purposeful data gathering techniques (26 percent). ERIC/AE is, of course, especially alert to obtain documents of this latter type; nonetheless, this proportion almost certainly reflects a growing research orientation both in the developing discipline or "field of study" and in many of the action agencies. Guides, handbooks, and other "how-to-do-it" materials (16 percent) and program descriptions (17 percent) are the other major categories. (ERIC/AE makes no organized effort to collect curriculum materials used in adult classes, though these are occasionally included if they seem outstanding or unique and come easily to hand.)

Canadian and other English language documents from foreign countries make up about 14 percent of the document files. ERIC/AE collects foreign language documents extensively, but because of translation problems has found no way to abstract and index them. Other Clearinghouses in the ERIC network are already contributing about 8 percent of the documents entering the ERIC/AE files, including many of the utmost importance which would never otherwise have come to the attention of the adult education profession.

Implications

Publication and other forms of transferring information through graphic records are sensitive indicators of the stage of development and the general condition in any professional field. Had we no other indicator, this cursory analysis of adult education document flow would tell us much about the field. The sheer size of the endeavor is apparent. The role of adult education in the solution of social problems, the diversity of sponsoring agencies and their relative isolation, the mass and turnover of workers, the emergent core of common interests, and the growing cadre of professional scholars, researchers and trained leaders are all clearly evident. Recent years have brought a proliferation of forms and sources of publication; this trend will continue and will accelerate as new and inexpensive forms of publication become available, as resources grow, as new agencies develop, and as there emerge new groups of workers having something to communicate.

Redundancy, the seemingly endless repetition of familiar things, which can be so annoying, is in fact functional and necessary, for it informs and perhaps inspires a constantly changing army of part-time, voluntary and transient workers on whom the field depends. In the distant future, however, we shall need to grow ever more analytical of our publication programs to ensure that they serve a definite purpose in an economical manner. The demise of publications is often as commendable as their establishment. Forms of publication to some extent determine as well as reflect the field.

Status of Information Services in Adult Education

Adult education has developed an elaborate set of communication mechanisms for the sharing of common interests among those in the field, and between adult education and the professional areas and academic disciplines on which it depends. Though this chapter focuses on the use of written (or more generally, "graphic") records, we should not imagine these are the only, or even the most important, communication forms.

The adult educator who learns to analyze deliberately and consciously the information needs that arise in doing his job well, will realize how dependent he is both on personal communication and on record keeping and other data producing mechanisms in his own organization. Every need for information related to a task is to some extent unique to the situation in which it arises. Often the best, and sometimes the only way to handle it is by some form of personal consultation, whether it be talking to a colleague at the next desk or writing or telephoning others who may be helpful. In some other professions, these mechanisms of personal communication have been studied and their influence charted to some extent. They include meetings and conventions with their attendant "corridor talk" and the webs of personal communication which grow in any profession, based on perceived common interests, "old school ties," and personal friendship. That these mechanisms with all their implications, both functional (sharing information) and dysfunctional (excluding the outsiders), play an important role in adult education is apparent to casual observation. In general, these communication forms are relatively expensive and time consuming, though for some purposes they are the most economical, appropriate, or even the only means available.

Since information needs are often unique to the particular organization or local situation in which they arise, many adult education organizations develop their own management data systems, based on precise analysis of the information needed to facilitate operations and using data processing techniques adapted from business and industry or other sources. In addition, pressing information needs usually will arise which are specific to "adult education." Channels must be developed to a variety of local agencies, other educational institutions, and a host of other information sources having nothing to do with adult education. This "mission-oriented" information gathering role is increasingly recognized as a vital staff function, requiring planning as well as specialists trained and assigned to this purpose.

In addition to information needs which are unique or amenable only to local handling or personal communication, every adult education worker will perceive needs which he shares with some or many others in the field. These are the "subject-oriented" information problems which are most efficiently handled by publications and by document-based information services. When the need or interest is common to enough persons, publication becomes the most economical answer. As photocopying, duplicating and other forms of "publication" multiply, it becomes possible to handle more information problems in this way. This accounts for the burgeoning array of forms of publication noted in the analysis of current document flow in adult education. A key characteristic of this type of communication is that initiative lies in the hands of the producer, who publishes what *he* perceives to be relevant. Though his perceptions may be modified by various feedback mechanisms, including the rise or fall of sales or subscriptions, he retains basic control of what is being said to the audience. For many purposes, publication in one form or another is the most or only appropriate and efficient method of information transfer. It can be grossly uneconomical or ineffectual, but publications often have many other, sometimes almost symbolic, functions, which must be evaluated along with the ostensible purpose of transmitting knowledge.

Adult education publications, when the proper conditions prevail, can form a mass of knowledge indispensable both to the improvement of adult education practice now and in the long run as experience and research accumulate to result in even better methods of teaching, program planning and administration. The conditions required to make this mass of knowledge truly useful are at least four: (1) means for discovering what documents exist on a subject and for judging their relevance or use for particular purposes; (2) means of obtaining either the documents themselves or their intellectual content in some usable form; (3) special arrangements and agencies for analysis and synthesis of information and the provision of user initiated and guided reference services; and (4) user sophistication in integrating document-based information resources with other methods of inducing planned change in adult education practice.

How to Find What Has Been Written

Publications must be assembled, analyzed and organized in some manner before their content can be readily retrieved. Means for this range from the table of contents or index of a book to the complex computer-based retrieval system now serving many fields. The instrumental first step is to capture current publications for systematic scrutiny and to record their existence in simple form. Given the diversity and scattered sources of adult education publications, it is not surprising that this service has been the weakest link in the chain of adult education information services. Nonetheless, there do exist some important tools of this type. *Education Index* and other Wilson Company periodical indexes have for many years provided subject access to a limited number of journals important to adult education. The British journal, *Adult Education*, produced a ten-year cumulation of its index and the *Journal of Cooperative Extension* has recently distributed a five-year cumulation of its index.

Over the years a profusion of simple citation listings by subject have appeared, many of which are found in this and previous editions of the *Handbook of Adult Education*. Many more lie buried in the literature review chapters of university dissertations. Long, undiscriminating lists of publications are at once a blessing, if nothing else is available, and a nuisance, since the user cannot obtain everything on the list and has no way of judging which titles are important. Using them becomes a battle of wits in which the user seeks clues (in number of pages, publisher, phrasing of the title and so on) as to which items may be worth his trouble. Much more useful, of course, are listings which contain annotations or abstracts to help readers assess the relevance and consequence of each document. Happily, an increasing number of annotated bibliographies are being produced. The *Review of Extension Research*, no longer being published, was a notable example of an on-going inventory with excellent analysis. Another is the annual register of adult education research which appeared in each Summer issue of *Adult Education* from 1955 to 1967 and now is a separate annual publication of the Adult Education Association of the USA.

At the capstone of the bibliographic "pyramid" stands the analytical review or state-of-the-art report by an expert, pointing to outstanding publications, analyzing trends, summarizing content, or suggesting new directions for research and development. These range in scope from modest reviews on narrow topics to the more comprehensive coverage in the adult education issues of the *Review of Educational Research* and Brunner's comprehensive, but now outdated, *Overview of Adult Education Research*. In style and purpose these analytical reviews range from compilations of program descriptions and other material intended to be of practical use to teachers, leaders and administrators to research reviews intended to consolidate knowledge and to stimulate or guide further investigation. In the past, and even now, production of such reviews, undoubtedly the most useful of the content access tools, has been made inordinately difficult by the need to search out relevant documents in dozens of obscure sources with no assurance that all important contributions have been reviewed. Since future researchers and reviewers use these secondary reviews as their basic sources, important documents missed in the first canvass are usually lost forever. Such problems have inevitably compromised the quality of most reviews, sometimes only slightly, sometimes drastically. Again, some of the best of this analytical review work lies forgotten in dissertations.

Guidance to literature is especially important at those critical junctures where adult education problems intersect with basic areas of knowledge and practice in other parts of education and in the behavioral sciences generally. Those publications which open up these adjacent fields, or bring us interpretations and insights which can be related to adult education work are among the most valuable. An example is *Adult Education: Outlines of an Emerging Field of University Study*, in which several chapters are based on analysis of the potential contribution of various disciplines to adult education as a field of study.

At best, the tools of content access to literature in adult education are inadequate to the degree that many persons probably no longer even try to use what is available. The time pathetically wasted in inefficient search efforts is a drain the field cannot afford.

How to Obtain Needed Documents

The problem of obtaining relevant publications may be viewed in two parts. There is first a need for constant flow of *current* information, thinking and "news." For most adult educators, it is feasible to identify the most pertinent journals, newsletters and publication series and to obtain them regularly at reasonable cost. Specialized newsletters and similar current information sources serve the needs of specialized audiences. Anyone who desires to keep track of several parts of the sprawling adult education enterprise will, however, have trouble finding the array of publications required for this purpose. A second, more troublesome need is for retrieval of the information in documents related to the user's interests. Since the information or intellectual content of documents rather than, necessarily, their presence as physical objects is what is needed, the preparation of reviews, digests and interpretations of the content of documents would seem to be the most direct, immediate and economical way to speed information transmission. Reviews and digests not only save the user the trouble of trying to collect the relevant documents, but also his time in reading them. Analytical work of this type should be recognized as a valuable contribution to the field.

For some purposes, carefully prepared abstracts may be adequate. Studies have shown, for example, that more can sometimes be learned and retained by studying good abstracts than from reading the documents themselves. However, exploratory studies by the ERIC Clearinghouse on Adult Education suggest that the person with a vital personal

Information Resources and Services

interest in a document cannot be well served by an abstract, however well prepared. These users will accept no substitute. There is, furthermore, low tolerance for reading or even scanning masses of abstracts with only tangential pertinence to the reader's interests. However, for the reader who wants to inform himself about several areas related to his interests, succinct summaries of content may be quite adequate. Similarly, extracts or well organized sets of brief quotations from texts will often be useful. In general, any effort to abbreviate, condense or summarize documents is likely to be a boon for a high proportion of those who are interested in the subject. The ten-page summaries of dissertations required by some universities are excellent examples; probably 95 percent of the potential readers of the dissertation will be well served by such digests.

At the agency level, every worker must have some minimum set of books and other materials for almost daily reference. Thus, a shelf of books and some personal files will be found in any office, often accumulating to substantial collections which the worker laboriously assembles to protect himself against the lack of backup library services. Staff libraries and materials centers in school systems and other agencies employing adult educators sometimes become important resources and would more often if the needs were more firmly expressed and if the relevant core of materials could easily be identified, obtained and updated.

Local adult education councils and libraries are often concerned and sometimes effective in developing extensive collections serving the local community. Some of the most usable collections of adult education materials are maintained in metropolitan public libraries. Audiovisual collections, including 16mm films, together with reference services on how to obtain such materials, are also found in public libraries for the explicit purpose of serving adult education programming needs. In recent years, in many localities, these public resources have been improved by regional cooperation and by cooperative arrangements between public and university or special libraries. Additional help is coming from the Title III resource centers in many areas.

At the state and national levels, supplementary services are available from state departments of education, state library systems and, sometimes, through the state chapters of national associations such as the National Association of Public Continuing and Adult Education and the Adult Education Association of the USA. Directories and guides to audiovisual or other resources are occasionally compiled.

At the national level, the use of microform publications in the ERIC and the University Microfilm systems makes adult education documents physically available on a scale unknown until recent years. Selective or standing order buying of adult education documents from ERIC, for example, enables anyone, anywhere, to build sizable resource collections at low cost, with no need to catalog, index or otherwise process the documents locally. Interlibrary loans, though costly to the institutions involved, can make unique resources of university libraries available, when need is imperative. Finally, national organizations in adult education, as their resources permit, are beginning to develop specialized collections and information services for their memberships. Notable among these is the NEA Adult Education Clearinghouse, which in cooperation with the ERIC Clearinghouse on Adult Education, has initiated a wide range of services, including assistance to state and local agencies which wish to develop resource centers in basic and secondary education for adults. Many agencies of the federal government provide direct information services or indirectly support their development. (Directories of some federal information activities are listed in Appendix II.) The activities range from production of materials suited to adult education purposes, through the publication of literature guides and maintenance of demonstration libraries, to active stimulation of information service centers with the resources, guidance and training programs required for their operation.

The Library of Continuing Education of Syracuse University, as a result of years of collecting and of gifts from many agencies and individuals, has come to be recognized as a central "library of record" for the maintenance of archival materials of many national organizations and the manuscripts or personal papers of outstanding adult educators. Other special collections have been identified in various places, notably the records of the Cooperative Extension Service and other federal programs in the U.S. National Archives, and the labor education materials in the Wisconsin Historical Society.

Access to foreign adult education literature, especially in foreign languages, is poor, but the seeds of improvement may be detected in such activities as: the publication and translation programs of *Convergence,* an international journal of adult education; long-range planning in the ERIC system for international acquisition and processing of foreign documents, perhaps in cooperation with educational documentation centers in foreign countries; the exchange programs and foreign collections in the Library of Continuing Education and the ERIC Clearinghouse on Adult Education; the UNESCO related work of the International Congress on University Adult Education, with its *Journal,* its *Newsletter,* and its encouragement of regional documentation centers; and the growth of foreign collections in a number of universities.

Specialized Information Needs in Adult Education

There is an obvious need for a number of other specialized information services.

Program and Curriculum Materials

Locating texts, discussion courses, audiovisual aids, programmed instructional materials and other resources for use in adult education programming is presently a task of almost insuperable difficulty. We are largely dependent on the various listings and access tools designed primarily for other levels of education. In these listings, description and evaluation of items especially designed for adult use are at best cursory and too often dependent on the word of the commercial producers of the materials.

We note many specialized guides to curriculum and audiovisual materials for particular program areas and the initiation of special curriculum resource centers, particularly for adult basic education. These efforts are hindered by the lack of comprehensive listing, inspection and evaluation of the mass of materials as they emanate from hundreds of sources. Though data processing techniques make it entirely feasible to maintain and update massive files economically, the methods for acquisition, meaningful description, and evaluation of curriculum materials are still a problem. Progress in this area in the next few years probably will be in improved listings in particular program areas together with better access to these guides themselves.

Educational Opportunities

As the educational opportunities for adults proliferate, the problem of finding the course that one needs becomes ever more pressing. The directories of the NUEA Correspondence Study Division and the National Home Study Council are examples of attempts to help with this problem. *Continuing Education* aims at systematic listing of conferences and institutes, whether university based or commercially sponsored (especially scientific, technical and professional offerings). With Carnegie Corporation assistance, the College Entrance Examination Board has in preparation a layman's directory and guide to continuing education opportunities for wide distribution in a paperback edition. Similar directories to courses available in particular cities or regions often appear as cooperative listings published in newspaper supplements; others have been compiled for special target groups (e.g., women).

Again, setting up the reporting system and standardizing brief, meaningful descriptions of the offerings are the chief obstacles. However, the demand for these services, and the development of information handling and updating techniques which make them feasible, should lead to many more in coming years.

Special Services

A small but growing number of persons and agencies require quick and direct access to information in highly specialized forms. As there are increases in comprehensive planning for federally supported programs, state-wide coordination of public school and higher education, and similar developments, the need for these specialized services will accelerate. By-product exploitation of ERIC and other information systems may make feasible the tailoring of many services to individual needs. These new services may include: selective dissemination of abstracts on the basis of personal or institutional interest profiles; data banks of enrollment and other statistics; computer search systems for efficient retrieval of documents in response to user initiated queries; information analysis centers where specialized personnel search out, synthesize or "repackage" information for particular needs; information service centers manned by trained personnel in various agencies at state and local levels; and service oriented clearinghouses in national adult education organizations.

Improvement in Information Dissemination

Much time could be saved and the improvement of information services in adult education accelerated by better coordination of present efforts, by study and research into information problems, by improved understanding and use of existing services and by the training of a cadre of adult educators as specialists in information interpretation and dissemination.

Document-based or data-based information systems, however sophisticated, are in themselves only weak instruments for aiding innovation or improving educational practice and research. When expertly exploited for purposeful change in adult education, however, they powerfully reinforce these efforts. Ultimately, knowledge must be mediated through personal interpretation in every stage of the process of engineering theory into practice. As the services themselves become more effective, we may expect they will be used more widely and efficiently— perhaps through "information officers," adult education staff members specially trained to locate and exploit all kinds of information resources.

National Information Systems in Adult Education

Educational Resources Information Center (ERIC)

Sponsored by the U.S. Office of Education in cooperation with 19 universities and professional associations, ERIC is a large-scale, and long-range, effort to improve information services throughout the field of education. It has four basic purposes. The first is to make a wide range of significant educational documents easily available to the educational community. Each of the clearinghouses in this decentralized system collects and analyzes (i.e., catalogs, abstracts and indexes) documents in its field of subject competence. Documents from all clearinghouses are processed by North American Rockwell Corporation into computer tapes from which *Research in Education* (RIE), the monthly announcement bulletin, is produced for publication by the U.S. Government Printing Office. Semiannual and annual author and subject indexes are available. By June, 1968, about 12,000 documents had been processed into the system, with from 800 to 1000 being added each month. *RIE* circulation then exceeded 4000 and it was widely recognized as the best single tool for access to the current flow of educational literature.

ERIC is sponsoring publication of *Current Index to Journal in Education* (CIJE) which will cover some 250 key educational journals. Analysis of the journal articles will contain citations and standard ERIC indexing of not more than five terms. Supplementing RIE and CIJE are several special ERIC document collections covering: education of the disadvantaged; manpower training and development; projects funded under Title III of ESEA; and all research funded by the Cooperative Research Program during the years 1956–1965. Some of these special collections are updated periodically and all contain important adult education documents.

ERIC processed documents, if not prohibited by copyright restrictions, are available for sale in microfiche or hardcopy reproductions by the ERIC Document Reproduction Service, operated by the National Cash Register Company. Microfiche is a 4 x 6-inch filmsheet containing up to 70 pages of text with an eye-readable title for filing. Each microfiche costs 25 cents; a standing order to the entire collection reduces the price to about 10 cents each, and the entire collection is now commonly available in education libraries and a wide range of educational agencies. Compact, inexpensive microfiche readers and reader–printers are now available. Hardcopy reproductions in 6 x 8-inch page size can be obtained for 5 cents per page.

The ERIC Clearinghouse on Adult Education (ERIC/AE) at Syracuse University acquires, analyzes and processes documents for the ERIC system on the education and training of adults. By January, 1969, about 1225 documents from ERIC/AE had been announced in *Research in Education* with about 70 per month being added to the file; many other documents were being processed for local files and use in ERIC/AE publications; nine adult education journals were being covered for CIJE.

A second major purpose of ERIC and of ERIC/AE is to produce bibliographies, literature guides, and interpretative summaries of information from many reports for use by educational decision-makers, researchers and practitioners. By June, 1968, more than 160 of these publications had been produced throughout the system; ERIC/AE had issued 22 subject bibliographies with abstracts in its Current Information Source series. All such publications from ERIC clearinghouse, often prepared in cooperation with agencies or subject experts in the field, are announced in *Research in Education* and are for sale through the ERIC Document Reproduction Service.

ERIC works to strengthen existing educational channels. Thus, each clearinghouse makes its publications available to journals and newsletters and prepares material especially for these established media. Various other forms of assistance are provided; ERIC/AE, for example, produces "add-on runs" of its publications for distribution by various agencies to their members, sometimes jointly sponsors publications with other agencies, provides reference services for high priority projects (e.g., this Handbook), and compiles the *Annual Register of Research and Investigation in Adult Education* for publication by the Adult Education Association of the USA.

Finally, ERIC helps to provide a base for developing a coordinated national educational information network in which the ERIC clearinghouses as information *analysis* centers build the document base and produce an array of publications and bibliographic tools for use by information *service* centers in educational agencies at all levels. Toward this end ERIC stimulates state departments of education, national associations, resource centers and other agencies to think through the information needs of their constituencies and to develop information services which make maximum use of ERIC and other resources. ERIC has produced a guide to educational information sources and helped develop summer institute training programs for staff members of educational information centers. It coordinates its activities with other information systems in the federal government and in related disciplines. As resources permit, ERIC/AE also aids the development of improved information services in adult education by serving as an informal center for studying information problems and by providing assistance to other agencies seeking to initiate or improve services for their members. The

Information Resources and Services 89

NEA Adult Education Clearinghouse, for example, has been developed in close cooperation with ERIC/AE in order that its services may make best possible use of the resources in the ERIC system.

How to Use ERIC

The key to using ERIC is *Research in Education* and the document collections it represents. ERIC collections and indexes are now commonly available in education libraries and agency information services to which one naturally turns for information. Effective use of the system requires some familiarity with the detailed post-coordinate indexing based on the *ERIC Thesaurus*, for this indexing differs from the broad subject heading approach to which we are accustomed. *Research in Education* is also the guide to ordering documents from the ERIC Document Reproduction Service.

Though the ERIC Clearinghouse on Adult Education cannot, except in unusual cases, provide search and reference services, it will inform the field through newsletters and other communications of the growing ERIC resources and will give all possible help to adult education and training agencies seeking to improve their own information service activities. In turn it is hoped that persons in the field will routinely forward to ERIC/AE two copies (one is destroyed in making microfiche) of all useful documents, regardless of form, whether published or not, for this document base is the foundation of all other ERIC services. ERIC/AE is located at 107 Roney Lane, Syracuse, New York 13210.

Other National Information Services

The National Educational Associations' Adult Education Clearinghouse (NAEC) provides many services to teachers and administrators in adult basic and secondary education. Working in cooperation with ERIC/AE, NAEC draws documents from ERIC and supplements this collection with other types of practical materials. From these files it responds to requests for information and prepares newsletters and other materials. It provides assistance in setting up similar resource centers and conducts special projects in the area of publicly sponsored adult education. NAEC is located at 1201 Sixteenth Street, N.W., Washington, D.C. 20036.

The School Research Information System (SRIS) is operated by Phi Delta Kappa, whose members throughout the nation serve as scouts for documents to supplement its files of materials obtained from other services. SRIS also provides search services and sells document reproductions. Its services supplement ERIC coverage by emphasis on reports of innovative practice in the public school systems. SRIS is located at Eighth and Union Streets, Bloomington, Indiana 47401.

Several other national information services useful to adult educators are the Science Information Exchange, the National Referral Center, and DATRIX. Finally, many governmental agencies with an interest in adult education serve as information centers, with services that range from maintenance of staff libraries to the large scale provision of curriculum materials and guides. Directories of these agencies are listed in Appendix II.

Chapter 6

Technology in Adult Education

EUGENE I. JOHNSON

A rising tide of change in the methods employed in the continuing education of adults was apparent as the seventies opened. While the tide was swollen by many tributaries, three seemed of particular significance: (1) growing confidence in the unique features of *adult* as opposed to childhood or adolescent education and a consequent increase in sophistication in the use of methods peculiarly appropriate to adults; (2) the technological explosion that loosed an avalanche of new educational equipment and materials; and (3) the vigorous movement of the federal government into the field, particularly through the so-called "War on Poverty." While a national survey would doubtless reveal continued reliance on traditional adult education methodology, the probable developments of the next decade or two are foreshadowed by these basic shaping forces.

To restrict the discussion of methods in this chapter to a cataloging approach would be to adopt a static stance and miss the exhilaration of a dynamic field coming into its own. Such an approach would not be directly relevant to many important questions: Methods for whom? At what point in time? Under what circumstances would various methods be most appropriate? A basic assumption of this chapter, therefore, is that the selection of method is relevant to many variables—among them: the stage in program development; character of the institution; numbers and availability of participants; time; cost; and access to special equipment.

The selection of method can perhaps best be viewed from the perspective of program development. The person concerned with the choice of method should first decide where he is in the process of program planning, for the same method or technique may be appropriate to several steps but the form or emphasis may change from one step to another. The relevance of program development as the framework for viewing method emerged clearly during the 1960's. It can be found in the comments of Schmidt and Svenson in an earlier edition of this Handbook [24]. The importance of clearly understanding the steps in program planning has been affirmed by Verner [28] and Houle [7] and a flood of pamphlets issued by agencies of the federal government, national voluntary organizations and universities. More recently, Knowles, in the *Modern Practice of Adult Education,* describes seven steps in the program development process and cites conditions and methods appropriate to each step [13].

Definitions: Method, Technique, Device

The attempt to bring conceptual order into the field of adult education has touched the issue of methodology along with others, but no generally accepted definitions have emerged that clearly distinguish methods from techniques. Verner would solve the problem by reserving the label of "method" for those administrative decisions of institutions or agencies offering programs that determine the basic format of the education activity (for example, classes to serve groups of people and correspondence study or apprenticeship to serve individuals)[28]. Thus the choice of method would be administratively determined by the nature of the educational task and the availability of the students. Verner would reserve the label "technique" for those procedures selected by the instructor to assist in reaching the educational objectives. Despite its obvious merits, this approach has not yet won universal acceptance.

In our discussion here the following definitions will be used:

> *Methods* are the activities selected or developed by the instructor to reach the educational objectives. They may include discussion, lecture, reading assignments, programmed material, interview, games or simulations, debate, tour, demonstration and many others.
>
> *Techniques* are considered as attributes or methods or procedures for introducing variety, focus and clarity. They are the catalytic agents in method. Thus, the asking of a question is a technique that may be useful in several methods—conducting discussion, test-

ing comprehension and others. They differ in scope from method; they require less time to carry out.

Devices refer to physical equipment used to facilitate the learning process. They may include videotape recorders, slide and film projectors, record players, easels, blackboards, typewriters and the like.

Because of the evolving nature of the field of adult education, these terms cannot remain constant in their reference to either procedures or equipment. One hesitates to call the computer a device. Properly programmed, it can direct a learning experience in such a manner that it is simultaneously a method, a technique and a device. Indeed at a computer-assisted instruction terminal, there may be a cluster of devices—a cathode tube, typewriter and voice track. Similarly, slide projectors and tape recorders may be linked together in a single system, as Long describes, so that the instructor's role is that of assembling these materials and equipment and arranging for their presentation [15]. Is this arrangement then a method, a technique or a device? Obviously it is all of them.

These terms must be used with sensitivity and common sense in order to organize learning experiences for adults and to enable adult educators to communicate with each other. Depending on the complexity of the educational situation, the various elements may be so interrelated as to make classification into methods, techniques or devices both arbitrary and somewhat pointless.

There are classifications, however, that are based on the definition of the task and the number and accessibility of the learners. Thus Verner distinguishes between those methods appropriate for individuals as opposed to groups. Aker believes it is useful to categorize methods by their appropriateness for large or small groups [1]. As in all other attempts at definition, the purpose in seeking standard meanings for such elusive terms is to facilitate communication and not to inhibit innovation in a highly volatile area, nor to place the field in a conceptual straitjacket.

The New Technology

Technology, sometimes called the *new media,* is a powerful yeast working in education today and will probably become even more potent in the decades just ahead. The advocates of more extensive use of technology share an almost religious fervor, while the dissenters (and the indifferent) still largely control the channels of influence that allocate funds and shape policies. As Wedemeyer observes, "Education's rejection of technology has created the void into which big business and big industry is now moving [30]." Alone of almost all of the areas of human endeavor, education has been singularly reluctant to keep pace with the development of technology, and singularly resistant to the radical notion that conventional educational means are insufficient, perhaps even incapable, of serving society's needs in the latter half of the twentieth century.

The field of adult education stands in sharp contrast to the rest of education with regard to the new technology. This was clearly evident in the responses of participants to a series of workshops in the new media offered at the 18th Annual Conference of the Adult Education Association of the USA in November, 1968. On a rating scale of one to five, the median expression of willingness to use the various pieces of "hardware" and the educational systems demonstrated was four. The reason most frequently given for not using the new technology was "cost," with lack of access to training opportunities ranking second. Since many programs of continuing education are dependent for policy and financial support on educational agencies whose primary purpose is not the education of adults, the use of new technologies has been limited by the prevailing policies of the educational establishment.

The term "revolution" is appropriately applied to the impact of the new technology on the educational scene. It is a revolution in hardware, in concepts, and in organization. The dramatic transformation is seen in a new industry that took form during the sixties through the merger of electronic companies and publishing houses. Thus General Electric and *Time* have joined to create General Learning, headed by Francis Keppel, former U.S. Commissioner of Education. Science Research Associates is a subsidiary of International Business Machines and General Telephone & Electronics has joined with *Reader's Digest,* to mention only a few of the new giants described in *The Phi Delta Kappan* [22]. The development of this powerful new industry and its relation to continuing education and to other elements of the educational field will unquestionably be one of the chief forces shaping education in the decades ahead.

The revolution in "hardware" which has led to the new education industry and the accompanying effort to develop appropriate "software," or programs and materials, began to receive adequate attention from adult educators toward the end of the sixties. Any listing of the new hardware employed tends to be obsolete before it appears in print. However, the ERIC Clearinghouse on the New Educational Media (at Stanford University) provides several useful listings and studies. Among those technological developments with which the field of continuing education is actively concerned at the present time are the following: the computer; several major developments in the television and radio broadcasting field; the uses of videotape and audiotape recorders; improvements in the 8mm film loop; the dial access information storage and retrieval system; projected media and various systems that link several devices together with appropriate built-in programming. Each of these will now be discussed along with examples of use in continuing education programs.

The Computer

The computer looms as potentially the most significant of all the products of the technological revolution because of the range of educational tasks it is capable of performing. It can facilitate research, keep records, monitor performance, activate almost any other electrically operated device, and assist in the instructional process. Its chief use for the latter task is to individualize instruction, by providing skill practice at the level needed by each learner and tutorial services that enable students to grasp the meaning of key words and concepts. For example, the Learning Center operated by North Carolina State University in a disadvantaged area of Raleigh is equipped with computer terminals that enable adults in basic education programs to proceed at rates most satisfactory to each student. The terminals include a display screen through which the computer instructs the student, a keyboard by which the student activates and responds to instructions, and earphones for audio reinforcement of images displayed on the screen [23]. The Armed Forces make use of similar arrangements in training men admitted under a special program for those with minor educational or physical handicaps to military service.

The storage capacities of the computer are not significantly affected by different kinds of curricular materials; it can handle with equal ease materials in foreign languages, mathematics, the physical sciences and the arts. Since the greatest value of the computer appears to lie in individualizing instruction, the chief problem at the moment appears to be not "technological but pedagogical; how to devise curricula that are suited to individuals rather than groups [27]."

Although the computer is widely used for administrative and research tasks, it has made little impact to date on the actual practice of education at all levels; its potential significance is under study at approximately ten universities throughout the country. The work at North Carolina State University in Raleigh and the Southwest Educational Laboratory in Albuquerque is of special interest to the field of continuing education. From this effort should come research results and guidelines that will help define the circumstances in which the computer can be most effectively used in the instruction of adults.

Major Developments in Broadcasting

The use of television and radio channels to carry instructional programs at every grade level from elementary through college is no longer a novelty. A report compiled by McKune indicated that enrollments in college level courses incorporating television reached almost a half million in 1967 [16]. More than a thousand universities, colleges, seminaries, institutes and television stations offered courses. Some 12 different subject areas were reported, with science the most popular and business the least popular. While few of these broadcasts have been developed especially for adults, many adults do watch them. Some agencies working with adults—the migrant and seasonal farm workers program in basic education, for example—encourage teachers to draw on the fund of programs prepared for children and college students.

Chicago's TV college is probably the most elaborate and comprehensive example of how television can, to a large extent, replicate the functions of a traditional two-year college. A full range of credit courses is offered to those who will not or cannot attend classes in person. Broadcast by Chicago's educational television station WTTW, these courses have enrolled more than 115,000 individuals between 1956 and 1968. Of these, 55,000 have followed TV courses as noncredit students. In the same period, a total of 225 students completed the entire two-year program exclusively on television. The typical TV college student has responsibilities of family and employment, and thus must study and participate for a three- to five-year period to complete his requirements. In a 1966 report, *Learning By Television*, the TV college was described as "a highly successful experiment," which demonstrated "that television has . . . matched and often surpassed the effectiveness of conventional classroom teaching [14]."

Many of the nation's 180 educational TV stations, especially those operated by universities, offer telecourses both for credit and non-credit in a great variety of subjects. Effective and appropriate to the television medium are those activities in which broadcasts are combined with printed and published materials, and frequently also with discussion groups meeting throughout the reception area of the broadcast. In these cases it is possible to use the vast outreach and ready availability of television to create what amounts to a totally new educational environment, and then to enhance the broadcast message with the permanence of print and the stimulation of face-to-face contact.

One of the earliest successful enterprises of this type was *Metroplex Assembly*, organized by Johnson in St. Louis in 1958 [9]. On this program, a series of television broadcasts was projected primarily to organized viewing groups that met to watch the first half of the program (usually a half-hour documentary on a subject of great importance to the metropolitan area), who then discussed for an hour the issues raised, and finally telephoned to the studio the questions that grew out of their discussions. These questions and the discussion in the television studio formed the substance of the second half of the program. The groups were given training in discussion and were supplied with background reading materials, discussion guides and opinion ballots to provide an additional feedback mechanism.

The basic ingredients of *Metroplex* were later used successfully in other programs and in a broader viewing area. *Great Decisions,* a reading and discussion program developed by the Foreign Policy Association, and conducted annually over an eight-week period, stimulated many ETV stations to offer programs keyed, in subject matter as well as timing, to the national FPA program. In 1962, National Educational Television (NET) offered eight *Great Decisions* programs to its national network of affiliated ETV stations, a practice which was repeated for the next seven years, during which the NET affiliate family grew from just over 50 to 150. It is clear that these broadcasts must have added dramatically to the 300,000 persons normally reached face to face by the FPA program.

In 1964, a program committee of the University Council on Education for Public Responsibility, combining forces with NET, presented a multimedia program on urban problems, *Metropolis: Creator or Destroyer?* Here, a book of readings and several auxiliary publications were combined with eight television films to enable more than 50 universities (some in Canada) to offer a broadly based consideration of urban problems [6]. The noteworthy element in this effort was that a number of stations, in cooperation with the universities, produced local follow-up programs focusing on the issues in terms of their respective communities.

Another significant example of the cooperation of university extension and educational broadcasting was the 1968 public affairs program "The Inner Core: City Within A City." In this case, the problems of the inner city in Milwaukee, Wisconsin, became the subject of a saturation television and radio treatment which took place over an entire week. Nightly, there was a documentary film dealing with one particular problem, such as housing, education, business, police, etc., followed by an open forum in which the leadership of municipal government, the business community, education and the various groups representing the residents of the core city engaged in a no-holds-barred discussion of Milwaukee's urban crisis. Characteristic of this effort was the fact that the discussants were people who themselves had the power to affect the outcome of the issues in dispute. One such outcome was the passage of an open-housing law which had been debated for more than a year.

Other stations in the non-commercial network have conducted similar projects on their own, that is, without the primary involvement of agencies of continuing education. Two notable examples occurred in consecutive years in the coverage area of WITF, Hershey, Pennsylvania, which includes the city of Harrisburg. In 1967, WITF conducted a series of broadcasts, with massive prior organization of discussion groups and with carefully prepared related print components, "Sons and Daughters," a sensitive and down-to-earth discussion of sex education and related issues. In 1968, the station turned its attention to the urban plight of the Harrisburg area and came up with another saturation treatment, "A Time for Action," similar in pattern to the Wisconsin programs. In this case, however, the utilization was even more intensive, including a network of "neighborhood forums" whose nightly discussions were summarized in a large weekly "open-forum," which was televised.

It must be stressed that the foregoing were merely examples of some of the leading experiments in this area. Similar efforts are being made by many of the educational stations in a wide variety of subject areas. One highly significant project is the Minneapolis "Town Meeting" in which educational television and radio combine with virtually all of the area's colleges and universities in the study and analysis of local problems ranging from air pollution to consumer protection to minority participation in local and regional government.

An act of Congress established, in 1967, The Corporation for Public Broadcasting, whose primary responsibility is the channeling of public as well as private funds to educational television stations and national and regional production centers. In 1969, the CPB commissioned a study of comprehensive new approaches to the needs and opportunities for continuing education through the broadcasting medium. This study, prepared by the National Instructional Television Center, was under consideration by the CPB as this book went to press. It seems certain, however, that the CPB will act decisively in the early 1970's to make continuing education an increasingly important part of public broadcasting, along with the areas in which it already functions: public affairs, public culture and programs for children not related to their classroom activities [4].

Recent Innovations in Broadcasting

The search for greater flexibility, reduced costs and increased audience size have generated several major technological developments in broadcasting that hold promise for the future of continuing education. *Multiplex* is a means for dividing the FM radio band into four or five subcarriers, each of which can carry a separate program; yet all can be broadcast simultaneously. An adapter on the radio receiver permits the individual to switch to any of the programs carried on the same band. The economic benefits of this are obvious, but the educational benefits lie in the possibility of interrelating the programs on the subcarriers to perform separate but integrated educational tasks.

Slow Scan Television. In 1966 slow scan television made its appearance and immediately offered hope for reaching individuals or groups in isolated situations. This innovation uses regular telephone wires for transmitting pictures and thus requires no expensive transmitting equipment. While it cannot carry motion pictures, it can transmit still pictures at controlled intervals. The technique will be useful for continuing education activities in which motion is not essential. The Medical Communications Center at the University of Wisconsin plans to add slow-scan to its other media to diversify its approach to educational planning. While considerably less expensive than open or closed circuit equipment, a slow-scan receiver still costs in the neighborhood of $15,000 to $20,000. It is not, for that reason, practical for individual home use. It is, however, a device that could be usefully employed in schools, libraries, universities, clubhouses, community centers and other places where numbers of people might come for individual study or discussion in small groups. It is generally less expensive than television at any distance over one mile, according to ITT who manufacture a system called VIDES. The University of Wisconsin, as noted, plans continuing medical education through the medium of slow scan TV [10].

The first use of a satellite in instructional television occurred in 1965 when an elementary school class in Paris was linked for an hour to a class in Wisconsin via Early Bird Satellite. This technique has not been applied yet to the field of continuing education. However, with interest and support from several of the major foundations in the United States, a satellite communication system for education may be in operation in the seventies and possible uses of such a system for continuing education was on the agenda for discussion at the Galaxy Conference of Adult Education Organization in December, 1969.

John Ohliger at Ohio State University reports regularly on developments in the mass media field through a newsletter going to members of the Mass Media Section of the Adult Education Association of the USA and other interested persons [20].

Dial Access Information Storage and Retrieval System. More commonly referred to as dial access library, this versatile device is serving a variety of educational functions. Essentially, it is an electronic system for distributing audio and video materials and programs which are stored in locations remote from where they are received. According to Donald Moon, the recorded materials can be useful in almost any kind of an educational situation and with almost any kind of subject matter [17]. Dial Access may be used, for example, to provide "enrichment" in such subjects as art, music and drama; to describe symptoms of a disease for physicians located in isolated areas; to allow some students to hear lectures at times convenient for them; and for drill in such subjects as typing and shorthand. Receiving stations may be conveniently located throughout a college campus (Ohio State University has about 400). For continuing education, all one needs is access to a telephone. In Wisconsin, students enrolled in correspondence instruction use the telephone to listen to tapes which they request by number. Transmission costs have retarded the spread of the dial access library, but future research and experimentation are expected to reduce the cost.

Audiotape Recorders. These recorders are now widely employed in continuing education programs. They are used for enrichment purposes in many courses, to provide a stimulus to discussion, and (mounted in automobiles) to provide music, self-guiding tours and basic information while driving in one's automobile. The Canadian Association for Adult Education is seeking to develop the same idea—recorders mounted in automobiles—for a more serious purpose. The Canadians hope to develop a practical plan whereby a major oil distributor (at any of its stations) will rent to drivers tapes on the history, economy, politics and culture of areas through which they plan to travel. The driver will be able to turn the tape in at another station of the same company on arrival at his destination [12]. As a training aid, recorders can enable the student to study the content and style of his performance, to analyze group activities and to record for later use presentations he might otherwise miss.

Videotape Recorders. This type of recorder first came into use for teaching such skills as skiing. By reviewing his performance, the student and his instructor are able to identify errors, diagnose difficulties and formulate new approaches or procedures to test in the future. The recorders have become popular in many other situations, including executive development programs, in-service training for nurses and sensitivity training as conducted by the National Training Laboratories. In the last connection, they are regarded as especially helpful in enabling trainees to grasp the importance of process and understand the impact of the trainee's style of behavior on individual and group behavior.

8mm Film Loop. Recent improvements have placed within the reach of every educator the capacity to make and use short, single concept films [29]. In its simplest form the equipment consists of a camera—automatic and as easy to load and operate as a snapshot camera—a projector about the size of a shoe box and a small screen. By anticipating points at which concepts or operations may be difficult to grasp, the educator can prepare a short (up to four minutes) film and introduce it at the appropriate moment in the instructional situation. Moreover, the total cost of the equipment is under $300 and little training is required for an experienced educator to become quite skillful in its use. Thousands of titles have been produced in recent years and are available from the sources identified by Volker [29].

Multimedia Programs

Different products of the technological revolution have led adult educators to a variety of experiments in combining the media for structuring educational activities. The influence of these efforts was seen in the sixties in the creation of new patterns ranging in length and complexity from single meetings to an entire curriculum or training program. A common concern in all these efforts has been to determine the appropriate role for each element in the educational system so that the new technology effectively serves educational purposes and does not become a mere gimmick. Five examples of the successful application of new technology at different levels follow.

In the Single Meeting

Long's work at the State University of Iowa illustrates an effective fusing of visual and sound tracks for the purpose of changing attitudes [15]. Using a variety of images projected on three different screens by slide projectors, Long dramatized many contemporary situations in which education has a role. The accompanying sound track sought to stimulate an audio response that would correlate with the power of the visual images. Other experiments have employed similar combinations in a number of educational activities—for example, providing an overview and review of a course or single programs for PTA and adult student body meetings.

In Subject Areas

Several systems have been developed to facilitate the teaching of reading, mathematics and other subjects. MIND, a business-oriented educational enterprise that began as an offshoot of the National Association of Manufacturers, employs a portable electronic machine programmed to help employees with limited reading comprehension master the essential vocabularies and concepts in their work. At least two publishing firms have developed systems that package programmed learning in automatic machines for English language instruction.

In Restructuring the Curriculum

The University of Wisconsin, through its project AIM (Articulated Instructional Media), has assisted students who could not come to the campus to acquire their college degrees. Organized as correspondence instruction, AIM enrolls students in college level courses in which they are served by telephone calls, packets of programmed materials, radio broadcasts, and correspondence with the instructor. The instructor may prescribe films, tapes, slides, books and other materials to help the student reach his educational objectives.

In a Company-Wide Training Program

The Eastman Kodak Company has incorporated the computer, along with other products of the new technology, in a comprehensive training program for its employees. Training is individualized through the storage of materials in the computer together with case histories of the achievement level of each employee in those skills critical to the operations of the company.

In the Health Manpower Field

The U.S. Public Health Service, engaged in a vast reorganization program during the last years of the 1960's, singled out the manpower needs of the health industry for special attention. Calling attention to the fact that three million workers are employed by hospitals and other health-serving agencies, the PHS was supporting a number of promising efforts to speed up the pre-service and in-service training of health personnel. As the results of these experiments become available in the seventies the role of the new technology in continuing education will become more clear.

The Role of the Federal Government

The vigorous activity of the federal government in adult education during the 1960's, supported by several landmark pieces of legislation, has affected both the extent and practice of adult education. From the standpoint of methodology, the impact of the federal government undoubtedly has been considerable, if difficult to delineate.

Adult Basic Education

The chief effect of federal support on the methodology of adult basic education to date has been to bring large numbers of teachers of adults within the scope of professional training programs rather than to introduce major changes in methodology. The vast majority of teachers employed in the adult basic education program serve on a part-time basis; few of them had training in the teaching of adults as opposed to the teaching of children or adolescents. The chief methodological advance in the 1970's is likely to be a continuation and widening of the effort to retrain these teachers in tested methods for helping adults to learn. In time, research and experimentation with the new technology—of the kind underway at North Carolina State University in Raleigh—will undoubtedly affect the methodology of adult basic education, but any widespread change in present patterns in the near future seems unlikely.

Community Education Programs

Passage of Title I of the Higher Education Act of 1965 increased the importance of viewing the entire community as the client for adult education services. It also underscored the difficulty of developing an effective methodology for so complex an educational task as helping a community to end air pollution, develop effective coordination of the activities of many overlapping governmental jurisdictions or improve relations among its many diverse economic, religious, racial and ethnic groups. While a strong case may be made on a logical basis for the use of broadcast media as the major method in community education, there is as yet no conclusive evidence to support its feasibility. The experience of the Extension Service of the University of California at Los Angeles with community seminars directed toward bringing white and black citizens together for a confrontation in an educational context indicates that effective educational work can be done—and on a fairly large scale—with conferences and discussion groups in which the broadcast media play no role.

The Arts and Humanities

Another piece of federal legislation—the Act to Create a National Foundation for the Arts and the Humanities (1966)—has implications for technology and methodology. The National Endowment for the Humanities has maintained that effective educational programs for the general public should be channeled through all institutions and agencies that have an educational mission. Thus it has made grants to television stations, newspapers, libraries, museums, as well as public schools and institutions of higher education. It is still too early to pass judgment on the success of these efforts and the contributions they may make to methodology.

Training Local Public Officials

Title VIII of the Housing Act of 1964 and Title IX of the Demonstration Cities and Metropolitan Development Act of 1966 provide funds for education and technical assistance for local governmental personnel. Several programs funded by the Department of Housing and Urban Development under these acts reveal a change in emphasis and methodology from earlier programs for these officials. Much less reliance is placed on lectures by experts and much greater emphasis is given to the concept that public officials have much to learn from each other. In the programs of the Institute of Public Affairs at the University of Iowa and the University City Science Center in Philadelphia, for example, careful attention has been paid to the structure that will best facilitate an effective interchange among officials and the circumstances under which content provided by an expert can most effectively be used. Once again a result of federal support has been to increase the number of professional adult educators involved in and conducting programs.

Some Conclusions

The new technology, while immediately useful for many adult education purposes, cannot be easily fitted into existing practices and systems. Needed are reorganization of educational resources and the provision of training activities to equip educators for tasks of differing complexity. Experience with the computer has shown that its greatest service to education probably lies in individualizing instruction. Yet few educators have been trained to program this enormously useful servant of the future. Additional obstacles are the resistance of professional personnel to change in the method of education as well as institutional and organizational rigidity.

The technological revolution is a continuing one. Many of its products will be difficult to fit into current patterns. Continuous research and evaluation will be necessary; this in turn will introduce the need for changes in administrative and teaching procedures. The continuing education of adult education personnel to function adequately in the technological age is a challenge and a necessity. The colleges and universities, especially those with graduate professional programs in adult education, should accept this challenge by developing and testing new patterns for organizing and conducting continuing education programs.

As the decade of the seventies opens, the stage is set for massive growth in adult education. To a considerable degree there seems to be a readiness to call on the services of adult educators, a readiness which stem from several decades of careful attention to developing methods appropriate and successful for adult learning. Adult educators seem eager to employ new devices and to incorporate research findings in their programs. The limitations are largely those of finance, lack of access to the products of the new technology and lack of training in their use. The fragmentation that has plagued adult education in the United States from its inception is still present, but a common concern for effective methods constitutes one of the major forces linking the field—and one of the brightest hopes.

References

1. Aker, George F. *Adult Education Procedures, Methods and Techniques.* Syracuse, N.Y.: Library of Continuing Education, Syracuse University, 1965.
2. Alter, Henry C. *Of Messages and Media: Teaching and Learning by Public Television.* Syracuse, N.Y.: Center for the Study of Liberal Education for Adults, Syracuse University, 1968.
3. *Annotated Bibliography on Professional Education of Teachers.* Washington, D.C.: Association for Student Teaching, 1968.
4. Carnegie Commission on Educational Television. *Public Television, A Program for Action.* New York: Bantam Books, 1967.
5. Carpenter, William L. *Twenty-Four Group Methods and Techniques in Adult Education.* Washington, D.C.: Educational Systems Corporation, 1968.
6. Freeman, Leonard, ed. *Metropolis: Values in Conflict.* Belmont, Calif.: Wadsworth Publishing Company, 1964.
7. Houle, Cyril O. *The Inquiring Mind.* Madison, Wis.: University of Wisconsin Press, 1961.
8. Johnson, Eugene I. *Extending the Educational Influence of Television Broadcasts.* Boston, Mass.: World Peace Foundation, 1967.
9. Johnson, Eugene I. *The Metroplex Assembly: An Experiment in Community Education.* Boston, Mass.: Center for the Study of Liberal Education for Adults, 1965.
10. Johnson, Eugene I. *The New Media in Public Affairs Education.* Washington, D.C.: Adult Education Association of the USA, 1967.

11. Johnson, Eugene I. *Public Television and Public Affairs Education.* Washington, D.C.: Adult Education Association of the USA, 1967.
12. Johnson, Eugene I., ed. *The New Media in Adult Education.* Washington, D.C.: Adult Education Association of the USA, 1968.
13. Knowles, Malcolm S. *Modern Practice of Adult Education.* New York: Association Press, 1970.
14. *Learning by Television.* New York: Fund for the Advancement of Education, 1966.
15. Long, Robert. "New Directions with Technology." *The New Media in Adult Education.* Washington, D.C.: Adult Education Association of the USA, 1968.
16. McKune, Lawrence E. *Compendium of Educational Television.* East Lansing, Mich.: Michigan State University Press, 1964.
17. Moon, Donald. "Dial Access Information Retrieval System." *The New Media in Adult Education.* Washington, D.C.: Adult Education Association of the USA, 1968.
18. National University Extension Association. *Evaluation and Final Report: National Adult Basic Education Teacher Training Program, Summer, 1966.* Vols. I and II. Washington, D.C.: National University Extension Association, 1969.
19. National University Extension Association. "The Instructional Media," *The Spectator,* XXXIII (June–July, 1968), pp. 4–13.
20. Ohliger, John, ed. *Mass Media Newsletter.* Columbus, Ohio: Department of Adult Education, Ohio State University.
21. *Patterns of Educational Use of a Televised Public Affairs Program.* New York: University Council on Education for Public Responsibility, U.S. Office of Education, New York University, 1966.
22. *The Phi Delta Kappan.* January, 1967. Bloomington, Ind.: Phi Delta Kappa.
23. Poos, R. W. "Some Points Regarding Computer Assisted Instruction." *The New Media in Adult Education.* Washington, D.C.: Adult Education Association of the USA, 1968.
24. Schmidt, Warren, and Svenson, Elwin V. "Methods in Adult Education." *Handbook of Adult Education in the United States.* Edited by Malcolm S. Knowles. Washington, D.C.: Adult Education Association of the USA, 1960.
25. Schramm, Wilbur. "Programmed Instruction Today and Tomorrow." *Four Case Studies of Programmed Instruction.* New York: Fund for the Advancement of Education, 1964.
26. Schramm, Wilbur, ed. *The Research on Programmed Instruction: An Annotated Bibliography.* U.S. Office of Education, Bulletin No. 35. Washington, D.C.: Government Printing Office, 1964.
27. Suppes, Patrick. "The Uses of Computers in Education." *Information: A Comprehensive Review of the New Technology of Information.* San Francisco, Calif.: W. H. Freeman, 1966.
28. Verner, Coolie. "Definition of Terms." *Adult Education: Outlines of an Emerging Field of University Study.* Edited by Gale Jensen, A. A.

Liveright and Wilbur Hallenbeck. Washington, D.C.: Adult Education Association of the USA, 1964.
29. Volker, Roger. "Super 8 Film Loop Production and Utilization." *The New Media in Adult Education.* Washington, D.C.: Adult Education Association of the USA, 1968.
30. Wedemeyer, Charles A. "The Future of Educational Technology in the U.S.A." *Teaching and Television, ETV Explained.* Edited by Mori Gutherie. Oxford, England: Pergamon Press, 1967.

Chapter 7

The Educators of Adults

CYRIL O. HOULE

Herzog, the central character of Saul Bellow's novel, is a part-time teacher of adults. He describes Smithers, the director of the program, by saying, "He looks like Thomas E. Dewey. The same gap between the front teeth, the neat mustache." To Smithers, Herzog writes an imaginary letter: "Look, Smithers, I . . . have a good idea for a new course. You organization men have to depend on the likes of me. The people who come to evening classes are only ostensibly after culture. Their great need, their hunger, is for good sense, clarity, truth—even an atom of it. People are dying—it is no metaphor—for lack of something real to carry home when day is done. See how willing they are to accept the wildest nonsense." Then Herzog turns away from his imaginary letter and says to himself: "O Smithers, my whiskered brother! What a responsibility we bear, in this fat country of ours! Think what America could mean to the world. Then see what it is. What a breed it might have produced. But look at us—at you, at me. Read the [news] paper, if you can bear to" [2, p. 28].

Look at us—at you, at me; at the volunteers, the part-time teachers, the administrators, the designers and promoters of programs; at all of us who try to aid the education of our fellow citizens. How can we make each learning episode more rewarding for those who trust in us? How do we ourselves use study, practice, and continuing self-examination to build clarity of thought, expertness of technique, and some measure of wisdom? How can we come closer to achieving the vision of our colleague, Herzog?

The Diversity of Careers

These questions confront a large and complexly organized body of people. Wherever adult education is more than the effort of an individual to teach himself, two groups of people are differentiated: those who try to provide focus and direction and those whose activities are thereby shaped and led. This duality has many patterns: the teacher and the student; the leader and the participant; the counselor and the person counseled; the administrative staff of an agency and the persons it serves; or the planner and the man or woman who is guided by his plans. Every such relationship has its distinctive pattern of interaction. Simple didactic teaching is relatively rare in adult education. In many settings, planning is shared and sometimes roles are reversed, the teacher becoming the taught; but at any given time the roles are clear. It is hard to deal adequately with this diversity of terms and practices, but, in arbitrary fashion, the first party in each of the above pairs may be given the generic term of "leader" or "educator of adults."

In the education of young people, the fact that there are only a few dominant institutional forms—e.g., the university or the K–12 program of the public school—means that relatively clear-cut categories of leaders can be identified and the patterns of their careers followed as they move through the processes of selection, pre-service training, induction and a lifetime of work. Many other agencies (such as churches, young peoples' associations and summer camps) also educate youth but their efforts tend to be overshadowed by those of the dominant institutions.

In the education of adults, however, no such central instructional forms exist. To study the leadership of adult education, it is necessary to examine simultaneously the career patterns of people at work in many institutions whose basic similarities are often obscured by their great variation of scope and purpose. In this respect, adult education is like many other major enterprises of mankind. A Smoky Mountain craftsman weaving rugs on a hand loom in his cabin is engaged in industry; so is General Motors; and between the two extremes of complexity lie countless producers of many kinds of wares, all of whom have their places in the total industrial enterprise of the nation.

In adult education the range of endeavors is not as great in scope or function as it is in industry, but the spread is wide enough to make difficult any generalizations about the basic concerns of the total field. A solitary piano teacher meeting adult students in her parlor and a giant university extension service with thousands of full-time, part-time and volunteer workers are both engaged in the same kind of enterprise —as are all educators of adults in ventures of intermediate size. As yet,

The Educators of Adults

many of those who work in the manifold forms of adult education are so caught up in the immediacies of their particular purposes or the special natures of their organizations that they make no effort to understand their own work better by studying that carried on for other purposes or in other organizations. Increasingly, however, the leaders of adult education are trying to look beyond the supposedly unique problems of each institutional form to discover the essential unities of the field.

The Pyramid of Leadership (Houle)

Insofar as a pattern may be discerned amid the bewildering variety of forms of leadership in adult education, it takes the general shape of a pyramid. This pyramid is divided into three levels which are essentially different, although at their edges they blend into one another, so that no sharp lines can be drawn to differentiate them.

The widespread base of the pyramid is made up of lay leaders in a great variety of community settings; for example, the major work of the Cooperative Extension Service is undertaken by more than a million volunteers whose contribution of time, even if estimated at only a minimum legal wage rate, might well be greater than the direct financial cost of the program. Many agencies use such volunteers; their number is legion and their influence enormous. They are indigenous to the community and yet, as Godby found in a study of 267 such people, the volunteer is somewhat different from the "average" citizen:

> He is better educated, he works at a profession or other vocation which in itself requires more education and probably provides better income than the "average," and if he owns and occupies a home, it has more rooms than has that of the "average" citizen. In age, however, he is about the same as other citizens, not being markedly older or younger. . . . These volunteers, it would seem, are persons with well-developed social consciences, and the training and means to do something about them. These volunteers have determined in large measure what is the desirable relation of themselves to the society of which they are parts. This relationship includes service to others above and beyond minimum standards set by law and custom. [3, pp. 50–51, 61]

At the intermediate level of the pyramid is a smaller but still very large group of people whose adult educational service is part of their regular jobs or who accept supplemental employment in that field; among them are most evening school and extension teachers, public librarians, museum curators and information and education officers in the armed services. An intensive study of some English representatives of this group led Styler to a feeling toward them he said he could "only describe as admiration." He reported that:

Frequently they say things which show that they know that through their studies students may achieve something greater than competence, or even excellence, in a few fields of activity; a better balance in living and a deeper insight into the qualitative aspects of life. [7, p. 32]

They had, that is, the same feeling as their American counterpart, Herzog.

At the apex of the pyramid is the still smaller but sizable group of people who have made adult education the focus of their careers and plan to spend their lifetimes as specialists in it. They include, among others, those who direct the adult educational activities of public schools, universities, churches, community colleges, libraries, museums, social settlements, prisons, and other institutions; professors of adult education; adult educational specialists on the staffs of voluntary associations or agencies concerned with health, safety, or other special interests; directors of training in government, industry, professional societies, or labor unions; and most of the staff of the Cooperative Extension Service. Not all of the people whom others might identify as being in this apex group consider themselves to be "educators of adults." One of the great challenges of the field is to create a sense of common identification and community among these leaders who will then influence the workers at the other levels of the pyramid.

Some adult educational specialists call themselves "professionals," but they do so with an uneasy air. Lawrence Allen has shown, from a content analysis of the literature, that adult education has moved steadily toward professionalism, but that it has not yet achieved the attributes accepted as essential by most contemporary definers of the term and which are characteristic, for example, of law, medicine, theology and engineering [1, pp. 157–158]. At present the specialist in adult education can be considered as a professional only in a loose and analogical fashion, such as that which distinguishes the trained from the amateur historian or the political scientist from the politician. By study and experience he has acquired a body of knowledge, a discipline and an expertise which sets him apart from other people, but he is not yet a member of a consciously defined company of men who have achieved the socially recognized and legally protected stature of a profession.

The job market for those adult educational specialists is highly complex. In elementary, secondary or higher education, the size of the basic institutions leads to clear-cut patterns of selection, training, placement and career advancement. Thus a young man may receive a Master of Arts in Teaching, join the faculty of a high school, return later on to the university for an Ed.D. in school administration and subsequently move up the promotional ladder from assistant principal to superin-

The Educators of Adults 113

tendent. The educators of adults in a few institutions (most notably the public library) have similarly clear-cut career progressions. More characteristically, adult educational specialists follow the pattern of most of the other professions. A doctor, nurse, architect or social worker may be employed in countless different settings, and may move from one to another, using his basic expertise in each. A specialist in adult education sometimes follows a similarly diverse pattern, being successively, for example, an evening school director, an extension staff member, an employee of a state department of education and a director of training in industry.

Nobody knows how many people are at each of the three levels and therefore how flat or how tall the pyramid of leadership in adult education may be. Anecdotal evidence and a few statistical tabulations indicate the number at each level is increasing and it is likely the overall proportions will remain in some kind of rough balance, since the three groups of leaders are intimately interrelated. Neither a volunteer corps nor a body of part-time leaders can maintain itself for long without the guidance and direction of specialists and they, in turn, tend to grow isolated or ineffective if they do not have help in carrying knowledge to the community. Also, there is constant movement both upward and downward within the pyramid. Volunteer and part-time leaders become intrigued with their adult educational responsibilities and extend their range of knowledge and competence. Meanwhile some specialists go on to broader institutional responsibilities (such as superintendencies or presidencies) or change to some other form of employment but still devote part of their time to adult education either as paid workers or as volunteers.

An Analysis of Adult Education Leadership

Educators of adults also may be classified in terms of the basic functions they perform, most such people fitting within one or more of four categories.

Most part-time and volunteer workers and some specialists are concerned with the direct guidance of learners. The most familiar term for such people is "teacher" but they are also called by many other names, such as tutor, advisor, counselor or lecturer. Classroom and group discussion activities provide the most common settings in which such people work, but it is characteristic of adult education that instruction is provided in many different forms ranging from a one-to-one relationship of leader and learner to the instruction of large audiences, either directly or by the mass media. The educators of adults who guide learners require two forms of expertise: the mastery of the "content" to be conveyed, content being interpreted in a broad way to include skill and effective learning as well as cognition; and the mastery of the instructional techniques required in the particular setting to achieve the desired objectives.

The other three functions ideally should be undertaken only by specialists, though large numbers of part-time workers and volunteers are now performing them. The central expertise required in the second function, the design and promotion of program, is an ability to use a basic theory of how to build sequential learning activities for adults (moving through all the stages from the determination of aims to the final appraisal of results); a knowledge of how this theory is applied in particular settings; and the capacity to guide and direct the educational program itself. Specialists must also be able to carry out the program they plan—if circumstances require that they do so. Thus the home advisor in the Cooperative Extension Service must not only know how to shape a total county program but she must also be capable of leading discussions, giving demonstrations or guiding individual homemakers.

The second function often merges imperceptibly into the third, the administration of program, in which the educator of adults is primarily concerned not with the guidance of learners or the shaping of instructional designs but with such skills as budgeting, staffing, organizing, controlling and public interpretation. Such a man (in Herzog's eyes, at least) was the gap-toothed Smithers. Ideally the administrator progresses through the ranks of those who perform the other two functions so that he understands intimately the nature of the work he directs, but (just as generals or industrialists are sometimes made presidents of colleges) people are sometimes appointed to head adult educational services because of their generalized administrative skills or for other reasons. In most cases adult education is the function of sub-units of larger organizations so that an ambitious administrator often moves on to assume responsibilities which transcend the education of adults, as when an industrial training director becomes a vice-president of personnel or the head of continuing education in a community college becomes the dean of academic affairs.

The fourth function, the advancement of adult education as a field, is one which enlists the talents of a relatively small but crucially important group of leaders, such as: professors of adult education; staff members of national, state and local associations and councils of adult education; and certain persons employed (part-time or full-time) by foundations, research units, state departments of education and various federal agencies. For such people, adult education itself becomes the focus of attention and is not merely a means of achieving other ends. Legge, who independently from the present writer developed the same

The Educators of Adults

functional analysis which is here being presented, calls this group the *animateurs* of adult education [5, p. 51]. They advance the field in many ways, among them writing and research, the training of leaders, the coordination of community efforts and the stimulation of activity by providing money or engaging in public relations endeavors.

The Training of Leaders

Most leadership training, like most adult education, is self-directed and therefore is undertaken with varying degrees of thoroughness and continuity. An individual confronted with the responsibility of becoming an educator of adults may learn almost entirely by trial and error, adopting certain practices and modifying them as a result of reflection about the results he achieves. He also may use other resources, studying books, pamphlets or manuals, talking with others in similar situations, attending meetings, asking for supervisory assistance or observing other programs.

The largest volume of organized (as distinguished from self-directed) training of adult educational leaders occurs within the institutions which sponsor programs, such as industrial and commercial establishments, public schools, substantive government departments and voluntary associations. Some of these agencies have clear-cut patterns of advancement in responsibility, and training is often a prerequisite for taking each step. Among the techniques used are: assistance by supervisors; internships; short courses, conferences, and workshops; staff seminars; collaborative training with other agencies; and the deliberate use of decision-making processes in such a way as to broaden the horizons of staff members (as when program planning is done by a group rather than by the head of the agency acting alone). Some institutions (most notably the Cooperative Extension Service) have accepted staff training and development as a major institutional function and maintain a special corps of people to undertake it.

The whole world of knowledge provides content for those who guide learners. While the availability of cultural resources varies greatly from place to place, educators of adults ordinarily have some access to the bodies of knowledge required to discharge adequately their responsibilities. Less readily available are the opportunities to gain expertise in the transmission of this content, although many community institutions offer courses or other programs designed to teach public speaking, discussion leadership, use of teaching aids or the mass media and other similar skills. In England in 1968, the British Broadcasting Corporation provided a series of ten programs on how to teach adults, broadcast over the entire network twice a week (once in prime evening time, and once on Saturday morning). While no similarly extensive opportunity has been available in the United States, many efforts at general or specialized training are offered by community colleges, public schools, libraries and similar institutions. The federal government has made provisions for training leaders in many programs and some enactments of Congress (such as the Educational Professions Development Act and legislation providing for adult basic education) provide substantial funds for this purpose.

More and more books, programmed courses, films and multimedia devices are being issued to provide training for people at all three levels of the pyramid, particularly the lower two. Among the best-known volumes are Miller's *Teaching and Learning in Adult Education*, Bergevin, Morris, and Smith's *Adult Education Procedures*, Stenzel and Feeney's *Volunteer Training and Development*, Lynton and Pareek's *Training for Development*, and the *Training and Development Handbook* of the American Society for Training and Development. In addition, many books and other materials are focused on particular techniques and approaches such as discussion leadership, sensitivity training, and the use of education in change theory and community development. Many of the instructional aids now available are at a simple how-to-do-it level, while others are based on learning theory and try to convey insight as well as skill.

The University as a Trainer

As is the case in many fields of work, the university is the major institution concerned with training educators of adults. While this function is still emergent, not being as fully crystallized in form as, say, the education of chemists, lawyers, or engineers, a general pattern of instruction is taking shape at four levels.

At the uppermost level, adult education is *a field of graduate study*. A fully developed curriculum leading to the doctorate was offered in 1968 by at least 20 universities in the United States and Canada. (So far as is known, the only other country with a similarly advanced offering was Yugoslavia.) By January 1, 1969, 726 Ph.D.'s and Ed.D.'s in adult education had been awarded at North American universities. An unknown number of additional universities provide the master's degree in adult education. Most of the work offered, at least for the doctorate, is graduate study rather than professional training, leading to the Ph.D. rather than the Ed.D. The student is supposed to master fundamentals in courses and other learning experiences and make his original contributions to knowledge by writing a thesis. The inherent purpose of the program is to prepare him for a life of continuing productive scholarship.

Much of what is known about adult education has, in fact, been produced in such graduate programs either by university professors or by their students. The great majority of the authors of this Handbook hold doctorates in adult education or are teaching in programs which award such degrees. In a sense, adult education as a graduate field is rather like sociology before the emergence of social work, or botany before the development of agriculture or forestry; fundamentals are being explored but have not been crystallized yet into fully developed professional training programs.

At the second level, such programs are emerging in several *university departments*. As noted above, some graduate departments of adult education award the Ed.D. as well as the Ph.D. and, while the requirements for the two may not differ greatly from one another, preparation is being provided for specialists who are somewhat analogous to school administrators or curriculum directors. In other university divisions, most notably public health, librarianship, social service, agriculture and home economics, some institutions are beginning to provide professional instruction in adult education.

The graduates of all these university programs do not yet make up a highly significant number of the career workers in the field. While the proportion may change gradually if trained specialists can demonstrate their superiority over those who have learned by trial and error or apprenticeship, it is likely the professions which cluster around the concepts and practice of adult education will be open rather than closed, more akin to business administration than to medicine. Society rigidly restricts the right to practice in the health professions, but it does not require the executive of an industrial corporation to hold the MBA. Despite this fact, schools of business thrive on most campuses and perhaps eventually so will graduate and undergraduate programs in adult education.

Most of the students in these advanced degree programs are men and women who have already had substantial experience in the field; the typical recipient of the doctorate is in his late thirties. Most of these people originally prepared for other careers but later found themselves engaged in some form of adult education and returned to the campus to acquire a more disciplined competence. While these experienced workers still make up the majority of the students, an increasing number of younger people are entering the graduate programs either directly from their undergraduate schools or soon thereafter. Since these students have had little or no experience, their graduate programs must incorporate internships or other forms of guided practice not required by older students who have already had years of service. It is possible that as the designs of present master's and doctoral programs change to accommodate the needs of young, relatively inexperienced students, the trend toward professional study will be accentuated.

At the third level, courses in adult education are being provided to persons whose central professional focus may be elsewhere but who anticipate becoming *part-time or career leaders*. Thus a young woman may be preparing to become a public school teacher of art or music and anticipate that she will teach classes for adults as well as for children; she may therefore take a course or two to provide the necessary preparation. In other parts of the university which develop special professional curricula, these special optional or required courses also may be offered.

Finally, many universities or individual professors offer special training opportunities for part-time and volunteer leaders. Thus the Bureau of Studies in Adult Education at Indiana University offered more than 200 institutes between 1953 and 1968, using this means to train mental health personnel, librarians, pastors, officers of volunteer organizations, and other similar workers. These institutes performed both a service function for the field and a means of testing educational concepts. Individual professors of adult education sometimes work in this same way; for example, Malcolm S. Knowles has developed his theory of *andragogy* in part by his work with the Girl Scouts [4]. The extension divisions of many universities, including some which do not have graduate programs in adult education, provide courses, conferences, correspondence instruction, group discussions and other means for helping to prepare the vast number of part-time and volunteer leaders required in their programs.

A Growing Stability

Many educators of adults enter upon their work with great enthusiasm because they believe it provides the answer to the world's ills. If the goals sought are limited and readily capable of accomplishment, the hours or years educators spend guiding learners or devising and administering programs are filled with a sense of accomplishment. But as Herzog—and perhaps Smithers—knew, the deeper difficulties caused by the unrealized potential of men and their societies are so obdurately resistant to change that educators of adults who try to cope with them are prone to frustration and despair. Part-time and volunteer workers abandon their efforts. Specialists enter other fields of work. Still other people are swallowed up by the bureaucracies which employ them and spend their days thinking only about the forms and processes of their programs. They seem almost afraid to look beyond the boundaries of their institutions, being content to consider themselves only as librarians, extension workers, training directors or holders of other specific titles.

Some specialists who once had a broad perspective of adult education lose it and concentrate on some tiny area of service.

Slowly, however, all too slowly, the leaders of the field of adult education are abandoning their reliance on intuition and imitation and are acquiring a body of tested knowledge on which it is possible to build expertness in attacking illiteracy, disease, intolerance, narrowness of viewpoint, incompetence and the other handicaps man encounters as he tries to build a better world. Those who conduct the Indiana institute report "a growing sophistication about adult education on the part of the trainees" and an increasing willingness to accept it as a generalized field of human endeavor [6, p. 90]. More and more educators of adults (specialist, part-time and volunteer) are extending their careers because they have a confidence born of observable accomplishment. The pyramid of leadership is probably not only increasing in size but also becoming more stable than before. As it does it will gradually become a more visible and coherent entity both to those who compose it and to the general public. Educators of adults will find their work to be relevant not just to the immediate present but to all the tomorrows of mankind.

References

1. Allen, Lawrence A. "The Growth of Professionalism in Adult Educational Movement, 1928–1958: A Content Analysis of the Periodical Literature." Unpublished doctoral dissertation. Chicago, Ill.: University of Chicago, 1961.
2. Bellow, Saul. *Herzog.* New York: Viking Press, 1964.
3. Godbey, Gordon C. "The Volunteer in Adult Education." Unpublished doctoral dissertation. Boston, Mass.: Harvard University, 1958.
4. Knowles, Malcolm S. "How Andragogy Works in Leadership Training in the Girl Scouts." *Adult Leadership,* XVII (October, 1968), pp. 161–162, 190–194.
5. Legge, C. D. "Training Adult Educators." *Journal of the International Congress of University Adult Education,* VI (June, 1967).
6. Smith, Robert M. "One Hundred and Fifty Institutes in Adult Education." *Adult Leadership,* XIV (September, 1965), pp. 90–91.
7. Styler, W. E. *Further Education Part-time Teachers Speak.* Hull, England: Department of Adult Education, the University of Hull, 1968.

Chapter 8

Philosophical Considerations

THURMAN J. WHITE

The central question of this chapter is: How has philosophy helped to solve the problems of adult education? Before the philosopher cries "foul" and complains that we have raised a question of utility about a non-utilitarian discipline, may we say: Admittedly, adult education is a practical art—an art dedicated to changing the behavior of humans. The changes may hurt humans or evoke in them the truly beautiful and the good. And if that is not the concern of philosophy, by what name shall we call it?

Philosophy has an immediate and intense attraction to the adult educationist because of its promise of high utility. Philosophy is concerned with such basic problems as freedom and social justice, equal opportunity—in civil rights and power—and the participation of citizens in great decisions. So is adult education.

The term "adult educationist" refers to all kinds of practitioners in the field of adult education—teachers, administrators, trustees, discussants, rapporteurs, tutors and the like. (It is not a synonym for the more commonly used term "adult educator.") The use of this term is intended to emphasize the studied practice of adult education. By so doing we enlarge the audience for whom the central question is relevant and at the same time make the central question more difficult to answer (i.e., we are asking about the relevancy of philosophy to practical problems). In an effort to come to the central question, three subsidiary questions will be raised in the following order:

What are some of the important problems in adult education?
What resources does philosophy offer the adult educationist?
What have philosophers said about the problems of adult education?

Before turning to these problems we will report briefly on what some adult educationists have said about philosophy and adult education during the past decade. A lengthy report is not required, although there is a greater volume of such writing than is usually recognized.

The Educationists' Views

Many who comment on adult education have deplored the scarcity of philosophic writing; but some like John S. Diekhoff have argued that the situation is not necessarily lamentable:

Year after year groups of educators sit in convention and committee and nod in solemn agreement when someone says that there is a crucial need for a philosophy of American education, or for a philosophy of adult education. Fortunately, in our society and in our tradition, we can't have it. As long as we are a pluralistic society, as long as our public is made up of many publics, we shall continue to have philosophies of education in conflict with one another. Meanwhile, educators will continue to muddle along as best they can (which is very well indeed) on the basis of different philosophies (or different assumptions), often not formulated at all; and they will continue to feel pressure from different individuals and publics with varied philosophies and assumptions. It has been said that the United States does not have an ideology; it is one. The same may be said of American education. Like the American ideology, the philosophy of education is tentative, changing, and eclectic. [14]

In a chapter in the 1960 *Handbook on Adult Education* entitled "Philosophies of Adult Education," the authors, John Walker Powell and Kenneth D. Benne, concur with Diekhoff: "The truth is that people in this field of endeavor have done much more educating than philosophizing about it. This is probably as it should be in a group enterprise, and it is certainly characteristic of the American way of getting things done." But they conclude, "There arise critical occasions, critical times, when disorder will not serve, when choices must be made, with the enhancement or degradation of important human values hanging upon the choice. Then, the kind of philosophizing that examines assumptions, the value consequences of alternative decisions, that seeks objectivity in the critical scrutiny of one's own beliefs as vigorously as in that of others', becomes a vital concern of the adult educator [35]."

The chapter in the 1960 Handbook examined differences among the philosophies "that now obtain within the blooming, buzzing confusion that is adult education in the United States," particularly those

Philosophical Considerations

that may be identified as rationalist, community development and human relations. This present chapter is concerned with any philosophy that speaks cogently about problems of adults who are learning. It assumes there is a continuity in learning best expressed in the notion of *education permanente*, as lifelong learning that begins in the cradle. But it also assumes one can look meaningfully at adulthood as a special period. As John Powell put it "there is an adult mind, different from those of the youth and the undergraduate; that the adult has a qualitatively different way of using his mind, of relating ideas to experience [34]."

At the end of the sixties every adult educationist, as every other thoughtful American, was expressing concern about the relationship between learning and the great social goals of America. For example, while the book *Administration of Continuing Education*, published in 1969 by the National Association for Public School Adult Education, does not even have a chapter on goals or philosophy, it is permeated by philosophical questions. The last words of the introduction read: "Do we have the courage to sift the strictly political from the educational values? As a society do we have the soul to help people help themselves?"

Problems

Here are four important questions which require daily answers by adult educationists everywhere:

1. Who, in the adult population, should learn?
2. Who should be responsible for adult learning?
3. What should adults learn?
4. How should adults learn?

Who Should Learn?

The question of who should learn is especially nagging. At the present time, the practical answer is, usually, anyone who can pay for it. The consequence is that the poor through ignorance have less and less chance of becoming anything but poor and ignorant.

The question has a social answer too. One need not have 20/20 vision to see the reactionary efforts of some to thwart the learning of others because many learning efforts are threatening. Labor education threatens management; executive training threatens labor. Ghetto education threatens landlords; real estate courses threaten consumers. The poor are threatened by bankers' institutes; the private economy is threatened by the training programs for welfare workers; public employees are threatened by the taxpayers' study of public expenditures; the extreme left is threatened by the teaching of the extreme right; and the Christian Church is threatened by the teaching of comparative religion. Neither the emotional commitments of the adult student body nor the general public's commitment to education for all can be taken for granted. Under fire are the values of centuries.

Who Is Responsible?

Perhaps the most sensitive question in adult education is, Who should be responsible? We might be tempted to say the question is automatically answered if the answer to the question, "Who should learn?" is "Everybody." The responsibility would thus become everybody's—and perhaps met through the United Nations. If we could give such an automatic answer, would we then be forced to wonder about the nature of man and of the cosmos? Especially about the influence of man's competitive, aggressive nature on the management of the responsibility? Clearly, conflict and disagreement cannot be separated from the question.

Adult education councils have been born out of this issue; occasionally they flourish, but most frequently they have perished by the subtle treason of their adversary members. Colleges and universities are engaged in a never-ending process of extension reorganization as aggressive leadership emerges on the campus. Teachers insist on authoritarian responsibility in their classes and sometimes move from teaching rebellious faces to looking at rooms filled with nonresponsible and non-responsive chairs. State governments seem delighted to have the federal government or business or voluntary organizations or just anyone relieve them of the responsibility.

The question is perplexing, perhaps in part, because we tend to be perplexed about the kind of people we seek to produce. To paraphrase a line from a television program, are we suggesting that each adult say to himself, "will the real me please stand up?" Or do we aspire to as much personal perfection as possible in an imperfect world? Or is the refinement of taste a task to be commonly enjoyed? Only when we are able to describe the kind of person we seek to produce, are we able to describe the qualifications of the parties who should be responsible.

What Is Important?

When we try to find out what adults should learn, we have answers ranging from "What they should know as parents and citizens," to "How to solve their problems." Sometimes the answer is "How to earn a living," and other times the answer is, "What was missed in childhood education." Or as the Durants' would have it, "How the environment can be increasingly controlled by life [16, p. 98]." Is it too simpleminded to say adults should learn the truth? Even though some truths are more true than others?

All such answers are right. But they are also wrong. Or more precisely, each such answer is wrong to the degree it pretends to be the ultimate, or even in a lesser sense, the most important aim of education. Actually, the answer may finally turn on a notion of the nature of knowledge. It may be there are eternal and unchanging truths to be discovered and learned by adults. Or it may be that knowledge is so chimerical that nothing is learned forever for certain. Or it may be that Thoreau had the matter well in hand when he remarked that he stood precisely where two eternities met—the eternity of the past and the eternity of the future. His stance at any moment was an absolute truth, but as he bit into the eternity of the future it changed. So did the eternity of the past as days and experiences were added to it. Thus it may be that what adults should learn may change, subject to the absolutes of the present. The very special problem of the adult educationist is to establish the truth about change and absolutes and to be able to tell the difference.

The Proper Method

There are a variety of approaches to the question "How shall adults learn?" The approaches tend to go from the extreme of "This is the best" to the extreme of "Use every way you have time for." But the question goes deeper than a simple turning to techniques for answers. It goes to a notion of the nature of the learner. For many years adult educationists have been fond of quoting Dewey on this subject though they usually march to the sound of different drums. Their enthusiasm of new approaches and theories of learning is almost notorious. An example is John Walker Powell's enthusiasm for "communication" as he states it in his *Learning Comes of Age.*

The absolute requirement for a society is *communication*. This means, literally, making common certain matters of knowledge, of purpose, of belief, of feeling, and of action. Everything which is the enemy of communication is subversive of society, and is opposed by education. Lying destroys communication; so the educator may take no part in the propaganda of false gospels, and must constantly invent ways of helping people seek for facts. Prejudice corrupts communication; so the educator is committed to the reduction of prejudice. Ignorance prevents communication; so knowledge must be made available, and attractive, and desirable. Anger and fear sever communication; so education has to create forces and habits that substitute reasonable inquiry for blind controversy, and carry the habits of inquiry right to the sources of fear. Partiality cripples communication; so education has the responsibility of helping people recognize all of the factors that must be taken into account in reaching decisions which affect them in common.

And behavior which contradicts precept (do as I say, not as I do) denies communication; so the educator must himself be a gatherer of knowledge, a foe of prejudice, a patient seeker of truth; and, in every way he can make himself so, a member of the family of Man.

By these examples I mean to say that the values on which the work of adult education is based are not just *asserted;* they are the most obvious and necessary requirements, implicit in the task of serving society through communication. [*34,* pp. 232–234]

People like Mortimer Adler take a different tack. They believe the communication of an idea is only the beginning. What is really important in the learning process is what a person does with an idea once he has it. The method required for this emphasis is discussion [*1,* p. 16].

Questions about methodology are becoming sharper. At least one recent study concludes that when measured by performance on written examinations, the large lecture section is as effective as small group tutoring; closed circuit television is as good as supervised independent study; and non-supervised independent study is as effective as any other method [*15*].

One is led to speculate that how adults are taught depends on a syndrome of purposes. When the adult educationist is means minded, he must at the same time be ends minded. And he ought not to deceive himself about what he is trying to accomplish. Most of us have noble goals but not every act we perform causes the angels to sing. John Diekhoff speaks of those who delude themselves about achieving spectacular ends:

How many programs of continuing education profess to strengthen the democratic way of life? Most of us, whenever we make a speech, say that this is one of our aims. This is conventional wisdom, in the sense that it is always said at conventions. When we have said it, we sometimes assert that everything we do contributes to that end; and thus we justify everything that we do in a neat circular argument. The director of one program of adult education once assured me that his class in ballroom dancing was the best education for democracy that his program included. People danced together who would not even meet one another in other circumstances.

People wish to dance, and if they wish to dance they must learn to do it.

Philosophical Considerations

They will learn more easily with a teacher, and I have no objection if someone wants to teach them, not much objection to calling it adult education, and no objection to calling it adult. But the central object of dancing lessons is to learn dancing, not democracy. If people in a dancing class broaden their acquaintance, develop tolerance for toe-treaders, shin-kickers, and other majority groups and special social classes, or manage to overcome the frustrations of past social failures, these are collateral benefits and not the benefits on which we should base our judgments of the success of a dancing class. I am sure of this: if we depend on dancing classes to produce an informed citizenry, to bring us nearer to the Jeffersonian ideal in which every man is his own statesman, we shall fail. We shall still have our failures if we accept ends more commensurate with our means, but they will not be such dismal failures and they will not be predestined. [13]

Philosophy as a Resource

Sometimes it seems the adult educationist is preoccupied with scrounging clients, finding people to teach, getting money to pay bills and otherwise taking effective action to get the job done. And if this is true, then philosophers will indeed have a hard time getting his attention. On the other hand, it may say something about a philosophical assumption of adult educationists: what they are doing is in and of itself a good.

The *doing* of adult education is an end which is not subject to tests outside of itself. But it does not necessarily follow that our ultimate wish is to do what we can to help people make of themselves, and of their society, what they will. Or that our ultimate wish is to do what we can to help people become what their corporation or organization want them to be. Or perhaps to become what our employers want them to be.

For, where does one find an amoral paragon who never questions the propriety and rightness of what he is doing? Where is the man who will thoughtlessly help others learn whatever they want to? Or like a robot, help others to learn what somebody else—corporation, organization, employer—wants them to learn? Does it not go without saying that the adult educationist will only help people to learn something if he himself thinks what they are learning is worthwhile? Or conversely, will he help people to learn something he thinks is bad? Which brings us back to philosophy. The adult educationist obviously is more than an automated machine; he is party to the ends served by his doing. He thinks not only about what he is doing, but also where his doing leads to.

While philosophers disagree with one another in a bewildering world of jabberwocky, they probably would come close to a consensus on this point: the ends of any adult education program cannot successfully run counter to the nature of reality, validly derived knowledge, the *summum bonum*, and logical reasoning.

Much of philosophy has been concerned with a "world view." A look at the various world views contains suggestions for contributions by philosophers to adult education. Typically related to education are idealism, realism, pragmatism and, more recently, linguistic analysis and existentialism.

The Concerns of Philosophy

In the discipline of philosophy there are the branches of metaphysics, epistemology, ethics, logic and aesthetics. Kenneth Benne has illustrated the relevancy of the discipline in an article on "Some Philosophic Issues in Adult Education." He argues that all education works on the basis of three clusters of assumptions and that it is the task of educational philosophy to clarify these differing clusters of assumptions and to discover or construct the rational bases on which choices among them can be made. The first cluster of assumptions has to do with the nature of man. The second cluster has to do with the nature of learning, the nature of knowledge and the ways knowledge is acquired and claims are validated. The third cluster of assumptions has to do with the nature, source and limits of pedagogical authority [5].

At least two authors—one a professor of adult education and the other a professor of philosophy—sharply remind us that philosophy is of critical significance in the lives of adult educationists. In *Adult Education: Outlines of an Emerging Field of University Study*, A. A. Liveright writes about the aims of adult education as a graduate field of study:

In view of the variety of tasks and responsibilities of practitioners in the field of adult education and the fact that most students for some time to come will be recruited from persons already working in the field, a graduate program is likely to emphasize content and subject matter which concerns itself primarily with broad knowledge and understanding and the development of a sound philosophy and code of ethics rather than with specific skills and a high degree of specialization related to only one task, one kind of agency, or one specific job in a particular agency. [25, p. 100]

Liveright says (and who is to refute him?) the graduate program is to emphasize the development of "a sound philosophy"; however, the references at the end of his chapter do not include any to meet this need.

The second reminder is both persuasive in impact and subtly directive toward a "sound philosophy." Frederick C. Neff, in *Philosophy and American Education* says:

> it seems fairly clear that some formal knowledge of general philosophy is necessary to the conduct of education, if only to lend logical responsibility to discussions of a predominantly educational nature. If education is inescapably a value-centered activity—by virtue of the fact that it is deliberately conceived, selectively structured, and actively prized—then, perforce, it must concern itself with a consideration of values, the nature of the good life and ideal ends. We are thus impelled toward an examination of axiology and morals at the quasi-philosophical level. If the prospective teacher needs to reflect upon what kind of world he would prepare young people to live in, then he must give some consideration to ontology, metaphysics, and cosmology. And if education is to aid the student in distinguishing between truth and myth, between reliable assertions and propaganda statements, then he must acquire skill in methods of recognizing and obtaining evidence, formulating and testing hypotheses, gaining and utilizing knowledge. And such matters have to do with epistemology and logic. [30, pp. 3–5]

While Neff is seemingly oriented to a readership of childhood educators, he is easily understood by adult educators. As Robert Blakely points out, "We can—and usually do—refrain from asking philosophical questions, but we cannot avoid acting according to philosophical assumptions. Our only choice is whether we do so in awareness, with examination and criticism, or in ignorance [7]."

Philosophers on Adult Education

In the literature of adult education published since 1960, there are many expressions of convictions, "oughts," "musts" and, oftentimes, penetrating opinions. The notable writings of a philosophical bent are still conspicuously absent although we can report on some worthwhile formulations.

A singular contribution was made by R. W. K. Paterson in an article published in the Rewley House Papers at Oxford University. While his paper was concerned with university adult education in England, it has had some impact in the United States. Paterson made a careful analysis of the ways in which the tutor's "normative framework" influences his judgment. His main argument is that the tutor performs his educational mission in concord with his values. He then argues that the tutor's system of values is rooted in the tutor's world view: "My main suggestion has been that so-called 'adult educational' values are in fact nothing but our religious, moral, social and other general values restated within the adult educational setting." Paterson illustrates his position by choosing a world view "which might broadly be called 'existential.'" In his frame of reference he refers to metaphysical, epistemological, and moral conditions and derives social, aesthetic and educational values.

From these sets of values are derived, Paterson asserts, value judgments on specifically adult educational issues:

Since every value judgment represents an indivisibly personal commitment, there can be no uniform set of value judgments which is "objectively true" for everyone concerned with adult education, even given the common framework sketched above. The judgments of the individual (let us say, a particular tutor) are expressions of his private and unique engagement to his adult educational vocation. He must make them from his own personal standpoint, from which alone the issues can have meaning for him.

   i. The tutor will refuse to give a general answer to questions about the role of universities in adult education, about their alleged responsibilities to the community, for it is his own role which the tutor is throughout concerned to define. He finds himself in the midst of a group of inquiring minds, and it is with his responsibility to these, the students by whom he is nightly confronted, that he must come to terms.
   ii. However the tutor sees his role, it will not be confined to that of an academic exercise or statable within the patronizing formula of "social service." His work is essentially "education" in the sense defined above.
   iii. The tutor will rescind the professed dichotomy between strictly "educational" and merely "educative" experience. The educational significance of an experience is to be judged, not by its literal content or its formal origins, but by its contribution to the individual's growth in authenticity as a self-acknowledging person.
   iv. Where a discussion topic raises controversial moral or political issues, the tutor will not shelter behind a neutral pose of academic detachment. . . .
   v. By what criteria is an adult educational enterprise to be judged successful or abortive? The answer must be that no objective or determinate criteria can do justice to the quality of adult educational work. Statistics of student numbers or class programmes are little better than desiccated accountants' sheets; charts of the intellectual territory covered during the academic session amount to no more than pedagogic time-and-motion studies; the worship of students; subsequent professional, political, or other public achievements is at best an insidious form of idolatry; while to make some undefined educational 'standards' the criterion is to beg the whole question. The

depth and quality of an individual's self-realization are not open to calculation.... [32, pp. 48–51]

Paterson obviously sees nothing special in a philosophy of adult education. He sees only adult educationists who operate with a philosophy, and who may very well turn to philosophers for help. His explicit articulation of existentialism with the problems of the adult education practitioner is remarkably useful. We are able to deepen our understanding of existentialism by casting it in our frame of reference. We also are able to see the transferability of philosophical thought into the market place; the utility of philosophy could hardly be more clearly demonstrated. It is singular that a philosopher should do this for adult educationists. It is possible, of course, that other philosophers have done something similar for other world views. If so, their writings could well be included in future issues of the publications commonly read by adult educationists.

An American philosopher, Horace M. Kallen, continues to make important contributions [21]. In four essays he examines adult education with the eye of the social philosopher. His approach is stated in four questions. What is it? What good is it? What is to be done about it? How do we know? His philosophical view is of adult education as a means of freeing the adult mind. On the issue of freedom–authority in the teacher–pupil relationship, he comes down hard on the side of the teacher as facilitator. He quotes Lao-tzu to make the point, replacing "leader" with "teacher."

> A leader is best
> When people barely know he exists.
> Not so good when people obey and acclaim him,
> Worst when they despise him
> 'Fail to honor the people,
> They fail to honor you';
> But of a good leader, who talks little,
> When his work is done, his aim fulfilled
> They will say, "We did it ourselves." [21, p. 45]

During the past decade a committee of the Adult Education Association of the USA has been continuously reviewing a range of philosophical considerations. These have been debated in annual conferences and reported systematically in the journals *Adult Education* and *Adult Leadership*. It is a rare issue when the latter journal has no article or report on philosophy, and these papers, when collected, will represent an important contribution. In most conferences on adult education philosophical papers have been presented—some searching and leading to vigorous debate. If fresh, provocative writing appears in the "seventies," we can document its origins with greater care than has been yet accorded such work. Possible seed-beds of future philosophical writing about adult education are the graduate courses in adult education now offered in many universities.

Finally, during the past decade, there appeared a book entitled *A Philosophy for Adult Education,* by Paul Bergevin [6]. The author is not an academic philosopher; he is a former industrial engineer, now a professor of adult education. Bergevin tries to formulate and test theories to guide practice. He is particularly concerned with selected goals of adult education:

> To help the learner achieve a degree of happiness and meaning in life
>
> To help the learner understand himself, his talents, his limitations, and his relationship with other persons
>
> To help adults recognize and understand the need for lifelong learning
>
> To provide conditions and opportunities to help the adult advance in the maturation process spiritually, culturally, physically, politically, and vocationally
>
> To provide, where needed, education for survival in literacy, vocational skills, and health measures.

Bergevin reviews adult education as a systematically organized program in an organized institution, as independent study, as participation training, as random experiential learning and as a special field of study. This leads him to examine a number of special problems, such as: (1) The Pursuit of Materialism; (2) The Fears of Ideals—The Desire to be Practical; (3) All Men Are Created Equal; (4) The Marginal Citizen; (5) Teaching Subjects Rather than Persons; and (6) Resistance to Change. Bergevin places a great deal of emphasis on the philosophical proposition that programs of adult education are to be designed and conducted to help adults see themselves as maturing beings seeking wholeness.

Changes in the Future

By and large, the philosophers of this decade have neglected adult education. Such neglect surely does not spring from a conviction that there are no philosophical problems in adult education. Perhaps philosophers have simply been preoccupied with their own problems and have concentrated on what they deem to be the central problems of philosophy. Credence to the explanation is given when it is remembered that philosophers have been developing new divisions among the emerging classifications of analytical, speculative and normative philosophers. The few new connections to education are notable. Frankena, for example, has placed carefully selected writings of Dewey, Whitehead, Maritain, and Peters in a contrasting juxtaposition. He maintains that a shift is underway by education from a dependency on the metaphysical and epistemological philosophers to a primary dependency on the moral and social philosophers [18].

It is difficult to see why philosophers should continue to ignore the needs of adult educationists for uniquely designed contributions. After all, engineers, social reformers, politicians, corporation executives, artists and systems analysts have all contributed mightily to adult education. Why not philosophers? Perhaps the adult educationists would do well to explain their problems to the philosophers (especially if the explanations are given by philosophically literate adult educationists). It seems probable they will. Also probable is that the burning social questions of the day, questions about how human dignity is fostered, how opportunities for human growth are maximized, how destructive passion can be curbed or transmitted, will be at the core of philosophy and practice.

References

1. Adler, Mortimer J. *Adult Education.* Chicago, Ill.: Great Books Foundation, 1955.
2. Adler, Mortimer J. *The Difference of Man and the Difference It Makes.* New York: Holt, Rinehart & Winston, 1967.
3. Ayres, C. E. *Toward a Reasonable Society.* Austin, Tex.: University of Texas Press, 1961.
4. Barton, George. *Ordered Pluralism.* Chicago, Ill.: Center for the Study of Liberal Education for Adults, 1964.
5. Benne, Kenneth D. "Some Philosophic Issues in Adult Education." *Adult Education,* VII (Winter, 1957), p. 68.
6. Bergevin, Paul. *A Philosophy for Adult Education.* New York: Seabury Press, 1967.
7. Blakely, R. J. "The Path and the Goal." *Adult Education,* VII (Winter, 1957), p. 93.
8. Blakely, R. J. *Toward a Homodynamic Society.* Boston, Mass.: Center for the Study of Liberal Education for Adults, 1967.
9. Brickman, William W., and Lehrer, Stanley. *Automation, Education, and Human Values.* New York: School & Society Books, 1966.
10. Brinton, Crane. *Ideas of Men.* Englewood Cliffs, N.J.: Prentice-Hall, 1950.
11. Bugental, J. F. T. *The Search for Authenticity.* New York: Holt, Rinehart & Winston, 1965.

12. Burke, John G., ed. *The New Technology and Human Values.* Belmont, Calif.: Wadsworth Publishing Company, 1966.
13. Diekhoff, John S. *We Need a Philosophy.* Occasional Papers/6. Chicago, Ill.: Center for the Study of Liberal Education for Adults, 1963.
14. De George, Richard T. *Ethics and Society.* New York: Doubleday, 1966.
15. Dubin, Robert, and Taveggia, Thomas C. *The Teaching–Learning Paradox.* Eugene, Ore.: University of Oregon Press, 1968.
16. Durant, Will, and Durant, Ariel. *The Lessons of History.* New York: Simon & Schuster, 1968.
17. Fletcher, Joseph. *Situation Ethics.* Philadelphia, Pa.: Westminster Press, 1966.
18. Frankena, William K. *Philosophy of Education.* New York: The Macmillan Company, 1965.
19. Goldschmidt, Walter. *Exploring the Ways of Mankind.* New York: Holt, Rinehart & Winston, 1960.
20. Jensen, Gale; Liveright, A. A.; and Hallenbeck, Wilbur. *Adult Education: Outlines of an Emerging Field of University Study.* Chicago, Ill.: Adult Education Association of the USA, 1964.
21. Kallen, Horace M. *Philosophical Issues in Adult Education.* Springfield, Ill.: Charles C Thomas, 1962.
22. Kaplan, Abraham. *American Ethics and Public Policy.* New York: Oxford University Press, 1963.
23. Kelley, William L., and Tallon, A. T. *Readings in the Philosophy of Man.* New York: McGraw-Hill, 1967.
24. Knowles, Malcolm S. "Philosophical Issues That Confront Adult Educators." *Adult Education,* VII (Summer, 1957), p. 234.
25. Liveright, A. A. "The Nature and Aims of Adult Education as a Field of Graduate Education." In: *Adult Education: Outlines of an Emerging Field of University Study.* Edited by Gale Jensen, A. A. Liveright and Wilbur Hallenbeck. Chicago, Ill.: Adult Education Association of the USA, 1964.
26. Margolis, Joseph. *Contemporary Ethical Theory.* New York: Random House, 1966.
27. Maslow, Abraham H. *Toward a Psychology of Being.* Princeton, N.J.: Van Nostrand, 1962.
28. Matson, Floyd W. *The Broken Image.* New York: Doubleday, 1966.
29. Montague, W. Pepperell. *The Ways of Things.* Englewood Cliffs, N.J.: Prentice-Hall, 1940.
30. Neff, Frederick C. *Philosophy and American Education.* New York: Center for Applied Research in Education, 1966.
31. Novak, Michael. *American Philosophy and the Future.* New York: Charles Scribner's Sons, 1968.
32. Paterson, R. W. K. "Values in Adult Education." *Rewley House Papers.* Oxford, England: Delegacy for Extra-Mural Studies, Oxford University, 1964.
33. "Philosophical and Social Framework of Education." *Review of Educational Research,* XXXVII (February, 1967).

34. Powell, John Walker. *Learning Comes of Age.* New York: Association Press, 1956.
35. Powell, John Walker, and Benne, Kenneth D. "Philosophies of Adult Education." *Handbook of Adult Education in the United States.* Edited by Malcolm Knowles. Washington, D.C.: Adult Education Association of the USA, 1960.
36. Randall, John Herman, Jr. *The Making of the Modern Mind.* Boston, Mass.: Houghton Mifflin, 1940.
37. Richardson, Herbert W. *Toward an American Theology.* New York: Harper & Row, 1967.
38. Woozley, Anthony Douglas. *Theory of Knowledge.* London, England: Hutchinson & Company, 1962.

Chapter 9

Research and Theory

BURTON W. KREITLOW

Adult educators have been more practical than theoretical, more oriented toward asking "What is the answer?" than "Where are we going?" or "Why are we going there?" It is this that accounts for the years that research and theory building were put aside while programs were expanded. The pattern of growth in adult education has not been a great deal different from the pattern of growth in other "helping" professions where the goal is service and the programs involve direct contact with people. This focus on the practical was natural enough. Adults needed both organization (arrangements for learning) and instruction in order to continue to learn. Both adult educators and agencies, without the guidelines of tradition, responded directly to this need. It wasn't long before the cadre of adult educators was large enough to give them a sense of visibility. However, they weren't quite certain what or who they were. Prior to 1960, those in the field carried on long discussions about whether they were part of a "profession" or a "field of study." By 1960 the number of adult education programs in the United States was so great that a re-evaluation was made. New questions were being asked, questions dealing with long-term goals and the philosophical basis of the promotion of continued learning.

The need for research and sound theory in American adult education was recognized by such leaders as Lindeman [26] and Overstreet [30] in the 1920's and 1930's. As programs expanded, those who tried to describe this growing edge of American education began to implore leaders of the field to take long, hard looks at the directions of this growth. Was there a theoretical goal for the field? Was there a visible structure to reach that goal? Were the rapidly expanding programs in the thirties, forties, and fifties a "topsy-like" extrusion in a random direction from some indescribable organism called the field of adult education?

These questions were asked many times and in many ways before anything of consequence was done to answer them. Authors contributing to the *Review of Educational Research* issues on adult education in 1953 [13], 1959 [20], and 1965 [23], emphasized again and again the need for research. Brunner [8] in 1959, and Kreitlow [24] and Hendrickson [14] in 1960 reiterated a challenge to the leaders of the field to put more of their efforts into research and theory building.

The social–educational climate and demand for adult education in the 1950's and 1960's prompted graduate programs in adult education to expand. Where only one or two students completed an institution's doctoral program in adult education in any one year before 1955, the numbers quadrupled thereafter. There were 100 doctorates granted in adult education in the twenty-year period from 1935 to 1955. In the five years between 1956 and 1960, 140 more degrees were granted and between 1961 and 1965, an additional 241 graduate students received doctoral degrees in adult education [15]. On the record, adult education had become a field of professional study. Any careful observer of that development had to ask again—where is the research? Where is the theory? It was recognized that adult education was here to stay and that some kind of cohesive force was needed to bring the field into sharper focus.

Research began to appear, not in great quantity nor with any consistent quality, but it took root as an adjunct to the developing programs of graduate study. Theorizing about adult education also grew from these programs, shaping them and being shaped by them. The need for sound theory and more research was expressed so often that adult educators finally believed it—and believing it, did something about it. There is evidence that the field of adult education is on the move in ways other than in the size of program.

Aker asked graduate students and persons who held doctorates in adult education to identify important areas of competence for the field of adult education [2, p. 276]. "The behaviors for which the highest percentage of both graduate students and doctorates expressed a need for more competence were those in which the adult educator, 'identifies, critically evaluates, and discusses scholarly work by investigators in adult education and related fields,' and in which he, 'uses the processes of appraisal to evaluate programs and to help clarify and change objectives.'"

A review of the research efforts reported in the *Adult Education* journal covering the 1963 through 1966 period indicates increased emphasis on such functions of adult education as evaluation, program planning and methods and techniques [*34; 35; 36; 37*]. The foundations of adult education that received emphasis were clientele appraisal and teachers and leaders. The number of studies reported on these functions climbed from 22 to 46 and from 9 to 28 respectively for the four-year period 1963 through 1966.

Where We Are

The move to active concern for theory and research began on many fronts. Review of developments between 1960 and 1965 showed the changing focus of the Professors of Adult Education, new dimensions in leadership and service of the Adult Education Association of the USA, developing potentials for research supported by the United States Office of Education and a broader recognition of the role of adult education in society by leadership in both the public and private sectors. With these visions and efforts united, additional forward steps were made.

The Professors of Adult Education, after preparing a 12-page document [*33*] on "the new imperative," struggled for four years to put into writing [*18*] a description of the field and a body of knowledge useful for graduate training programs for adult educators. Although this painful process led to no classic document, it stimulated institutions with graduate programs to examine their program goals and reasons for being.

During this same period, the federal government developed a new stance toward adult education. There was a tradition of extensive federal aid for adult education in the Cooperative Extension Service in the U.S. Department of Agriculture, but only limited aid (and this in vocational fields) through the United States Office of Education (USOE). The first developments based upon a new perception of adult education by those in the USOE appeared in the 1950's with such adult education activities as were possible under the Vocational Rehabilitation Act of 1954, the Cooperative Research Act of 1954 and the National Defense Education Act of 1958. Between 1960 and 1965, a much more complete perception of the role of adult education in the U.S. was evident in the programs then approved. Among the major acts of that period, the following clearly indicated an awareness of the performance potentials in adult education: Manpower Development and Training Act of 1962,

Vocational Educational Act of 1963, Economic Opportunity Act of 1964, Elementary and Secondary Education Act of 1965 and the Higher Education Act of 1965. Indeed, so much recognition of the field had been given during this period that in 1966, the Adult Education Association of the USA published a 111-page directory of federal support for adult education [1].

The development of government programs which recognized adult education as part of a national responsibility was more in response to a changing society than an effort at leadership. Yet these programs did provide leadership of a sort. With the availability of new sources of funds for research and for programs, the practitioner was forced to ask about goals for his activities and to consider the nature of the field as he applied for funds. The positive research developments which stemmed from this period of growth and goal examination by adult educators are summarized by Liveright:

Positive Developments. Among the positive developments in Adult Education research are:

1. The National Opinion Research Center study provides, for the first time, sound facts and figures covering participation, and important data about motivation, attitudes, and recruitment.
2. The study by Brunner and Associates provides future researchers with an excellent overview of what has been done and what needs to be done.
3. A recent study by Burton Kreitlow of the University of Wisconsin, under a grant from the Cooperative Research Program of the U.S. Office of Education, performs a useful initial effort in relating adult education to other disciplines and proposes priority areas for research in adult education. "Relating Adult Education to Other Disciplines," Burton Kreitlow, Mimeographed, 1964.
4. Professor Harry Miller of Hunter College was requested to prepare a working paper for this study dealing with the development of a method or conceptual framework for examination of motivation and participation. This working paper (published by CSLEA in 1967) uses Maslow's needs analysis and selected pressures to look at forces for and against participation in different kinds of adult education among differing socio-economic groups. Miller suggests a fruitful method for participation analysis and creating experimental programs to stimulate greater participation.
5. An Ad Hoc Committee for the Study of Research in Adult Education (now known as the Adult Education Research Conference) headed by William Griffith, Associate Professor of Education at the University of Chicago, includes some 30 to 40 active adult educators; there were two

Research and Theory 141

hundred members by 1969. This group meets at least once a year "back to back" with the American Education Research Association. It has produced some interesting reports based upon discussions at the meetings.

6. The increasingly active Research Commission of the AEA is seeking to focus greater attention upon research among adult educators.
7. Adult education professors are placing greater emphasis upon research and more educators with research backgrounds are becoming professors. Because of these developments, the quality of doctoral dissertations is expected to improve greatly and the number of theses is expected to mount.
8. Evan R. Keisler, Stanford University member of the Committee on Learning and Educational Process of the Social Science Research Council, recently prepared a study of adult education research at the request of the Committee. Keisler found that although it "would seem reasonable" to give some attention to "the process of adult learning in relation to instruction," there is small evidence of "the existence of a separate field of adult learning." Nonetheless, Keisler suggested the following areas for discussion:

   a. The learning process and adult motivations.
   b. The learning process in adult reading instruction.
   c. The learning process among unemployable youth.
   d. Non-English speaking adults.
   e. Learning in late adulthood.

   Despite Keisler's findings of lack of research for adult learning, the possible interest of the Social Science Research Council is important. It is recommended that it be involved in future research activities and committees set up in the field of adult education.
9. The new research arrangements in the U.S. Office of Education—the establishment of a Division of Comprehensive and Vocational Education Research in the Bureau of Research, and the appointment of a highly qualified staff for this unit—can be an important step in furthering effective research. [27, pp. 37–38]

For the first time in the development of the field of adult education, adult educators had the resources at their disposal to carry out programs, examine past performances and take a serious look into the future.

The attempts to explain the role of adult education, identify its basic philosophy, clarify its overall objectives and describe the processes by which adult educators relate to their publics have all aided in obtaining a theoretical picture of the field. This picture has been described in a number of ways. The structural model developed for research in adult education encompasses the key ingredients identified in the literature and by interviews with national leaders in the social sciences. This schema identifies the three major and interrelated categories of application. They are:

1. The adult as an individual and a learner
2. The adult's response to social–cultural phenomena
3. The adult education enterprise.

Knowledge of these three categories is seen as a reasonable expectation for those who are to enter the profession. It is reasonable to expect the disciplines that help adult educators study the adult as an individual and as a learner (psychology, educational psychology, etc.) also will aid the person entering the field to strengthen his approach to both the organization and the operation of programs. In Dickerman's integration of the chapters in *Adult Education: Outlines of an Emerging Field of University Study* is the suggestion that adult educators get help from the other disciplines [12].

Chamberlain suggested administrators are ". . . more concerned with knowing things that work than in knowing why they work although he recognizes some inadequacies in this view [9, p. 78]." Through a factor analysis Chamberlain reported that the adult education professors place a higher value on concepts or intellectual aspects than do directors of adult education in voluntary organizations and the observers of adult education [9, pp. 82–83]. Directors also highly regard relationships to the group while observers emphasize the relationships with society. Directors of evening colleges downgrade concepts while emphasizing skills—the practical approach—and the deans of general extension divisions follow a similar pattern but also give positive emphasis to values.

Studies of the Cooperative Extension Service showed a somewhat different pattern. Biever concluded that the county agricultural committee perceived the agricultural agent's most important activity as dissemination of information [5, p. 110]. Schlutt [32, p. 220] found that both the beginning agents and their district leaders perceived "public and working relationships" and "leadership development" as having the highest values.

Knowles describes elsewhere in this book how rapidly and positively the field has moved in recent years. This movement has been in response to changes in society that have focused on the need for continued learning and led organizations engaged in adult education to examine their goals and in many instances to drastically change their structures (e.g., cooperative extension and vocational adult education). This push opened administrative doors for university faculties to establish or revise graduate programs for advanced study in adult education and pulled adult education into the mainstream of education from its former station on the margins of acceptance.

How We Got There

Whence came the financial and moral support to move? What stimulated those on the margin of the educational establishment to develop programs for adults? Numerous reasons have been noted in the literature, but rising above all others was the need to respond to a society that demanded learning as an input to its continued development. The changing electro–technical environment in communications, factory, and home demanded of an adult the ability to adjust, to change, to learn. There was a response in the central agencies of education—elementary schools, secondary schools, colleges and universities. There was an even greater response by the agencies of adult education. The climate for growth of adult education had reached a point where it could stimulate growth with or without cultivation. Institutions with both direct and indirect ties to the field began to respond. Agencies that were initially concerned with the education of young people now assumed the additional task of educating adults; agencies which had been created to serve adult students expanded their programs; community-serving agencies expanded their educational services to outside groups [19]. Many other agencies such as business and industry, government and labor unions recognized the need for their own adult education programs as a basis for growth and, at times, survival.

It is within this same environment that graduate study and research in adult education began their climb to visibility and impact. Houle charts the quantitative aspects [15; 16]. Some growth in graduate programs occurred in much the same way as the field itself grew—a job needed doing and someone responded. The organization of graduate programs was a response to demands of the field, but as programs were installed in major universities, justification on the basis of more than numbers of potential students was needed. The rationale of the field and its theoretical base had to be examined in relation to long established graduate programs in both the Schools of Education and Colleges of Agriculture.

The number of doctoral degrees in adult education granted by U.S. universities grew from 2 degrees in 1945 to 48 degrees in 1966 with a peak of 68 degrees in 1965. Prior to 1945, only 14 doctorates in adult education had been granted in all universities. It should be noted that the 246 degrees granted in the five-year period (1961–1966) is only 20 short of the total number of all previous degrees granted. Also encouraging is the fact that 95 percent of all recipients of doctorates in adult education are still employed in adult education or related fields.

The Changing Social Atmosphere

Why is adult education, so long on the margin of the field, now an integral part of life in the United States? First, because the social–technical climate demands continued learning and institutions of higher learning have accepted the challenge to prepare scholars to deal with the demands. Second, associated with this motivation for graduate study is the need to know more about the process of organizing continued learning. Graduate programs in American universities have traditionally provided the major operational research base in the field of education and so it has come about in adult education. It is here that graduate faculty members can organize for continuing research on major problems of the field and graduate students can contribute to an expanding body of knowledge.

No definitive study of the quantitative research output in adult education has been made, but there is evidence the upward spiral of completed studies each year parallels that of the expanding graduate programs. DeCrow reported in 1967 for the ERIC Clearinghouse on Adult Education the completed studies and studies in progress were so extensive that the practice of abstracting both for the quarterly journal, *Adult Education,* was no longer feasible [11]. There were too many for the space available. Thus 177 abstracts of completed research were published and 150 résumés of research-in-progress were sent to Science Information Exchange (SIE).

It should be clearly stated that the increase in graduate study and the advance in research was not accomplished solely by a response on the part of the universities to the social climate. Leadership from the great foundations (Ford, Kellogg, Carnegie) and the federal government was essential. The universities were concerned, but there is little evidence to show they would have made the major advances without the federal government and the foundations teasing them along. A typical example is that of the University of Wisconsin where the Kellogg Foundation, in 1956, helped underwrite a ten-year program of graduate fellowships, in-service education and research that established the National Agricultural Extension Center for Advanced Study. During this same period, funds from the National Defense Education Act provided fellowships to those seeking Ph.D. degrees in Adult Education from the School of Education. In 1956 there were five full-time graduate students in Adult or Extension Education on the Wisconsin campus; in 1965 there were 100.

Research and Theory

Although the major support for research and graduate program development came from foundations and the federal government, additional impetus was supplied by business, industry, professional organizations and state and local municipalities. Sabbaticals or leaves of absence to conduct advanced study in adult education were no longer rare. The Adult Education Association established a Commission of Professors of Adult Education in 1956. During its first years, the Commission focused on and developed the theoretical framework of the field and the organization of advanced study programs that would support that framework.

As a field of professional study, adult education borrows and reformulates knowledge from other disciplines. In his cogent chapter dealing with this reformulation process, Jensen clearly shows how knowledge from other disciplines is used and how phenomena studied by other disciplines—such as the social action process—become unique content for adult education [17]. Jensen's analysis of the process is followed by an identification of the relevance of such fields as sociology, social psychology, psychology, administration and history, and adult education practice. In his investigation, Kreitlow identified major concepts from the above and other disciplines and charted their relationship to both the curriculum for graduate study and the research needs of the field [21; 22].

New Ideas About Adult Learning

A number of key ingredients and concepts are finding their way into the adult education literature and receiving implementation by the agencies operating programs. Practicing adult educators are more aware of social change and its impact upon learners and potential learners. The works of Tyler [39] and Bloom [6] on curriculum development have been adapted by adult educators and are widely used in developing programs by adult education agencies. Socialization throughout the life span, long neglected by sociologists, is of great concern to adult educators and now that researchers and theoreticians like Brim and Wheeler [7], Becker [4] and Neugarten [29] are giving it their attention there will be additional impact made as adult educators translate the concepts into terms usable for program development.

Adult education would never be attempted were it not for a belief that adults can learn. Research into the nature of adult learning has only recently provided a base for making operational judgments. Early reports by Thorndike [38] of cross-sectional students are of historical significance, but the longitudinal (through the life span) studies of Lorge [28], Bayley and Oden [3] and Owens and Charles [31] give definitive guides to the areas of intellectual development that are maintained, hold firm, or decline through the life span. Adult instruction should be adjusted to what we know about the experiences of adults, their intellectual abilities and motivations. This phase of the field is only beginning to develop.

Adult education has been growing and changing; its base has been established. With the exception of status studies of the institutions of adult education, no serious examination has been made of the process of change, solely with adult education institutions in focus. Indeed, it is only recently that models for change in education have been examined as to their implications for an agency such as University or Cooperative Extension. Building upon what is known about the process of change in agriculture and its associated adoption process, and relating this to the change process in education as diagrammed by Guba and Clark [10], Kreitlow and MacNeil [25] designed a model to describe the improvement process in any educational institution. The key ingredients of the Model for Educational Improvement are organized into three dimensional space, including such critical factors as: a source of internal and external input; channels to move from research to development to diffusion to adoption; an improvement module where interaction among those with key roles can take place (administrator, citizen, teacher, student); and space where improvement ideas can move to the appropriate channel toward adoption or stagnate for lack of commitment or leadership. Models are used as a means of appraising the process of change as it relates to adult education, to give structure and visibility to theory, and to appraise an observed process (institutional change in this example) as it relates to the development of the field.

Toward the Future in Theory and Research

Adult education has been a "following" field of study. Long sitting at the margin of universities and public schools, it has only recently become sufficiently structured to have its own identity. The move forward has often been held back by the traditions of teaching and administrative practices organized for elementary, secondary or higher education. Adult education has an opportunity to be a "leading" field of study. Evidence suggests that the change from "follower" to "leader" has been made. The field has expanded rapidly in its mission and scope, in the development of graduate programs and in its research. During this time, adult education has been fortunate in having national professional organizations of long standing watch over it and lead the way. The National Association for Public Continuing and Adult Education, the groups associated with University and Cooperative Extension and the Adult Education Association of the USA's Commission of

Professors of Adult Education have played a watching and leading role. An example of this concern is noted in the joint efforts made to outline the research priorities to be used as guides for future investigations. The identification of research priorities was a joint undertaking of the U.S. Office of Education, Federal Extension Service, Commission of Professors of Adult Education and the University of Wisconsin. A field of study developing its theory and rationale in response to today's social setting would be doomed if it did not take advantage of its concerned parent institutions and those disciplines to which it is related. Adult education is doing this and must continue to do so.

References

1. Adult Education Association of the USA. *Federal Support for Adult Education*. Washington, D.C.: Adult Education Association of the USA, 1966.
2. Aker, George F. "The Identification of Criteria for Evaluating Graduate Programs in Adult Education." Unpublished doctoral thesis. Madison, Wis.: University of Wisconsin, 1962.
3. Bayley, Nancy, and Oden, Melita H. "The Maintenance of Intellectual Ability in Gifted Adults." *Journal of Gerontology*, X (January, 1955), pp. 91–107.
4. Becker, Howard S. "Personal Change in Adult Life." *Sociometry*, XXVII (1964), pp. 40–53.
5. Biever, Lawrence J. "Roles of County Extension Agents as Perceived by County Agricultural Committee Members in Wisconsin." Unpublished doctoral thesis. Madison, Wis.: University of Wisconsin, 1957.
6. Bloom, Benjamin S., ed. *Taxonomy of Educational Objectives*. New York: Longmans, Green, 1956.
7. Brim, Orville S., Jr., and Wheeler, Stanton. *Socialization After Childhood: Two Essays*. New York: John Wiley & Sons, 1966.
8. Brunner, Edmund de S., and others. *An Overview of Adult Education Research*. Chicago, Ill.: Adult Education Association of the USA, 1959.
9. Chamberlain, Martin N. "The Competencies of Adult Educators." *Adult Education*, XI (Winter, 1961), pp. 78–82.
10. Clark, David L., and Guba, Egon G. "Understanding Social Change." *SEC Newsletter*, I (October, 1965), pp. 1–4.
11. DeCrow, Roger. "Research and Investigations in Adult Education." *Adult Education*, XVII (Summer, 1967), pp. 195–258.
12. Dickerman, Watson. "Implications of This Book for Programs of Graduate Study in Adult Education." In: *Adult Education: Outline of an Emerging Field of University Study*. Edited by Gale Jensen, A. A. Liveright and Wilbur Hallenbeck, Washington, D.C.: Adult Education Association of the USA, 1964, pp. 307–326.
13. Essert, Paul L. "Adult Education—An Overview." *Review of Educational Research*, XXIII (June, 1953), pp. 195–201.

14. Hendrickson, Andrew. "Adult Education." In: *Encyclopedia of Educational Research* (3rd ed.). Edited by Chester W. Harris. New York: The Macmillan Company, 1960, pp. 30–42.
15. Houle, Cyril O., and Buskey, John H. "The Doctorate in Adult Education, 1935–1965." *Adult Education*, XVI (Spring, 1966), pp. 131–168.
16. Houle, Cyril O., and Lappin, Ivan M. "Doctorates in Adult Education Awarded in 1966." *Adult Education*, XVII (Spring, 1967), pp. 132–133.
17. Jensen, Gale. "How Adult Education Borrows and Reformulates Knowledge of Other Disciplines." In: *Adult Education: Outlines of an Emerging Field of University Study*. Edited by Gale Jensen, A. A. Liveright and Wilbur Hallenbeck. Washington, D.C.: Adult Education Association of the USA, 1964, pp. 105–111.
18. Jensen, Gale; Liveright, A. A.; and Hallenbeck, Wilbur, eds. In: *Adult Education: Outlines of an Emerging Field of University Study*, Washington, D.C.: Adult Education Association of the USA, 1964.
19. Knowles, Malcolm S. "The Field of Operation in Adult Education." In: *Adult Education: Outlines of an Emerging Field of University Study*. Edited by Gale Jensen, A. A. Liveright and Wilbur Hallenbeck. Washington, D.C.: Adult Education Association of the USA, 1964, pp. 41–67.
20. Kreitlow, Burton W. "Adult Education—An Overview." *Review of Educational Research*, XXIX (June, 1959), pp. 225–229.
21. Kreitlow, Burton W. *Educating the Adult Educator: Part 1. Concepts for the Curriculum*. Bulletin 573. Madison, Wis.: University of Wisconsin, College of Agriculture, March, 1965.
22. Kreitlow, Burton W. *Educating the Adult Educator: Part 2. Taxonomy of Needed Research*. Theoretical Paper No. 13. Madison, Wis.: University of Wisconsin, Research and Development Center, May, 1968.
23. Kreitlow, Burton W. "Needed Research." *Review of Educational Research*, XXXV (June, 1965), pp. 240–245.
24. Kreitlow, Burton W. "Research in Adult Education." In: *Handbook of Adult Education in the United States*. Edited by Malcolm S. Knowles. Chicago, Ill.: Adult Education Association of the USA, 1960, pp. 106–115.
25. Kreitlow, Burton W., and MacNeil, Teresa. *An Evaluation of the Model for Educational Improvement, An Analytical Tool for Describing the Change Process*. A Working Paper. Madison, Wis.: University of Wisconsin, Research and Development Center for Cognitive Learning, 1968.
26. Lindeman, Edward C. *The Meaning of Adult Education*. Montreal, Canada: Harvest House, 1961.
27. Liveright, A. A. *A Study of Adult Education in the United States*. Brookline, Mass.: Center for the Study of Liberal Education for Adults, 1968.

28. Lorge, Irving. "Capacities of Older Adults." In: *Education for Later Maturity*. Edited by Wilma Donahue. New York: Whiteside, 1955.
29. Neugarten, Bernice L., and others. "Age Norms, Age Constraints, and Adult Socialization." *American Journal of Sociology*, LXX (1965), pp. 710–717.
30. Overstreet, Harry A. "No Previous Training Required." *Journal of Adult Education* (June, 1936), pp. 241–246.
31. Owens, William A., and Charles, Don C. *Life History Correlate of Age Changes in Mental Abilities*. Cooperative Research Project No. 1052. Lafayette, Ind.: Purdue University Press, 1963.
32. Schlutt, Edward F. "The District Extension Leader's and the Beginning County Agent's Perception of the Beginning Agents' Role Definition and Role Fulfillment." Unpublished doctoral thesis. Madison, Wis.: University of Wisconsin, 1959.
33. The Commission of the Professors of Adult Education. "Adult Education: A New Imperative of Our Times." Chicago, Ill.: Adult Education Association of the USA, 1961.
34. Thiede, Wilson B., and Draper, James. "Research and Investigations in Adult Education." *Adult Education*, XIII (Summer, 1963), pp. 195–216.
35. Thiede, Wilson B., and Draper, James. "Research and Investigations in Adult Education." *Adult Education*, XIV (Summer, 1964), pp. 195–225.
36. Thiede, Wilson B., and Meggers, John. "Research and Investigations in Adult Education." *Adult Education*, XV (Summer, 1965), pp. 195–234.
37. Thiede, Wilson B., and Meggers, John, "Research and Investigations in Adult Education." *Adult Education*, XVI (Summer, 1966), pp. 195–238.
38. Thorndike, E. L., and others. *Adult Learning*. New York: The Macmillan Company, 1928.
39. Tyler, Ralph W. "New Dimensions in Curriculum Development." *Phi Delta Kappan*, XLVIII (September, 1966), pp. 25–28.

Chapter 10

A Glance at the Future

PAUL A. MILLER

Adult education has endured although it has not been fully understood. It is an endurance noted for its lack of visibility and its quietness. One recalls a memorable scene in *Goodbye Mr. Chips*, when Mr. Chips makes a reassuring speech to a boy named Robertson who is conjugating Latin verbs in the midst of an air raid:

It may possibly seem to you, Robertson—at this particular moment in the world's history—that the affairs of Caesar in Gaul, some two thousand years ago, are of secondary importance—and the irregular conjugation of the the verb *tollo* is . . . even less important still. But believe me . . . my dear Robertson—that is not really the case. You cannot judge the importance of things by the noise they make.

This is one view of the meaning of endurance. It describes perhaps the most important comment to be made about continuing adult education: It has endured. But, in order to endure, one must come to prevail. The endurance that has enabled adult education to prevail, in both its eternal and daily meanings, is a most important legacy for anticipating its character for the next several years. This legacy has not been built up without scars—scars which only now are beginning to heal. The deepest wound in the character of adult education, a result of the struggle to win more than marginal status, was an underlying suspicion—a kind of paranoia—that learning in later life was only partially welcome in the main body of educational activity. Indeed, for many

151

years, it was *de rigueur* at adult education assemblies to air complaints about inhospitable colleagues at home and hostile administrators everywhere. However, as the preceding chapters of the Handbook reveal, the age of paranoia for adult education has come to an end and its demise in the sixties is sure to release creative energies on behalf of lifelong learning—energies long contained in the struggle of the field to prevail.

Changes in the Society

The ability to throw off this old bondage is not alone due to the growing confidence of adult educators. Forces in contemporary society are setting up conditions which point increasingly to the necessity of adult learning. In short, what is happening to modern life stands on the side of adult education. The swirls of change in education itself inexorably move the balance of interest toward the informal, out-of-school side. In the whole of society, human institutions are either in such upheaval or so stagnated that human competence (at least for the production and distribution of social goods and for the discovery of human identity) is impossible without some pervasive arrangement for continuous learning. Such forces color any view of the future, since the future of man depends upon how adaptive man can make himself and his institutions.

A Growing Disparity

The change in education generally is at once a paradox and a revelation concerning the future of adult education. Public policy places education high upon the agenda of the nation at a time when the efficacy of education is doubted. This disparity produces some remarkable expansions in the context of educational discussions. Education is reflected in the desire of the public to eradicate poverty, to extend equal opportunity, to make it possible for every person to live his life with dignity and to help the underdeveloped nations to share the technological benefits of the developed nations. These expansions in the idea of education move it from the enclosures of schools and colleges, into the currents of life. Small wonder adult education edges closer to the center of the stage.

This displacement in the meaning of education, rapidly becoming a conception of human development, has become more massive and widespread than anyone, even a decade ago, could foresee. And we look forward to successive explosions of human activity, forced outward by technology, sprawling across the ramparts of old and outmoded institutions, withering still further the vestiges of the primary community, centralizing man and his activity in cities (and raising those questions about who he is). There are few doors to keep people out of education. There are few if any doors closed to adult education.

Equal to or greater in importance than the shifts in the idea of education are far-reaching turbulences in the fabric of society. These turbulences flow from the reorganization of society from rural to urban life, from the imbalance between social and technological invention, and from confusion and discord about where the changes are leading us. The issues are many, but some may be singled out as having greatest bearing upon the usefulness of education in general, and upon the future promise of adult education in particular.

Perhaps the central paradox is the success of the United States in producing and distributing economic and technological goods contrasted with its lack of success in producing and distributing social goods. Much of the American genius, including that in education, has been arrayed on the side of economic goods. It is likely the disparity will grow more acute in the future unless education in all of its forms is joined with the policy-making process to achieve better understanding of the *origins* of social technology (rather than continuing the historical emphasis upon the social effects of mechanical technology). This shift in emphasis is impossible without greater belief in and expansion of adult education.

A Loss of Individuality

Another issue concerns the rapid growth in the importance of the public sector, and the resulting effect it has on advancing group decisions at the expense of individual decisions. This is a vast and still new problem of reconciling social choices with individual values—in decisions about cities, education, health care and environmental quality. Even as an evident strain exists today between the citizens and a centralized government which emphasizes collective action, only wise participation in the future will avoid deepening alienation of people from their governing authorities—a profound challenge to education, whatever its form may be.

A related problem concerns the large functional units of administrative action—in education, health, housing, agriculture, labor, welfare, and commerce. Stretching from local to national levels, the communicaion within these blocs is more effective than that which occurs among them. Accordingly, people tend to become social functions rather than complete persons. To the medical specialist, a person is a medical disorder; to the teacher, a slow or rapid learner; to the highway engineer, a driver of automobiles; to the legislator, a voter; to the farmer or manufacturer, a consumer. Public institutions organize themselves around these functions, and compete over resources for them. Learning about these inefficient systems of citizen transaction which are characteristic of our day is learning that cannot be legislated into existence. Only self-study—by individuals and groups, that is to say, adult education—will make it possible for administrative practice to be so continuously reshaped as to serve not itself but the ends of people.

Such imperfections in the social fabric provide one among many starting points for anticipating the future of adult education. Of one thing we may be certain, adult learning will be shaped by both those forces at work within education as well as those which tear the social fabric. At the same time, adult educators may be expected to help effect the needed reformation of the whole of education. Formal learning will be increasingly released, like some long-contained genie, for absorption into the whole of life, to serve people of all ages, of all needs, of all hopes. And just beyond is the tempting mystery of how education may help the search for personal identity to prevail over corrosive distrust among individuals and between the groups to which they attach allegiance.

Commitments to Program

The authors of this Handbook stress the importance of program to the drama of adult education. Growing and maturing as it is, the field strikes one as amorphous, especially if he is looking for a way to gain a sense of direction. But the content of this Handbook, and the manner in which several authors have honed down their conclusions, suggests at least a partial outline of things to come in the decade or so ahead.

Basic Citizenship

The future program commitment of adult education, everywhere in the world, is likely to be influenced by one quite substantial dissatisfaction—the traditional emphasis upon the refinement of occupational skills. The 1980 Handbook may call the seventies a decade which saw the change from stress on occupational symbols of success to values capable of superseding the hitherto dominant ethic of work. Adult education will be seeking ways to update family and community life at the expense of vocational skill. As the Handbook suggests, new and stronger guidelines for learning more about basic citizenship seem already to be visible.

Public Responsibility. The next decade will doubtlessly fan the present debate over the restraints to individuality of post-industrial technology. The outcome is already involved in present day suggestions that technology may indeed enlarge the individuality and choices of persons if the individual is capable of performing in a *community of organizations.* During the next decade, the meaning of community will continue to shift away from the direct relationships of persons toward transactions of individuals through economic, political, religious, educational and public service organizations. This will mean diverse groups providing equally diverse opportunities for people to contribute inputs of time, energy and money, and to receive diverse outputs of goods, services and cultural satisfactions. To bring minority groups into the mainstream involves more than distributing benefits; it also will require, as in the black ghettoes of urban America, new structures as well as new skills.

There is another dimension of education for public responsibility that almost certainly will be increasingly important in the decade ahead. This is the rediscovery of the importance of the *community professions.* Whether teaching in the schools or serving as an appointed or elected official, those who take part in local government will play increasingly significant roles. As the sixties come to a close, a widespread awareness of the inadequacy of local government is found throughout the land. While there are vast imperfections in the performance of the federal government, the past decades have seen rising performance levels of national leaders charged with such complex assignments as managing the economy and working out national programs in health and transportation. But at the state, county and city levels officials are hamstrung by forms of governance which were developed for earlier and simpler times. This incongruity is now so apparent that no more urgent business exists in the United States than to encourage more young people, by means of improved preparation and working conditions, to choose local government as their life's work. But even this will accomplish little unless adult educators find new ways to reach both the people and their officials with learning opportunities designed to inspire them to perform the critical acts that the public sector requires.

Still another aspect of forthcoming public responsibility is found in the need to strengthen the *helping professions* and to find new forms for their activities. As expressive values make inroads into instrumental values, helping and nurturing at the community level is bound to be taken up by more people, either as paid professionals or as volunteers. There is no greater challenge to adult educators than to help people learn how to reach out to the poor, teach the infirm, and encompass the needs of the wounded. In the process, more attention is likely to be called to the need of creating "careers for the poor" in order that those who understand their own people may take up nurturing roles and move through them to higher levels of professional practice. From teacher aide to teacher is but a single example.

Continual Learning. Such new horizons will not of course reduce the burden of providing continuing in-service education to those who practice the standard professions. The "Service Society" places the solution of human needs in the hands of the professional practitioner. With the expansion of knowledge, this is a terrifying prospect unless continuous learning and relearning comes to be seen as a part of professional practice. This is an enormous challenge to both pre-service and in-service professional training.

Family Life

The second requirement of basic citizenship stems from the performance levels of families. The decade ahead is not likely to see a revolution in family–life education. But some discoveries will be made as the search for an elusive human identity continues. Among them most likely will be something more than lingering doubt that formal education has done very much to help individuals fulfill themselves through living with others in family groups. It also seems likely we shall learn that instruction and practice about how one works at making a family, compared with how one is taught to succeed in an occupation, is everywhere given the back of the educator's hand. And we shall better understand how educators and family members share these common illusions: something in the process of growing up is sufficient to make one a good wife or husband or parent; there is little to be taught about it; it rather happens to one; and anyway it is either a bit too ordinary or private to be tampered with.

Adult educators in the next few years may be expected to do better at applying modern theories of organization to the family. They will be asking themselves what families contribute as useful outputs to society and what they need back as inputs. Adult education can thus be used to bring family development a bit closer to its central interest, recognizing that the family is yet the best way of socializing the young; providing intimate, consistent, dependable, and secure relationships between male and female; between two human beings; and providing finally that microcosm of living which tests continually how conflict may be resolved without destroying a system of social relationships. Similarly, the field of adult education, if it proposes larger intentions for family life, will need to acquire more ideas about how families link up with communities. Moreover, as the mass media and other features of learning technology become more accepted extensions of adult education, the family will come to be viewed as a fundamental and natural host of continuous human growth and development. Within the decade it would be surprising if a few enterprising adult educators failed to work with the learning console idea in the family residence, setting forth the blueprint of an era in which the educational influence of the family is understood at last in conjunction with the educational influence of the school and the community.

The Urban Strategy

In the next several years, as it has been in the immediate past, American education will be urgently asked to contribute to the solution of problems in urban society. If they hope to find new forms of public financial support, adult educators will be called upon, by host institutions and agencies and by national and local centers of governmental power, to outline strategy for applying the education of adults to critical urban issues. In the bargain, an old dilemma of adult education will be revealed again: Is it to be addressed to individuals interested in some form of personal fulfillment or to groups desirous of effecting social change, or to some combination of the two? How to balance these two elements—intervention in the life of an individual and intervention in the community—will be among the important problems in the years ahead.

In higher adult education, for example, the swing to a strategy of social change (or even devising a form of social technology or engineering) just now is following in the wake of earlier extensions of university resources for cultural enrichment and occupational enhancement. Whatever the outcome of this swing, it will encounter the historical bias of adult education to middle class interests. One must wonder what the seventies will bring to the field as it considers how best to assist the policy-making tasks of people holding posts of urban power, on the one hand, and how to enlarge educational opportunity, on the other hand, for people whose lives are blunted by poverty and racial and other forms of discrimination. In the least, it is safe to predict, one may expect closer communication among leaders of adult education, those committed to community action and the practitioners of such community professions as social work and the religious ministry.

Continued anxiety over urban ills will result in all of education becoming more experimental and more willing to take risks. This is an especially acute need where adult education is concerned, because its traditional financing—basically a fee for service system—has allowed few if any funds for experimental and evaluative purposes. Something will have to be done soon about this if genuinely multidisciplinary efforts are to characterize the field. There is urgent need in urban society to test ideas which proved useful in other situations. This is a challenge for Cooperative Extension, which needs risk capital for testing the youth development programs of rural society in many and varied urban settings. Less standard fare will doubtlessly characterize adult education in the next decade. But risky investments will be much in order.

During the course of the sixties, education found it difficult to relate to the changing currents of urban life. Confused, though its meaning and application remained, adult education nevertheless has carried on as perhaps the most self-conscious tie of the schools and colleges to the larger community. This is a resource that will stand adult education in good stead, especially as its leaders bring themselves to understand that these linkages need more study and codification. Such efforts will improve the meaning attached to adult education and enable educational leaders in general to learn more about how institutions may define their relationships with society. There are few questions in need of more conscious, more creative and more committed responses.

The Educable Patron

Even as many would doubt the efficacy of contemporary education, it surely provides more educational opportunity in the absolute sense and more quality of learning as well, although perhaps not in proportion to the need for it. Moreover, recognizing the number of people who now have had extensive educational experience, evidence seems rampant on every side that these same people fail to understand the relationship of educational activity to them and to their communities. The importance of education has created an already large and growing popular constituency for schools and colleges, a constituency which on the whole has been neglected, either as continuing learners or as informed patrons of the institutions. These popular constituencies, not always seen as educable patrons, are frequently politicized, not educated, in order to enlarge specific institutional fortunes. It makes no matter whether the conflict is over the management of the school or over the issue of how far the university should go in servicing society. In both instances, the very graduates of these schools and colleges are frequently not prepared to lend their insights to the perilous exigencies which now spring up in educational development.

There are clashes of opinion, sometimes violent, on every side. One needs only to mention the tortuous response to ridding the society of separate and unequal schools. The conflict is no less real and no less violent as one observes the fragility of higher education, surrounded as it is by rebellious and undifferentiated constituencies, each pushing for responses to issue resolution no longer capable of discharge by the instruments of academic governance. In this instance, the university seems to be undergoing some vast technological institutionalization in society without a meaningful conversation among those whose experience with the process is extensive.

These critical drifts of educational institutions suggest that adult educators must gird themselves for the task of providing continuous education about education. As education within the educational family becomes more feasible, the school is likely to become more of a community center than it now is, and the university may discover adult education is much less the delivery of an educational service to a given clientele than it is the convening of discussants about critical societal issues, with the process, not the delivery, the aim of highest fidelity. Adult education about education will be among the foremost challenges of the future.

Commitments to Competence

Several directions are identified in the Handbook. None surpasses in importance the professional development of adult education. For the first time, significant numbers of leaders appear who have chosen adult education for their life's work. The field possesses a burgeoning literature, although more descriptive than analytical. The centers of research and graduate study grow in number and size and are likely to continue their growth. Their location has become common knowledge as they have come to influence the field. Adult education is on the way to becoming professionalized, both at home and abroad. Some major substantive designs for competence are visible, to which these remarks now turn.

Resource Organization

Thinking of urban society as a community of organizations (and acting accordingly) will have increasing impact upon institutions and agencies, like those in adult education, that propose to match specialized resources with generalized problems. A major problem of complex societies, requiring the most creative assessment, concerns how technical resources are discovered and deployed for use. Struggling with issues of resource management will be among the major professional challenges of adult education in the immediate future.

Internal Organization. As more and more people experience the decay of social institutions, and suffer the crises of institutional neglect, they will become increasingly willing to run the risks of setting up entirely new forms. More tools to help them also are available, such as systems analysis. All of education will be interested in the techniques of adaptation, perhaps more than ever before in history, and adult education will be no exception. It will be good for adult educators to look squarely at an old strain—how to establish their activities as a part of some sponsoring institution or agency. Administering and budgeting for adult learning, especially in the schools and colleges, have been sufficiently marginal to the main body of practice that adult educators had ample reason in the past to link poor acceptance of their work to the flimsy arrangements provided for it.

Throughout the history of adult education, experience and discussion have organized about two modes within schools and colleges. The first argued for the importance of decentralizing resources, on a wide institutional basis, with a small and frequently marginal office to conduct managerial tasks. This mode assures that adult education is seen by all members of the institution as a normal everyday part of *educational* duty. The other mode of organization, its proponents insist, defers to the growing specialization of function; it makes necessary specific resources and decision-making centers for the conduct of adult education. The first mode secures legitimacy for the field in the parent group; the second mode speaks more to sensitivity of client needs.

One senses, perhaps from the new confidence of adult educators as well as their greater access to professional opinion, that arguments polarized around these two modes are breaking down. While it is not likely these major ways of conducting adult learning programs will be overthrown, the next few years should see the addition of and the widening out of new forms. It is likely specific settings will produce equally distinctive modes, and a mood of relaxation will grow about how best to organize for the adult education task. Continuing experience with such approaches as the campus conference center will make the search for some ideal way of establishing adult education much less important.

If one attempts to chart the direction of the drift, however, adult education would seem to be moving toward new forms of incorporation within institutions as wholes. Here it is influenced by events in the whole of education—an edging toward informal, independent study, the use of the community as the learning space and greater stress on "learning how to learn." Education generally is incorporating the old tenets of adult education within its theories and methods of learning. The notion of continuous learning is becoming more acceptable, if not necessary, to pedagogy, from kindergarten to the graduate school. It can mean but

A Glance at the Future 161

one thing: Adult education in the schools and colleges will become stronger substantively and less distinct as an organizational datum.

As the idea of education expands into human growth and development, "education" and "continuing education" rise to a closer interface with each other. An anachronism is exposed: Why do institutions whose sole function is education see fit to sponsor divisions of "education" and "continuing education"? As such anachronisms become visible, and as new questions about educational efficacy are raised, the leaders of institutions may be expected to consider new centers devoted to human learning in its broadest and most dynamic sense. When the "school of education" becomes the "institute for human learning," adult educators may find their own modes less clear for awhile, but, having joined a larger mission, they will be better able to influence the relationship of learning to life.

External Organization. The organization of adult education also involves the community beyond the educational institution or agency. During the past decade, enormous proliferation of structure occurred in the local community. Responding to popular confusion over national systems of delivering human services, latent public demand, and sometimes overt hostility, some people were stimulated to clothe such old ideas as "community action" with new creeds and to make use of such extensions as "store-front centers," "street academies," "neighborhood centers," "free universities," and "city churches." Notwithstanding the fact that these ideas were connected to helping a submerged black minority to move forward, they also speak to the great public determination to meet needs of community identity.

If it is true that the megalopolis will characterize human living in the future—and one may hope adult educators will help raise the question as to whether or not this trend is right or necessary—the problem of access to educational opportunity, for all people and for many purposes, is among the post-sixties challenges. Such structures as have risen in the sixties will doubtlessly be continued, reviewed, and modified in the seventies. Among the interesting prospects is that the adult educator will try his hand at creating a distinctively urban institution of continuing education, designed especially as a community institution to encourage adults to learn through independent study, group study, community participation, group problem solving, and the recreative and cultural arts.

Such a new institution for adult education, given present trends in the field, could be welcomed on a free standing basis, or as an extension of some other center. The need for such an institution is on the way to becoming clear. First, extensive educational facilities on the wealthy side of the city are not being used by people on the poor side. Second, educators must learn more about how learning can better connect with the hopes of deprived people and how to dedicate effort, not to remaking others in one's own image, but to the reduction of lostness, to the method of seeking, to the joy of human fulfillment. Third, the new "college in the city" would spin new ties to existing schools and colleges, and open the gates to people of all ages and of all walks of life and interests. Fourth, a new instrument of off-campus education will serve as the rallying point of education for adults, whether sponsored by educational institutions, social agencies, libraries, government groups, industries or churches. Lastly, it would assist if not enable the talent of a total metropolis to be identified and mobilized for service, enlivened with the dream that all may come to teach as well as to learn.

It is extraordinary how American society sponsors educational institutions which produce such unintended consequences and problems without insisting that those very institutions employ their talents to help in the solutions of those problems. Manpower planning is so awkward today that stocks of talent are not ordinarily located where the problems are (illustrated in such a helping profession as nursing). With the impact, still muted, of cybernetics on urban life, the design of a new life style seems in the making, a style that will enable both productive and service chapters in the life cycle of the citizen. Such a change will not only transform every aspect of education, but will also lead to new kinds of continuous learning. This possibility is clearly seen in the promise of womanpower. Certainly the next decade will find educational centers opening themselves to mature women in less begrudging fashion than they do today, fusing group learning with independent study and community service with instruction. Before long the practices of housewifery and motherhood will not exact the price of intellectual stagnation.

Finally, as a kind of outward-facing competence, whether as part of newly created institutions for adult education or not, the management of programs of continuous learning will require greater willingness on the part of educators to master media technology. In many ways, the media constitute the leading opportunity for adult educators to establish revolutionary connections between the community and educational opportunities. Mastery of the media cannot be left to business and the military. Possibilities are clearly visible: state-wide networks that give access to information available in many data banks; city-wide plans employing decentralized computer-access learning centers that would be available to any resident; a college-wide curriculum extended through computer access into the community, with the goal of creating a total information environment; a computer-based grievance center, giving citizens access to spokesmen of government—local, state or national.

A Glance at the Future

As the world moves along a precipice of international disaster, educators everywhere are challenged to make up their minds about the media technology—produced by the same laboratories, including their own, that yielded the weaponry capable of contemporary destruction. It is to be hoped some of the centers for graduate study in adult education will prepare a generation of dreamers competent to consider the profound implications of telecommunications.

Educational Systems

Conversation about education today refers casually to computers, television, teaching machines, multiplex radio bands, consortiums, nation-wide compacts and team teaching. New and special structures abound: Regional laboratories; the Teacher Corps; manpower centers and community service centers. All together they are coinciding to form the era of systems: state systems; consolidated university systems; regional network systems; new systems of federalism; community information systems.

This era, moving across urban communities now lacking identity and a unifying force, shouts a message to education, the loudness of which can no longer be denied: isolated and unilateral approaches on the part of individual institutions of education are becoming both obsolescent and counterproductive. For good or ill, all human endeavor will be increasingly transformed by the age of systems. How to become more skillful with multilateral approaches in community education is a major challenge to adult education: it is an important and urgent theme for the decade ahead.

The magnitude of social problems in the urbanizing century, when placed beside the money, knowledge and talent available for solution, exposes to full view the remarkable lack of connection between the various levels of education. Even with almost everybody participating in some way in education—all ages, all aptitudes and at all times—educators persist in defining the most careful distinctions among educational levels. One must wonder if this is not at bottom the cause of the lock-step which lingers on after almost everyone agrees that great numbers of students are never touched in terms of their unique potentialities. No reform holds more promise to widespread adult education systems than the tendency here and there of fostering a fellowship between the university, the community college and the public school.

The University. The contemporary university is caught between its own traditional expectations and those of its popular constituencies. As the outward explosions of the technological age found so many human institutions wanting, it was assumed the center which provides the knowledge upon which the technological age is based would fill the gap. The university, geared to centuries of nurturing a necessary independence, elected to take up this challenge quite on its own, at the very time when cooperative approaches seemed the only antidote to social fragmentation.

Has the university gone far enough, *as a unilateral force,* with its intervention on behalf of continuous learning? Shouldn't the university devote more of its resources to strengthening the entire fabric of education in the community? Should it not be creating new institutional forms, supporting them, preparing personnel for them, devising research and development plans, demonstrating, evaluating, all with the hope that every school and college might become attuned to a more zestful, varied, individualized form of community learning? A more viable system of education in the United States awaits the sympathetic fellowship of the university. Adult educators can help secure this fellowship and, in the bargain, encounter profoundly positive opportunities for their own work.

The Community College. As the saga of lifelong learning unfolds, it is difficult not to assign the community college a centrally important place. The distribution and growth of these institutions suggests that education of the future will be enormously influenced by the chain of them now springing up across the country. The community college movement will introduce the most students to higher education in the future.

Having emerged as an inventive response to the egalitarian ideals of mass higher education, the community college has grown up with a comfortable feeling about being part of its local area. This is true in a way never characteristic of the university. In one sense, however, the full impact of the community college upon adult education will not arrive until it takes deep root in urban centers. When it does, new instruments of adult education will surely be in the making.

Recent writing about the community college suggests that, having matured in its academic and technical options, it is arriving at fresh insights and commitments about community service. Several hundred strong, with new institutions added by the month, and leaders proud of the movement, community colleges will capture many of the headlines of the next decade for persistent, widespread adult education and community service. Not to be overlooked as well is the location of the community college between the public schools and higher education, a position that ironically it did not always enjoy. Accordingly, insofar as educational systems influence adult education in the future, the community college turns out to be the strategic link between the two other major elements of the formal educational enterprise. With good luck, the community college will join Cooperative Extension as a unique instrument of community-based continuous educational service.

The Public School. Urban pathologies show that vital centers of neighborhood life are more needed than before. On every side a redefinition of the school is under way. It has been largely a place for children, but many now believe the school must return to its ancient role as a civic center—as town hall, cultural center, "center club," a place of local identity. Everywhere there is a search for ways of reorienting schools to community needs. Some believe the school should be the nexus of urban community life, especially for the central cities. The growing experience of teaching disadvantaged children convinces more and more people that the community as much as the school becomes the learning arena. The school of the future will likely cooperate more closely with industry, cultural and recreational centers and municipal agencies. And once the school employs the entire community as the domain of learning, the process of "learning how to learn" will at last entice adult educators to connect their work with those early ages when the process begins. As this happens, the theory of continuous learning will become more than theory, and the learning community will come into sight.

Educational Service Agencies. There is an even more complex kind of coordination than that needed within the educational enterprise. This becomes apparent when active forms of adult education are proposed as interventions to effect social change or create new forms of social technology. Standing in the midst of the social upheavals of our day, educational institutions are involved with social problems whether they like to be or not. However, pressures of growth and financial uncertainty, along with the deadweight of established practice, hold back improved communications between the educational establishment and the community. Neither of them can do much alone, even knowing what the problem is. No community has found the way to merge the concerns of both so that educational and non-educational agencies may work together and yet not impair the special functions for which each was established.

Accordingly, adult educators will have special opportunities for unusual public service in the future by joining with leaders from public and private life to plan and execute "metropolitan educational service or development agencies." Until such system approaches are devised, much of education will not be responsive to human potentials in all their variations, and will continue, as an exception indeed among major sectors of activity in society, on a trial-and-error basis.

Some such format will be required if the urgent need is to be met for a new collaboration between higher education, the public schools, community government, and community organizations. These educational service agencies will promote comprehensive planning and evaluation, as well as community education, work–study programs, and the training and retraining of teachers for every aspect of the educational task. They will also identify and develop new relationships between education and family and community life, including housing, health services and employment opportunities. Adult educators must be in the middle of this movement, since their own ties extend in this direction, and because adult education on behalf of all education is among the crucial emphases of the future.

A National Observatory. As adult educators incorporate in their plans an interest in a *system* of education, it is certain their thoughts will turn increasingly to a better way of crystallizing the national interest in their own field. Already it is difficult to keep various adult organizations conversing on common plans, to link the effort of adult education to legislative development and to communicate to constituent agencies in the field how adult education is related to national goals and values.

Moreover, given the improvements in systems analysis, perhaps the next decade will see the development of a major instrument for measuring progress, for defining adult education, for describing how one part of the field interacts with others and discerning what influence adult education exerts upon American society. Assessments of progress and failure in education are retarded on every front, due perhaps to deep felt beliefs in pluralism and local control. Adult education is somewhat free of these constraints. As part of the "national observatory," or under some other auspice, and as the borders between various levels and kinds of education grow less distinct, adult education leaders will continue the move toward measuring the field in more analytical terms.

The Future of Adult Education

Reading the Handbook gives one the view that the idea of continuous lifelong learning is no longer in doubt. Even the old paranoia, of not being accepted in the main camp of education, is fading. Accordingly, it seems safe to state that adult education will not perish, even as adult educators become more relaxed and confident, more given to forsaking old modes of program form and method. No field of education will be immune in the years ahead to risk and failure. But one way or the other, adult education will prevail. The context of its vision, which is no longer very different from that of education as a whole, is sufficient calling for any educator.

A Glance at the Future

Finally, perhaps more than any other part of education, adult learning is sensitive to changes in social procedure. It is today. The gales of change are sweeping across the entire world. New forces—in Europe, in Asia, in Africa—are trying to shift the balance of power within their societies. New populations are demanding more voice in the management of society, as students are demanding more voice in the conduct of their own education. The United States among other countries is moving toward an entirely new life style, toward a more open society, and temporarily a more explosive one. One is led to say that education does not change bceause some reformer demands it. Education changes only under the impact of profound forces of change within the society itself. This is what is happening today, and what adult educators must continue to explore together.

Part II

Some Institutions and Organizations

Chapter 11

Adult Education Institutions

WILLIAM S. GRIFFITH

Adult education is typically conducted by individuals trained in other specialties working in institutions established to serve some other primary purpose [17, pp. 91–92]. Consequently, those who attempt to discern the boundaries of the field are frequently perplexed by the absence of a dominant institutional form such as can be found in all other levels of education. They are further confused because there is no professional society of adult educators, since, in other fields lacking a common institutional form, members of a professional society define the limits of the field. The lack of a professional society of adult educators and of a dominant institutional form accounts for the difficulty that both academicians and practitioners encounter when they try to get a clear image of the adult education field.

Part II of this handbook has been designed to assist the reader in developing an overview of the field by presenting him with general and specific information on the institutional forms and arrangements in adult education. This introductory chapter deals with the relative importance of the various institutions and with ways of examining their similarities and differences. It also treats the problem of interinstitutional coordination with emphasis on the role of the government. The chapter concludes with a discussion of the growing influence of professional adult educators on the institutions. In the subsequent 11 chapters detailed descriptions of the organization and operation of selected adult education institutions will be presented.

The Variety of Major Adult Education Institutions

In the United States a great many institutions carry on adult education programs. For centuries Americans have been building institutions and their efforts often have demonstrated more enthusiasm than rationality. Over 130 years ago Alexis de Tocqueville observed that:

> Americans of all ages, all conditions and all dispositions, constantly form associations. . . . If it be proposed to inculcate some truth, or to foster some feeling by the encouragement of a great example, they form a society. Wherever, at the head of some new undertaking, you see the government in France, or a man of rank in England, in the United States you will be sure to find an association. [7, p. 198]

This propensity to form associations which subsequently become formalized and develop into institutions has characterized the efforts of those who have sought to educate adults. The history of American adult education may be written as an account of the founding, growth, development and demise of institutions which have served special interests.

The individuals who have had the greatest influence on the field were men who were devoted to the accomplishment of a given objective and who were successful in establishing institutions that worked toward attaining that objective. Holbrook is remembered because of the Lyceum; Vincent, because of the Chautauqua; Harper, because of correspondence instruction; Van Hise, because of university extension; and Knapp, because of the Cooperative Extension Service.

This tendency to develop a new institution whenever a new purpose is identified that can be served through adult education, does not result in an orderly development of the institutional structure of the field. A second factor which tends to make the field appear disordered to the casual observer is the offering of adult education programs by institutions having some other central purpose. Accordingly, it is difficult for anyone who is not well acquainted with the field to imagine its institutional complexity.

Perhaps the first step to be taken in demonstrating the institutional structure of the field is the listing of the major institutions of adult education together with the number of adults they serve.

Relative Importance of Major Adult Education Institutions

The relative importance of the various adult education institutions is not necessarily revealed by a tabulation of the number of adults each reaches. But, lacking a better index, this tabulation provides one indication of importance. Based on interviews conducted in 11,957 households

Adult Education Institutions

in 1961–62, Johnstone estimated the number of adults attending the educational programs of various institutions (see Table 4).

Table 4. *Estimates of Adult Education Courses Attended at Different Sponsoring Institutions* [9, p. 61]

Sponsoring Institution	Number of Courses Reported	Estimated Number of Different Persons Who Attended Classes, Lectures, Talks or Discussion Groups
Church and synagogues	692	3,260,000
Colleges and universities	689	2,640,000
Community organizations	488	2,240,000
Business and industry	406	1,860,000
Elementary and high school	383	1,740,000
Private schools	246	1,120,000
Government (all levels)	235	1,050,000
Armed forces	116	480,000
All other sponsors	50	240,000
(Total)	3305	13,360,000[a]

[a] Does not total number of persons listed in column because some persons studied at more than one sponsoring institution.

The most important facts shown in Table 4 are that the majority of adults learn in institutions that are not popularly regarded as adult education institutions and that adults do most of their learning in institutions that are not primarily educational. A second fact illustrated by the table is that the institutions listed appear to have little in common, a situation which may not trouble adult educators but which is likely to be confusing to others.

Rich Profusion or Muddle?

Frank Jessup, secretary of the Delegacy for Extra-Mural Studies at Oxford University, said the field of adult education could be described either as a rich profusion, or as a muddle. Further, he comments that adult education in a pluralistic society ought to be pluralistic in aim, in content and in method. It would be impossible to impose a single pattern on the variety of institutions, and from a value position it would be wrong to do so, he concludes. But if there were no similarities among the institutions it would not be possible to identify them as adult education institutions.

Yet because the institutions are so diverse an observer may note only disparate forms and have great difficulty in distinguishing common elements. Further, unless he has some way of reducing the number of kinds of institutions conceptually, he will be unable to think systematically about the field of adult education.

Approaches Used in Dealing with the Variety of Institutional Forms

Two approaches have been used by students of adult education in their efforts to deal with the variety of adult education institutions. The first approach is the development of a typology or classification system. At least two professors of adult education have constructed schemes for classifying the apparently disparate institutions.

The Classification Approach

Malcolm S. Knowles has developed a quadripartite typology of institutions providing adult education: (1) those created primarily to serve adult students; (2) those initially concerned with the education of youth but which are now assuming the secondary task of educating adults; (3) those created to serve the whole community; and (4) those primarily concerned with non-educational goals but which use adult education to achieve them [10; pp. 42–60]. This framework has already been presented above in some detail by Wayne Schroeder.

The framework developed by Cyril O. Houle includes both those agencies that provide adult education and those associations whose members are either adult educators or adult education institutions. This framework, which will be presented in detail in a forthcoming book by Houle, divides the agencies providing adult education into two groups: those that are primarily educational and those that are partly educational. In the first group adult education may be a dominant, coordinate or subordinate function. In the second group adult education may be either a coordinate or a subordinate function.

Even though the agencies that conduct educational programs for an adult clientele are popularly regarded as the only institutions of adult education, such a view gives a restricted impression of the institutional complexity of the field. In Houle's framework the societies or organizations of adult educators such as the National Association for Public Continuing and Adult Education or the agencies employing them such as the Association of University Evening Colleges are treated as institutions of equal or greater importance.

The associations of adult educators tend to be oriented toward one or more of the following five bases:

Adult Education Institutions

1. *Content.* Adult educators who have a commitment to a particular message which they wish to deliver to all adults form groups. Religious adult educators, adult educators working for world peace, and adult educators working in the family planning area, come together to discuss ways of achieving their common objective.
2. *Sponsoring agency.* Adult educators who are identified with a specific agency that offers adult education. These adult educators have created groups which serve as a forum for the discussion of the special problems faced by those who conduct programs in that agency. Examples of such groups are the Association of University Evening Colleges, the National Association for Public Continuing and Adult Education, the National University Extension Association, and the National Community School Educational Association.
3. *Method.* Adult educators who are committed to the use of a single method form organizations. Examples are the National Home Study Council, the residential adult education groups within the Adult Education Association (AEA) and the National University Extension Association, and the National Association of Educational Broadcasters.
4. *Place.* Adult educators who form groups on the basis of their common concern for a given geographic location. Examples of such groups are the Northern Illinois Round Table of Adult Education, the Denver Adult Education Council, the Illinois Adult Education Association, the Missouri Valley Adult Education Association, the Adult Education Association of the USA, and the Canadian Association for Adult Education.
5. *Clientele.* Adult educators who form groups on the basis of their identification with a particular clientele. Examples of such groups are labor union educators, prison educators and industrial training educators.

Because these five categories are not mutually exclusive an adult educator may be a member of more than one group. Accordingly, there appears to be no logical basis for hypothesizing systematic differences among the five kinds of institutions. If the classification is to be of value for purposes other than describing the multitude of institutions, then it must be demonstrated that significant differences exist among the kinds of adult educators who belong to the five kinds of institutions, with regard to (1) the process of program development, (2) procedures for securing resources, (3) methods of evaluation, (4) routines for program modification, (5) procedures for arriving at objectives or (6) other significant variables. The research has not yet been done to demonstrate that such systematic differences exist among the categories.

The Developmental Model Approach

The second approach which has been used in an effort to provide a systematic way of thinking about the uniformities and differences in the institutions of adult education is that of comparing their patterns of establishment, growth and development. James Carey used this approach in studying the development of university extension divisions and succeeded in producing a scheme for categorizing their growth stages [3, p. 11]. William Griffith sought to develop a growth model for adult education institutions and constructed a five-stage growth prototype based on data from five apparently dissimilar institutions [5, pp. 276–287]. Organization theorists are continuing to search for characteristics which apply to organizations of various kinds at different points in their development [20, pp. 451–533]. Because so little is known about the growth characteristics of adult education institutions, a great deal of research must be conducted before adult educators will be able to move beyond their present intuitive methods in developing and modifying their institutions.

At the present time neither the classification approach nor the developmental model approach has been sufficiently refined to make it of practical use. Even though it is possible to classify an institution of adult education on the basis of the relative importance of adult education in the priority listing of institutional objectives or on the basis of its stage of development, neither of the approaches affords any appreciable power of prediction.

There are, however, certain tendencies in the development of adult education institutions which have been observed in a number of settings and which appear to mark the growing maturity of the field. One of the most important of these is the change in the perception adult educators have of the physical facilities of their own institutions. In the developmental process the adult educator changes from an approach based on the use of a part or all of a given set of institutional facilities to an approach in which the program planning process comes to include a step in which a decision is made about which facilities are to be used.

Institutions established for purposes other than that of providing learning opportunities for adults sometimes have facilities which may remain idle for part of the time. These institutions may also be searching for ways of improving their income. Accordingly, an adult education program may be established to take advantage of idle facilities or to produce additional income. In either case, the charge to the adult educa-

Adult Education Institutions

tor is not primarily to develop whatever program is best suited to the needs of the adults in the community but, rather, to offer a program which will take advantage of the existing idle space.

Eventually, however, the person who administers such a space-filling program is likely to become interested in serving educational needs that cannot be taken care of in the existing facilities. If he succeeds in developing programs that entail the use of additional facilities, then he has progressed to a higher professional plane where the decision concerning which facilities to use is based upon their merits as learning environments rather than upon their ownership.

The authors of the chapters in Part II describe specific institutional programs and ways in which adult educators have begun using an increasing variety of physical facilities to enable them to do a better job of serving their intended audience. Stokes discusses a seminar on wheels and a church without a building as examples of a changing perspective toward religious education facilities. Harlacher paraphrases the statement that the boundaries of the university campus are coterminous with the boundaries of the state, saying that the community college campus is the community college district. This notion requires the use of a variety of physical facilities based on program needs. Monroe presents evidence to show that libraries, museums and art galleries have improved their adult education efforts by making their collections available at a number of locations, thereby greatly increasing accessibility. Finally, Finch asserts that a great strength of adult education in the public schools is its willingness and ability to take education directly to the adult audience in their own neighborhood. These examples illustrate change in the adult educator's attitude toward physical facilities. Where previously he would have thought in terms of developing programs to use the institution's facilities, he now selects the appropriate facilities only after considering the audience and the intended content of the program. Even so, increasing accessibility is not a magic formula for increasing participation in adult education. Correspondence instruction and educational television have made it possible for adults to study in their own homes, but it is clear these institutional learning arrangements have attracted only a small segment of their potential audience [9; 13; 17]. Perhaps the next step in this developmental process will be the consideration of the adult education needs and resources of the total community.

Interinstitutional Coordination

In the absence of reliable methods of predicting the behavior of adult education institutions, it is extremely difficult to devise workable schemes to bring about effective interinstitutional coordination. Such coordination as may be found now is primarily the result of the workings of the free enterprise system. Increasingly, however, it seems that more deliberate efforts will be required if a well-rounded program of adult education is to be provided.

The Free Enterprise Approach

Each institution is created and maintained to serve a particular set of goals. The leaders of each institution, thinking only of their own programs, attempt to reach a specific audience. It is not surprising many of the institutions serve essentially the same group of adults. Some institutions are more successful than others, and there is a continuing process under way of establishing new institutions and closing out unsuccessful ones. In most cases the only force guiding this process is what Adam Smith called the "invisible hand."

Amid the myriad of institutions involved in adult education in any American city it might appear that of all possible ways to develop a full range of adult education opportunities the *laissez-faire* approach would be the least desirable. On the other hand it can be argued that the individual learner is the most appropriate judge of the quality of his own educational experience and that he will support the institution which offers the best combination of price and service. Further, it can be assumed the alert adult education director acting out of a profit motive will be sensitive to unsatisfied learning needs and will move promptly to satisfy the perceived learning needs of the community.

But since many of those who presumably have the greatest need for education to improve their competence as parents, consumers or workers are both least inclined and least able financially to participate, the free enterprise approach seems inadequate. Only with the support of tax funds does it seem possible to make adult education accessible to all.

Voluntary Cooperation and Coordination

Each institution is concerned for its own autonomy and there is a slowly dawning realization this autonomy may be enhanced through cooperative efforts with other institutions. In the detailed reports on the individual institutions in Part II there are accounts of modest cooperative efforts. Rogin emphasizes the cooperative activity of labor unions and university labor education centers. Finch mentions the growing acceptance of the practice of developing contractual relationships for adult education between the public schools and other community agencies. Harlacher points out the synergistic and catalytic capabilities

Adult Education Institutions

of the community college as it works with other institutions in its district. Boone notes that the expanding role of the Cooperative Extension Service is leading directly to increased interinstitutional program development. Additional examples could be given but they, like those already listed, would fall short of a plan for the establishment of a coordinated program of adult education for the total community.

One of the consequences of the uncoordinated approach to adult education program development is that potential students have quite a task if they attempt to find out what opportunities for coordination exist. Nevertheless, the only adults who are able to participate in programs are those who have both the desire to participate and the knowledge of the location of an accessible institution.

John Johnstone estimated that while 71 percent of American adults know of something they would like to learn, only about 50 percent participate in adult education after leaving school [9, p. 2]. Possibly this 21 percent difference can be explained by a lack of information about learning opportunities on the part of the public. Johnstone calculated that 55 percent of adults in the United States know of at least one place an adult can go for instruction. Approximately 12 percent believe that no such opportunities exist and 33 percent are uncertain of the existence of such institutions [9, p. 201]. An obvious conclusion which may be drawn from these data is that adult education participation can be increased by improving communication between the institutions and those they seek to serve.

Adult Education Councils and Neighborhood Centers

Two kinds of arrangements have been developed in an effort to provide information on learning opportunities to interest adults. These two approaches are also expected to facilitate communication among adult education institutions and between institutions and their students.

Adult educators have attempted to develop viable adult education councils in a number of cities, and in some cases they have secured foundation backing to initiate the effort. Generally, however, these voluntary coordinating groups have not been successful in building a sound financial base, and those which have survived lead a precarious existence. Because the member organizations generally have modest budgets, they are unable to bear the cost of operating the council. The use of foundation grants to assist in establishing councils has not been a fruitful investment because when the grants were exhausted the councils were frequently allowed to die.

If a council is to offer sustained service it will usually require the full-time efforts of an executive secretary and secretarial assistance.

The council must then engage in fund raising activities to support the staff salaries, and these activities can consume the greater part of the staff's time, while only peripherally related to the educational objectives of the council. Yet, the staff must give such efforts their primary attention as the price of maintaining the council. There is virtually nothing in the literature at this point to indicate a practical division of efforts between fund raising and service for a viable adult education council. Income for a council should be provided without requiring the selling of information to those who need it; otherwise, it seems unlikely that the adult education council approach will be an adequate means of making the full range of adult learning opportunities known to the people of the community.

Congress has enacted legislation establishing neighborhood centers as a result of concern over the inability of adult education and other institutions to work together to increase the effectiveness of their services to the poor. The personnel of the centers are supposed to be fully informed about the learning opportunities in the community. Because they are located in the neighborhood of those to be served, the centers should be effective in providing assistance to individuals who would not otherwise be aided. Although it has not been demonstrated yet that these centers can build a bridge from the institutions of adult education to their potential disadvantaged clientele, the idea seems eminently sound. If the centers are wisely administered, their efforts should lead to the increased utilization of existing resources.

Although it is conceivable that adult educators might learn how to design and operate adult education councils which would facilitate communication and voluntary coordination, it seems more likely that government supported information centers will both make learning opportunities more widely known and provide information to the leaders of the institutions which will facilitate and encourage cooperative program planning. Increased governmental involvement in adult education is likely in the future for two reasons: (1) adult educators have been unable to develop an economically viable model council which can support branch centers accessible to those who live in disadvantaged areas; (2) legislators view adult education as a means of accomplishing social purposes and they will take steps to see that the institutions and those they may be able to help are brought together by whatever mechanism seems workable.

Federal and State Government Influences

Both the federal and state governments have influenced the development of adult education by establishing special institutions and

Adult Education Institutions

by providing financial support to selected institutions. Many of the largest and most influential institutions were either created by the federal government or have been supported by it [8, p. 170]. In 1914 the passage of the Smith-Lever Act created the Cooperative Extension Service as an adult education monopoly in agriculture and home economics in the land-grant colleges. Other institutions have the right to develop adult education programs in the same subject areas, but to do so without the special subsidy is to work at a marked financial disadvantage. It was not considered unusual for the federal and state legislatures to show special interest in the land-grant colleges and state universities by supporting special programs for them.

During the Johnson administration legislation was enacted to support specific programs rather than a special group of institutions. Although the federal government will continue to support the institutions which have received aid in the past, new programs are likely to be enacted in ways that show no favoritism for special kinds of institutions [8, p. 182]. However, when legislators become convinced that a particular educational need is not being met by the established institutions, they may conclude that new institutions are needed. The tax support for community colleges has come out of this kind of perception.

Government Support for Community College Adult Education

Federal and state funds are now being used to support community colleges with mixed results. For example, in Iowa in 1965 the General Assembly authorized the establishment of 16 area community colleges and vocational technical schools. The vocational technical schools do not offer the arts and science courses which are required in programs for students who wish to transfer to four year colleges. The area community colleges generally offer high school completion programs for adults in the daytime or evening, utilizing local school buildings to make the program readily accessible to the students. When the state legislature took the step of encouraging the establishment of area schools, the junior colleges which had been operated by local school districts were reorganized to take advantage of the special state support.

Legislation has both intended and unintended results. One of the unintended consequences of the legislative incentives to new institutions such as the community college to provide adult education programs is that there may be a reduction of number of programs in the community rather than an increase. If the special incentive leads to a relocation of programs from institutions receiving little or no state reimbursement to institutions which received a higher state subsidy, there may be a decline in the total number of institutions and programs in adult education.

The legislation may have been developed to answer the wrong question. Instead of asking how community colleges can be encouraged to offer adult education programs, the question should be how can the community college be encouraged to develop adult education programs in a way that will complement the total adult learning opportunities of the community? In states where a progressive department of public instruction has developed a system for reimbursing adult education programs in secondary schools, the introduction of equivalent programs in the junior college with a higher rate of reimbursement tends to produce a shifting of programs from the high schools to the junior colleges.

Legislative Influence on Program Coordination

Those who seek to strengthen adult education through legislation must ask themselves: "How can a new institution strengthen the total adult education program within a community, and how can it conduct a program without weakening or eliminating other institutions which are performing a useful service by conducting adult education programs which might also be provided by the new institution?" This question is complex because there is an assortment of adult education institutions in each community and their programs vary greatly. Accordingly, the approach needed to provide a community with the full range of adult education opportunities is one which rewards a new institution for conducting programs which are not already available. Those who set public policy and those who administer programs should consider the many adult education institutions and programs in relation to community needs. Given this approach, the whole attitude toward the development of the community college or any other institution entering the adult education field is affected. Rather than requiring an institution to have an open door and to be all things to all men, an unrealistic and misleading goal at best, the more reasonable approach is one which calls for the college to do only those things in adult education which it can do better than other institutions or which it alone is willing to do. Program development which fails to consider the availability of programs in the community as well as community needs can scarcely be regarded as exemplifying a sense of professional responsibility.

The federal government in the future will be more likely to foster cooperation. The government requires plans for the state's use of federal funds in order for the state to receive funds from the community services title of the Higher Education Act of 1965. A group of individuals who are able to represent all of the institutions of higher education, both public and private, in the state carry out the development of the state plan. Similar provisions in the State Technical Services Act and in basic adult education legislation indicate that the federal government has taken some responsibility for promoting cooperation and coordination among the institutions of adult education.

But the needs perceived by legislators are not always the same as those perceived by adult educators, and the result is frequently something other than what the adult educators expect.

In any field the personnel of the established institutions naturally and understandably think of themselves as the appropriate persons to conduct the work of the field. The leaders of institutions which have worked in a given way over a period of years develop a proprietary interest in their work. They resent the intrusion of new institutions and that resentment is magnified if those new institutions have access to special sources of support not available to the older institutions.

An example of the difference in the perception of legislators and of adult educators in university extension divisions may be seen in the case of Title I, the community services title, of the Higher Education Act of 1965.

Institutional Accommodation to Federal Legislation

From 1940 until 1965 the National University Extension Association sought federal legislation to provide a relatively modest appropriation to subsidize the activities of the established university extension divisions. These adult educators showed little or no interest in promoting legislation which would encourage additional universities to conduct adult education. When the Higher Education Act was passed in 1965, the intent of the Congress was not to support extension divisions but, rather, to encourage as many of the institutions of higher education as possible to assist urban areas in the solution of their problems. Even though it appears reasonable to assume that the established extension divisions could expand and modify their programs more readily than other institutions could initiate adult education programs, the Congress decided to support projects rather than institutions. The result, after twenty-five years of promotional work for federal aid to general extension divisions, was an act which supported special projects and for which all instituions of higher education were eligible regardless of their experience. But the actual effect was somewhat different from that anticipated by the legislators.

All institutions of higher education in the state had to be given an opportunity to propose projects in the development of each state plan. Despite this requirement, less than 20 percent of the 2400 institutions of higher education became involved in conducting programs under Title I. The most convincing explanation for this situation is that the larger extension divisions with personnel who had had considerable experience in developing proposals both drafted proposals in anticipation of the passage of the legislation and also prepared the soundest proposals. Smaller institutions with less sophisticated personnel will require additional time and experience in proposal development before they will be able to take advantage of this legislation.

Although the legislation has not led to the involvement of the majority of the institutions of higher education in adult education programs designed to solve community problems, it has encouraged involvement well beyond the state universities and land-grant colleges. And it is worthy of note that the relatively modest sum of 10 million dollars nationally was sufficient to stimulate the modification of over 300 programs.

Institutional Change

The willingness of over 300 institutions of higher education to conduct programs of community service is an illustration of one way in which the programs of adult education institutions are modified. Because of their precarious financial situation adult education institutions frequently behave in an opportunistic fashion, expressing a desire to become involved in whatever kind of educational work some sponsor is willing to underwrite. This willingness to accept new programs is not restricted to the smaller, less affluent institutions. Wayne Ringer, in his study of program planning in the Cooperative Extension Service, found that the largest institutions, which he had expected to be most highly bureaucratized and least able to accept new programs, were in fact more willing to try new programs than were the institutions with the smaller budgets and staff [19, p. 150].

Efforts to modify educational institutions seldom demonstrate the highest degree of rationality. Presumably, in an ideal situation a decision to modify an institution would be based upon the examination of evidence relating to the attainment of institutional goals. In actual practice the decision to make a change is rarely based on evidence of an educational nature. Instead, as John Apel found, the willingness of adult educators to accept a proposed change is likely to be influenced more by their perception of the effect of the proposed change on specific situational variables than on the extent to which the change would further the goals of the institution [2, pp. 134–135].

Just as efforts to modify an institution are influenced by a great many factors in addition to the popular impression of the relationship of the change to the objectives of the institution, the modification of the educational program itself is likewise subject to powerful influences

Adult Education Institutions

other than measurements of the cognitive attainments of the individual learners. If one is to have an appreciation of the functional value of evaluation to an adult education institution, he must be aware that there is an institutional perspective of evaluation which differs markedly from that taught in courses on program planning and improvement.

An Institutional Perspective of Evaluation

The Adult Education Association of the USA has criticized evaluation practices, stating that they frequently do not measure progress toward student goals; but that they merely indicate the number of adults enrolled and retained in a program, or that they are opinion polls of student reactions [14, pp. 204-205]. In practice, the students' attitude toward the course, which may have little to do with the amount of cognitive gain, is the major determinant of program decisions in the prevailing enrollment economy. Student opinion, including their preferences for certain formats and their liking for individual instructors, is of greater functional value to an institutional program than are objective assessments of cognitive gains. Practical administrators are fully aware that the existence of their programs is dependent upon a satisfied clientele or sponsor group who will continue to provide the essential financial support. Accordingly, a "happiness index" which tells the program administrator what the participants liked and what they disliked is of greater practical importance to the immediate survival concerns of an adult education institution than is the assessment of the amount of learning which has been achieved.

The evaluation of the cognitive achievement of adult students is a complex activity which consumes resources and must therefore be justified if it is to be supported by institutional leaders. Certainly the evaluation of individual learning achievements is not considered to be an essential activity in adult education institutions today. For evaluation to be carried out there must be statements of the desired learning goals expressed in measurable terms and a comparison of the actual terminal behavior of the students with the intended behavior. Such efforts require the investment of staff time and money. If the results of such an evaluation are not required for institutional survival, then the expenditure of resources in evaluation must be justified on some basis other than economic. Unless the results are helpful in attracting new students or in maintaining the participation of those already in the program, the efforts expended in evaluation are an expense which reduces the ability of the institution to compete with those who do not evaluate.

Perhaps the strongest case which can be made for evaluation is that its lack is incompatible with the idea of professionalism. If an adult educator wishes to regard himself as a professional educator, and not simply an institutional entrepreneur, he will regard the assessment of learning outcomes as an indispensable activity. Accordingly, any educational activity, regardless of its public acceptance and profitability, which did not include provisions for evaluation would be looked on as commercialism rather than education. But professionalism is still at an early stage of development in adult education.

Professionalism and the Institutional Structure of Adult Education

Adult education has been more a movement than a profession. The absence of universally applicable professional standards—measures of proficiency and accomplishment—makes it difficult for the public to recognize competency in adult educators. As a consequence, those who have studied to prepare themselves to work in the field are not accorded the status in the public mind that is given to other professionals.

The development of institutions which regard the provision of adult education as a major objective is increasing the demand for professionally prepared adult educators, and professional preparation is gradually becoming equated with professional study. Yet the field seems reluctant to move to a stronger emphasis on professionalism.

Lack of a Professional Society

In Lawrence Allen's study of professionalism in adult education he included the following as one of the fifteen criteria of a profession: A profession organizes its members into an association which tests competence, maintains standards, establishes training opportunities, and thereby gains societal recognition and status for the profession [1, p. 19]. If Allen's criteria are valid, and if the testing of competence, maintaining standards and establishing of training opportunities are the functions performed by a professional association, then it is clear that no such organization exists in the field of adult education.

Although there are many institutions in adult education, there is no professional society of adult educators. Membership in the AEA is open to all who wish to join. Membership in the National Association for Public Continuing and Adult Education is open to "present and former members of the adult education staffs of state and local public school systems and professors of education teaching classes in which public school adult education administrators or instructors are enrolled . . ." [16, p. 145]. In the latter organization, however, an effort

Adult Education Institutions

is being made to upgrade the preparation of teachers and administrators of public school adult education programs [16, pp. 137–144]. This effort is limited to the listing of desirable qualifications and no effort is being made to drop members who lack such qualifications or to refuse the membership applications of those lacking the recommended preparation. Other adult education institutions follow similar practices with regard to qualifications for membership. Many of those who work in the field seem to have an almost pathological enmity toward the idea of a professional society for adult educators, a society that had qualifications for membership which would make it exclusive. Yet, without the development of a professional society, it seems unlikely that the career workers in the field who have pursued graduate study will be accorded a professional status by the members of other professions or by society at large.

A Growing Sense of Professionalism

However, the number of individuals holding graduate degrees in adult education is continuing to increase. As these individuals move into positions of responsible leadership in the field, they will likely think in terms of the totality of the field rather than focusing exclusively on the kind of institution in which they are working. The professionally oriented adult educators have accepted the fact that the learning needs of American adults cannot be met through the independent, uncoordinated efforts of institutional leaders who think only in terms of their own institutions. In almost every one of the following chapters the reader will find examples of interinstitutional cooperation. Although these efforts typically involve only two or three institutions, the acceptance of the principle of cooperative planning is unmistakable, and fuller implementation of the principle may reasonably be anticipated at local, state, and national levels.

Within the last five years the likelihood of developing a rationally conceived national scheme of adult education involving all of the institutions of adult education has increased appreciably. Institutional leaders who saw the need for cooperative planning realized that an entirely new national organization was required. Hence, the Ad Hoc Committee of Adult Education Organizations (now called the Coalition of Adult Education Organizations) was created expressly to work on matters of concern to the whole field. The fact that the *ad hoc* has since been dropped from its name suggests that its members are committed to its work. Never before in the history of adult education have so many professionally oriented leaders of such a wide variety of adult education institutions made a continuing commitment to work together. On the basis of the desire to cooperate exhibited by the members of this Committee, and their stature in and broad grasp of the field there is reason to be optimistic concerning the ability of the members of the family of adult education institutions to work together for the common good in the decade of the seventies.

Conclusion

Adult education has typically been conducted by individuals trained in other specialties employed by institutions established to serve some other primary purpose. Although it seems unlikely that the number of institutions established primarily to serve the educational needs of adults will increase markedly over the next decade, it is likely that new coordinating mechanisms will be developed. The men who provide the leadership for the institutions of adult education today seem more aware of this need for cooperation and coordination than has any preceding generation of leaders. In the following chapters the readers will find the specific examples of this growing awareness of the interdependence of the institutions. This recognition of mutual concerns and a willingness to work together will characterize the decade of the seventies for the institutions of adult education.

References

1. Allen, Lawrence A. "The Growth of Professionalism in the Adult Education Movement, 1928–1958: A Content Analysis of the Periodical Literature." Unpublished doctoral dissertation. Chicago, Ill.: University of Chicago, 1961.
2. Apel, John Dale. "Prediction of Adult Educators' Attitudes Toward Institutional Changes." Unpublished doctoral dissertation. Chicago, Ill.: University of Chicago, 1966.
3. Carey, James T. *Forms and Forces in University Adult Education*. Chicago, Ill.: Center for the Study of Liberal Education for Adults, 1961.
4. Glaser, William A., and Sills, David L., eds. *The Government of Associations*. Totowa, N.J.: Bedminster Press, 1966.
5. Griffith, William S. "A Growth Model of Institutions of Adult Education." Unpublished doctoral dissertation. Chicago, Ill.: University of Chicago, 1963.
6. Harrison, John Fletcher Clews. *Learning and Living, 1790–1960; A Study in the History of the English Adult Education Movement*. Toronto, Canada: University of Toronto Press, 1961.
7. Heffner, Richard D., ed. *Alexis de Tocqueville, Democracy in America*. New York: American Library Association, 1956.

8. Houle, Cyril O. "Federal Policies Concerning Adult Education." *The School Review*, LXXVI (2) (June, 1968), pp. 166–189.
9. Johnstone, John W. C., and Rivera, Ramon J. *Volunteers for Learning: A Study of the Educational Pursuits of American Adults*. Chicago, Ill.: Aldine, 1965.
10. Knowles, Malcolm S. *The Adult Education Movement in the United States*. New York: Holt, Rinehart & Winston, 1962.
11. Knowles, Malcolm S. "The Field of Operations in Adult Education." *Adult Education: Outlines of an Emerging Field of University Study*. Edited by Gale Jensen, A. A. Liveright and Wilbur Hallenbeck. Washington, D.C.: Adult Education Association of the USA, 1964.
12. Knowles, Malcolm S., ed. *Handbook of Adult Education in the United States, 1960*. Chicago, Ill.: Adult Education Association of the USA, 1960.
13. MacKenzie, Ossian; Christensen, Edward L.; and Rigby, Paul H. *Correspondence Instruction in the United States*. New York: McGraw-Hill, 1968.
14. McMahon, Ernest E.; Coates, Robert H.; and Knox, Alan B. "Common Concerns: The Position of the Adult Education Association of the USA." *Adult Education*, XVIII (3) (Spring, 1968), pp. 197–213.
15. March, James G., ed. *Handbook of Organizations*. Chicago, Ill.: Rand McNally, 1965.
16. National Association for Public School Adult Education. "Constitution, National Association for Public School Adult Education, as Amended November 21, 1965." *Public School Adult Education 1968 Almanac*. Washington, D.C.: National Association for Public School Adult Education, 1968.
17. Powell, John Walker. *Channels of Learning; The Story of Educational Television*. Washington, D.C.: Public Affairs Press, 1962.
18. Powell, John Walker. *Learning Comes of Age*. New York: Association Press, 1956.
19. Ringer, Wayne B. "Bureaucratic Character of Adult Education Organizations and Innovativeness in Program Development." Unpublished doctoral dissertation. Chicago, Ill.: University of Chicago, 1968.
20. Starbuck, William H. "Organizational Growth and Development." *Handbook of Organizations*. Edited by James G. March. Chicago, Ill.: Rand McNally, 1965.

Chapter 12

Colleges and Universities

KENNETH HAYGOOD

In 1960, A. A. Liveright wrote:

The past 20 years have been pioneering, exciting ones in the field of college and university adult education. The period has been characterized by growth in the number of institutions active in higher adult education, in the quantity of students enrolled in college and university adult education, in the scope of offerings, and especially in an increase of imaginative innovation. A growing number of persons especially concerned about adult education and trained for it have been attracted to the field; and a new type of student—one who is interested more in continuing higher education than in remedial training—is increasingly welcomed on the evening college campus and in various extension programs. [15, p. 203]

These characteristics continue to describe college and university adult education. Excitement, innovation, the sense of growth and development, make adult education one of the most interesting fields of higher education. Also, in the past decade, a new characteristic has begun to emerge: maturity. Some of the experimentation and proliferation of the past has settled into programs which have become models of excellence in higher adult education. In spite of ups and downs, there is now a greater financial stability in higher adult education than ever before. Improvements in theoretical analysis and research and the growth in the number of fully trained professionals are additional signs of increasing maturity in the field.

The interaction between youthful growth and increasing maturity characterizes the field of adult education at this time. Houle describes the present day milieu as follows:

> We are now well launched on the greatest forward surge of growth which higher adult education has ever known, more broadly based, more maturely conceived, and more universally accepted than at any other time in our history. The social determinist would find no root cause to explain this growth, in the same sense that the end of a long world war created the last major thrust. We have, instead, only the maturing of many trends, which, interacting together, have created wide-spread support for advanced forms of adult learning. The ideas of 15 years ago have come into their own. We were prophets. . . . we have worked hard and successfully to create programs, and now we reap the reward. We sense that we are still nearer the beginning than the end of a spurt of growth whose culmination we cannot yet see. [10, pp. 3–4]

As the forces at work in the field of higher adult education continue to converge, its importance in colleges and universities will become accepted. Educators and administrators of higher adult education programs will become valued and respected as they effectively combine scholarship with innovative approaches to provide educational activities for the diverse needs of the adult population.

Background

With a few noteworthy exceptions, adult education has sprung up like a weed in the university rather than being planted there purposefully as a part of the garden. Once there, it often has been treated as a weed, given little nurture or concern though admired for its vitality.

Summer schools, started as early as 1869 at Harvard and well established by 1910 at many institutions, have generally been viewed as supplementary activities to the regular program, as is evidenced by the flight of the faculty from the campus during the summer. The evening college, whose main periods of growth and development Dyer identified as occurring after World War I and then again after World War II, grew out of the need to meet specific educational needs of urban communities [5]. The demand for educational opportunities for part-time evening students and adults was first met by making available existing educational programs in the evening and on Saturdays. The decision to design programs especially for adult audiences was made gradually over the years, rather than as an institutional commitment to a new kind of student [8]. The university extension concept, borrowed from England during the last quarter of the nineteenth century, at first appeared as a commitment to meet the educational needs of adults and off-campus

Colleges and Universities 193

students. However, extension's many setbacks in the early years suggest the institutional commitment did not go so far as to provide the resources needed to design new curricula and teaching methods suitable to adult audiences. The Cooperative Extension Service, the largest adult education program ever created, was established in 1914 to provide education for rural America. Even this university-based program evolved from needs that were nonacademic. Indeed, it is possible that if funds had not been provided for establishing agricultural colleges, universities might not have supported Cooperative Extension programs at all.

These examples suggest that although educational activities for adults are among the fastest growing programs at colleges and universities, the increase in the number of programs doesn't necessarily indicate the institutions have a major commitment to the education of adults. Colleges and universities often did not establish adult programs; they were instead the work of a few persons who sensed particular educational needs or responded to new forces at work in society.

As higher adult education programs evolved and grew by accretion within the university establishment, several institutional forms emerged such as General University Extension which dealt with a variety of degree and non-degree activities; Cooperative Extension which first concerned itself with agriculture in rural areas, but more recently with urban areas as well; Evening Colleges which served large municipalities; Residential Continuing Education which provided short-term learning experiences, often in special conference facilities; Correspondence Education which was conducted primarily by mail but recently in combination with television and other activities; and Mass Media Programs which range from college-credit courses and community-wide study-discussion groups utilizing television to in-service professional education by radio. These are the forms that currently dominate the field. Experimentation is constantly under way, however, and new forms will be devised as universities and colleges respond to new conditions. Shannon and Schoenfeld mention this experimentation as they discuss university extension, but their remarks apply to other forms of higher adult education as well:

It has always been extension's role to pioneer, to fill the gaps, and then to "work itself out of a job" by creating or encouraging substitute agencies. This role general extension has performed with an aplomb that is amazing in the light of the resistance an institution ordinarily exhibits to changing directions. Vocational schools, community colleges, branch campuses, professional organizations, lecture bureaus, traveling library services, public health associations, welfare departments, little theatres, municipal reference centers, discussion clubs, school standards agencies, debate societies, urban leagues—these and many other activities and organizations have been "mothered" over the years by university extension and then prodded out of the nest. [19]

Higher adult education constantly raises fundamental issues for the institutions it is part of, because it is responsive to new situations and seeks to fulfill the needs of adult learners.

Current and Recurring Issues

After almost a century of higher adult education activities, many fundamental questions still have not been resolved. Even the terms used to describe the field are not definitive, a symptom of confusion in higher education over whether or not there should be special programs for adults. For example, *extension* and *evening college* refer to activities which are not necessarily directed to the education of adults. Many evening colleges concentrate their efforts on developing degree-credit courses for students who are able to study only in the evening or part time, or for students not eligible to attend the full-time day programs. The average age of such students is similar to their full-time day college counterparts. Their objectives are the same. Extension programs often serve comparable off-campus degree needs and in some cases are intentionally aimed at youth, as in the case of 4-H Club activities. Thus, one cannot equate the terms *adult education* with *extension* or *evening college* programs. Furthermore, the term *continuing education*, which implies the concept of lifelong learning, is often used to designate administrative units which contain evening college and extension functions but which only incidentally stress continuous learning.

A Question of Purpose

Still to be resolved is the question of the purpose of higher adult education. Many programs go beyond traditional college or university courses because adult learning needs transcend these limited offerings. But how far should an institution of higher education go in meeting the variety of adult education needs? Few people today believe a college should be concerned only with youth, and scarcely anyone holds that adult education is not a legitimate part of the purpose of the university. However, many argue that higher education for adults should use institutional resources and tax funds only if it does not interfere with the full-time, daytime, degree students. This laudable concern with the education of young people sometimes perverts common sense, as in the case of providing state support for the young student who is unmotivated, unprepared, undirected or apathetic, but who nevertheless is urged to remain in school and get a degree.

At the same time, a highly motivated, goal-directed older person can often take advantage of educational resources only if he can be admitted as a regular degree student in programs designed primarily for regular full-time college students. Only a handful of institutions have developed college degree programs specifically to meet the needs of adults. Many states do not subsidize non-degree students, and there is very little scholarship money for part-time adult students. Higher adult education programs are often expected to break even or make a profit. Without begrudging young people a full opportunity, it seems reasonable that governmental and institutional support for adult students would be an equally profitable investment.

A third issue is the conflicting demands made on the university by the traditional activities of research and scholarship as opposed to adult education and community service. Some people feel universities and colleges should not be involved in community service at all. However, almost all universities have moved beyond traditional on-campus programs to become involved in a variety of activities [9]. Consultative services, information referrals, applied research, field studies, speakers' bureaus, conferences, medical and psychological services, testing and counseling programs, community projects—these and many others constitute the normal range of activities of contemporary institutions of higher education.

The Proper Method

Since it is virtually impossible to find an institution of higher education that does not, in some way, relate to the community through programs, studies, or services, there really is no issue as to whether an institution of higher education should provide service to the community. The issue is rather how the institution interprets its objectives, defines its clientele and serves that clientele. In determining how an institution functions, the following objectives apply, particularly to universities: (1) The discovery of new knowledge, through research and scholarly activities; (2) The accumulation and storage of information in books, libraries, museums, computers, among others; (3) The dissemination of accumulated knowledge through teaching, publications, films, and so on; (4) The application of knowledge and skills to specific situations.

These basic functions can be directed to any number of ends including the education of youth or adults, the application of knowledge to immediate and long-range community problems, research on basic scientific and social questions, as well as to the examination of fundamental philosophical questions. The resolution of the question of how and to what ends these functions are directed is a highly sophisticated matter requiring, first of all, sensitive analysis of the university as an institution in a highly complex and rapidly changing social system. The second requirement is a continuing analysis and evaluation of the various categories of people to be served and their relative order of priority. For example, it is conceivable that by the twenty-first century the primary participants in programs of institutions of higher education no longer will be young adults, but continuing learners who are constantly seeking new knowledge and who are permanently associated with educational institutions. Third, a more precise approach to the allocation of the resources of institutions of higher education is required, one which results in a better balance between what such institutions should do and what they can actually achieve. In the event that institutions take this more refined approach to defining and implementing their purposes, then the issue of community service will be placed in a framework more relevant for our time.

The Petersens, in a major study of university adult education, stated they were concerned that it had failed to realize its potential for providing needed programs consistent with institutional objectives [18]. They noted that adult education and extension functions were often scattered about the institution rather than combined into a "total extension function." This function, they believe, should comprise all the university's activities other than its two core purposes of scholarly research and the education of the young toward a degree. As they interviewed university administrators they found this concept was not often understood. While the Petersens did not advocate complete reorganization around the major areas of research and degree activities on the one hand and extension functions on the other, they did suggest that:

every institution ought to establish an accounting system capable of measuring the portion of its budget that goes into adult education, as well as the allocation within this among various types of programs. Unless this is done, there is no possibility of real control, either in the sense of banning unsuitable types of activity or of setting a schedule of priorities among those that are suitable but of greater or lesser importance. [18, p. 132]

Some Significant Developments

The necessity for continuing education is a fact of modern life. Increasing awareness of its importance has led to the rapid development of continuing education throughout society. Many businesses, governmental agencies, and other organizations recognize that, unlike the college degree programs, continuing education is becoming everybody's business. While many people still feel the colleges and universities are best equipped to provide learning experiences for adults, others challenge that notion. Some of the most innovative and effective continuing education goes on outside of the institutions of higher education—in industry, government, churches and in special settings such as the Esalen Institute. The growth of adult education at institutions of higher education is matched if not exceeded by its growth under other auspices.

The Universities' Role

While other agencies are increasing their activities in continuing education, the universities are developing as significant foci for leadership. First, they are emerging as the training centers for professional development in the field. Second, adult education research, which has been gaining momentum in the past decade, is based primarily in the universities. Third, as research efforts in higher adult education mature, universities will undertake more systematic analysis of the needs for continuing education in their communities as a part of overall efforts to gather sophisticated data on the populations they serve. Fourth, institutions of higher education are providing leadership to the field by undertaking the development of curricula and materials for continuing education, and this function may expand in the years ahead to serve all adult education agencies and organizations interested in expanding and improving their programs. A fifth significant development is occurring at institutions of higher education which are providing testing, counseling and referral services for adults to help them with their educational and vocational plans. In the future, the emphasis in university adult education may shift from developing programs for their own students to providing help to other organizations and agencies as they develop appropriate programs for their adult clients. This change in emphasis would be consistent with the role of a university in training others for leadership. It would also make it possible for the universities to balance their program development activities with the more scholarly areas of research and the training of professionals.

Reading Material Available

Another indication of the increasing growth and stability of higher adult education is the emergence of a substantial body of literature relative to this field. Commercial publishers have taken an active interest in books about education for adults in recent years. These publications supplement the literature emanating from The Center for the Study of Liberal Education for Adults and from the professional associations. Also very important is the work of the ERIC Clearinghouse on Adult Education, at Syracuse University, which has done an outstanding job in preparing annotated bibliographies and reviews of the literature such as the useful "University Adult Education: A Selected Bibliography, 1967, Review and Topical Index."

Much of the future experimentation and growth of higher adult education will take place in institutions serving major metropolitan areas. These areas are apt to be the focal point for the resolution of some of the major social problems of the coming decades, and metropolitan institutions of higher education will find themselves increasingly involved in finding solutions to the problems of urban society. Furthermore, the "typical adult education participant" as defined by Johnstone "lives in an urbanized area and more likely in the suburbs than inside the large city [11]." Those institutions which relate themselves effectively to the metropolitan community will draw many of their adult participants from this group.

These developments, as well as new legislation, signify a growing interest in and acceptance of higher adult education. In a period of increasing demand for programs and services, higher adult education has a unique opportunity to clarify its goals, coordinate its efforts and emerge into a phase of productive maturity.

Adult Education Within Institutions of Higher Education

Because evening colleges, extension divisions, correspondence programs, credit programs through television, and so on, admit both adults and regular college students, administrative responsibility and control of adult education activities is often unclear. Adult education administrators responsible for these heterogeneous programs are usually loath to separate the adult students because many adult programs could not stand alone financially. James Carey indicates that within universities 75 percent of the evening colleges and 95 percent of the extension divisions are separately organized; whereas in liberal arts colleges, approximately 50 percent of the units containing adult programs are separately administered [4].

Carey also identified a pattern of growth or life cycle in evening colleges and extension divisions. In the beginning of the cycle there is departmental domination, when adult education is primarily the activity of campus departments with no independent unit for adult education; then there is autonomous development, when a separate unit exists and major emphasis is placed on differentiating this unit from regular campus

Colleges and Universities

operation; then integration, when the extension division is not threatened by close ties with the university and becomes an integral part of it; and finally assimilation, when the adult education division, although still separate, becomes fully accepted as an essential element of the university. Carey does not imply these are necessarily ideal stages, for each institution must develop the pattern most appropriate to its own needs. However, it is clear those divisions that are integrated or assimilated into the institutional structure are likely to have the greatest capacity for producing strong programs of adult education. Those divisions in the second, autonomous stage, appear to be most expendable and insecure.

The Organization of Adult Education

As adult education programs grow into full-scale administrative units, directors of adult education are brought in to take over decision-making responsibility from the departments. In Carey's study, published in 1961, 41 percent of the evening colleges and 31 percent of the extension divisions were found to function much like colleges under the direction of deans. These autonomous units had almost twice the amount of liberal education programming of those under the control of the departments. With reference to attitudes toward community service, Carey found there was no neat correlation between control and commitment to community service. While state-supported institutions had a more active outlook toward their communities than private universities did, institutions regardless of the locus of control maintained a passive outlook toward adult education activities [4].

There is also a relationship between the size of staff and type of institutional organization. Evening college organization is usually smaller and less complicated than that of extension divisions, particularly if the evening college program is primarily devoted to credit programs which are similar to daytime offerings. A typical evening college has one or two staff members; only 10 percent of them have more than five. Extension divisions, often serving entire states, are more complex. About 60 percent employ at least five staff members, with many of them having ten times that number. Also, the evening college staff is generally not divided into departments, whereas the extension division sometimes develops a complex administrative arrangement consisting of many highly specialized units. In the small liberal arts colleges, adult education programs often are part-time responsibilities of regular faculty members or administrators whose major concerns are other matters.

It is clear there is no set form for organizing the adult education component of the institutions of higher education. Much depends on the type of institution and its particular resources and mission. However, it is also clear that unless there is a special unit for maintaining a concern for adult education programming, the task will not be carried out effectively, or even at all. There are two opposing views on the matter of organization and the decades ahead will see increasing experimentation with both forms. One view holds that the adult division should be primarily an administrative unit that serves adults by drawing on the resources of the whole university. With this model there should be heavy involvement of faculty, students and members of the community. This approach encourages simplicity of administration, keeps costs at a minimum, and also leaves control of degree and credit programs in the regular departments with the director of adult programs serving as an advocate of adult needs and as an innovator in program development.

Another view, which appears to be gaining strength, holds that adult education activities should be organized separately from the regular program, with freedom to develop resources and programs uniquely suited to serve the burgeoning educational needs of adults. This type of organization would not have a discrete body of subject matter, but would have its own specialists available to develop programs especially for adults. Some people feel that as long as adult education programs are tied to the youth-oriented institutions of higher education it will not be possible to develop the full range of activities required to implement relevant programs for adults. The ultimate development of this concept would result in the establishment of a "university for adults." The New School for Social Research in New York City closely approximates this model.

Arrangements for faculty also vary widely. Overload teaching by regular university faculty members is the most common practice. However, as an increasing number of programs are developed for adults, some departments are assigning faculty members to teach in adult programs and releasing them from teaching in the undergraduate or graduate divisions. Some joint appointments have developed to assure continuity of faculty involvement between academic departments and adult programs. Full-time separate evening or extension faculties have been advocated, but they are found at very few institutions. Part-time non-faculty teachers from the community at large are extensively used in adult programs particularly in urban areas. Non-degree programs make the most use of these teachers, whose appointments are usually subject to the approval of the academic departments.

With the growing number of faculty members teaching part time in adult programs there is increasing concern that the part-time faculty are not adequately integrated into the academic community. Faculty orien-

Colleges and Universities

tation, training and evaluation activities have been initiated but are still sparse. Perhaps the most fundamental problem associated with teaching in adult programs concerns differentials in salary and incentive as compared to regular college teaching. This disparity is sometimes due to the requirement that adult programs pay their own way, so that teaching and administrative costs are kept at a minimum.

Current Program Areas

Credit and Degree Programs. About 900,000 individuals enroll each year in credit courses offered by extension divisions or evening colleges in programs leading to a first college degree. The pressure for degrees is such that this major function of university adult education will continue to grow in the foreseeable future. Another 800,000 persons each year are engaged in part-time studies for higher degrees. As the educational level rises, this extension function becomes very important.

Few, perhaps no more than 5 percent, of the part-time students studying for degrees ever achieve them. Perhaps many of these students have no real interest in degrees. Degree credit courses often are the only ones available in their area of interest, and some students believe credit status reflects seriousness of purpose or guarantees the quality of instruction. Insofar as the faculty is concerned about quality and academic standards, they tend to focus their attention on credit courses, leaving the non-credit courses to the discretion of the director of the adult program.

Some universities have moved to return credit courses to control of the regular campus departments, leaving non-credit work of all types under the administration of a separate adult division. In the meantime, a new category, "non-degree credit," is emerging. This credit may in some cases serve as an elective course toward a degree, be applied toward a special certificate, or may fulfill the requirement for tuition remission by an industry or business, but is not designed as a part of a degree sequence. This type of enrollment will probably increase considerably in the coming years.

The regulations governing degree credit activity are varied. However, almost all institutions limit the amount of degree credit that may be earned in the evening college, extension division, or by correspondence studies. Because the credit system and residence requirement are often too rigid for part-time students seeking degrees, a number of degree programs expressly designed for these students are being tested with great success at several universities [16]. Also, systems of credit by testing have been developed as a part of the college level examination program, administered by The College Entrance Examination Board.

Non-Credit Programs. AUEC-NUEA institutions report 1,800,000 registrations in non-credit classes, short courses, correspondence courses and conferences during the 1967–68 year [2]. Registration by subject matter is as follows:

Education	15%	Interdisciplinary	7%
Humanities	14	Health professions	5
Business	12	Law	4
Agriculture	9	Physical sciences	3
Behavioral sciences	9	Biological sciences	1
Engineering	8	Other	13

Non-credit programs in liberal education range from the substantial four-year program at the University of Chicago to conferences and short courses. Occupationally oriented non-credit courses are often organized in certificate or diploma sequences and aimed at retraining workers or upgrading skills on the job.

In non-credit programs a great deal of innovation and experimentation is possible. New approaches and forms can be developed without concern for the regulations applied to credit programs by the institutions or by accrediting agencies. For this reason, much of the creativity and experimentation in the field of higher adult education can be found in the non-credit programs. Further, individual faculty members do not develop the same kind of vested interest in non-credit courses as they do in credit programs, making it easier to eliminate obsolete activities and start new ones. Non-credit programs, in general, cause less friction within the academic community, although they are often challenged as not being appropriate to the university's mission. With the variety of needs being met by non-credit programs and the great number of offerings, the range of quality is great. Successful innovation and crass commercialism exist alongside each other, and improving quality without destroying flexibility and relevance is one of the great challenges to the contemporary adult educator.

Continuing Professional Education. Some of the earliest programs of higher adult education were for professionals, and recent years have seen a dramatic growth in continuing professional education. The concept of continuing education is particularly appropriate for professionals, many of whom are graduating into a world where a college education soon becomes obsolete. Colleges and universities have not been able to meet all the growing demands in this area and many of the professions have set up substantial and high-quality programs on their own. Where programs are developed by colleges and universities they are well

Colleges and Universities

attended. For example, in 1963 there were enrolled in the University of California Extension professional programs:

   1 out of every 3 lawyers in the state;
   1 out of every 5 dentists;
   1 out of every 6 doctors;
   1 out of every 8 engineers;
   1 out of every 12 teachers in the state [3].

Because continuing professional education receives unquestioned acceptance as an appropriate university function, few of the issues raised about non-credit activities are applied to this area. In most cases, the professional associations are involved in the planning of programs, which helps to assure that the offerings are of high quality and appropriate to the needs of the profession. On the other hand, because continuing professional education programs are often highly specialized, institutions of higher education need to be concerned about the liberal education aspects of their offerings.

Liberal Adult Education. This is one of the most important and yet difficult areas to develop, largely because liberal education programs are seldom self-supporting from tuition and fees. Taxpayers do not demand liberal education, and they are not inclined to support it as they would vocational or professional education.

The natural audience for liberal adult education has been identified as the middle-aged, middle-class, largely professional group. This group is being served in a number of ways, but very little is done for many other adults who could benefit from programs of liberal education. For approximately sixteen years, the Center for the Study of Liberal Education for Adults attempted to promote and assist in the development of liberal adult programs at institutions of higher education. While the Center no longer exists, it left a legacy of ideas, programs, and a body of literature available through the Library of Continuing Education at Syracuse University.

Special Clientele Groups. Higher adult education programs are developed for a wide variety of audiences: foremost among these are programs for labor, management, public employees, the aged and women. Each of these groups has special characteristics and particular needs that can be served through adult education, and special programs for them wax and wane. In years past, for example, labor education programs were very common and in some countries constituted a national movement. Recently, there has been less activity in this area, while there has been a considerable increase of programs for the aged and for women, particularly for those women re-entering the labor market after their children are in school or leave the home.

Currently, new client groups are emerging. Law enforcement officials are seeking to develop greater professionalism through educational programs that stress liberal arts content as well as technical skills. Many programs have been developed for the educationally disadvantaged and for professionals and paraprofessionals working with such groups that formerly were excluded for racial or economic reasons. Obviously, such programs have raised questions about the appropriate role of the university in providing educational programs that are not necessarily college level.

The decisions to enter such special program areas as those just mentioned are usually based on insight, sensitivity to emerging needs and past experience, with a minimum of theoretical analysis of needs and resources. With notable exceptions, higher adult education programs have neither money nor staff time for systematic program analysis and development. Most offerings are either taken from the regular curriculum or are developed in response to expressed demands from a clientele which can pay for programs not subsidized by institutional, foundation or governmental funds. For these reasons, programs often lack continuity and progression. Adults cannot find many of the educational opportunities they need and therefore cannot develop long-range continuing education plans. Until higher adult education receives institutional and financial support for program development, it is unlikely the current approaches will be changed. This does not, however, mean higher adult education will not serve the needs of a great number of adults, for its sheer growth and proliferation will provide many new opportunities.

Urban Extension and Community Education

The Cooperative Extension Service traditionally provided highly successful community education programs in rural areas. In recent years, there has been a major effort to reorient Cooperative Extension to serve urban communities. Cooperative Extension dealt with its rural clientele largely in connection with their economic interests as producers, marketers, homemakers and future farmers. If it were to serve metropolitan citizens comparable to those in the rural areas, work would go on primarily in the middle-class suburbs. Therefore, if Cooperative Extension is to be effective in the "inner city," it will have to change its program and approaches to meet the needs of a new clientele. If it is successful, Cooperative Extension will be one of the most important educational influences in the urban areas of the future.

Colleges and Universities

General Extension Programs

General university extension has conducted many community development programs. The content of these programs includes formally organized educational experiences for community leaders, applied research on community problems, activities to stimulate community self-education efforts and technical and advisory services to local governments, voluntary organizations and other groups. Recently, some evening and community colleges have become engaged in one or another aspect of this type of activity.

Like Cooperative Extension, general extension tended to root its community development programs in rural communities and to foster life styles and values tied to a small-town view of life. The agrarian life, however, has been replaced by urbanization and industrialization, and most Americans have become city dwellers in fact if not in spirit. Industrialization requires the development of technological and professional skills for technical and mechanical work. Urbanization requires the development of a sense of community among large numbers of heterogeneous people. It requires a recognition of the fact that these diverse people are also interdependent, and that their common destiny is determined by how well they reconcile their differences and build a society that serves their individual and collective needs. The role of the university in developing such a sense of community, Charles V. Willie believes, is:

> to educate leaders from and for all levels of community—partly because all levels of community need leaders and partly because truth comes only from the fusion of a number of viewpoints—and that university education must become involved with current controversial community issues. The university must teach activists the benefits of reasoned thought and thinkers the methods and techniques of effective action. [21, p. 70]

A further responsibility of the urban university is the interpretation of the meaning of urban events to the people. J. Martin Klotsche states this responsibility as follows:

> The university located in the city has the broader task of informing citizens about all aspects of urban America. This is clearly within the tradition of university responsibility. Since education must fit the requirements of the culture in which it operates, a new kind of education designed to help people understand the urban environment is necessary. [13, p. 36]

The essential function and approach of urban community education programs has been one of the major topics of discussion during the last ten years. During this period university interest in urban community education was greatly stimulated by a series of Ford Foundation grants for urban research and extension [6], by university involvement in community action programs of the Economic Opportunity Act and by funds from Title I of the Higher Education Act of 1965 for "Continuing Education and Community Service."

Some urban extension approaches have been concerned with the human and social consequences to potential urban users of the use or non-use of available technical knowledge. Others have emphasized the importance of simply transmitting existing and new knowledge to the urban population wherever it may be needed: how to repair a house, how to get a job, how to buy foods and prepare a nutritious meal, how to obtain welfare services. Still other approaches have concentrated on urban community leaders: educating them about the facts of urban life; an understanding of urban policy questions; or training them in roles such as decision-makers, communicators, legislators and administrators. A few approaches have concentrated on setting up programs within a metropolitan framework, recognizing that the metropolis is the most important social, economic and political unit and the arena in which most of the people will work out their destiny as the twentieth century draws to a close.

In spite of encouraging efforts to urbanize higher adult education, there is still no resolution of the conceptual problem of how to allocate the resources of the institution. As colleges and universities increasingly direct their efforts to the urban community, they have to reconsider the composition of their clientele, the purposes of the programs, and the consequences of the present and future offerings. What is perhaps the key issue is pinpointed by Milton R. Stern:

Whatever it was in the past or will be in the future, the core of the urban problem is race. In the view of large numbers of Negroes, the university is but one more racist institution among many. What evidence can most universities offer to the contrary? [20]

Traditional higher adult education programs have served upwardly mobile populations. Even agricultural extension, despite its practical orientation, has, by and large, ignored or failed to reach the migrant worker, the poor farmer, the unemployed and groups with special needs, such as the American Indian. While a number of adult poor people have managed to attend institutions of higher education and even obtain degrees by part-time study, on the whole higher adult education has tended to serve the privileged; thus it has contributed to the widening gap between the white, educated, increasingly affluent suburban population and the non-white, educationally and economically deprived central city population.

Colleges and Universities

A Variety of Programs

Expressing concern through action, a wide variety of urban extension activities have appeared that at least dramatize the issues even if they do not resolve the problems. Store-front university extension centers have been established in ghetto areas; new careers and manpower development programs have been initiated; programs to help law enforcement personnel improve their understanding of inner-city residents have sprung up across the country; urban policy seminars for community leaders have been offered in many areas; continuing education programs for professionals have dealt with new approaches for youth, the aged, the indigent, the unemployed and the multi-problem families; programs for public officials and public employees—these programs and many others have involved universities and colleges with a new urban clientele.

In the meantime, numerous conferences, studies, training programs, and special projects have been conducted to assist institutions of higher education in thinking through how they can best relate to the urban community. It is hoped these practical efforts will enable institutions to work through tough operational questions and ethical problems related to the provision of educational resources to appropriate populations of the urban community. Because the urban complex is fraught with political hazards and philosophical dilemmas it is unlikely colleges and universities can either escape unscathed or come up with instant solutions. But the growing presence of institutions of higher education in the centers of metropolitan communities attests to their commitment to the task. The next decade, which will be characterized by great upheaval and innovation, will provide higher adult education with its greatest test to date; and urban extension efforts may well determine the main direction of adult education for generations to come.

Future Approaches to Adult Learning

Residential Conferences

Short-term conferences and institutes in a residential setting have increased dramatically, due in large part to the support of the Kellogg Foundation. The Foundation has provided more than $20 million since the early 1950's for buildings, training and research at ten institutions of higher education, with four more in the planning stage [1]. In 1964, it was reported that 130 conference centers were in operation and it is likely many more actually exist. In the future virtually every higher adult education program will have such a facility or ready access to one, even though it may be commercially owned and operated.

Independent Study Programs

Johnstone reported that 8 percent of adult learners were engaged in independent study in 1962 [12]. With programmed learning, television and radio and improved correspondence study programs integrated into other learning activities, this area may greatly expand in the future.

Community Learning Centers

With the development of computer-aided instruction, closed-circuit television, more flexible learning formats and a greater willingness to develop off-campus educational activities, institutions of higher education will experiment with the establishment of local learning resource centers where adults can come for independent study, tutoring and direct instruction in small groups. The development of such centers, built in preference to branch campuses, will give institutions of higher education a low-cost, flexible approach to reach a new clientele in the central city and suburban areas who would not normally come to the main campus. While centers could be established quite easily in libraries and public schools, they are more likely to arise in shopping centers, industrial parks, multi-purpose community centers, and other locations not now associated with the educational establishment.

Comprehensive System of Continuing Education

As the demands for adult education increase, the various institutions, agencies and organizations devoted to adult education may begin to link their programs in a metropolitan system that ultimately could be even more extensive than what is now available to young people. It should not be a monolithic system, but rather one that brings existing elements together into an articulated whole. To do this might require developing the following elements:

1. Metropolitan-wide organization to link the system together.
2. A center for testing, counseling and referral for adults interested in education. If necessary, there would be branches. Preferably the referral system would be computerized.
3. A center for curriculum and program development to assist all adult education agencies to improve their offerings.
4. A laboratory for basic research on the adult learning process and for experimentation with methods and equipment.
5. A research program to identify characteristics, needs and resources of the adult population.

Colleges and Universities

6. A program of professional development for adult education personnel of all agencies centered in a local university.

While the establishment of such a comprehensive, coordinated system would take some time, in some communities many of the intermediate steps have already been taken and exist in isolation. It will most likely be the universities that take the leadership in designing, implementing, and monitoring it when such a system comes into being.

Financing Higher Adult Education

A fiscal fact of life is, as the Petersens put it, that "University adult education almost always has to pay its own way in an extraordinary proportion [18]." The heavy dependence on student tuition leads to a "market economy" approach, a lack of funds for adequate program development, and avoidance of high cost or high risk programs even if the clientele are of great social consequence.

Cooperative Extension is in the most secure financial position because it is jointly funded by federal, state and local levels of government. General extension, which sometimes receives state subsidies, is occasionally in a better financial position than the evening colleges or private institutions. The latter almost without exception are self-supporting and very often are expected to make a profit. These private institutions acquire an average of 81 percent of their income from tuition and fees, while urban public institutions report 75 percent and community colleges 45 percent of their total costs come from fees and tuition.

Liveright, in gathering data for his forthcoming study, averaged the size of the continuing education budgets of types of institutions (whose budgets ranged from $10,000 to $16,000,000) and identified the following [17].

Type of Institution	Average Size of Budget	Percent of Total Budget for Adult Education
The pacesetters	$3,440,000	5.1%
Nonurban public institutions	2,506,000	6
Urban public institutions	1,100,000	5
Private institutions	860,000	8.5
Community colleges	237,000	1.7

Besides tuition, fees and state subsidies, higher adult education relies on foundation grants for financing. The major foundations have tended to direct their resources for adult education into particular channels as have the Ford Foundation into urban extension; the Carnegie Corporation into surveys of adult education, correspondence study, education of women, special degree programs for adults; the Kellogg Foundation into capital funds for residential centers, research and training in residential education; and the defunct Fund for Adult Education into educational television and liberal education.

Through allocation to states for special training institutes federal legislation has stimulated a number of areas of adult education, particularly adult basic education. Title I of the Higher Education Act of 1965 has provided approximately 10 million dollars per year for continuing education and community service programs. It was hoped originally this legislation would do for general extension what the Smith–Lever Act did for Cooperative Extension. In addition to these federal sources, many special purpose funds, estimated by some to total as much as one billion dollars annually, can be directed to adult education activities.

Coordination

Professional Associations

There are two important associations that provide for effective communication within the field of college and university adult education. The National University Extension Association (NUEA) was organized in 1915. Membership is restricted to colleges and universities in the United States which direct a variety of extension operations both on campus and away from it. The large university typically belongs to NUEA; at present there are 155 member institutions. The other important association is the Association of University Evening Colleges (AUEC) which includes in its membership almost all urban colleges and universities in the United States (and several in Canada) offering evening college programs for adults. AUEC was organized in 1939 and now has a membership of 76 institutions.

Cooperative and General Extension

The obvious need for these two branches of higher adult education to work more closely together has led to many attempts at mergers, collaboration, coordination and containment policies with varying degrees of success. The Petersens point out that past attempts to bring the two extension services together were on a basis of common interest when, in fact, the two services are quite different [18]. Each has certain strengths and weaknesses and plans for cooperation must take their

Colleges and Universities

differences into account. No pattern of coordination or amalgamation has yet arisen that is applicable across the country, and it is likely developments in this area will be quite slow. However, where an effective union of cooperative and general extension does take place, it will have the potential to release a great educational force.

Local, State and Regional

Many new approaches are being tried to bring about greater coordination within the field in general. To cite a few: Title I of the Higher Education Act requires a coordinated state plan which involves all interested colleges and universities; AUEC has admitted junior college members; New England has a regional continuing education center; Ohio has created a Council on Higher Continuing Education that is carrying out a cooperative statewide project among state-assisted universities; AUEC and NUEA joined with other national adult education organizations for a Galaxy Conference in 1969.

Conclusion

Impelled by the needs of adults for continuous learning opportunities that are high in quality, relevant, geographically and economically accessible, colleges and universities will not only maintain their present level of commitment to higher adult education, but also will find more effective means for implementing their efforts. With more experience, a better financial base, and greater numbers of professionally prepared adult education personnel, the field can look forward to continuing the rapid growth and the development of maturity that characterized the past decade.

References

1. Alford, Harold J. *Continuing Education in Action*. New York: John Wiley & Sons, 1968.
2. Association of University Evening Colleges. *Programs and Registrations, 1967–68*. Washington, D.C.: National University Extension Association.
3. *California Extension in a Decade of Transition: A Report to the Combined Academic Senate Committee on University Extension Covering the Years 1952–1962*. Berkeley, Calif.: University of California, 1963.
4. Carey, James T. *Forms and Forces in University Adult Education*. Chicago, Ill.: Center for the Study of Liberal Education for Adults, 1961.

5. Dyer, John. *Ivory Towers in the Market Place.* Indianapolis, Ind.: Bobbs-Merrill, 1956.
6. Ford Foundation. *Urban Extension: A Report on Experimental Programs Assisted by the Ford Foundation.* New York: The Ford Foundation, 1966.
7. Frandson, Phillip E. *Higher Adult Education: Its Present and Future.* Washington, D.C.: Association of University Evening Colleges–National University Extension Association, 1967.
8. Haygood, Kenneth, ed. *A Live Option: The Future of the Evening College.* Boston, Mass.: Center for the Study of Liberal Education for Adults, 1965.
9. Haygood, Kenneth. *The University and Community Education.* Chicago, Ill.: Center for the Study of Liberal Education for Adults, 1962.
10. Houle, Cyril O. "From Craft Toward Profession." *The Continuing Task.* Boston, Mass.: Center for the Study of Liberal Education for Adults, 1967.
11. Johnstone, John W. C. "Adult Uses of Education, Fact and Forecast." *Sociological Backgrounds of Adult Education.* Chicago, Ill.: Center for the Study of Liberal Education for Adults, 1964.
12. Johnstone, John W. C. *Volunteers for Learning: A Study of the Educational Pursuits of American Adults.* Chicago, Ill.: Aldine, 1962.
13. Klotsche, J. Martin. *The Urban University: And the Future of Our Cities.* New York: Harper & Row, 1966.
14. Liveright, A. A. *Adult Education in the United States.* Boston, Mass.: Center for the Study of Liberal Education for Adults, 1968.
15. Liveright, A. A. "Adult Education in Colleges and Universities." *Handbook of Adult Education in the United States.* Edited by Malcolm S. Knowles. Chicago, Ill.: Adult Education Association of the USA, 1960.
16. Liveright, A. A., and DeCrow, Roger. *New Directions in Degree Programs Especially for Adults.* Chicago, Ill.: Center for the Study of Liberal Education for Adults, 1963.
17. Liveright, A. A., and Mosconi, David. *Continuing Education in Institutions of Higher Education.* Unpublished study. The Academy for Educational Development.
18. Petersen, Renee, and Petersen, William. *University Adult Education.* New York: Harper & Row, 1960.
19. Shannon, Theodore, J., and Schoenfeld, Clarence A. *University Extension.* New York: Center for Applied Research in Education, 1965.
20. Stern, Milton R. "Trends and Tangents: Continuing Education." *Journal of Higher Education* (April, 1968), pp. 230–233.
21. Willie, Charles V. "Educating the Urban Student for the Urban Way of Life." *Political Backgrounds of Adult Education.* Boston, Mass.: Center for the Study of Liberal Education for Adults, 1967.

Chapter 13

Community Colleges

ERVIN L. HARLACHER

The community college is a uniquely American institution. As such, it incorporates many educational traditions of long standing together with other concepts so recent and ill-defined they are difficult even to discuss, let alone implement. Central among these new concepts is *community service*.

There is no disputing the fact that most junior and community colleges perform some (and sometimes many) traditional adult education services. It is also a fact in many small colleges community service programs are administered by a local public school adult education administrator, past or present. This situation is often unavoidable and may be desirable. On the other hand, the close overlapping between traditional adult education programs and community college service programs regrettably obscures the fact that the community college is developing its own unique approach to serving the adult community. This chapter accepts as a given the important role community colleges play in traditional adult education programs. The emphasis here, instead, is on the new concept of community service and how such services may be planned, developed and provided.

Essential to understanding the community service concept is a realization of the difference between the junior college and the community college. The difference is not always —perhaps not even often—comprehended by those outside the field, yet it is a critical difference. Not every junior college is truly a community college. A "junior" college is an institution that primarily duplicates organizationally and fulfills philosophically the first two years of the four-year senior college. On the other hand, a true community college connotes an institution that has developed beyond an isolated entity into an institution seeking full partnership with its community. In the process, the community college becomes for its district community a cultural center, a focal point of intellectual life, a source of solidarity and a fount of local pride.

It is out of this broader concept of involvement with the community that community service emerges as a focal point for the community college. While many of the particular services offered may be provided by other institutions as well, the central service thrust of the community college affords a characteristic and valuable posture to this new institution that is peculiarly its own. The soundly conceived community service program recognizes the college's obligation to accept the following responsibilities:

1. Become a center of community life by encouraging the use of college facilities and services by community groups when such use doesn't interfere with the college's regularly scheduled day and evening programs.
2. Provide educational services for all age groups which utilize the special skills and knowledge of the college staff and other experts to meet the needs of community groups and the college district community at large.
3. Provide the community with the leadership and coordination capabilities of the college, assist the community in long-range planning, and join with individuals and groups in attacking unsolved problems.
4. Contribute to and promote the cultural, intellectual and social life of the college district community and the development of skills for the profitable use of leisure time [8, p. ii].

Accepting these objectives as its mission, the community college service program encompasses but extends far beyond formal, on-campus instruction for adults. The program aims at the whole person in the whole community and sees no one as unworthy because of his present level of development, his ideas, or his current status in the culture. The community college service program is founded on the bedrock of the following principles:

1. The "campus" is coincident with the length and breadth of the college district. Community service is a process and not a place.
2. The college is obliged to go to the community at least as aggressively as the community is encouraged to come to the college.

3. Education cannot and must not be limited to formalized classroom instruction.
4. The community college should be a catalyst for community development.
5. Community college service programs should meet community needs while avoiding useless duplication of existing services.

The pressures promoting the rapid growth of educational demand at all levels are keenly felt by junior and community colleges. On the average, a new two-year college will open its doors about once a week for the next several years, as has been the case for the past several years. It appears, therefore, that community service movement now getting under way will have an enormous impact on the adult education field, because of the size, growth rate and scope of present and projected community service programs.

Organizing and Administering the Community Service Program

With the financial assistance of the Alfred P. Sloan Foundation and on behalf of the American Association of Junior Colleges, the author in 1967 made a national survey of community college service programs [8]. Thirty-seven community college districts in thirteen states were visited, and field studies were supplemented by extensive correspondence with 28 other college districts in twelve states. Altogether, the districts surveyed operated 104 campuses in nineteen different states. A number of other administrators active in or knowledgeable about community college service programs were also queried. Suggestions and recommendations made in this chapter are based on the AAJC study and on the author's own experience.

With respect to organizing and administering the community service program, experience has shown the following principles to be critical. First, a community service program cannot be successfully developed without a sound knowledge of what the needs and interests in a given community are now and what they can be expected to be in the future. Adequate long-range planning is essential; this in turn implies that resources and qualified personnel must be provided to study community needs, whether through surveys, polls or advisory committees. Furthermore, a means must be provided from the outset to re-examine constantly shifting needs and desires on a continuous basis.

Once community needs have been determined with some degree of confidence, program purposes and objectives should be defined, refined and reduced to formal, written statements that can be discussed and debated by all those in the community and the college whose support and cooperation are required. Properly pursued, the program definition phase can provide not only a clear focus for the program, but a mechanism for communication and education about the program.

The challenge of preparing the program statement is a stern one: The statement must be specific enough to indicate clearly what is to be done by whom and broad enough to avoid limiting the program to the routine, obvious missions and audiences already being served by others. Program statements should encompass written policies, regulations and procedures, including procedures for continuous review and evaluation.

Providing for community service program staff is a critical step in program development. Experience demonstrates that a successful program requires the full-time service of an able administrator unburdened by teaching, public relations, or other administrative duties. Community service administration is not only a full-time task, it is a vital one, and must be regarded as such. The administrator should report directly to the administrative head of the college; this direct relation simplifies management of activities that transcend departments and also provides needed status for the program in the eyes of other faculty and staff members. Depending on the size of the program, its rate of growth, and the resources available, the community services administrator should be provided with sufficient full-time staff. Depending on the program, the administrator's assistants may range from clerical help to auditorium managers, publications personnel, radio–TV station managers, recreation coordinators and community development specialists. In community service programs, as in all else, nothing can be had for nothing, and a strong program requires adequate staffing.

Vigorous community participation in the program—from survey of needs to post-program evaluation—is also essential. The means used to secure community participation vary from setting to setting, although some form of advisory committee or network of committees is typically encountered. If they are to be effective, advisory bodies will also require adequate staff support and consultation services. The temptation to make community advisors "rubber stamps" must be avoided at all costs. Any successful community service program must be *of* the community and not merely *for* it. Persons selected to speak for the community, and the methods used to articulate their activities, must be based on a sound, comprehensive knowledge of the community and its leadership structure. But, to repeat for emphasis, effective community participation in developing and operating the community service program is indispensable.

Financing the community service program is never simple, but programs that are truly the community's rather than the college's will find it easier to obtain funds. In some states, as in California, the law permits a community college district to increase its maximum tax rate to finance community services. Other funds may be available from local public school districts, state departments of education, federal agencies, or other public and private agencies at all levels. Many community service programs can be made to support themselves, in whole or in part. Extreme caution should be exercised, however, in requiring a program or service to pay for itself. Many important community needs are unmet partly because the people who need or want them are unable or unwilling to pay for them. On the other hand, free use of community facilities or services which are donated can make important in-kind contributions to the community service program budget. One further word of caution is indicated at this point. If staff and faculty of the college are asked regularly to perform extra services without compensation in time or money, badly needed on-campus support for the program inevitably will lag.

Methods and Approaches in Community Service Programs

It is difficult and not overly useful to make many generalizations about the methods and approaches used in community service programs. A few observations can be made, however, and augmented with specific examples.

The most successful approaches stem from the programming principles enunciated at the beginning of the chapter. Services should be delivered throughout the community rather than only on campus or at a few, scattered sites. Furthermore, services should be oriented away from formalized classroom situations and toward the realities of the community itself. Community service programs should aim toward contributing to long-term growth and participation as well as providing for the needs of the moment.

Relevant Program Planning

Translated into approach, these principles imply programming methods which are mobile and flexible, and quickly applicable in varied settings with a minimum of effort. Programs should be inclusive rather than exclusive to the fullest practicable extent, making room insofar as possible for the broadest range of ages, previous levels of attainment, styles of learning and interests. Many individual programs will require an extremely narrow focus suited to highly immediate and specialized needs. Nonetheless, the community service administrator should build into every program the maximum feasible degree of openness and flexibility. Some specific examples taken from the 1967 study [8] may spark some useful ideas in the reader's mind in this connection.

Oakland Community College in Michigan proposes to establish a network of "Think–Links" in urban slum areas. These multiservice outreach operations will be based in empty neighborhood stores and in mobile units located on urban renewal land. Each Think–Link will offer realistic literacy and basic skills training; a community student action corps composed of neighborhood grass-roots leaders and college students; service by one or two educational and vocational counseling centers; cultural and educational enrichment programs; and volunteer faculty and community consulting services.

Hudson Valley Community College has operated mobile recruiting vans in ghetto areas to enroll clients for its Urban Center pilot project. Oakland (Michigan) Community College offers a traveling science museum, complete with short courses throughout its 900-square-mile district, in cooperation with a local science institute.

El Centro College in Texas offers in-plant training courses in fire stations, hotels, insurance companies, savings and loan companies, and so on. A work simplification course given at St. Paul Hospital in Dallas by El Centro College is estimated to have saved the hospital $750,000 in operating costs during the first year.

Los Rios Junior College, which serves a 2600-square-mile area in Northern California, established a satellite campus 40 miles from the main campus and is planning a series of smaller centers. During 1967, 270 students were enrolled in college credit courses in 35 different subjects at the satellite campus. Los Rios is considering the use of closed-circuit television between campuses, and has developed a program to bring plays and other cultural events into remote communities in its district.

San Bernardino Valley College (California) and St. Petersburg Junior College (Florida) operate home discussion group programs. The California program focuses on neighborhood, community and area problems and extends to sponsorship of workshops, seminars, weekend residential conferences and round tables. The Florida program concentrates on semi-monthly informal meetings in which groups select moderators from their own members and exchange facts, ideas and opinions on topics as diverse as modern art and the impact of technology on society.

Many community colleges use the short-course method with great success. Typical of these is the program at the Center for Community Educational Services, established by the State University of New York Agricultural and Technical College at Farmingdale. In 1966–67, the Center offered 720 special programs and served 32,000 people. In-service training programs are also widespread among community colleges—offered on campus, at the work site or elsewhere. Indicative of how much room for innovation there is, even in relatively traditional methods, is one in-service training program developed by Abraham Baldwin College in Georgia. The Baldwin College effort attracted 25 missionaries working in 16 different foreign countries to a weekend program entitled "Agricultural Missions."

Reaching out to serve people where they live and work, and employing, whenever appropriate, modern technology (e.g., remote computer consoles, telelecture, educational television, videotape recorders) the effective community service program is readily accessible to people on their own terms. For the most part, droning lectures given in chalk-dusty classrooms at odd hours miles away from home cannot provide the service required. At the same time, no amount of slick packaging will make successful a service program that fails to address itself to the needs and interests of those being served.

Planning Learning Activities

The initial suggestion for a new program might come from many sources: from an advisory committee member; as a result of a routine contact between the program staff and a member of the community (individual citizen, employer, service agency and so on); from a faculty member; or from within the program staff itself. The suggestion is then formally submitted for consideration according to written procedures governing the program. Usually, procedures entail an investigation of need and interest in the community, followed by staff and community advisory committee review and decision in the light of the overall program objectives and policies.

Once it has been determined a given program will be offered, program planning begins. It cannot be emphasized too strongly that adequate lead time must be allowed for thorough planning. A weak or entirely unsuccessful new program diminishes the community service effort as a whole by lowering its esteem in the eyes of the community and of college faculty and staff. Clear responsibility for planning each program must be assigned or assumed by the community services administrator. At the same time, planners should have active participation from all parties who will be involved in the program whether as participants, as staff, or in supporting, coordinating and facilitating roles.

It is important that objectives of new programs be spelled out in detail and thoroughly understood by all persons concerned. Important also are formal agreements whenever the expenditure of funds, use of facilities, provision of services or other valuable resources are required.

Planners must provide for adequate communication about the program within the college and community. Of course, one should determine in advance the criteria and procedures to be used to evaluate the program —and follow through on them without fail. Dates, commitments and other details of the program require coordination with other agencies in the community, to avoid possible conflicts and to insure joint programming whenever possible and desirable. Finally, planners should strive for programs of the highest quality—even if it means fewer programs.

Techniques and Resources

Traditionally, educational institutions have been thought of as vertical or concentrated resources, that is, as a "pile" of facilities and people at a central point to which people come for service. The community college, however, properly regards itself as a horizontal or distributed entity. Its physical campus may be logistically important, but its actual campus is the college district. The college welcomes and encourages maximum use of its own physical and human resources by all individuals and groups in the community. In turn, the techniques of community service concentrate on tapping every other resource in the community in support of its activities.

The community is a valuable laboratory for the enrichment of the total college curriculum. Field trips to art galleries, business and industry, local government offices, public and private service agencies— all are educational resources that can be incorporated into community service programs. The community can be the object of special studies, surveys and polls initiated through the program. Joint programs with business, government and other educational agencies at all levels— public and private—can provide unique and valuable service. Community leaders can be used as resource persons in a variety of ways.

Community colleges are finding community resources of great value in offering programs requiring costly special facilities. This trend is apparent in the health services fields where many colleges jointly sponsor training programs with hospitals and medical laboratories for both professional and non-professional personnel. Such cooperative ventures permit the college to avoid buying costly equipment that may quickly become obsolete.

In other fields, Rockland Community College in New York is developing its college library as a strong, community-serving central reference and research library to complement existing library services in the county. Jamestown Community College (New York) displays on its campus at all times 100 paintings provided by the Chautauqua County Society of Artists. A non-profit cooperative nursery school operates on the campus of the State University of New York Agricultural and Technical College at Farmingdale. Rock Valley College (Illinois) offers a career advancement program in cooperation with 33 firms that place employees in each of a variety of designated positions on a work–study basis.

Taken collectively, these few examples represent a trend toward what has been called *institutional synergism*. Working closely with other agencies in the community, the community college is able to help accomplish what no single institution could hope to achieve on its own.

Evaluating Community Service Programs

Program evaluation in every field of endeavor today represents an exciting opportunity and a stiff challenge. In community service programs, as in others, needs and desires continuously to outstrip resources. Consequently, there is a growing awareness of the need to determine the practices and programs that are effective. Without adequate evaluation, it is impossible to expand sound programs or to improve poor ones. Relying as it does on the community for its advice and support, the community service program is in a better position than many to know how well it is doing.

As every professional realizes, serious evaluation must be something more than "what the community will buy." Many important community needs may not be widely felt, let alone demonstrated. At the same time, many sincere individuals, groups, firms and agencies often do not know what they need, what they want, or what they are getting through existing programs. It is up to the community service administrator and his staff to devise, test and constantly improve useful methods for program evaluation.

Routinely, of course, all participants in specific programs should be asked to evaluate the activities, either upon termination or at specified intervals. This kind of appraisal can be useful in identifying (or verifying) program weaknesses. Strong endorsements by participants, however, should be viewed with caution. People often are reluctant to admit their errors of judgment in entering a weak program. Some think it bad manners to criticize a program, particularly if they have rapport with program staff. Advisory committees are useful in evaluating community service programs if the committees are used intelligently.

Comprehensive community surveys on an annual or semi-annual basis can provide useful information for evaluative purposes. The use of outside consultants for evaluation is sometimes justified, but tends too often to be regarded as an easy path that allows local personnel to avoid hard choices and critical decisions.

A checklist that may be useful in deciding upon evaluation procedures for community service programs was developed by the author in an earlier study [10, pp. 69–76].

A State Survey

A survey was made in 1966–67 of California community colleges, long leaders in the community service field. Of the state's 66 college districts 51 were studied. The 51 districts operated 60 campuses. Of the 60, 41 had at least one full-time community service programmer and 12 anticipated hiring a full-time administrator within the year. The 60 campuses reported the following community service activities (the numbers in parentheses after each category indicate the number of persons taking part in that activity during the survey year): Community use of facilities (1,808,000); recreation (808,000); community forums and lecture series (269,000); fine arts series (224,000); community performance events (199,000); planetarium and museum shows (78,000); non-credit short courses, seminars, workshops, conferences and institutes (72,000); arts festivals (50,000); and community research and development projects (18,000).

On 16 of the campuses it was estimated that from 50 to 99 community organizations used the campus facilities during the year, while 9 campuses reported from 100 to 299 and 4 institutions indicated from 300 to 699 organizations had used the campus facilities.

Some Sample Programs

Following are some examples of programs throughout the country. Regretfully, it will be feasible to give only the barest hint of the vast number and variety of these activities.

Provision of Physical Facilities and Services. Foothill College in California makes its facilities available for a wide range of cultural events, from an annual concert series by the San Francisco Symphony to youth symphony concerts, opera, ballet and modern dance, chamber music, drama, vocal concerts, appreciation concerts for children and art exhibits. Three community symphony orchestras make their home on the Foothill campus.

Montgomery Junior College in Maryland provides rent-free laboratory and classroom space and other facilities for the Metropolitan

Washington School of Printing, which offers non-credit courses in printing technology for county students.

Mount San Antonio College in California provides library service for residents of the community college district.

The State University of New York Agricultural and Technical College at Farmingdale through its Center for Community Educational Services opens its campus to farm tours. Three guides are employed to conduct lecture tours of the botanical gardens, farm areas, and animal complex. Nearly 32,000 persons—most of them elementary school students from 147 different schools—took part in these tours in a single year.

Community Educational Services. Since 1940, Abraham Baldwin Agricultural College (Georgia) has offered a series of short courses for Georgia farmers. Courses are usually limited to one day and concentrate on one facet of a given topic. They are tailored to fit expressed needs and offered without charge. In 27 years, 743 short courses have been conducted for a total of 98,699 people.

A similar short course program has been developed in the metropolitan area by Milwaukee Institute of Technology. Some 127 courses were presented to 31,160 persons in 1966 as a service to area businesses, industries and homemakers.

Miami-Dade Junior College (Florida) offers extension credit courses in many local centers, including airline companies, public agencies, hotels and an Air Force base. In a recent fall semester, some 600 persons were enrolled.

New York City Community College (Brooklyn) offers one of the nation's most comprehensive in-service training programs for the human service occupations. Training for building inspectors, preparation for civil service promotion examinations, training for hospital aides, training for housing code inspectors are only a few examples. Del Mar College (Texas) has a similar program.

Community Counseling. Rockland Community College, cooperating with the State University of New York, operates the New York State Guidance Center for Women, serving women in their thirties and forties who are seeking help in choosing vocational goals. The Center served 365 clients in its first year of operation, providing individual and group testing and counseling services, supported by an outreach program concentrating on low income areas. Other substantial programs that provide educational or vocational counseling for persons not formally affiliated with the institution are operated by Cuyahoga Community College in Ohio and North Florida Junior College.

Human Resource Development. Community college service programs are numerous in the area of human resources development. New York City Community College through its Urban Center helps disadvantaged Brooklyn high school graduates in the lower quarter of their classes secure job training and placement services. At Peralta College (California) the East Bay Skills Center (funded under the Manpower Development and Training Act) served 1400 students in 1967. Oakland Community College (Michigan) has Project SERVE, which counsels and places senior citizens in need of additional income.

Campus Radio–Television Stations. Chicago City College operates a "TV college" for 26 hours each week, offering both credit and non-credit courses. These courses have been formally participated in by 170,000 persons since the program's inception in 1956. Nearly 75 percent of those enrolled for credit complete course requirements. Milwaukee Institute of Technology, cooperating with the Milwaukee Public Schools, assists in presenting more than 800 telecasts annually to 70,000 students and teachers in more than 130 Milwaukee schools. Long Beach City College (California) students operate and maintain radio station KLON, which serves 100,000 elementary and secondary public school students.

Community Development. Abraham Baldwin Agricultural College (Georgia) began Project SURGE in 1964. The project uses a network of 14 committees representing many aspects of community life. These committees prepare goals and objectives for five-year periods. Through committee meetings and annual county-wide meetings, the community makes plans to achieve its objectives and to evaluate its progress. Cerritos College (California) undertook a socioeconomic study of its district and followed this with a comprehensive community opinion poll. The Cerritos survey was undertaken jointly with a citizen's advisory committee composed of city managers, chamber of commerce managers, school superintendents and coordinating council presidents. Essex Community College in the suburbs of Baltimore uses a series of workshops and seminars to convey information and knowledge about such matters as local government, planning, renewal and community organization.

Cultural and Recreational Activities. It is difficult even to suggest the broad scope and variety of community college service programs in the cultural and recreational field. Foothill Junior College (California) is exemplary if not typical. Its public events programs attract more than 25,000 persons annually to four series of events in the fine arts, lectures and forums, art exhibits and films. Each series is planned by a separate student–faculty committee. As mentioned earlier, the college is also the home of three community symphony groups, and its annual concert series by the San Francisco Symphony has become an important local tradition. The lecture series has presented such national figures as General Maxwell Taylor, Robert Hutchins, Erich Fromm and Cleveland Amory.

Flint Community Junior College (Michigan) conducts a Tours and Trips program which last year involved some 1300 persons in such excursions as the Shakespearean Festival in Ontario, a Mediterranean Holiday and Highlights of Europe. Cerritos College (California) operates a community art gallery which in 1967 was visited by 26,000 persons. Typical of another activity in this category, Cerritos developed an imaginative summer recreation program embracing aquatics, fine arts and sports events staged throughout the college district. More than 110,000 persons participated in this program in the summer of 1967.

In the field of science, Foothill College is again exemplary. Its Space Science Center houses a planetarium, an observatory and is permanent host to the Peninsula Astronomical Society. Members of the Amateur Research Center (60 high school and college students and technicians) are affiliates of the Center. A daily lecture–demonstration program at the planetarium had an attendance in 1966 of 21,000 school children and 5300 adults. The observatory is a key unit in a worldwide network participating in the NASA Argus Moonblink Program. Project OSCAR has developed a complete satellite tracking station.

Festivals of various sorts are also common. Cabrillo College (California) in cooperation with the Cabrillo Guild of Music, offers a Music Festival of ten concerts during two weekends in late August. The festival —attended by 5000 persons in 1966—was covered by *The New York Times*, and was videotaped for 12 hour-long television programs in San Francisco and Salt Lake City.

Community performing groups find a natural home on community college campuses. Del Mar College (Texas) has the 45-member Del Mar Chamber Orchestra, together with an 80-voice community symphonic choir, and the 30-voice Schola Cantorum. The Corpus Christi Symphony was founded at Del Mar College and has become strong enough to take on an independent status. Flint Community Junior College (Michigan) sponsors an annual ten-week summer theater program employing a professional resident theater company in four major productions.

Some Problems in Development

Needless to say, the rapid development of community service programs in community colleges is not without its problems and difficulties.

The author's 1967 study discusses at greater length eight problems or issues which can merely be mentioned here [8, pp. 80–117]:

Problems

1. *Communication.* "Communication" refers to reaching all those in the community who need or desire services, and to reaching all those on campus and in the community who collectively possess the resources required to provide services. It is a never ending task to identify and maintain contact with those key groups, opinion leaders and decision-makers in every field who can get the word out and bring the people in.
2. *Support from boards of trustees, administration and faculty.* A question often heard in this quarter is "But is this really a *college* program?" It is sometimes difficult for those whose past experience encompasses only "pure" subjects "taught" in formal "courses" to appreciate the requirement for diversity of approach and address in community service programs. It is the program director's task to organize and provide effective orientation on a continuing basis. A tested technique for achieving this end—easier said than done—is to identify the target group's own needs and interests and to assist in developing programs to meet them.
3. *Coordination of services with other community and regional groups.* In this field as in so many others, interagency planning and coordination on a regional basis is becoming essential. The problem has two principal aspects: The first is communication. The second is the need to devise innovative ways for all concerned parties to meet their several needs and receive suitable credit from their respective constituencies.
4. *Identification of community needs and interests.* The naïve community services administrator is certain he knows what the community needs. The cynical administrator is sure the community does not know what it wants. The effective administrator is certain of nothing but is dedicated to trying to find out.
5. *Planning and evaluation.* These vital activities are too often neglected or ignored, in the interest of "getting on with it." Furthermore, planning and evaluating are perhaps the most abstract, complex, and difficult aspects of any educational program. The burden of leadership here falls especially heavily on the shoulders of the program administrator. If he does not insist on adequate time and resources for program planning and evaluating—and if he does not keep up with current efforts to improve these functions—no one else will, and overall effectiveness will suffer.

6. *Philosophy and objectives*. Often, the needs a community service program should address itself to are those the community for whatever reasons has "swept under the rug." It is difficult to gain community recognition for such needs. In this area, the spadework done to establish and maintain intensive community involvement in program planning will yield especially fruitful results. It is also important to provide continuing communication about program philosophy and objectives as well as the program activities themselves.
7. *Administration and supervision*. Community service is a field in formation and one that requires unusual degrees of maturity, experience, judgment, initiative and flexibility. Such talent is rare and is in intense demand. On the other hand, the nature of the program lends itself to a wide variety of administrative approaches and styles. More than a few extremely successful community service administrators were recruited in unlikely places.
8. *Physical resources*. Community service demands on college facilities must compete with older, better established programs in an era when community colleges are working desperately to accommodate floods of students. For this eminently practical reason as well as philosophical ones, community service is rendered at or near the point of need in the community whenever possible, thus making a virtue of necessity.

Seven major trends are apparent in community college service programs:

- The community college will develop aggressive multiservice outreach programs designed to extend its campus throughout the entire college district.
- The community college will place increased emphasis on community education for all age levels and all groups.
- The community college will utilize a great diversification of media in meeting community needs and interests.
- The community college will increasingly utilize its catalytic capabilities to assist its community in the solution of basic educational, economic and social problems.
- The community college will be increasingly concerned about the cultural growth of its community.
- The community college will place greater emphasis on interaction with its community.
- The community college will increasingly recognize the need for cooperation with other agencies.

The community college is becoming a dynamic force affecting the thought processes, habits, economic status and social interaction of people from many walks of life throughout the country. It is becoming a major, integral component of our national educational structure. But this is just the beginning, for (as noted earlier) we are now establishing a new community college every week of the year. Through its program of community services, the community college will insert into the life stream of its people forces that can stimulate, change, and unify the individuals and organizations it serves, ultimately affecting the tone of mind of the entire community.

References

1. Bevlin, Marjorie. "The Junior College as a Community Art Center." *Junior College Journal,* XXX (April, 1960), pp. 442–445.
2. Brownell, Baker. *The College and the Community.* New York: Harper & Row, 1952.
3. Clark, Burton R. *Educating the Expert Society.* San Francisco, Calif.: Chandler, 1962.
4. Donham, Dan J. "We Can Serve Welfare Recipients." *Junior College Journal,* XXXVIII (March, 1968), pp. 74–76.
5. Gleazer, Edmund J., Jr. "AAJC Approach: Summer Community Services." *Junior College Journal,* XXXVIII (March, 1968), p. 9.
6. Gleazer, Edmund J., Jr. *An Introduction to Junior Colleges.* Washington, D.C.: American Association of Junior Colleges, 1960.
7. Harlacher, Ervin L. "California's Community Renaissance." *Junior College Journal,* XXXIV (May, 1960).
8. Harlacher, Ervin L. *The Community Dimension of the Community College.* Washington, D.C.: American Association of Junior Colleges, 1967.
9. Harlacher, Ervin L. *Critical Requirements for the Establishment of Effective Junior College Programs of Community Services.* Unpublished doctoral dissertation. Los Angeles, Calif.: University of California, 1965.
10. Harlacher, Ervin L. *Effective Junior College Programs of Community Services: Rationale, Guidelines, Practices.* Junior College Leadership Program, Occasional Report No. 10. Los Angeles, Calif.: University of California, 1967.
11. Harlacher, Ervin L. "New Directions in Community Services." *Junior College Journal,* XXXVIII (March, 1968), pp. 12–17.
12. Harlacher, Ervin L. "The Obligation of the Junior College for Community Service." *Junior College Journal,* XXX (May, 1960), pp. 502–516.
13. Johnson, B. Lamar. "Is the Junior College Idea Useful for Other Countries?" *Junior College Journal,* XXXI (September, 1961), pp. 3–8.

14. Koch, Moses S., and Libenstein, Saul E. "A Community College Attracts the Aging." *Junior College Journal,* XXXV (October, 1964), pp. 26–27.
15. Koch, Moses S., and Wolley, Priscilla M. "Established: A Curriculum to Train Urban Professional Assistants." *Junior College Journal,* XXXVII (October, 1967), pp. 20–24.
16. Medsker, Leland. *The Junior College: Progress and Prospect.* New York: McGraw-Hill, 1960.
17. Menefee, Audrey G. "There's a Meeting Here Tonight." *Junior College Journal,* XXXI (March, 1961), pp. 387–390.
18. Newman, Fred M., and Oliver, Donald W. "Education and Community." *Harvard Educational Review,* XXXVII (Winter, 1967), pp. 44–46.
19. Putnam, Howard. "The College Community-Service Program as an Agency of Social Action." *Junior College Journal,* XXXI (December, 1960), pp. 221–223.
20. Reynolds, James W. "Community Colleges and Studies of Communities." *Junior College Journal,* XXXI (October, 1960), pp. 63–64.
21. Reynolds, James W. *An Analysis of Community Service Programs of Junior Colleges.* Washington, D.C.: U.S. Office of Education, 1960.
22. Rollins, Charles E., and Appleson, Wallace B. "Accent on a Cultural Commitment." *Junior College Journal,* XXXVIII (October, 1967), pp. 30–31.
23. Steinberg, Shelson S., and Shatz, Eunice O. "Junior Colleges and the New Careers Program." *Junior College Journal,* XXXVIII (February, 1968), pp. 12–17.
24. Thornton, James W., Jr. *The Community Junior College.* New York: John Wiley & Sons, 1960.
25. Vaccaro, Louis C. "The Manpower Development and Training Act and the Community College." *Junior College Journal,* XXXIV (November, 1963), pp. 21–23.
26. Verner, Coolie. "The Junior College as a Social Institution." In: *Community Services in the Community Junior Colleges.* Proceedings of the Annual Florida Junior College Conference. Tallahassee, Fla.: Florida State Department of Education, 1960.
27. Vines, Eugene T. *Community Service Programs in Selected Public Junior Colleges.* Unpublished doctoral dissertation. George Peabody College for Teachers, 1960.
28. Waggoner, Ann Carr. "Venture into Continuing Education." *Junior College Journal,* XXX (September, 1960), pp. 44–49.

Chapter 14

Greater change has taken place in public school continuing education within the past few years than has occurred in over a century. And the momentum of change is increasing. The changes within the next few years may be destined to make those of the recent past seem insignificant by contrast.

Changes in the Past and Future

Six years ago, educators only envisioned the full-time adult high schools of today. They only dreamed of well-equipped, 12-month adult education centers, community colleges and vocational–technical institutes devoted exclusively to the education of out-of-school youth and adults. And today's broad range of programs from adult elementary to post-college refresher courses was then unheard of in most communities. Similarly, few schools had full-time administrative and counseling staffs, and fewer still provided health and social services. Practically unheard of were funds for program planning, curriculum development, individualized study through programmed learning and materials centers, and in-service training for teachers.

If anyone, even a few years ago, suggested that city transit buses would be taking students, free of charge, to and from adult centers or that continuing education would be on a tuition-free basis, he would have been open to ridicule. Today, these dreams are becoming realities.

Approximately 70 Manpower Development Training (MDT) centers, largely in urban areas, were in opera-

Public Schools

ROBERT E. FINCH

tion during 1967. Many of these centers operated two 8-hour shifts—a few had programs operating 24 hours a day, six days a week.

These centers met the following criteria:

A centralized facility, generally under public school administration, especially designed to provide on a continuous basis, counseling and related services, work orientation, basic and remedial education, and institutional skill training in a variety of occupations for trainees recruited from a broad area. The center provides maximum utilization of physical and instructional resources and a high degree of flexibility, serving all types of trainees and all types of MDTA projects, including multioccupational and single projects, individual referrals and classroom components of coupled institutional OJT [on-the-job-training] projects. [7, p. 24]

Currently, emphasis is on beginning-level training although centers may also offer upgrading training and retraining for workers whose skills have become obsolete. The total enrollment in MDT institutional programs was reported at 176,500 in 1967 with many of the trainees enrolled in full-time centers.

In the cities as well as in a growing number of rural areas, the quiet evenings of part-time adult education are gone. Enrollments in full-time programs of continuing education are now equaling part-time enrollments in many communities. Community colleges account for a great deal of the growth [8].

It is not at all unrealistic to anticipate that by 1975 enrollments in public school continuing education programs will be one and one-half to two times those of day high school enrollments. In many communities, adult education is now the third dimension of public education—along with elementary and secondary education. Directors of continuing education hold the same status as the directors of elementary and secondary education and operate on a division basis with a full-time supervisory and administrative staff. Today the question is not *why* public adult education should provide millions more with the opportunity for education—but *how*.

Education has always been considered the key to a good job, housing, adequate food and other advantages. A crucial question today is: "Do the majority of our citizens, including many educators, really want to offer an educational opportunity to one fourth of the black and white population of our country who are now in virtual economic bondage because of the lack of education and training?" Many directors of continuing education feel the public schools, the community colleges and vocational–technical institutes, if given the opportunity to do so, could triple current educational and training efforts. Several years ago President Johnson said our public schools represent an 85 billion dollar in-

Public Schools

vestment which is only being used 30 percent of the time. That value is probably closer to $100 billion now. The great strength of public school adult education is its willingness and ability to take education—especially basic education—directly to the people in their own neighborhoods.

Dropouts—Young and Old

The changes in continuing education, as notable as they are, are only a token effort in relation to the backlog of uneducated and undereducated people. It is not uncommon to have an enrollment of two or three thousand people in adult basic education in a city of a half million —a city where there are more people with less than a fifth grade education than there are college graduates. One out of four persons in America lacks a high school education. Few federal dollars and limited local and state dollars are being expanded for the high school completion of the dropout. In too many communities high school completion for the dropout is still limited to those who can afford to pay, making tuition nothing more than a selecting and screening-out device.

The unemployed dropout has no well-organized lobby. It is usually the professional organizations that testify before congressional education committees on his behalf. Seemingly, the militant, the radical and even the irresponsible elements in our society understand this better than do many of our so-called responsible citizens. The former are capitalizing on the indecision and the failure of the majority to provide an educational opportunity for all.

The fact that many cities are in serious financial difficulty and that continuing education is not required by law cannot be ignored. Tragically, it is the wealthy industrial states of the North that have the largest number of high school dropouts. In some states those dropouts are left in the deep educational void between public supported day schools and public supported colleges and universities. Until the majority of people decide that public education must: (1) provide basic elementary education for all, including millions of adults who have never gone beyond the fifth grade; (2) place the same emphasis upon preparation for the world of work as is now placed upon preparation for college; and (3) offer the high school dropouts—both young and old—a second chance to complete their high school education and acquire marketable skills, there will be no lasting solution to our socioeconomic problems.

When the Cincinnati Board of Education established its first evening high school in 1856, it wrote in the records a simple statement of purpose: "The perpetuation of our superior form of government depends upon an intelligent and informed citizenry. If this is not looked to, power will gradually pass from the many to the few and in the lapse of time this great fabric of government will find a common grave of all the great republics of history." Now the impact of scientific advances is placing upon education, and continuing education in particular, challenges unheard of a few years ago. Perhaps it is time to remind ourselves that our system of public education came into being as a direct reflection of our fundamental belief in the personal worth and dignity of the individual—be he an illiterate from a Southern farm, a high school dropout, an unemployed worker, or a high school or college graduate seeking to continue the education acquired during his earlier years.

Technology has eliminated many of the routine jobs high school dropouts and graduates with few marketable skills depended on for employment. Routine jobs, from setting pins in a bowling alley to telephone switchboard operation, from digging ditches to putting crackers in a box, have been eliminated.

Many of the young people who have withdrawn from day school and lost routine jobs face a dilemma. As one of them, a 19-year-old male, said, "I can't go back to day school with those young kids. All my friends are gone—I don't fit. Besides, in the middle of the school year I can't make up what I've missed." For thousands of youth and adults an effective public supported program of continuing education in the public schools and the community colleges is the best answer to the so-called dropout problem. Armed with a marketable skill, plus the necessary English, mathematics and other academic subjects, they may have an even chance in the competitive labor market. Dropouts who have faced the world of work for a year or two can come back to evening and day adult high schools for a second chance. Usually they are determined to do something about the opportunity they missed. No citizen, regardless of age, should be denied the opportunity to resume or continue his education.

The Nature and Scope of Activity

The public schools offer a very wide variety of courses in response to local community wants and needs. According to staff personnel of the National Association for Public School Adult Education, subjects in the following areas are most commonly offered:

1. General Academic Education: Common high school subjects and general classes, such as economics, creative writing, public speaking, languages.
2. Civic and Public Affairs Education: Forums, discussion groups, informal classes, institutes, and other group activities that seek

Public Schools

to develop an understanding of local, state, national and international problems.
3. Americanization and Elementary Education: Classes and activities emphasizing naturalization and integration of foreign-born adults, or literacy and fundamental skills for the foreign born who need education below the high school level.
4. Fine Arts: Music, drama, painting, sketching, art appreciation, orchestras, bands, choral groups and TV production.
5. Practical Arts and Crafts: Block printing, photography, leather, art metal, ceramics, furniture refinishing, and other non-vocational and hand-skill activities.
6. Business and Distributive Education: Typing, shorthand, bookkeeping, office machines, salesmanship, business management, window decorating, display advertising.
7. Agriculture: Vocational agriculture courses.
8. Vocational and Technical Education: Apprentice training, occupational extension, service and domestic trades, and other classes designed for job improvement.
9. Homemaking Education: Sewing, cooking, nutrition, consumer buying, household and budget management, interior decoration, home repairs, home landscaping, gardening.
10. Parent and Family Life Education: Parent study groups, classes that deal with social and psychological aspects of parenthood and family life, child care and development, child guidance, family relationships, premarriage problems, home and school relationships.
11. Health and Physical Education: First aid, home nursing, food handling, physical fitness, health education.
12. Personal Improvement: Personal psychology, personality improvement, charm, poise, social adjustment.
13. Recreational Activities: Sports, dancing, bridge lessons, and other activities primarily designed for leisure time.
14. Safety and Driver Education: Driver education, water safety, first aid, civil defense, accident and fire prevention.
15. Remedial Special Education: Classes for handicapped adults, lip reading, Braille, speech correction, remedial reading and other courses [4, p. 22].

Some idea of the scope of adult education in the public schools can be gained from a 1968–69 survey which dealt with school systems of 6000 or more pupils [17]. About 1200 systems provided data. Almost 60 percent reported adult education activities. Just over 1.3 million adults were enrolled. They were taught by about 35,000 part-time and

6700 full-time teachers. The school systems reporting granted about 3000 elementary and secondary school diplomas together with some 85,000 "Certificates of Equivalency."

Another study published in 1967 reported 2 million adults enrolled in 338 school districts [6]. Of this total, one-half million were enrolled in high school credit classes, with about 37,000 receiving high school diplomas. The elementary school enrollment had some 231,000 adults.

Teacher stipends have undergone a steady growth over the past two decades (though they may not have significantly outstripped inflation) [20]. The median wage was $2.00 per hour in 1945; $5.00 per hour in 1964; and $6.00 per hour in 1969. The present range is very broad—from $3.00 per hour to a maximum of $25.00 per hour. The chief administrators of public school adult education programs also exhibit a broad annual salary range—from about $6,000 to about $24,000 yearly with a median of some $13,000.

At present it is impossible to ascertain exactly how many persons are enrolled in continuing education activities in public schools. The United States Census Bureau estimated that about 2 million were enrolled in such activities in 1957. Higher estimates had appeared before that time. Knowles cites a U.S. Office of Education study that projected 4.4 million enrolled in 1958 [13]. The Johnstone and Rivera [11] estimate is 1.7 million enrolled for the category "Elementary and High School." The 1969 Public School Adult Education Almanac verified 3.7 million persons definitely in attendance, and James Dorland, of the National Association of Public Continuing and Adult Education (NAPCAE), called this figure "conservative."

Another sign of growth is the dramatic increase in the number of states with full-time directors of adult education—an important leadership position usually located in the state department of education. In 1959, only 25 states employed such a person and many of those functioning were only part-time appointments [15]. All 50 states and Puerto Rico now have full-time directors. The state directors are already served by a professional organization, The National Council of State Directors of Adult Education.

The Role of NAPCAE

Considerable credit for progress in continuing education in the public schools can be given to the National Association for Public Continuing and Adult Education. The Association offers leadership through conferences, publications and consulting services. A. A. Liveright credited NAPCAE with a major role in the establishment of adult education agencies in state departments of education and in furthering

Public Schools

adult basic education (through helping to increase federal appropriations for this activity). He calls the organization "an important influence in the field [14, p. 65]."

Some Trends

The concept of the full-time, 12-month adult education center, community colleges and area vocational schools, devoted exclusively to the education of out-of-school youth and adults, is gaining acceptance throughout the country. The impetus for the full-time center has been gained through manpower development and training programs, adult basic education, and other federally and state funded programs. These new, full-time adult centers are not found in abandoned elementary school buildings or in abandoned firehouses. They are in good buildings with good lighting, good equipment, good food prepared by food service training classes, and above all, have qualified instructors who enjoy teaching in an atmosphere conducive to adult learning.

Many counties and states are discovering that the full-time adult education center offers advantages in flexible program planning and operation on an area basis. The combining of adult programs—accelerated high school programs, basic education classes, occupational skill training, upgrading training for the underemployed, refresher training for college graduates, parent education programs, and so on, into a coordinated daytime program, provides several advantages. Sound student health services, maximum impact counseling and guidance services, effective follow-through on student adjustment problems, a programmed learning and materials center providing guided individualized study, teacher in-service training, and better curriculum development—all of these become feasible under a combination and coordination of local, state and federal financing.

Community Partnerships

Scores of agencies and programs—including county welfare departments, Metropolitan Housing Authority, Opportunity Industrialization Centers, Neighborhood Youth Corps, Community Action Agencies, Pilot Cities, Model Cities and various youth service agencies—can secure substantial federal grants for the education and training of out-of-school youth and adults. The public schools are increasingly conducting adult classes on a contractual agreement basis with these community agencies, enabling them to fully utilize the federal funds available to them. Few agencies have the buildings, equipment, teaching staff or technical know-how to conduct adult classes—especially in the area of vocational–

technical education. Through their clientele, they do, however, have direct contacts for the recruitment of students in need of education and training.

Contractual agreements to conduct classes for these agencies on an instructional cost basis, plus overhead charges, provide a realistic and workable community partnership. They enable both the schools and the agencies to do the things for which they have expertise. In addition, this approach enables the school to utilize fully its teaching, counseling and administrative staff on a continuous basis.

Individualized Instruction

A major change in the traditional classroom learning process is slowly gaining momentum through individualized instruction. In continuing education in particular—where time for study is frequently at a premium, student motivation high and what is learned has immediate application for job opportunities or promotion—the new approach has gained rapid acceptance.

Encouraging the student to accept greater responsibility for learning has been talked about for years. What is new are the methods and techniques which make it easier for this to take place. Learning is an individual process. Students learn at different rates. Individualizing instruction allows the student to discover his own errors, correct his mistakes, and retest himself before his efforts are checked by the teacher.

Individualized instruction is a direct move away from the imitation and memorization of facts which characterize much classroom learning today. Many educational authorities have long believed that learning can be enhanced by relating facts to problem situations that have meaning for students. Unfortunately, it was difficult to apply this long-talked-about principle when the lecturer or textbook simply dispensed facts and students were tested upon their assimilation of facts with little emphasis upon problem solving. Under individualized guided study it is easier for the student to succeed rather than fail. It is not surprising that many less able students, including those in their teens, appreciate this "special privilege." And the more able students appreciate the privilege of moving ahead at their own pace.

Course Offerings

As predicted by the U.S. Department of Labor in 1960, job opportunities and corresponding training are centering increasingly in the service occupations—from health services to auto body and fender repair. With the rapid change to more sophisticated job opportunities, mathematics and English proficiency have become essential in many types of job preparation, such as drafting and electronics. For the man who is struggling to understand fractions and how to use a ruler, our new world of electronics with its minimal mathematics requirement of trigonometry is as far away as the moon. He sees the enticing full-page advertisements for electronic workers, draftsmen and hundreds of other unobtainable jobs. Lacking the education needed to secure these jobs he feels cheated, and rightly so.

Efforts are being made to overcome this crucial problem. The trend is toward teaching basic education (grades one to eight in connection with job training. Basic mathematics is being taught in relationship to the particular skill being learned. Under an eight-hour instructional day, for example, a student may spend one hour in group counseling, two and one-half hours in basic education, and four and one-half hours in skill training. Also, personal economics, as applied to home and family living, is receiving greater attention in basic education classes. Major companies are concerned about the inability of many workers to live within their incomes.

The Coming Challenge

If and when public institutions engaged in continuing education receive a mandate to expand their programs still further, following are areas for which planning and development will be crucial if the challenge is to be met.

1. Local and state directors must learn the full responsibilities of staff leadership in administering and supervising continuing education. Full-time leadership is entirely different from that of part-time leadership. School systems throughout the country are undertaking intensive studies of curriculum and self-evaluation of the total educational program. If necessary, local and state directors must insist that continuing education, as the third dimension in education, be included in all such research and developmental studies.
2. Undergraduate programs to prepare teachers in the field of continuing education for the public schools are virtually nonexistent. Teacher training institutions in our colleges and universities must begin undergraduate programs to prepare teachers for the instruction of out-of-school youth and adults.
3. Now is the time to further expand and develop new methods of instruction. We know individualized instruction works exceptionally well with highly motivated out-of-school youth and

adults. Learning laboratories show promise along with other new kinds of technology. Why hesitate to discard outmoded teaching techniques and methods?

4. Professional associations will need to extend their research and development programs and consider new services for teachers, counselors and administrators. This will require a much broader financial base than they now enjoy.

5. Regional accrediting associations and state departments of education will need to adopt standards for high school completion. Most day high school state standards were written when men and boys were laying railroad ties by hand and girls were operating manual switchboards. In 1968 the North Central Association of Colleges and Universities adopted new criteria for adult high school completion. Other accrediting associations are considering the same step.

6. Publicly supported continuing education will need to intensify and expand programs of community partnership with business and industry and other community agencies, fully utilizing all available local, state and federal funds. Such partnerships can develop an area-wide, tuition-free, full-time concept of continuing education rather than a limited school-district approach on a part-time instructional basis.

7. Emphasis is being placed upon technical–vocational education for the 60 percent of day school youth not going on to college. Adult vocational–technical programs for the unemployed and underemployed are vital to our economy, which may require training and retraining workers several times in a lifetime. Leaders of continuing education must remember the importance of a balanced educational program. Learning how to earn a living is essential, but learning how to effectively utilize and protect one's earnings is equally important. Continuing education programs in home and family living, parent education, consumer education and short-term general education courses must not be pushed aside as we enter a new era of vocational–technical competence for all.

8. It will be necessary for the states to assume a greater share of the cost of educating and training out-of-school youth and adults both in high school completion and adult vocational–technical programs. Some states are now merely the bookkeepers and overseers of combined federal and local expenditures, expending at most only token state funds for the education of out-of-school youth and adults. It is becoming increasingly essential that local boards of education maintain a financial

Public Schools 241

interest in continuing and vocational education by providing the necessary matching funds for both state and federal programs and otherwise providing for continuing education programs not financed under state and federal projects—such as high school completion and short-term general education courses. Without a reasonable financial investment, a local board of education may lose enthusiasm, interest and control over the very type of educational programs that have become essential for urban areas.

The federal government should more fully plan for utilizing the educational capacity of our public schools. It has been clearly demonstrated over the past five years that the public schools can educate and train tens of thousands of adults at a reasonable cost.

9. We know that millions of people are migrating to the cities in search of economic betterment. It is essential to develop effective continuing education programs "at home" in the rural areas. This will require a combined local, state and national effort.
10. In promoting adult continuing education, it will be important to gain the active involvement of the decision-makers on the local, state and national level. School superintendents, members of boards of education, state legislators and congressmen tell the story far better than do local and state directors of continuing education [4].

Conclusion

The fact that an increasing number of out-of-school youth and adults are seeking to improve themselves is one of the most encouraging signs of our times. We know that continuing education for out-of-school youth is one of the least expensive investments our society can make, to say nothing of the dignity and self-respect gained by the individuals involved. Education means effort, but the economic rewards to the individual for self-improvement remain a prime factor in our heritage. We know that age is a relatively unimportant barrier to learning and that the ability of an individual to learn must not be confused with lack of previous education. We know that motivation and the experience of the individual are two great assets for learning by out-of-school youth and adults.

Continuing education has become a third dimension in public supported education because the "time for learning" is no longer reserved for school-age children. We can only surmise and guess at public school adult education as it will be a few years from now. Our educational dreams of tomorrow, however, rest on one question: As a society, are we willing to make the financial commitment necessary to help people help themselves?

References

1. Aker, George F., and Carpenter, William L. *What Research Says About Public School Adult Education.* Tallahassee, Fla.: Department of Adult Education, Florida State University, 1966.
2. Borus, Michael E. "The Economic Effectiveness of Retraining the Unemployed Based on the Experience of Workers in Connecticut." Unpublished doctoral dissertation. New Haven, Conn.: Yale University, 1966.
3. Burkett, J. "Comprehensive Programming for Life-Long Learning." *Adult Education,* X (Winter, 1960), pp. 116–121.
4. Cortwright, Richard W., and Dorland, James R. "In 1-2-3 Order: How to Set Up an Adult Education Program." *American School Board Journal* (February, 1969), pp. 19–22.
5. Dobbs, Ralph C. "Self-perceived Educational Needs of Adults." *Adult Education,* XVI (Winter, 1966), pp. 92–100.
6. Dorland, James R., and Baber, Gaye, compilers. *Public School Adult Education Program Study.* Washington, D.C.: National Association for Public School Adult Education, 1967.
7. *Education and Training/Learning for Jobs.* Washington, D.C.: U.S. Department of Health, Education and Welfare, 1968.
8. "The Fantastic Growth of the Two-Year College." *Changing Times* (September, 1968), pp. 35–38.
9. Hill, T. M. *Poverty Programs.* Washington, D.C.: Vocational Rehabilitation Administration, U.S. Department of Health, Education and Welfare, 1965.
10. Houle, Cyril O. "Back to New Francisco." *Adult Leadership,* XV (February, 1967), pp. 261–262.
11. Johnstone, John W. C., and Rivera, Ramon J. *Volunteers for Learning: A Study of the Educational Pursuits of American Adults.* Chicago, Ill.: Aldine, 1965.
12. Knowles, Malcolm S. "Role of Adult Education in the Public Schools." *Journal of Education,* CXLIV (April, 1962), pp. 3–36.
13. Knowles, Malcolm S. *The Adult Education Movement in the United States.* New York: Holt, Rinehart & Winston, 1962.
14. Liveright, A. A. *A Study of Adult Education in the United States.* Boston, Mass.: Center for the Study of Liberal Education for Adults, 1968.
15. Luke, Robert A. "Public School Adult Education." *Handbook of Adult Education in the United States.* Edited by Malcolm S. Knowles. Washington, D.C.: Adult Education Association of the USA, 1960.
16. National Association for Public Continuing and Adult Education. *Tech-*

niques for Teachers of Adults. Published eight times a year. Washington, D.C.: National Education Association.
17. National Education Association. *Adult Education Statistics, 1968–1969.* NEA Research Memo 1968–16. Washington, D.C.: Research Division, National Education Association, 1969.
18. New York State Education Department, Bureau of Adult Education and Bureau of Educational Finance Research. *Adult Education, The Relationship of Program Development to State Fiscal Policy.* Albany, N.Y.: New York State Education Department, 1964.
19. Potts, Alfred M., compiler. *Educationally Disadvantaged—Bibliography.* Alamosa, Colo.: Center for Cultural Studies, Adams State College, 1965.
20. *Public School Adult Education Almanac.* Washington, D.C.: National Association for Public School Adult Education, 1969.
21. Scott, Carl A., and others. *Family Life Education.* New York: Child Study Association of America, 1965.
22. Torrence, Preston E. "The Tuskegee Experiment in Adult Training." *Adult Leadership,* XV (September, 1966), pp. 83–84.
23. U.S. Department of Health, Education and Welfare, Office of Education, Division of Vocational and Technical Education. *Educationally Disadvantaged.* Washington, D.C.: Government Printing Office, 1965.
24. U.S. Department of Labor. *Report of the Secretary of Labor on Research and Training Activities Under the Manpower Development and Training Act.* Washington, D.C.: Government Printing Office, 1963.

Chapter 15

Public Libraries and Museums

MARGARET E. MONROE

Public libraries and museums represent collections of materials essential to a community of men who are to share in the past and hold links to the present and the future. While preservation of the past was a major purpose of their original establishment, availability to the elite and the expert has become a chief concern. The libraries have come—in the context of mass democracy of the twentieth century—to recognize their educational function in society. The adult education movement of the early twentieth century articulated and reinforced a growing desire of librarians, curators and docents to see that larger proportions of society shared the fruits of the arts and the mind. In the past fifty years each of these institutions has developed educational philosophies and techniques that have enhanced its effectiveness as an adult education agency.

Public Libraries

Founded with educational objectives, the early public libraries of the United States were designed to serve the educated public (Boston Public Library in 1852), the young school student (Salisbury, Connecticut in 1833) or the urban working youth (Mechanics Institute libraries throughout the East and Midwest in the 1830's to 1850's). Developing from settlement house origins, public library branches in large cities at the turn of the century served clientele with the same problems and characteristics (illiteracy, foreign language background, unemployment, unique cultural values) as the inner-city population of the 1960's [27].

The library adult education movement from the 1920's through the 1930's focused on the advisor guiding the reader in individual reading programs; "Reading with a Purpose" booklets supplemented the librarian's proposals to readers of "what to read next." Motivation for self-improvement during the depression years made the advisory service especially relevant. During the 1940's and 1950's, library adult education —in the wake of World War II and a growing internationalism—turned to group discussion of human values and social problems through such programs as Great Books Discussion, American Heritage Programs and Great Decisions. Beginning in the 1950's and carrying through the 1960's, the adult education programs of public libraries refocused on the study of the particular needs of special groups in the community [10; 27].

While the adult education movement provided a framework for these public library services, the message came to most librarians and library directors with keenest impact from major social events: the depression, war and social revolution.

Community Study

While public libraries became conscious of the need to study their communities in the 1920's, it was not until the development of the American Library Association's Library–Community Project (supported by a grant from the Fund for Adult Education from 1955 to 1960) that librarians generally gained the techniques and accepted the importance of this preliminary step to planning library services. Helen Lyman Smith's survey in 1953 found there was little activity and little interest in community study [37], while a 1968 survey by Robert Ellis Lee reports that 220 of the 328 responding librarians felt community study to be of major importance [16]. The move from 10 to 70 percent interest in community study has been accompanied by an important difference in the kinds of adult education services offered and the methods by which they are developed.

Community study led to rejection of the concept of "the general reader" and to development of services for more clearly identified groups: students; teachers; the aging; labor; the handicapped; the disadvantaged. Close study brought to light large numbers of potential library users of whose interests and needs the library has been unaware. Increased sensitivity to the potential patron, as well as social unrest, led to the development of outreach programs.

Outreach Programs

Society's dropouts—the illiterate, the unmotivated, the disaffected, the rejecting and rejected—are a major social concern today. Public libraries, like other educational agencies, have come to view these groups as not the unreachable, but the unreached. Joining with other educational and social agencies in community-wide effort to help the social dropout back into society, the public library has reassessed the contribution of its resources and its program of service. Librarians, like educators, social workers and even law enforcement officers, are coming to sense society's share of responsibility for the decision to drop out, and (in agreement with Marshall McLuhan and Karl Menninger) to accept a degree of responsibility for the "crime" and for rehabilitation of the "criminal" [24; 25]. Lowell A. Martin, reporting on the outreach program of the Enoch Pratt Free Library, wrote: "The problem is as much what society makes of these individuals as what they make of themselves [22]."

Public library programs of outreach to the disadvantaged (low-education, low-income, cultural minorities) have tended to emphasize reaching the children and young adults, recognizing that the unreached adult is truly the "hard core" of the problem. Nevertheless, film showings and conversation about books and community resources to meet pressing adult problems have been successfully developed for mothers of preschool children in Head Start programs throughout the country. Colorful holiday festivals (Cinco de Maio in Los Angeles Public Library) that use films and musical recordings to attract adults in family-type programs have been scheduled, with significant involvement of the target audience themselves in the planning and performance. With teen-age dropouts—the embryo disaffected adult—library field workers stress contact. A field worker in the San Francisco Public Library, whose work is entirely on a street corner, seeks to develop a dialogue in honest communication and sincere concern for these young adults as individuals of real potential. Book and film discussion of critical social problems (drug addiction, sexual promiscuity, racial tensions) attract young adults by getting down to real life as they experience it.

Library services to the adult illiterate and new literate have stressed collections of easy-to-read materials and the introduction of adults enrolled in basic education classes to the resources and services of the library. Tutorial assistance in the library, usually developed under a volunteer program or in cooperation with school training programs, provides personal assistance in reading and other study problems [12; 21].

Because contact and two-way communication lie at the heart of reaching the unreached, public libraries have used indigenous leaders as staff members to relate the library to the concerns of the disadvantaged.

Joint planning of educational programs—long an adult education principle—is an increasingly accepted practice in public library outreach service. Close cooperation among agencies on community-wide programs is increasingly recognized as essential to the success of any one agency's program, but the old obstacles to such cooperation still remain—agency rivalry, agency traditions, a limited view of professional practice. Nevertheless, programs in the Rochester Public Library, Denver Public Library, Enoch Pratt Free Library (Baltimore), among others, are based on community-wide cooperation.

Federally funded community action, New Careers, Job Training and related programs have brought funds directly to public libraries or fostered the growth of programs in other agencies with which libraries cooperate. The prestige and the financial support provided by federal legislation like the Economic Opportunity Act, the Manpower Development and Training Act, and the Library Services and Construction Act —all legislation of the 1960's—are of inestimable value to stimulating programs of public library adult education.

The outreach concept has not been limited to bringing library service to the economically and socially disadvantaged. Federal funds have encouraged special attention to the handicapped, home-bound and institutionalized through the Library Services and Construction Act [32]. The building of hope—the move from apathy to aspiration by the members of these groups is the focus of book, film and recording services of public libraries. Cooperation with educational directors of various institutions and social agencies has been important both in identifying the group to be served and in planning the services. The aged, the mentally ill, the blind, the convicted criminal are being helped toward effective independence with the aid of reader's guidance, book talks, and book and film discussions. Such long-established programs as those of the Cleveland Public Library and the Enoch Pratt Free Library are serving as prototypes for wider development of this service.

Now that major urban libraries are meeting increasingly sophisticated demands for information service made by research organizations and industry, a reading public of increasingly high education and a burgeoning student population, the outreach philosophy is beginning to permeate the whole vision of adult service. As the St. Paul Public Library director commented: "The attitude of sitting back waiting to serve whoever happens to come into the library has changed to planning for service to special groups of adults and young people outside the library, to find and serve them. This is the big change since 1954 [39]." Another public library director, quoted in *Social Change and the Library, 1945–1980*, said: "The war on poverty has been a tremendous

Public Libraries and Museums

opportunity for the library to become involved in cooperative efforts of many community agencies and to understand the interrelationship of people, institutions and political realities [15]." The outreach philosophy, it would seem, can go far beyond the service to the disadvantaged which gave it impetus in the 1960's.

Service to Individuals

Public libraries traditionally have been self-service institutions, and it has been their genius to devise as many catalogs, indexes and information services as possible to enable the reader to help himself. Increasing attention is now given to self-instruction in the use of the library through taped audio explanations and audio-visual learning programs. The work of Paul Wendt of Southern Illinois University has inspired other explorations into this area of adult education. Similarly, reading improvement programs for adults, for which the Brooklyn Public Library offers a prototype, is another way of providing the adult with effective tools for personal growth [14].

Individual reading guidance in public libraries has become closely related to information service in subject or general reference departments. Its focus in adult services is less on personal development and increasingly on the suggestion of the appropriate book for the reader's purpose. Relatively few libraries today have staff members designated as "readers' advisor" (most rely on all public service librarians to perform this service); the result is a tendency to relate reading guidance more closely to reference service from which it originally developed [1].

Readers' advisory service, nevertheless, is designated as such in some public libraries; those persons concerned provide the patron with reading lists, assistance in book choices and aid in planning reading programs for special purposes (travel to a foreign country, catching up on science and so on). The wide availability of paperbacks, the stimulation of intellectual curiosity by some television programming and the increasing availability of adult education courses in various institutions have relieved the reader's advisor of some pressures to provide guidance for these purposes. To some extent, advisory services attempt to provide supportive reading programs related to television programs and adult classes.

Reading for an Age of Change, a series of reading programs in pamphlet form, provides a sound readable introduction to such topics as "Space Science" (by Ralph E. Lapp), "Freedom of the Mind" (by William O. Douglas), "Cultural Anthropology" (by Walter Goldsmidt) and "The World of Economics" (by Robert L. Heilbroner). Published during the period 1962–1968 under a grant from the Carnegie Corporation of New York, these reading programs were intended to serve as the highly popular *Reading with a Purpose* series (1925–1933) had done. Careful studies of their use, however, have shown only the mildest public interest, and adult educators are forced to conclude that, lacking the active guidance of the earlier period, reading programs did not serve a ready-made public in the 1960's [8].

Group Service as Adult Education

Two distinctive types of group services are adult education oriented and are increasingly accepted as a normal part of public library programs; programs sponsored by the library and designed for adult groups in the community and planning and materials services to community organizations and agencies. Robert Ellis Lee says the major development of public library adult education during the period 1957–1964 was "the gradual acceptance by libraries of services and programs for groups [16]." A survey of public library group services shows both types of services being built firmly into the educational and public relations programs of a number of libraries [39].

During the period 1951–60, major financial support by the Fund for Adult Education to public library group activities provided many librarians with training in discussion leadership through Great Books and American Heritage discussion programs. Additional benefits were experience in program planning with the local communities (through Experimental Projects in Adult Education) and the building of an enlarged public for discussion of public issues and human values. In the 1960's, without special funding on a national scale, similar programs continued to serve the public interest; of 49 public libraries responding to the 1967 group services survey, over 70 percent reported offering some type of adult discussion program [39]. The liberal arts programs were most generally represented by Great Books discussion groups, and the public issues programs by Great Decisions discussion groups. Local variations were many. The New York Public Library reported high interest in discussion programs on "Significant Modern Books of the Twentieth Century" and "Today's American in an Age of Technological Change" [30].

Group learning activities using films and informal conversation, exhibits with lectures (following a pattern established by the Enoch Pratt Free Library), book talks with coffee and conversation are increasingly developed for specific segments of the community; e.g., the aging, young mothers, business executives, high school teachers. Potential clientele in these groups are extended invitations as individuals, through their group affiliations, and by the technique of getting them involved in planning the programs. The practice of "participative leadership" is growing in public library adult education [10; 30].

In 1943, Ralph A. Beals, later director of the New York Public Library, challenged librarians with the adult education task of "infusing authentic information into the thinking and decision-making of the community [6]." This has been the primary orientation of the program of services to community organizations.

Detroit Public Library and Seattle Public Library have, for almost thirty years, taken the initiative in developing program planning institutes for leaders of community organizations. Joint planning and sponsorship of these events has kept the institutes relevant to organizational needs. In other libraries (such as Dallas and Cleveland), film departments, heavily used by program chairmen, have taken leadership in program planning. The Enoch Pratt Free Library built a major service of counseling individuals about program ideas. Typically the library service involves: (1) sharpening the focus of programs on topics important to the particular organization; (2) suggesting materials and resources (films, speakers, books) and techniques for using them (panels, lectures, discussion); and (3) assisting in provision of materials, reading lists, book talks and/or discussion leaders. The institutes on program planning tend to select a program theme and, over the period of a day or two, amplify the theme, illustrate relevant resources and demonstrate appropriate ways of programming.

A second important aspect of library service to community groups is that cited in relation to the Outreach programs. Information services to other community agencies are becoming of major importance. Bringing research-based information to the specialists who are shaping community decisions in the areas of education, economics, government and welfare is to truly "infuse authentic information into the thinking and decision-making of the community." The experience with the poverty programs has provided the most intensive and sustained experience of this function in recent years, and has created a vision of similar service in other areas of community planning.

A framework of adult education philosophy, theory and practice is operational in public libraries today. For many librarians it provides, as R. Russell Munn puts it, the basic inspiration, "like the words of Henry V to his troops at Harfleur [28]." For others, it provides the practical vehicle by which library service may be made to move through the chaotic and confused communities of our times.

Size of Clientele

An attempt to estimate the number of adults regularly using public library adult education services has apparently never been made. Such an attempt would face the great difficulty that the "adult education" aspect of these services varies in intensity so that a form of service (e.g., the exhibit) might be considered adult education on a particular occasion and be almost void of any educational element on another occasion. Liveright, in his 1968 study of adult education, deplores the lack of statistics in the public library field [*18*, pp. 81–83]; but it is important to recognize that more precision and uniformity in planning and describing library adult education must precede the gathering of statistics if they are to be considered reliable.

Museums

"The American museum is the child of nineteenth century liberal thought," wrote Henry Francis Taylor, pointing out that the idea of a public museum open to the non-specialist layman and general citizen, rather than to the experts and favored few alone, came in the Napoleonic era, some fifty years after the founding of the British Museum. "The American museum is, after all, neither an abandoned European palace, nor a solution for storing and classifying the accumulated national wealth of the past. It is an American phenomenon developed by the people, for the people, and of the people [*39*]."

Basically a museum is concerned with objects, often with unique objects. Ideally, verbal interpretations are kept to a minimum and the viewer confronts the object directly. To be sure, in order for him to understand the object, he may need to know where it came from, what its purpose is, its inner construction or function, and so on. Interpretation of the object, then, is an important part of museum work; but basically the object remains in central focus, whether it be a Peruvian water jar, Betsy Schuyler's wedding dress or a model of the planets rotating around the sun.

Museums are categorized typically as art, historical or science museums. The concept "historical museum" is broad indeed, including a wide range from the local historical society's collection of Indian arrowheads to Madame Toussaud's Wax Museum and the splendid new educational Museo Nacional de Anthropologia in Mexico City. Museums of art have likewise a great range in size and quality of collections. The science museum may best represent the tendency of museums in the mid-twentieth century to specialize, abandoning the attempt at comprehensiveness and focusing on a special aspect to which it can do justice.

Very few museums attempt to cover all three fields, although the Newark (N.J.) Museum and the New Jersey State Museum are exceptions. Of the some 5000 museums in operation today, about half are concerned with history, and the remainder are divided more or less equally between art and science.

A History of Museums

In 1930 Carnegie Corporation of New York commissioned Paul Marshall Rea to study the museum as an agency of adult education. Rea concluded that, in contrast to public libraries in the early 1930's, museums were not clear in their adult education purposes, had not organized to carry out their goals, had little professional direction, and could not be said to achieve consistent results. He identified three serious defects in museum educational services:

1. As a result of operating from a single location, museum accessibility was very low.
2. The per-viewer cost of exhibitions tended to be high.
3. Museum management, untrained for public service, had no consistent commitment to this area of service [34].

From this report and the subsequent foundation support of museums, the modern science of museum management and educational service gained major impetus.

Ten years later Theodore Low, Director of Education of the Walters Art Gallery in Baltimore, analyzed the educational techniques and achievements of museums. Recognizing the concept of the museum as a social instrument, Low concluded:

The fact is that museums have devoted a disproportionate amount of time and energy to the cultivation of the upper circles, both of intelligence and of society. More often than not they have been extremely fearful of getting "the wrong kind of people." It does not take any statistics to prove that people who now frequent museums form a minute fraction of the total population of any one community. What becomes of the vast majority of the people? Are they not members of the public? Hasn't the museum a definite duty to fulfill toward them?

There is only one answer to the above questions. It is here, in the field of popular education that the museum belongs today. [19]

However, it should be pointed out that not all museum administrators (some of whom pay little more than lip service to adult education) would agree with Low. While progress was made during the thirties and forties in the development of lectures, planetarium demonstrations, classes, field trips, nature trails, clubs for children and adults, loan collections and radio education, it was not until the 1950's that the greatest changes took place in educational programs. Museums, like ballet, theater, and orchestra, responded to the general public need that grew with the shorter work week, the higher level of educational achievement, higher income in the post-war economy, and greater sophistication of taste through increased mobility and travel.

Display Methods

Electronic technology and skilled display techniques revolutionized exhibition techniques in the 1950's and 1960's. The provision of a film, filmstrip or slide series as an introduction to the exhibit ensures that the forest will not be missed for the trees. Adapting the techniques of the full-scale habitat group of the natural history museums, historical museums as well as science museums has made a high art of the diorama—the miniature model portraying a scene in authentic detail, with the three-dimensional foreground blending almost imperceptibly into the painted background. The Museum of the City of New York and the Chicago Historical Society have long led the field in the use of dioramas. The presentation of the "period room" (consisting of an assemblage of authentic objects and furnishings) came close to perfection with the opening in 1951 of the Winterthur Museum near Wilmington, Delaware [2].

Museums of science have developed exhibits around working models and functioning experiments that wait to be triggered by the visitor's press of a button. In the Chicago Museum of Science and Industry the visitor experiences a descent in a cage to a coal mine and a ride in an electric car through the mine gallery. At the Cranbrook (Michigan) Institute of Science, exhibitions present principles rather than objects in an "open laboratory" of models-in-motion to illustrate various laws of physics. The Franklin Institute (Philadelphia) and the new Smithsonian Institution's Museum of History and Technology offer equally fine examples of this approach. These innovations derive from the famous Munich Deütsches Museum, where a typical exhibition is a laboratory demonstrating the principles of falling bodies and projectile motion, with a full-scale replica of Galileo's study adjacent.

The popularity of such participative exhibits proves that involvement in experiment and demonstration are a vastly more effective means of instruction than the "cabinet of curiosities" approach to museum education. The world's fairs in Seattle and Montreal underscored the fascination which learning in this form holds for adults as well as for young people. In terms of per-viewer cost, these highly effective exhibit techniques justify the expenditure for their preparation. The putting of art into action in an "audience-activating environment" is a major focus of the Chicago Museum of Contemporary Art, opened in 1967. Learning and experiencing through participation is increasingly emphasized in our world of advanced technology.

The museum tour has been released from the limitations of the small group led by a low-voiced docent, who feared to disturb the solitary viewer while he instructed his flock. The viewer-activated lecture related to each exhibit (whether listened to through an individual receiver or projected to serve all persons in the immediate area) enables the museum-goer to choose to listen or not. On a nature trail, a pre-taped commentary, which a visitor carrying a small fourteen-inch receiver may turn on, provides a more flexible and useful lecture than could be delivered in person by an educational staff member.

Our great mobility as a society has made possible the development of field trips as part of a museum program (bringing the viewer to the object) and distribution of loan collections and use of mobile exhibitions (bringing the objects to the viewers). Further, this mobility has encouraged the National Park Service to develop a vast network of "site museums": historic houses, trailsides (illustrating the local geological, botanical, zoological and anthropological history of the area). Then there are more elaborate historical reconstructions like Williamsburg in Virginia and Sturbridge in Massachusetts.

The regional museum and the "indigenous museum" attempt both to preserve and to emphasize the beauties of the local region and lead the native viewer to see his daily environment freshly and with enhanced appreciation. An introduction of participation and personal involvement of people in the indigenous museum goes well beyond the traditional museum functions, and in museums of glass-blowing, fisheries, and so forth, it verges on vocational education. One of the best illustrations of the indigenous museum (without vocational education overtones) is the Museum of the Cornwall Countryside in New York [31].

Because museums emphasize "seeing," they have an increasing appeal to those oriented primarily to the viewing media, and they are especially effective with adults who lack formal education. The UNESCO experiment with educational museum technique in Mysore, India, stressed the combination of films, objects, posters and sound recordings. UNESCO found that the opportunity for the illiterate adult viewer to return again and again to the museum strengthened his absorption of knowledge and provided an opportunity to reflect between visits [29].

With an increasing concern for the educational outcome of museum programs, some museums are cooperating closely with libraries, historical societies, colleges and social agencies. The Cleveland Museum of Art engages in cooperative programs with Karamu House, Music

School Settlement, the Cleveland Public Library and the Council on World Affairs. The Walters Art Gallery of Baltimore has a long history of cooperative programming with the Enoch Pratt Free Library. The Detroit Institute of Arts has cooperated since 1959 with the University Center for Adult Education (of Wayne State, Michigan and Eastern Michigan universities) in offering courses in art appreciation, art history, exhibition study and studio art. The strength of such joint programs lies not only in the shared effort, but also in the promotional power that arises from the common front which a group of important agencies projects. Further, the events (festivals, happenings, concert–exhibit–lecture programs) which such cooperative ventures bring about can be attractive to a wide segment of the community.

Perhaps the acme of adult education through museums comes in the Roberson Memorial Center of Binghamton, New York, which is concerned solely with explaining, teaching and stimulating interests and not with research and scholarship. Although the Center has a very limited collection, it borrows many exhibitions (which, in turn, are lent to schools). The Center offers classes of all kinds; it sponsors a ballet company, civic theater, symphony orchestra, opera and a writers' workshop. Serving 11 counties, this cultural center is a museum only in part, but well represents the active and activating role developing among museums.

During the 1960's, museums and museum education were given impetus, some financial support and promise of further support by three pieces of federal legislation. In 1964 an Arts and Humanities branch was added to the U.S. Office of Education. (Funds and programs emanating from this office are routed through local school boards, a factor that limits the positive effect on museums.) The 89th Congress passed, but did not fund, Public Law 89-674, "The National Museum Act of 1966," which authorized programs to train museum employees, distribute publications and improve museum techniques. The National Foundation for the Arts makes funds available directly to museums and art centers for the purpose of promoting exhibitions, strengthening collections, training personnel and extending museum resources to school and community. These developments are helping to strengthen the role of the museum educator specialist and, hopefully, will soon bring this professional educator into more active association with other adult educators at the local and national level.

Museums of Art

Museums of art, like public libraries, developed in the United States during the great cultural surge of the early and mid-nineteenth century.

Public Libraries and Museums

Between 1858 and 1870 five major art collections were organized and opened to the public: Walters Gallery of Art in Baltimore (1858); Albright Art Gallery of Buffalo (1862); Corcoran Gallery of Art in Washington, D.C. (1869); Metropolitan Museum of Art in New York City (1869); and the Museum of Fine Arts of Boston (1870). The purpose of the Metropolitan Museum of Art was to "afford to our whole people free and ample means of innocent and refined enjoyment . . . and the cultivation of pure taste in all matters connected with the arts [40]." These important and increasingly comprehensive collections were conceived as lending their educating influence to society through their availability. Their organization for public use made them an important force in cultural life in the second half of the last century.

The rich collections of art built by the wealthy, to reflect and indulge a personal taste in private collections, have become a public resource as they are bequeathed or made available for public display and study. The Isabella Stewart Gardner Museum (Boston), built as a collection for Mrs. Gardner with the advice of Bernard Berenson, is a fine example; the Phillips Collection in Washington, D.C., is another; and the Frick Collection in New York City is yet another. These exquisite collections have no obligation to comprehensiveness, but are the display of an educated personal taste in art.

The educational concept behind the public art museum of the nineteenth century was that the visitor could develop his appreciation and understanding of art through contemplation of the best examples. The weakness of this concept lay in the fact that the layman, lacking knowledge of artists and their development, art history or art technique, had no tools to aid his understanding and confronted art as pure experience. Curators of art museums came to realize that art, if it were to contribute more than sensation, and if it were to become an instrument for interpretation of the past providing a sense of cultural continuity, must not only be felt but must be understood. The educational programs of art museums developed to seek this dual achievement.

Selectivity in display was enhanced by departmental development around cultural eras (e.g., Egyptian, modern French and early American). Exhibitions of schools of painting—cubism, and its forerunners, for example—were designed to educate the public's understanding and appreciation. Comprehensive retrospective exhibitions of the work of a single famous painter (such as the epoch-making exhibition of Van Gogh's work in the late 1940's) combine an intense aesthetic experience with art history and an introduction to art technique. The Cloisters, a branch of the Metropolitan Museum of Art, constitutes a permanent exhibition with focus on a specific period, combining such features as architecture, painting, sculpture, textiles, music and other arts to illustrate medieval culture. These principles of exhibition have become basic to education of public taste.

To supplement the exhibition, tours conducted by the museum docent (or "teacher") and published catalogs were the earliest established educational techniques. Lecture programs related to exhibitions and to the permanent collections of a museum likewise remain a standard part of museum programs. The elaborate educational programs of such museums as the Metropolitan or the Albright Art Gallery make place for lectures and tours designed for different levels of art sophistication chiefly through instituting memberships in the museum and cultivation of special interests within the membership. Thus the casual and intermittent contact of the museum with most of its users has been supplemented by educational programs for the more interested.

Art museums in the United States, from the early twentieth century, have seen the importance of bringing innovative technique and concept to the public at an early stage, allowing the educated art amateur to participate with the art connoisseur in evaluating contemporary art. John Cotton Dana, librarian and museum curator for Newark, New Jersey, led the way in this effort; his Newark Museum was the first to give definite and consistent encouragement to the newer tendencies in art. The Whitney Museum of American Art was founded with this function as one of its purposes.

The Museum of Modern Art, founded in New York City in 1929, has been an important popularizer of modern art. Not only was it established to focus on bringing contemporary art to the general public, but it has consistently sought to interpret the aesthetic values in objects of daily utility. Design of such objects as the chair and the saucepan in the memorable exhibit of 1933 focused on industrial objects, and in the six years following, nine such exhibitions were arranged. The influence on public taste and industrial design has been notable. Further, the Museum of Modern Art led the way in clear, concise, informative labeling of objects on exhibit, and established a pattern of sequential viewing of objects in an exhibition so that planned aesthetic and educational insights could be achieved. And taking the electronic and mass media age in stride, the museum has placed considerable emphasis on the film as an art form.

Art objects for loan and for sale have become major extensions of the museum to the daily life of the adult. Art reproductions—from postcards to full-scale sculpture—are an important concern of art museums. Art classes, begun on a broad scale under the Depression Era's Works Progress Administration, have made a sustained contribution to appreciation of technique and to satisfaction in artistic expression. The collaboration of art museums with such popularized adult programs

Public Libraries and Museums

as the Book-of-the-Month Club "art seminars" can be cited as encouraging. Growth of community art associations, commercial and cooperative art galleries, and the contribution of corporations to the support of the arts are further indication of expanded interest in the arts in the mid-twentieth century. The charge that there is danger of deterioration through popularization of the arts (rather than the broadening of the public to appreciate the best) may have some substance; but it is hard to deny that the great activity and interest in the arts—a product of leisure, technology, and educational effort—have moved the public taste to greater sophistication than ever before. The museum's intensive lecture series and courses together with field tours to art in nearby communities or foreign countries give promise of building an adult audience with discriminating taste in the arts.

Size of Clientele

"It is commonly known that more people visit art museums than witness baseball games. A few years ago over one-and-a-half million people saw Leonardo's 'Mona Lisa' [41]." Hopefully the World Series and Mona Lisa on television could divide the viewing audience evenly between them. The 1965 survey of museum use made by the American Association of Museums found that museums were conducting formally organized classes and lectures for 8,000,000 school children; 4,500,000 adults; 56,000 art students; 14,000 undergraduates registered for college-credit museum courses; and 4,000 graduate students engaged in joint museum–university projects in art, history and science [4]. About 14 percent of all museums reporting had programs for adults, while 20 percent offered programs for children. It is clear that museum educational services to adults are substantial.

Training Adult Educators for Library and Museum Staffs

The importance of educational services for adults in public libraries and museums is not yet fully reflected in the professional staff for these professions. Leadership in the two fields has accepted the service innovations developed under the impetus of the adult education movement and absorbed these services as fundamental approaches without integrating adult education philosophy into the basic orientation of their professions.

Museum workers specializing in educational services will find no programs or courses devoted to learning adult education work within the museum context [3]. Courses and laboratories in museum methods, however, deal with exhibit techniques as well as administrative and curator functions. Museum educators tend to rely on course work taken directly in university schools of education for acquiring expertise in educational programming [36].

Working under the direction of museum educators, volunteers often carry the major responsibility for guiding tour groups through the museum. Such volunteers are usually given a training program, often of two years' duration, to prepare them to interpret the collection and conduct tours. The training programs at the Art Institute of Chicago and the Los Angeles County Museum of Art are the responsibility of the museum's educational director.

Library educators have made more self-conscious efforts to prepare public librarians for adult education work. A three-day conference was held in 1954 to analyze the elements that should be incorporated in library education. The conclusion was reached that much of the special knowledge and skill to be acquired for adult education services should be gained in university departments of education, sociology, psychology and mass communications (or on the job) and stressed the responsibility of library education for the perfection of the more traditional services of community study and librarian-to-reader book interpretation. The adult education orientation of public library service, however, was seen as essential in library education [5].

Eight years later, Lemke identified "only eight or nine" library school curricula that included a course directly dealing with adult education [17]. A study, now in progress by the author of this chapter, will show that response in library education to the development of educational services to disadvantaged adults has been even more limited. A thorough review of library education for adult education services in public libraries has not been made since 1959 [26], but a 1965 survey of library school catalogs led Purcell to conclude that "some form of course in adult education is now available in nearly all accredited graduate schools of library education [33]." This generous assessment can be considered indicative of a broad, general orientation to adult education.

The departments of adult education in university schools of education, then, are probably serving as the major sources of preparation for those whose work in museums and public libraries is in the educational services to adults.

References

1. Adult Services Division. *An Exploratory Study of Adult Services and the Adult Services Librarian.* Chicago, Ill.: American Library Association, 1968.

2. Alexander, E. P. *The Museum, a Living Book of History.* Detroit, Mich.: Wayne State University Press, 1959.
3. American Association of Museums. *Museum Training Courses in the United States and Canada.* Washington, D.C.: American Association of Museums, 1965.
4. American Association of Museums. *A Statistical Survey of Museums in the United States and Canada.* Washington, D.C.: American Association of Museums, 1965.
5. Asheim, Lester, ed. *Training Needs of Librarians Doing Adult Education Work.* Chicago, Ill.: American Library Association, 1955.
6. Beals, Ralph A. "The Public Library as an Agency for General Education." In: *The Library in General Education.* 42nd Yearbook of the National Society for the Study of Education, Part II. Chicago, Ill.: University of Chicago Press, 1943, pp. 99–112.
7. Cahill, Holger. "John Cotton Dana and the Newark Museum." In: *A Museum in Action.* Newark, N.J.: Newark Museum, 1944.
8. Eason, Helga H. "What Has Happened to the Reading for an Age of Change?" In: *Ways with Books.* Edited by Ruth W. Gregory. ASD Guide to the Literature of Adult Services, No. 3. Chicago, Ill.: American Library Association, 1968.
9. Finn, B. S. "The New Technical Museum." *Museum News,* XLIII (November, 1964), pp. 22–26.
10. Gregory, Ruth W. "The Search for Information about Community Needs." *Library Trends,* XVII (July, 1968), pp. 14–21.
11. Grove, Richard. "A New Federal Program." *Museum News,* XLIII (March, 1965), pp. 20–21.
12. Hiatt, Peter, and Drennan, Henry, eds. *Public Library Service for the Functionally Illiterate.* Chicago, Ill.: ALA Public Library Association, Committee on Services to the Functionally Illiterate, 1967.
13. Katz, Herbert, and Katz, Marjorie. *Museums, USA: A History and Guide.* Garden City, N.Y.: Doubleday & Company, 1965.
14. Keller, Richard L. *Manual of the Reading Improvement Program, 1955–1960.* Brooklyn, N.Y.: Brooklyn Public Library, 1960.
15. Lacy, Dan, and Mathews, Virginia H. *Social Change and the Library, 1945–1980.* Washington, D.C.: U.S. Office of Education, Bureau of Research, 1967. (Mimeographed)
16. Lee, Robert Ellis. *Continuing Education for Adults Through the American Public Library, 1833–1964.* Chicago, Ill.: American Library Association, 1966.
17. Lemke, Antje B., ed. *Librarianship and Adult Education, a Symposium.* Syracuse, N.Y.: Syracuse University, School of Library Science, 1963.
18. Liveright, A. A. *A Study of Adult Education in the United States.* Boston, Mass.: Center for the Study of Liberal Education for Adults, 1968.

19. Low, T. L. *The Museum as a Social Instrument.* New York: Metropolitan Museum of Art, 1942.
20. Luhde, E. T. "Stamford Museum Installs Electronic Guide System Along Its Nature Trail." *The Museologist,* No. 82 (March, 1962), pp. 19–22.
21. MacDonald, Bernice. *Literacy Programs in Public Libraries.* Chicago, Ill.: American Library Association, 1967.
22. Martin, Lowell A. *Baltimore Reaches Out: Library Service to the Disadvantaged.* Deiches Fund Studies of Public Library Service, No. 3. Baltimore, Md.: Enoch Pratt Free Library, 1967.
23. Martin, Lowell A. *Students and the Pratt Library: Challenge and Opportunity.* Deiches Fund Studies of Public Library Service, No. 1. Baltimore, Md.: Enoch Pratt Free Library, 1963.
24. McLuhan, Herbert Marshall. *The Medium Is the Message.* Coordinated by Jerome Agel. New York: Random House, 1967.
25. Menninger, Karl. *The Crime of Punishment.* New York: Viking Press, 1968.
26. Monroe, Margaret E. "Educating Librarians for the Work of Library Adult Education." *Library Trends,* VIII (July, 1959), pp. 91–107.
27. Monroe, Margaret E. *Library Adult Education.* New York: Scarecrow Press, 1968.
28. Munn, R. Russell. "Library Leadership Through Adult Group Services." *Library Trends,* XVII (July, 1968), pp. 86–95.
29. "Museum Techniques in Fundamental Education." *Educational Studies and Documents.* No. 17. Paris: UNESCO, 1956.
30. O'Brien, Katherine Lord. "The Library and Continuing Education." *Library Trends,* XVII (July, 1968), pp. 22–35.
31. Parr, A. E. "The Indigenous Museum." *The Museologist,* No. 89 (December, 1963), pp. 3–9.
32. Phinney, Eleanor. "Trends and Needs: The Present Condition and Future Improvement of Group Services." *Library Trends,* XVII (July, 1968), pp. 96–107.
33. Purcell, Gary R. "An Adult Education Course." *Journal of Education for Librarianship,* VI (Summer, 1956), pp. 43–47.
34. Rea, P. M. *The Museum and the Community.* Lancaster, Pa.: Science Press, 1932.
35. Rosenberg, Harold. "Museum of the New." *New Yorker* (Nov. 18, 1967), pp. 225–228.
36. Schwartz, Alvin. *Museum: The Story of America's Treasure Houses.* New York: E. P. Dutton, 1967.
37. Smith, Helen Lyman. *Adult Education Activities in Public Libraries.* Chicago, Ill.: American Library Association, 1954.
38. Stevenson, Grace T., ed. "Group Services in Public Libraries." *Library Trends,* XVII (July, 1968).
39. "Survey of Trends in Group Services in Public Libraries, August, 1967." *Library Trends* (July, 1968).

40. Taylor, H. F. *Babel's Tower: The Dilemma of the Modern Museum.* New York: Columbia University Press, 1945.
41. Wittmann, Otto. "The Museum and Its Role in Art Education." *Art Education,* LXIX (February, 1966), pp. 3–6.

Chapter 16

The Cooperative Extension Service

EDGAR J. BOONE*

*With the collaboration of Professors Emily H. Quinn and Robert J. Dolan, Department of Adult Education; and Robert E. Honnold, Graduate Fellow in Adult Education, North Carolina State University.

The Cooperative Extension Service, often referred to as "Agricultural Extension," is the world's largest publicly supported, informal adult education and development organization. Its history has been one of innovation. With over half a century of recognized achievement, it is America's first (and only) *national* system of adult education. Its programs have enabled both rural and urban people to acquire knowledge and skills needed to adapt to changing social, economic and cultural conditions.

The Cooperative Extension Service is dedicated to "the development of people themselves, to the end that they, through their own initiative, may effectively identify and solve the various problems directly affecting their welfare [17]." This goal is met primarily by extending and interpreting the research findings of the U.S. Department of Agriculture and state Land-Grant institutions to the people through county and area Extension offices.

The name "Cooperative Extension Service" was derived from a tripartite arrangement of cost-sharing by federal, state and local units of government. The term "Cooperative" is used to describe the special relationship between the Department of Agriculture and Land-Grant universities that evolved from the passage in 1914 of the Smith–Lever Act. This act established the grant-in-aid principle at the core of Cooperative Extension. A Memorandum of Understanding specified the elements of the fiscal relationship between the Department and the universities [16].

The term Cooperative Extension is also appropriate because county Extension workers, state Extension staff members, and federal Extension staff members share in the development of programs at local, county, state and federal levels. The term "Extension" denotes the process of extending the education resources of the U.S. Department of Agriculture and Land-Grant universities to all citizens of the United States. The term "Service" has come to connote an educational role.

The distinguishing features of the Cooperative Extension Service are:

> Informal teaching that is designed to make knowledge relevant and help individuals, families, businesses, and communities to identify and solve their problems.
> The extensive use of lay advisory committees or councils to assist with planning, executing, and evaluating the educational program.
> The extension of its reach and effectiveness by working with (and through) new and existing organizations.
> The training of local lay leaders.
> The support by different levels of government which has encouraged responsiveness to national, state, and local problems.
> The reciprocal relationship between services and research, which provides channels for new knowledge to flow to the people and allows human needs and problems to be transmitted to the scientists [14].

Evolution, Legislation and Finance

To understand the Cooperative Extension Service, one must first understand the economic and social impetus from which the system evolved. First, off-campus education in agriculture and home economics was a growing concern of the administrators of Land-Grant institutions at the turn of the century. Second, rural leaders throughout the nation were pressing for educational assistance. Consequently, President Theodore Roosevelt appointed the Country Life Commission in 1908. This group recommended the creation of a service that would provide every person on the land with both information and inspiration [10]. Third, Extension came into existence when the United States was predominantly rural oriented, and the farmers faced many pressing social and economic problems.

Several basic legislative acts influenced the establishment of the Extension Service: the Organic Act of 1862, the first Morrill Act of 1862, the Hatch Act of 1887, and the Smith–Lever Act of 1914 which, respectively, established the Department of Agriculture, Land-Grant

The Cooperative Extension Service

institutions, experiment stations, and Cooperative Extension Service. Ahlgren states these acts resulted in the most interesting and effective partnership of its kind in the world today [2]. This legislation linked the USDA, the experiment station, and the Land-Grant institution to provide the educational system (i.e., Cooperative Extension Service) for successfully communicating relevant research findings to the people in all walks of life. The Smith–Lever Act specified that the mission of this new educational system was "to aid in diffusing among the people of the United States useful and practical information on subjects related to agriculture and home economics, and to encourage the application of the same [15]."

The Smith–Lever Act further authorized Congress to appropriate funds for carrying out this intent. The Act and subsequent amendments provided the following formula for allocating grant-in-aid funds:

1. First, an equal amount is allocated to each state on a matching basis.
2. Second, 4 percent of the remaining funds is allotted to the Federal Extension Service for administrative, technical, and other services, and for coordination of the Extension work.
3. Of the remainder, 20 percent is allocated to the states in equal proportions, 4 percent is paid to the states in proportion to the rural population of each state to the total rural population, and the balance is distributed on the basis of farm population of each state to the total farm population according to the Census.
4. A special fund is appropriated to the Secretary of Agriculture for allocation in accordance with special needs in certain agricultural areas [15].

In addition the Cooperative Extension Service receives monies under the Agricultural Marketing Act of 1946; these funds are allocated on a project basis.

The Land-Grant universities worked through the legislatures in each of the 50 states and Puerto Rico in formulating comparable state acts authorizing Extension and its means of support. These acts vary from state to state, but the usual arrangement for state funding involves some type of cooperative cost-sharing by state and county governments. Hence, the finances for the Cooperative Extension Service come basically from three sources: federal, state and county tax appropriations. In addition, a small amount of funds comes from nontax sources and from some municipalities. The federal funds available during fiscal year 1968 for Extension work under the Smith–Lever Act and the Agricultural Marketing Act totaled $81,136,000; state legislatures provided $96,752,-000; county governments allocated $46,600,000; and nontax sources supplied $4,243,000. These four sources total $228,731,000, which represents an increase of $100 million over the 1958 appropriation.

In recent years, there has been a sharp decline in the percentage of Cooperative Extension funds coming from federal sources. For example, in 1936 the proportions contributed at the federal, state and county levels were 59, 19 and 19 percent, respectively, while in 1968 the corresponding percentages were 36, 42 and 20. This trend implies an awareness by state and local officials of the impact of Extension educational programs resulting in the willingness to support Extension. The trend also provides an excellent example of federal grants-in-aid inducing local units of government to undertake programs to solve problems in the national interest.

Payments of federal funds are made directly to the state Extension office in accordance with the budget and plans of work submitted by the state Director of Extension and approved by the Administrator of Federal Extension Service. A similar arrangement is common between the respective state governments and the state Extension offices. County appropriations are disbursed in a variety of ways. More than 80 percent of the total Extension Service budget is allocated to salaries of professional staff, including 15,044 Cooperative Extension agents and 232 Federal Extension personnel.

Scope and Objectives

One of the major factors contributing to the success of the Cooperative Extension Service as an agency of change has been its willingness to undergo rigorous internal and external evaluation and make adaptations in organization and programs consistent with societal needs. Although the basic mission of Cooperative Extension has remained essentially the same, social, technological and economic changes have broadened its program scope in terms of clientele, methods and techniques.

To understand the scope and objectives of the Extension Service it is necessary to review legislative and policy statements setting its direction and boundaries. Sanders suggests the following dimensions may be used to examine the scope of the Service: "the people to be served, the subject matter to be included, and the methods to be used [14, p. 29]."

The Smith–Lever Act identifies Extension's clientele as the people of the United States, its possessions and territories who are not formally "attending or residents in colleges in the several communities." The clientele was made more specific by the *Joint Committee Report on Extension Programs, Policies and Goals* of 1948, the Scope Report of 1958, and the 1968 report of the Joint U.S. Department of Agriculture–National Association of State Universities and Land-Grant Colleges Study Committee [17; 11; 18]. The 1948 report emphasized that Extension responsibilities are not limited to farm people or even to rural residents, but include all interested people regardless of race, creed, socioeconomic status or group affiliation; the clientele groups identified in the 1958 *Scope Report* and the 1968 USDA–National Association of State Universities and Land-Grant Colleges Study Committee Report encompass farm families, non-farm rural residents, urban residents, farm commodity and related organizations, and individual firms and organizations dealing with agri-business services.

The reality of its broad charter can be substantiated by the fact that in 1967 the Cooperative Extension Service provided learning experiences for 14 million rural and urban families and 3,235,000 young people. About 2.3 million disadvantaged adults were reached while 240,000 of the young people served came from ethnic minorities.

The second dimension of the scope and objectives of the Extension Service is related to the subject matter or content of the learning experiences provided. The Smith–Lever Act, as amended in 1962, specifies content as "agriculture and home economics and subjects relating thereto." Even though the emphasis is on agriculture and home economics, the words "relating thereto" provide latitude for adult educators to design experiences to fit the ever changing needs of the people. This latitude is quite evident when one analyzes the history of Extension. The Scope Report of 1958 states that in the early days Extension efforts were vocational in character; however, as the needs of rural people changed, so did the emphasis of the Extension program. Knowles adds that "following World War I, with the problem of agricultural production diminishing in importance, emphasis gradually shifted to problems of marketing and conservation [12, p. 91]." He goes on to mention that during the depression the Extension Service was called on to manage state and federal emergency rural relief and farm programs. World War II added other emergency activities which diverted energy from Extension's central mission but which also added to its prestige and its "reality orientation." Since 1950 only about one-third of the efforts of county Extension workers has been directed toward agriculture, one-fourth to educational programs of rural organizations and training local voluntary leaders, and the remainder to human resource development [12].

The 1948 report emphasizes the importance of planning Extension education in relation to people's needs and gearing objectives, content, and methods to problems resulting from changes in needs [17]. Ten years later, the Extension Committee on Organization and Policy suggested the framework within which objectives could be determined by each state and by each county Extension service. This guide to Extension programs delineated nine areas of interest: efficiency in agricultural production; efficiency in marketing, distribution, and utilization of farm products; conservation, development, and use of natural resources; management of the farm and home; family living; youth development; leadership development; community and resource development; and public affairs. The first four program areas pertain to agriculture while the last five are concerned with education of family members for life in a changing society. A recent development has been the identification of four major program categories by the 1968 Joint USDA–National Association of State Universities and Land-Grant Colleges Committee: agriculture and related industries, social and economic development, quality of living, and international Extension. Within the context of these content areas, the Extension staff and lay leadership of each state and county can identify instructional objectives through a systematic diagnosis of the needs of the people.

The third dimension involves the methods used to reach people. The act mentions "demonstration, publications, and otherwise." Again Congress demonstrated that it did not intend for Cooperative Extension to be hampered by undue restrictions in methodology. In keeping with the spirit of this legislation, the contemporary Extension staff utilizes an extensive array of methods and techniques.

In summary, the overall program objective of Cooperative Extension is to plan, execute, and evaluate learning experiences that will help people acquire the understanding, the abilities and capabilities, attitudes, and skills essential for solving farm, home, and community problems. This objective is met through educational programs that make use of research findings emanating primarily from the U.S. Department of Agriculture and the Land-Grant institutions.

Organization and Structure

The Cooperative Extension Service consists of three levels of organization—federal, state and county. The heart of the Extension Service is the Land-Grant college system, which is unique in higher education. The National Association of State Universities and Land-Grant Colleges provides the vehicle for state Land-Grant institutions to work with one another and with the U.S. Department of Agriculture (USDA).

The overall role of the Federal Extension Service, as specified in the Memoranda of Understanding between the states and the USDA, includes basically three major functions. Lloyd Davis delineates these as:

The "education" aim function, involving responsibility for leadership in and coordination of all educational programs of the department.

The state program support function, involving stimulation, planning, and execution of Extension programs within the state.

The establishment and maintenance of relationships with other governmental agencies germane to the national Extension function. [8]

In this role, the Federal Extension Service contributes directly to the programming efforts of each state. Heading the Federal Extension Service (FES) is an Administrator appointed by the Secretary of Agriculture. Supporting the efforts of the Administrator is a relatively small staff of administrators and program and subject-matter specialists.

The state Extension Service performs somewhat similar functions to those performed by FES except that it serves as the educational arm of both the USDA and the Land-Grant institution. Its primary role is that of providing leadership in developing and administering an Extension program within the state. The state (i.e., the Land-Grant institution) determines the type of organizational structure best suited for achieving this broad mission; consequently, the type of organization varies from state to state. The most common type of organization is closely aligned with colleges of agriculture and home economics within the Land-Grant institution. Heading this type of organization is a director selected by the institution with the approval of the Secretary of Agriculture. Under the director are usually several assistant directors, various middle-management supervisors, the program and subject-matter specialists, and the county Extension staff members. Several states have changed from this conventional system to area systems (e.g., Michigan, Kentucky and Indiana). A few state universities—Missouri, West Virginia, Oklahoma, and Virginia—have merged their Cooperative and General Extension services. Under this arrangement, the top administrator may be designated Vice-President or Dean of Extension and must be approved by the Secretary of Agriculture.

The county is the basic unit in the Cooperative Extension Service. It constitutes the level at which most programs are developed. Here the resources of the USDA, the Land-Grant institutions, and of related groups are brought to bear in seeking solutions to problems. A typical county is staffed with three to four professional Extension educators. Supporting the efforts of the county staff is a cadre of trained volunteer leaders. In 1962, more than 1.3 million volunteer leaders devoted an average of 11 days to Extension programming [1]. County staffs are permitted considerable latitude in program development.

How can the administration of this tripartite organization provide for freedom in decision-making and at the same time achieve coordination? Davis asserts that the system requires bilateral policy formulation with understanding of the need to give the interests of both parties full consideration [8]. Ferguson partially answers the question by stating that "Extension administration is influenced by policy decisions at each level of the government" [10, p. 117]. Necessary is the involvement of numerous people in policy-making at each level. At the national level, the Extension Committee on Organization and Policy (ECOP) of the National Association of State Universities and Land-Grant Colleges gives leadership to policy formulation. Examples are the 1948, 1958 and 1968 policy statements, which Ferguson contends are not binding on any state despite their general acceptance and marked influence on state policy. ECOP helps achieve a national consensus on goals and changing responsibilities and helps to harmonize local and state problems with national concerns.

Davis feels that regional meetings of state directors are useful in studying and discussing various national policies and procedures within the states [8]. These meetings and other means such as the Memoranda of Understanding, project agreements, plans of work, and budgets at all levels of the organization are partially responsible for the coordination and communication achieved throughout the Extension Service. In addition, the competent staff has undoubtedly helped this decentralized organization to function effectively.

Being primarily an agency concerned with effecting change in a complex society, Extension requires skilled personnel. This requirement has resulted in periodic reformulation of objectives, modification of structure, and redefinition of responsibilities. Personnel management systems instituted by many state Extension services have resulted in the development and utilization of job and position descriptions, professional improvement programs, and personnel appraisal systems.

The number of staff members employed at the state and county levels is illustrated in Table 5 [13, p. 223; 16, p. 417]. On July 1, 1967, there was one or more paid worker in each of 3150 counties in the 50 states, Puerto Rico and territories of the United States. Table 5 reveals an increase of only 162 professionals in nine years or slightly over 1 percent. However, a significant increase in the number of specialists should be noted (along with a significant decrease in the number of agricultural agents).

Programming

The Cooperative Extension Service has developed an ingenious system of programming that utilizes the collaborative efforts of profes-

Table 5. *Comparison of Extension Agent Positions by Numbers, 1958 and 1967*

Position	1958	1967
Director and Assistant Director	120	164
Administrative officer	82	130
Specialist:		
State	2,528	3,031
Area	(unknown)	706
Supervisor:		
Agriculture	253	286
Home economics	230	180
4-H Club	264	252
Agricultural agent	7,064	6,171
Home economics agent	4,271	4,054
	14,812	14,974

sional and lay leaders in developing educational programs designed to meet immediate and projected needs of the people. The elements of programming and the environmental forces that influence programs can be conceptualized within the total framework of the Cooperative Extension Service. At each level of the Extension Service there is an interrelation of the internal and external forces that affect program decisions. The external forces include national, state, and local organizations (e.g., farm, labor, business, education and civic organizations, and the clientele in each community). The legal forces are the legislative acts, the laws of national, state and local governments, and the policies of the Land-Grant institutions. Other external forces influencing program are the effects on social and cultural changes on the clientele. Reciprocal, cooperative and collaborative relationships among all levels of the Extension Service provide channels for these forces and make possible a coordinated program effort. However, in terms of specific objectives, the program evolves primarily from the county Extension agents' interaction with lay people.

Ways of approaching programming vary somewhat from state to state; however, the different strategies have certain common elements:

> Formation of a broad program framework which delineates the national and state program objectives, policies, procedures and practices.
>
> Adaptation and linkage of the program framework to area and county units.
>
> Formation and maintenance of lay leadership structures essential for planning, executing and evaluating Extension programs at area and county levels.

Utilization of lay leaders in diagnosing, analyzing and interpreting problems.

Development of a long-range program prospectus which: depicts the cultural, social and economic situation for a designated program area; identifies the major problems of the clientele; and outlines plans for the involvement of staff and lay leaders in coping with these problems.

Development of an annual plan of work, which is the educational strategy for meeting specific short-range and instructional objectives within a designated period of time.

Implementation of the plan of work, which includes execution of educational tasks and learning situations.

Evaluation of accomplishments in relation to specified objectives and plans.

These common elements are perceived as sequential steps in which the Extension staff and lay people carry out the programming function of the Cooperative Extension Service. In this sense, programming consists of three major phases: planning, executing and evaluating. Planning refers to the continuous process by which decisions are made with regard to what is to be done before resources are committed. The execution phase includes development of the program prospectus and annual plans of work and implementation of these plans by action. Evaluation is the process of determining the extent to which program objectives have been attained. This process also involves appraising staff member performance.

Methods

The methods utilized by Extension adult educators to provide learning experiences for the clientele can be classified as *individual contact*, *group* and *mass media* methods.

Individual contact methods are those in which the Extension educator and the individual learner interact in relation to a problem. These include farm, home or business visits; personal office calls; and correspondence.

Group methods are those in which Extension educators have direct verbal or visual contact with at least two or more persons. These can be classified as lecture in person or by recording, telephone or telelecture; lecture utilizing visual aids and other techniques; discussion; forum and panel discussions; result demonstrations; tours and field days; method demonstrations; workshops; in-depth schools; and combinations of two or more of the preceding.

The Cooperative Extension Service

Mass media methods are those used by Extension to communicate with large, unassembled portions of a population. Such methods include newspapers, magazines, radio, television, publications, displays, exhibits, circular letters, telephone tapes and answering sets. The Cooperative Extension Service has developed a vast array of research-based bulletins, booklets and circulars to supplement and enrich learning situations regardless of the method used.

Evaluation

Evaluation is the third major process included in programming; it is the process of determining the extent to which the objectives of the programs of the Cooperative Extension Service are attained. This process also is concerned with evaluating professional staff members' level of performance in relation to defined role expectations. All Extension staff members, individually and collectively, are responsible for evaluating program accomplishments. In addition, periodical reports are required at each level of the organization.

The Cooperative Extension Service has continuously assessed its accomplishments throughout its history and sought improved methods of evaluation. Recently the Federal Extension Service has worked with California, North Carolina, Iowa and Massachusetts in installing a computerized systems analysis program for reporting Extension educational accomplishments in relation to the stated objectives of the program. When completed, this reporting system will be a rapid, efficient means of attaining feedback about program impact at county, state and national levels. Eventually the Extension Service at all levels should be able to adapt programs and resources to changing needs. Some examples of educational programs resulting from effective programming are briefly described below.

Agriculture. In 1967, the USDA and the soybean industry estimated that 1 billion bushels of soybeans were needed to meet domestic and foreign requirements. The Cooperative Extension Service initiated an educational program to help farmers in 30 soybean-producing areas to develop an understanding of relevant economic considerations and the latest technology to apply to their farms. As a result, in large part, of county Extension meetings, individual contact methods, and demonstrations, farmers achieved a production of 985 million bushels of soybeans in 1967 [7].

Community Development. For many years, the Extension services have developed educational programs to stimulate leadership and foster cooperation among local organizations. During the six-month period ending June 30, 1967, the state Extension services worked with more than 14,000 county and area committees and organizations. Extension sponsored 739 training schools, seminars, workshops and conferences for local government officials; 3338 for citizen leaders; and helped prepare 1950 Overall Economic Development Plans during that period. Concurrently, the Extension Service assisted people in planning economic development projects which created nearly 50,000 new jobs, and 5636 community facility and service projects in such areas as recreation, water and sewage and health facilities. The staff also cooperated with many agency programs and over 9283 projects concerned with such matters as job-training, watersheds and air and water pollution [7].

Anti-poverty Activities. An example of an Extension Home Economics program designed to help break the cycle of poverty occurred in Lake County, Indiana. Three approaches were used to help people make better use of their resources for family living and to improve their income. Three groups of women were trained to teach disadvantaged homemakers: 24 middle-class women from Extension homemaker clubs, 18 volunteer leaders among the lower-income group, and 41 volunteers from Aid for Families with Dependent Children (AFDC). They were trained to be Department of Welfare Homemakers and Home Management Assistants assigned to the Cooperative Extension office. The first group taught over 3675 disadvantaged homemakers such subject matter as time and money management, use of donated foods, clothing construction and housekeeping. The second group was trained to teach various lessons at settlement houses and Head-Start parents' meetings. Of the final group, 32 are now employed, 7 have enrolled in night classes to complete high school, 4 have completed training for other jobs, and 6 have become independent of public welfare [7].

Youth Through TV. Nearly three-quarters of a million boys and girls in 35 states participated in 4-H Club activities through television in 1967. These program series dealt with such subjects as emergency preparedness, automotive care and safety, and dog care. In an effort to inject more science or "why" into 4-H projects, North Carolina specialists developed a series of nearly 100 science exercises, each demonstrating one or more scientific principles relating to one of the traditional 4-H projects. A majority of the exercises are suitable for urban boys and girls as well as rural youth. As a follow-up to this effort, the 10-program, 4-H TV Science series, produced by Michigan State University, is telecast over the University Educational Television Network and five commercial stations. Recruitment is coordinated through the public schools with some counties enrolling all fourth, fifth and sixth grade students. Total enrollment is expected to approach 100,000.

Professionalism

Cooperative Extension Service has amassed perhaps the most competent cadre of professional adult educators in the world. Basic educational requirements for staff are high. Employment in the Service at the county level requires the baccalaureate degree. Positions at the state or area level call for at least the Master's degree. These policies are under continuous scrutiny, and several states now demand the master's degree for employment at the county level. Table 6 shows how college degrees are apportioned among Extension's professional staff.

Table 6. *Level of Formal Education of Cooperative Extension Personnel (1968)*

Level of formal education	Number	Percentage
Baccalaureate degree	9,383	61.9
Master's degree	4,623	30.5
Doctoral degree	1,153	7.6

The Extension Service also has a comprehensive professional development program. This program is based upon a continuing analysis of the training needs and desired levels of staff competency in relation to changing job expectations and requirements. This program provides three kinds of opportunity for Extension staff members:

Orientation and induction for newly employed personnel and for those changing positions within the organization.
Opportunities for experienced personnel to better understand their clientele, the program content, and the teaching process.
Learning experiences related to leadership and management for administrative personnel.

Most of the 50 state Extension services have employed highly trained staff development personnel to conduct personnel development programs. These training specialists are expected to involve administrative and supervisory personnel (and subject-matter specialists) in the continuing study of training needs of staff members and the development of programs designed to satisfy such needs.

Further evidence of the Cooperative Extension Service's continuing effort to raise the level of professional competence of its staff is reflected in the following data. In 1967, 1800 in-service education meetings, workshops, and conferences were conducted for Extension professional staff members. This activity encompassed more than 100,000 man days. Over 1300 Extension professionals were enrolled in graduate courses. During this period there were 125 persons pursuing master's degrees and 400 persons pursuing doctoral degrees [7].

The Journal of Cooperative Extension began publication in 1963. The purpose of this journal is to provide the 15,000 professionals in the Extension Service a synthesis of research findings, theories and principles that undergird the field. The journal is sponsored and supported by the American Association of Agricultural College Editors, Epsilon Sigma Phi, National Association of County Agricultural Agents, National Association of County 4-H Club Agents, National Home Demonstration Agents' Association and the federal and state Extension services.

More than 1400 Extension employees are members of the Adult Education Association of the United States. And a high percentage of Extension workers are members of learned societies closely identified with their area of specialization.

Problems, Trends and Opportunities

A factor contributing to the success of Cooperative Extension work has been the system's capacity to modify its programs to meet the needs of people in a rapidly changing society. Changes in occupational structures, population shifts, increasing vertical and horizontal mobility and the emergence of new patterns of interaction all necessitate educational programs to equip people to function effectively and to perform productive and satisfying roles in a democratic system. Such programs require flexibility and innovation on the part of Extension staff and volunteer leaders.

To remain a progressive and effective force for educational change, the Cooperative Extension Service will need to do the following:

1. Intensify programming efforts and develop far-reaching long-range programs.
2. Develop or recruit professional educators who have the knowledge and proficiency to become effective change agents.
3. Recruit and train more subprofessionals or program aides to assist professional educators in planning, executing and evaluating education programs.
4. Modify organizational structures for maximum program effectiveness.

The Extension program must remain a people's program that will progressively permeate all levels of society and continue the active

The Cooperative Extension Service

involvement of voluntary leadership. However, there will be increased emphasis on the adoption of systematic and productive programming processes. The programming process will become more efficient through the use of rational planning processes, experimentation and improved technologies for implementing programs.

The demand for assessment of behavioral changes in relation to established objectives will necessitate the development of reliable and valid instruments for measuring effectiveness. Both systems analysis through use of computers and a more extensive application of present and new knowledge about the learning processes of adults should accelerate this evaluative dimension of programming.

With increased emphasis on efficiency and effectiveness of programming, the Extension Service can concentrate on both short- and long-range educational programs directed at the most relevant problems of society and people at all socioeconomic levels. The approach to education can no longer be segmented if it is to achieve maximum benefits for the individual, the community and the organization.

The Extension worker will enjoy an increasingly important position in American society as a change agent. Professional advancement will be enhanced by his commitment to continuing education, the acquisition of relevant behaviors for effective performance through in-depth graduate study, and the development of a converging body of educational theory and practice.

Staffs will become more highly competent and specialized in subject areas but concomitantly will become highly proficient in facilitating the teaching–learning, programming, and social action processes. The staff will be recruited in large numbers from the behavioral and social science fields, as well as technical fields, and will be rigorously trained for change-agent positions.

Pilot projects, studies, and experiences in many states have indicated that program aides or subprofessionals can assist adult educators and extend the competency and skill of the professional staff to larger numbers of people. Program aides or subprofessionals are persons who live in the community served and who have less than a college education. They are given special training by county Extension agents and work under their supervision. They are also on a lower salary schedule than professionals.

These program aides, when properly trained, have proved effective in communicating with, motivating, and instructing people in the lower socioeconomic groups. They can also perform many routine tasks. In fact, this trend might eventually lead to a new position role in adult education known as "Adult Education Technician."

Organizational structures will be changed to facilitate maximum program effectiveness. Closer linkages will be established within the Land-Grant institution to bring the total resources of the system to bear on the major concerns of people. These ties may be formal or informal, but will bring into focus the objectives of General Extension Service and Cooperative Extension Service. Research, teaching, and extension dimensions of the Land-Grant institution will offer stronger mutual support in the solution of problems.

Cooperative Extension will coordinate its programs more closely than in the past, not only with traditional educational and service agencies, but also with new and emerging systems such as the community college.

References

1. Boone, E. J., and Ferguson, C. M., eds. *An Image of Cooperative Extension.* Madison, Wis.: National Agricultural Extension Center for Advanced Study, 1962.
2. Boone, E. J. *Changing Dimensions in Agriculture and Home Economics.* Madison, Wis.: National Agricultural Extension Center for Advanced Study, 1962.
3. Boone, E. J., and Kincaid, James. *The Cooperative Extension Programming Function.* Raleigh, N.C.: North Carolina Department of Extension Training and Studies, 1963.
4. Boone, E. J., Quinn, E. H., and Dolan, R. S. "A Conceptual Schema of the Programming Process in the Complex Adult Education Organization with Special Emphasis on Its Sociological Aspects." An unpublished paper. Raleigh, N.C.: Department of Adult Education, North Carolina State University, 1965.
5. Federal Extension Service. *The Cooperative Extension Service Today: A Statement of Scope and Responsibilities.* Washington, D.C.: U.S. Department of Agriculture, April, 1958.
6. Federal Extension Service. *Amount and Percent of Cooperative Extension Funds Available to States and Puerto Rico, by Source, from Fiscal Year Beginning July 1, 1914,* MO-256. Washington, D.C.: U.S. Department of Agriculture, 1967.
7. Federal Extension Service. "Cooperative Extension Service's Budget Estimates and Report to Subcommittee on Appropriations, House of Representatives." Washington, D.C.: U.S. Department of Agriculture, 1968. (Mimeographed.)
8. Ferguson, C. M. *Collected Papers on Administration in Government.* Madison, Wis.: National Agricultural Extension Center for Advanced Study, 1964.
9. Ferguson, C. M. "Innovation in Extension." *Journal of Cooperative Extension,* II, No. 3 (Fall, 1964).

The Cooperative Extension Service 281

10. Ferguson, C. M. *Reflections of an Extension Executive.* Madison, Wis.: National Agricultural Extension Center for Advanced Study, 1964.
11. Kearl, B. E., and Copland, O. B., eds. *A Guide to Extension Programs for the Future: The Scope and Responsibilities of the Cooperative Extension Service.* Raleigh, N.C.: North Carolina State University, 1959.
12. Knowles, Malcolm S. *The Adult Education Movement in the United States.* New York: Holt, Rinehart & Winston, 1963.
13. Matthews, J. L. "The Cooperative Extension Service." *Handbook of Adult Education in the United States.* Edited by Malcolm S. Knowles, Chicago, Ill.: Adult Education Association of the USA, 1960, pp. 218–229.
14. Sanders, H. C., and others, eds. *The Cooperative Extension Service.* Englewood Cliffs, N.J.: Prentice-Hall, 1966.
15. *Smith–Lever Act as Amended in 1962.* Public Law 83, 83rd Congress, 1st Session, S. 1679, Chapter 157, 1962.
16. U.S. Congress, House of Representatives, Committee on Appropriations. *Department of Agriculture Appropriations for 1969.* Hearings before Subcommittee, 90th Congress, 2nd Session. Washington, D.C.: Government Printing Office, 1968.
17. U.S. Department of Agriculture and the National Association of State Universities and Land-Grant Colleges. *Joint Committee Report on Extension Programs, Policies and Goals.* Washington, D.C.: Government Printing Office, 1948.
18. U.S. Department of Agriculture and the National Association of State Universities and Land-Grant Colleges. *A People and a Spirit.* Report of the Joint USDA–NASULGC Study Committee. Fort Collins, Colo.: University of Colorado Press, 1968.

Chapter 17

The Armed Forces

NATHAN BRODSKY

Education as a lifelong process is an accepted objective of the armed services of the United States. Therefore the policy of the Army, Navy, Air Force and Marine Corps is to look upon education not merely as an extension of schooling, but as a continuing necessity for service personnel. The services provide education for better job performance, preparation for higher responsibility and for a fuller life during service and after return to civilian status.

The Scope of Defense Involvement in Education

By any standard, the Department of Defense (the composite of the Office of the Secretary of Defense, the Organization of the Joint Chiefs of Staff, the defense agencies, and the military departments) conducts the world's largest adult education programs. Of the ten cabinet departments and more than fifteen other agencies supporting or conducting education, only one has a larger training establishment than the Department of Defense (DoD). In 1968, for example, DoD was responsible for $2.2 billion, or 20 percent of all government outlays for training (and this sum excludes training such as recruit and pilot training). More than $1.6 billion went into training that was estimated to have value in civilian life. In 1969, the Department of Defense provided training for approximately 800,000 military personnel and 25,000 civilians. The range of Defense educational interests extends from overseas schools for dependent children to full and part time graduate study for professional military education.

Goals

The Department of Defense has established education standards for military personnel. Regardless of service arm, each officer is encouraged to attain at least a baccalaureate degree, each warrant officer at least the equivalent of two years of college and each enlisted man at least a high school degree or its General Educational Development (GED) equivalent. DoD is committed to continuing education not only because the technological and managerial requirements in the armed forces make education a lifetime process, but also because the Department recognizes that continuing education for servicemen and women must be concerned with personal fulfillment and with making contributions toward better citizenship.

Former Secretary of Defense Clark Clifford, in describing attainment of national security, identified the basic elements as the unity of the American people, the power of the weapons of the armed forces, and the quality of the training and leadership of those forces. With respect to training, Clifford stated that as one of the world's largest educators, the Department of Defense should be one of the world's best. "The training obtained during military service has been for many Americans the open sesame to a fuller life," he said. "Now and for the indefinite future, millions more must serve to guard our country against external threats to its security. We can serve them and add immeasurably to that security by seeing to it that they leave military service equipped to accept a larger share of the problems and the rewards of American society." Robert McNamara, Clifford's predecessor, also stressed support for education and launched several major educational efforts to improve the quality and capability of the serviceman. He enunciated policies designed "to assist and encourage military personnel to develop educationally and professionally through voluntary participation in off-duty educational programs." Educational opportunities should be provided, McNamara directed, to assist the individual to: perform his service job more effectively; prepare himself for more responsible service jobs and increase his chances for promotion; maintain continuity in the academic or vocational training which he began before entering the service; prepare himself to continue his education after he leaves the service; increase his value in the civilian manpower pool.

Clientele Being Served

The educational levels of service personnel range from those who need to learn how to read to those who need post-doctoral programs. Thus, the armed services are developing an integrated Core General

Educational Development program for those who either must learn how to read or who seek to attain eighth grade or high school equivalency. Servicemen are encouraged also to take courses (full or part time) at the graduate level either at service schools such as the war colleges or at "in-house" accredited postgraduate institutions or at civilian institutions.

For all of the services, it is estimated that approximately 70 percent of the officers and 3 percent of the enlisted men are college graduates. An additional 18 percent each of the officers and enlisted men have completed some college. On the other hand, 21 percent of the enlisted men have completed less than four years of high school. For enlisted men, the trend during the 1960's was toward an increase in the number of high school graduates and a decrease in the number of college graduates (as a result of draft deferments for college students).

Overview of Educational Activities

The scope of the adult education programs offered servicemen is so broad that, given the varying definitions of adult education, one might well include all of the service training schools, professional schooling and off-duty educational activities. If one accepts the definition of Verner that ". . . a relationship . . . in which the agent selects, arranges, and continuously directs a sequence of progressive tasks that provide systematic experience to achieve learning for those whose participation in such activities is subsidiary and supplemental to a primary productive role in society [17]," then truly, most of the training and education provided by DoD may be considered adult education.

Of the more than 3 million military personnel employed in the Department of Defense, almost one out of every ten is in a formal training environment at any one time. Skill training is provided to meet the needs of 1500 occupational specialties. Half of the enlisted men receive training in technical skills, the majority in the maintenance and repair of electronic, electrical and mechanical equipment. About 33 percent are trained in supply and administrative occupations and about 5 percent in medical and dental specialties. Only 12 percent receive training in skills directly associated with the firing of weapons.

More than 300 Army schools exist throughout the United States. Clark and Sloan identified over 4000 separate resident courses [4]. Additionally, training is provided in hospitals and through correspondence centers.

When an officer enters the armed services, he has in most instances already acquired a baccalaureate degree. He will, however, be required to continue his education to broaden his horizons and prepare him for increasing responsibilities. And because only one out of five officers continues in the service for a full career, taking advantage of his educational opportunities will also provide training for a second career.

Approximately 27,000 officers attend basic courses each year to learn about exercising the role of leadership and the technical fundamentals related to their assignments. About 8800 of the more experienced are selected to attend an advanced program at branch schools to prepare for duties at higher levels. The pyramid begins to narrow and approximately 3100 officers with approximately 10 to 15 years of service attend courses which prepare them for command and staff positions. Finally, the most promising officers (approximately 950) are selected for senior colleges (i.e., the Army War College, the School of Naval Warfare, the Air War College, the National War College and the Industrial College of the Armed Forces).

Some military positions require knowledge in such specific areas as oceanography, economics, language and international relations. As a result, as many as 2800 officers may be selected to attend civilian universities and colleges to pursue academic programs. Additionally, about 1700 students have the opportunity to study at in-house graduate institutions (the Naval Postgraduate School and the Air Force Institute of Technology) whose curricula are tailored to meet specific needs in science, technology and management.

Similar programs tied to the career needs of enlisted men exist for continuing education on duty either at in-house schools or at civilian institutions. Recruits in the Navy, for example, may get schooling to enable them to become postal clerks or electronic technicians. As they progress in the service, they may receive advanced training that is career related. The Navy also is sponsoring an Associate Degree Completion Program which provides full-time technical and vocational education for career enlisted men. This program enables enlisted men to attend junior college to obtain an associate degree.

Off-Duty Education Programs

A wide variety of off-duty educational opportunities is available to servicemen. These programs have been developed in response to varying needs for continuing education. They include tuition assistance for courses at civilian educational institutions, educational benefits available through Public Law 89-358, on-base continuing education classes, correspondence courses and various degree-completion programs.

The armed forces will give tuition assistance to personnel to encourage their taking courses at approved civilian educational institutions. A provision in the appropriations act each year allows reimbursement up

The Armed Forces

to 75 percent of cost. This tuition assistance enables the serviceman to take courses which may be either career related, or a continuation of education begun before entering the service or applied toward a trade, profession or other occupation which he intends to pursue after leaving the service.

The Veterans Readjustment Benefits Act of 1966 and subsequent modifications applies to those who served on active duty since January 31, 1955. This act enables members of the armed forces who have served at least two years of active duty to use educational benefits while still on duty. Thus, many servicemen have the choice of applying for either tuition assistance or for educational benefits under the veterans assistance acts to support their continuing education. Educational counselors in the military services advise servicemen about these programs.

In addition to the above methods, many military bases are able to hire instructors and counselors to meet specific educational needs. These instructors may teach such subjects as reading, typing, foreign languages and various high school or college courses.

All members of the armed forces have access to a wide range of correspondence courses regardless of which branch of the service offers the course. The subjects range from technical and vocational to academic. Many of the courses are voluntary in nature; others are required in order to increase one's proficiency and to qualify for promotion.

Airmen may enroll in the Extension Course Institute to take courses in aeronautical maintenance and other job related topics. In the Army, a home-study plan is provided which parallels, as closely as practicable, the corresponding resident courses given at Army service schools. Approximately 1430 subcourses are included in that program. The Marine Corps Institute similarly emphasizes job related study as does the Navy Correspondence Course Center.

United States Armed Forces Institute

The United States Armed Forces Institute (USAFI) is a major phase of the educational program offered to servicemen. The USAFI was established in 1942 to provide, through correspondence, academic courses to all members of the military service. Initially established under the Army, USAFI was transferred to the Office of the Secretary of Defense in 1949. USAFI provides correspondence courses ranging from elementary through college levels. It currently offers about 200 courses with almost half of these at the college level. There are over 300,000 enrollments in USAFI yearly.

In addition to the courses developed by USAFI, agreements exist with almost 50 colleges and universities to provide some 6000 correspondence courses to servicemen. This participating college and university program consists of separate contracts with each university to develop and provide the educational materials and guide the student through the course. A serviceman who is fairly certain he will be enrolling in or returning to a college after his service is completed is particularly well served by this program. He can begin or continue study at the college he chooses to attend.

An important aspect of the USAFI program is its testing activity. Most courses use a USAFI subject standardized test as the final examination. These tests are based on several of the commonly used textbooks in a subject matter area, so that they provide indication of the student's achievement regardless of the text he has used. USAFI provides test specifications and the textboks to an educational institution (a university or a testing service) which conducts the test development. A rigorous procedure is followed which includes use of the test in civilian schools to permit the establishment of norms. When this evaluation is completed, the test is submitted to the American Council on Education for determination of a passing score and for use in recommendation for course credit.

Special Programs for Beginners

The services seek to be responsive in their educational offerings to the needs of the servicemen. Thus, when "Project 100,000" was launched, USAFI redirected a portion of its effort to meet the educational needs of that project. In launching Project 100,000, Robert McNamara talked about the "unused potential of the Department of Defense—potential for contributing to the solution of the social problems wracking our Nation."

Project 100,000 was announced in August, 1966, at a time when one-third of 1.8 million men reaching military service age were failing to qualify under draft standards. Some of these men failed for medical reasons, but most failed because of educational deficiencies. Under the 100,000 program, 40,000 men were accepted for the year ending September 30, 1967, with a goal of enrolling 100,000 each year thereafter. The "new standards men" (as they are called for identification purposes, though they are not separated from the other men in the service) are not necessarily men of low ability. They are often men who lack the educational background which is measured by qualifying tests. They may have failed in their formal education, but the designers of Project 100,000 believed these men could be made into fully acceptable soldiers by providing them with effective training activities.

Project 100,000 men train with other recruits. Their work assign-

The Armed Forces

ments are made on the basis of demonstrated ability. Some have progressed to non-commissioned officer schools. Most seem to be gaining self confidence and a sense of achievement which should serve them well as they return to civilian life.

The increasing requirements for educational materials to support Project 100,000 led to the development of an integrated program for general educational development of servicemen from basic literacy through high school equivalency. This program was designated the USAFI Core-GED Program; it seeks to assist the trainee make up for educational deficiencies so as to attain either eighth grade or high school equivalency. The (Core-GED) program provides educational support at three levels: from beginning student to functional literacy; from the pre-high school student to eighth grade equivalency; and from high school student to high school equivalency. Except at the beginning level, the program does not require classroom teaching. It is a self-teaching method under the guidance of a resource person who is available to help the student who enters at his own level and progresses at his own rate. Tests are administered to the student when he is ready for them. Records of his accomplishments accompany him as he changes station.

One of the areas of major concern to Project 100,000 has been that of training functional illiterates to read. Traditional literacy training usually grouped functional illiterates together and used classroom techniques which previously had failed with such men. In evolving the literacy program to be used in the Armed Services, it was concluded that providing more of the same would not lead to the desire to learn. The content of the materials must be meaningful to the learner. It must be planned for men and not for boys. The Core-GED Program, therefore, is based on the premise that men will learn best from those materials which are related to their adult experience and which are adult in tone and subject matter.

The Army is establishing its reading program at all basic combat training centers. Among the 1939 graduates as of July, 1968, the gain in reading level had ranged from one to three grades. (It is recognized that elementary grade classifications are unsatisfactory measures for adults; nevertheless, these are the only criteria now available.) Approximately 28,000 recruits received reading training as of June, 1969.

In constructing the Core-GED program to provide educational support for students ranging from beginners to high school equivalency, a systems approach was utilized. The system includes development of the educational materials, instructor training seminars, placement and achievement testing and evaluation. A guidebook offers suggestions concerning facilities, time schedules, duties of tutors, placement of students and related matters. Through a continuing process of development, evaluation, feedback and refinement, it is anticipated that an ever-evolving program will be geared to meeting the educational needs of those servicemen who have not completed high school.

Other Educational Activities

A variety of programs are conducted through civilian educational institutions. The Navy Enlisted Scientific Education Program, for example, provides 4 years of college at any one of 22 participating institutions to selected persons who upon graduation attend the Navy Officer Candidate School.

The Army permits a maximum of 1200 servicemen who can complete a baccalaureate degree within one calendar year or an advanced degree within six months to attend school full time for that purpose. The trainee receives full pay and allowances, but must pay his own tuition and fees. The Air Force has a similar degree-completion program, as do the Navy and Marine Corps.

Local arrangements are made for educational support by neighboring institutions. Thus, for example, the naval base at Key West has arranged on-campus courses through the Florida Keys Junior College. These offerings can lead to a high school diploma, technical–vocational competency and a two-year college certificate.

At Camp Lejeune, North Carolina, arrangements have been made with a neighboring school system to conduct high school classes during off-duty hours. This program has been accredited by the State Department of Public Instruction. USAFI textbooks and study guides are used and guidance counselors are provided.

Within the United States a variety of college programs is available to servicemen. These programs include opportunities to pursue associate certificates, technical certificates, baccalaureates and graduate degrees. Thus, for example, an airman stationed at Selfridge Air Force Base in Michigan may take courses at any one of seven institutions of higher learning. An airman in the less populous state of North Dakota still can complete his undergraduate education at the University of North Dakota or at Minot State College.

A number of opportunities exist for continuing college level education overseas. In 1950 several universities were invited by major overseas commanders to provide servicemen with college level, resident, off-duty courses. The University of Maryland offers courses leading to a baccalaureate degree in Europe, the Middle East and the Far East. Florida State University provides similar opportunities in the Caribbean; the Universities of Hawaii, Alaska and the Philippines serve military personnel in those areas. The Sophia University provides a program in

The Armed Forces

Tokyo. Master's programs are available in Europe through Boston University, the University of Southern California, and the University of Utah; and in Japan through the University of Southern California and the University of Hawaii.

General and College Level Examination Programs

One of the significant areas of armed services contribution to adult education is its cooperation in the development of the General Educational Development Testing Service of the American Council on Education. With the growing recognition of the importance of educational achievement for employment, union membership, college admission and many other purposes, the General Educational Development (GED) tests were developed initially for veterans and service personnel. They have since been made available to all who are interested.

In the armed services, USAFI not only offers courses in preparation for the GED testing program, but also administers the test under stringent conditions to assure the integrity of the process. Each year, approximately 90,000 servicemen earn GED equivalency certificates by completing the USAFI program. This significant accomplishment has been the passport to college or employment for several million servicemen since the inception of the GED testing program.

Another activity receiving wide support in the armed services is the College Entrance Examination Board's (CEEB) College Level Examination Program. This program was established in 1965 and has been incorporated into USAFI. The examination measures the extent to which the student has attained the equivalent of a portion of a college education. Thus, the examination is designed to provide a means to qualify for advanced placement or credit for the more mature student just as is provided on most campuses for the abler students. The College Level Examination Program (CLEP) is supported by the armed services because it helps provide the flexibility needed if American education is to continue to be vital. CLEP recognizes that individuals learn in many ways and that traditional methods of assessment may be supplemented while preserving the integrity of academic standards. This need for flexibility is particularly evident in the armed services where there is increasing demand for continuing education by a large segment of the population but for whom the traditional approaches are often barriers to achievement.

Evidence that the CLEP merits greater acceptance as an instrument of adult education is contained in the findings of the College Entrance Examination Board concerning the results of the CLEP tests. A total of 43,877 USAFI candidates were tested during the period July, 1965 to

December, 1966. As reported by the CEEB, "the average USAFI candidate exceeded the score levels recommended by the Commission on Accreditation of Service Experiences for consideration for college credit in three of the five tests, and in the other two, for all practical purposes, equalled the level recommended." The number of USAFI candidates whose achievement was beyond freshman year varied from test to test, ranging from 18,000 to 24,000. As the CEEB stated: "The USAFI data substantiates the CLEP premise that educational achievement among American adults is substantial and beyond that which might be indicated solely on the basis of records of formal college attendance."

Evaluating Educational Experiences

The Commission on Accreditation of Service Experiences (CASE) was established by the American Council on Education in 1945 at the request of civilian educational institutions and the regional accrediting associations to assist institutions in assessing credit for military educational programs. World War II and Korean War veterans benefited from such assessments, and the educational institutions found these students were on the whole highly motivated and good academic performers. The Veterans Readjustment Benefits Act of 1966 and subsequent related legislation provide educational benefits for post-Korean veterans, thus promoting increasing demand for higher education by servicemen and the need for a continuing means for evaluating their service education. Consequently, the American Association of Collegiate Registrars and Admissions Officers requested that CASE prepare a new edition of *A Guide to the Evaluation of Educational Experiences in the Armed Services* and such an edition was published in September, 1968, partially financed by the Department of Defense [15].

How does the Commission on Accreditation of Service Experiences evaluate service educational experience? CASE consists of members appointed by the American Council on Education from the academic community and a professional staff. The Commission has enunciated policies which define the conditions under which courses and educational programs are evaluated. CASE selects civilian educators to make evaluations of each training program and course in terms of academic credit. At least three educators make recommendations on each course or program. The Commission then makes credit recommendations to civilian educational institutions which are either published in the Guide or provided to the institution in response to its request. Each institution is provided an objective assessment which it may use in evaluating the serviceman or veteran returning to continue his education.

The CASE advisory role in evaluation of educational experiences

The Armed Forces

in the Armed Services facilitates the task of educational institutions and motivates servicemen to continue their educational development while in the service. The thousands of young adults whose education is continued as a result of this process are substantive evidence that learning may take place in many forms and that, if their efforts are properly assessed and credited, increased numbers are motivated to continue their education.

Summary of Major Available Programs*

Tuition Assistance

> *Eligibility:* All active duty personnel except officers within two years of controlled separation.
> *Assistance:* Pay 75 percent of tuition fees for off-duty study at accredited schools.
> *Education and Location:* Studies leading to bachelor's and advanced degrees. Most military bases.
> *Further Information:* Education office at any military base.

United States Armed Forces Institute (USAFI)

> *Eligibility:* All active duty service personnel.
> *Assistance:* Reduced fees for correspondence courses offered by colleges and universities through USAFI. After $5.00 initial enrollment fee, normally no charge for additional courses listed in USAFI catalog. Testing Service is provided at no expense to the serviceman.
> *Education and Location:* Elementary school subjects through college level courses. All military bases.
> *Further Information:* Education office at any military base.

Army Enlisted Schooling

> *Eligibility:* All active duty military personnel; training must meet an Army requirement.
> *Assistance:* Normal pay and allowances, plus tuition, books, training supplies, and related fees.
> *Education and Location:* Accredited universities, colleges, graduate schools or other civilian educational institutions.
> *Further Information:* Office of Personnel Operations, Department of the Army, Washington, D.C. 20310.

* Excluding in-house training and education.

Army General Educational Development

Eligibility: All active duty personnel.

Assistance: Academic and vocational at little or no cost; counseling and testing free; training for civilian employment under Project Transition for terminating servicemen.

Education and Location: Approximately 300 Army Education Centers worldwide.

Further Information: Director of GED at any Army Education Center.

Army Degree-Completion Program

Eligibility: Active duty commissioned officers or warrant officers with three years' service, or enlisted personnel with one year of service who can obtain a baccalaureate degree in twelve months or a graduate degree in six months of full-time college attendance.

Assistance: Ordered on permissive temporary duty (TDY) to college; receives normal pay and allowances; student pays all school expenses.

Education and Location: Baccalaureate or graduate degree. Any accredited college or university.

Further Information: Director of GED at any Army Education Center.

Navy Enlisted Scientific Education

Eligibility: Navy or Marine Corps enlisted men and women in pay grade E-4 or above with high school educations. Top percentile is chosen from annual examination. Minimum ages: 21 for Navy, no minimum for Marine Corps.

Assistance: Full pay and allowances, plus tuition and related fees.

Education and Location: Four consecutive years; B.S. degree in science or engineering; 22 colleges.

Further Information: Personnel office of any Navy or Marine Corps command.

Navy College Degree Program

Eligibility: Active duty officers who can obtain a baccalaureate degree in 12 months or less through full-time attendance at a civilian college.

Assistance: Full pay and allowances; officers pay all educational expenses.

The Armed Forces

Education and Location: Baccalaureate degree. Any accredited college or university.
Further Information: Personnel office of any naval activity.

Air Force Airman Education and Commissioning Program

Eligibility: Career-minded active duty airmen with at least one year active duty and 30 semester hours of college credit.
Assistance: Full pay and allowances, plus tuition and related fees, for maximum of two years residence study followed by Officer Training School (OTS).
Education and Location: Studies leading to bachelor's degree. Selected civilian colleges.
Further Information: Education office on any Air Force base.

Air Force "Operation Bootstrap" Terminal TDY Program

Eligibility: Dependent on career status, length of service, fields of study.
Assistance: Permissive Temporary Duty to complete course requirements for degrees. Student pays for all tuition, fees, books and transportation.
Education and Location: Qualifying baccalaureate or higher degrees.
Further Information: Education Services Officer at any Air Force Base.

Air Force "Operation Bootstrap" Non-terminal TDY Program

Eligibility: Dependent on career status, length of service, fields of study.
Assistance: Permissive Temporary Duty to take courses related to jobs or career fields. Student pays for all tuition, fees, books and transportation.
Education and Location: Improve job proficiency or study in areas of concern and value to the Air Force.
Further Information: Education Services Officer at any Air Force Base.

Air Force "Operation Bootstrap" Tuition Assistance

Eligibility: All academically qualified personnel except officers within two years of controlled separation.
Assistance: Maximum of 75 percent of tuition fee.

Education and Location: Off-duty education for undergraduate, graduate, or technical courses at approved schools.
Further Information: Education Services Officer at any Air Force Base.

Marine Corps College Degree Program

Eligibility: All regular and reserve officers in the grade of warrant officer through lieutenant colonel who have sufficient credits to enable them to complete their baccalaureate degree requirements in a maximum of 18 months.
Assistance: Ordered to college for maximum of 18 months depending upon type of degree pursued. Personnel receive regular pay and allowances. Students pay all school expenses.
Education and Location: Studies leading to baccalaureate degree at any accredited civilian college or university.
Further Information: Commandant of the Marine Corps, Code DSL, Headquarters Marine Corps, Washington, D.C. 20380.

Marine Corps Off-Duty Program

Eligibility: All active duty personnel.
Assistance: Tuition assistance or free of charge. Professional college counseling available.
Education and Location: Off-duty education for undergraduate, graduate, or technical courses at accredited schools.
Further Information: Commandant of the Marine Corps, Code DSL, Headquarters Marine Corps, Washington, D.C. 20380.

Professionalization of Adult Educators

To direct the adult education programs, the armed services employ educational officers and counselors. These persons are required to provide a variety of services, including: counseling; information on education and occupations; testing and evaluation; advisement; registration and enrollment; and follow-up.

Approximately 3600 persons are assigned to education positions in the armed services. This number includes civilians and service personnel. In order to assess what is being done and by whom, the armed services initiated in late 1967 a comprehensive survey of the off-duty educational services. The results of the study were to be used to help establish professional standards and training programs for adult educators and to estimate resources needed to support the off-duty programs.

The increasing demand for competent professional counselors, which exists throughout the educational community, is also present in the military services. Counselors are needed at all levels from elementary through higher education to assist servicemen in planning their educational programs. Recognizing the need for new techniques, the services are investigating the automation of some counselor functions to provide quick access, particularly in areas such as career-oriented information.

In-service seminars and workshops are being conducted to provide educational officers with opportunities to update their skills and knowledge. Liaison is maintained with professional organizations and with educational institutions. Some consideration is being given to encouraging civilian institutions to offer courses which would be of value to educational officers throughout the world. As professional standards increase, there will be growing demands for in-service training to keep educational officers qualified for their task. The adult education professional in the armed services faces unique challenges—remote locations, mobility of clientele, priority of military missions. Yet there is abundant evidence these difficulties can be overcome if the armed services are committed to extending the capabilities of their training personnel.

Research in Adult Learning

The armed services conduct continuing research on personnel development including adult learning. A number of research organizations are used such as the Naval Personnel Research Activity, the Air Force Human Resources Laboratory and the Human Resources Research Office of George Washington University which performs its research under contract with the Army. The range of adult learning activities undertaken by such research organizations extends from the development of self-instructional materials to the design of instructional systems.

Research is undertaken to develop significant knowledge concerning learning processes. Courses are developed to meet specified training objectives and often include procedures for testing, evaluation and feedback. Innovations such as programmed instruction and computer assisted instructional programs are being developed and tested. There is concern for ways of improving the readability of materials. Some research is directed toward developing and testing training strategies whch may be appropriate for varying levels within an operational training context. Research is under way to determine the reading, listening comprehension, and arithmetic skills required for major occupational specialties.

Particular attention is being devoted to simplification of written materials, particularly for basic training and for occupational training. Thus, for example, the Navy rewrote its *Bluejacket's Manual* to include techniques for simplifying the non-technical language, for making wider use of illustrations and photographs and the sequencing of material.

Looking Ahead

A testimony to the commitment of continuing education is the fact that the military services are able to conduct such a variety of educational activities. One must view these programs in the context that in the short run they place demands upon military commanders unrelated to their immediate mission, absorbing manpower, facilities and time that may be needed for military purposes. It is the long-run benefits to the military services and to the individuals in terms of professional development and personal fulfillment that are the incentives for extending adult educational opportunities.

Those who are making the service a career know that education is essential to their advancement. Commanders and managers within the services are required to plan for the serviceman's being away from the job for short courses. For extended courses, provisions are made in programming and budgeting to provide "personnel spaces" for educational use. Off-duty programs are planned by local commanders, making facilities available whenever possible.

The in-house schools have been responsive to new developments in instructional methods. Innovations have been introduced using programmed instruction, educational television and computer assisted instruction. The military services have learned to structure courses to meet learning objectives. They are applying a systematic approach to the learning process, placing strong emphasis on good teaching. The service schools accept the fact that instructors must be trained to teach and must be observed in order to assess performance. There exist several outstanding teacher training programs which not only deal with the philosophy of learning, but also incorporate know-how concerning educational technology.

As military–civilian differences become less significant in a number of areas relating to national security, a larger common utilization of instructional materials and techniques will be possible. Thus, for example, the services have pioneered in areas such as systems analysis, resources management and cost effectiveness techniques which have application to civilian endeavors. The development of curricula and teaching aids to teach such tools of analysis is of direct interest to many civilian schools of business.

The Armed Forces

There will be a continuing need for civilian educational institutions to supplement in-house schools of the armed services. Tuition assistance, veterans' benefits, degree-completion programs, requirements for higher education and graduate programs, high school equivalency—these and many other programs will require continuing interface between the services and the educational community to promote the best opportunities for continuing education. The increasing exposure of servicemen to educational programs will result in motivation for continuing one's education. The challenge to educational institutions to meet these needs with flexible and imaginative offerings is most immediate.

References

1. Brodsky, Nathan. "The Professional Education of Officers." *Phi Delta Kappan* (May, 1967), pp. 429–432.
2. Bureau of the Budget. *Budget of the United States, Fiscal Year 1968.* Special Analyses G—Federal Education, Training and Related Programs, Washington, D.C.: Government Printing Office, 1968.
3. Bureau of the Budget. *Budget of the United States, Fiscal Year 1969.* Special Analyses H—Federal Education, Training and Related Programs, Washington, D.C.: Government Printing Office, 1968.
4. Clark, Harold F., and Sloan, Harold S. *Classrooms in the Military.* New York: Teachers College, Columbia University, 1964.
5. College Entrance Examination Board. *College-Level Examination Program—Candidates Tested Through the United States Armed Forces Institute, July 1965–December 1966.* New York: College Entrance Examination Board, March, 1968.
6. Commission on Accreditation of Service Experiences, American Council on Education. *Granting Credit for Service School Training.* Bulletin No. 8 (3rd ed.), September, 1968.
7. Commission on Accreditation of Service Experiences, American Council on Education. *Opportunities for Educational and Vocational Advancement: GED Testing Program, Comprehensive College Testing Program, USAFI Courses and Tests.* Bulletin No. 10 (3rd ed.), June, 1965.
8. Department of the Air Force. *Operation and Administration of the Air Force Education Service Program,* AFM 213-1, 1968.
9. Department of the Army. *General Educational Development,* AR 621-5, 1964.
10. Department of the Army. *Marginal Man and Military Service.* Washington, D.C.: Government Printing Office, 1965.
11. Department of Defense. *Off-Duty Educational Services Programs for Military Personnel,* DoD Directive 1322.8, May 1, 1967.
12. Department of the Navy. *Educational Services Manual.* NAVPERS 15229, 1967.

13. Lyons, Gene M., and Morton, Louis. *Schools for Strategy.* New York: Frederick A. Praeger, 1965.
14. Masland, John W., and Radway, Laurence I. *Soldiers and Scholars.* Princeton, N.J.: Princeton University Press, 1957.
15. Turner, Neil, ed. *A Guide to the Evaluation of Educational Experiences in the Armed Services.* Washington, D.C.: American Council on Education, 1968.
16. United States Marine Corps. *Marine Corps Education and Library Manual.* MCOP 1560.16, 1967.
17. Verner, Coolie. "Definition of Terms." In: *Adult Education: Outlines of an Emerging Field of University Study.* Edited by Gale Jensen, A. A. Liveright and Wilbur Hallenbeck. Washington, D.C.: Adult Education Association of the USA, 1964.

Chapter 18

Labor Unions

LAWRENCE ROGIN

Unions comprise a major institution in the United States. There are more than 18,000,000 unionists organized into about 180 national and international unions (the latter including members in Canada) which have approximately 75,000 local units. The American Federation of Labor–Congress of Industrial Organizations is comprised of 13,600,000 members from 125 unions. Local units of AFL–CIO affiliates form state and local central bodies.

National policy accepts unionism and collective bargaining as a basic method of dealing with employer–employee relations, and it is here the unions make their greatest impact. But union concerns go far beyond the work place. Unions are active in politics and legislation at all levels of government. They participate in a wide variety of non-governmental activities not related to bargaining. If education is meaningful in a democratic society, then the education of unionists about their problems as unionists and citizens is significant to the quality of their participation as individuals, and the quality of the participation of unions in American life.

The education of unionists in the United States is the function of that branch of adult education known as labor education, or workers' education; in this country the terms have identical meanings. Labor education is the attempt to meet workers' educational needs and interests as they arise from participation in unions. It is education directed toward action. Its programs are intended to enable workers to function more effectively as unionists, to help them understand society and fulfill their obligations as citizens and to promote individual development. It does not include training in job skills for the labor market, commonly known as vocational education.

Labor education differs from the more traditional forms of nonvocational adult education because it involves workers in education through a functional organization, the union. By using the union as the recruiting mechanism, programs can be developed around the needs that emerge from union activity. Once involved in education the unionists often extend their educational interests beyond these immediate needs; but, the original interest is aroused through them. Almost all labor education is voluntary.

Sources and Goals of Labor Education

Two institutions conduct most labor education in the United States: unions and university labor education centers. Some Catholic institutions conduct courses for unionists. There is also some labor education, a small part of the total, conducted by universities without labor education centers, U.S. Government departments, libraries, public school adult educators and by a few voluntary organizations with other primary purposes.

Because labor education reaches workers through their unions, nearly all the programs conducted by other organizations are jointly sponsored with a union, and the union may play a major role in planning as well as in recruiting. The initiative for a particular program may come from a union or from a university labor education center or other organization, but the result is a cooperative effort. Considerable labor education is conducted directly by unions without the assistance of other educational institutions.

Structure of Available Education

In the United States there is no national comprehensive system of labor education. Each institution develops its own priorities, its own method of operation and its own program identity. This is true for the individual unions as well as for the other organizations that conduct labor education. As has been indicated, unions and universities cooperate on specific programs, and there are examples of cooperation among unions and university centers, but these few do not change the general picture.

Opportunity for labor education is not equally available to unionists in different unions or different geographic areas. The variations are so

Labor Unions

great that for some unionists in some places there are a great number of programs, while for others differently situated there are none at all. The major determining factors are whether the union to which the worker belongs sponsors education, and how much; what the state and local central bodies do; and, often most important, whether there is a university labor education center in the area and the amount and character of its activities.

Almost all labor education is directed toward those unionists who are active in their organizations, either as volunteers, or as paid staff. The major emphasis is on local union activities. These include local officers, members of bargaining committees, stewards who have the responsibility for contract enforcement at the work site, and members of other committees, such as those concerned with politics, legislation or community affairs. This group makes up about 10 percent of the total union membership. However, there are very few unions, if any, in which 10 percent of the membership are engaged in education. In general, the proportion would be far less. Much labor education is open to those members who are not active, but few attend, except in those unions like the Garment Workers, Meat Cutters, or United Auto Workers (UAW), which attempt to educate new members. An increasing amount of education is being conducted for full-time union staff. Very little labor education is directed to nationally elected union officials, but there have been two recent programs, the first conducted by the Brookings Institute on an inter-union basis, and the second by the Steelworkers for the national officers and executive board.

Since most labor education is directed toward increasing the students' competence to function in the union, many courses deal with such problems as collective bargaining, union administration, communications, trade union history and structure and politics and legislative issues. Almost all staff training has this practical purpose.

Some labor education is directed toward broad social problems, such as civil rights, urban affairs, poverty and international relations. In general these are parts of more functional programs, although there have been a few intensive programs delving into social problems. Examples include training in the problems of poverty at West Virginia University and the University of Massachusetts, and an urban affairs project run by Cornell University in New York City.

There is an increasing number of courses in the social sciences. These were the focus of a series of experimental ten-week resident schools for union staff sponsored by the National Institute of Labor Education in 1961 and 1962, and form the basic curriculum for evening classes run by a number of university centers. Recently there have been attempts to help unionists achieve formal educational goals, such as a high school diploma or college credit. The UAW cooperation with community colleges in Michigan to establish an associate degree program in labor studies is a pioneering effort of this kind.

A few unions offer programs which emphasize cultural interests. The Garment Workers have stressed these activities over the years, and more recently the Cornell center in New York has developed a number of such programs with unions in that city.

Labor education uses forms common to adult education: short intensive conferences; resident schools, mostly for one week, but occasionally for longer periods; and evening courses, most of them running seven to ten sessions, but some for a full semester, or, rarely, a full academic year. There is almost no correspondence education. The short conferences are probably the most numerous and draw the largest enrollments. One week resident schools are also widely used. Evening classes make up the largest part of the education conducted in the home communities of the workers.

Most labor education is in self-contained units: that is, each conference, course or resident school has a specific function which is completed when the program is over no matter what its length. However, in recent years a number of university centers have sponsored long-term evening programs consisting of a series of courses which provide opportunity for broad continuing education. The intensive training programs dealing with the problems of poverty have included a series of resident schools and conferences.

Union Education

The greatest amount of union education is conducted by national and international unions. About 40 of more than 180 such unions in the United States sponsor some consistent educational activity. These include some of the largest unions, so in fact they represent more than half of the nation's unionists. Most of these unions conduct a few regular education activities, but only a few make a serious attempt to reach throughout the union. By far the most complete program is that of the UAW. Among the other unions for which education is an important concern are the Communication Workers, the Steelworkers, the Ladies Garment Workers, the Amalgamated Clothing Workers, the Machinists, the Meat Cutters, and the State, County and Municipal Employees.

There is no typical national union education program. Those unions which provide major support for education generally make an effort to sponsor education for local union activities throughout the union, but both the form and content of the education will vary. The greatest variation in content relates to the amount of emphasis on political and social issues.

Some indication of the amounts and kinds of nationally sponsored union education are shown in the following figures from the most recent survey of labor education in the United States, which covers calendar years 1965 and 1966 [9]. Full-time conferences lasting one to three days are the most common activity, with 34 unions holding them; but figures are not available for the total number held or the number of participants. Twenty-two unions conducted 253 one-week resident schools for local union activists with an enrollment of 19,085. Seven large unions ran just over 200 of these. Eighteen unions held specially organized sessions for the training of full-time staff, with a total enrollment of 2511. The staff training sessions ranged from two-day conferences to one instance of a six-month combination of academic and union training, provided by the Communications Workers for new staff. Two large unions, the UAW and the Steelworkers, have set up special staff training centers which provide regular three-week sessions with the union staff members participating in small groups.

Some local unions and other subordinate units of national and international unions conduct educational activities. In most unions the initiative for local education comes from the local unit, but there are a few which nationally encourage and support such activity. In one union with a long interest in education, the Ladies Garment Workers, education of local unionists is sponsored by subordinate units, while the national education department concentrates on staff training.

In general, locals of unions with national education programs are more likely to carry on their own education, but some of the most imaginative education programs are in locals of unions that have no nationally sponsored activity. Teamsters Local 688 in St. Louis, for example, has established a residential education center which draws students without regard to their union role. Local 3 of the International Brotherhood of Electrical Workers, in New York, conducts a varied program which includes residential education and a great variety of part-time courses, a number of which are directed toward cultural subjects and individual development.

Some special programs are conducted by the AFL–CIO Department of Education, but the primary function of the department has been to promote labor education, coordinate activities among unions and between unions and universities and assist AFL–CIO affiliates. The department is a major source of labor education materials. Its areas of greatest concern have been staff training and one-week schools. One other AFL–CIO department, Community Services, conducts a major educational program—mainly in cooperation with state and local central bodies—dealing with the out-of-plant problems of workers. In 1966 there were 197 community services courses enrolling 7556 and 115 conferences enrolling 11,125 in 87 different communities.

In addition to community services education some AFL–CIO state and local central bodies carry on other educational activities, with the state organizations taking greater initiative. The variations are great, with a few central bodies, like Texas and Michigan, doing a great deal, others a little and many nothing at all. One-week resident schools are the main activity of state central bodies; 26 of these enrolled 2444, in 1966. In the South and in the Rocky Mountain area, state central bodies pool their efforts in support of such resident schools. Active state central bodies run a number of educational conferences.

University Labor Education

There are 27 formally established university labor education centers in the United States, extending from New England through the industrial East and Midwest, then jumping to Colorado, California and Hawaii. There is one center in the South (Virginia) and another in Puerto Rico. Two of these have special purposes: the Brookings Institute conducts special conferences for elected national union officials, and Harvard University runs a 13-week resident training program for union staff. All of the others sponsor a variety of educational activity, including part-time courses, usually in the evening, conferences, and resident schools of varying length. Most of these are for local unionists, but some are for full-time union staff.

All but four of the university centers are attached to state supported institutions; the exceptions, in addition to Harvard and Brookings, are Roosevelt University in Chicago, and the American University in Washington, D.C. The centers share no common structure within the universities. Some are in industrial relations institutes which also run management programs, some are located in extension divisions, and others are in, or are attached to, academic departments. They vary greatly in size and in the amount of financial support. There is also variation in emphasis, with some centers concentrating on programs to meet the immediate needs of unionists while others are emphasizing broad-gauge training. Many centers do both, and this trend is increasing. All of these centers have formal relationships with unions through advisory committees. In addition, almost all of the learning activities are jointly sponsored with a union, a central labor body, or the AFL–CIO.

The labor education survey previously mentioned obtained statistics concerning the work of 23 centers—all of which functioned in 1965 and

1966 except Puerto Rico [9]. During that two-year period these centers conducted 1066 short courses for local unionists with an enrollment of 27,433. Eleven centers ran long-term evening courses providing continuing non-credit study. These enrolled 5884. There were 419 conferences ranging in length from one to four days with an attendance of 23,433. Some of these were on campus, others in the home communities of the workers. Eighteen centers worked with unions on 138 one-week resident schools which enrolled 9645. A variety of programs for full-time union staff included short courses, conferences, one-week resident schools, some that were two weeks in duration and a few which ran a full semester.

Some of the university centers also ran projects with a special purpose, usually financed by government or foundation grants. These included the poverty training programs at West Virginia University and the University of Massachusetts and others at Rutgers, Penn State and the University of Minnesota; a 13-week residential school for the Steelworkers at Indiana University; the training of labor education instructors by Penn State and the Cornell Urban Affairs project.

Other Programs

During the 1940's about 100 Roman Catholic institutions of various kinds—universities, parishes or dioceses or special organizations—conducted education programs for trade unionists, sometimes in joint activities with management. The number of such efforts has declined sharply in the past two decades, so that there are at the present time only ten such programs, all with their origins in the earlier period. Six of the present programs are attached to Catholic institutions of higher education, the others variously sponsored. Catholic labor education differs from most others in that the courses are initiated directly, rather than in cooperation with a union or group of unions. The recruiting is generally through the unions, similar to that for other labor education. The content is also quite similar, except that some schools include courses in social ethics, based upon the social teachings of the encyclicals.

Two agencies of the U.S. Government regularly carry on educational activity with unions. The Federal Mediation and Conciliation Service conducts courses for shop stewards as part of its effort to reduce friction in labor–management relations. The Bureau of Labor Standards of the U.S. Department of Labor conducts training to help develop union sponsored safety programs. A few other governmental agencies carry on labor education projects, or supply learning resources to unions and universities.

Some labor education projects arise out of cooperation between unions and public libraries. The American Library Association sponsors a Joint Committee on Library Service to Labor Groups, on which librarians and unionists are equally represented, and a few major libraries have specialized staff to work with unions. A wide variety of local projects have been developed, mostly of a service or promotional nature; but some are organized for more formal educational purposes.

One public school district in Philadelphia has a special program for unions as part of its adult education effort. This program operates quite similarly to those of the university centers. The same is true of the one state department of vocational education (Alabama) which has a specialized labor education staff.

Labor Education Staff

Unions and universities employ labor education specialists as administrators and teachers. Reports from unions indicated that 34 national and international unions employed 192 education personnel, of whom 94 worked full time on education [9]. Forty-two of these worked for one union, the UAW, and no other union had nearly that many. Data from the same survey indicated that 156 persons were employed by local units of unions for education, of whom 53 were full-time educators. Of the total, 50 were employed by one union, the Ladies Garment Workers, which has a large decentralized program. Twenty-one university centers reported a total of 126 staff members.

Labor education specialists require expertise in program development, subject matter competence in major areas of labor education content and the ability to teach adults. Most of them have become skilled through experience. A large number of union educators have risen to their present positions through the union ranks, while others have been brought in from other unions. Almost all those working for universities have considerable academic training, and many have union experience as well. In most centers there is an effort to employ persons with advanced degrees.

At present there is no formal channel for the training of new labor educators. A few institutions have established intern programs for this purpose, but these provide only a small portion of the new entrants to the field. Since labor education is expanding, this means most of the new staff members learn while doing.

Part-time teachers provide much of the labor education instruction, in both unions and universities. These instructors are chosen for subject matter competence and the ability to teach adults; they may be unionists, academicians, government officials or independent professionals. Some

Labor Unions

university centers and some unions train local unionists to teach certain basic courses. Penn State has had a major project of this type, and the American Federation of State County and Municipal Employees has developed a nation-wide steward training scheme which uses local unionists as instructors. The Cornell center has been the academic resource for this effort.

Financing of Labor Education

The major costs of labor education are met by the unions which sponsor or co-sponsor the activity. Some public funds come into the field through the university centers attached to state institutions. Usually, but not always, the university meets administrative costs. Most of the centers provide some subsidy for instruction, but the amount varies among institutions—from Cornell which provides a limited number of courses free of charge to those institutions which recapture all of their instructional costs. There is no general pattern.

In recent years there have been some grants from federal agencies for special purpose labor education. Rutgers, West Virginia, Massachusetts, and Penn State Universities received Office of Economic Opportunity grants for the training of trade unionists in the problems of poverty. Rutgers also received a grant from the Department of Health, Education and Welfare for work with unionists in vocational rehabilitation, and Massachusetts one for education about the problems of juvenile delinquency. A number of university labor education centers received grants under Title I of the Higher Education Act. Some of these were used for expansion of traditional programs, but in other cases special programs were developed in urban affairs or community problems.

While the Ford Foundation's Fund for Adult Education functioned, it financed a number of labor education projects including some of the early programs of the National Institute of Labor Education. Other foundation grants have gone to the University of Chicago, now no longer involved in labor education, and UCLA. Cornell's current urban affairs project in New York City is partially funded by the Ford Foundation as was the experimental residential program for the Steelworkers at Indiana University. But most foundations have not been willing to make grants in this field.

In both the unions and universities the shortage of funds has been a major factor in holding back the expansion of labor education. Where funds are available, programs expand and grow in sophistication. The UAW is the best example of this among the unions, and Cornell is probably the best supported university center.

Evaluation

Since labor education is action oriented, it is difficult to apply the traditional measuring sticks of evaluation. The test of success is not solely what the student has learned, or even what attitudinal changes have occurred; rather it is what actions have resulted from the educational experience. This is not only difficult to measure, but also difficult to attribute to a specific educational cause. The result has been an extremely limited effort to evaluate traditional labor education. Most of the evaluation has been of the special purpose programs, such as the few longer residential schools and the poverty training sponsored by the Office of Economic Opportunity. The evaluative techniques used for these projects are not necessarily applicable to other aspects of labor education.

There has, however, been some increase in the attention paid to evaluation as a result of the availability of government grants. A major project at Penn State is taking a very close look at participants in the long-term program conducted by that university and should be generally useful.

Organizations of Labor Educators

There are four organizations of labor educators, but none of these is all encompassing, nor does any one serve to relate labor education to the general field of adult education.

The largest is Workers Education Local 189 of the American Federation of Teachers. This is a national local union which includes both union and university educators, but not all of either. Local 189 performs some union and some professional functions.

Educators working for unions affiliated with the AFL–CIO are brought together by the AFL–CIO Department of Education in annual meetings, though they have no formal organization. Until the expulsion of the UAW in 1968, the AFL–CIO affiliates included all unions which took education seriously on a national basis.

The University Labor Education Association founded in 1961 is made up of the staffs of the university centers. It deals with common problems of the centers and liaison with the AFL–CIO, as well as the professional concerns of labor education.

Labor educators who belong to the Adult Education Association of the USA designate the Labor Education Section as their area of interest. In theory this should form the link between labor educators and the general adult education movement, but this has not proved to be the case. Many labor educators have not joined AEA, and most of those who have joined have not been active. As a result the ties between labor education and the general field of adult education have been very tenuous.

Some Trends

In the past ten years there has been an expansion of labor education conducted by the two major institutions in the field, the unions and the university centers, while the work of the independent agencies has declined. A number of unions which had previously ignored education turned to it, particularly unions of public employees, such as the American Federation of State County and Municipal Employees, the Fire Fighters, the American Federation of Government Employees and the unions of Postal Workers. The number of university labor education centers doubled during the same period. Three new centers have been established in the past two years, including the first one in the South, at Virginia Polytechnic Institute. There also has been greater support for some existing centers, so that their activity has been expanded.

During the same period the American Labor Education Service, the last of the independent labor education agencies, ended its activity when it was no longer able to raise financial support. The number of Catholic labor education centers also declined. A new organization, the National Institute of Labor Education, was established in 1957 as a joint venture of the unions and university labor educators in an effort to attract foundation funds for experimental projects. NILE did receive support for several projects, but its purpose was not achieved. Its primary activity at present is the development of a labor education materials center.

Unions have increased their efforts in the training of full-time staff. Some of them have established special centers for this purpose, while others have relied on university resources. The UAW Leadership Studies Center is the most ambitious of these projects. It has its own faculty and has developed carefully prepared training materials. The AFL–CIO is now planning the establishment of a staff training center.

The past decade has seen the expansion of long-term evening classes conducted by the university centers. These concentrate on broad subjects, particularly in the social sciences rather than on skills training. Thirteen universities now conduct such programs, and others are considering them.

Curriculum content has shifted to include more attention to social problems, particularly related to poverty, civil rights and urban affairs. The specialized projects noted earlier have been part of this trend.

There are two developments just starting which may affect the future character of labor education. One is the opening by the UAW of the first of a series of family education centers which will bring residential education within driving distance of this large union's membership. These centers are intended to provide facilities for a wide variety of educational programs directed to the members of the union, their spouses, and their children. This is probably the first effort of its kind in the United States.

The second development is quite different. Some universities and some unions are seeking to establish credit programs for unionists which will lead to academic degrees. The Michigan experiment has already been noted. It is too soon to say how successful these efforts will be.

Conclusions

Labor educators have demonstrated the ability to involve unionists, mostly blue-collar workers, in non-vocational, voluntary adult education. Unionists do respond to educational opportunity when they are approached through their unions; when the education is conducted under auspices in which they have confidence, in a style that involves them in the learning process; and when the subject matter is relevant to their concerns. Once they are drawn into education activity and have a successful experience, many worker–students are motivated toward education that is broader in scope, has long-range goals, or deals with controversial social issues.

Very few unions that initiate educational activity give it up. Rapidly growing unions and unions facing new problems turn to education to help them. The number of university centers continues to increase; some that have had difficulties have reorganized in order to continue to function.

Yet labor education remains peripheral to the adult education movement in the United States. Very few unions take it seriously enough to invest sufficient funds for a meaningful program. The total number of unionists involved is only a fraction of the potential audience. Most university centers operate under financial restrictions which prevent the development of a broad-based, truly experimental program.

Unless there is a major breakthrough in scale, based on a massive infusion of union or public funds, or both, the present situation will continue. In some unions, and for some unionists, labor education will be meaningful. But for the total union movement and for the nation, labor education will represent an indication of what might be done rather than a major accomplishment.

References

1. Barbash, Jack. *Universities and Unions in Workers' Education.* New York: Harper & Row, 1955.
2. *Challenges to Labor Education in the 60's.* Washington, D.C.: National Institute of Labor Education, 1962.
3. Cook, Alice H., and Douty, Agnes. *Labor Education Outside the Unions.* Ithaca, N.Y.: Cornell University Press, 1959.
4. *Labor's Public Responsibility.* Washington, D.C.: National Institute of Labor Education, 1960.
5. Liveright, A. A. *Union Leadership Training.* New York: Harper & Row, 1951.
6. Mire, Joseph. *Labor Education.* Madison, Wis.: Inter-University Labor Education Committee, 1956.
7. *Reorientation in Labor Education.* Chicago, Ill.: Center for the Study of Liberal Education for Adults, 1962.
8. Rogin, Lawrence. "How Far Have We Come In Labor Education?" *The Labor Movement, A Re-examination.* Madison, Wis.: University of Wisconsin Industrial Relations Research Institute, 1967, pp. 121–126.
9. Rogin, Lawrence, and Rachlin, Margorie. *Labor Education in the United States.* Washington, D.C.: National Institute of Labor Education, 1968.
10. "Symposium on Labor Education." *Industrial Relations,* V, No. 2 (February, 1966), pp. 53–106.
11. *Workers' Education in the United States.* Fifth Yearbook of the John Dewey Society. New York: Harper & Row, 1941.

Chapter 19

Business and Industry

LEONARD NADLER

Business and industry in the United States have been involved in adult education since pre-colonial days. The term commonly applied to this involvement is "training"; however, in recent years other words have been gaining acceptance, and we now hear: development; training and development; human resource development; and manpower resource development. Any definition of the word training would be very close to some of the accepted definitions of adult education. Liveright offered this definition:

Adult education is a process through which persons no longer attending school on a regular, full-time basis undertake activities with the conscious intention of bringing about changes in information, knowledge, understanding, skills, appreciation, and attitudes.... [14]

A trainer would want to add: to make the person more effective on the job. (However, employers are recognizing that to make a person effective on his job may require more than job-related training.) For purposes of this chapter, "adult education" and "training" are used interchangeably.

Training has focused on two groups. The prime group consists of employees. With the rapid advance of technology, as well as other influences, training programs have expanded to serve the customers and client systems of the business or industrial organization. Furthermore, since 1960 there has been a growing trend for business and industry to become involved in the social scene, and we now see companies engaged in training persons who are neither employees nor customers.

315

Statistics on adult education in business and industry are almost impossible to find and the validity of those available is highly questionable. Liveright indicates the frustration involved in such an endeavor and many others have met with similar experience [14]. One difficulty is in the definition of terms, as not all those engaged in training activities even agree they are functioning in the field of adult education. In contrast to public sectors of our society, business and industry have not been anxious to publicize their statistics except when required by law. This is understandable and defensible but it does preclude the gathering of valuable data. Another difficulty arises from the fact that some activities, such as on-the-job training, do not readily lend themselves to data gathering.

Clientele

By far the largest group involved in training is the employees. The kinds of programs offered to these employees vary greatly, but the major emphasis is on job-related activities. Companies usually have some form of induction and orientation programs for new employees, ranging from one hour lectures to programs extending over a period of several months. No one model satisfies all the needs, but there appears to be general agreement on the desirability of a well-organized and conducted induction and orientation program.

Closely allied are opportunities for skill training concerned with job-related skills. These encompass such areas as machine operation, sales and office procedures. In many cases, the personnel department will have hired persons who have the minimum skills for entry but require additional training to achieve desired skill on the particular equipment used by the employer. A typist, for example, may be able to meet the minimum standards for employment but may never have typed on the particular machine nor have used the particular dictating equipment available in her new office. Organizations hire new employees with engineering degrees and then devote considerable time to helping the new employee relate his previous education to the requirements of his new job. No criticism of the educational system is implied, but rather recognition that differences in specific skill requirements among employers are great.

For many years we have had apprenticeship training and this practice proved satisfactory during our emerging years as an industrial nation. Today, apprenticeship training is still with us but mounting problems strongly indicate the need for newer approaches to keep apprenticeship as a meaningful method of entry into the labor market.

Business and Industry

At the other end of the work force is the training—often costly—of the supervisors and managers who have become crucial to the growth and survival of organizations.

Training for customers is one of the major changes resulting from the impact of technological advance. Products have become more complicated, requiring manufacturers to provide training for their customers on installation, operation and maintenance of the product. Since World War II, purchase contracts awarded by the defense establishment have usually included provisions for the supplier to provide training to the government using the equipment. In the consumer products field, training programs may be conducted by a specific company to encourage customers to use their products. There are department stores in which auditoriums are available for consumer training conducted by store personnel or by manufacturers' personnel using the store facilities.

Training conducted for customers may take place on the customer's site or at special schools provided by the manufacturer. Telephone companies throughout the country have a packaged program they will bring to the office or plant of a subscriber to train personnel in telephone manners and telephone usage. Training for switchboard operators on the specific type of equipment installed in the subscriber's officer is usually held in a special training facility attached to the telephone company. Firms in the field of electronic technology have customer schools in strategic cities throughout the United States. IBM, Honeywell and RCA are among the leaders in this field who have various kinds of permanent installations to serve the training needs of customer personnel.

Another emerging clientele group is the trainer's own organization. The way man is organizing to get his work done is rapidly changing. Organizations are discovering they must develop greater flexibility and be more amenable to change than in the past. New needs are becoming evident for the organization as well as for the individual. As this chapter is being written the approaches to "organization development" are still in their infancy and it is not possible to foretell directions, but the concept of the organization as a total system needing "education and development" is a challenging one.

Some companies have begun to train persons who are not employees, customers or representatives of the organization. An outstanding example is the involvement of some of our leading companies in establishing Urban Job Corps Centers. The expertise of companies in training their own employees has been brought to bear on the needs of individuals who are not yet in the labor market and who would not be able to enter without special assistance. Most of the activity in this area has resulted from government contracts under legislation concerned with poverty and civil rights.

Organization and Finance

Methods of organizing adult education in business and industry are varied. As a part of a larger organization, the training unit is usually affected by the way the company has organized to meet its need for similar staff services. Training has usually been located under the personnel division with the training director reporting to the personnel director. This arrangement is being questioned, but it is too early to see any real movement of training to a position outside the personnel office. An individual in charge of training may have any one of a number of titles. The most common is "Training Director" but this is by no means universal.

The organization for training can be centralized or decentralized. A centralized training unit is concerned with the bulk of the training, and the trainers will be either regular employees of the training division or on assignment to that division. In a decentralized training organization, the training division is likely to be exceedingly small and do very little training, with the bulk of the training being conducted by persons outside of the training division.

A company having many geographically dispersed locations may have a centralized training office at the corporate level but a decentralized operation in relation to the individual plants. An element of confusion can arise when the trainer at the plant level reports administratively to somebody within the plant while relating professionally to the corporate training office.

The form of organization will also reflect how the trainer sees himself. His professional capabilities, background, and self-image strongly influence the organization of training in his company. The major roles have been identified as learning specialist and instructor, administrator of training programs and contributor to organizational problem solving [13]. If the organization accepts him in the last role, as well as the others, his placement will be closer to that of top management.

Mobility among trainers is high and there is a lack of agreement as to the professional credentials for a person filling the position of training director. Full-time personnel on training assignments may be selected either because of their knowledge of the field of education or because they performed well on a particular job. A good engineer may be withdrawn from his line position and assigned to training, the rationale being that a good engineer should be able to train other engineers. He may join the central training staff for a few months or for several years. By contrast, where there is a small central staff, most of the training may be done by people "on the line." Non-training personnel are utilized by either assigning them temporarily to training positions for the duration

Business and Industry

of a particular program, or assigning them as part-time trainers while they stay on their line job. Temporary personnel are also used; one source is the university adult educator on leave or vacation.

The most common method of financing training is through a budgetary allocation, which may take either of two forms. An allocation may be made to the training department, which is then responsible for all training funds. An alternative approach is to give the central training unit a small budget and have other units of the company include training expenditures in the department budget. Then, as the departments utilize training, they pay for it. In essence, the training unit charges for its services. For example, the Civil Service Commission in the U.S. Government provides training for employees in various government agencies.

Where a central unit must charge, there is a strong influence on the training staff and the entire organization. A company may establish the policy that when training of a similar quality can be obtained at a lesser cost from an outside source, the department is free to go outside the company to meet its training needs. This makes it incumbent upon the training unit within the company to be competitive when offering services to other parts of the organization.

Methods and Techniques

When one realizes the variety of situations and personnel involved in adult education in business and industry, it is not surprising that the methods and techniques likewise present a wide spectrum. The mobility of trainers and the lack of cohesion in the field have made it highly susceptible to gimmicks and crazes. The training director is constantly beset by an overwhelming tide of literature and salesmen offering him the answer to all of his training problems. All too frequently the products and gimmicks being offered to him are poorly researched and inadequately field tested. Despite the variety of pressures, trainers have been remarkable in their efforts to provide valid educational experiences.

A way of looking at the methods and techniques of trainers is through (1) group learning situations; (2) individual learning situations; and (3) the impact of educational technology.

The organized class is the most prevalent form of group learning in business and industry. For purposes of scheduling, control and budget a group learning situation in a classroom is by far the easiest to administer. The methodology ranges from the lecture to the laboratory [4; 22]. There is a trend toward actively involving the learner in the learning process. Particularly, the training of supervisors and managers has relied heavily on simulation, role-playing, gaming and sensitivity training.

Extensive use is made of audio-visual media, particularly the 16mm film. Several companies are now engaged in producing films for use in training programs and regular Hollywood-made commercial films are also used. Commonly used equipment includes the overhead projector, the tape recorder, and more recently the videotape recorder.

The most frequently used method for individual learning is on-the-job training (OJT) which is a system whereby the learner is counselled and coached while he works. In an OJT program there should be a regular sequence of tasks to be performed. The learner does not proceed to more complicated tasks until he has mastered the accepted standards on the earlier ones. OJT is used not only for new employees, but also to teach employees new procedures, product lines or technology. It is usually under the direction of a supervisor and only infrequently is a regular trainer used.

The assignment of reading materials is another way to provide for individual learning. This is particularly helpful where there is specified printed material which the learner needs to become familiar with in order to perform efficiently. Safety rules, company policy and department directives can be learned in this fashion. Managerial literature and periodicals might be on the reading list for a group of managers, who now have a flood of material directed to them. Evaluation and feedback must be built in so the learner and his supervisor can be assured learning has taken place.

Job rotation is frequently used to enable the learner to prepare for a higher level job or to gain knowledge of other aspects of his own job. The objective may be for the learner to experience the process of production before products reach his work station or the disposition of the product after he has accomplished his work. A dramatic and effective use of this technique was during World War II when aircraft mechanics were required to fly in the planes on which they had worked. Job rotation requires a good deal of advance preparation and provision for evaluating the learning that has taken place. As a technique for individual learning it is extremely significant but quite time consuming.

Educational technology has been emerging rapidly and has resulted in the formation of a variety of groups endeavoring to identify the relationship of new techniques to the trainer. In 1961 the American Society for Training and Development formed a National Committee on Programmed Instruction—a significant development in educational technology. The Committee completed its work in 1965 with a series of recommendations [23]. The heightened interest in educational technology has also resulted in the formation of the Industrial Training

Directors Division of the Department of Audio-Visual Instruction and the National Society for Programmed Instruction. There are undoubtedly other organizations which will emerge with a particular interest in educational technology. The American Management Association started an annual conference program in 1965 which has emphasized educational technology in its program content and exhibit areas.

Computer-assisted instruction is becoming more significant as we learn to use it. The cost is still too high for most practical applications but major breakthroughs in time sharing and other concepts will bring it within the range of more training budgets. Closed-circuit television is another application of technology which holds much promise. Through the 1960's there was a shortage of sufficient material, particularly designed for the manager [6]. As the decade drew to a close more organizations were developing materials specifically for this medium.

Program Planning

There are no agreed-upon approaches to program planning in this area of adult education. It is understandable, when one examines the academic disciplines to be found among training directors, that there should be varied approaches to program planning. One approach is to view the planning of programs as a process which revolves around critical events [18]. Systems models also have been developed and are being successfully used in an education–engineering approach. Extensive use is made of flow chart and mathematical models to provide a closed system for program planning [24]. Another attempt at model-building along psychological lines has been reported by John D. Folley, Jr. [5].

There is still extensive use of a technique evolved during World War I by Charles Allen which utilizes a four step method: preparation; presentation; application; and verification. The slogan of this program has been, "if the worker hasn't learned, the instructor hasn't taught." There may be some controversy over this by educational purists, but for the supervisor it provides the impetus to critically examine his training techniques.

Models for program planning range from those which respond to specific needs to those which offer packaged programs designed to meet broadly identified needs. Training directors have been very sensitive to the necessity for determining needs before developing training programs. If there has been a weakness in program planning by training directors, it is in translating needs into learning experiences. Trainers appear to be comfortable with the approach of involving others in the learning situation. Extensive use is made of steering committees, bracketing several levels of management, and other devices for involving various elements of the organization in planning the educational experience.

Resources and Facilities

The essential resource that training directors use is people—themselves and others. Other members of their organization may be used in training and these are referred to as in-house people. At times, the trainer will choose to use those who are not of his own company and thereby relies on out-of-house people. Instead of people he may choose to use a "package," which usually includes people but in a structured sense. In addition to people, there is the need for the necessary facilities to conduct training.

More and more the private sector has begun to use university faculty as one of their out-of-house resources. This has been monetarily rewarding to the professor and of benefit to his students as the professor brings the real world back to the campus. Faculty members are called upon to consult on education problems within the organization, to develop programs or assist the training staff in developing programs, to conduct all or a segment of a program, and in some rare cases to help in research and evaluation of training programs. Within universities there have been special forms of organizing to meet this need. At Harvard University a private company was brought into existence. At the University of Michigan a Bureau of Industrial Relations has been quite active in offering their services nation-wide to business and industry as they confront training problems. Companies of varying sizes have come into existence, composed of various mixes of individuals, both academic and non-academic, and the growth during the middle 1960's has been astounding. These companies provide various services in training and consultation, depending upon the individuals concerned, their location, outside interests, capitalization and related factors. In the rush of acquisitions, many of them are bought up by larger corporations seeking to enter the education industry.

Packaged training programs have had a significant degree of acceptance. In the early 1950's, for example, when a technique known as "brainstorming" became popular, packaged programs were developed so organizations could conduct their own brainstorming sessions [20]. In the early 1960's an application of sensitivity training was packaged in a program known as the managerial grid [3]. There have been other programs, most of which have not been objectively evaluated. Often they appear to be sold on the strength of going along with the crowd, rather than on their applicability to a specific training need.

Business and Industry

Rarely does a company have a physical facility designated only for training use. Trainers often use conference rooms or other multi-purpose facilities. Companies with large turnover or those requiring special entry level training may make special provision for a training facility. The size of the facility may be no indication of the commitment of the company to training, since a vast amount of training is conducted away from the place of work. Status has evolved in this area and sometimes overrides the expense and lack of benefits that may derive from a facility away from the work location. However, the concept of the "cultural island" has proved helpful, particularly where attitudinal change is desired.

Extensive use has been made of university facilities such as Residential Centers for Continuing Education, of which there are now more than 65. Hotels and motels have been added to the burgeoning industry by providing off-site facilities for training, particularly at the supervisory and managerial levels. Many country clubs encourage the use of their facilities for training and conferences during the off-season.

Another off-company approach is the use of a training trailer, which is a special mobile unit ranging from a mini-bus to a large tractor-trailer equipped with appropriate learning aids. The organization can take the training directly to the employee. Trailers are useful in situations where the employee is in constant contact with the public and where it would be too expensive to take him away for training—for example, in supermarkets and catalogue stores.

Evaluation

Evaluation of training in business and industry is complicated by many factors. There are the questions of what to evaluate and of cost effectiveness. The evaluation of any learning experience must be related to its objectives. In business and industry the overall objective of training is the more effective performance of the individual as an employee. Therefore, the ultimate evaluation must be in terms of job performance. However, there are so many other factors affecting job performance that it is frequently easier to evaluate what has happened in the learning situation, rather than performance on the job.

Methodology for evaluation must be related not only to the objectives but also to the process of program planning utilized by the training director. No matter which program planning approach is used, evaluation needs to be built in. Kilpatrick suggests that evaluation be in four areas: reaction; learning; behavior; and results [10]. There is little agreement, however, on what should be evaluated or on the appropriate methodology. Criteria for evaluation are also related to the ways in which the evaluation might be used.

As we move up in the organization, there is a decreasing tendency to evaluate training programs. More evaluation is done of skill training programs than of those conducted for supervisors, and even less for managerial training. The reasons for this are not clear, but may be related to the ease of evaluating skill training as against the difficulty of evaluating training related to attitudinal change or problem solving skills.

Most training is conducted without any direct relationship to cost effectiveness. There is a constant search for techniques which will bring about this relationship; so far it has proven unrewarding. Training does not exist in isolation from the total organization. Reinforcements on the job are equally as important as the training experience itself and can seriously influence the trainee's use of skills developed during training. Trainers have tried to link their programs to reduced absenteeism, lower turnover rates, or similar measures used by the personnel department to evaluate results. When the trainee is on a production line, in sales, or in some other position where output is measurable, trainers have endeavored to relate training to production.

There is a tendency to accept training—despite its inability to relate to cost effectiveness—simply on the implication of its usefulness to the organization. A quantified measure may not be available and the results not amenable to statistical analysis—much depends upon what the trainee does as a result of the training. Infrequently will the trainer evaluate merely for the sake of evaluation, as it can be costly and time-consuming. The trainer is more likely to avoid evaluation unless it relates to budget, facilities, staff, or some other aspect of the administration of the program.

Research

Adult educators in business and industry, more than other adult educators, come to the field of adult education from other disciplines. They bring to the training field the research orientation of their respective backgrounds, among which are psychology, personnel and administration. Research is conducted upon those aspects of training with which they feel the most comfortable. Research is reported in a variety of journals depending upon the particular background of the researcher and the professional field with which he identifies. There is a lack of coordinated effort and, unfortunately, no generally accepted clearinghouse for coordinating the research or sharing the results. Educational technology and sensitivity training are two areas that have been

Business and Industry

widely researched. For the latter it is possible to find much of the research gathered in one place [11].

Instances can be cited where companies have conducted research projects. These have usually been in-company activities and the results generally have not been made available to outside professional groups. Research projects have also been conducted by individual university teams and some of these have been reported in the journals.

The need exists to identify more clearly some of the specific research needs. Some of the questions asked by Kreitlow should be explored [12]. To stimulate research, the American Society for Training and Development (ASTD) has established a Research Fund, but at this writing it is too early to know what impact this fund will have on research in training.

Training Adult Educators

Training Organizations

Few membership organizations have been concerned with adult education in business and industry as a major focus. However, there are membership organizations in a variety of areas which make certain provisions for their members who have an interest in training. The major, and possibly only, organization concerned specifically with trainers is the American Society for Training and Development. The Adult Education Association of the USA has made provision within its structure for trainers, and other organizations have likewise developed organizational forms to meet the needs of trainers in their ranks.

The ASTD has a history going back to 1942 when it was formed by various state training organizations then in existence. The growth was slow and by 1967 it had reached 6000 members; but by the end of 1968 it was well on the way to 8000 members. It is estimated that this is still far below the number of persons actually engaged in the field of training as a full-time responsibility. ASTD has a national office which provides services to local chapters and a few overseas chapters composed largely of American trainers serving with companies or with government agencies.

Their monthly publication (edited by Robert Craig for many years) is the *Training and Development Journal*. ASTD is currently contemplating an expanded program of publications. At this time it is the leading organization of adult educators in business and industry, but it is doubtful if the bulk of the membership consider themselves as adult educators. However, it is significant that during the annual conferences of 1967 and

1968, sessions on adult learning conducted by Malcolm Knowles drew large audiences and the evaluation of the 1968 conference indicated the desire of the members for more information in this area.

The Adult Education Association of the USA has long contained within its ranks members who are involved in adult education in business and industry. In 1958 an attempt was made by Tenho Hermanson of IBM to help this group clarify its objectives and explore the relationships between AEA and other organizations concerned with the problems of training directors. One positive result was the formation of a special interest section at the annual AEA conference. This interest section still lives, but only barely. Attendance at its meetings is highly variable. It has not yet found its role in the total context of adult education, although it is quite likely the growing interest of trainers in adult education, and adult educators in training, may well prove the impetus needed for this group to become a vital force in the professionalization of training.

A new organization in the field is the National Society for Programmed Instruction (NSPI) which is principally concerned with educational technology. It does not draw its members exclusively from business and industry but from educational institutions and agencies as well. However, its main leadership comes from training directors or persons working for companies active in the educational field. At the present time, NSPI is too young to reveal the impact it may have. While efforts are being made to encourage this organization to become part of one of the existing organizations, it appears unlikely that such efforts will be successful.

Other organizations have begun to set up special interest sections, consonant with their internal organization. This is seen in the areas of psychology and vocational education where the membership includes persons actively engaged in the field of adult education in business and industry.

Preparation of Trainers

The emergence of training in the 1940's stimulated the growth of opportunities for persons to develop training skills. Among the earlier programs was that conducted at the University of Wisconsin in conjunction with ASTD, which started in 1953. At the Cornell School of Industrial and Labor Relations there has been an annual one-week training institute since 1950. Other universities have offered special programs, but not on a continuing basis or in the depth available in these two programs. The special institutes are not designed to improve the overall competencies of the trainers but rather to focus on particular areas of need. The annual conference of ASTD, which has been held continuously since 1943, has also provided opportunities for the professional growth of trainers. A program of regional institutes sponsored by ASTD National and Regional also focuses on the growth needs of training directors.

Since the middle of the 1950's there has been increasing pressure for university-level degree programs related to adult education in business and industry. Departmental brochures are beginning to include training directors as one of the audiences served by their programs. One of the first programs in the field of industrial education concerned directly with the needs of training directors was developed at Purdue University under Harry Belman. This program was geared to needs of the vocational instructor though in recent years, under Thomas Hull, it has included emphasis on administration. It is essentially an undergraduate program.

Since 1955, The George Washington University has offered a graduate program in both adult education and employee development. Until 1965 the program, under the School of Education, did not have a full-time professor assigned to it, although an experienced faculty was available. In 1965 the University appointed a full-time professor in the areas of adult education and training and since then the program has grown very rapidly. Separate courses are available for those pursuing the graduate degree in Employee Development, although, as might be expected, there are several courses which are essential for both the general adult education major and the training director [17].

There is coordination among other universities regarding offerings designed to meet the professional growth needs of training directors. Future efforts in this area may bring about vast changes in the entire field of training.

Degrees and professionalism are closely intertwined. One of the hallmarks of a profession is agreement on a body of specialized knowledge. The program at The George Washington University puts the core of the subject matter in education, but there is a lack of agreement on this. Others see training as subsumed under personnel, administration or labor relations. Attempts have been made to establish some criteria for professionalism, and the ASTD formed a national committee designated as the Professional Development Committee to explore the situation and make recommendations. The committee was in existence for about two years but was unable to develop recommendations which would move the trainer closer to professionalism. Different levels of membership has been one approach to this problem and is still under discussion within ASTD as one step toward standardization and professionalization.

Training in Government

The training of employees is conducted at all levels of government. There is entrance level training for those entering the job market for the first time, as well as in-depth executive development conducted in specialized schools such as those at Kings Point, New York, and Charlottesville, Virginia. Training can range from a few hours to several weeks and from the simplest skills to those needed in the space program. In this section emphasis will be placed on the training of federal employees by the civilian arm of the government.

Much of what has been said earlier in this chapter, about training in the private sector, applies to training conducted by the government. The differences are minor and private sector trainers find the transition to government training positions to be less traumatic than anticipated. The flow of trainers from government to the private sector has also been a practice, though for some time the private sector has been less likely to accept the government trainer. As the trainers have met at conferences, institutes and meetings of their professional organizations the movement between government and the private sector has been facilitated.

Training of its employees by the government has a long though clouded history, not unlike training in private industry. By the 1930's, training in various federal agencies had become commonplace and the training function was part of the operation of at least some of the elements of government. By 1938 the need was expressed among these trainers to meet and exchange ideas and experiences. That year the Training Officers Conference started in Washington, D.C., and in 1968 the TOC celebrated its 30th anniversary. By 1968 it was no longer the vital organization it had been in its earlier years, although it now included representatives from industry and universities, as well as from government, in the Greater Washington area. As other organizations emerged to serve the field and appealed to a nation-wide membership, the role and purpose of the TOC became less clear. It still stands as a landmark in the history of training and provides concrete evidence of the involvement of the government in training as far back as the 1930's.

Officially, training for government employees was not legitimized until 1958 by the passage of the Government Employees Training Act (GETA). Prior to that time, some individual and isolated agencies had training responsibilities as part of their enabling legislation. GETA encouraged all elements of government to assume responsibility for the training of their employees. By the end of fiscal year 1966 (June 30), the cost of training federal employees was estimated to have reached about $180 million per year.

Business and Industry

The central unit for federal training is found in the Civil Service Commission. As with similar central units in private industry, this one has little or no administrative control over the training conducted by the various departments. In 1967 The Presidential Task Force on Career Advancement submitted its report to the President. The report recommended strengthening the central training unit while allowing it to assume more leadership in a variety of areas including interagency training [8]. The Congress also looked into government training, and in 1967 the Subcommittee on Manpower and Civil Service issued a Report [21]. Though highly critical of the Civil Service Commission, the Subcommittee urged the extension of Civil Service Commission operations and influence on training activities of various government agencies.

The federal training programs are moving in some new directions. There is evolving a relationship between the uniformed services and the civilian arms of the government concerned with the absorption of veterans into regular civil service. In a wide variety of activities designed to focus on social problems, the federal government is in the massive business of training people in a patchwork of programs in 11 sections of the country. In many of these programs trainers from the private sector are working with the federal programs in a blending of relationships including straight profit contracts as well as the detailing of private trainers to assist in government training programs. However, the multitude of training activities carried on by the federal government in support of social and economic problem-solving are too diffuse and complex to describe accurately at this time.

The role of the federal government in training is changing even more rapidly than that of the private sector. As with the private sector, government faces the challenge of developing training personnel. The Task Force found that 40 percent of the employee-development officers in the federal government were over 49 years of age. Unless steps are taken soon, there is little hope of satisfactorily replacing these trainers in a market competing for innovative and capable young people.

Problems and Trends

Pressure is beginning to emerge for some kind of international exchange in the field of training. For years we have been exporting our knowledge and experience in training and by the middle of the 1960's the tide had begun to turn. Other countries were now pursuing developments based on their own expertise and national problems. At the 1968 Conference of ASTD more than 20 foreign countries were represented and many of them could well have been sharing information rather than receiving it. Books written about training in foreign countries indicate interesting variations on some of the practices familiar to American trainers [9; 15; 16]. The United States Department of Labor has encouraged studies in various parts of the world and this has proven stimulating to an exchange. As trainers from other countries develop, experiment and innovate, it becomes incumbent upon adult educators in the United States to improve communications and exchanges with their colleagues in other countries.

Federal Legislation

Beginning with the Manpower Development and Training Act of 1962 the federal government has had an increasing impact on adult education in business and industry. Companies previously opposed to "federal interference" have begun to recognize that the job is too difficult to be done by any one group and requires some form of federal assistance. Grants and contracts are not necessarily the only approach, but some form of support such as that given for capital investment might be in order. A Human Investment Act was presented to Congress in 1967 and again in 1968, but by the end of the 90th Congress no action had been taken. Additional legislative action is almost assured as the result of numerous legislative hearings on the relationship between the federal government and the role of business and industry in training [7].

Professionalism

The question of professionalism is becoming critical for those working as trainers in business and industry. One aspect relates to identification. As long as training is not seen as a profession the high mobility of trainers is not only to be expected but is actually to be encouraged. Lacking a professional identification, the individuals so assigned look for the day when they can return to the position in the professional field for which they have been trained.

Education Industries

Many companies that formerly trained only their own employees, and possibly their customers, are now seeking new markets in the field of education and training. These "spin-off" companies have discovered that the needs for education and training in business and industry are growing and the budgets for this activity are likewise increasing. Organizations such as Ford–Philco and Westinghouse Learning Corporation, which have provided training within their own corporations, are now servicing outside companies. These companies are not only looking for customers in the private sector but are also exploring possibilities in the public schools, as well as colleges and universities. Predictions are that in the decade to come, the "education industry" might well equal the military–industrial complex which loomed so large ten years earlier.

In the early 1960's there was the emergence of many companies, particularly those who plunged into the teaching machine field. By 1965 it was estimated that over 70 percent of those in business five years earlier had ceased to exist. Customers now found that a teaching machine they had purchased was meaningless for there was nothing to put in it. This has tended to make the market suspicious of the offerings or products of those engaged in the education industry.

Social Responsibility

The rise of a feeling of social responsibility within the American population began in the early 1960's and with the Economic Opportunity Act of 1964, the United States became committed to a program which involved all elements of the population. By 1967 it became evident that the entry point into society rests on economic viability. A person who does not have a job or economic resources cannot be a contributing member of society. In his State of the Union Message in January, 1968, President Lyndon Johnson challenged the private sector to provide the necessary jobs. By the spring of 1968, a National Alliance of Businessmen had been formed which involved more than 1500 companies throughout the United States pledging 100,000 jobs by June, 1969, and 500,000 jobs by 1971. At present it is still too early to assess the movement as to its success or failure. It is not too early to indicate that there will be a lasting effect on the concepts of social responsibility held by leaders in business and industry.

The implications for the training director are almost staggering. He will now find himself involved with adult learners who are different from those he has known before. Adult illiteracy has previously been the province of the public school adult educator, and now the adult educator in business and industry finds that he likewise must know something about adult illiteracy and its implications for the adult learner in work situations. The training director is finding himself more involved with minority groups and social movements than he ever contemplated. It is heartening at this time to see the steps being taken by adult educators in business and industry to meet the challenge.

Coupled with this is the need for involving more minority group members as trainers. Some of the work on new careers for the poor have indicated that we may have to explore ways in which we can develop the paraprofessionals in business and industry much as some public schools have been experimenting with teacher aides and teaching assistants.

References

1. *Assessing and Reporting Training Needs and Progress.* U.S. Civil Service Commission, Personnel Methods Series, No. 3. Washington, D.C.: Government Printing Office, 1961.
2. Bennis, Warren, and Slater, Philip. *The Temporary Society.* New York: Harper & Row, 1968.
3. Blake, B. B., and Mouton, Jane S. *The Managerial Grid.* Houston, Tex.: Gulf Publishing Company, 1964.
4. Bradford, Leland; Gibb, Jack R.; and Benne, Kenneth D. *T-Group Theory and Laboratory Method.* New York: John Wiley & Sons, 1964.
5. Folley, John D., Jr. "The Learning Process." In: *Training and Development Handbook.* American Society for Training and Development. New York: McGraw-Hill, 1967, pp. 34–54.
6. Gladmon, William T. "Management Training via Television." *Training and Development Journal* (May, 1967), pp. 6–10.
7. *Hearings Before the Subcommittee on Employment, Manpower, and Poverty.* Washington, D.C.: Government Printing Office, 1963.
8. *Investment for Tomorrow.* Presidential Task Force on Career Advancement. Washington, D.C.: Government Printing Office, 1967.
9. King, David. *Training Within the Organization.* New York: Barnes & Noble, 1964.
10. Kirkpatrick, Donald L. "Evaluation of Training." In: *Training and Development Handbook.* American Society for Training and Development. New York: McGraw-Hill, 1967, pp. 87–111.
11. Knowles, Eric S. *Explorations in Human Relations Training and Research. Part 2. A Bibliography of Research.* Washington, D.C.: NTL Institute for Applied Behavioral Science, 1967.
12. Kreitlow, Burton W. *Educating the Adult Educator: Part 2. Taxonomy of Needed Research.* Madison, Wis.: University of Wisconsin, 1968.
13. Lippitt, Gordon, and Nadler, Leonard. "Emerging Roles of the Training Director." *Training and Development Journal* (August, 1967), pp. 2–10.
14. Liveright, A. A. *A Study of Adult Education in the United States.* Boston, Mass.: Center for the Study of Liberal Education for Adults, 1968.
15. Lynton, Rolf P., and Pareek, Udai. *Training for Development.* Homewood, Ill.: Richard D. Irwin, 1967.
16. Nadler, Leonard. *Employee Training in Japan.* Los Angeles, Calif.: Education and Training Consultants, 1965.
17. Nadler, Leonard. "Professional Preparation of Training Directors." *Training and Development Journal* (April, 1966), pp. 12–18.

Business and Industry

18. Nadler, Leonard. *A Process of Training.* Washington, D.C.: Leadership and Resources, 1968.
19. Nadler, Leonard. "What Is Sensitivity Training?" *Manage* (May, 1968), pp. 22–28.
20. Osborn, Alex F. *Applied Imagination.* New York: Charles Scribner's Sons, 1953.
21. *Report Covering the Effectiveness of the Implementation of the Government Employees Training Act.* Subcommittee on Manpower and Civil Service of the Committee on Post Office and Civil Service, House of Representatives. Washington, D.C.: Government Printing Office, 1967.
22. Schein, Edgar H., and Bennis, Warren G. *Personal and Organizational Change Through Group Methods: The Laboratory Approach.* New York: John Wiley & Sons, 1965.
23. Silvern, Leonard. "Recommendations for Programmed Instruction." *Training and Development Journal* (January, 1966), pp. 27–34.
24. Silvern, Leonard. *Systems Engineering of Education 1: The Evolution of Systems Thinking in Education.* Los Angeles, Calif.: Education and Training Consultants, 1968.
25. Stout, Ronald. *Local Government In-Service Training.* Albany, N.Y.: Graduate School of Public Affairs, State University of New York, 1968.
26. Wolfbein, Seymour. *Education and Training for Full Employment.* New York: Columbia University Press, 1967.

Chapter 20

Health and Welfare Agencies

JOE R. HOFFER

Voluntary health and welfare agencies sponsor an impressive amount of adult education as an "end in itself" (e.g., through recreation and other informal activities as well as professional and technical training). However, their major contribution to the field is their use of education as a "means to an end" (i.e., better health, socialization, legislation and services of all kinds). It is necessary, therefore, to describe both the nature and substance of the health and welfare fields and the educational component of the programs and activities of health and welfare agencies.

Covering two distinct and large fields such as these—and doing justice to each—in anything short of a separate book, poses problems of its own, even though there is a growing number of common elements between them. Further complicating such a task are the following two problems. First, there does not exist a central depository for the myriad data on how these organizations educate their own membership, or on their contribution to the education of the public at large. Second, there is a tendency for the educational activities of voluntary organizations in these fields to be of such a peripheral nature or so interwoven with the total program as to make inaccessible much of the desired information.

To overcome some of these difficulties it has been necessary to set some arbitrary boundaries and to make some assumptions with which the reader may or may not agree:

1. To use the *Encyclopedia of Social Work* as a major resource [12].

2. To limit the scope of coverage primarily to *national voluntary organizations*.
3. To stress the common educational elements of health and welfare.
4. To refer the reader to the 1960 *Handbook of Adult Education* for background and historical data.
5. To highlight the significant recent developments in health and welfare.

National voluntary health and welfare organizations have developed either because local agencies need stimulation, guidance and support from the national source, or because some needs can best be met by a national service. This national–local partnership is essential in effectively meeting individual, group and community social and health needs. There are, therefore, a number of systems and subsystems operating in the health and welfare fields which in turn must be related more directly to other major systems such as education, communication, planning and social action.

The Organizational Structure

National voluntary agencies vary considerably in their objectives, structure and relationships. Like local organizations, they are the products of history and tradition, as well as of social, economic and political forces. They are differentiated to some extent according to their functions, but these differences cut across fields, age groupings, races and religions, ideologies and methods of practice.

As with many types of agencies, programs and services in health and welfare can be classified in numerous ways. The educational programs are usually directed to the professions, the patient or client or his immediate family and the public at large. Most programs can be classified under one of the following headings:

Individual Services

1. *Counseling and Guidance:* educational, vocational, social, emotional, religious, health, cultural, recreational.
2. *Casework:* sociocultural and economic adjustment in the family, group and community; resettlement services, social functioning of individuals and groups.
3. *Nursing Services:* bedfast patient, educational, health.
4. *Clinical Services:* detection, education, medical, health, family planning.
5. *Casefinding:* door-to-door home visits.
6. *Educational:* fellowships, scholarships.

Health and Welfare Agencies

Group Services

1. *Clubs:* social friendship groups with varied health and welfare activities, usually determined by the members themselves with the help of the leader. Interest is usually first on being together and second on the activity.
2. *Classes:* for learning special skills or health and welfare knowledge in both formal and informal settings.
3. *Special interest groups:* The activity itself is the primary attraction rather than who else is participating.
4. *Sports and athletics:* on a competitive team basis.
5. *Troops:* as in scouting.
6. *Informal, individual use:* lounges and game rooms with varying degrees of leadership.
7. *Resident camping:* overnight camping, usually from one to eight weeks.
8. *Facilities:* usually with no direct service leadership such as parks, zoos, museums, and similar services.
9. *Committees:* for planning or administrative purposes.

Community Services

1. *Leadership or continuing education training:* developing leaders and officials, voluntary and career, through participation in solving community problems.
2. *Forums, Conferences and Seminars:* local, state, national and international educational forums and conferences on a wide variety of health and welfare problems, issues, trends and methods.
3. *Community Development:* processes by which the efforts of the people themselves are united with those of government authority to improve economic, social, health and cultural conditions of communities.
4. *Professional Education:* professional practitioners (physicians, nurses, therapists, psychiatric and medical social workers, group workers, and family case workers) in health and welfare make a considerable contribution in teaching both in the classrooms and in field work.
5. *Life-Centered Community Schools:* offer a flexible curriculum focused on community problems to younger citizens and adults through the use of school facilities by local groups.
6. *Military Social and Medical Services:* provided in a variety of military settings around the world including mental hygiene con-

sultation clinics, hospitals, disciplinary facilities, combat organizations, schools and research centers.

A national organization serves the total field or a specialized field by informing the public on goals and achievements and on the nature and extent of problems with which the field is concerned. Its educational services include the operation of speakers' bureaus for local groups; the study of community or agency programs; planning and administering regional conferences and training institutes. It also operates programs, provides guidance and training for local groups, designs master plans for special problems (e.g., older adults, camping, and employment). The national health organizations are primarily health related in that each is organized to combat a particular disease, disability, or group of diseases and disabilities, or to improve the health of a particular group of people. The aim of national social welfare agencies is to assist local affiliates in helping individuals, groups and communities toward a mutual adjustment of individuals and their social environment. In recent years, there has been increasing emphasis on changing the social environment to meet better the multitude of existing health and social problems.

While the nature, scope and purposes of national voluntary health and welfare organizations may not have changed drastically in recent years, there have been some developments that may indeed change the complexion of these two fields in the next ten years. These include:

1. The impact of new governmental programs (e.g., the antipoverty programs, the Model Cities Program, Comprehensive Health Planning, aging and juvenile delinquency programs).
2. The impact of new non-governmental programs (e.g., Urban Coalition, new community planning structures, the Civil Rights Movement, and the rapidly expanding and activist youth population).
3. The acceleration of "participatory democracy" on the local levels in both governmental and non-governmental agencies.
4. The acceleration of advocacy or reform processes on all levels of government and in non-governmental organizations.
5. A degree of alienation of the citizenry from the present political parties in the United States.
6. A conflict in the priorities of values.

Clientele

An individual who seeks a starting point from which to comprehend the complicated network of health and welfare services in a modern community should grasp two fundamental ideas. First, agencies and

Health and Welfare Agencies

services are concerned primarily with four basic human problems: dependency, ill health, maladjustments and recreational needs. Second, these four problems tend to converge, in one combination or another, on the individual, family and community, with each problem intensifying the destructive consequences of the other.

Comprehensive statistics on clients and participants are not available, but the number of individuals, groups and communities served or involved as volunteers (volunteer participation is regarded as a key to the success of educational effort) in the wide ranging services by voluntary health and welfare organizations is considerable. These persons include: normal and healthy people, the crippled, the deaf and hard of hearing, the mentally retarded, migrants, transients and non-residents, narcotics addicts, unmarried parents, aliens and the foreign born, working mothers, racial and minority groups, the aged, delinquents and offenders and the poor.

Finance

The wellspring of our vast modern health and welfare enterprise arises from the Judeo-Christian imperative of man's responsibility to his fellow man. Increasingly in recent years the American public has been urged to do more for what loosely are catalogued as the social services, more for education, more for individual security, more for public assistance, more for health, and more for low income housing. And the public has responded positively.

Calculations by the American Association of Fund Raising Counsel estimated that, in 1968, a record $15.5 billion from foundations, $1 billion from corporations, and another $1 billion from bequests would be received. In 1967, the total was $14.5 billion; in 1960 it was $8.9 billion. For health and hospitals, the 1968 estimate is $3 billion. In 1960 the donations for this purpose were only $1 billion. Religion will receive $7 billion—an increase of $2.5 billion over 1960—and education an increase of $1.6 billion over 1960, or $3 billion. In the social services, the increases are equally encouraging. In 1960 the American Red Cross collected $83 million from its campaign for contributions; in 1967, it collected $109 million. The various "Community Chests" and "United Funds" across the country raised $458 million in 1960, but by 1967 they had increased it to $669 million.

Even more significant perhaps are the spending statistics for government in health, education and welfare. In 1960, all government outlays (federal, state and local) for social insurance, public assistance, health, education, war veterans, housing, and similar items was $52 billion. By 1967, this outlay had nearly doubled—in just seven years, it was more than $100 billion. In 1967, this type of government spending amounted to more than 13 percent of the Gross National Product, which is the total value of all goods and services produced in the country.

Governmental and Voluntary Agency Relationships

Relationships between various government entities and private social welfare agencies in the 1960's are widely disparate and highly fluid. The march of events over the preceding thirty years has worn thin the shibboleths about these relationships. Questions at issue range from the highly pragmatic—how to secure the increased care urgently needed by one group or another—to those involving fundamental philosophies. Among the latter are the nature of the "good society," pluralism, private enterprise, optimal means and rates of social change and progress, government, bureaucracies (private, whether sectarian or non-sectarian, and governmental), the social roles of justice, philanthropy, and charity, and church–state relationships.

On one point, however, there is virtually unanimous agreement: that only the resources of government are sufficient for health services, public assistance and other income-maintenance programs. Private agency support for this principle, sometimes begrudgingly accorded, is granted on the grounds that only the taxing power of government is adequate to the task. Thus, there is little acceptance of the value of social justice or of the importance to a democratic society of the entire society's concern for all its disadvantaged citizens.

Terminology is debated almost as vigorously as are underlying concepts. The distinguishing terms of public and private or governmental and voluntary agencies are no longer unquestioned. The former dyad appears to some to understate the public interest and trust that is vested in private or voluntary organizations. Use of the term "voluntary" to characterize private activities, while appropriate to the philanthropy and charity concepts underlying these services, is thought to downgrade the voluntary elements inherent in democratic government. Examples are freedom to support or oppose legislation, to serve on boards and commissions, to volunteer advice to governmental bodies, and to volunteer for services in governmental institutions and programs. Conversely, the possibly involuntary nature of some allegedly voluntary actions deserves attention.

Agency Sponsorship and Approach

National Voluntary Organizations

The National Health Council, in cooperation with the American Public Health Association, sponsors the National Commission on Community Health Programs, established for a critical review and evaluation of community health services. In 1962, the Council and the National Social Welfare Assembly (now the National Assembly for Social Policy and Development) established a joint uniform accounting project for the health and welfare fields. The Council carries on important projects in the health careers field, conducts school health conferences, maintains contact with state and local health councils in an effort to stimulate effective community health planning, and sponsors meetings of executives of member agencies. One of the Council's most significant activities is its Annual Health Forum, which brings together governmental and voluntary leaders in the health field. Topics discussed in recent Forums include: "Health Resources—A Public and Private Responsibility"; "Accident Prevention and Emergency Care"; and "Positive Health for Older People."

Cooperative activities in health and welfare have moved forward substantially in the national field in recent years. In particular, there has been progress in relating the roles of governmental and voluntary organizations, in establishing closer communication and common interest patterns between national and local planning bodies, and in the active participation of national organizations in these undertakings.

The National Assembly for Social Policy and Development (formerly the National Social Welfare Assembly) was reorganized in March 1968. In addition to a major change in function (from social welfare planning to social policy formulation and action) the new Assembly has a 300-member citizen corporation instead of the previous national agency control. It is the national organization with major responsibilities in the broad field of social policy of which social welfare is a part.

In addition to these two national organizations, there are five major so-called "Umbrella Agencies" (i.e., individual and/or organizational members representing the various functions, services and interests in health and welfare) which have major educational functions: the National Association of Social Workers (NASW), the American Public Welfare Association (APWA), the Council on Social Work Education (CSWE), the National Conference on Social Welfare (NCSW) and the American Public Health Association (APHA).

Sectarian Agencies

Programs and activities under sectarian auspices, usually open to all, represent a respectable segment of voluntary health and welfare services. There are approximately 350 Jewish Community Centers and YMHA's and YWHA's in the United States. Jewish cultural services have received greater local and national attention in recent years. Emphasis has been on the development of research, archives, libraries, publications, scholarships for graduate and postgraduate studies in universities financed in part by Jewish Federations. The National Jewish Welfare Board provides a wide variety of services to Jewish Community Centers and YMHA's and YWHA's.

Historically, Protestant denominations in the United States started with preaching and worship programs—and later initiated specialized programs in home and foreign missions, parish and higher education and—most recently—social education and action.

National Council of Churches affiliates are engaged in programs of social education and action in such areas as international affairs, race relations, economic life and housing. Settlement houses and community centers have been historic expressions of Protestant social concern. More recently group service centers have been developed by churches in rural areas and especially among isolated populations. In addition to recreational, educational and intercultural activities, most of these agencies offer some form of organized religious program.

The National Catholic Welfare Conference (NCWC) was established in Washington in 1919 by the Catholic Bishops of the United States in order to meet more effectively the socially related problems occurring with greater frequency in the program of the Church. Within the structure of the NCWC there are seven departments concerned with the solution of many demanding community problems. For example, the Social Action Department deals with labor–management cooperation, interracial justice, community organization, urban renewal and housing.

Group work as a social service in the Catholic field is exemplified by the existence of Catholic settlements located in large metropolitan areas to which Catholic immigrants have moved. A large part of the group work in Catholic social services can be found in the Catholic Youth Organizations (CYO)—a nationally coordinated program of the Youth Department of the National Catholic Welfare Conference, settlement houses and parish centers. CYO programs provide organized athletics, craft programs, religious and cultural experiences, study groups and occupational training. The CYO program is found in most of the 148 dioceses of the United States.

In addition to organizations with a religious focus, the following designate in some sense the wide variety of auspices and approaches used to classify health and welfare agencies: Organizations that are focused primarily on serving a neighborhood or local community; including such agencies as settlement houses, neighborhood centers, boys clubs, community health centers, clinics, mobile health units.

Apart from independent efforts by groups aimed at clarification and refinement of definition, some of the most useful and relevant definitions

Health and Welfare Agencies

in the field of social welfare and the social work profession have been formulations and reformulations undertaken at and in preparation for meetings of the International Council on Social Welfare (formerly the International Conference of Social Work) and the International Congress of Schools of Social Work. Modest beginnings were made in Madras (1952) and in Toronto (1954), more recently in Brazil, at Recife, Belo Horizonte and Petropolis (1962), in Japan at Osaka and Tokyo (1958), in Rome (1961), Athens (1964), Washington, D.C. (1966) and Helsinki (1968). In all these conferences, national position papers submitted to pre-conference working parties provided a basis for identifying underlying assumptions, guiding principles, patterns of organization, operational problems, and issues relating to both social policy and practice. Examination of the proceedings of these meetings indicates that community development and social development have received continuing attention both in plenary session papers and commission reports.

There has been a growing partnership during postwar years between the U.S. Government and American voluntary agencies with regard to international programs. Through contractual agreements the Agency for International Development (AID) has enlisted the experience and know-how of voluntary agencies in a manner that has been beneficial in achieving goals. Voluntary agencies are providing welfare, education, housing, rural development, health and agricultural services to people in so-called "underdeveloped" areas.

Approaches and Methods

Voluntary health and welfare organizations use a wide variety of approaches and methods in discharging their educational function. A partial listing follows:

1. *Self-Help Groups:* to increase community participation in affecting health, social, educational, therapeutic, community and legislative action.
2. *Recreation Activities:* as a means of improved use of leisure time, through development of hobbies, avocational "do-it-yourself" training, social clubs, sports, as well as educational and public service projects.
3. *Educational Activities:* including adult education and research as well as staff training and field work supervision. In addition, courses in human relations, training for teacher's aides and work with the emotionally disturbed.
4. *Volunteer Committees:* to encourage individual participation in

health and welfare organizations and public service projects.
5. *Case Records Maintenance:* as a source of factual data as a basis for staff training, general education and research.
6. *Published Materials:* books, educational pamphlets, journals, industrial and house organs, newspapers, manuals and "how-to-do" booklets as a means of education and interpretation.
7. *Family Life Education:* the dissemination of information about family relationships, personality development and social adjustments largely through family social workers.
8. *Public Communication Media:* the press, radio, television, films, the live theater through such productions as "Plays for Living" on themes of American family life and tele-lectures and interpreters of educational activities.
9. *Casework and/or Counseling:* to provide individuals with a means for expressing attitudes and feelings and for the development of new perspectives for handling problems of social functioning through discussion.
10. *Work with Groups:* group discussion as a mutually helpful means of achieving normal social functioning through the use of the relationships and resources of appropriate reference groups, and of educating both patients and family members in families whose children may be affected by mental retardation, cerebral palsy, muscular dystrophy, or other neurological disabilities.
11. *Study Tours:* educational tours sponsored by health and welfare organizations usually planned in conjunction with international conferences.
12. *Conferences* (local, state, national and international): serve as a unique means of communication and of informal education for growing and constantly changing fields [8]. As in any developing profession, the new departures in thinking and practice in health and welfare and its experiments and demonstrations are usually first presented at a forum, then are reflected in proceedings and articles in periodicals and much later appear in books.

Planning

There are three major levels at which governmental and voluntary health and welfare efforts are directed toward meeting the four basic human problems (i.e., dependency, ill health, maladjustment and recreational needs). Nationally, the Department of Health, Education and Welfare and national professional and voluntary health and welfare

Health and Welfare Agencies

associations serve primarily to stimulate, support, guide and standardize the efforts of local and state organizations. State health and welfare departments and state voluntary organizations are, in a sense, line organizations which offer varying degrees of direct service and activities. At the same time, they provide stimulatory, supportive and standardizing functions to the local governmental and voluntary agencies within their purview. On the local scene, one finds an impressive array of governmental and voluntary health and welfare agencies which directly serve the needs of the local population.

However organized, each national association develops a national understanding and policy with respect to its own aspect of health and welfare. In educational work aimed at the public at large, the goal is to stimulate action either for individual or community health improvement. The process is designed to impart information and motivate people to promote their own and their families' health, take adequate preventive measures, recognize danger signals, seek competent advice and services, or work together to assure the availability in the community of needed services or facilities.

The adult education programs grow out of the aims and objectives of each national association which are based on the specific need(s) for which the association was established. Learning activities are planned with specific target groups in mind depending on their needs and interests (e.g., health or disease prevention). "The maintenance and enhancement needs of a large formal organization" wrote Edward Banfield "can seldom be well served if at all, by tactics which aim narrowly at the aggrandizement of the organization or which cynically disregard the interest of a larger public [2]."

One local professional social work organization expressed its objectives in these words:

The Chapter should undertake a major educational campaign directed to the public at large, through the media of newspapers, radio, TV and a speaker's bureau to present to organizations and various community groups the realities of inadequate health and welfare standards and the pressing needs of clients. The Chapter should enlarge its direct lobbying and other forms of social action [13].

"Participatory democracy," Paul Goodman suggests, "is grounded in the following social-psychological hypothesis. People who actually perform a function usually best know how it is done. By and large, their free decision will be efficient, inventive, graceful and forceful. Being active and self-confident, they will cooperate with other groups with a minimum of envy, anxiety, irrational violence or the need to dominate [7]."

Volunteers have always been an integral part of the health and welfare systems but with the growing emphasis on social action and change, this term has been expanded to encompass users of services and neighborhood control.

"Social action" is the term commonly applied to that aspect of organized health and welfare activity directed toward shaping, modifying or maintaining the social institutions and policies that collectively constitute the social environment. But even this term has been expanded and some of the trends are discussed below. Confrontation with people in problem situations is a normal technique today—an extension of dialogue and the use of advisory groups.

Skills in work with groups are a necessary requirement for adult education in health and welfare. Group-work practitioners are now serving a wide range of health and welfare organizations. The problem-solving process provides participants with opportunities to display their talents and tap their individual competencies. Among those prime personal qualities which appear to be essential for effectiveness are: demonstrated conviction about community improvement; vital interest in the immediate problem or program; and enough imagination to see that merely talking about the possibility of change does not actually bring about change.

Evaluation

There seems to be no overall scheme for evaluating learning activities in health and welfare agencies. Informal evaluation does go on, however, by national organizations and by local planning and research organizations. In essence, the adult education programs in health and welfare are becoming organized around the real-life problems of individuals and society. Voluntary agencies must continue to receive financial support either through their own efforts (as many national health organizations do), or as participating members of community or united funds. Evaluation methods may vary depending on the nature of the money raising efforts.

As competition for funds increases and as the giving public becomes more sophisticated, large formal organizations or united funds must offer their contributors (employees, members, recipients and so on) non-material incentives, like the opportunity to be of service to the community or to perform what Barnard has called "ideal benefactions." Thus the voluntary health and welfare organizations try to design evaluation techniques that measure (1) the extent to which individual, group and community educational objectives are met; (2) effectiveness in meeting agency objectives; and (3) effectiveness of fund raising activities.

Health and Welfare Agencies

Problems and Trends

In the eyes of health and welfare leaders the current social problems can be met only by massive programs to end poverty, enlightened policies against racism and vigorous efforts for world peace. Many professionals and citizens agree on the implied objectives but differ strongly on the means to achieve them. Education, and especially education used as the basis for effective social change, can play a crucial role in reaching agreement on the methods.

Getting people to change values, or to recognize disparity between conditions and ideas, has been the work of the reformer. Organization and provision of services were the task of health and welfare organizations. But each alone can be sterile; they must work together for maximum achievement. In a social action-oriented community organizing effort, a number of major practice issues must be faced. These include: recruiting and retaining members; selecting the most relevant health or social issue; moving the membership as a group; and adjudicating conflicts between short- and long-range objectives.

Two developments which present problems and opportunities for health and welfare organizations of the future are: (1) *Participatory Democracy*—public health officials are being urged to support community control of health institutions as a simple and old-fashioned solution to the problem of health care in the cities. Community control is the thrust in many communities and people are moving in on all institutional services, whether they be education, sanitation, police, welfare, or health; (2) *Advocacy and Social Reform*—an increasing number of professional practitioners strongly sympathize with the movement for social change and are playing a more aggressive leadership role. These developments provide the ingredients for new trends and emphases in the future.

New strategies and techniques are being used in health and welfare to encourage environmental and institutional changes on behalf of the disenfranchised poor (e.g., bargaining, picketing, demonstrations, confrontation, use of power, building democratic skills, protests, therapeutic involvement, issue-oriented pressure on institutions, dialogues). The principal question that must be faced is: Should the worker use these new strategies as the group's leader or negotiator, or should he be a "behind-the-scenes" advisor and teacher? These workers are being subjected to great strains by a group whose major focus is radical change. This is especially true of those social workers whose personal values may not be in tune with emerging separatist sentiment in neighborhood or community groups.

The climate produced by an overwhelming array of social and health problems and developments in methodology and structure has resulted in many new program innovations and emerging ideas in health and welfare. These include:

1. *Alcoholism Control*—Preventive efforts have mainly been centered about educational approaches to young persons in society in an effort, not necessarily to achieve abstinence from alcohol, but rather to encourage moderation in consumption.
2. *Accident Prevention*—An educational program that approaches accidents from several points of view, with efforts directed toward changing behavior associated with accident causation.
3. *Home Nursing Services*—Visiting nursing services (as opposed to full-time care for a bedfast patient) which may involve repeated and frequent calls to the houses of clients for the purpose of administering therapeutic and educational nursing procedures.
4. *Early Detection of Chronic Illness*—Involves both educational and clinical functions aimed at discovering incipient chronic illness by relatively simple and inexpensive clinical tests.
5. *Direct Medical Care Services*—A full program might include clinics, probably for disadvantaged sectors of the population, with free or part-pay medical service.
6. *Family Planning*—Birth control, or family planning, programs containing both clinical and educational features designed to develop public recognition and appreciation of the desirability of some method of family planning. Includes all the social and economic aspects implicit in "planning."
7. *One Social Work Method*—There is a growing recognition there may be little basic distinction between and among the so-called methods of social work practice (i.e., casework, group work, and community organization).
8. *Use of Non-professionals or supporting personnel*—A new army of people has moved into recently created jobs in social welfare and health.
9. *New Planning Structures*—Recognition that a broad frontal attack must be made on social and health problems which will result in new planning structures called planning coalitions. New structures will be built at all geographic levels—local, state, regional, national and international.
10. *International Activities*—At this stage of history, American health and welfare personnel are inevitably concerned with the international aspects of their fields. Many domestic health and social problems are actually phases of international or worldwide conditions that require international approaches.
11. *Information Science*—It is becoming evident that an attempt to

classify the services and activities in health and welfare under any of the existing conventional classification schemes (such as the Dewey, Library of Congress or the Brussels systems) using a hierarchical structure is impractical and ineffective. Nonconventional methods of indexing and informational retrieval offer possible alternatives.
12. *Data Processing*—The field is accepting the increased efficiency of machine systems as a valuable tool for workers and organizations. Computers are proving useful and economical for handling mailing lists, bookkeeping and accounting, fund-raising, case records and research data.
13. *Allied Professions and Fields*—Recent sociological analysis of social and health problems suggests that concentrated attention is in order. The increasing necessity for interdisciplinary research and inter-professional practice forces us to examine our methods and to find ways of meshing our efforts with those of related fields.

Adult education if it is to be effective must be based upon an understanding of significant social and health trends and the nature of the criticism that has been directed at the health and welfare organizations. There are some individuals and groups that feel time is running out on the great problems—war, racial injustice and poverty. John Gardner has pointed out that "the modern belief that man's institutions can accomplish just about anything he wants, when he wants it, leads to certain characteristic contemporary phenomena [6]." He continues by raising some pertinent questions that have implications for adult education in all health and welfare, "all of this leaves us with some crucial and puzzling questions of public policy. How can we make sluggish institutions more responsive to human need and the requirements of change? How can we mobilize the resources to meet the grave crises ahead?"

A basic purpose of adult education, as of education in general, is to help equip the individual with the knowledge, insight, and skills which will enable him to make the wisest decisions in his social, health, economic and political life, as well as to contribute to his personal enrichment. The present tenor of health and welfare is one of advancement to new problems. Ours is not a static society. New needs and problems emerge constantly, and the ideals we seek to achieve, themselves, advance. Thus the new policy, the new program, carries within itself the generative seeds of new aspiration and new adaptations. Education is basic to solving these problems and therefore those responsible for learning activities must also change and adapt.

The challenge and opportunity for voluntary health and welfare agencies is highlighted by the VISTA slogan, "If you're not part of the solution, you're part of the problem."

References

1. Andrews, F. E. *Foundations—20 Viewpoints.* New York: Russell Sage Foundation, 1965.
2. Banfield, Edward C. *Political Influence.* New York: The Free Press, 1961 (paperback, 1965).
3. Council on Social Work Education. *Public Health Concepts in Social Work Education.* Proceedings of Seminar Held at Princeton University, Princeton, New Jersey, March 4–9, 1962. New York: Council on Social Work Education, 1962.
4. Council on Social Work Education. *Personnel in Anti-Poverty Programs: Implications for Social Work Education.* New York: Council on Social Work Education, 1967.
5. *Education for the Allied Health Professions and Services.* Report of the Allied Health Professions Education Committee of the National Advisory Health Council. Public Health Service Publication No. 1600. Washington, D.C.: Government Printing Office.
6. Gardner, John W. *No Easy Victories.* New York: Harper & Row, 1968.
7. Goodman, Paul. *The New York Times Magazine* (July 14, 1968), p. 16.
8. Hoffer, Joe R. "The Large Forum in the Social Welfare System—Planning and Action." *The Social Welfare Forum 1967.* New York: Columbia University Press, 1967, pp. 86–103.
9. Hoffer, Joe R. "The Relationship of Natural and Social Sciences to Social Problems and the Contributions of the Information Scientist to Their Solutions." *American Documentation* XVIII, No. 4 (October, 1967). A reprint of the American Society for Information Service.
10. *Innovation in Local Health Services.* Public Health Service Publication No. 1664-2. Washington, D.C.: Government Printing Office, 1968.
11. Knowles, Malcolm, ed. *Handbook of Adult Education in the United States.* Washington, D.C.: Adult Education Association of the USA, 1960.
12. Lurie, H. L., ed. *Encyclopedia of Social Work* (15th ed.). New York: National Association of Social Workers, 1965.
13. National Association of Social Workers. "Memorandum." New York: National Association of Social Workers, 1968.
14. *N.H.C. Member Organizations.* New York: National Health Council, 1968.
15. National Commission for Social Work Careers. *Manpower—A Community Responsibility.* Annual Review. New York: Arden House Workshop, 1967.
16. Naylor, H. H. *Volunteers Today: Finding, Training and Working with Them.* New York: Association Press, 1967.
17. *Professional and Supporting Personnel.* A reprint from the 1967 Man-

Health and Welfare Agencies 351

power Report, "Social Work" and "Health Manpower." Washington, D.C.: U.S. Department of Labor, Manpower Administration, 1967.
18. *Quality in Health Care.*Vol. 1: *Challenges and Definitions.* Report of the 1968 National Health Forum, Los Angeles, March 15–17. New York: National Health Council, 1968.
19. *Quality in Health Care.* Vol. 2: *Action Proposals and Discussions.* Report of the 1968 National Health Forum, Los Angeles, March 15–17. New York: National Health Council, 1968.
20. *Quality in Health Care.* Vol. 3: *Priorities and Resources.* Report of the 1968 National Health Forum, Los Angeles, March 15–17. New York: National Health Council, 1968.
21. *Report on the Executive Program.* A Program of In-Service Training in Administration and Management for Supervisory Personnel in Boys' Clubs Through the United States. New York: Boys' Clubs of America, 1968.
22. *Selected Bibliographies on Social Welfare.* Columbus, Ohio: National Conference on Social Welfare, 1968.
23. *Social Welfare as a Career.* A Bibliography of Recruiting Materials for Social Welfare Positions. New York: Committee on Personnel, National Social Welfare Assembly, 1966.
24. Stenzel, A. K., and Feeney, H. M. *Volunteer Training and Development: A Manual for Community Groups.* New York: Seabury Press, 1968.
25. *The Changing Voluntary-Governmental Partnership.* New York: United Community Funds and Councils of America, 1965.
26. "The Non-Governmental Organization at Bay." Reprint from the 1966 *Annual Report of Carnegie Corporation.* New York: Carnegie Corporation of New York, 1966.
27. *The Role of Community Health and Welfare Councils.* New York: United Community Funds and Councils of America, 1965.
28. *This Is the NCSW.* Columbus, Ohio: National Conference on Social Welfare, 1968.
29. U.S. Department of Health, Education and Welfare. Public Health Service. *Comprehensive Mental Health Planning in Six States.* Public Health Service Publication No. 1686. Chevy Chase, Md.: National Institute of Mental Health, 1965.
30. *Voluntaryism and Health: The Role of the National Voluntary Health Agency.* New York: National Health Council, 1962.
31. *The Volunteer Board Member in Philanthropy. Some of His Responsibilities, Achievements, and Special Problems.* New York: National Information Bureau, 1968.
32. Woods, D. E. *Adult Education in the YWCA.* Geneva, Switzerland: World YWCA, 1966.

Chapter 21

Religious Institutions

KENNETH STOKES

Religious organizations, apparently, not long ago constituted the largest category of participation in the field of adult education. Precise statistics are not available, but Malcolm S. Knowles estimated that 15,500,000 adults participated in adult educational activities in religious institutions in 1955 [23, p. 251]. *Volunteers for Learning*, a major statistical study of the educational pursuits of adults, estimated that 3,280,000 adults were taking courses in "Religion, morals and ethics" in 1962 [21, p. 49]. This seeming discrepancy comes from the fact that Knowles based his estimate on figures reported by the religious institutions themselves (which undoubtedly included organizations of various degrees of educational, service, and social orientation), while *Volunteers for Learning* projected an estimate for learning experiences in "Religion, morals, and ethics." A more precise figure undoubtedly lies somewhere between these extremes and would be dependent upon the definition of "adult education" employed.

But numbers may be misleading, for Knowles also comments on the development of adult education in religious institutions during the first half of this century with these words:

> The Protestant and Catholic churches, and to a somewhat lesser degree the Jewish temples and synagogues, continued to lag behind many other institutions in the expansion and differentiation of adult education well into the modern era. [23, p. 145]

This is probably a fair generalization, though signs of improvement began to appear in the 1950's and were clearly evident during the 1960's.

To describe adult education in religious institutions, it is necessary to see it in the context of the larger changes taking place in the whole of religious society during recent years. The 1960's were a period of far-reaching reexamination of the role of religion in a changing society. The tremendous membership growth in religious institutions which followed World War II leveled off. Social patterns underwent major change with the development of Sunday shopping habits, the proliferation of opportunities for weekend outings and the increasing affluence to make them possible, and a high mobility that loosened institutional ties. All of these factors contributed to a growing feeling on the part of many persons, particularly young adults, that the church was not keeping pace with the changing culture. As a result, two things happened: there was a lessening of active participation in the nation's religious communities, together with a growing awareness on the part of astute churchmen of the drastic need for many changes in the program and image of the religious institution.

If any word were to symbolize the growing edge of religious thinking in the sixties, it would be *renewal*. The concept of evangelism has taken on new meaning. Less and less the emphasis is on converting the non-churched; more and more the concern is with a renewal and deepening of commitment within the ranks of the vast majority of the population who claim a religious faith, but whose relationship to the church or synagogue is nominal, to say the least.

The activity in civil rights has caused thoughtful churchmen to look with shame at the fact that the hour of religious worship is still, for the most part, the most segregated hour in the week. All over the country, men and women are struggling to reconcile their emotional upbringing and prejudices with what they know to be the valid objective demands of their faith. Progress has been slow, but leadership has been vocal in this area of concern, and renewal is increasingly taking place.

The ecumenical movement grew to significant proportions in the 1960's. Vatican Council II, which brought about sweeping changes in the life of the Roman Catholic Church, has had a profound effect not only upon its own people, but upon all of society. The growing mobility of the population necessitates increasing and more frequent changes of religious affiliation. Less and less do people feel the necessity to hold allegiance to denominational loyalties; more and more they are finding that more than one religious group can fulfill their spiritual needs. Increasingly as people move they relate to new churches in new communities, and another ecumenical step is taken. The renewal of the church manifests itself in many new forms of religious cooperation.

Finally, because of the changes taking place in the religious community, there has been an increased desire on the part of many to rethink the basic tenets of their faith. Renewal has spawned a new interest in theology—not just the reiteration of traditional formulations, but rather a grappling with the meaning of faith itself in the contemporary culture.

It is in the context of these sweeping changes in the religious community that adult education has played a significant role. But, it is not the traditional adult education one usually associates with religion—sermonizing, indoctrination, rigid formulizations. Rather, a new adult participation is manifesting itself in countless forms. The renewal of religion takes a forward step when a Sunday morning class looks up from its lesson book to discuss, and subsequently to act upon, a problem in its own community. The renewal of religion is seen in small groups of men meeting at 6:00 A.M. for breakfast and discussion of their common spiritual problems. The renewal of religion takes place through the increasing use of weekend retreats, lay schools of theology, study groups in homes and factories as well as churches and synagogues, and coffee houses where folk music and table talk provide the evening's major program.

The marked change that appeared in many religious institutions of the 1960's came about because the people began talking together—about their faith and their personal problems and their corporate problems—and then began taking action. Adult education, therefore, plays an important role in religion today. However, the generalizations made here take different forms in the major religious communities.

Judaism

Adult education has been an important part of the Jewish tradition dating back to biblical times. Knowledge of the Torah was of utmost importance to even moderately well-educated Jews throughout history. But it was not until after World War II that adult education came to be recognized as a clearly defined discipline within the overall program of Jewish education.

Dr. Samuel I. Cohen, who made a major study of adult Jewish education [7], sees this growing awareness of adult education within Judaism as stemming from the new role of the American Jew:

> By the end of World War II, it was apparent that a major upheaval had taken place in American Jewish life. This period marked the turning point in the whole pattern of American Jewish education. The decade that witnessed the destruction of 6,000,000 Jews in the Nazi holocaust and the subsequent

establishment of the State of Israel witnessed also widespread uninhibited Jewish identification, record synagogue enrollments, and increased interest in Jewish education on all levels. The decade and a half, 1940–1956, has been described as the period of "Jewish revival" in this country.

On the adult level there were increasing numbers of people seeking guidance and resources to help them to better accept their Jewishness, to participate in the affairs of the Jewish community, and to find self-fulfillment in their Judaism. By the early 1950's, it was obvious that adult Jewish education was coming to the fore as an important new development in the American Jewish community. [8]

In 1964, the American Association for Jewish Education conducted a major national study on adult Jewish education; this culminated in the First National Conference on Adult Jewish Education in February, 1965. This study surveyed not only the three major synagogue groups of Judaism, but also major national mass-membership Jewish organizations, such as the American Jewish Committee, American Jewish Congress, B'nai B'rith and Hadassah, all of which utilize adult education in their programs [36].

The 1964 survey revealed wide variations of objectives, content and methodologies. Much Jewish adult education still held to a strong emphasis on Jewish tradition, but increasingly this emphasis was seen in the context of a positive reaffirmation of Jewish consciousness within the culture of the times. Julius Schatz of the American Jewish Congress described the contemporary Jewish stance as being "a secular curiosity in the validity of religious experience." The study also indicated that, despite the growing interest in adult education and the proliferation of activities, there were still widely diverse educational objectives underlying the programs. There appeared to be no accepted "adult Jewish educational methods," per se, but the more formalized lectures and courses of the past were giving way to forums, discussion groups and more informal patterns of presentation. For the most part, the study revealed most educational leadership to be provided by rabbis, although the lay educator role has begun to emerge increasingly since the study was completed and the national conference was held.

Many individual synagogues, particularly in affluent communities and near institutions of higher learning, have developed extensive adult education programs, some involving professional full- and part-time teachers. The courses run the gamut from biblical history and Yiddish to the problems of minorities in contemporary society.

It is obvious adult education is playing an increasingly important role in the life of the Jewish community. Its major theme extends in two directions—both vitally important to the Jew—outward to an increased understanding of an involvement in the crucial issues of American culture, and inward to reaffirm a definition of Jewish identity within the larger culture.

Roman Catholicism

The Roman Catholic Church's focal point throughout its existence has been the liturgy of the Mass. Until recent years, the doctrines of the Church were clearly defined and relatively unquestioned. The educational program of the Church, for the most part, was concerned primarily with the training of children in the parochial school system. Because of this educational structure, adult education played a relatively small role in the life of the Church, except as Inquirer's Classes were held for those adults wishing to know more about Roman Catholicism.

However, with the increasing mobility of population, the upswing in interfaith marriages, the emerging ecumenical movement and, above all, the tremendous influence of Vatican Council II on Roman Catholic thought and practice, adult education is rapidly becoming vital and significant in the life of the Church. Vaile Scott writes:

> Vatican II has undoubtedly been the primary motivating force for much of the interest in Catholic adult education. The Council itself was, in a sense, a large scale adult education program, and for many it has become the prototype for future Catholic adult education programs. [40, p. 4]

In the realm of theology, the trend has been away from traditional scholasticism to a more biblical approach, which, in turn, seeks to find its place within the context of existential philosophy. An increasing concern with social issues and the "secular society" has marked the trend. In liturgics, the increasing use of the vernacular and the involvement of the laity in the Mass have stimulated lay interest in a better understanding of the experience; and from this need has grown a significant opportunity for adult education which is being fulfilled in parishes across the country.

With Roman Catholic elementary and secondary education moving increasingly away from parochial schools and into public schools, a greater religious educational burden is being placed on parents. For this reason, parent education is fast becoming an important element of the adult education of many parishes.

In terms of method, more and more the traditional lecture is giving way to a variety of informal types of discussions, short courses, and small group activities, including experimentation with different forms of sensitivity training. The retreat has always been an important part of Roman

Catholic devotional life, but primarily for the clergy and the members of religious orders. Now, lay retreats are finding increasing favor and utilization as opportunities for reflection and discussion of personal faith in a changing time.

Although much Roman Catholic adult education is taking place in the local parish, an impressive new direction in this field is seen in the development of diocesan adult education centers in such major cities as Chicago, Detroit, Baltimore, Los Angeles and San Francisco. The tightly knit organizational structure of the diocese within the Roman Catholic system makes such a community-wide program readily workable. A glance at one of the more successful centers gives an idea of the types of activities.

The Catholic Adult Education Center in Chicago (CAEC) was founded in 1955 as an experiment in continuing liberal education for adults with special concern for issues related to faith and belief. In the first year, five adult centers were established throughout the city (usually in parochial schools) and approximately 1000 persons participated. By its 11th year, the CAEC was reaching over 2500 people through 12 centers. Courses have included everything from "The Bible" to "Insights from Modern Psychology," from "Great Issues in Education" to "The Negro in America" and "The Crisis in Public Morality." These courses are scheduled for periods of 8 to 10 weeks in the fall, winter, and spring. During the summer, extended institutes for clergy and laity are held. The program of the Catholic Adult Education Center is enhanced by the appearance of speakers of national stature from widely diverse fields of specialization. By utilizing the resources of the entire diocese and staffing the Center with full-time professionals to develop, organize, and oversee the total program, CAEC provides a significant opportunity for high caliber adult education to thousands of people who would not have these opportunities within the context of their local parish [40].

Roman Catholic adult education is just beginning to emerge as a significant aspect of the life of the Church. There is no doubt that it will play an increasingly important role in the years ahead.

Eastern Orthodoxy

Father Ernest A. Villas, the director of the Department of the Laity of the Greek Archdiocese of North and South America, summarizes the place of adult education in his Church succinctly:

The term "adult education" is a relatively new phrase, new concept and new concern for the educational program of the contemporary Orthodox

Church. In Orthodox circles the term "education" is usually equated with the younger generation. . . . Rarely is education conceived as an ongoing process that begins in the early years and continues on into later life.

Yet our need for education never stops. The growing realization of this by industry, science and the arts is evidenced by an increasing trend toward adult education programs, a trend which the Church cannot afford to overlook. [15, p. 6]

With the establishment of the Department of the Laity in 1961, there began to emerge the first concepts of an ongoing program of adult education in American Eastern Orthodoxy. A preliminary concern has been to provide programs of basic religious education to second and third generation members who were deprived of adequate religious education in their childhood due to the relative scarcity of churches in the "new country." For the most part, content and methodology have been of the traditional mold, but increasingly new forms are being tried. A new form which has been quite successful is the Church Family Conference, many of which are being held regionally throughout the Church. In these conferences, parents and children participate in a one-day session which includes worship and study (together) related to the faith and meaning of Orthodoxy.

Ten years ago, little could be reported concerning adult education in the Eastern Orthodox Church. However, clearly defined indications of a significant program can now be seen.

Protestantism

Adult education in the Protestant perspective is more diverse than in other religious groups. With more than 200 denominations, each with its own particular theological emphasis and educational philosophy, Protestant adult education reveals no single pattern of adult educational activity. However, certain examples can be described which, taken as a whole, give something of a cross section.

Much of Protestant adult education programming during the years from the 1930's into the 1950's, when adult education as a relatively clearly defined discipline was in its infancy, was done interdenominationally. Activities in the thirties and forties tended to stem from the International Uniform Lesson Series and the United Christian Adult Movement, both interdenominational. By the time of the formation of the National Council of Churches in 1950, most of the major denominations had organized staffs of specialists in adult education who, increasingly, did their own research, writing and programming, with decreasing emphasis on interdenominational planning.

In the 1950's and 1960's, interdenominational efforts focused increasingly on the provision of resources to undergird the denominational programming. Interdenominational Strategy Conferences were held during this period. They were sponsored by the National Council and dealt with such topics as "Christian Parenthood," "Young Adults," "The Aging," "Education and Vocation," "Use of Radio and Television" and "Controversy and Conflict." To these conferences came adult educators from many denominations, and on the basis of the insights gained they developed program materials for their respective denominations.

In the 1960's, adult education began to be perceived less as an age-group division in religious education and more as a means by which the renewal of the church might take place. During this period a rebirth of interest in theology occurred in many Protestant churches. It was not the traditional biblicism of personal piety as much as a search for the link between the divine and the secular, between the Christian message and the ugliness of much of our "Christian culture," between God and man increasingly estranged. The "God is dead" theology which emerged in the sixties never really captured the allegiance of most Protestants, but it stimulated a new concern for the reconstruction of a more meaningful theology. Books like *Honest to God* by John Robinson, *The Secular City* by Harvey Cox and *The Christian Agnostic* by Leslie Weatherhead shattered many of the traditional images of the church and, increasingly, Protestants find themselves grappling with the implications of a new approach to faith.

More and more this encounter is taking place through small groups. Although ministers continue to preach sermons, they are finding these sermons discussed in "talk-back" sessions or seminar groups over coffee after the service. "Dialogue," "engagement" and "encounter" are becoming word-symbols of the new philosophy of contemporary religious adult educators. Churchmen are finding much in the behavioral sciences that is relevant to the search for spiritual meaning, and the works of Fromm, Howe, Maslow, Allport and Erikson are utilized increasingly as bases for discussions in the church. Sensitivity training and the expanding understandings of group dynamics give a new dimension to religious study groups as, more and more, groups organized around interpersonal experience, in contrast to pure content, play an important role in the church. Many churches sponsor "T groups" or "growth groups" and regard them as significant parts of their programs of adult education. Technology is also having its impact on the educational program for adults. Films and filmstrips, recordings and even television tapes are being utilized.

For the most part, much of the pioneering in new forms of adult

Religious Institutions

education in the churches is taking place in the local church where a creative ministry and laity are combining their efforts to develop programs which speak to the needs of the times. Some examples of such activities will be discussed shortly. Before that, however, it should be noted that denominational boards of education, long tied to traditional forms, have begun to develop new kinds of programs, and to publish new materials which seek to breathe relevance and renewal into the life of the church.

The United Methodist Church, for years a leader in the field of adult education among the major denominations, has, for example, recently developed a new series of books for adult study focusing on the contemporary meaning of religion. One of these books, *Man's Search for a Meaningful Faith* by Robert C. Leslie, is based on Erik Erikson's concept of the stages of man's life—a concept drawn from the field of psychology. Leslie uses illustrative material from everywhere—cartoons from the *Saturday Review*, quotations from the Broadway play *J.B.*, some of Dylan Thomas' poetry, Betty Friedan's *The Feminine Mystique*, and an occasional *Peanuts* cartoon.

The Lutheran Church–Missouri Synod offers a variety of study opportunities ranging from pure Bible study to such topics as "Population Growth" and "Teenagers Need Parents."

The United Presbyterian Church, USA, has developed a new series of paperback adult study materials, Decade Books, for "the person who finds that his childhood church school education isn't sufficient for today's questions of faith."

The United Church of Christ has combined its program for men's and women's groups into a new form which emphasizes the total role of the laity in the church, in effect replacing the traditional organizations. *Lay Life and Work*, as it is called, seeks to stress the concerns in the world of lay people and develop programs designed for day-to-day living.

These examples could be duplicated several score times in describing new programs and materials being developed in other denominations. Some are mentioned to give an idea of new developments at the national denominational level.

But perhaps even more exciting are the new forms of adult education activity taking place in the local church. Hundreds of churches of many denominations around the country have developed and continue to experiment with a variety of forms for adult involvement in the process of learning and doing. Four examples are cited—almost at random—as indicative of the kind of adult education taking place in these churches.

Seminars on Wheels

Since about 300 members of First Congregational Church in Chappaqua, New York, commute daily to their respective offices in downtown Manhattan, 35 miles away, arrangements have been made with the New York Central Railroad for a special car to be added to the end of the 7:05 A.M. limited on certain Monday mornings. Men of the church, and anyone else who is interested, gather in that car for discussion of the previous morning's sermon. By turning over alternate seats in the coach, small groupings of four men can be arranged for easy conversation. Such topics as "The Triangle of Job, Religion, and Me" and "Business Ethics" have been explored and well received. The Seminar on Wheels imaginatively utilizes a previously untapped period of time for a unique kind of adult learning activity [34, p. 26].

The Potter's House

Sponsored by the Church of the Saviour in Washington, D.C., the Potter's House is a coffee house with a purpose. At its tables almost any evening of the week sit all kinds of men and women—artists, businessmen, politicians, beatniks and sophisticates, Ph.D.'s and plumbers. Many of them carry on animated conversations trying to outdo others with their talk; some seldom speak; others listen and then respond. Underlying the varieties of personal viewpoint is a sense of community set up by the spirit of the Potter's House fellowship. The image of the potter is biblical, referring to him who shapes the clay with his hands into cups, vases and works of art. Similarly, according to the Rule of the Potter's House, "Your life is to be so yielded to the hand of the Potter that you shall be to those who gather in the Potter's House the bearer of this message, a witness to God's redeeming love in Jesus Christ [35]." For many Washington residents—and visitors from all over the country—the Potter's House, with its opportunity for meaningful dialogue and conversation with a purpose, *is* the church, and its coffee tables are the pews.

The Church Without a Building

When Presbyterians in North Burlington, Vermont, were invited to begin a new church in that community in 1955, the usual patterns were expected—the construction of a building and the development of a typical church program. However, the people of the church took another course. First, adult membership classes, running the gamut of personal and corporate interests, grappled over a six-month period with the fundamental question: "What is a church?" There followed planned and disciplined study of the Bible and of ethical questions pertaining

Religious Institutions

to vocation. As the people became more open toward one another, they found in their small groups a mutual ministry of support and love. But, they also moved out into the community. Some of the men of the church visited inmates in the jail; some of the women got to know girls in the home for unwed mothers. They started a coffee house; they became involved in the problems of the slums. They've been so busy over these years *being* the church that they still haven't had the time to *build* a building [19].

"On Stage" Learning

In San Lorenzo, California, the people of the Episcopal Church of St. Christopher enjoy reading plays; they find meaning in discussing the implications of these plays. A group in the church meets monthly for a play-reading followed by discussion. After "living the parts" for an hour or two, the group members explore the play's implications. There is a camaraderie which makes discussion of life's sensitive, yet fundamental, problems come more easily. Careful selection of plays is important, of course. The people of St. Christopher have found new meaning in their faith through the medium of the drama [19].

The four examples cited above *are* unusual, although they are representative of the experimentation that is taking place. Countless local Protestant churches have moved away from the traditional adult class into new forms of adult learning, and countless others have retained the traditional class, but revitalized their adult Sunday school programs with new materials and techniques. In the reference section at the end of this chapter several volumes are listed which tell some more of these stories [3; 4; 19; 34; 35; 37].

Religion in a Larger Context

Adult education has been explored here primarily as it is found in the context of the nation's four major religious groups. But much that is happening lies outside the local synagogue, parish or church. Much of it involves members of several religious communities. The few examples are of experiments in which the religious communities are in dialogue with each other and/or with the world at large.

The Ecumenical Movement

There is a new spirit of conversation among the various religious groups. A prime example of this is seen in the development of "Living Room Dialogues."

Living Room Dialogues are an effort to give direction to a spontaneous grass-roots desire among many lay people to become involved in the ecumenical movement at the point of discussion or conversation about religious issues related to Christian unity. They are small, informal groups of Christian lay people meeting together in homes (usually once a month for a period of 6–8 months). Wherever possible, representatives of Orthodox, Roman Catholic, and several Protestant groups are involved. Normally, there is no clergy present, for much of the value of the program stems from its lay character. These groups follow a guidebook, prepared jointly by the Paulist Press and the National Council of Churches, which presents resource material for seven dialogues:

1. Concern, Prayer, Love: Foundation for Dialogue
2. Good Conversation in Christ
3. How Do We Worship?
4. Our Common Christian Heritage
5. Renewal of God's People
6. Our Common Christian Witness
7. Why We Don't Break Bread Together

The experience of persons participating in Living Room Dialogues has resulted in new insights into the traditions of others, the elimination of false stereotypes, and openness to cooperation and understanding between Christian groups. Many Dialogue groups continue beyond the structured sessions and explore other areas of concern [13].

The Consultation on Church Union (COCU), a clearly defined program of exploration of realistic possibilities for church unity, has been gathering impetus. Although COCU is still basically in the planning stage at this writing, many of the progress reports of this endeavor are being studied, discussed and evaluated in the local churches and interdenominational study groups across the nation. The United Presbyterian Church, USA, has developed a study and action project with representatives of the Jewish community known as "Encounter for Reconciliation" which provides opportunity for exploring the differences of faith and practice of these and other groups.

The Ecumenical Movement has been strengthened greatly by the openness of most religious bodies to new relationships, and adult education has had an important role in this process.

Religion and Secular Society

American society has been undergoing profound changes. The issues of civil rights, the impact of automation, the problems of affluence and poverty have been "front page" concerns and, because of their

Religious Institutions

moral and ethical overtones, they have become priority concerns for members of the religious communities also. Religious adult education increasingly has sought to relate the fundamentals of faith and belief to the problems of the day-to-day world, and where renewal in the church is perceived, much of it is due to this new relevance to the times.

The *Report of the National Advisory Commission on Civil Disorders* (the Kerner Report), issued in 1968, has probably been studied and discussed in churches more than any other secular publication in history. A group of American Baptist churches in Santa Monica, California, for example, grappled with the issues of this report, and from their discussions came the development of an interracial day camp, youth retreats and adult seminar programs which have markedly strengthened their community relationships.

Nearly all the major religious bodies have prepared and made available study guides and program material on the problems of racism in our society. The American Jewish Congress provides numerous pamphlets and study guides designed to help the participants better understand the nature of prejudice. Many Protestant denominations have social action agencies (by one name or another) which promote discussion and action in this area. The Southern Baptist Convention, with its major constituency in the South, has prepared a hard-hitting study on the problems of civil rights that is being used for frank discussion by concerned church members [43]. The programs of many Roman Catholic adult education centers also deal with these issues.

Much of the encounter between religion and society takes place outside the walls of the church. A good example is the Detroit Industrial Mission which seeks to stimulate discussion of significant issues in groups of men and women involved in industry in management offices, on the assembly line, in the engineering laboratories, at the union hall and in the executive dining room. Often members of an individual church or several churches in similar vocations are gathered together, with the help of the staff members of the Detroit Industrial Mission, to talk about their problems on the job. Other programs involve representatives of management, technology, and labor in common discussion not just about the problems of industry and business, but about the relationship of their personal faith to their daily work [3].

Many churches take action concerning a community problem and contribute to adult education by sponsoring literacy classes. Volunteer teachers in Methodist churches use the Laubach system ("each one teach one") to tutor illiterates. In Tallahassee, Florida, church leadership has guided a program called Volunteers for Basic Education for Adults. A very large literacy program in Mississippi stems from the efforts of the Church Women United.

Increasingly, churchmen are relating themselves to centers of continuing education which are not religiously oriented in the traditional sense. One such center is the Esalen Institute in California, which seeks to "explore those trends in the behavioral sciences, religion and philosophy which emphasize the potentialities of human existence." Esalen conducts a year-long program of seminars and human relations laboratories on a wide variety of topics. Those participating often find their religious attitudes enriched and broadened [39].

Continuing Education for Laity and Clergy

Various types of lay schools of theology emerged in the 1960's primarily in theological seminaries. These programs are usually of one- or two-weeks duration and held during the summer. Lay people find in such experiences a vital opportunity to work with the same professors, books and ideas their clergymen know and are guided by. Many laymen indicate the lay schools have been experiences of major importance in their lives. In addition to seminaries, some large churches and synagogues (and dioceses and other clusters of churches and synagogues) sponsor lay schools.

Most of what has been written here has focused on the adult educational experiences of laymen. Opportunities for the continuing education of the clergy have also developed rapidly. Many of the major theological seminaries sponsor programs in which clergymen return to the campus for reading and intensive dialogue with members of the faculty for periods of from two to fifteen weeks. Another type of continuing education is illustrated by the Institute for Advanced Pastoral Studies in Bloomfield Hills, Michigan—a center for pioneering in communication and continuing education with special emphasis on church leadership. This center has developed a creative approach to help clergymen cope with the unique problems of the ministry in American culture.

Training Adult Educators

A prime example of a program for training voluntary and professional religious adult educators is the Indiana Plan, so named because of its development at Indiana University [2]. The Plan emphasizes changing adult behavior through group learning activities designed and conducted by the learners themselves. Since its inception in the mid-1950's, over 250 Indiana Plan Institutes have been held throughout the United States, involving thousands of adult educators in intensive training. The Episcopal Church and the Disciples of Christ have adopted the

Indiana Plan as an official part of their adult education programs. Many other Protestant denominations and the Roman Catholic Church have utilized its insights and approach in much of their educational programming. The Indiana Plan is viewed by many adult religious educators as probably the most valid approach to adult education in the religious perspective to have been developed to date.

Most of the leadership for adult religious education has come from clergymen whose graduate training has been primarily in the seminary and from laymen whose professional training has come from a variety of sources. Relatively few persons of professional religious orientation have completed graduate degrees in adult education. A survey of research projects completed and some 600 doctorates received in adult education through 1966, as reported yearly in *Adult Education,* uncovered fewer than 30 persons clearly identifiable as professionally oriented to religion and adult education. (Obviously some persons with such orientation may have pursued research or be in positions not so designated.) It is true the number of such persons has been increasing in recent years; however, this is due in large part to the funds made available by the Lilly Foundation for the pursuit of degree programs in adult education at Indiana University for those of professional religious orientation. Approximately half the doctorates in adult education granted at Indiana University in the 1960's were earned by churchmen. But, considering the number of persons involved in adult education in religious institutions, there is still a paucity of trained leadership at the professional and scholarly level. Only a few large local churches and synagogues have engaged staff persons with full-time responsibility for adult education.

Summary

Adult education in religious organizations took on many new and diverse forms in the 1960's, many of them unheard of, or certainly not considered applicable to the religious community a decade before. Today the rapidly expanding role of the laity in religion is playing an important part in the development of still other new patterns. There is much evidence to indicate that the maturing of the adult education movement in America and the new openness to change which has recently characterized religious bodies have come into confluence. And there is a new enthusiasm and confidence that adult education will continue to play an important role in the renewal of the church which is so important and necessary to the American culture.

References

1. Anderson, Philip A. *Church Meetings That Matter.* Philadelphia, Pa.: United Church Press, 1965.
2. Bergevin, Paul, and McKinley, John. *Design for Adult Education in the Church.* New York: Seabury Press, 1958.
3. Casteel, John L., ed. *The Creative Role of Interpersonal Groups in the Church Today.* New York: Association Press, 1968.
4. Casteel, John L. *Spiritual Power Through Personal Groups.* New York: Association Press, 1957.
5. Clemmons, Robert S. *Dynamics of Christian Adult Education.* Nashville, Tenn.: Abingdon Press, 1958.
6. Cohen, Samuel I. "Adult Jewish Education." *American Jewish Yearbook,* LXVI (1965).
7. Cohen, Samuel I. "History of Adult Jewish Education in Four National Jewish Organizations." Unpublished doctoral thesis. New York: Yeshiva University, 1967.
8. Cohen, Samuel I. "Organizational Adult Jewish Education." *Adult Leadership,* XVII (May, 1968), p. 24.
9. Deffner, Donald Louis. "The Church's Role in Adult Education." Unpublished doctoral dissertation. Berkeley, Calif.: University of California, 1957.
10. Ernsberger, David J. *Education for Renewal.* Philadelphia, Pa.: Westminster Press, 1965.
11. Ernsberger, David J. *A Philosophy of Adult Christian Education.* Philadelphia, Pa.: Westminster Press, 1959.
12. Fry, John R. *A Hard Look at Adult Christian Education.* Philadelphia, Pa.: Westminster Press, 1961.
13. Greenspun, William B., and Norgren, William A. *Living Room Dialogues.* Glen Rock, N.J.: National Council of the Churches of Christ in the USA, and Paramus, N.J.: Paulist Press, 1965.
14. *Guide to Select Adult Jewish Educational Materials, A Resource for Adult Jewish Education Leaders.* New York: American Association for Jewish Education, and National Council on Adult Jewish Education, 1966.
15. *Guidebook to a Program of Adult Education in the Greek Orthodox Church.* New York: Greek Orthodox Archdiocese of North and South America, Department of the Laity, 1967.
16. Havighurst, Robert J. *The Educational Mission of the Church.* Philadelphia, Pa.: Westminster Press, 1965.
17. *How You Can Conduct a Small Leadership Group: A Christopher Handbook.* New York: The Christophers, 1961.
18. Howe, Reuel L. *The Miracle of Dialogue.* New York: Seabury Press, 1963.
19. *It's a Great Time to Be a Christian: Experience and Experiments with Parish Programs of Lay Christian Education.* New York: Seabury Press, 1968.
20. Janowsky, Oscar I. "Adult Jewish Education—Analysis of a Survey."

Address delivered at the First National Conference on Adult Jewish Education, New York (February 28, 1965).
21. Johnstone, John W. C., and Rivera, Ramon J. *Volunteers for Learning: A Study of the Educational Pursuits of American Adults.* Chicago, Ill.: Aldine, 1965.
22. Khoobyar, Helen. *Facing Adult Problems in Christian Education.* Philadelphia, Pa.: Westminster Press, 1963.
23. Knowles, Malcolm S. *The Adult Education Movement in the United States.* New York: Holt, Rinehart & Winston, 1962.
24. Koenig, Robert E. *The Use of the Bible with Adults.* Philadelphia, Pa.: Christian Education Press, 1959.
25. Little, Lawrence C. *A Bibliography of Doctoral Dissertations on Adults and Adult Education* (revised). Pittsburgh, Pa.: University of Pittsburgh Press, 1963.
26. Little, Lawrence C. *The Future Course of Christian Adult Education.* Pittsburgh: University of Pittsburgh Press, 1959.
27. Little, Lawrence C., ed. *Guidelines for the Development of Christian Education Curricula for Adults.* Pittsburgh, Pa.: University of Pittsburgh Press, 1961.
28. Little, Lawrence C. "Some Recent Research Contributions Toward Our Understanding of Religious Adult Education." *Adult Leadership,* XIII (March, 1965), p. 272.
29. Little, Lawrence C. *Wider Horizons in Christian Adult Education.* Pittsburgh, Pa.: University of Pittsburgh Press, 1962.
30. Maves, Paul B. "The Christian Education of Adults." In: *Religious Education: A Comprehensive Survey.* Edited by Marvin J. Taylor. Nashville, Tenn.: Abingdon Press, pp. 132–142.
31. Maves, Paul B. *Understanding Ourselves as Adults.* Nashville, Tenn.: Abingdon Press, 1959.
32. McCune, Shirley D., and Mills, Edgar W. *Continuing Education for Ministers: A Pilot Evaluation of Three Programs.* Washington, D.C.: National Council of the Churches of Christ, 1968.
33. McKinley, John. *Creative Methods for Adult Classes.* St. Louis, Mo.: Bethany Press, 1960.
34. McLane, Edwin D. *The 7:05 and the Church Alive: Dynamic and Successful Programs in Today's Churches.* Englewood Cliffs, N.J.: Prentice-Hall, 1963.
35. O'Connor, Elizabeth. *Call to Commitment.* New York: Harper & Row, 1963.
36. *Proceedings. National Conference on Adult Jewish Education. February 28, 1965. New York City. A Summary Report.* New York: American Association for Jewish Education, 1965.
37. Raines, Robert A. *New Life in the Church.* New York: Harper & Row, 1961.
38. Reinhart, Bruce. *The Institutional Nature of Adult Christian Education.* Philadelphia, Pa.: Westminster Press, 1962.

39. Schutz, William C. *Joy: Expanding Human Awareness.* New York: Grove Press, 1967.
40. Scott, Vaile. *Adult Education: A Proposal for Catholic Education.* Oak Park, Ill.: Privately published, 1968.
41. Stokes, Kenneth Irving. "Major Trends in Cooperative Protestant Adult Education." Unpublished doctoral dissertation. Chicago, Ill.: University of Chicago, 1965.
42. Thorp, Nathan D. "Programming for Adult Religious Education." *Adult Leadership,* XVII (November, 1968), pp. 217–220.
43. *We Hold These Truths. . . .* Nashville, Tenn.: Sunday School Board of the Southern Baptist Convention, 1968.
44. Zeigler, Earl F. *Christian Education of Adults.* Philadelphia, Pa.: Westminster Press, 1958.

Chapter 22

Some Other Institutions

H. MASON ATWOOD

The examination of adult education programs according to their institutional sponsorship obviously poses a number of problems in classification. Most institutions that provide learning experiences for adults do so in more than one of the program areas described in Part III. At the same time, no program area is the responsibility of only one institution. It should also be noted that even the institutions treated in Part II are not discrete units (e.g., a large part of the Cooperative Extension Service is in universities, as are some programs of labor education). All told, then, many widely varied institutions are involved in the provision of adult educational programs. As William S. Griffith observed earlier, they are referred to as adult education institutions although very few have been established for, or have as their primary purpose, adult education. Much information is available about some of the institutions. Generally, these are the subjects of the preceding chapters.

Prominent among the "other institutions" are the correctional institutions. Because of the extent of their programs, the number of adults involved, and the magnitude of the social problem with which they deal, correctional institutions will be discussed in some detail. Hospitals—general, special and mental—have significant concerns in the area of adult education. In addition, there are the proprietary schools and the independent and residential schools. All these institutions and their adult educational programs will be examined, however briefly.

There are several populations that make up the clientele of most institutions. It seems safe to say that all institutions provide educational activities for their own personnel—employees, staff, volunteers. Such activities usually come under the heading of in-service education. In addition most institutions exist to serve certain well-defined groups of persons—students in schools and colleges, patrons of libraries, members of churches and labor unions. A major function of the institution may be to provide educational programs for these groups. For some institutions there also are external populations toward whom educational efforts are directed. These may include the public at large or particular publics.

Correctional Institutions

Within America's vast criminal justice system the term "corrections" has reference to all prisons, reformatories, jails, workhouses, penal farms, and so on; to juvenile training schools and detention centers; and to the probation and parole machinery. In a narrower sense, "correctional institutions" are those congregate living arrangements in which about one-third of the corrections population is incarcerated.

Scope and Purpose of Correctional Education

It has been said that the primary goal of corrections is just that—correction—and that in modern correctional institutions there is a major commitment to rehabilitation [12, p. 42]. Within the total area of rehabilitation or treatment, education has been assigned a major role and, since 85 percent of the incarcerated offenders are adults, the correctional institution is a major adult education agency.

However, rehabilitation of the incarcerated offender has not always been accepted as the most important purpose of penal institutions; even today its acceptance, in many instances, is more in theory than in practice. Not many persons today subscribe to William Paley's eighteenth-century theory that confining the criminal in a separate compartment "is calculated to raise up in him reflections on the folly of his choice and to expose his mind to such bitter and continued penitence (hence 'penitentiary') as may produce a lasting alteration in the principles of his conduct [25, p. 258]." There remains, however, the widely held conviction that confinement, punishment and retribution are the major concerns of penal institutions. The following statement from the report of the President's Commission on Law Enforcement and Administration of Justice confirms this observation: "The most striking fact about correctional apparatus today is that, although rehabilitation of criminals is presumably its major purpose, the custody of criminals is actually its major task [27, p. 12]."

Data concerning offenders may be confusing in regard to classification. Also each survey or study has certain limitations, e.g., the National Council on Crime and Delinquency's survey did not include federal agencies [22]. Nevertheless, the report of the President's Commission bolstered by the NCCD survey, furnishes more reliable statistics, as of 1965, then had previously been available [27]. The information makes the nature and scope of adult education needs in this institutional setting quite clear.

The Clientele for Correctional Education

In 1965, the average number of offenders under correctional authority was about 1.3 million. (Projections show an expected increase of more than half a million by 1975.) Two-thirds of the total number were "community based"—that is, they were on probation or parole. Of the more than 425,000 incarcerated offenders, about one-sixth were in institutions primarily for juveniles. Nearly 363,000 were adult prisoners. Add to these numbers the more than 121,000 people employed in corrections, for whom in-service education is extremely important, and the task for adult education becomes even more formidable. In 1965, less than 20 percent of the corrections personnel had treatment and rehabilitation as their primary function, and nearly two-thirds of them were probation and parole officers in the community. The others were educators, social workers, psychologists, and psychiatrists in the institutions. The remaining 80 percent of correctional manpower had major responsibilities for custody and maintenance.

The Characteristics of Offenders

Although there are great differences among offenders, they exhibit certain predominant characteristics. A great majority are male, most are between 16 and 30 years of age, and they are severely handicapped educationally. Many have dropped out of school. They tend to have unstable work records and a lack of vocational skill. For one reason or another the typical offender has been the victim of material failure in a society which places a high premium on material success and he has little self-esteem. In fact, he has been described by some authors as a double failure for he has not been successful even in his criminal activity.

Commitment to prison, in most cases, symbolizes the double failure of the prisoner. For the more than 90 percent whose crimes were the taking of someone else's money or property, recourse to crime implies some failure in the satisfaction of materialistic desires by legitimate means. Subsequently, commitment to prison indicates failure in crime also. [8, p. 263]

It is a commonplace of correction practitioners that these offenders as a group are not merely vocationally incompetent. They are criminally incompetent too. The evidence lies, of course, in the fact that they were caught, convicted, and committed. [12, p. 6]

The level of formal education is much lower among correctional institution inmates than in the general population, according to figures reported for 1965. About 55 percent of the federal and state felony inmates had completed no more than eight years of school and less than 17 percent were high school graduates. These figures for the general population were 34 percent and about 45 percent, respectively.

As concerns the previous work experience of male federal and state felony inmates (correctional institution population is 95 percent male), nearly one-third were laborers, a category that accounts for about 11 percent of the general labor force. The categories of "service workers, including household" and "operatives" accounted for somewhat higher percentages of inmates than of persons in the general labor force.

Correctional Education

Nearly forty years ago, Austin MacCormick pointed out that "education of prisoners is fundamentally a problem of adult education" and that "the penal institution should make use of all that is known about the education of adults [17, p. 9]." He listed six "facts" to be emphasized in formulating an aim and philosophy for prison education. They are not much different than admonitions currently expressed. In abbreviated form his facts were:

1. We must not expect too much in the way of quality or quantity production.
2. We must not assume that programs and routine in and of themselves are accomplishment.
3. Education for prisoners must be individualized.
4. Education for prisoners must be "adultized." They are adults, with adult interests, concepts, and experiences.
5. Education for prisoners must be broadly inclusive in its offerings.
6. Compulsion should be applied sparingly.

MacCormick suggested the following aim of education for adult prisoners:

Some Other Institutions

> Its aim is to extend to prisoners as individuals every type of educational opportunity that experience or sound reasoning shows may be of benefit or of interest to them, in the hope that they may thereby be fitted to live more competently, satisfyingly, and cooperatively as members of society. [17, pp. 11–12]

The types of educational opportunity recommended by MacCormick were fundamental academic education, vocational education, health education, cultural education and social education. With varying degrees of emphasis, more recent recommendations for prison education appear to echo MacCormick's thinking.

The President's Commission on Law Enforcement and Administration of Justice makes the following recommendation:

> Correctional institutions should upgrade educational and vocational training programs, extending them to all inmates who can profit from them. They should experiment with special techniques such as programmed instruction. [27, p. 175]

The last part of the recommendation is new, of course. Programmed instruction was not in vogue in 1931, but MacCormick did advocate using "every type of educational opportunity that experience or sound reasoning shows may be of benefit."

Most suggestions for education in correctional institutions emphasize vocational training although in this regard Daniel Glaser adds the following:

> It should be stressed that employment opportunities promoted by education do not come exclusively from vocational training. Linguistic and mathematical facility from more purely academic education may also enhance a man's performance at many jobs. [8, p. 279]

Social education is an area of continuing concern. According to Glaser, "special courses frequently are conducted in prison to deal exclusively with questions of values and with adjustment in interpersonal relationships, marriage, alcoholism and other personal behavior matters not bearing directly on any vocation [8, p. 281]." He reports that "late in 1961 the U.S. Bureau of Prisons initiated an experimental intensive social-education program in the federal reformatory at Englewood, Colorado." Note that this "experimental" program was initiated more than 30 years after MacCormick's statement of aims for prison education.

Until recently, programs of education in correctional institutions, with few exceptions, have not been highly innovative although there is an increasing number of modifications in already existing programs. To a very great extent, obviously, the nature and magnitude of programs depend upon the financial support provided. Other considerations include the philosophy of the administration and the nature, size and location of the institutions.

Vocational training in prisons, as in adult educational offerings generally, has gone through cycles with varying degrees of emphasis. At this writing, it is receiving much attention. In the National Council on Crime and Delinquency survey, 70 percent of all institutions reported some vocational training efforts. Funds made available through several federally subsidized programs have had a stimulating effect.

Academic education follows fairly traditional lines. In large institutions, elementary and secondary schools are usually maintained with high-school completion being the principal objective. If they meet state standards, and often they do, the high schools are accredited like those in surrounding communities. However, not many prison schools offer all subjects usually found in the curriculum.

Elementary schools, or their equivalent, now have instituted expanded programs of basic education, including literacy education, with the aid of funds from the Adult Education Act of 1966. In the past, many illiterate inmates had available to them only the well-intentioned, but rather sporadic, assistance of volunteer teachers.

In the past, college-level courses have been part of an institution's program only because of particular circumstances—a nearby college or university that provided instructors or, in a few cases, the presence of a prison staff member or inmate qualified to teach. There are indications that college-level courses are becoming more commonly a regular part of prison programs. A 1965 survey reported that such programs were in effect in 11 states and planned in 13 more [21].

Most educational programs are not full-time assignments for inmates. Some are offered only in the evening. Vocational training is more likely to be on a full-time basis than is academic education. Some institutions arrange for work assignments, vocational training and academic classes in combinations designed to supplement one another.

Correspondence study is used extensively to provide instruction in subjects or areas not included in the prison's own program. Instruction from private correspondence schools includes a high percentage of vocational subjects. That provided by state and private universities is more often for high-school completion, personal improvement or college credit. Except where correction departments themselves have correspondence courses, the inmate usually is expected to pay the course fee. For those who depend entirely on their prison earnings, regular correspondence course fees are likely to be prohibitive. Some state schools offer reduced fees to inmates. Indiana University's Correspond-

Some Other Institutions

ence Study Bureau provides any of its courses to inmates of Indiana institutions for only $1.00.

Provisions for social education are difficult to summarize. Often they are provided through treatment activities other than those classified as education—counseling by chaplains and psychologists, group therapy and recreation. Many of the programs are experimental in nature and often cease to exist once the experiment is concluded. Some social education is provided by volunteer groups anxious to assist in prisoner rehabilitation. In some small institutions the volunteer guided activities are virtually the only provisions for social education. They may include Dale Carnegie courses, discussion groups, Great Books, art instruction and other kinds of self-improvement educational activities.

Many persons are convinced that social education holds the greatest promise of help for the inmate when he is returned to society. They argue that it was the offender's inability to adjust to the society in which he lived that led to his deviant behavior and subsequent commitment.

Methods, Techniques and Resources

Education in correctional institutions makes use of about all the methods, techniques, instructional arrangements and educational aids found in other adult educational programs. The traditional class and laboratory experiences are common in vocational education, for example. Individual methods of study include correspondence study and programmed instruction. Lectures and discussions are commonly used techniques of instruction with, perhaps, less dependence on the former than in schools generally. Other techniques employed are role-playing, demonstration, forum and the question period. Occasional use of a panel or symposium, with outside resource persons, is reported.

Programmed instruction has met with mixed reactions. The Task Force on Corrections was guardedly optimistic: "One promising approach to this problem (making learning a more relevant and rewarding experience for inmates) is that of programmed learning." According to the Task Force report, "research and experience in the application of programmed instruction to correctional education have been extensive." Yet the report describes only two examples which have gained considerable attention [28, p. 53].

The Draper Youth Center, Elmore, Alabama, conducts a wide variety of courses and educational activities using programmed materials. The other institution is the National Training School for Boys, recently moved to Morgantown, West Virginia, from Washington, D.C. It should be noted that both institutions have innovative programs of which programmed instruction is only a part. The National Training School is especially for young offenders. The Draper institution has inmates of all ages. The word "Youth" in its name refers to the age of the offender at the time of commitment. At Draper, the education program is integrated with efforts to change the social climate of the entire institution. Intensive vocational and personal counseling are provided. Inmates who have progressed well help others and students from Auburn University work with inmates. There are provisions for inmates who complete high school and qualify for trial release to become students at the university. At National Training School the inmates earn points for accomplishments including progress in school and exemplary behavior. With the points they purchase certain comforts not otherwise provided.

The Task Force on Corrections calls the programmed learning experiments "dramatic" in motivating inmates to learn, but it quickly qualifies its enthusiasm as follows:

But while programmed learning is the core of both programs, it has been accompanied by quite radical changes in the whole approach of the respective institutions and the addition of substantial numbers of able and imaginative staff members. Neither project has attempted to substitute machines for personal contact; indeed counseling and instructional help have been substantially increased, and the presence of program innovation attracted more able and imaginative staff. Under such conditions, the potential of more conventional educational methods would undoubtedly be much greater too. [28, p. 54]

Evaluation of Correctional Education

Evaluation of correctional education, often cited as one of the major needs, has been very difficult. Attempts have been made, but, at best, the results are inconclusive. Difficulty in evaluation begins with lack of agreement on and lack of clarity and testability of goals. Even when goals are stated and understood, the data necessary for evaluation are not always available.

It is common to equate the goal of correctional education to the general goal of corrections—rehabilitation—even though rehabilitation, if accomplished, is the result of the total treatment program. Education can be expected to furnish the tools—knowledge, skills and attitudes—that make rehabilitation possible. Ultimately, correctional education, like any education, should be evaluated in terms of its products, and those products are the inmates for whom the education has been provided. However, even on the description of the desired product there seems to be disagreement. MacCormick, as quoted earlier, wrote that "we must not expect too much in the way of quality or quantity." Toward the

Some Other Institutions

opposite extreme, Conrad says that it is not enough to transform an offender into a non-offender, but that "the task of correctional rehabilitation is the transfer of the criminal careerist to the pursuit of a conventional career [12, p. 7]."

A general goal of correctional education is said to be the reduction of recidivism. Writing on the testability of correctional goals, Sherwood points out the difficulties with this goal. He suggests two important questions: "(1) what is meant by it—that is, how is it to be specifically defined? and (2) however defined, is this a sensible goal for corrections?" He asks first if "reduced recidivism" means that the offender commits no more crimes or fewer crimes, and he then refers to the difficulty attached to the meanings of recidivism.

The narrowest definition of recidivism is in terms of whether or not the same individual comes back into the same institution or correctional system after having been released from that institution or system at some time in the past. The broadest definition is in terms of whether or not he commits another crime anywhere, whether or not he is apprehended and convicted. The first is testable but unsatisfactory; the second is more satisfactory but untestable in practice. An acceptable, testable definition must therefore be somewhere in between. [12, pp. 44–45]

Whatever the expectations, and even with the difficulties of definition, the success of rehabilitation, and hence of the educational programs, is measured in terms of non-recidivism. There are, of course, intermediate goals and most lend themselves more readily to appraisal. Some concern the development of desirable behavior and attitudes within the institution. Others are in terms of tasks with easily measured outcomes—to become literate, to complete high school or to learn a trade.

Very often, then, the educational program is evaluated in terms of these task goals. Another practice in prison schools, as in many public schools, is the appraisal of certain observable facets of the total school operation—curriculum, teaching staff, physical facilities and equipment, length of instruction time, and so on. To use either of these, the degree to which task goals are achieved or the appraisal of the several parts of the school operation, is to make certain assumptions about correlation. Such assumptions, for example, are that completion of high school or learning a trade results in, or at least contributes to, reduced recidivism; or that a well-qualified corps of teachers, modern facilities and well-rounded curricula do the same.

The problem of evaluation is compounded by what has been described as the deplorable state of information bases [12, pp. 28–33]. The most obvious difficulty is that of collecting information on released offenders. Not only is such information often non-existent, where it is available the lack of uniform reporting adversely affects its usefulness. Within correctional institutions themselves much information in systematic form is collected. Yet even here the information, since it is kept in individual case files, has been of limited use in evaluating programs. Modern information retrieval methods may solve the latter problem.

Evaluation of correctional education, with all of its problems, does receive attention in the educational programs themselves and in well-organized research projects. Although all the latter do not show conclusively that prison education is reaching its goals—in fact some studies show that it has the opposite effect—there are indications that it generally is beneficial. Results of evaluation research must be interpreted with care. Some studies that compare post-release experiences of offenders who were inmate students with those who were not fail to take into account differences in other characteristics of the subjects. But even with matched groups of students and non-students, studies have shown that correctional education does reduce the chances that the releasee will return to prison.

From the data collected in studies of prison education and recidivism. Glaser presents three "tentative and highly qualified conclusions":

For most inmates, prison education is statistically associated with above average post-release success only when the education is extensive and occurs in the course of prolonged confinement.

For most prisoners, especially for those with extensive prior felony records, the usual duration and type of involvement in prison education is associated with higher than average post-release failure rates; while

A small amount of education in prison frequently impairs post-release prospects on inmates indirectly, by inspiring them with unreasonable aspirations, or by the education's being pursued instead of alternate preparation for post-release life. [8, pp. 282–283]

More encouraging is Glaser's concluding comment:

Many individual cases of reformation encountered by us, in which prison training and education were clearly major assets in a new way of life for the released offender, demonstrate a great prison education potential. [8, p. 283]

Also encouraging are the results of a study by S. J. Saden, who compared students with non-students in a follow-up of 1000 men paroled from Michigan State Prison at Jackson some 12 to 15 years earlier. Among the students, 74 percent were successful on parole as were 64 percent of the non-students. Among those with previous criminal records, 66 percent were successful as compared with 55 percent of the non-students [29].

Some Problems in Correctional Education

The problems that accompany the adult education effort in correctional institutions, as in any institution, are a result of its nature and history, tradition, and the expectation of the publics served.

Personnel Problems. There is a shortage of qualified personnel to man correctional education programs. The President's Commission recommended that "states should, with federal support, establish immediate programs to recruit and train academic and vocational instructors to work in correctional institutions [27, p. 175]." But there is need for in-service training for all correctional personnel.

One of the major obstacles to the effective operation of rehabilitation programs has been the division between the functions of custody and treatment. The National Council on Crime and Delinquency survey report points out the following:

> Most institutional programs are shaped to meet the requirements of custody and control. Custody and control are the nucleus, the paramount consideration of the entire institutional apparatus. That is why two-thirds of all adult institutional employees are engaged in custodial tasks. [28, p. 182]

Custody personnel often have felt that educational programs and other treatment efforts have interfered with the custody function. Treatment personnel have contended that the opposite is true. Neither side has understood well the function and problems of the other. The current trend, one that hopefully will eliminate this obstacle, is to make both custody and treatment the responsibility of all prison personnel. In-service training will be necessary if this approach is to succeed.

Inmate Motivation. Inmate motivation must be understood if one is to comprehend correctional education. Education as an opportunity to compensate for past failures has been suggested as a motivating factor. It assumes, however, that the inmate recognizes his failures and develops a rational outlook including long-range goals. Long-term rewards, however, can seem distant and unreal. In fact, they often become unreal when released offenders have difficulty in getting jobs for which they have been trained. On the other hand, with two exceptions, immediate rewards for learning are meager. The major short-term incentive for participation in educational programs is the hope that it will reduce the duration of the offender's incarceration. Inmates are quite aware that a self-improvement effort usually has a favorable effect on parole boards. The other immediate reward, at least in some institutions, is the opportunity to substitute schooling for some less desirable assignment.

The Corruptibility of Prison Education. Glaser states that malpractices arise chiefly when programs must rely on inmates as teachers and in the accrediting of correspondence study [8, pp. 268–269]. Inmates merely seek evidence of having completed educational courses. There is likely to be a relatively large amount of cheating. This problem is not unique to prison education, however.

Correctional Institutions for Women. Women's correctional institutions present special problems in the design and conduct of educational programs. Though there are some differences in the educational needs of men and women, the major difficulty encountered is the small population typical of the institutions for women. The kinds of programs generally found in the large prisons and reformatories are usually judged to be too expensive in terms of cost per inmate. The conflict of educational programs with work schedules and the shortage of staff for such programs are other difficulties. Women's prisons are not without educational activities, however. There are many examples of innovative efforts involving the use of part-time staff, volunteers and inmates as instructors. Small-group techniques and individual instruction, such as correspondence study, are used. Programmed instruction may be particularly useful in these institutions.

Education for Misdemeanants. Education for persons convicted of misdemeanors, as compared to that for felons, receives little attention. The misdemeanant, if he is incarcerated, has a shorter sentence and most often is in a city or county institution. The high population turnover has made the provision of educational programs difficult and, in general, almost nonexistent. Yet there are about twice as many commitments for misdemeanors as there are for felonies. Among the misdemeanants there are many first-time offenders who are good prospects for early rehabilitation programs, making the need for imaginative educational efforts even more acute.

Research in Rehabilitation. Research in correctional rehabilitation has been increasingly in evidence during the last decade. As shown in the discussion on evaluation, the lack of agreement on what constitutes rehabilitation is a major obstacle to research. Other difficulties cited are those found in the conflicting theories of correction, the ethics and methodology involved, the observation of programs, and the interpretation of data [12, pp. 51–52]. Another apparent problem is translating the findings of research into improved rehabilitation programs.

Some Other Institutions

A Change in Public Opinion. The attitude of the general public constitutes a major problem that must be solved if correctional education and the rehabilitation of prisoners is to be successful. So long as society sees the purposes of correction primarily as punishment, retribution and confinement, there will be extremely limited opportunities for the released offender no matter what rehabilitative efforts have been expended.

Hospitals

Hospitals have not received as widespread attention as adult education institutions. In A. A. Liveright's study of adult education in the United States there is only one brief mention of hospital adult education programs and that is in regard to continuing education for physicians [16]. Yet educational programs have been and continue to be important concerns in these institutions. For this brief examination, hospitals are classified as general, special and mental.

The primary purpose of all hospitals is to provide "patient care." The objective of hospital adult education programs is to help make such care as effective as possible. To that end, almost all hospitals conduct programs of in-service education, some of which are very extensive. These programs are provided for all levels of personnel, including the several groups of volunteers common to most hospitals. Patient education programs, including those for the patient's family, constitute another important activity. Finally, hospitals conduct educational programs for the public.

General Hospitals

General hospitals traditionally have helped to train certain medical and paramedical personnel, including nurses and physicians. There are programs to train X-ray, medical laboratory and operating room technicians; inhalation therapists; and practical nurses. Training for chaplains and hospital administrators is also provided. All of these may be more akin to higher education than to adult education. They are chiefly pre-service education and lead to degrees, diplomas, certificates or licenses. Among the many other kinds of educational programs for hospital personnel that clearly fall within the province of adult education are pre-service and in-service programs for such personnel as nurses' aides, orderlies and ward secretaries—persons who now do many routine jobs once required of registered nurses.

Patient education in general hospitals has taken many forms, but, in the main, it has been limited to that provided for patients with chronic health problems. Exceptions are classes for new parents and expectant parents. The short hospitalization period for most patients has limited the kinds of educational programs largely to instructions given the patient or his family. In general, the purposes of patient education are to assist in adjustment to hospitalization and treatment, understanding of condition or disease, and adjustment to the post-hospitalization period.

As yet general hospitals have not engaged in extensive educational programs for the public except for some activities in the realm of public relations. Health education of the public has been seen as the responsibility of government agencies and voluntary organizations. It has been suggested, though, that hospitals are in a particularly advantageous position to assume such responsibility.

An example of educational programs in a large general hospital is furnished by a 1968 survey of educational programs at Deaconess Hospital, Evansville, Indiana. The report of the survey lists, in addition to the formal accredited programs (e.g., school of nursing, and training for technicians) the following: four formal internal programs of training—nurses' aides, orderlies, unit clerks and management services; twelve continuing education programs for hospital personnel; nine patient education programs; and seven specialized educational activities and services [32].

Deaconess Hospital is in the beginning stages of a project to determine its possible role as a community agency for the health education of adults. First steps in the project were diagnostic studies by interns doing graduate study in adult education at Indiana University. An education coordinator and a director of nursing, both of whom hold doctor's degrees in adult education, are on the hospital staff. Although hospitals typically have not filled such positions with professionally trained adult educators, recent lists of job opportunities indicate that such a trend may be developing.

Special Hospitals

Special hospitals provide care for patients with specific kinds of diseases or other health problems, usually of a chronic nature (e.g., tuberculosis) or for patients in particular age groupings. The educational programs needed for personnel in these institutions are much the same as those in general hospitals. Programs include orientation for staff at all levels, in-service education and other continuing educational opportunities.

A distinguishing feature of special hospitals is the relatively long period during which the patient is hospitalized, or at least has a con-

Some Other Institutions

tinuing relationship with the institution. Thus patient education, including programs for families of the patient, can be planned for substantial periods of time. Much of the treatment for the rehabilitation of patients is under the rubric of therapy and certainly therapy and education are not synonymous. But if some educational programs are therapeutic, or if some therapy is educational, it seems unnecessary to distinguish sharply between the two functions.

Special hospitals have even more limited concern for community education than do general hospitals. In part, this is due to the fact that most special hospitals actually are not community institutions. Some are operated by federal agencies, for example the Veterans Administration; others are state operated or may be part of a state or private medical school complex.

Mental Hospitals

The history of mental hospitals in some ways has been similar to that of penal institutions. Although the ideas of punishment, retribution, and penance were not present, the concept of protecting society by confining the mentally ill was common. Thus the responsibility of the institution was primarily that of providing custodial care.

Although there are non-governmental institutions for the mentally ill, and large general hospitals have psychiatric wards, most institutionalized treatment in the area of mental health is in state-operated mental hospitals. Most states have mental health departments responsible for such operations.

Mental hospitals, like other hospitals, require broad programs of in-service education. Orientation programs and opportunities for continuing education of hospital personnel are among the educational needs, which differ from those in other hospitals only because of the special nature of the patients. In mental hospitals, as in general hospitals, the increased demand for well-trained personnel, along with manpower shortages, has made in-service education a crucial concern. Also contributing to the need for such programs are the changing philosophy and methods in the treatment of the mentally ill, especially as they are reflected in patient education.

The education of adult patients in mental hospitals has taken on new meaning in recent years. Potential students include all those who are educable or trainable, and the terms are now applied to many more patients than in the past. The purposes of such education are the habilitation or rehabilitation of the patient and, whenever possible, his return to the community. The concept of commitment with no hope of leaving the institution is no longer commonly held among mental health officials. Even for those patients who have no prospects for return to the community there are possibilities for educational programs, largely for the purpose of helping them meet problems of living within the institution.

Education of the families of mental patients is also a major concern. If a patient eventually is to be discharged from the hospital, his family will have an important role in his continued recovery and in maintaining his mental health. Such a role requires an understanding of the nature of the mental illness and the kinds of attitudes and behaviors that help prevent its recurrence.

In the matter of education of the public, mental hospitals face a great challenge. In at least one respect the similarity of mental hospitals and correctional institutions reappears. The returned mental patient is accepted in the community with about as much enthusiasm as the paroled convict. Thus a primary objective of public education programs by mental hospitals is a society that understands the nature and treatment of mental illness and can modify its behavior and attitudes so they are consistent with that understanding. Fortunately the hospitals receive considerable assistance in programming for public education. Voluntary organizations, community groups and other agencies provide many such programs.

Mental health as a major program area for adult education is not widely recognized. However, at least one example of the potential of adult education in this field is available.

Since 1960, Professors Paul Bergevin and John McKinley of Indiana University's Bureau of Studies in Adult Education have conducted a developmental study of adult education in mental health. A variety of experimental educational programs have been conducted with patients and staff of state mental hospitals. Graduate interns majoring in adult education have been assigned to identify the needs of several hospital groups and to plan programs to meet the needs. Several doctoral dissertations in adult education have resulted from these activities [1; 3; 7; 19].

The most significant result of the Indiana study so far has been the reaction of the State Department of Mental Health. The Department established two positions in state hospitals requiring the doctorate and the master's degree respectively—the director of training and education and the training officer. Adult education is recommended as a field of study for both positions. Four hospitals now have persons in these positions, three of whom hold the doctorate in adult education. The superintendent of one hospital and the director of the Division of Education and Training of the State Department of Mental Health also have doctorates in adult education. The Department offers grants-in-aid for per-

Some Other Institutions

sons pursuing higher education and study in adult education is receiving increased support under this program.

Proprietary Schools

The term "proprietary" connotes a venture undertaken for profit and the proprietary school is just that. It may be a single-owner enterprise, a partnership or a corporation. Some incorporated institutions are included even though they disclaim the profit motive. In any case, the schools are independently financed and the operators assume the risks of free enterprise.

In the 1966 report *Classrooms on Main Street*, the term "specialty schools" is used to describe schools other than conventional public and private institutions at the elementary, secondary, and college or university level [5]. They are private, non-degree-granting institutions preparing students for vocational or avocational pursuits in the specialty for which each has been established. The description appears to be the same as that for proprietary schools, with two exceptions. It avoids the profit criterion and it excludes some institutions that do not specialize, notably correspondence schools.

The chapter on proprietary schools in the 1960 edition of the *Handbook of Adult Education in the United States* furnishes information that is still useful [14, pp. 339–344]. *Classrooms on Main Street* is more comprehensive and it is recommended as a reference to supplement this account. In addition to the history of specialty schools and the regulations to which they are subjected, the volume discusses the following: business schools; training in selected industries (e.g., construction, transportation, retailing); skilled trade preparation (e.g., truck drivers, repairmen); semi-professional occupations (e.g., airplane pilots, radio announcing, commercial art); personal—and protective—service occupations (e.g., barbering, private policemen and detectives); and leisure-time activities (e.g., physical fitness, arts and crafts, personality development).

The Johnstone report, *Volunteers for Learning*, provides data on participation of adults in the educational activities of privately sponsored schools [11]. However, statistics on proprietary schools are conflicting and difficult to interpret. According to Liveright, "the lack of exact figures of the participation in proprietary institutions education results in widely varying estimates of adult education in this sector [16, p. 89]." Examples of such variation are his own estimate of some 32,000 private and proprietary schools of which about 8000 are proprietary, and the finding of Clark that there are more than 35,000 specialty schools [5, p. 4]. Both authors quote the 1960 Handbook in reporting that proprietary schools have "current" enrollments of over 5,000,000, but this figure was taken from a 1953 survey [14, p. 147]. Figures from the Johnstone report, on the other hand, indicate that in 1961–62 the number of adults who attended courses sponsored by private schools was 1,120,000 [11, pp. 61–62]. Since in that study "the category of 'private schools' consists of profit-making institutions of all types" presumably it includes most proprietary schools. At any rate, one can conclude that proprietary schools reach significantly large numbers of adults. Estimates of tuition paid annually range upward from $125 million.

Quite naturally proprietary schools are concentrated in the more densely populated areas of the country. Most are located in downtown districts, a fact obviously responsible for the title of the volume by Clark and Sloan [5]. For certain vocations these schools are the only sources of training. For some young adults the schools build upon preliminary training received in high school. For the school dropouts proprietary schools provide a second chance, at least in job preparation. Also of importance is the role of these schools in the updating of knowledge and skills of adults threatened with loss of work because their jobs have become obsolete. In the area of leisure-time education, the proprietary schools have developed extensive programs, many of which are not to be found in more conventional institutions of education. Such programs are becoming more and more in demand with increasing amounts of leisure and earlier retirement.

Perhaps the key to the success of the education-for-profit institutions is simply that they are profit-making enterprises. To prosper, in fact even to survive, they must be flexible and extremely sensitive to the needs of adults and the demands for a variety of training opportunities. They must, of course, furnish that training satisfactorily if they are to stay in business.

Correspondence schools are a special kind of proprietary educational institution. Figures from a 1967 survey by the National Home Study Council showed that over 5,000,000 persons were enrolled in all types of correspondence institutions. Private home study schools accounted for more than 1,579,000 of the students, second only to those in federal government and military establishments. A 1966 Carnegie Corporation-financed study of correspondence instruction in the United States included an examination of "home study schools which are in business for profit [18]." The report of the study presented arguments of both the critics of the profit motive in education and those who defend it. Among the practices questioned was the spending of 40 to 45 percent of the total budget on sales and promotion (compared to 17 percent on instruction). The report, mildly critical of the proprietary home study schools,

Some Other Institutions

made note of "the importance of the profit motive in determining such important issues as public acceptance of the correspondence method, the percentage of operating revenue that can be spent on instruction, and the attention a school can and will pay to the problems of the individual student [18, p. 80]."

The private home study schools, however, claim that they should be judged by their performance. The number of enrollments and the length of time many have been in business seem to indicate that they play a substantial role in the education of adults. The schools are subject to a variety of regulations. Some are in the form of local ordinances and state laws. Others are indirect controls such as licensing in certain vocations (which means that the training must be of a quality that will enable graduates to qualify for such licenses). There is also a small amount of private control in the form of accrediting agencies. Among those recognized by the U.S. Office of Education are the Accrediting Commission for Business Schools, an Accrediting Commission for Home Study Schools, and a subcommittee of the Committee on Engineering of the Engineers' Council for Professional Development.

The profit motive tends to be the object of some suspicion and certain proprietary schools have been guilty of behavior that is at least unethical. Clark points out two chief sources of malpractice—the manner in which job opportunities are presented and instances where the training involves no specific trade skill. Misleading but not illegal advertising terms and phrases are another abuse [5, pp. 32–33].

The problems faced by proprietary schools, as might be expected, relate to the profit motive for which they are established. One of the more persistent is the general lack of awareness of the schools on the part of the potential students. This results in the expenditure of large sums for advertising. All the schools are plagued by suspicion of their education-for-profit status as well as by the unethical behavior of a few. However, proprietary schools continue to fill a gap in adult education, particularly the vocational area. Their chief asset is their flexibility, which may enable them to become even more significant forces in adult education.

Independent Adult Schools

In the last *Handbook of Adult Education in the United States* [14], the authors of the chapter, "Adult Education in Independent and Residential Schools," concerned themselves with non-residential and residential, independent adult centers. The two kinds of institutions, according to the 1960 account, are responsible for "a small but significant fraction of adult education."

Non-residential Centers

By definition, the non-residential, independent, adult centers are not affiliated with other institutions. It seems that this category would not include the proprietary schools described in the preceding section. Some other agencies (e.g., art galleries), although they may be independent, properly belong elsewhere in this book.

There appear to be relatively few institutions that meet the criteria for non-residential, independent, adult schools. Generally they are supported by foundations, endowments, gifts or income from gifts and bequests; they derive only part of their income from fees or tuition. The schools are non-profit and, although their structures vary, they typically are governed by some group of concerned citizens such as a board of directors. The courses of study are non-credit although some do provide for high-school equivalency certificates, usually using the General Educational Development test scores as criteria.

The oldest of the non-residential adult centers is the Junto in Philadelphia which has survived since it was founded in 1727 by Benjamin Franklin. It has changed in form over the years and is, according to Klein, "the extreme independent [school], with its tailor-made board, faculty, program, and building [14, p. 264]."

The Watkins Institute in Nashville, Tennessee, has been operating since 1885. The school meets its expenses from gifts and rental income from property placed in trust with the state of Tennessee by Samuel Watkins. Instruction was provided free for many years, but modest fees are now charged. The institute is governed by a three-member Board of Commissioners. Courses are offered in a variety of subjects including art, business and home economics, as well as those leading to a high school equivalency diploma. More than 4000 students are enrolled annually.

Other examples of non-residential, independent, adult centers are the McCall Industrial School and the Baker–Hunt Foundation in Cincinnati; the Boston Center for Adult Education; and the Cambridge (Massachusetts) Center for Adult Education.

Residential Centers

In the 1960 Handbook, Schacht wrote that "unaffiliated residential centers of adult education in the United States are admittedly few and largely the results of the conviction and devotion of a few individuals [14, p. 272]." In his concluding statement he said that "the odds in today's society seem to be against any major development of residential

Some Other Institutions

adult education which does not have the money, personnel, facilities and prestige of the institutionalized agencies of our culture [14, p. 273]." Ten years later there is no evidence upon which to differ with Schacht's observations.

Chautauqua stands out among the residential, independent, adult centers. Apparently it acquired the characteristics of an "institutionalized agency." Founded in 1874 at what is now Chautauqua Lake, New York, its origin and growth are part of any history of adult education. Nearing its centennial year, it continues to draw adults and families to its summer programs with their emphasis on culture, education and recreation.

Among the schools Schacht characterized as "too much a personal possession of their founding individuals to be considered well-established institutions with a future," the John C. Campbell Folk School and the Penland School of Handicrafts, both in North Carolina, are very much alive. Both have heavy emphasis on arts and crafts programs with the Campbell school also active in some kinds of manual skills and folk music. Another of this group was the Highlander Folk School, Monteagle, Tennessee, whose controversial programs were under almost constant attack. The school came to its demise when it lost its tax-exempt charter in 1960. Its successor, the Highlander Center in Knoxville, cannot really be called a residential school. The Cold Spring Institute, 60 miles north of New York City, is dedicated to the problems and needs of older adults. Its major contribution may be more in the area of aging than in residential adult education.

There are other residential schools, but more are affiliated with some larger institution. The whole area of residential adult education, unlike the independent residential school, has continued to grow and to involve increasing numbers of adults. University facilities for housing participants in conferences, conventions, workshops, institutes and other adult educational activities are being strained to meet the demands. But "residential" does not describe a particular adult educational institution, so the larger field of residential adult education is not a concern here. (It is a part of the institutional programs of colleges and universities, community colleges, business and industry and religious institutions.) In addition, many programs are conducted by professional associations using commercial facilities (e.g., hotels, motels and campsites).

Like the proprietary schools, the independent adult schools, both residential and non-residential, fill gaps in the adult education scene. Although they make up only a very small part of all adult education in the United States, persons who participate in their programs most likely regard them as significant.

References

1. Ackerman, Ora R. "Knowledge of and Attitudes Toward Mental Illness as Held by Three Populations Involved with the Mentally Ill." Unpublished doctoral dissertation. Bloomington, Ind.: Indiana University, 1963.
2. Allen, Richard G. "Application of Adult Education Methods to Hospital Training." *Adult Leadership,* XVI (May, 1967), pp. 20–22.
3. Arnold, H. Merrell. "An Experimental Public Education Program in Mental Health." Unpublished doctoral dissertation. Bloomington, Ind.: Indiana University, 1967.
4. Beck, Walter E. "Changing Systems—Mental Hospitals and Prisons." *American Journal of Correction,* XXXI (January–February, 1969), pp. 35–40.
5. Clark, Harold F., and Sloan, Harold S. *Classrooms on Main Street.* New York: Teachers College, Columbia University Press, 1966.
6. Conrad, John P. *Crime and Its Correction* (revised). Berkeley, Calif.: University of California Press, 1968.
7. Dollins, Curtis N. "The Effect of Group Discussion as a Learning Procedure on the Adaptive Social Behavior of Educable Adult Mental Retardates." Unpublished doctoral dissertation. Bloomington, Ind.: Indiana University, 1967.
8. Glaser, Daniel. *The Effectiveness of a Prison and Parole System.* Indianapolis, Ind.: Bobbs-Merrill, 1964.
9. Glaser, Daniel. "The Effectiveness of Correctional Education." *American Journal of Correction,* XXVIII (March–April, 1966), pp. 4–9.
10. Johnson, Elmer H. *Crime, Correction and Society.* Homewood, Ill.: Dorsey Press, 1964.
11. Johnstone, John W. C., and Rivera, Ramon J. *Volunteers for Learning: A Study of the Educational Pursuits of American Adults.* Chicago, Ill.: Aldine, 1965.
12. Joint Commission on Correctional Manpower and Training. *Research in Correctional Rehabilitation.* Washington, D.C.: Joint Commission on Correctional Manpower and Training, 1967.
13. Joint Commission on Correctional Manpower and Training. *Targets for In-Service Training.* Washington, D.C.: Joint Commission on Correctional Manpower and Training, 1967.
14. Knowles, Malcolm S., ed. *Handbook of Adult Education in the United States.* Washington, D.C.: Adult Education Association of the USA, 1960.
15. LaVallee, J. Edwin. "Education at Auburn Prison." *American Journal of Correction,* XXVIII (May–June, 1966), pp. 4–9.
16. Liveright, A. A. *A Study of Adult Education in the United States.* Boston, Mass.: Center for the Study of Liberal Education for Adults, 1968.
17. MacCormick, Austin. *The Education of Adult Prisoners.* New York: National Society of Penal Institutions, 1931.

18. MacKenzie, Ossian; Christensen, Edward L.; and Rigby, Paul H. *Correspondence Instruction in the United States.* New York: McGraw-Hill, 1968.
19. McKinley, John. "A Participation-Training Program in a Mental Hospital: An Experiment in Adult Education." Unpublished doctoral dissertation. Bloomington, Ind.: Indiana University, 1960.
20. Miller, E. Eugene. "Education at Bucks County Prison." *American Journal of Correction,* XXIX (March–April, 1967), pp. 22–25.
21. Morris, Roger R. "State Programs in College Education for Inmates of Correctional Institutions." *American Journal of Correction,* XXX (March–April, 1968), pp. 2–22, 36.
22. National Council on Crime and Delinquency. "Correction in the United States." *The Journal of Crime and Delinquency,* XIII (January, 1967), pp. 1–280.
23. Noble, Henry J. "The Center for Correctional Training and the New York City Department of Correction." *American Journal of Correction,* XXIX (March–April, 1967), pp. 8–13.
24. Office of Manpower Policy, Evaluation, and Research. *Training Needs in Correctional Institutions,* Manpower Research Bulletin No. 8. Washington, D.C.: U.S. Department of Labor, Manpower Administration, 1966.
25. Paley, William. "The Principles of Moral and Political Philosophy." In: *Eighteenth Cenutry Penal Theory.* Edited by James Heath. New York: Oxford University Press, 1963.
26. Pitkin, Royce S. *The Residential School in American Adult Education.* Boston, Mass.: Center for the Study of Liberal Education for Adults, 1956.
27. President's Commission on Law Enforcement and Administration of Justice. *The Challenge of Crime in a Free Society.* Washington, D.C.: Government Printing Office, 1967.
28. President's Commission on Law Enforcement and Administration of Justice. *Task Force Report: Corrections.* Washington, D.C.: Government Printing Office, 1967.
29. Saden, S. J. "Correctional Research at Jackson Prison." *Journal of Correctional Education,* XV (October, 1962), pp. 22–26.
30. Schacht, Robert H. "Residential Adult Education—An Analysis and Interpretation." Unpublished doctoral dissertation. Madison, Wis.: University of Wisconsin, 1957.
31. Schacht, Robert H. *Week-end Learning in the U.S.A.* Boston, Mass.: Center for the Study of Liberal Education for Adults, 1960.
32. "Survey of Deaconess Hospital Education Programs." Evansville, Ind.: Deaconess Hospital, 1968.
33. U.S. Department of Justice, Bureau of Prisons, "Prisoners in State and Federal Institutions for Adult Felons, 1966." *National Prisoner Statistics.* Washington, D.C.: Bureau of Prisons, 1968.

Part III

Some Program Areas

Chapter 23

Curriculum and Content

ROGER W. AXFORD

The central purpose of this section of the Handbook (Part III) is to bring alive the wide variety of program areas in adult education. To be more explicit, it attempts in a limited way to describe what is being learned in adult education.

We have examined adult education's recent history, discussed its terminology, identified some common concerns of adult educators, and described several of the major institutions and organizations that develop and conduct adult education programs. Now we shall consider the curriculum and content of selected program areas in adult education. Only a limited number of the major areas can be examined because the exhaustive nature of the concerns of adults results in a great variety of programs. Even of these, a few have been merged in the last decade.

In using the terms curriculum and program, we are aware of how commonly they are used, yet how elusive they really are. Thurman White has written about some of the difficulties:

We do not now have a continuing curriculum for adults. We do not now have an integrated curriculum. In no place in America can an adult do organized study of all his learning concerns. In no place in America can an adult pursue one learning concern through its many changes during his lifetime. In no one place in America can an adult integrate his efforts to fulfill several learning concerns during any phase of maturity. The adult curriculum is incomplete, discontinuous, and uncommitted. [15]

What differences in meaning or connotation are there between program and curriculum? Many people have pointed out that a typical difference is to employ the term curriculum for formal institutions. Alan Thomas writes:

Adult educators tend still to use the word program in preference to curriculum, in part because it contains more variables in practice than does the more formal system. In the formal system, place, time, and the organization of personnel are held relatively constant, while blocks of subject matter and exposure to them, generally described as the curriculum, are altered. In adult education there are few constants of any kind, except an interest in learning or behavioural change. [11, p. 244]

Recent attention has been given not only to planning and providing greater coherence and continuity in program, but toward the evaluation of results. Verner has said "the effectiveness of all educational experience can be evaluated by measuring the number of changes in behaviour resulting from it. In the last analysis, this is the only precise way of evaluating program [14]." Along with this concern for evaluation has come an increasing concern for stating the objectives of a program in measurable terms, in defining more precisely the audience for a specific program and in obtaining participation by the learner in planning and assessing the results of the program.

Changes in Emphasis

Changing times present new problems, and institutions of adult education need to program to meet these problems. For example, when the nation became aware that large numbers of persons lacked the basic skills of reading and fundamental education, adult basic education was brought into the elementary and secondary schools under federal support. When sufficient numbers of adults express needs to organizations or agencies with a capacity to meet those needs, new programs are developed. In the near future, we also may see new institutional forms emerge, as in the case of university residential adult education centers, where the content is frequently devoted to updating professionals, analyzing social problems, or identifying state or regional problems [1]. The curriculum and content offered by the institution is usually dependent upon the current concern of the adult students. As James Russell Lowell said:

> New occasions teach new duties
> Time makes ancient good uncouth;
> They must upward still and onward,
> Who would keep abreast of truth.

Curriculum and Content

What Do Adults Study?

Perhaps the most revealing findings in this connection are those of John W. C. Johnstone in *Volunteers for Learning* where he describes the types of subject matter studied by adults in broad categories [5, Chapter 3]. By far the largest number of adults indicated they were studying some job-related subject or skill. At the time of the research, 9 million persons were estimated to have been engaged in vocational study. They pursued subjects and skills used in the professional, technical, business, office and sales spheres of white-color occupations, and in the skilled trades, semi-skilled and service spheres of blue-collar occupations.

The second largest category of subject matter in Johnstone's study was that of leisure. It was estimated that 5.5 million adult Americans studied subjects and acquired skills relating to hobbies or to recreational pursuits. Athletics, decorative arts and crafts, dancing, music, art, technical arts and hobbies were included under this category.

Religion, morals and ethics (including Bible Study) was the third largest area in which adults sought knowledge and understanding. General education, including academic subjects of the sort adults would normally study as part of their high school or college education, came fourth. Excluded from this category were business, trade technical, vocational, professional, or other job-related courses.

Home and family life subjects came fifth with topics such as the establishment, maintenance and improvement of a home in this category. Sixth came personal development courses such as physical fitness, speed reading, and speech and public speaking.

Current events, public affairs and citizenship ranked seventh in the number of persons participating. This area includes subjects dealing with current social, political and economic affairs and includes courses in citizenship and Americanization. Agriculture ranked eighth with an estimated 320,000 adults participating. Ninth came miscellaneous subject matter including driver education and military science courses.

Where Do Adults Study?

Johnstone found that 66 percent of all general education subjects were studied in colleges and universities, and a total of 79 percent in either colleges, universities, secondary or elementary schools [5, p. 63]. Business and industry and local school systems shared the burden of providing vocational subjects. The largest single category was business and industry, accounting for 29 percent of the courses.

Recreational subjects, for the most part, were studied within the context of community organizations, with 40 percent in this category. However, 23 percent of the courses in this area were taken at elementary and secondary schools. It was found that 28 percent of home and family life subjects, like recreation, were programmed in community organizations with 25 percent undertaken in elementary or secondary schools.

Churches and synagogues accounted for nearly all religious studies, 96 percent. Public affairs were studied most often in community organizations, which accounted for 36 percent. Colleges and universities stood second with 20 percent [5, pp. 63–66].

Johnstone reported that significant numbers of men and women seem to develop their own learning plans, choose their own curricula and select courses, tutors or educational materials to obtain the goals they seek. Recent studies by Allen Tough indicate the numbers of persons who pursue significant projects of self-directed learning may be very large indeed, with a range of subject matter almost to defy description or analysis [12]. For such persons the enrollment in a course, or the selection of books in a library may be one part of a continuous and coherent project of self-learning. Tough believes most adults can be aided to embark on such projects and that, increasingly, the role of schools and colleges and libraries will be to facilitate autonomous efforts to learn.

Why Do Adults Study?

Every administrator of adult programs and curriculum planner wants better answers to this question. The reasons would appear to be extremely varied. They range from those of the man who attends an elementary school literacy class to learn to write his name to those of the woman who goes to a university extension class to learn how to invest wisely for retirement.

Cyril O. Houle investigated a small, but highly select sample of adults who seek additional learning [4, pp. 16–30]. Studying 22 cases in depth, he classified each of them into one of three categories: (1) the goal oriented; (2) the learning oriented; and (3) the activity oriented.

The goal-oriented adult has one or more specific objectives he wants to attain through the adult education program. Credit for a class, a certificate, knowledge of data processing, learning to type, any or all might be the goal of an adult coming to a continuing education class.

Learning-oriented adults are motivated by the desire to know. They seek learning for its own sake. The person who continues to attend Great Books classes because he enjoys learning just for learning's sake is an example. University extension curriculum planners find many

Curriculum and Content

people come back again and again. The present writer knows a dentist who takes a botany or biology course each semester and has for years; he says, "Just because I enjoy the learning."

The activity-oriented individual is attracted to such institutions as the YMCA and the YWCA. The content of the program often interests this individual less than the activity and social aspects. To meet people, to socialize, to escape from less desirable activity are reasons the activity-oriented individual may give for joining an adult class.

The curriculum planner should keep in mind that people with each of these primary orientations are likely to be enrolled in any given class. He will want to design the experience to be attractive and rewarding to persons of each orientation.

In the final analysis, a list of purposes for which adults study might be as extensive as the yellow pages of a telephone directory. Here is a condensed listing:

1. To develop a skill, to improve one's job.
2. To make up a deficiency, complete a certificate, diploma or degree.
3. To become a better citizen.
4. To broaden one's view of the world and of the people in it.
5. To learn about health and how to improve health habits.
6. To learn to be a more effective family member, father, mother, budget-maker, consumer, provider.
7. To develop skills in communication and human relations.
8. To deepen an understanding of a hobby, interest or latent ability.
9. To increase one's income.
10. To meet a requirement demanded by a business, industry or profession.
11. To fill leisure time with something meaningful [1].

The Vital Role of Content

Institutions and agencies of adult education are merely vehicles that adults use to get to the content of the curriculum, whatever it may be. It is the learning experiences offered through the curriculum that can bring knowledge and skills to the adult—and the probability of maturity and wisdom. It is the content, the curriculum arranged and structured by the program planner, that determines what shall be learned, retained and practiced.

The curriculum specialist and the program planner are pivotal in the learning process. What shall be included and what excluded in the learning process is a curriculum consideration. The teacher and the administrator must work hand in hand in curriculum planning.

Pearl Buck, a writer concerned with adult education, brings home the vital role of content. The material to be learned must be relevant, meaningful and applicable.

There is no time today for the trivial, the childish, immaterial program. Every hour that people are willing to give to come to a class or meeting ought to be most carefully used and planned to give the utmost in accurate information presented in the most interesting way.

We have no time to waste, as a nation. There is little time left in the world. It is true that our people as a whole do not realize the danger of being uninformed or misinformed, but it is the duty of the program planner to let them know. He has to combat not only ignorance but the reluctance of the average mind to be informed rather than amused.

. . .

The program planner must learn the skillful art of giving the people what they need to know, and indeed must know, while he is giving them what they want. It takes a high integrity, a profound knowledge of people and where they are as well as the techniques of popular education to be a good program planner. [3]

How Do Agencies Decide What to Offer?

Alert adult education administrators are continually looking for ways to improve their curriculum. If there are areas of adult learning not being served in a community, a visit to the local agency director will often bring a course into being. A community leader, a social worker or an extension agent often will provide the stimulus for a seminar, workshop or course. The faculty of adult education agencies also discover curriculum needs from their adult students. In an ever-changing society, the curriculum must continually be updated to keep in touch with the lives and needs of the adult population.

The administrator, the teacher, the clientele or any combination of the three, may make the decision of what is taught. Colleges and universities have curriculum committees and these tend to be centered in departments. Vocational schools utilize the experience of advisory boards, as do many YMCA's, to determine the content of the program offered the adult.

A revealing study was done in Illinois to ascertain what directors of public school adult education think the purpose of the adult program should be. The study was based upon replies representing 47 high school

Curriculum and Content

districts and revealed that the directors conceive of the program as serving adults primarily for purposes of leisure-time activity and recreation, the cultivation of vocational skills, continuing education and cultural development and community service [9, pp. 1–24].

Some agencies find a specialist in a certain curriculum area and then proceed to build a course around him. For example, an excellent musician in Chicago plays the recorder and the local YWCA has successfully employed him for many years to teach the recorder to adults. A reading specialist knows the curriculum of elementary reading and becomes the key resource for building a program of adult basic education. Some agencies survey the potential audience to find out their interests and needs and develop the content and curriculum accordingly. The Cooperative Extension Service tends to be clientele oriented and brings to adult groups specialists who can develop the programs desired in the communities. If the content is vital, the adults will attend. This is the premise upon which the program planner works.

How Do Adults Discover Learning Opportunities?

Adults learn of the opportunities for continuing their education from a variety of sources. Radio, television, and the mass media are continually announcing offerings for adult education [10, pp. 265–288]. The *Milwaukee Journal*, in cooperation with the Milwaukee Council for Adult Learning twice a year produces a supplement listing, all the adult education offerings in the county. The Racine, Wisconsin, Adult Education Roundtable produces a booklet that describes the agencies providing adult education opportunities and identifies the subjects offered and the persons to contact. The University of Maine produces a newspaper supplement each semester listing the available courses of 28 colleges and universities (both public and private) throughout the state. Numerous public school adult educators develop attractive brochures announcing the curriculum offerings of the semester or quarter. The Denver Adult Education Council publishes a directory of adult education offerings for the area. Finally, the word-of-mouth testimony of a satisfied adult has proved to be one of the best sources on what is available for continuing education.

Two Problems

Two problems have arisen in recent years to cause considerable speculation—the trend toward what Marshall McLuhan calls the "global village" and the concept often referred to as the "spiral curriculum."

Many writers have warned, for decades, that the educational technologies have given the power to a few to influence the minds of all. McLuhan, and perhaps others, have described a process of *tribalizing* by which those who form the audience for the mass media are all exposed to a curriculum of ideas, processes, events, attitudes and values. Sharing as they do this stream of stimulus and influence, they are gradually or rapidly becoming members of a few great "tribes" or "villages." This is a trend and the consequences, both for good and ill, are of such impact they should not be ignored.

However, the educational technologies may also have a different, reverse effect; they may also lead to the individualization of learning. Such media and devices as programmed learning, the new cassette that will plug into the television set, the computer, facsimile printing from electronic broadcasts, are making and will make possible an enormous range of individual stimuli drawn from everywhere, to be read or seen, or experienced by individuals in privacy. One immediate consequence is to bring about widespread plans to individualize learning. How students of all ages can be assisted to choose wisely their own program or curriculum will become a matter of urgency for the educationist.

The concept of the "spiral curriculum" has developed from the notion of *education permanente* or lifelong learning. It has long been recognized that the most important lessons of life cannot be taught well in atoms and segments. J. R. Kidd puts it this way:

One of the problems of the schools has always been how to teach certain ideas or achieve certain kinds of growth in an individual when a lengthy time span is necessary for maturation. How do you teach honour, or justice, or courage? How do you help students to welcome the innovator, to learn to be innovators themselves, and at the same time cherish the "eternal verities?" How do you arm people against propaganda and against crushing pressures to conform? How long does it take to assist a man to become healthily critical of society, of ideas, and of himself, without becoming a sceptic, one who has faith in nothing? Or how, in a curriculum, do you find time to get a hearing for ideas that are merely important against the clamour of those that are urgent? It is much too simple an answer to these baffling questions to say that the time span for education must be extended. But, as the Greeks knew, "time is a kindly God," and, only where education is available when and as needed, will some of life's most important problems be solved. [6]

Take such a sensitive area as "international understanding." From time to time, well-meaning, sometimes well-planned efforts are made in a single classroom or in a single course to deal with some aspect of this matter. Lectures are given or projects are planned, or sometimes

Curriculum and Content

field trips are taken—all of them fragmented, atomistic experiences, about a single country or a single event, or about the constitution of some agency of the United Nations. Each specific activity may be quite successful, but it does not constitute or result in international understanding. The activity may be well planned for a particular age group, but rarely, if ever, is it preceded (or followed up) by other experiences that would give meaning or context or support to this isolated event. This is not to criticize what is done through United Nations Associations, or Parent–Teacher Associations or by classroom teachers. It is simply to point out how difficult the task is under present circumstances, and how far short falls what we do from what we mean by education in international understanding.

Yet it is possible to conceive of a growing, developing, maturing program of studies leading to international understanding. Such a program might begin with songs, stories and games in early childhood, and continue to new, yet related, activities dealing with other countries and their peoples and acts of international cooperation in history, science, geography and the arts during the elementary and secondary school years. Coupled with these activities at the same age level could be film and television programs of many kinds, opportunities to travel abroad or attend sessions of any agency of the United Nations, or, if that were impossible, to take part in model assemblies or international conferences. Further extension of knowledge could take place in many phases of higher education where there is more opportunity for direct contact with people from other countries. All of this could be followed during adulthood by a wide range of learning experiences and engagement in actual projects of international cooperation. Although some objectives may be fulfilled by programs or curricula developed in a short time span, most of the great problems of living require nothing less than long-term designs and combined operations such as those proposed here.

With more leisure time available in our rapidly growing technological society, the programs for adults are proliferating. The following chapters describe some of the program areas that are now prominent in adult education. Among the areas examined are: remedial and basic education; human relations training; home and family life; education for social and public responsibility; vocational and technical education; continuing professional education; adult education for self-fulfillment; and continuing education for women. Each author has been chosen because of professional involvement in his particular program area, and although only selected major program areas are treated, others will be added in the years to come. The curriculum and content of adult education are continually changing with the interests and needs of our society.

References

1. Axford, Roger W. *Adult Education: The Open Door.* Scranton, Pa.: International Textbook Company, 1969.
2. Brunner, Edmund deS., and others. *An Overview of Adult Education Research.* Washington, D.C.: Adult Education Association of the USA, 1959.
3. Buck, Pearl S. *People.* Vol. 4, No. 8 (April, 1945). Published by the East–West Association.
4. Houle, Cyril O. *The Inquiring Mind.* Madison, Wis. University of Wisconsin Press, 1961.
5. Johnstone, John W. C., and others. *Volunteers for Learning: A Study of the Educational Pursuits of American Adults.* Chicago, Ill.: Aldine, 1965.
6. Kidd, J. Roby. *The Implications of Continuous Learning.* New Delhi, India: Caxton Press, 1966.
7. Knowles, Malcolm. *Informal Adult Education.* New York: Association Press, 1950.
8. McGlothlin, W. J. *Patterns of Professional Education.* New York: G. P. Putnam's Sons, 1960.
9. Mann, Thomas W. Office of the Superintendent of Public Instruction, State of Illinois. Circular series A-192, July, 1966.
10. Miller, Harry L. *Teaching and Learning in Adult Education.* New York: The Macmillan Company, 1964.
11. Thomas, Alan. "The Concept of Program in Adult Education." In: *Adult Education: Outlines of an Emerging Field of University Study.* Edited by Gale Jensen, A. A. Liveright and Wilbur Hallenbeck. Washington, D.C.: Adult Education Association of the USA, 1964.
12. Tough, Allen. *Learning Without a Teacher.* Toronto, Canada: Ontario Institute for Studies in Education, 1967.
13. Tyler, Ralph W. *Basic Principles of Curriculum and Instruction.* Chicago, Ill.: University of Chicago Press, 1957.
14. Verner, Coolie. *Some Considerations of Evaluation in Adult Education.* Extension Papers. Alberta, Canada: University of Alberta, 1960.
15. White, Thurman. "The Emerging Curriculum in Higher Education." *CSLEA Newsletter.* Chicago, Ill.: Center for the Study of Liberal Education for Adults, May 10, 1962.

Chapter 24

Adult Basic Education

RICHARD CORTWRIGHT

EDWARD W. BRICE

This is a time of educational revolution—a time when adults of all ages and from all walks of life are returning to the education they missed when they were of "school age." On the other hand, many school-age learners are dropping out. Unless some amazing changes occur in the whole fabric of American education and society many more young people will become school dropouts. These dropouts will in turn be potential recruits for remedial and basic education programs for adults. The problem of educating the undereducated is compounded by the population explosion; in the next sixty years the density of the population across the world will be similar to that of present-day Japan.

The 1960's have placed remedial and basic education for adults in a place of hitherto unequaled importance in the field of adult education. This is the sector of adult education described by such various titles as fundamental education, Americanization, English for the foreign born, social education, literacy education, and now adult basic education (ABE). According to the *Standard Terminology for Instruction in Local and State School Systems*, adult basic education is defined as:

Instruction in communicative, computational and social skills for adults whose inability to effectively use these skills substantially impairs their getting or retaining employment commensurate with their real ability, in order to lessen or eliminate such inability, raise their level of education, and enable them to become more productive and responsible citizens. This usually is considered to include instruction for adults whose educational attainment is below the eighth grade level. [21]

An emphasis in this definition is that ABE is not just basic reading skill or basic computational skill, but a knowledge of these skills related to and integrated into an educational plan for adults that equips them to function on an eighth-grade level. ABE is concerned with learning basic social, economic and scientific concepts as well as with attitudes and values that will help the adult in his personal development.

The question of whether or not a modern society can proceed without functional literacy has been asked by Ginzberg:

Can a democratic society function effectively in the contemporary world unless the citizens are literate? How can an individual discharge the responsibilities of citizenship unless he can inform himself on the issues of the day and express his opinions with respect to them? How can a free press, on which a democratic society depends, flourish without a literate populace? [12]

There are signs the subject of adult basic education has come of age. International and national organizations, public and private, have committed themselves to attacking the problem of undereducation. What was once conceived as a problem removed from America is now considered a significant American problem, and various disciplines are now involved in developing new educational strategies toward decreasing undereducation [6].

The interest of UNESCO in literacy is reflected in a series of influential documents beginning in 1957 with *World Illiteracy at Mid-Century* and including such studies as *The Teaching of Reading and Writing* by the late William S. Gray. UNESCO has also periodically compiled statistics concerning the extent of illiteracy in the world. UNESCO estimates show that:

In 1950, of 1579 million adults, 700 million were illiterate.
In 1960, of 1881 million adults, 740 million were illiterate.
In 1970, of 2335 million adults, 810 million will be illiterate, if the current rate of eradication of illiteracy is maintained [22].

When historians of the American twentieth century look back on the 1960's, they may characterize the decade by three developments of profound historical significance: the civil rights struggle; the extraordinary reshaping of our federal–state–local governmental relationships; and the maturing of responsibility for quality education for all citizens of all ages and at all instructional levels [3]. It is a long walk from the moonlight school of 1911 in Kentucky to the charismatic leadership of Dr. Frank C. Laubach and the pioneer work of South Carolina's Will Lou

Adult Basic Education

Gray begun in the 1920's, to the adult program of the International Ladies Garment Workers Union in the 1930's, to the "Private Pete" Army program during World War II, to volunteer programs like those of the General Federation of Women's Clubs in the 1950's, to the leadership of Dr. Ambrose Caliver in the 1940's, to the Literacy Councils in the 1950's and 1960's, to a systematic national program of ABE in the 1960's and the programs planned for the 1970's and beyond.

Legislation has inaugurated a range of educational programs whose characteristics create a new dimension for federal management and state and local involvement. Under these programs, the federal government has sought to extend the principle of "creative federalism" by involving people at federal, state and local levels in the planning and execution of the programs.

Recent Developments

In the 1960's ABE was no longer the struggling infant of adult education. For example, in a poll of public school teachers, more than 80 percent responded that the schools themselves should provide adult education programs. The educational climate had been sufficiently conditioned to begin to meet the fact of undereducation in America. In a society that had become technologically complex at an exponential rate, there was little space for those at the bottom rungs of the educational ladder to advance economically. Among 321 selected occupations in the United States, a review of the median number of school years completed showed that none of the occupations had employees with less than eight years of schooling.

It has been discovered that potential ABE students have special educational needs whether they be sub-population Negroes, Mexican-Americans, Puerto Ricans, Indians, poor whites, seasonal farm workers, migrants, Cuban refugees or others. One-third of the unemployed have not gone beyond grade school and two-thirds of the unemployed do not have a high school diploma. The majority of undereducated are Negroes whose unemployment rate is about two and one-half times the national average. Seventy percent of those who fail the Armed Forces Qualifying Tests have parents who did not go beyond high school. In 1970 there will be close to 7.5 million dropouts of whom one-third will not have completed the eighth grade. Many of those who complete high school will not be able to function on a twelfth grade level.

Adult education became a direct concern of the federal government early in the 1960's and was included as a part of legislation, enacted earlier in the decade, that dealt with manpower development and training and vocational education for adults.

Federal legislation for adult basic education reflects action on the part of government to meet the education needs of the undereducated: the Manpower Development and Training Act of 1962; the Vocational Education Act of 1963; the Economic Opportunity Act of 1964; the Adult Education Act of 1966 and subsequent amendments to this Act. The fact that the U.S. Office of Education was spending $45 million a year on ABE in 1967 meant that the people and the government were paying serious heed to educating the undereducated.

Scope of the Problem

But is adult undereducation still a problem in America? How important will reading really be for a society saturated by mass media communication? About 23 million people 25 years of age or older were the educationally disadvantaged population in 1960 (see Table 7). Undereducated adults make up about 13 percent of the total population. Even this figure may not represent the extent of the problem of adult undereducation, however, since many adults who have gone to school for eight years cannot function at that grade level. In addition, the educationally disadvantaged population is not limited to any age level, even though the older the group, the larger the number of potential ABE students (see Table 8). Perhaps 40 percent of high school graduates read below the eighth grade level. In the 1970's the potential ABE student will probably be younger, will return sooner to relearn ABE-type skills, and will be more receptive to learning. There will probably be more flexible programs to meet his needs.

The passage of the Economic Opportunity Act in the summer of 1964 triggered the important legislative breakthrough the adult educators had so long anticipated. It was followed later that year by the creation of the Office of Economic Opportunity as an autonomous federal agency. In April, 1964, the National Association for Public Continuing and Adult Education, nationally representative public school adult educators, in cooperation with the U.S. Office of Education, met in Washington for the purpose of assessing the most pressing needs that face the field of adult education. From this meeting came the decision to hold three regional adult basic education institutes during the summer of 1965. Due to the unavailability of federal funds for that particular purpose, the Ford Foundation financed workshops held at the University of New Mexico, the University of Maryland, and the University of Washington. These were the first ABE "summer institutes."

In 1966 came the significant decision by Congress to transfer adult basic education programs from the Office of Economic Opportunity to the U.S. Office of Education. This action was accomplished by repealing

Table 7. *Persons 25 Years Old and Over with Less than Eight Years of School Completed (1960 Census) Resident Population 25 Years Old and Over*

State	Total (thousands)	Less Than Eight Years of School Completed			Median School Year Completed		
		Number (thousands)	Percent of Age Group	Rank of State	Total	White	Nonwhite
Total							
United States (50 States and D.C.)	100,375	22,732	22.6				
	99,438	22,056	22.2	—	10.6	10.9	8.2
Alabama	1,670	643	38.5	47	9.1	10.2	6.5
Alaska	105	16	15.7	17	12.1	12.4	6.6
Arizona	661	138	20.9	30	11.3	11.7	7.0
Arkansas	964	331	34.4	43	8.9	9.5	6.5
California	8,869	1,300	14.7	13	12.1	12.1	10.5
Colorado	941	126	13.4	10	12.1	12.1	11.2
Connecticut	1,482	274	18.5	26	11.0	11.1	9.1
Delaware	246	48	19.6	28	11.1	11.6	8.4
District of Columbia	461	98	21.2	31	11.7	12.4	9.8
Florida	2,845	650	22.8	34	10.9	11.6	7.0
Georgia	2,015	811	40.3	48	9.0	10.3	6.1
Hawaii	309	82	26.7	38	11.3	12.4	9.9

Table 7. (continued)

State	Total (thousands)	Less Than Eight Years of School Completed Number (thousands)	Less Than Eight Years of School Completed Percent of Age Group	Less Than Eight Years of School Completed Rank of State	Median School Year Completed Total	Median School Year Completed White	Median School Year Completed Nonwhite
Idaho	340	37	10.8	2	11.8	11.8	9.6
Illinois	5,808	1,048	18.0	24	10.5	10.7	9.6
Indiana	2,550	432	17.0	19	10.8	10.9	9.6
Iowa	1,541	211	13.7	11	11.3	11.3	9.5
Kansas	1,216	159	13.1	8	11.7	11.8	9.6
Kentucky	1,610	535	33.2	42	8.7	8.7	8.2
Louisiana	1,639	688	41.9	50	8.8	10.5	6.6
Maine	534	84	15.7	16	11.0	11.0	10.7
Maryland	1,693	461	27.2	39	10.4	11.0	8.1
Massachusetts	3,011	523	17.4	20	11.6	11.6	10.3
Michigan	4,219	739	17.5	21	10.8	11.0	9.1
Minnesota	1,845	269	14.6	14	10.8	10.8	9.9
Mississippi	1,065	403	37.8	46	8.9	11.0	6.0
Missouri	2,493	535	21.5	32	9.6	9.8	8.7
Montana	356	47	13.3	9	11.6	11.7	8.7
Nebraska	791	96	12.2	7	11.6	11.7	9.6
Nevada	160	17	10.9	3	12.1	12.2	8.8
New Hampshire	345	56	16.3	18	10.9	10.9	11.7

New Jersey	3,600	739	20.5	29	10.6	10.8	8.8
New Mexico	445	108	24.2	37	11.2	11.5	7.1
New York	10,124	1,969	19.4	27	10.7	10.8	9.4
North Carolina	2,307	956	41.4	49	8.9	9.8	7.0
North Dakota	324	59	18.4	25	9.3	9.3	8.4
Ohio	5,378	954	17.7	22	10.9	11.0	9.1
Oklahoma	1,300	304	23.4	35	10.4	10.7	8.6
Oregon	996	121	12.1	6	11.8	11.8	9.9
Pennsylvania	6,606	1,425	21.6	33	10.2	10.3	8.9
Rhode Island	498	118	23.6	36	10.0	10.0	9.5
South Carolina	1,136	493	43.4	51	8.7	10.3	5.9
South Dakota	360	50	13.8	12	10.4	10.5	8.6
Tennessee	1,912	666	34.9	44	8.8	9.0	7.5
Texas	5,031	1,514	30.1	40	10.4	10.8	8.1
Utah	419	38	9.0	1	12.2	12.2	10.1
Vermont	213	31	14.6	15	10.9	10.9	10.5
Virginia	2,083	756	36.3	45	9.9	10.8	7.2
Washington	1,577	185	11.7	5	12.1	12.1	10.5
West Virginia	1,000	305	30.5	41	8.8	8.8	8.4
Wisconsin	2,175	387	17.8	23	10.4	10.4	9.0
Wyoming	174	20	11.6	4	12.1	12.1	9.3
Guam	28	11	38.8				
Puerto Rico	925	656	70.9				
Virgin Islands	14	9	61.2				

Table 8. *Educationally Disadvantaged Population (EDP) (1960 Census)*

Age Group	\multicolumn{8}{c}{Years of School Completed}									EDP in Each Age Group (thousands)	People in Each Age Group (thousands)	Percent of Each Age Group in the EDP	Percent of the Total EDP in Each Age Group
	0	1	2	3	4	5	6	7				
18	12	5	10	8	10	16	31	62	157	2,498	6.3	0.6
19	13	3	8	11	12	17	29	55	151	2,275	6.6	0.6
20	12	3	5	9	12	17	29	53	142	2,190	6.5	0.6
21	11	3	5	8	12	19	30	54	146	2,203	6.6	0.6
22	12	3	6	9	13	20	34	57	157	2,158	7.3	0.7
23	14	3	6	10	15	21	36	60	169	2,106	8.0	0.7
24	13	4	6	11	16	22	37	65	178	2,144	8.3	0.8
25–29	73	23	42	68	95	132	221	368	1,026	10,870	9.4	4.4
30–34	87	30	55	95	134	178	299	487	1,368	11,951	11.4	5.9
35–39	100	37	67	121	171	212	354	541	1,608	12,508	12.9	6.9
40–44	103	41	73	134	189	231	387	619	1,782	11,567	15.4	7.7
45–49	127	48	86	161	228	283	473	758	2,167	10,928	19.8	9.3
50–54	153	52	93	179	253	299	500	767	2,229	9,696	23.7	9.9
55–59	209	62	111	213	300	325	545	769	2,538	8,595	29.5	10.9
60–64	260	59	106	215	303	303	507	646	2,404	7,111	33.9	10.3
65–69	372	67	121	234	331	293	491	553	2,467	6,186	39.9	10.6
70–74	347	55	98	198	279	234	393	400	2,007	4,661	43.1	8.6
75 and over	438	66	119	246	369	280	470	471	2,440	5,359	45.5	10.5
Total[a]	2,365	571	1,025	1,940	2,729	2,909	4,876	6,795	23,213	116,015		100
3% Adjustment for Census Error	2,438	589	1,057	2,000	2,814	2,999	5,027	7,005	23,933	119,495		

[a] Totals differ from sums due to column rounding.

Adult Basic Education

Title II-B of the Economic Opportunity Act, and by enacting the Adult Education Act of 1966 as Title III of the Elementary and Secondary Education Act Amendments.

The implementation of ABE programs requires the instruction of millions of undereducated adults by trained teachers. Particular effort has been made to expose teachers to various kinds of audio-visual technology. Subject-matter specialists from adult education, educational administration, educational psychology, psychology, sociology, testing, counseling, urban affairs, reading, teaching English as a second language, and other disciplines are being used extensively in ABE teacher training programs. In addition to the university-based summer short course, state ABE directors have developed year-round in-service teacher training at state and local levels.

Teacher Training

Previous to the enactment of federal legislation, several universities conducted programs to train administrators and teachers of ABE: Syracuse University, Baylor University, Indiana University, San Francisco State College, Tuskegee Institute, Florida State University, Virginia State College at Norfolk and the American University. Funds from Amendments to Title III of the Elementary and Secondary Education Act, also called the Adult Education Act of 1966, made possible an extended, in-depth series of summer institutes for teachers and administrators of ABE. The first federally supported institutes were held in 1966: 9 were held that year, 20 the following year, and 25 in 1968.

These institutes were designed to provide an overview of the concepts and procedures useful in conducting adult basic education programs. A typical institute was two or three weeks in length, had from 50 to 100 participants, and dealt with such concerns as:

Philosophy of adult basic education
Teaching adults to read
Establishing instructional objectives
Programmed instruction
New ideas and technology
Organization and administration of state and local programs
Counseling adults

In 1967 the summer institutes were strengthened by a Pre-Institute Seminar conducted at Wayne State University. This week-long course served as preparation for the persons staffing the 20 institutes to be conducted that summer across the country.

A major objective of the summer institutes was to prepare the participants to conduct in-service training for teachers, administrators and volunteers involved in their programs "back home." It is estimated that participants in the nine 1966 institutes alone gave pre- and in-service training to 12,000 teachers.

In 1969 a workshop was held at the University of Chicago to assist professors of adult education and adult education researchers to address themselves more effectively to the vast problems of preparing the quantity and quality of instructional personnel needed for ABE.

Sponsoring Agencies

The principal federal agency which has taken responsibility for ABE programs is the United States Office of Education in the Department of Health, Education and Welfare. In addition, ABE programs have been administered by the Department of Defense, the Department of Labor, the Department of the Interior, the Department of Justice, the Office of Economic Opportunity and the Veterans Administration. The data in Table 9 show the number of eligible enrollees as well as the actual enrollments in federally supported adult education programs in fiscal year 1967. For example, during fiscal year 1967 an estimated 40,000 adults enrolled in adult education programs administered by Project 100,000 in the Department of Defense.

In the late 1960's ABE programs were also sponsored by other agencies: the Model Cities Program of the Department of Housing and Urban Development; the Department of Labor financed Job Opportunities in the Business Sector program (JOBS) administered by the National Alliance of Businessmen (NABS); other manpower-oriented programs in the Department of Labor such as the Concentrated Employment Programs (CEP) and the Work Incentive Now Program (WINS). In addition more than 600 non-governmental agencies—such as Laubach Literacy, Inc., Church Women United and volunteer Literacy Councils in the National Affiliation for Literacy Advance (NALA)—were actively engaged in ABE. NALA, in 1968 for example, trained 1600 tutors (in 268 workshops) who were teaching about 3500 adults. All of these programs are in addition to the 1,023,788 adults enrolled in the adult education programs reported in Table 9.

Special Projects

From the funds available from the Adult Education Act, the United States Office of Education also funded Special Projects in ABE. The first Special Projects undertaken by the United States Office of Education in ABE were: (1) a demonstration project providing remedial education,

Table 9. *Eligibles and Enrollments in Federally Supported Adult Education Programs, Fiscal Year 1967*

Administering Agency and Program	Estimated Number of Eligibles	Estimated Enrollments in Adult Education Programs
Department of Defense		
Project 100,000	100,000	40,000
Project Transition	150,000	NA
Off-Duty Educational Services Programs for Military Personnel	500,000	210,000
Department of Health, Education and Welfare		
Adult Basic Education	18,220,000	380,838
Vocational and Technical Education	NA	NA
Work Experience and Training	1,326,000	33,400
Community Work and Training	300,000	NA
Cuban Refugee Program	44,000	5,500
Vocational Rehabilitation	4,000,000	NA
Department of Labor—HEW		
Manpower Development and Training Programs	10,065,000	46,000
Institutional, MDTA for RAR Residents		
On-the-Job Training, Coupled		
Department of Interior		
Bureau of Indian Affairs		
Adult Education Programs	367,000	25,000
Employment Assistance Programs	367,000	NA
Department of Justice		
Citizenship Education and Training	3,088,133	136,000
Educational and Vocational Training for Federal Prisoners	20,000	12,000
Department of Labor		
Concentrated Employment Program	Same as MDTA	NA
Operation Mainstream	Same as MDTA	NA
New Careers	Same as MDTA	NA
Specific Impact	Same as MDTA	NA
Neighborhood Youth Corps	2,485,000	12,500
Office of Economic Opportunity		
Community Action Program		
Adult Basic Education	11,000,000	50,000
Indian Training Program	367,000	19,400
Migrant and Seasonal Farm Workers Program	1,800,000	28,000
Job Corps	(2,485,000)	20,000
Veterans Administration		
Veterans Readjustment and Training Program (GI Bill)	4,500,000	4,750

counseling and on-the-job training; (2) an occupationally oriented program for union members; (3) a program for the parents of summer Head Start students; (4) an experimental program conducted by the Opportunities Industrialization Center in neighborhood homes in informal settings; (5) the determination of suitable materials for teaching undereducated migrants and the use of mobile schools to accompany migrants; (6) a television series for Spanish-speaking migrants; (7) a research and demonstration center for Appalachia; (8) a project to test and evaluate instructional materials; (9) a demonstration to test new and innovative approaches to teaching adults in an urban industrial area; and (10) a demonstration project using educational technology for instruction. Ten more Special Projects were funded in 1968 and a similar number for 1969.

Goals and Resources

ABE is considered more than teaching the beginning skills of reading and writing or arithmetic. The purpose of specialized ABE curricula is to lead the ABE student from basic literacy—the manipulation of beginning-level reading, writing and arithmetic skills—to a variety of knowledges such as understanding the world of work (reading a help-wanted column, answering an advertisement by telephone, using the classified telephone directory to get a job, using employment services, making out an application form and learning about governmental jobs), labor unions, social security, getting along on a job, consumer education and improving health in the home.

It is also the purpose of ABE to bring participants up to the level of "functional literacy." Census statistics reveal that unemployment and illiteracy go together. Without basic learning skills the adult is severely limited in obtaining gainful employment. Often vocational training programs fail or have been of limited usefulness because adults do not have sufficient skills to benefit from vocational instruction. Therefore, long-range programs aim to provide adults an opportunity to improve communication as well as personal, social and economic skills.

To meet the need for special educational materials, publishers are producing a wide range of instructional materials. It appears the more effective materials are directly related to the present interests of adults, specific jobs and simple directions for adult problem situations. The best of these materials are adult, multi-racial and stress action in clear vivid language packaged attractively either in programmed-learning sequences or in more conventional textbooks. In addition, the education industries, often the result of mergers of software and hardware manufacturers, have entered the ABE market. A national conference of an

Adult Basic Education

adult education association, such as the National Association for Public Continuing and Adult Education or the Adult Education Association of the USA, is not complete without wide-ranging displays of ABE instructional materials.

Also related to the development of adult remedial and basic education is the Adult High School (AHE) or High School Equivalency Education (HSE), as well as special college degree programs for adults. In the mid-sixties some 58 million adults did not have a high school diploma. During World War II the United States Armed Forces Institute Test of General Education Development (GED) was first prepared. The well-known GED tests, after extensive revisions, are now offered nationally. Passing the GED leads to the awarding of a high school diploma. By 1970, 50 percent of Americans will need at least a high school diploma and up to two years of college or technical training for job purposes. Another 25 percent will need a high school or vocational school diploma. Only about 6 percent of the jobs will be filled by unskilled workers. Adult High School Diploma Programs will probably consider granting credit gained from armed forces schools, community colleges, correspondence courses, adult school credit courses and work experience.

In order for ABE teachers and administrators to carry on more effective programs two national resource organizations were organized in the late 1960's: the ERIC Clearinghouse on Adult Education (ERIC/AE) and the NEA Adult Education Clearinghouse (NAEC).

Directors, counselors, supervisors and teachers of ABE are encouraged to take advantage of the services of the ERIC Clearinghouse on Adult Education which is sponsored by the Educational Resources Information Center (ERIC) of the U.S. Office of Education and by the Library of Continuing Education of Syracuse University. ERIC/AE is one of the 19 education clearinghouses in the national ERIC network of information analysis centers [8]. ERIC/AE abstracts, indexes, and retrieves substantive documents which are made available through *Research in Education,* the monthly abstract Bulletin published by the United States Office of Education. ERIC/AE also publishes newsletters, Current Information Sources, Annual Research Reviews and Information Analyses.

The NEA Adult Educational Clearinghouse (NAEC) was established by the National Education Association to provide easier access to information useful in the education of adults and out-of-school youth. Particular attention is placed on elementary and high school level completion programs for adults. NAEC supplies written answers to requests for information about adult education by citing references, providing copies of documents and summaries of information. In addition to supplying written responses to requests, NAEC makes its services available by conducting workshops on information utilization, by distributing multi-media programs on resources and research information, by maintaining a referral system of consultants on adult education, and by publishing broadsides of adult education information. Arrangements for collaboration with the ERIC Clearinghouse on Adult Education have been established so the two services complement and reinforce each other. NAEC uses ERIC and other materials in developing a range of information services.

Research

Serious research in adult basic education has increased substantially in recent years. Examples of research on characteristics of students, dropouts, readability levels of instructional materials and program financing follow.

Characteristics of Students

A study of characteristics of ABE participants indicated that adults who participate in stipend programs differ significantly from those who participate in non-stipend programs, and that all undereducated are not alike. Those adults with a high degree of alienation differ significantly from those who exhibit a lower level of alienation. In addition, the undereducated do participate in social activities. They have marked social problems, but they do not make use of formal agencies to help themselves. They learn about ABE classes from many sources. However, all adults with characteristics of deprivation, subordinate racial status and limited education are not highly alienated [9].

Dropouts

A study of ABE dropouts, about half Puerto Rican and half Negro, indicated most of the dropouts to be in their thirties, married, at low reading levels, and out of class after less than 50 hours of instruction. The main reasons for dropping out were change of residence and instruction's interference with work responsibilities [14].

Readability Levels of Instructional Materials

A study of the readability level of instructional materials used in a Job Corps camp indicated that materials dealing with language and money management tested at about the fourth, fifth or sixth grade levels.

Adult Basic Education

The adult students, it was concluded, should have been able to read these materials since they also tested at about these levels [5].

Program Financing

A study of the financial needs to carry out a national program of ABE over twenty years offered a plan to reach 13 million illiterate adults between 18 and 64 years of age. The plan would cost from $55 million to $235 million per year. It was projected that the economic gains of the participants would be four times the cost of the program [23].

The Future

The National Advisory Committee on Adult Basic Education has made seven recommendations for ABE through 1972 [1]. The committee recommends:

1. That the immediate Adult Basic Education Program focus on the nation's educational priorities including, but not limited to, civic participation, jobs, home and family life. The appropriations recommended are:
   Fiscal year 1970—$100 million for 1 million adults,
   Fiscal year 1971—$150 million for 1.5 million adults,
   Fiscal year 1972—$200 million for 2 million adults.
2. That the Office of Education be strongly urged to look with favor on requests from the state education agencies for additional funding of the Adult Basic Education Program in areas of urban crisis; that $20 million in additional funds be appropriated immediately for this purpose.
3. That the Office of Education develop a ten-year national plan for adult basic education with provisions for coordinating and consolidating all federal programs with adult education components; that $250,000 be appropriated to cover the estimated cost for the preparation of the plan.
4. That immediate steps be taken to strengthen the National Advisory Committee on Adult Basic Education so that it may:
   Provide the leadership needed for developing, implementing, and reviewing the ten-year plan
   Provide the leadership for coordinating and consolidating the functions of adult basic education with related programs administered by other federal agencies
   Develop supporting services
   Recommend future legislation.
5. That an appropriation of $200,000 be authorized annually to sup-

port a committee staff, special data-gathering services, and the preparation and publication of an annual report.
6. That a continuing training program for teachers, administrators, counselors, and other leaders be strengthened, with increased emphasis on the training of aides and volunteers to meet the requirements of the expanding Adult Basic Education Program. Recommended appropriations are:

 Fiscal year 1970— $5 million for 5,000 enrollees,
 Fiscal year 1971—$10 million for 10,000 enrollees,
 Fiscal year 1972—$15 million for 15,000 enrollees.
7. That support for special projects and funds for the experimentation and demonstration essential to the rapid improvement of adult basic education be continued. Recommended appropriations are:

 Fiscal year 1970—$20 million,
 Fiscal year 1971—$30 million,
 Fiscal year 1972—$40 million.
8. That the Adult Basic Education Program be extended beyond the present eighth-grade functional level through legislative action; that additional funds be appropriated for this purpose.

Total appropriations required by the above recommendations for the Adult Basic Education Program are:

1970—$125 million,
1971—$190 million,
1972—$255 million.

There is now a great seriousness of purpose to implement programs of remedial and basic education for adults. Within the historical perspective of the adult education movement in the United States, however, the questions will be: Did ABE reach its peak in the 1960's; Will adult high school education supplant adult basic education in the 1970's? Whatever the answers, it is clear that remedial and basic education for adults has come of age.

What has been reported in this chapter are revolutionary beginnings. Yet, significant and encouraging as they are, they provide but a glimpse of the task remaining. We have come to the time when there is general agreement that we can no longer neglect to utilize the vast resources inherent in the large groups of undereducated adults found in our population.

References

1. *Adult Basic Education—Meeting the Challenges of the 1970's.* First Annual Report of the National Advisory Committee on Adult Basic

Education to the President of the United States and the Secretary of Health, Education and Welfare (August, 1968), pp. 2, 3.
2. Brady, Henry G., Jr. *Adult Basic Education—A Summary of Activities July 1, 1967–June 1, 1968.* Tallahassee, Fla.: Department of Adult Education, College of Education, Florida State University, 1968.
3. Brice, Edward W. "The Importance of Adult Basic Education in Today's Society." *Perspectives in Adult Basic Education for Administrators.* DeKalb, Ill.: Northern Illinois University, 1967, pp. 1–5.
4. Bureau of the Census. *U.S. Census of Population: 1960 General Social and Economic Characteristics.* Final Report, PC 1 series for each state. Washington, D.C.: Government Printing Office, 1960.
5. Carroll, A. *A Readability Analysis of Randomly Selected Basic Education and Vocational Education Curriculum Materials Used at the Atterbury Job Corps Center as Measured by the Gunning Fox Index.* Bloomington, Ind.: Indiana University, 1967.
6. Cortright, Richard W. "American Literacy—a Mini-Analysis." *Convergence—An International Journal of Adult Education,* I (September, 1968), pp. 63–67.
7. Cortright, Richard W. "Professional Preparation in Literacy Education." *Journal of Teacher Education* (September, 1965), pp. 290–293.
8. DeCrow, Roger and Grabowski, Stanley. "Sources of Information About Adult Education." *Adult Leadership,* XVII (June, 1968), pp. 75–77.
9. Dutton, Marion Donnie. *A Description and Analysis of Selected Characteristics of Participants in Adult Basic Education in Hillsborough County, Florida.* Unpublished dissertation. Tallahassee, Fla.: Florida State University, 1967.
10. ERIC Clearinghouse on Adult Education. *Adult Basic Education, Current Information Sources.* Syracuse, N.Y.: ERIC Clearinghouse on Adult Education, 1967.
11. Fitzgerald, Hunter. *Adult Basic Education National Teacher-Training Institute, July 10–28, 1967.* Los Angeles, Calif.: University of California, 1967.
12. Ginzberg, Eli. "10,000,000 U.S. Illiterates." *Americas,* C (November, 1958).
13. Greenleigh Associates. *Inventory of Federally Supported Adult Education Programs.* New York: Greenleigh Associates, 1968.
14. Moss, Doris, and Richardson, Robert. *A Study of Students Who Have Discontinued Attendance in the F.S.E.T. III Adult Basic Education Program.* Brooklyn, N.Y.: New York City Board of Education, 1967.
15. National Association for Public School Adult Education. *The Administration of Adult Basic Education, A Manual of Training Materials.* Washington, D.C.: National Education Association, 1967.
16. National Education Association, Research Division. *Teacher Opinion Poll, 1967–1968.* Washington, D.C.: National Education Association, 1968.
17. National University Extension Association. *Materials for the Adult Basic*

Education Administrator and Teacher, Bibliography. Washington, D.C.: National University Extension Association, 1967.
18. National University Extension Association. *Materials for the Adult Basic Education Student, A Bibliography.* Washington, D.C.: National University Extension Association, 1967.
19. Oakland Public Schools. *Evaluation of the EOA Basic Education Program, 1965–1966.* Oakland, Calif.: Oakland Public Schools, 1966.
20. Pearce, Frank C. *Basic Education Teachers, Seven Needed Qualities.* Stanislaus County Multi-Occupational Adult Training Project, Teacher Characteristics, Report 4.1. Modesto, Calif.: Modesto Junior College, 1966.
21. Putnam, John F., and Chrismore, W. Dale, compilers. *Standard Terminology for Instruction in Local and State School Systems: An Analysis of Instructional Content, Resources and Processes.* Office of Education, U.S. Department of Health, Education and Welfare. Washington, D.C.: Government Printing Office, 1967.
22. UNESCO. *Illiteracy and Human Rights.* Paris: UNESCO, 1968.
23. Venn, Grant, and others. *A Comprehensive Plan for Solution of the Functionally Illiterate Problem, A Report on the Present, A Plan for the Future.* Washington, D.C.: Management Technology, 1968.
24. Wheeler, Hubert. *Adult Basic Education, A Guide for Teachers* (revised). Publication 134-G. St. Louis, Mo.: Missouri State Board of Education, 1967.

Chapter 25

Human Relations—Sensitivity Training

GEORGE K. GORDON

One of the most distinctive educational inventions of the mid-twentieth century is known as "human relations training" or "sensitivity training." There seems to be little agreement between authorities in distinguishing between the two terms. For practical purposes they have become interchangeable. Regardless of the name, this type of training is an important part of the educational program of many institutions and organizations. It will be referred to here as human relations training—with apologies to those who prefer sensitivity training.

Human relations training is sometimes called "the group dynamics approach." This is a misleading and obsolete label—but it is a clue to the origins of human relations training. For centuries, students of human nature have observed that individual behavior is powerfully influenced in both positive and negative ways by the groups to which people belong. It was well into the twentieth century, however, before investigators began to develop ways to overcome the technical difficulties involved in small-group research. By then the problems of technological, economic, social and political change were mounting rapidly. It became increasingly important to understand how groups influence individuals, and vice versa, and the role groups play in promoting or suppressing change. Consequently, money became available chiefly through private foundations, industry and government to finance research in small-group life. The resulting body of research findings and theory became loosely identified as "group dynamics."

The study of this new body of literature not only cast light on the inadequacies of many common social practices but also suggested innovative alternative practices to be explored. These innovations and attempts to explore their usefulness are especially associated with such organizations as the National Training Laboratories, which began conducting training programs in the summer of 1947.

Early training programs were obviously exploratory in nature. They were sometimes awkward in design; they were sometimes flawed by inappropriate procedures; and they were often saturated with group dynamics jargon. It was out of these origins that today's human relations training programs emerged.

Understanding Human Relations Training

For the person who has never participated in human relations training, the attempt to understand what it is can be frustrating. An inquirer may quickly conclude that the proponents of human relations training are more blessed with enthusiasm than with clarity of exposition. He may even suspect they are deliberately obscure or evasive when describing human relations training.

Such reactions are not unusual. In fact, their commonness points to a basic problem of human relations training—it is indeed difficult to define and describe without resorting to equivocal and conditional statements as well as other kinds of strained and circuitous language. It is important to understand why this happens. The following observations are pertinent to the communication problem:

1. Human relations training is a relatively new invention. Even those who have been involved in it from its beginnings do not agree on the boundaries within which it falls. Moreover, it seems premature to set rigid boundaries at the present time.
2. Human relations training is conducted in an action research framework. The training is constantly evolving and changing.
3. As training centers and institutions experiment in adapting the training to the special needs of specific learners, unique training formats emerge. As a result, there are several kinds of programs known collectively as human relations training.
4. Human relations training resembles several other areas of human endeavor which are better established such as traditional education, study–discussion programs, leadership training and group therapy. Human relations training is often perceived only in terms of a few selected characteristics that it shares with one of

Human Relations—Sensitivity Training

these other kinds of endeavors. On this basis, human relations training is liable to appear to be a fumbling attempt at group therapy, an ill-conceived approach to leadership training, or a scatter-gun educational strategy with no substantial content.

5. Human relations training is focused on personal experience. It is relatively easy to describe the mechanics of program designs, techniques and procedures, but something is always lost in trying to communicate about the diversity of human experience.

These observations and their implications account for the vague or elusive quality of much that is written and said about human relations training.

Common Program Characteristics

Human relations training programs generally share three common characteristics: (1) they are focused on learning about self and relationships with others; (2) the learning is based on the personal experience of the learners themselves as they associate with one another during the training; (3) the learners become collaborative investigators accepting increasing responsibility for directing their own learning. A specific training event has the potential for promoting learning in all of its phases; however, time limitations usually mean that only a restricted number of the potential learnings can be developed adequately. (Moreover, specific groups of learners and sponsoring organizations are more concerned with some learnings than with others.) Therefore, a particular training event is usually designed to place primary emphasis on two or three of the potential learning categories while the other categories are dealt with tangentially, if at all.

Regardless of focus or format, all human relations training events share a common educational strategy. They are designed to encourage each learner, with the help of his fellow learners, to become involved in a careful scrutiny of his own thought patterns, perceptions, feelings, value system and actions in order to discover whatever incongruities or inadequacies may exist. They are designed, furthermore, to encourage each learner, with the support of his fellow learners, to invent and experiment with better integrated patterns of functioning.

Training Design Components

The session-by-session schedule of human relations training programs usually includes combinations of the following kinds of activities:

Training Groups. Training groups are known by various names. They are most widely called "T-Groups," containing between eight to twelve people who meet as a continuing group during the training event. The training group is the core of the training experience. Membership is in a relatively unstructured situation with no imposed direction other than to "become a group." They thus meet in a vacuum regarding structures, procedures and objectives—which is quite unlike the social situations they are used to encountering. In this dilemma, individual members usually attempt to fill the vacuum with their standard repertoire of social behaviors. The group thus becomes a microcosm for observing, analyzing, diagnosing and evaluating personal behavior and interpersonal relationships.

Theory Sessions. Organized presentations of research findings and theoretical formulations are offered by theory sessions. These sessions help orient the trainees to what is about to happen to them or clarify and systematize what they have already experienced. Such presentations are usually scheduled in general (large group) sessions; but they may also be made informally in the training group as occasion demands.

Focused Exercises. Exercises are devoted to carefully planned demonstrations and practice opportunities. They may focus on patterns of influence, intergroup competition and group member roles—or on such special skills as observation, communication, planning and supervision. Role playing and simulation are frequently used; so are such creative or projective techniques as finger painting, fantasy, tactility training and body awareness exercises.

Other Activities. Additional activities may be introduced (often improvised) as the need arises. These have included "bull sessions," dyadic or triadic conversation groupings, video or magnetic tape analysis, and individual study, projects and reports.

The word "laboratory" is another term frequently associated with human relations training. This refers to the methodological relationship between the learners and the educational agency which conducts the training. The laboratory method calls for the learners to be temporarily isolated, physically and psychologically, from everyday work and home relationships. Participants usually take up residence at the training location for the duration of the training event. However, the word "laboratory" was chosen for its common meaning, a place where experiments are conducted. The great bulk of human relations training is conducted in the laboratory setting.

Human Relations—Sensitivity Training

The Trainer Role

In most cases, the training procedure is guided by an educational agent called a "trainer." This is an unfortunate choice of terminology, since it suggests animals jumping through hoops to the crack of a whip. The term was chosen, however, to distinguish the role which the trainer plays from the role of the traditional teacher. The trainer usually does not impose agenda, organization or procedures on the training group. His primary purpose is to encourage the members to learn for themselves.

The trainer accomplishes his assignment through carefully chosen interventions in the life of the group. Depending on the group's development and the problems it faces, the trainer interventions take two basic forms: (1) the trainer may intervene as an expert "process observer," drawing attention to what is happening in the life of the group and posing analytical questions for consideration by the group; or (2) he may enter in essentially as a consultant with methodological expertise to place at the group's disposal.

Skillfully conducted interventions serve to establish in the group conditions which support personal learning by the group members. These conditions include:

Observant Participation. The trainer's process observations and the process analysis which they engender establish the legitimacy of such behavior in the group; this is a departure from standard social conventions. Establishment of the legitimacy of process analysis makes it possible for all group members to begin functioning as observant participants—observing, analyzing and experimenting with their own group life.

Here-and-Now Focus. The group's attentions are directed to behavioral events actually occurring within the shared experience of the training group.

Psychological Safety. A climate of acceptance among the group members is cultivated. This minimizes individual defensiveness and allows each person to display and examine realistically his own typical patterns of behavior and to experiment with new behaviors under conditions of minimum personal risk.

Feedback. The effectiveness of learning efforts is greatly enhanced if the learner receives immediate and direct knowledge of results as he attempts to use newly acquired learning. In human relations training, the process through which knowledge of results is obtained is called *feedback*. It involves the development of means for gathering data on the effects of individual behavior. Through intervention, the trainer establishes the acceptability of both seeking and giving feedback in the training setting.

Models and Conceptual Frameworks. As the training group develops, the members are confronted with needs not only for data gathering and analysis, but also for such activities as diagnosis of difficulties, problem solving, decision making and planning. The group must develop procedural models for carrying out these activities. And as the learners accumulate experience and new understandings during the training, these must be integrated in light of previous experiences and future expectations. The new learnings must be conceptualized, generalized and organized into a viable framework in order to sustain appropriate application of new learnings. While models and conceptual frameworks are suggested in general session presentations and learners are encouraged to develop or invent their own, the trainer's relationships with the training group should demonstrate: (1) that he himself uses such models and conceptual frameworks; (2) that he continues to weigh and test them; (3) that he is aware of alternatives; and (4) that in spite of his relative expertise in these matters he continues to be an open and inquiring co-learner in the training group.

The trainer's role is complex. The person filling this role must have great personal security as well as genuine expertise. The skill and ease with which he performs as trainer is the key to what happens in the training group and, as has already been pointed out, the training group is the core of the training experience. Each person brings his own unique personality, understandings, values and personal needs to bear on the trainer role. Each trainer, therefore, develops his own special style of training. There are marked differences among trainers as to what constitutes sound trainer style. The definition of the trainer role and acceptable standards of trainer behavior constitute one of the most controversial aspects of human relations training.

The Congenialities of Training Groups

It would be wrong to assume the trainer is the sole determinant of what happens in human relations training. The peculiar mixture of people attending a training event allows the group to focus on certain kinds of learnings. For example, the more homogeneous the learners the more congenial the group is likely to be toward training that is focused on group and organizational performance.

Heterogeneity among the learners tends to limit the possibilities of meaningful mutual learning about groups and organizations. Each learner discovers too many irrelevancies, incongruities, contradictions and exceptions to the particulars of his own organizational frame of reference. There is too much frustration in constantly translating ideas and information from one learner's unique situation to another's. In such groups, personal growth and development of the members is the obvious commonality which they can fruitfully explore together. Such predilections are not inevitable, but they are natural likelihoods which can be taken into account in designing human relations training events.

Varieties of Training Designs

It is apparent human relations training varies somewhat with the setting. It can be anticipated that a particular group of learners will be most congenial toward certain kinds of learning objectives. A training staff can be selected that will match the training styles, skills and interests of the trainers to the objectives of the potential learners. And the components of the training design can be variously combined, arranged and modified to accommodate the needs of the learners.

Three training programs will now be described briefly to reveal the variety that exists in the design and conduct of human relations training.

The Instrumented T-Group. The systems approach to human relations training was developed by the Southwest Human Relations Training Laboratories and the Esso–Humble Oil Company and is especially well adapted for learning about groups and organizations. In this approach, the T-Group is initiated in the standard unstructured dilemma. However, the trainer role is minimized by the use of a battery of self-administered data-gathering instruments (rating scales, ranking instruments, inventories) that the group uses periodically. Responses to the instruments are summarized and plotted visually before the group, session-by-session or day-by-day. These shared data become the basis for self-evaluation and diagnosis in the group as well as for the development of face-to-face feedback (e.g., sharing one's perceptions of another person's behavior with him and the group).

The action-research aspect of human relations training is clearly demonstrated in the instrumented T-Group. The learners quickly assume responsibility for gathering their own data, analyzing it, evaluating their situation, diagnosing their own needs, setting objectives, planning a course of action, and proceeding. Group development is augmented by carefully prepared theory sessions and focused exercises selected well in advance to coincide with the most likely chronology in which problems and issues arise in the life of such groups. The use of a fairly stable battery of instruments can facilitate comparative studies of groups.

Participants in such training are expected, at the very least, to acquire a set of concepts and skills which they can use to clarify the various interpersonal, group, and intergroup problems which they meet in everyday life. Ideally, trainees can acquire a training model which is transferable *in toto* to other situations.

Therapy for Normals. The human relations training program developed through the Graduate School of Business Administration at UCLA and the Western Training Laboratories is focused primarily on learning about self and relationships with others. The more clinical and individual focus of this approach is reflected in the label "Therapy for Normals" by which it is often identified. The gross objective of this training is to promote optimum personal growth of people who are "normal" by accepted social standards but who may, nevertheless, be stultified by the limited personal expectations embodied in accepted social standards.

The training is expected to contribute to the total enhancement of the individual by helping him to: (1) transcend his own routine ways of perceiving and thinking; (2) enter into a fuller and richer experience of people and events; (3) develop intimate and accurate knowledge of himself; (4) reassess the meaning and significance of his own life; and (5) initiate sustained growth toward increasing personal adequacy. Group variables are largely ignored in favor of the exploration of individual dynamics, the unfolding of a fully functioning personality, the strengthening of self-image, and the cultivation of ego strength.

Training designs for these events tend to be quite innovative, including a wide variety of activities intended to promote individual exploration of new modes of self-expression, projection of the internal self, intensified awareness of the varieties of sensory experience, critical analysis of personal effectiveness and experimentation with life styles. Training is aimed at breaking up the "lonely crowd" syndrome and the "gamesmanship" of mass culture that alienate people from one another and from their own authentic selves.

At the least, such training events may be viewed as retreats, opportunities to disengage from gamesmanship and to reconstitute one's own unique selfhood. But many advocates of Therapy for Normals see it as offering a viable alternative to gamesmanship. In any case, the hoped-for outcome is that the participant makes a deep commitment to continued growth toward integrated, authentic personhood in his relationships with other people.

In Therapy for Normals, learning about *self* and *interpersonal rela-*

tionships receives primary emphasis. The instrumented T-Group approach includes special adaptations for learning about *groups and organizations*. A training approach which emphasizes *learning how to learn* is exemplified in "Participation Training" as developed by the Bureau of Studies in Adult Education at Indiana University. Though Participation Training is not generally identified as human relations training, it fits the genre.

Participation Training. Participation Training events are usually designed with reference to a specific institutional setting and the learners —e.g., a church or a hospital—are usually affiliated with that institution. Learnings about self, relationships with others, groups and organizations are explored in terms of how these contribute to helping the learners learn better. The training design focuses successively on: (1) the cultivation of collaborative learning skills (e.g., listening, clarifying, setting goals, keeping discussion relevant); and (2) the mastery of procedures for planning and conducting group educational activities for adults.

Training group, theory session and focused exercise components are included in the training design. The training groups, however, are not initially thrown into the classic, unstructured dilemma which is typical of T-Groups. Instead, minimal task and procedural structure is introduced by the trainer. This structure is rapidly assimilated by the group members and elaborated thereafter to suit their needs. But the trainer has the complex assignment of initiating process analysis and observant participation while at the same time introducing task and procedural structure. Because of the imposed task and procedural structure, Participation Training events are identified as "institutes" rather than "laboratories."

Learners in Participation Training are expected, at the least, to gain a command of conditions that should be activated in planning and conducting adult educational programs and personal skills and procedures which are appropriate in activating the educational conditions. At the optimum level, learners can expect to acquire command of training design components which can be applied in a variety of institutions and organizations [3, 4].

These three programs briefly described represent efforts to educate and train (or reeducate and retrain) people in selected categories of human relations training. It should be understood, however, that specific training events can be designed to focus on almost any combination of learning outcomes. Moreover, if given enough time and continuity, an extended training program can explore systematically the whole range of human relations learnings. An interesting example of such an extended training effort is the YMCA Organizational Development Project, conducted during the years 1961–1966 [2]. This was an in-service training program for YMCA executives. Specific learning objectives and program designs were revised annually and ultimately included elements such as learning about marital relationships and use of management games.

The variant types of training programs have been employed in a wide variety of institutions and organizations. Programs have been conducted with industrial managers as well as production-line foremen. The training has been used with social service agencies, religious groups, community leaders, college students, the Internal Revenue Service, juvenile court judges, public school teachers and teacher aides, the unemployed, mental health institutions, correctional institutions and law enforcement personnel.

Training Outcomes

Typically there are positive and negative results in human relations training. On the positive side, individual learners frequently report great personal satisfaction in having become "reacquainted with themselves"; they also report exhilaration in the sense of renewed personal worth—gained as accepted members of a training group. Many report gratification in the development of greater interpersonal skills. There are reports of marked attitude changes associated with expanded understanding and insight into what makes people and groups function as they do. And there are some dramatic reports of the achievement of a radical reorientation to life.

On the negative side, some people are simply frustrated by the training experience; they report they learned nothing or that their sense of self-organization was so disrupted by the training they were left with more problems and questions than they started with. Some report the training only served to alienate them further by sapping their willingness to come to terms with the realities of everyday life. There are some dreary reports of defeat, and perhaps career disaster, in attempts to apply training procedures and techniques to everyday life. Some contend the training is merely a form of "brainwashing"—erosion of individual autonomy through the subtle manipulation of group culture. And there are some accounts of severe personal breakdowns linked with training experiences.

Current Trends and Issues

There are several fascinating trends in current human relations training program development: unfortunately, only a few can be singled

Human Relations—Sensitivity Training

out for mention here—those that seem to be most significant for the future.

Training programs designed specifically for public school personnel are expanding rapidly. This clientele has been a particular concern of the National Training Laboratories through the years. But only recently has there been a burgeoning of interest in human relations training among public school personnel themselves. The training programs have become an object of controversy in professional education journals [11]. At this writing, plans are being consolidated for the introduction of human relations training throughout the public school system of Orange County, California.

Human relations in the troubled cities of the United States have been a national issue during recent years. Many agencies are experimenting with ways to resolve some of the problems. The University Center for Adult Education in Detroit is an example. The Center has been experimenting with a wide array of human relations training programs; much of the effort is directed to the inner-city. During 1967–1968, some 500 people were trained and the scope of the program continues to expand.

For several years, advocates of human relations training have attempted to promote what may be called a "systemwide" approach to training in specific institutions. It is contended that the sporadic training of isolated individuals or groups is relatively ineffective in promoting organizational change, since one side of a relationship cannot be changed without also changing the other side at the same time. Programs are being developed for introducing human relations training systematically throughout the component parts of entire organizations. The YMCA Organizational Development Program included some explorations of a system-wide approach. Plans for the Orange County, California, schools include training for children and youth as well as for the faculty and staff.

The programs developed at Esalen Institute, Big Sur, California, and the "Human Awareness" concepts and techniques of William C. Schutz [10] are currently the center of great interest in human relations training circles. Schutz and his associates place great emphasis on the physicalness of human nature. They contend that man's capacity for verbalization tends to displace, and become a pallid surrogate for, experience. As this displacement progresses, the individual becomes insulated from acquaintance with the fundamental realities of his own human nature. He may develop elaborate intellectualizations about human nature and attribute more significance to these than to the physical realities from which they are abstracted. Such a person may become increasingly dehumanized in that he becomes increasingly insulated within his own intellectualizations about reality and less able to maintain contact with real people. The Schutz techniques are designed to help people become reacquainted with their own sensory–physical nature. Human relations trainers have become increasingly enamored of these techniques and have been incorporating them selectively into human relations training programs for several years. There is considerable controversy over whether, or how, such techniques fit into the educational standards of human relations training [1].

There are knotty issues involved in human relations training. Most of these emerged early in the history of training and continue to remain unresolved. The incorporation of Human Awareness techniques was identified as a training trend, but it also bears on the issue of training standards—which is perhaps the most persistent and controversial issue in human relations training. At stake in this issue are answers to questions such as: What are the functions of the trainer? What are the boundaries of acceptable trainer behavior in carrying out his functions? How should trainers be trained? Should certification of trainers be professionalized? [9]

Transfer of learning is another resilient issue. Training programs are admittedly and purposefully conducted in relative detachment from the everyday life of the learners. During the training, groups develop their own unique culture, value system, behavioral norms and work relationships. These training phenomena are not ends in themselves, however. They are meant to provide the experiential base for developing sound insight into interpersonal phenomena. Each learner must generalize these learnings into more appropriate ways of dealing with the particulars of his own unique situation. A learner who seizes upon the training phenomena as ends in themselves and attempts to perpetuate them into everyday life is almost certain to meet with resistance, resentment, hostility and failure; and he may seriously disrupt his home, community and work relationships. This particular problem accounts for many of the negative training outcomes mentioned earlier.

A well-known aftereffect of training is called "fade-out." Learners frequently report that following the training they discover they are exquisitely aware of the flow of human relationships in which they live and they astonish themselves by the ease and adeptness with which they find themselves functioning. In the course of time, however, their sensitivity to people gradually becomes blunted and they begin interacting in standard, routine ways. The effects of the training have faded out. This is a well-documented phenomenon and is usually interpreted as pointing up the need for follow-up support of training. But if the training outcomes are so perishable, do they constitute worthwhile learning? Or does fade-out merely demonstrate that the training effects are mostly a matter of psychic contagion generated by the intensive interactions of training groups?

The fade-out pattern points to the difficult issue of verifying the effectiveness of human relations training. Up to the present, justification of human relations training is based mostly on anecdotal data [7]. Such reports of what people think has happened to them as a result of training are likely to be influenced by self-delusions, rationalization, wish fulfillment, auto-suggestion and the desire to please. Evidence of cause–effect relationships derived from carefully controlled investigations is rare in human relations training [6]. The multiple systems within which people live and work are too complex and subtle to be investigated by existing research techniques. One must either accept a clinical approach to the study of individual cases or assume that phenomena occurring in the laboratory setting reflect what can and does happen in everyday life.

The issues of human relations training will continue to be targets for concentrated efforts toward resolution. And the outcomes of current training trends will be carefully scrutinized. Results of these investigations will need to be weighed carefully for implications for the broad field of adult education.

References

1. Argyris, Chris. "On the Future of Laboratory Training." *Journal of Applied Behavioral Science*, III, No. 2 (1967), pp. 153–183.
2. Batchelder, Richard L., and Hardy, James L. *Using Sensitivity Training and the Laboratory Method.* New York: Association Press, 1968.
3. Bergevin, Paul; Morris, Dwight; and Smith, Robert M. *Adult Education Procedures.* New York: Seabury Press, 1963.
4. Bergevin, Paul, and McKinely, John. *Participation Training for Adult Education.* St. Louis, Mo.: Bethany Press, 1965.
5. Bradford, Leland P.; Gibb, Jack R.; and Benne, Kenneth D. *T-Group Theory and Laboratory Method.* New York: John Wiley & Sons, 1964.
6. Durham, Lewis E.; Gibb, Jack R.; and Knowles, Malcolm S. "A Bibliography of Research on Human Relations Training." In: *Explorations II.* Washington, D.C.: National Training Laboratories Institute for Applied Behavioral Science, 1967.
7. Miles, Matthew B. "Changes During and Following Laboratory Training: A Clinical–Experimental Study." *Journal of Applied Behavioral Science*, I, No. 3 (1965), pp. 215–242.
8. Paris, Norman N. "T-Grouping: A Helping Movement." *Phi Delta Kappan*, XLIX, No. 8 (1968), pp. 400–463.
9. Schein, Edgar H., and Bennis, Warren G. *Personal and Organizational Change Through Group Methods.* New York: John Wiley & Sons, 1965.

10. Schutz, William C. *Joy: Expanding Human Awareness*. New York: Grove Press, 1967.
11. Thomas, Donald. "T-Grouping: The White-Collar Hippie Movement." *Phi Delta Kappan*, XLIX, No. 8 (1968).

Chapter 26

Education for Family Life

NOREJANE HENDRICKSON

ANDREW HENDRICKSON

If asked why we need family life education we may point out, as Eleanor Braun Luckey has, that our newspapers and books, our ministers, teachers and parents, and our movies and plays constantly remind us how little we know about ourselves, and how the social ills threaten family life [31].

One way to assess the needs and problems of the field is to look at the conditions in society affecting it. Technological advances have come so rapidly and have been of such import that the twentieth-century family has found itself surrounded by change. What at the turn of the century was science fiction is now reality. Man has visited outer space, has transplanted vital organs in the human body, has split the atom and has invaded the privacy of the fetus in the confines of the uterus. There has always been change, but now there is a difference in the amount and rapidity of it. Brzezinski terms our age the "Technetronic Age" [9]. He says the change process is so telescoped that the impact of change may have a shock effect on the human being. The gap between the scientific evolution and biological evolution is vast. Biological evolution is a slow process. The problem of fitting the twentieth-century family to the culture determined by scientific evolution is not only challenging but also overpowering.

Human beings in a changing world live in many environments. In a few hours, a traveler can visit an underdeveloped agrarian culture, an urbanized–industrialized culture, and a technologically oriented, electronically controlled military or industrial base. The many inventions, conveniences, and luxuries of the twentieth century should have made life more rewarding. Great strides have been made in transportation. Improved medical facilities and techniques, along with drug discoveries, have brought improved health and longer life spans. Women are free to vote, hold public office, and work outside the home. Secondary education is available to all and some higher education is available to most. Families own houses, automobiles, TV sets, much do-it-yourself equipment designed to make life easy. Why then has family stability declined?

In an urban society, individuals and individual families lose some of their identity. As individual members travel farther and farther from the home to school, work, church or social activities family life becomes less cohesive. Family patterns break down. Changes come too rapidly to be assimilated. New knowledge has brought about increasing sexual freedom. Youth have been given more freedom with fewer guidelines. They are marrying early and are having more premarital pregnancies. The divorce rate is high. The difficulties of communication between the generations, always a problem, seem to have increased with the new freedoms accorded youth. Family patterns valued by parents are frequently not accepted by their children.

Cottrell in discussing research in family life education states that research should be undertaken that helps to discover or uncover *elements of competence* (capacities or skills) needed by the individual to function effectively [11]. What elements of competence do functioning families have that non-functioning ones lack? Cottrell proposes an active, intervention type of research. The individual should be helped to develop new competencies and the effect of these on his ability to function would be measured. He believes adequate attention has been given to descriptive studies. With the many transformations in our lives there is need for more dependable guidelines to aid us in family living.

The challenge is not insurmountable but it is worthy of the best efforts of those who value families. Stroup has suggested the need for family life research following a long-range family life policy [43]. He asks the questions: How much value does our society place in knowing more about marriage and family life? How much of its research funds are allocated to these vital topics?

Our society is not unique in coping with problems of family life. Brannan reported the world problems of family and community living identified at the Eleventh International Congress on Home Economics as:

1. The increasing world population.
2. Population migration from rural to urban areas and from country

Education for Family Life

to country. Structural changes in the rural areas are having a marked effect upon this problem. Many countries indicated concern over problems connected with the adaptation of the rural population to urban centers.
3. Problems of the aging population and of the young.
4. Raising of economic standards.
5. Malnutrition and sub-nutrition.
6. Unemployment and underemployment.
7. Lack of appropriate attention being given to the status of women in some areas of the world.
8. Lack of suitable housing.
9. Lack of educational opportunities and the need for improving the quality of education generally.
10. Rapidity of social, economic, and technological changes.
11. Changing family patterns and changing roles of family members [5].

These problems are interrelated. It is far easier to identify them than to find constructive ways to meliorate or resolve them.

The complex society deemphasizes the family. Yet, in perspective, it can be noted that man has always wondered if he could survive. Part of his ability to do so has come from family life. The family is the oldest social institution. If man survives, it will, too. It may change structure and it may not. How the family survives depends on our wisdom.

Definitions and Terminology

In the agrarian society there was little need for formal education for family living. Beginning families turned to more experienced family members for advice. The family doctor, the teacher, and the minister were long-time associates of the family. They were available if needed. However, family problems usually were considered just that. The authoritarian role of the father weakened with migration to the cities; young couples felt less secure and had to look outside the family for information and assistance.

In its early days parent education was an excellent example of an American folk movement. Parents began to organize into groups for the purpose of deepening their understanding of children. Parent education had two qualities. It was geared to parents and it was voluntary. The organizations that grew steadily and stabilized the movement were lay initiated and dependent to a major extent on lay leadership. The strength of these organizations had been recognized as "grass-root" strength.

The movement started late in the nineteenth century through the interest of thousands of small, scattered women's organizations. By the end of the century most of these groups were amalgamated into national organizations, many of which still exist. According to Muriel Brown organized parent education stemmed from two main sources—parent meetings and the professional interest in child development created by psychological studies such as Miss Shinn's *Biography of a Baby.*

The experts had the scientific information and the parents desired to increase their effectiveness. Therefore at the beginning of the movement, the emphasis was on parents (later parents-to-be were included), and the educational approach was the expert telling the parents how to guide and care for children. Brown mentions the following six shifts of emphasis after the professionals became involved in parent education:

The expert:

1. Told the parents what to do and how to do it.
2. Taught parents the principles of child development.
3. Attempted to teach parent–child relationships to the parents.

The parents and specialists together:

4. Studied the nature of parent–child relationships.
5. Studied the inter-relationships with the family.
6. Studied the family and the family–community relationships. [8]

At present, the cooperative efforts of parents and specialists have broadened to include the study of family–community relationships with "community" expanded to include the nation and the world. However, as in all folk movements, parent education is maturing only slowly. If one examines programs of parent education, a number are still at the "expert tells" stage.

From interest in parent education came the broader concern encompassed in the title, family life education. In this Handbook, the discussion is related to family life education for older youth and adults. This broader term began to be used (perhaps one should say misused) about 1930. Courses such as Health, Parent Education, or Family Nutrition were designated Family Life.

As to definition, an uncomplicated one was used by Muriel Brown in the 1948 *Handbook of Adult Education:*

Education for family living is that branch of adult education which deals specifically with the values, principles and practices of family life. It has for its general objectives the enrichment of family experience through the more skillful participation of all family members in the life of the family group. Its offerings include learning opportunities for both sexes and all ages. [7]

Education for Family Life

A more comprehensive and recent definition comes from the National Commission of Family Relations of the National Council of Family Relations:

> Family life education is a fairly new educational specialty but one for which there is a steadily increasing demand. It is a multi-professional area of study which is developing its philosophy, content, and methodology from direct experience with families and the collaboration of such disciplines as home economics, social work, law, psychology, sociology, economics, biology, physiology, religion, anthropology, philosophy and medicine. It includes a number of specialized areas, among which are interpersonal relationships, self-understanding, human growth and development, preparation for marriage and parenthood, child rearing, socialization of youth for adult roles, decision making, sexuality, management of human and material family resources; personal, family and community health; family–community interaction, and the effects of change on cultural patterns. [15, p. 211]

This definition is very broad in scope. In essence the totality of the meaning of the term family life education is the basis for much of the difficulty in implementing functional programs at any level—classroom, community, state or national. Because the overall definition is comprehensive, it should be used that way. A system could be developed where the broad term family life education is stated followed by the specific topics to be concentrated on, if that be the case. Such a practice might prevent confusion. For example, "Family life education: sex education; family life education: parent education" would show the relationship between the broad and the specific areas.

It should be stated parenthetically at this point that where the authors, discussing programs, have used the terms parent education and family life education interchangeably they are following the terminology used in the sources cited.

Research and Practice

Through the years effort has been put into developing content, sharpening focus and building theory in the area of home and family life. As yet research on family life education is limited. However, in the special aspects covered under the broader definition of the field, there is much research. The problem is one of locating the research and seeing where there is an adequate amount and where there are gaps. Also, the quality of the research is often less than adequate. Useful approaches and instruments need to be developed. Theoretical frameworks should be constructed and more family life educators ought to be trained to conduct and interpret research.

Cottrell [11], Stroup [43] and others are asking for more realistic research. Stroup has suggested the resolutions from the 1960 White House Conference be studied as a basis for developing an overall family life policy that would serve as a guide to researchers. He has also suggested researchers follow a theoretical framework, so there would be fewer small isolated studies. He believes research findings would become more meaningful if this were done. There seems to be a trend for directing both the educational and research endeavors toward the family as a unit.

Government Agencies and Activities

Interagency Panel. To guide the development of preschool and day care programs an Interagency Panel in Early Childhood has been established at the federal level. This panel was created to improve and expand early childhood programs financed by federal funds. The panel is seen as a vital step in developing cooperative relations among federal programs concerned with early childhood and in furthering the efforts of the Social and Rehabilitation Service of the Department of Health, Education and Welfare to help families become self-reliant and self-supporting. Coordinator of the panel will be the Associate Chief of the Children's Bureau. The Panel will include representatives of the Departments of Labor, Housing and Urban Development, and Agriculture; the Office of Economic Opportunity; agencies of the Department of Health, Education and Welfare; and other agencies concerned with early childhood programs.

State Departments of Education. Twenty-eight responses to an inquiry form sent by the authors to 56 state and territorial Departments of Education showed that relatively little attention has been given to family life education at the state level. In 15 of the responding states, no state staff time had been devoted to this field. In the other 13 states from 1 to 12 staff members devoted part of their time to promoting the field. Most frequently these staff members were in vocational home economics. Two states revealed that where they had formerly had state staff in this field they now had none.

Adequate enrollment figures for class attendance are not available on a national scale, but usable figures from 11 states indicate there were approximately 108,000 adults enrolled in public school and junior college family life classes under general adult education, while more than 107,000 were enrolled in classes under vocational education.

Evidence of a growing awareness of the importance of the field in some states is revealed through various special efforts. Two states re-

Education for Family Life

ported working cooperatively with state universities and local TV stations to produce extended series of programs on family life. One of these was produced on videotape for use throughout the state. In other states, the state Department of Education had produced teachers' manuals and guideline bulletins to assist teachers in establishing family life classes. Several states were using the junior community college as the vehicle for developing family life classes. One state was promoting pre-natal and post-natal classes and classes for unwed mothers.

In California, courses in parent education are part of the general adult education program of the public schools, and are supported on an average daily attendance basis as are other adult education classes. Classes include those for expectant parents, for mothers of infants, and for parents of preschool and school-age children. In a recent year 22,725 adults were enrolled in parent education classes in Los Angeles schools.

In replying to a question about new thrusts or developments, several respondents called attention to the fact there was a unit on family life in the materials used in adult basic education (ABE) classes. This brings up the question of what specific benefits may come to families through gains made in literacy, arithmetic skills and elementary social studies (frequently called "Everyday Living Skills") on the part of the 500,000 adults enrolled in these classes. Although the overall effect of this program has yet to be determined, evidence is accumulating that learning to read, write, compute, and understand living skills up to or near the eighth-grade level has brought immense satisfaction to thousands of enrollees who are now able to use a telephone directory, read labels on goods in stores, write and read letters, follow their children's progress in school, and in some cases, get a job or be upgraded on the job. Of 3100 ABE students in Mississippi replying to a question about benefits of the program, 819 said they had obtained jobs; 274 had been discontinued from public welfare; 1071 had voted for the first time; 1488 were planning to enter a high school program; 1284 said their children were staying in school; 1988 were more attentive to personal habits, such as bathing; 2424 said they were getting along better with people; and 2189 said they had more respect for the law than before.

To assist public schools develop this area of knowledge in their ABE programs, the National University Extension Association has produced a manual with units covering such topics as health and safety, adult and childhood growth and development, homemaking skills, family relationships, and the family in the community [35].

Cooperative Extension Service. The most systematic attempts in family life education at the state level are the activities carried on by the Agricultural Extension Service and schools of Home Economics of the

Land-Grant universities. Home Economic Extension agents are attached to the universities but work at the county level. Among the many specialists who assist the county agents are the Family Life Extension Specialists. An example of an active program is that of the University of Illinois where these specialists during 1966–1967 held 91 meetings to train 2975 local leaders who in turn taught over 44,000 adults [38].

The University of Minnesota, in addition to the work of its Extension agents, is, through its Department of Home Economics Education, working in direct cooperation with the Department of Vocational Education of the state Department of Education to encourage and promote programs of Continuing Education in Home Economics in the public schools. Programs include such areas as child development, family relationships and family finances.

An innovative activity at the University of Missouri for making the services of the Home Economists available to lay persons wishing help in parent education is the "collage" series [32]. It consists of a series of 14½-minute videotapes (later copied on 16mm film), radio tapes, newspaper releases and phonograph records. To date several series have been developed, called *Growing Pains, Guiding Hand, Today's Teens* and *Empty Nest.*

Antipoverty Programs. Most Head Start and other community action programs designed to help children in deprived areas have the collateral aim of educating parents. But reaching parents caught up in the poverty syndrome is a new experience. Systematic study and reporting on this phase of parent and family life education has barely begun. Among the early experiments reported are those conducted by the public schools of Omaha, Nebraska [39], New York City [12] and those conducted by the Universities of Florida [19], Illinois [27] and Missouri [16].

Members of the Cooperative Extension Services of the Universities of Alabama [40] and Massachusetts [26] have studied ways of reaching low income families who are not connected with existing programs for preschool children. In both studies gains were noted in such skills as food buying, food preparation, housekeeping and child guidance. Methods used included one-to-one teaching, use of leaflets and newsletters, and small-group discussion. Highly personalized learning experiences seemed to produce the best results.

Kraft and Chilman reviewed parent education for low income families between 1961 and 1963 [29]. They found that certain programs such as discussion groups, recreation, social, or workshop type activities had been successful. Activity programs seemed to be more successful than discussion-type programs. Workers reported difficulties in organizing and sustaining programs. Although the absence of objective methods of evaluation made it impossible to report on the overall effectiveness of the parent education programs, success was frequently gauged according to certain inferred therapeutic side effects of participation, such as self-confidence.

Local Communities

Several notable programs are found at the community level. Family Life Councils have been organized in Utah County, Utah, and Niagara Falls, New York. The Utah Council developed a TV series that local people wrote, produced and acted in. The Council has sponsored conferences and formal classes in family life education. The Niagara Falls Council has sponsored a number of workshops including one on pastoral counseling [45].

In New York City the League for Parent Education, with 25 chapters located in the metropolitan area, conducts year-round parent education programs. Although behavioral changes are sought, many of the benefits relate to strengthened egos and lessened guilt feelings through associating with others with like problems.

In Denver and other cities in Colorado boards of education employ teachers to work with parents of pre-school children [33]. In addition to a college degree with a major in an appropriate field, teachers are required to have a knowledge of group processes and interpersonal relations and confidence in parents' ability to work out their problems. Informal assessment of the program indicates better home–school relations on the part of families participating that carries over in interest in other community enterprises.

Several local school systems, through their vocational home economics programs, are instituting parent education and home management classes for low income families. Local housing authorities cooperate in these programs. Examples can be found in Dallas, Gary (Indiana), Cincinnati and Chicago [24].

Voluntary Organizations

The National Congress of Parents and Teachers with its nearly 12 million members and a Congress in each state, has over the years been a strong influence in improving the lot of children and families. It has consistently supported legislation for child welfare, better working conditions for women and better school programs. It has stimulated parent education activities, especially study groups, through its publications (including the *PTA Magazine* which contains graded study outlines), a national radio project and university workshops.

Examination of the organization's annual meeting *Proceedings* for the past several years reveals some of its latest thrusts. It has sponsored radio and TV broadcasts to bring parent education to non-members. It has helped in efforts to correct social ills such as juvenile delinquency, pornography, child molestation and lack of sex education including education about venereal disease.

Most state PTA Congresses sponsor leadership training courses, the most effective being those held in cooperation with state universities. California, New York, Illinois and Ohio are outstanding in this respect. The authors of this chapter made an assessment of ten years of such workshops in Ohio and found that some 3500 potential lay leaders had been trained and that among the many positive results of the workshops were an increasing tendency to use democratic methods in conducting study-discussion groups and a tendency to use better prepared materials, especially the articles and graded study outlines in the *PTA Magazine* [22].

Other lay organizations that carry on family life education as part of their programs include The American Association of University Women, General Federation of Women's Clubs, National Council of Catholic Women, National Council of Jewish Women, National Society for Crippled Children and Adults, and Young Men's and Young Women's Christian Associations. Added to these are the many professional associations with varying degrees of interest in family life education.

Other Programs

College Courses. Many colleges and universities have courses in marriage and family living, and some have established marriage counseling clinics for their students. Barnett studied church-related colleges and universities in the South and found that 90 percent of them offered such courses [3]. Half were in sociology departments and the rest in other social science departments. In a study by Landis a decade ago, 80 percent of the colleges reporting offered courses in marriage and the family, and Landis estimated that over 100,000 students were enrolled in such courses at that time [30].

The American Social Hygiene Association [1] has prepared manuals for teaching family life courses in colleges of education. These are to prepare teachers to teach family life courses in high schools and colleges.

Family Planning. Because of the effect of the population explosion on national economies and on the welfare of individual families, considera-

Education for Family Life

ble interest in family planning has developed over the past decade. Chilman in an extensive review of programs, evaluation and research in this area summarizes by saying:

> There is general reason for concern about the rapidly expanding population in the United States and particular reason for concern about the close association between poverty and large family size. Early marriage, early arrival of the first child, and closely spaced children are also highly associated with poverty. Difficulties in effective family planning are particularly likely to occur for non-whites with less than an eighth-grade education and of rural residence or rural origins.
>
> . . .
>
> Further research of many kinds is indicated including evaluative studies of various family-planning service models; further and more sophisticated investigations of the knowledge, attitudes, and behaviors of particular groups; research as to the social–psychological side effects of family size limitation and contraceptive availability; and more basic studies regarding optimum family size and its relation to marriage, parenthood, and child development. [10]

One research program of significant breadth is the New Orleans Parish Family Planning Demonstration Program conducted by the Tulane University School of Public Health and Tropical Medicine and supported by a number of federal agencies and private foundations. Among its objectives are: (1) to develop and implement a patient-oriented program capable of identifying, contacting, educating and offering family planning information and service to the estimated 18,500 "high risk" or immediately post-partum indigent women between 15 and 44 years of age in Orleans Parish; and (2) a reduction in the infant, maternal and stillborn mortality rates, and in the incidence of mental retardation by reducing the number of premature births after a desired family size has been achieved [44].

Methods and Resources

Both Auerbach [2] and Brim [6] term mass media, counseling and group discussion as the three basic methods in parent education. Mass media includes the use of all printed materials, and radio and television. While relatively little use is made of radio and television in family life education, extensive use is made of printed materials.

Hundreds of books come off the presses each year, some written by individual authors, like Spock's *Baby and Child Care,* and others under institutional auspices, like *Child Behavior* by Ilg and Ames of the Gesell Institute. A decade ago Brim quoted estimates of 25 million a year as the number of pamphlets being distributed [6]. Some of these are commercial ventures; some are prepared by agencies like the Child Study Association and the National Congress of Parents and Teachers; while others are prepared by government agencies, such as the Children's Bureau and the Cooperative Extension Services of the state universities. The Cooperative Extension pamphlets are noted for their brevity, their aptness and their wide distribution.

Magazines are another source of parent and family life education information. *Parents' Magazine* is an example of a successful commercial venture. *Children,* published by the Children's Bureau, is an example of a non-commercial magazine of high professional quality. Several popular magazines—*McCalls, Ladies Home Journal, Family Circle, Reader's Digest,* and others—carry significant amounts of parent education material.

Newspapers are spotty and irregular in the amount and quality of family life material presented. The information ranges from the high quality offerings of such independent newspapers as *The New York Times* to the uneven material in local papers by doctors and psychologists. Studies have shown that while the quality of the latter material is improving, the small quantity and lack of regularity prevent its having any significant impact [14]. The vast popularity of such columns as "Dear Abby" and "Ann Landers" reveals an ocean of unmet family life education needs.

Little use seems to be made of radio as a means of parent education outside of occasional series put on as part of regular Cooperative Extension Service programs beamed to rural audiences. Television programs are mostly of two types—those addressed directly to parents and those (primarily for entertainment) that portray valued concepts of family relationships (examples: "My Three Sons" and "Family Affair"). References made elsewhere in this chapter to the few instances where television is being used by universities as a teaching medium for family life programs suggest the wide open possibilities of this medium.

Group discussion has been a major method in parent education since the beginning of the movement. The difficulty of collecting attendance data on informal groups makes it impossible to accurately gauge the extent this method is used. In recent issues of the *Proceedings* of the National Congress of Parents and Teachers it was noted that the number of child study groups is on the increase and that approximately 300,000 parents participate annually in such groups [34]. To these figures can be added the hundreds of thousands more who meet under such auspices as "Y" organizations, churches, settlement houses, school groups outside of the PTA and parent education groups recently organized in connection with many of the anti-poverty programs. The Cooperative Extension

Education for Family Life

Service, in assisting some 7 to 8 million farm families to improve their family living practices, also uses group discussion as a basic method.

Sources of subject matter for these discussions may come from the experience and concerns of the parents themselves; from a medium such as a film, a play or a case study; or from a packaged program prepared by an expert, of which Ethel Kawin's publications are an example [28]. The most identifiable tendency in the use of group discussion methods is the use of them in conjunction with some auxiliary source such as a film, a play or skit, role-playing or the presence of a resource person.

The greatest limitation on group discussion as a method for parent education is the shortage of trained leaders—both lay and professional. Ideally the colleges and universities should be training cadres of professionals, who in turn, would train lay leaders. But because of the shortages, the colleges and universities engage directly in training lay leaders. This is like eating one's seed corn because one is hungry. The ideal discussion leader is one who has enough knowledge to understand the issues being discussed and locate appropriate resources together with the leadership skill to see the discussion becomes a learning experience of the kind likely to cause a change in behavior.

Adequacy of resources seems no longer to be a problem. In addition to the vast and varied amounts of printed materials, the audio–visual departments of most city and county libraries, and those of colleges and universities and state Departments of Education carry numerous films, filmstrips, tape recordings, and graphic materials suitable for individual and group study in parent education. In addition, there are a number of excellent handbooks written particularly with parent groups in mind, most of which list a variety of resources [13; 18; 21; 36; 37].

A great deal of family life education transpires through counseling. Brim states that:

the parent's relations with the clergyman, the pediatrician, and the general practitioner, the pediatric and public health nurse, and, of course, the kindergarten and elementary schoolteacher, have provided natural settings in which parental questions regarding the child and counseling on the part of the professional have inevitably occurred. [6]

He raises the question of whether or not clergymen and medical personnel should be permitted to counsel parents outside of the areas of their respective competencies. Perhaps this problem is being mitigated by the fact that the clergy are receiving more training in psychology and doctors are now being trained in psychiatric aspects of medicine.

A certain amount of counseling goes on automatically when persons are exposed to the mass media or are members of a discussion group. In cases where a parent's problem is too embarrassing to be mentioned in a group discussion, or where the person is referred for deep counseling, he must seek and get help on a personal basis. This raises the issue of cost and of who should pay. Can the community afford the cost, or conversely, can it afford the consequences of not providing the services? One approach to the answer to these questions is found in the fact that most city school systems now have on their staffs one or more trained psychologists who make themselves available to parents. Gazda and Ohlsen [17] and Gene Harding [20] have reported on experiments in group counseling for parents.

Problems and Issues

The field of family life education is beset by a number of problems. Some of these have to do with logistics—how to produce more and better leaders and teaching materials and how to make them both more available to the field. This is not merely a matter of physical distribution. It is a psychological one of getting people to realize these resources are there *for them*. Other problems have to do with roles and responsibilities. Which organizations should serve which groups and under what circumstances? Related to the latter is the problem of organization and coordination in the field. In terms of present needs the problem is how to bring family life education to bear on the social tensions threatening to tear apart our democratic social fabric. Some of these tensions are increased "crime in the streets" and the broad intergenerational gap, racial tensions, bizarre forms of protest and shifts in social values.

The most fundamental problem of the field seems to be lack of organization and focus. Family life education, like the adult education field of which it is a part, is extremely diverse in both its theoretical and its practical aspects. This diversity has prevented any clear definition of the field and has kept any one educational institution or governmental agency from accepting responsibility for developing the field. This, in turn, has created problems in financial support and in coordination of programs.

If the social problems are ever to be solved it will be with the application on a broad scale of the principles and practices of sound family living. In spite of its loss of certain functions the family is still the basic unit of our society for socializing the young and stabilizing the adult personality. Making the needed impact on these social problems cannot be done on a piecemeal and sporadic basis as at present. Rather, what is needed are massive, coordinated attacks by numbers of agencies working together with each playing its own appropriate role.

If the problems of focus, organization and central authority could be solved, many other questions would become secondary and would fall

Education for Family Life

into place (e.g., who trains leaders, who does research, who develops materials and distributes them, and who provides support). Perhaps state councils of family life education with members drawn from all groups with a vested interest in the field would be the answer, especially if these were related to local councils on one hand and to national services on the other. For this to become an actuality some agency or agencies would have to take leadership, at least initially. Either the state Departments of Education or the Home Economics Extension Services of the Land-Grant universities would be appropriate agencies to take this role. If the field could be so united, the isolated and scattered efforts of the many dedicated persons and agencies would be brought together in a discernible pattern.

References

1. American Social Hygiene Association. *Strengthening Family Life Education in Our Schools;* and *Education for Personal and Family Living.* New York: American Social Hygiene Association, both 1955.
2. Auerbach, Aline B. *Parents Learn Through Discussion.* New York: John Wiley & Sons, 1968.
3. Barnett, Vera T. *A Study of Marriage and Family Living Courses.* Unpublished master's dissertation. Tallahassee, Fla., Florida State University, 1950.
4. Berger, Miriam E. "The Continuous Parent Education Group." *The Family Coordinator,* XVII (April, 1968), pp. 105–109.
5. Brannan, Betty Jean. "The Eleventh International Congress on Home Economics." *The Mockingbird* (Official Publication of the Florida Home Economics Association), Fall, 1968.
6. Brim, Orville, Jr. *Education for Child Rearing.* New York: Russell Sage Foundation, 1959.
7. Brown, Muriel. "Education for Family Living." *Handbook of Adult Education in the United States.* Edited by Mary L. Ely. New York: Columbia University Teachers College, 1948, p. 83.
8. Brown, Muriel. "Trends in Parent Education." *The Annals of the American Academy of Political and Social Sciences,* XL (November, 1935), p. 74.
9. Brzezinski, Zbigniew. "America in the Technetronic Age." *Childhood Education* (September, 1968), pp. 6–10.
10. Chilman, Catherine S. "Fertility and Poverty in the United States: Some Implications for Family-Planning Programs, Evaluation, and Research." *Journal of Marriage and the Family,* XXX (May, 1968), pp. 226–227.
11. Cottrell, Leonard S., Jr. "New Directions for Research on the American Family." In: *Sourcebook on Marriage and the Family* (2nd ed.). Edited by Marvin S. Sussman. Boston, Mass.: Houghton Mifflin, 1963, pp. 548–553.

12. Drescher, Ruth. *Head Start Parents' Adult Basic Education Project.* Albany, N.Y.: New York State Department of Education (March, 1968).
13. Duvall, Evelyn, and Duvall, Sylvanus. *Leading Parents' Groups.* Nashville, Tenn. Abingdon Press, 1946.
14. Evans, Helen H. *Fifteen Years of Advice to Parents of Young Children in Selected Newspapers and Magazines.* Unpublished master's dissertation. Columbus, Ohio: Ohio State University, 1966.
15. "Family Life Education Programs: Principles, Plans, Procedures, A Framework for Family Life Education." *The Family Coordinator,* XVII (July, 1968), p. 211.
16. Garrett, Pauline E. *Interdisciplinary Approach to Preparing Home Economics Leaders for Emerging Programs Serving Disadvantaged Youth and Adults. Final Report.* Columbia, Mo.: University of Missouri, 1967.
17. Gazda, George M., and Ohlsen, Merle M. "Counseling as a Means of Parent Education." *Adult Leadership,* XIV (January, 1966).
18. Goller, Gertrude. *When Parents Get Together.* New York: Child Study Association, 1955.
19. Gordon, Ira J. *A Parent Education Approach to Provision of Early Stimulation for the Culturally Disadvantaged. Final Report.* Tallahassee, Fla., University of Florida, 1967.
20. Harding, Gene. "Operation Family: An Experiment in Family Education." *Adult Leadership,* XVII (October, 1968), pp. 169–170.
21. Hendrickson, Andrew. *Handbook for Parent Education Leaders* (revised). Columbus, Ohio: Ohio State University, 1963.
22. Hendrickson, Norejane, and Hendrickson, Andrew. "Meeting Needs for Parent and Family Life Education." *Adult Leadership,* XII (May, 1963), pp. 2–3.
23. Hendrickson, Norejane. *A Brief History of Parent Education in the United States.* Columbus, Ohio: Ohio State University, 1963, pp. 17–49.
24. Hodge, Madeline C. "Housing and Family Life Education." *Adult Leadership,* XI (February, 1963).
25. Horning, Leora N. "Home and Family Life at the Des Moines Conference." *Adult Leadership,* XVII (September, 1968), pp. 135–136.
26. Hunter, Starley M. *Families and Their Learning Situations.* Amherst, Mass.: University of Massachusetts, 1967.
27. Karnes, Merle B. "An Approach for Working Mothers of Disadvantaged Preschool Children." Urbana, Ill.: University of Illinois, 1967.
28. Kawin, Ethel. *Parenthood in a Free Nation* (Vol. I, *Concepts for Parents;* Vol. II, *Early and Middle Childhood;* Vol. III, *Later Childhood and Adolescence*). New York: The Macmillan Company, 1963.
29. Kraft, Ivor, and Chilman, Catherine. *Helping Low-Income Families Through Parent Education.* Washington, D.C.: U.S. Department of Health, Education and Welfare, 1966.

Education for Family Life

30. Landis, Judson. "The Teaching of Marriage and Family Courses in the Colleges." *Marriage and Family Living* (February, 1959), pp. 26–40.
31. Luckey, Eleanor Braun. "Education for Family Living in the Twentieth Century." *Journal of Home Economics*, LVII (November, 1965), pp. 685–686.
32. McArthur, Arthur. "Missouri Specialists Take to the Air." *The Family Coordinator*, XVII (April, 1968), p. 956.
33. Moore, Lottie E. "Parent Education Pre-School Program." *Adult Leadership*, XI (May, 1962), pp. 7–9.
34. National Congress of Parents and Teachers. *Proceedings*. Chicago, Ill.: 1963 to 1967.
35. National University Extension Association. *Personal and Family Development in Adult Basic Education: Curriculum Guide and Resource Units*. Washington, D.C.: U.S. Office of Education (June, 1967).
36. *New Hope for Audiences*. Chicago, Ill.: National Congress of Parents and Teachers, 1954.
37. *Parent Education Handbook*. Curr. Bul. No. 96. Kansas City, Mo.: Public Schools, 1955.
38. Pepoon, Lucille. In a letter dated November 15, 1968.
39. Phelps, David W. "Project Headstart." *Adult Leadership*, XV (June, 1966), pp. 41–42.
40. Priester, Jeanne. "An Identification of Effective Methods to Employ in Conducting an Educational Program to Reach and Teach Low Income Young Homemakers in Rural Areas." Paper presented at the National Seminar on Research, Chicago, February 11–13, 1968.
41. "Services for Children and Families." Washington, D.C.: U.S. Department of Health, Education and Welfare, 1968. (Pamphlet.)
42. "The Story of the White House Conferences on Children and Youth." Washington, D.C.: U.S. Department of Health, Education and Welfare, 1967.
43. Stroup, Atlee L. *Marriage and Family, A Developmental Approach*. New York: Appleton-Century-Crofts, 1966.
44. *Studies in Family Living, Reprint No. 25*. Washington, D.C.: Population Council, December, 1967.
45. Wagner, Joseph. "A Community Council on Family Life Education." *Adult Leadership*, XII (March, 1964), pp. 267–269.

Chapter 27

Education for Social and Public Responsibility

HILTON POWER

There are several possible definitions of education for social and public responsibility, but the one used by Abbott Kaplan in the 1960 edition of this Handbook has the virtue of being explicit and inclusive. Moreover, adopting it allows us to make comparisons between one edition and the next and appreciate the changes that have occurred over a span of one, two or three decades. Kaplan says:

> Educational programs in social and public responsibility are those that are designed to develop understanding and knowledge of public issues and problems facing the country and its citizens domestically and internationally in political, economic, and social areas. [11, p. 513]

The most noticeable change in education for public responsibility has been in content; particularly affected has been the balance between domestic and international issues. This shift is a reflection of rapid changes and sharp conflicts that have emerged in the 1960's over policies relating to race relations as well as a dawning public realization of the plight of the major cities. These two domestic problems and the increasing involvement in Vietnam, with its spiraling costs in men and treasure, have become the dominant issues in the past decade.

It is not possible to chart accurately changes in interest because of the diversity of activity, the large number of responsible bodies originating programs and the lack of a national system of reporting adult education activities. The absence of periodic reporting using standardized data and definitions is understandable when one considers the variety and number of institutions and agencies both public and private, formal and informal. To identify changes which have occurred in the last ten years a careful search was made of several sources: "Continuing Education for Adults," published by the Center for the Study of Liberal Education for Adults; "Adult Leadership" from the Adult Education Association of the USA, and from files of "Techniques," "Administrators Swap Shop," and "The Pulse of Public School Adult Education," all published by the National Association for Public Continuing and Adult Education.

A Comprehensive National Study

With the assistance of the Carnegie Corporation, the National Opinion Research Center (NORC) undertook a national study, *Volunteers for Learning*, and provided the first reliable statistical basis for examining the role played by different types of institutions and associations [9]. This study provided a review of participation using a number of variables. More recently the National University Extension Association and the Association of University Evening Colleges published a useful five-year summary of enrollments obtained from the combined membership of more than 230 different institutions [4]. It was hoped this report would help provide a chart of trends developing in recent years. Unfortunately neither this report nor the NORC study provides a detailed breakdown of programs by subject matter except in rather broad categories.

Volunteers for Learning, however, provides the best available estimates of participation in adult education. Estimates are based upon an extensive national survey made in mid-1962. All subjects were grouped into nine different areas. The section on current events, public affairs and citizenship corresponds closely with the definition of social and public responsibility given above and results in the following estimate of participation:

General political education (includes political science)	310,000
Current events	280,000
Courses on communism	250,000
Civil defense	190,000
Americanization and citizenship	less than 180,000
All other public affairs courses	less than 180,000

The report gives a total of 1,080,000 for current events, public affairs and citizenship.

Education for Social and Public Responsibility

In a review of the study, Woock argued for the inclusion of participants in other categories who were enrolled in history and social sciences (excluding political science) [17]. These two subjects accounted for 790,000 additional participants. One can therefore estimate as follows the total audience to be educated for social and public responsibility:

Current events, public affairs and citizenship	1,080,000
History	490,000
Social sciences (excluding political science)	300,000
	1,870,000

This was about 7 percent of the total number of different adults engaged in adult education (which in that year was estimated at 23 million).

Methods of study by adults interested in Public Affairs were as follows:

	Percent
Talks or lectures	30
Attended classes	26
Self-education	23
Discussion groups	16

The rest were involved in educational television, correspondence or on-the-job training.

The distribution of courses and programs in public affairs by sponsoring institutions was:

	Percent
Public affairs organizations in the community	36
Colleges and universities	20
Churches and synagogues	11
Government	11
Elementary and secondary schools	10
Business and industry	7
Armed forces	4
Private schools and others	1

At the time of the study, education for social and public responsibility involved less than 2 million of the 110 million eligible voters. Of these participants 250,000 were interested in studies about communism and another 190,000 were involved in civil defense training. This meant that almost half a million participants were concerned about the necessity to be prepared for a possible attack by a communist power equipped with the means of mass destruction. Ironically, public interest was negligible in questions about pollution of the environment, conservation of resources, and the role of public policy in science and technology. Although excellent programs have been offered successfully in these fields they are far from being widely represented throughout the nation.

To account for the fact that a comparatively small segment of informed and active adults in the total population are engaged in public affairs study some weight must be given to the prevailing public apathy and caution toward controversial issues. Controversy can be and is dealt with in many programs offered by community organizations, schools, colleges, universities and churches. In some instances this has been done in the face of opposition from groups that often have strong financial backing and aim at stifling a dispassionate examination of foreign and domestic issues. Many organizations that might deal with controversial issues choose to exercise caution when confronted by this resistance to free discussion. There has also been a growth of radical action-oriented groups at either end of the political spectrum that have tried to drown out and end opposition by creating polarization of opinion on basic issues. There has been a regrettable retreat by some organizations, a lack of willingness to run any risks of public criticism when controversial activities represented only a small percentage of their total program.

Audience

Johnstone and Rivera's study provides a valuable base line for future efforts to measure involvement in education for social and public responsibility [9]. Of course, some who reflect upon an audience of 7 percent of all those involved in adult education might conclude this is a very satisfactory result. Also, there are no standards of comparison, either national or international. However, in terms of the issues dividing the nation at present and the extent of public understanding of such issues one must conclude that the record is far from adequate in terms of present needs. It is for this reason an assessment should be made of the potential audience for programs of social public responsibility.

V. O. Keys says that "no trustworthy information exists on variations in the size of the politically active sector of the population through time" [10, p. 594]. A. O. Hero considers less than one percent of the total population would qualify on the basis of his criteria of sustained interest, adequate information, rigorous analysis and purposeful action [6]. The task of adult education is two-fold—to sustain the tiny minority of one percent estimated by Hero and to enlarge that group by recruiting and equipping others who are active and interested but not

Education for Social and Public Responsibility

necessarily well informed. The numbers of people who are interested in such issues among those eligible to vote has been estimated by Hayes as between 6 and 7 million [5]. These are not large numbers but they do suggest there are significant numbers of people who are potential recruits for programs in the area of public responsibility. That this group may be increasing is supported by the NUEA-AUEC figures of registrations over the seven-year period 1960-1966 [4] and by a study of Rosenau where he concludes "that increasing numbers of people and a growing proportion of the overall population are attentive to public affairs in general and to international affairs in particular [15, p. 47]."

In the absence of supporting studies it is difficult to say whether this increase in the attentive public comes from the traditional pool of middle class white people who by virtue of their education and economic status have constituted the majority of the audience in the past. There are signs the "under thirties," who are not ordinarily considered to be motivated to devote much attention to public affairs, have become increasingly concerned about issues related to poverty, race and foreign policy. The under thirties have, as natural allies, activist elements in the black community who are working to obtain some sort of resolution of the same issues. If this guess is correct, the attentive audience is growing and the new recruits belong to two segments of the population formerly inactive and unconcerned about public affairs.

Trends and Developments

Foundation support and encouragement have helped adult education organizations to survive the period of waiting while the established, formal systems of education decide upon the admission of adult education to full partnership. Because of the importance and necessity of foundation assistance, the donors were criticized at times when they decided to make no further grants to a particular venture they had initiated—leaving the recipient the choice of becoming self-supporting or closing up.

Principles and practices of community development were encouraged and nurtured by the Carnegie Corporation and a wide range of such rural and urban programs that are now supported by federal funds. Theories, methods and practices of community development have infused the poverty program, the extensive rural development activities of the Cooperative Extension Service, the eight pilot urban-studies centers funded by the Ford Foundation and much of the work now being done under Title I of the Higher Education Act. Educational (and now public) television owes its existence to foundation initiative which has been continued through federal funds. International affairs education for adults would certainly not have achieved its present state, precarious though it is, without foundation support.

Contributions by foundations to the development of new approaches to adult education have had a major impact upon programs of education for public responsibility. Even if one were to list the specific programs that have failed after considerable encouragement by foundations, the balance sheet would still be heavily weighted upon the credit side. More important, the foundation investment of venture capital in public affairs education has resulted in its acceptance and incorporation in one way or another in federal and state supported programs that have in turn permanently strengthened adult education. Also the foundations have had the courage and wisdom to venture into study of issues that were emerging but not yet clearly established as key or critical areas for public concern. In the mid-sixties support by foundations for citizen education in world affairs tapered off but new areas were encouraged—relating to poverty, civil rights and equality of educational opportunity.

Another major development in the 1960's has been the recognition of the need for action that will lead to a retardation of the economic and social disintegration of large cities. In the 1950's the migration to the suburbs was an established fact, but the implications of these movements were not clearly or widely appreciated. People were aware the city constituted a complex and intricate problem with widespread ramifications for both those living within and without its borders; but the problems did not really come into sharp focus until the plight of racial minorities and the inequality of educational and economic opportunities contributed to riots in Watts, Newark, Detroit, Cleveland and other urban centers. Though federal intervention to alleviate the underlying conditions may be considered inadequate, the "poverty program," the funding of the Department of Housing and Urban Development and related federal programs at least demonstrated there are practical approaches. These programs, though directed at a specific audience and selected problems, had the effect of generating a variety of activities that involved and directly affected other concerned citizens. Leadership elements in a variety of organizations, particularly church groups, began to see some of the issues at stake and to realize the need for action. This led to the development of countless programs focusing upon aspects of life in the central city, some assisted by federal funds but many supported by voluntary contributions.

This spillover from federal programs—coupled with the responsiveness of organizations concerned with civil rights, racial equality and equality of educational opportunity—has focused the attention of a wider audience upon issues that otherwise are only part of the late news, a glimpse from a commuter train window or the morning newspaper headlines. In 1966 federal funds for programs related to adult education for the disadvantaged, largely literacy and vocational training, amounted to more than $700 million plus a further $323 million for community action programs—a total of more than one billion dollars. Some of these funds were used to train volunteers or professional workers and to encourage citizen workshops for planning and participation. Though the primary target was to better the economic condition of the poor, many other groups were involved and learned at first hand something of the causes of poverty and its effects upon society.

Part of the motive for federal intervention in the elementary and secondary fields of education was the desire to find a way to hasten integration in the schools and to equalize opportunities for the disadvantaged. This activity was only part of the public concern which has focused on race relations. In the last few years there has been a great ferment over whether or not 20 million blacks are, in fact, to be citizens of the country. Again, educational programs, reaching only a minority, have been initiated by a variety of institutions and organizations—the schools, the black people, churches, urban universities and many ad hoc neighborhood groups. The important point to be stressed, perhaps, is not the amount of activity that can be called education for public responsibility, but that a wide range of issues raised by the plight of the Negro are now considered important topics for colleges, universities, voluntary organizations and churches in their adult programs. Ten years ago these issues were barely recognized as legitimate subjects for adult education, and those who reminded us of the issues then were often considered radical.

Educational Institutions

Libraries and Television

Libraries play an important part in the encouragement of adult education and usually have seen their major purpose as encouraging and awakening citizen interest in public affairs. Perhaps the major change in recent years has been the impact of federal legislation which has provided much needed funds to improve and extend local and state library services, thus strengthening their basic mission and complementing the work of other community agencies and organizations.

Another important change not fully recognized in all its implications is the transformation of educational television into public television. An outcome of the inquiry undertaken at the behest of the Carnegie Corporation was a report, "Public Television: A Program of Action," which strongly argued that the "educational television" concept be replaced by the "public television" concept [2]. Although it is too early to assess the outcomes, the intentions are clear—to concentrate upon and report contemporary events in a personal and forceful way, to attempt to achieve understanding as well as knowledge. As H. C. Alter says, "television has outgrown the classroom to become a public forum, reflecting the issues and the culture of the nation as a whole [1, p. 3]."

Television has so often been accused of falling short of its critics' expectations that the improvements in quality and the range of public affairs programs are not always given due credit. National Educational Television, according to Alter, provided 135 hours of public affairs programs to its 140 affiliates in 1967 [1, p. 17]. The breakdown of these programs was as follows:

Public Affairs	Hours
World affairs	47
National affairs	34
Politics	12
Education	9
Race and poverty	9
Communications	8
Consumer affairs	6
Health	4
Others (ethics, technology, foreign trade, etc.)	6
	135

Commercial networks have improved and increased their contribution. As an illustration of what once would have been considered unthinkable, NBC in 1965 produced a three and one-half hour review of the nation's foreign policy for the period 1945–65.

Karl Mannheim pointed out two decades ago that the school of the past was a "training ground for imitative adjustment to an established society [12, p. 245]." He contended that today's school ought to offer "an introduction to an already dynamic society." Society has possibly arrived at the stage where the important emphasis must be to educate for greater adaptability because of the greater rate of change. Appropriate behavior for today may be far from adequate tomorrow. Since we are not sure what tomorrow is going to be like the only course is to educate for adaptability. Education for perceptive understanding of the social environment will become more important than for acquiring the patterns of behavior required today.

As the educational system moves towards education for adaptability

Education for Social and Public Responsibility

it may run the risk of weakening certain values in our cultural heritage. Clark has called this "the slippage of age old ideals [3]." Mannheim accurately forecast that attempts to provide education for flexibility would lead to some confusion and chaos. As a result of exposure to the mass media young people are quick to incorporate into their thinking new ideas many older persons will never fully assimilate. Today it is the young who are challenging openly the age-old ideals, raising in the minds of the old the spectre of chaos or anarchy. They are not only challenging the present social values but are doing so in a variety of imaginative and compelling confrontations completely outside the usual channels for arbitrating social and political issues. One young leader described his group's protests at the 1968 Democratic Convention in Chicago as being "televised in living color, in prime time and fully sponsored [14, p. 30]."

Though the activities and ends sought by such groups may prove to be of only passing interest in the next decade, there can be no denying that age-old ideals are passing away. These new styles of action to achieve immediate ends have been devised by people who are for the most part under thirty, many of them students. The group has also established as an issue for serious discussion the concept of the generation gap. In doing so they have given much greater prominence to the idea put forward by Margaret Mead that today "age and experience become not orienting factors but disorienting ones [13, p. 33]."

Federally supported programs relating to poverty and administered by the Office of Economic Opportunity, and the "seed money" provided by Title I of the Higher Education Act have visibly influenced the type and range of offerings in education for public responsibility throughout the country. The wide diversity of programs and their impact are impossible to catalogue but they range from concern about civic architecture, city and regional planning to experiments in recruiting and training volunteer urban agents, training community leadership, citizen education in urban affairs and the creation of community development service centers. Many of these programs reach beyond the major urban centers and also are found in small and medium-sized communities scattered across the nation.

A tremendous infusion of imagination and experiment marks these efforts exemplified in programs dealing with interracial problems where mixed groups of blacks and whites attempt to reach understanding about the nature of issues that have proved so divisive. To date, most of these efforts appear to concentrate upon exploring and identifying issues and creating a basis of understanding for voluntary cooperative action which, it is hoped, will lead to constructive resolution.

The Housing and Urban Development Department of the federal

government has a variety of programs which deal with the quality of urban life. For example, one program involved a community-wide review of a proposed set of priorities for a newly formed regional planning office in the Sacramento area. Home discussion groups were arranged and eight television programs were broadcast in prime time. A regional conference involved 1500 citizens in a revision of the priorities for the regional plan of development.

Colleges and Universities

The University Council on Education for Public Responsibility initiated programs produced by National Educational Television for use by informal discussion groups. One program was entitled "Metropolis: Creator or Destroyer," another "Technology and Human Values." The impact of the Council's work has been to provide basic educational materials for use by university and college extension departments throughout the nation. Unfortunately, Metroplex, an extensive and imaginative community program based upon the use of television for discussion groups, came to an end by 1964. This program had been conducted for several years by Washington University in St. Louis. As a demonstration it more than proved its effectiveness. This method of reaching relatively large audiences is still being used, most recently in programs developed jointly by CBS-TV and the National Council of Churches of Christ. Both series deal with the problems of the individual confronted by change and an uncertain future. Study programs designed for university alumni have also contributed a great deal to a heightened awareness of the role university graduates can play in helping to shape a humane society. Dartmouth, Chicago, Washington University in St. Louis and Massachusetts Institute of Technology have designed and conducted intensive residential programs that have influenced other universities and colleges.

In the area of world affairs education the sustained programs of high quality carried on in the World Affairs Centers at the University of Minnesota and the University of Wisconsin have continued to provide an example of what universities can do for graduates and the wider community.

Universities and colleges continue to provide some of the best programs of education for social and public responsibility. Their work has been enhanced by the support provided by both government and foundations, especially in those subjects which relate to the plight of the cities and to race relations. The nature of the support, however, tends to place the greatest emphasis upon technical problems and their solution. As Ziegler commented in reviewing the role of the universities in continuing

scope have had the effect of reducing efforts (also of long standing) directed towards education for social and public responsibility.

General education for adults, carried out independently or in cooperation with other educational institutions, has been an important feature of public school programs. These programs still continue, but it is difficult to maintain their relative importance in the face of the expansion of federally assisted basic education. Although this has been one of the unintended consequences of federal aid to adult education, the public schools still have a secure place in the field of education for public responsibility. They are in a position to expand their present contribution and efforts when resources permit.

National Organizations

It is not an easy task to estimate how many national organizations are involved in this area of adult education. An examination and comparison of directories published in both the 1950's and the 1960's show that the total number of organizations was around 400 in each period. What has changed is the emphasis. There are at present six organizations concerned with incorporating Africa in their titles, and in 1953 none was listed. New organizations have appeared and some old ones have disappeared from the scene. The best current listing is to be found in *Intercom* [7]. The problems and effectiveness of these organizations have been recently summarized by George Beebe:

They don't have much impact. . . . They have great overlap in their membership, programs, and hence their impact. . . . They remain important seedbeds for people and ideas. They tend to be catalysts, slow mass media, hidden persuaders. . . . Adult education in this field certainly bears out (the) contention that "reasonable debate about foreign policy brings very limited results." The process has to go on, however, since most people are slow learners and need much exposure of repetition. . . . Most of the organizations no longer have the illusion that they can achieve rapid social change, but neither do they believe they have raw power—only staying power. They believe in evolutionary change derived from lifting the level of sophistication and interest of the general public. Hence, crisis issues are left to *ad hoc* groups and energy is directed to "long looks ahead," "ethics and foreign policy," "world peace through world law," etc. [17, p. 31]

The demise of the Center for the Study of Liberal Education for Adults, one of the innovations sponsored initially by the Fund for Adult Education, is to be regretted. Its publications and influence encouraged new developments in public affairs education.

World Affairs Councils

In 1956 there were 31 Councils and today there are 59 with a total membership of more than 50,000, reaching an annual audience of more than 180,000, and with an annual budget exceeding $1.3 million. About half of the Councils have standard programs of lectures, but about a third maintain a wide range and variety of activities including regular mass media programs, foreign visitor hospitality programs, small-group discussions based upon the Great Decisions programs and other in-depth study groups and programs for secondary schools.

Churches

Churches have had an impressive tradition of concern for social and public issues. Many denominations have carried on extensive programs of education for their members. Through their national headquarters, as well as the National Council of Churches, they have sought constantly to place their views before the public and government alike. Concern about civil rights and the war–peace issue have caused church leaders to intensify their efforts at all levels. Besides taking positions on a wide range of issues church bodies have also been responsible for launching action programs with far-reaching effects.

Because of urban blight and decay and the attendant issues of race, school desegregation and poverty churchmen have focused their attention upon the need to develop an entirely new approach to the role of the urban ministry. Special training programs have been created to teach and train ministers for these new conditions with the purpose of providing competent lay and professional leadership. These intensified efforts to deal with relevant concerns have broadened the scope and effectiveness of many churches and their members and have contributed to a wider public appreciation of and support for social action. A 1965 issue of *Intercom* gave a comprehensive listing of the activities of major religious organizations as well as details of the types of program content and method [8].

Summary

If education for social and public responsibility is to merit support it is as part of the case for liberal education for adults in a free society. Clearly there is no widespread support yet, as demonstrated by the present situation. Vocational and recreational interests account for more than 50 percent of all programs, all forms of public affairs no more than 7 percent.

Chapter 28

Vocational–Technical Education

GRANT VENN

The vocational–technical education of adults is considered by many to be a process rather than a program—a process that involves the development of the individual for social, economic and occupational competence. It is carried on in institutions, on the job, in formal and informal situations, and elsewhere. The activity that takes place in educational institutions is planned and organized and may be distinguished as a program. Such programs have as their objective either the preparation of the individual to enter an occupation or the upgrading or updating of the adult already employed. Adult vocational–technical education, therefore, may be classified as either preparatory or supplementary in nature.

Non-Federally Aided Programs

Viewed from another angle, adult vocational–technical education may be divided into non-federally aided and federally aided programs. Among the former are the private for-profit schools, private non-profit schools, home study schools, and business and industry on-the-job training programs, to name but a few. The range of possibilities in this category is so great that no attempt will be made to do additional cataloguing.

To illustrate the point, the National Home Study Council in its directory of accredited home study schools indicates there are many separate courses available in each subject area. Courses vary widely in depth and scope. For example, one course in radio may teach a student to repair radios; another may teach him to be an engineer with a broadcasting com-

Another example of a program dealing effectively with community problems in a wide spectrum of activities including the vocational-technical, is the Mott Foundation (Flint, Michigan). It was founded for the purpose of supporting religious, educational and recreational activities for public benefit, and it offers 1200 adult education courses to approximately 70,000 registrants each year. More than 50 community schools and other community centers are utilized to carry out the program objectives. Courses include those in home arts, basic education, trades and industry, city beautification, recreation skills, parent education, music, art crafts and academic subjects. Language, economics and mathematics are included in the program as well. While some people enroll to meet hobby objectives, many others select courses for retraining and job-upgrading opportunities. Career development is an important objective of many program participants [8].

Federally Aided Vocational–Technical Education

Since 1917, the local-state-federal programs of vocational and technical education have been developed on the basis of grants-in-aid to the states to encourage and support vocational training. The original legislation, the Smith–Hughes Act, specified agriculture, home economics and trades and industries as the occupational categories for which state and local training costs and other expenses would be eligible for partial reimbursements by federal funds. Subsequent enactments continued this pattern by designating other occupational categories in which training could be supported by federal funds. The George–Deen Act of 1937 added the distributive occupations. It was superseded by the George–Barden Act of 1946 which provided for a major expansion in vocational education. Separate amendments of this Act in 1956 added practical nurse training and comparable preparation in other health occupations and authorization for training in the fishery trades and industries. Then came the National Defense Education Act of 1958 which authorized training of technicians in occupations necessary to national defense.

The Vocational Education Act of 1963 set a new pattern for federal support of vocational and technical education. It continued the previous authorization for training in specified occupational categories and added the office occupations, but it also permitted states, at their option, to transfer federal funds from one category to another. In addition the 1963 Act offered states additional funds for the training of specified population groups, regardless of the occupational objectives of the training. Population groups named in the Act are high school youth, post-high

approximately 3 million adults and out-of-school youth were enrolled in preparatory and supplementary courses. The 7 million persons served during the year exceeded by almost 1 million those involved during the previous year.

Areas of greater than average growth and development include the following:

Almost one-half million adults were enrolled in agricultural education in fiscal year 1967. Post-secondary programs in agricultural technology increased by 35 percent.

Consumer education and homemaking for working mothers and residents of low income housing areas experienced considerable expansion.

Office education almost doubled its enrollments, and significant numbers of nonwhites were among those trained.

Vocational–technical educators are continuing to seek increasing opportunities for the preparation of individuals for gainful employment. Linked with this objective is their awareness of the significance of supplementary programs that update and upgrade workers' skills and knowledge.

Occupational training is being made available to a steadily increasing number of adults. Of significance here is the fact that among the adults served is a growing number of persons with special needs—migrants, the educationally deprived, the economically disadvantaged, the physically handicapped, and many more. Programs funded under the Vocational Education Act, the Economic Opportunity Act, and the Manpower Training and Development Act have proved that persons with special needs can be prepared for employment and can successfully function on the job once trained.

Terminal-type courses in vocational agriculture were offered at the post-secondary level in 274 schools, including area schools, community or junior colleges, and universities in 40 states and Puerto Rico. A total of 413,454 adult farmers and farm workers participated in courses in "agricultural mechanics" and "farm management" in fiscal year 1967.

In distributive education, packaged programs in which course content is tailored to a given situation are gaining acceptance. Wisconsin has developed courses in real estate, hotel and lodging management, insurance and credit. These programs are taught by teachers who travel a circuit, each meeting classes in a cluster of cities, large and small, on a contractual basis. Georgia provides a 100-hour diploma program covering the career objective of the adult.

Courses for licensed practical nurses, nurse's aides, medical laboratory assistants, and dental assistants outstrip other courses in popularity

Vocational–Technical Education

in the health field. Of the 21 occupations for which preservice programs were offered, all but five were for adults on a supplementary basis. Enrollments in adult programs totaled 20,000 in fiscal year 1967. To better serve nursing homes, states trained many service aides, nurse assistants, and physical therapy aides. Shortages in hospital food service workers are being alleviated through courses offered to adult women.

Enrollments in home economics courses for gainful employment increased from 41,846 in 1966, to 62,245 in 1967, an increase of more than 48 percent. The greatest area of gain was in food management and production occupations. Training for institutional work increased over 250 percent from the previous year.

Adult homemaking programs broadened in content. Greater emphasis is now being placed on the dual role of the woman as a homemaker and a wage earner. Consumer education is receiving greater attention in programs for adult women. The needs of persons in public housing, migrants, low income groups, families receiving public assistance—all are being served by adult homemaking programs.

The Education Department of the Florida State Prison System made office education available to approved inmates to facilitate their rehabilitation. The Berkeley Adult School (California) developed and operated a program aimed at culturally deprived and low income adults interested in immediate employment as stenographers and clerk typists.

There was a 12.5 percent gain in fiscal 1967 of adult technical education enrollments over those of 1966, according to figures of the U.S. Office of Education. Adult programs enrolled many more students than secondary and post-secondary programs. Illinois has expanded and improved its technical education activities to a point where almost any employed person in the state can enroll in a technical course within easy commuting distance of his home.

Expansion has occurred in trade and industrial courses for adults which served 966,301 adults in fiscal 1967. The 1967 increase totaled 162,000, or 20 percent above 1966. There were more than 151,300 apprentices in related instruction courses offered in the trades field. The total number of adults served in trade and industrial education was 966,301. One state reported 3156 persons enrolled in a home study course in this occupational area. Another state reported a program in which 275 of a total of 285 machine operators were welfare recipients.

Manpower Development Programs

The consolidation and unification of federally funded programs that have evolved rapidly seem to be a present day phenomena. The *Manpower Report of the President* states as follows:

training institutions. Sixty-two thousand trainees have been enrolled in basic education since 1962.

Table 10. *Institutional Trainees by Occupational Category of Training, Fiscal Year 1967*

Occupational Category	Percent of Trainees
Machine trades	21
Clerical and sales	20
Structural work	18
Service occupations	17
Miscellaneous	23

Accomplishments in Manpower Development

The cumulative enrollment since the inception of the MDTA program in 1962 has reached 907,400. Those trained in the institutional phase of the MDTA program numbered 669,500, while the on-the-job phase handled 237,900 trainees. The Department of Health, Education, and Welfare arranges the institutional training through public private educational agencies. It is estimated some 27 other agencies are involved in some way. Improvement in coordination and cooperation among these agencies has been accomplished through the Cooperative Area Manpower Planning System (CAMPS).

Awareness of the Adult Education Process

Business, industry, trade associations, labor unions, private schools, even private citizens are becoming increasingly interested in providing services in the field of adult vocational–technical education. There are many examples of this involvement associated with programs of manpower development. Federal aid and federal subsidies tend to heighten this interest by providing funds for a variety of educational and training activities. Funding ranges from outright grants for research to reimbursement for spoilage created by trainees in on-the-job training situations. Courses range from basic skill development to basic education. Some adults must develop reading and writing skills to aid them in undertaking training in the basic skills of some semi-skilled occupation.

There is a growing awareness now on the part of adult education planners that adults can have a wide range of real handicaps that must be met and overcome before stable employment can be anticipated or training for employment undertaken. The array of auxiliary services

Vocational–Technical Education

needed is broad and the cost of providing a comprehen... be expensive. Services needed include such items as deb... consumer education, vocational counseling and guidance... habilitation, marriage counseling, family management, person... job-finding techniques and many, many more.

Thus, one sees the vocational–technical education of adult... ing as a process rather than a single program. Moreover, the p... tion of adults for entrance into the world of work becomes increas... intricate as business, industry and government increase in comple... While simple entry-level job skills acquired by a worker are helpf... the setting into which the individual will carry these skills, once he is on the job, is frequently so complicated that additional coaching and consultation must be given him by those who would provide sound vocational–technical education. State and local programs of vocational education funded in part by federal funds still remain the major permanent endeavor for preparing and propelling trained workers into the nation's labor force and for improving the productivity of those already there.

References

1. *Community Action—Adult Education.* Washington, D.C.: Office of Economic Opportunity, July, 1966.
2. *Directory, 1969.* Washington, D.C.: National Association of Trade and Technical Schools, 1969.
3. *Directory of Accredited Private Home Study Schools.* Washington, D.C.: National Home Study Council.
4. *Economic Report of the President.* Transmitted to Congress, January, 1967. Washington, D.C.: Government Printing Office, 1967.
5. *Education and Training—Learning for Jobs.* 1968 Report of the Secretary of Health, Education and Welfare to Congress on the Manpower Development and Training Act. U.S. Department of Health, Education and Welfare (OE-87020-68). Washington, D.C.: Government Printing Office, 1968.
6. *Fiftieth Yearbook.* Minneapolis, Minn.: William Hood Dunwoody Industrial Institute.
7. *Manpower Report of the President.* U.S. Department of Labor. Transmitted to Congress April, 1968. Washington, D.C.: Government Printing Office, 1968.
8. *Mott Program of the Flint Board of Education.* Flint, Mich.: Mott Program.
9. *Vocational and Technical Education: Annual Report, Fiscal Year 1966.* U.S. Department of Health, Education and Welfare. Washington, D.C.: Government Printing Office, 1968.

Continuing Education for the Professions

flexibility. The lifelong articulated learning process may be considered in four inter-related stages.

There is that level and quality of education decreed by society as being desirable for citizens according to their roles. The amount of education required may vary from basic literacy to a high school diploma or more. If one is considering the professions, the minimum expectation would be a high school diploma and the common requirement would be several years of college.

A second stage is the preparation for entering the profession. Using the law as an example, this stage might be undertaken in a law firm, but more likely, it will done through a university. The professional curriculum is usually developed and approved by the professions, the licensing boards and the universities. The extent of involvement by each of the groups is a complex matter subject to both tradition and change.

The third stage involves contact with the clients of the profession. This may take the form of internships, practice teaching, ward assignments and other experiences closely related to qualifying for licenses to practice. The student at this stage participates in real situations relating to the profession. Learning in these activities should be coordinated with the other aspects of education. The activities are under the supervision of a professional and the person in training has neither the authority nor the responsibility of the professional.

The fourth stage concerns the student's education after he has graduated and qualified as a professional. At this stage—the continuing education stage—he is given the authority and assumes the responsibilities designated by the profession and by various agencies of society. The curriculum of continuing education should not be a repetition of previous levels of education but should provide an opportunity to explore and study the new.

Built into each of these stages are alternatives relating to career objectives—such as administration, research and teaching. As Henderson points out, "an objective of the professional schools is also to provide for flexibility in career objectives [8, p. 291]."

Characteristics of Continuing Education for the Professions

Identifying the four not entirely discrete stages serves as a way of placing professional continuing education in perspective—of relating it to other aspects of the education of the professional. There are some characteristics unique to the continuing education stage and some all the stages share.

One significant characteristic is that there are frequently no legal or professional requirements to be met after certification or licensing. (An

rectories and catalogs available. *Continuing Education* (Philadelphia, Pa.: Data Bases), a quarterly digest, contains a general listing of the programs of the major professions. For specific professions, publications describing or listing programs are available on an annual basis—for example, *Continuing Education for the Chemist* (Washington, D.C.: American Chemical Society), *Post Baccalaureate Courses for Continuing Engineering Education* (New Providence, N.J.: Reference Publications) and *Interagency Training Programs Bulletin* (Washington, D.C.: Government Printing Office). Others are available, through the monthly *Research in Education* (Washington, D.C.: Government Printing Office), from the Library of Continuing Education at Syracuse University or through various professional associations.

Methods and Materials

Opportunities for innovation are readily available in professional continuing education. The professional fields have been so beset by rapid change and technological developments in substance and techniques that the professionals themselves have come to expect them. This may account for the general willingness to try the latest educational methods and materials. All types of methods and materials are used, some particularly appropriate to the specific professions. For example, Harvard Business School's Management Simulation Game was developed as a teaching device for classes of 20 or more students grouped into four- and five-man teams called "firms" [18]. Simulation was used to integrate various learnings into an overall strategy implementation exercise, to involve participants in the utilization of analytical techniques through problem-solving, and to require people to cooperate and communicate in order to solve a complex problem.

Other devices include role playing and confrontation, as well as workshops. Teaching machines, or "auto-instructional" devices, serve an information-presenting function and afford a means for the student to make appropriate responses to the material presented. In continuing education for physicians considerable use is made of closed-circuit television.

The Role of Government

The participation of government in professional education has long been evident at the state level where it has had considerable effect on curriculum by the allocation of funds either directly or through state universities. The licensing of professionals and other regulatory practices have been exercised at the state level rather than nationally.

The influence of government at both the state and national levels may be expected to increase. The funds available for professional continuing education may be expected to increase accordingly, and this increase will affect both the quality and the extent of continuing educational opportunities. Appropriating funds for specific purposes will determine the areas of a profession to be developed. Adult educators together with the professionals in specific fields, therefore, need to be knowledgeable about legislation and effective in its support.

Finance

The financing of professional continuing education activities is, of course, related to the overall financing of education for the professions. The first three stages of professional education are financed as are other school and university activities. Although the per student cost of education in the professions may be greater, the direct cost to the student himself is usually no greater than that borne by the student in other fields. Frequently, however, the student in the professions does not have time to work to help finance his education, and he usually requires a number of years of study and practice before realizing any substantial income.

Continuing education is usually paid for by the professional person himself, perhaps on the assumption that he is able to bear the full costs. But sponsors are increasingly bearing some of the burden. The sponsors may be the university, the professional association, the employer or base of operations—such as a hospital. In recent years the federal government has provided some funds for the continuing education of physicians.

Role of Professional Associations

Professional associations have a significant role in the development of continuing education programs. Their influence may become quite involved at times and it may be expressed in many ways:

> Through accrediting bodies composed of universities and colleges and professional schools with their various policies and programs.
> By the approving of university programs—done, for example, by the American Chemical Society and the Engineering Council on Professional Development.
> By joining with an educational institution to co-sponsor a program or an organization. An example would be a graduate school of Sales Management that develops a two-year program (perhaps three

way duplication may be prevented and gaps in programming avoided. Arrangements of this kind would enable limited educational resources to be effectively brought to bear on the needs of the professions.

As the sponsors of continuing education further develop programs for the professional, they have great opportunities for innovation. Adult educators can prepare for this task by informing themselves about the needs, issues and questions appropriate to each profession. Similarly, they can help to inform persons in the professions about the field of adult education. There are excellent opportunities to form task forces or teams that can develop creative activities and model programs of continuing education for all the professions.

References

1. American Management Association. *American Management Association Conference and Exhibit on Education and Training.* Third Annual Conference, August 8–11, 1967. New York: AMA, 1967.
2. Cockburn, Patricia, and Raymond, Yvonne R. *Women University Graduates in Continuing Education and Employment, an Exploratory Study Initiated by the Canadian Federation of University Women 1966 and LaFemme Diplomee Face a L'Education Permanente et au Monde du Travail.* Toronto, Canada: University of Toronto Bookstores, 1967.
3. Davis, Benjamin. *A Study of the Continuing Legal Education of Allegheny County Bar Association Members.* Doctoral dissertation Syracuse University, 1968.
4. Dryer, Bernard V. *Lifetime Learning for Physicians; Principles, Practices Proposals; a Report from the Joint Study Committee in Continuing Medical Education.* Evanston, Ill.: Association of American Medical Colleges, 1962.
5. Everly, Jack C. *Continuing Education Instruction via the Mass Media* Paper presented at the National Seminar on Adult Education Research, Chicago, February 11–13, 1968.
6. Flaherty, M. Josephine. *An Inquiry into the Need for Continuing Education for Registered Nurses in the Province of Ontario.* Master's dissertation. Toronto, Canada: University of Toronto, 1965.
7. Gage, N. L., ed. *Handbook of Research on Teaching* (a project of the American Education Research Association). Chicago, Ill.: Rand McNally, 1965.
8. Henderson, Algo D. "Innovations in Education for the Professions." *Education Record* (Summer, 1968), pp. 290–297.
9. Hospital Research and Educational Trust. *Programmed Instruction and the Hospital, A Report on the Use of Programmed Instruction in Health Care Institutions.* Chicago, Ill.: Hospital Research and Educational Trust, 1967.

10. Horwitz, Milton J. *Research in Professional Education with Special Reference to Medical Education.* New Dimensions in Higher Education, No. 22. Washington, D.C.: U.S. Office of Education, 1967.
11. Houle, Cyril O. "The Role of Continuing Education in Current Professional Development." *American Library Association Bulletin,* LXI (March, 1967), pp. 259–267.
12. Kidd, J. Roby. "Continuing Education in the Professions." *A Symposium on Continuing Education in the Professions.* Vancouver, Canada: University of British Columbia, 1962.
13. Liander, Bertil, ed. *International Study of Marketing Education.* Philadelphia, Pa.: Marketing Science Institute, 1967.
14. Liveright, A. A. *A Study of Adult Education in the United States.* Boston, Mass.: Center for the Study of Liberal Education for Adults, 1968.
15. Lysaught, Jerome P. *Research on the Use of Programmed Instruction Among Adult Learners in Professional Health Fields.* Paper presented at the National Seminar on Adult Education Research, Chicago, February 11–13, 1968.
16. Lysaught, Jerome P., and others. *Programmed Instruction in Medical Education.* Rochester, N.Y.: Rochester University, Clearinghouse for Information on Self-Instruction in Medical Education, 1965.
17. McGlothlin, William J. *Patterns of Professional Education.* New York: Putnam, 1960.
18. McKenney, James L. *Simulation Gaming for Management Development.* Boston, Mass.: Harvard University Business School, 1967.
19. Olean, Sally J. *Changing Patterns in Continuing Education for Business.* Boston, Mass.: Center for the Study of Liberal Education for Adults, 1967.
20. Pifer, Allan. *The Quasi Nongovernmental Organization.* New York: Carnegie Corporation, 1967. Annual Report.
21. Rossman, Parker. *The Clergyman's Needs for Continuing Education.* New Haven, Conn.: Yale University, Divinity School, 1964.
22. Rubin, Irwin M., and Morgan, Homer G. "A Projective Study of Attitudes Toward Continuing Education." *Journal of Applied Psychology,* LI (June, 1967), pp. 453–460.
23. Ruhe, C. H. William. "The American Medical Association's Program of Accreditation in Continuing Medical Education." *Journal of Medical Education,* XXXIX (July, 1964), pp. 670–678.
24. Ruhe, C. H. William. *Continuing Education Courses for the Physicians for the Period from September 1, 1966 to August 31, 1967 and from September 1, 1968 to August 31, 1969.* Chicago, Ill.: American Medical Association, 1966–1968.
25. Sheats, Paul H. "The Role of University Extension in Liberalizing Continuing Education in the Professions." *A Symposium on Continuing Education in the Professions.* Vancouver, Canada: University of British Columbia, 1962.
26. Wiegand, Richard. *Factors Related to Participation in Continuing Edu-*

Chapter 30

Continuing Education for Women

JANE BERRY

ROSALIND K. LORING

Among the most recent additions to the field of adult education are the activities primarily developed for the education of women. In the past decade these programs have more than doubled in size and in number [13]. While growth has been unhalting, controversy still centers upon questions of validity and feasibility. The dimensions of each institution's program have tended to reflect the convictions of the administration and the source(s) of funds; the content and form have depended upon the interests of individual program planners and their ability to assess individual and community needs.

Some socioeconomic and cultural factors relevant to educational programming are:

1. The roles of women—reflected in their activities, responsibilities, relationships and self-concepts—have changed dramatically in the past decade. Much has been written about these changes in popular and professional publications.
2. The discontinuity in women's lives becomes apparent in their educational patterns. Many more women than men return to school after an absence of from five to twenty years.
3. The educational attainment of women today when they take a "leave of absence" to marry and have children is greater than that of women in previous generations. This greater achievement provides a substantial base for continuing education.

4. Many women are now convinced of the overriding value of education regardless of the intended use for which it is acquired.
5. The diverse family patterns and varied schedules of women with home responsibilities make their participation in educational programs dependent upon appropriate timing and location.
6. Labor demands and labor shortages have given encouragement and frequently financial support to women who are motivated to continue their education and in a position to do so. Women are being trained for new fields ranging from Head Start teachers to computer programmers.
7. Our affluent society is urged onward by advertising so that almost every family desires more than it has. A second income has become acceptable in order to supplement the husband's earnings. The wife may work to make possible higher education for the children, or to acquire a luxury or simply to obtain more food and clothing.
8. Technological improvements have radically affected housekeeping; today it can readily be combined with an educational, community or employment commitment.
9. Education for leisure strives to promote fulfilling and productive use of leisure time. Americans are not comfortable using all their free time in play. A residual puritanism makes women want to feel needed and helpful in society as well as in the home.
10. The knowledge explosion in the behavioral sciences has encouraged women to be concerned about themselves as individuals and look for educational programs that will promote self-development.

These facts indicate why specialized programs for women are a vital support to our social structure. The new programs must relate educational efforts to the reality of women's lives in contemporary America.

Goals

The goals of continuing education for women have tended to be broad and unfocused, this at a time when the trend in adult education is toward specificity of goals. Selectivity has occurred as planners respond to expressed needs. The wide range of goals includes: strengthening society's view of what women can achieve; improving the abilities and competencies of women so they can embark upon second careers, or move from the home into the community, or move from the community to business and industry; rebuilding women's self-image and self-confidence so they are not underutilized; helping women to resolve the questions of personal identity and changing life patterns; educating men and the general community about changes in women's status, abilities and expectations and indicating ways in which these changes affect men and their enterprises.

In meeting this spectrum of goals, major emphases have been on:

> Training or re-training to enter specific educational or occupational areas (required credit classes, study techniques, business management, report writing).
> Personal enrichment (liberal arts, humanities, travel seminars, painting and allied arts).
> Improving abilities necessary for community leadership (discussion-group training, program planning or special subject matter such as political science and sociology).
> Understanding of self and family—Who am I? (Often these courses in expanding awareness, counseling and family communication are initial educational experiences for women returning to education and lead to additional programs.)
> Improvement or development of work or homemaking skills (child development, food preparation, interior decorating).
> Para-professional training for both minority/poverty women and middle-class women (for such positions as counselor aide, consumer education aide, teacher aide, and many others in the various "helping" professions).

As with other fields of adult education, the government's goals regarding the resolving of the urban crisis, race relations and poverty have become an important part of the goals of continuing education for women. There is a broad continuum of possibilities in government-sponsored projects which meet the needs of special female populations. Some examples are: Adult Basic Education programs for women; the Work Incentive Program, a joint venture of the Department of Labor and the Department of Health, Education and Welfare; and the New Careers Program sponsored by the Department of Labor.

Patterns of Sponsorship

A few colleges and universities have tried special arrangements integrating women into the regular campus program (e.g., the pioneer efforts of Sarah Lawrence College, Bronxville, New York in the early 1960's). Other universities (such as the University of Minnesota—the Minnesota Plan) have campus-based services that stress individual attention for women enrolled in regular university curricula. But most programs designated *continuing education for women* are sponsored either by a special division (extension, university college or a counterpart) or by an academic division such as home economics, human resources, or social sciences.

Junior–community colleges, in the past specializing in two-year vocational training for specific occupations (such as nursing), now have expanded to counseling courses, family related and liberal arts activities, and to credit courses to prepare women for transfer to a four-year college or university. The public adult schools, in addition to scheduling in the evening subjects of traditional interest to women, have extended their "day" to overtime classes designed to meet many of the goals described. The Los Angeles City schools have been funded for a demonstration school open from 9 A.M. to 9 P.M. offering subjects of interest to disadvantaged women.

In a few local communities, several institutions pool their resources to co-sponsor broad educational programs for women. An example is the innovative, highly successful Council for the Continuing Education of Women, which is composed of Barry College, Dade County Public Schools, Florida Atlantic University, Miami–Dade Junior College and the University of Miami.

Interdisciplinary sponsorship may occur within an institution, or may involve joint action between an institutional department and a community agency, business or industrial firm, or a governmental unit. Such joint sponsorship was evident in a special project developed in a New Jersey community college at the request of the business community. Middle-aged women recruited as clerk–typists received training which included clerical skills and the confronting of such human relations questions as, "How do I feel about making adjustments to a changed work environment?"

Specialized educational programs have been developed by a number of community agencies and organizations. National associations like the League of Women Voters, American Association of University Women and the American Foreign Policy Association plan and administer their own programs. They have educational staffs who occasionally call upon continuing-education-for-women departments in colleges or universities for consultation service, or the joint sponsorship of such activities as leadership training and courses concerning current problems (e.g., air pollution).

There are a few private, commercial programs of education for women. An example is Everywoman's Village in San Fernando Valley (a suburb of Los Angeles) which presents a complement of studies ranging from ethics to yoga. Although business and industry send women employees to programs scheduled by institutions, some companies also provide in-plant training much as voluntary agencies do. For example, Hughes Aircraft trained typists from hard-core poverty areas. After three or four weeks of classroom training, the balance of the thirty-week period was comprised of both on-the-job and classroom instruction.

Program Development

While many educational institutions have sizable departments responsible for planning and administration, others rely upon one person to initiate and implement special programs for women. In either case programs are initiated by faculty in cooperation with departmental staff, participants (who are always willing to make suggestions) and committees drawn from the community.

In voluntary organizations programs are developed by committees at the national level for use by individual branches or sections; but local planning is also widespread. Some volunteer organizations have advisory committees, either institutional or community-based, which are utilized for comprehensive programs or for certain projects, such as environmental control or community development. These voluntary organizations frequently seek consultant service from professional adult educators and directors of programs of continuing education for women.

Since the field is still new and exciting there are many people who are willing, even eager, to help. Among them are adult education colleagues, community leaders and representatives from business and government. Participant evaluation is frequently utilized to assist in planning. Another facet in the planning process is the cross-fertilization that occurs at meetings of professionals in the field, such as the Section on Continuing Education for Women of the Adult Education Association of the USA. Other national associations in recent years have developed sections or divisions with special emphasis on women's education—among them: The National Association of Women's Deans and Counselors, The American College Personnel Association, National Vocational Guidance Association and The Home Economics Association.

Competent Personnel

One problem the programmer faces is locating and utilizing teachers who are competent in subject matter and have the ability to interact with women of varied backgrounds. Frequently a content specialist is not able to relate information to the particular needs of women. For example, management theory is management theory regardless of the composition of the audience. But women students are entitled to examples, case studies, and materials that are oriented to women as well as to men. Potential female managers want to know how practicing female managers make decisions and handle personnel problems. Few men who teach management have such information readily available.

There are increasing numbers of well qualified teachers—university faculty members, adult public school teachers, various specialists in the community—who are engaged in teaching in continuing education programs for women. The Center for the Study of Liberal Education for Adults pamphlet, *Daytime School for Adults,* describes the enthusiasm expressed by many university faculty members who teach special classes for women [6].

Scheduling

Another concern is scheduling; programmers experiment to find the time block most convenient for women. Concentrated periods of time are preferred by many women to once a week sessions. Scheduling typically includes half day, or all day, sessions. Such a format simplifies such matters as transportation, arrangements at home, conflicting community commitments and parking problems.

Some programs allow women students to combine credit and non-credit learning activities in a flexible manner. It is helpful when participants can move easily back and forth between credit and non-credit courses, the same woman often enrolling in both types at the same time. Non-credit programming is vast and varied in terms of format. Programs can be anything from a lecture series or living room discussion group to a typical class. Some non-credit courses involve homework and substantial reading assignments. Others are experimental in method, utilizing sensitivity techniques designed to expand awareness. A sampling of titles and topics follows:

Group Counseling for Women
Developing Personal Potential
Study and Reading Skills
Contemporary Moral Issues
Tension Areas: The World Today
History Unearthed: An Introduction to Archeology
Investing in Securities
Feminine Response in Literature: From Philosophy to Gossip
Practical Speech Making
Sex Education: Whose Responsibility?
Stresses in Modern Marriage
Law in Everyday Life
The American Home as a Work of Art
Problems and Prospects of the Negro Movement

Greek Dance in Its Cultural Context
Introducing Mexico

As the titles indicate, many courses are inter-disciplinary with content selected to interpret and amplify major themes. UCLA Extension's one-day conference, "The Promise of Maturity: Fresh Options in the New Middle Years," used faculty members from the disciplines of history, psychology, public health, education and sociology in an effort to foster understanding of the process of aging.

In the total field of continuing education for women, credit courses have played a relatively small part. For some, however, they are a primary aspect of preparation for re-entrance to school. Credit classes, generally scheduled during daytime hours, provide opportunity to renew study habits and update information prior to campus matriculation. Often these courses are an answer to interrupted education with respect to the timing of credits. When credits are not allowed due to time elapsed, special considerations have been worked out for women who have recently performed satisfactorily in credit classes.

Supportive Services

More pressing in this field than in most other adult education specialities is the need for a wide range of supporting activities. These services range from providing occasional information about campus–community resources to intensive personal counseling or even referral for therapeutic help; they include education, vocation or skills counseling, scholarship aid, assessment or testing, placement and child care.

Counseling for mature women is provided in two general patterns: one in a group setting, usually as a non-credit course; the other is individual counseling, usually at an employment center, community center or in connection with an educational institution. Some counseling services for women continuing or planning to continue their education may be provided by the counseling bureau of a college or university. However, at many colleges student counseling service is not available until one has been accepted and enrolled as a student.

Frequently sought but difficult to find are scholarship funds. Even more than men, women in some socioeconomic groups find they cannot secure funds to continue their education. Many schools as well as families have policies of preference for men in scholarship funding. Other policies preclude scholarship assistance for a part-time student, but frequently the only way a woman can continue her education is as a part-time student.

Very few institutions provide formally for consultative services;

more often the program administrator informally consults over the telephone or in a meeting. Only infrequently do community agencies or business concerns compensate for this time. Requests to serve on advisory committees, provide information about speakers, or to function as speaker or trainer are usually made without monetary reward in mind. Unless the educational institution or agency has allocated funds for this use of program time, the staff person serves as a volunteer in the true sense of the word.

Finance

Sufficient funds to cover the costs of all desirable activities of continuing education for women are usually not budgeted by the sponsoring institution. Most programs conducted by university extension divisions are partially or wholly self-supporting by fees from participants. Where tax support is available, usually for public adult schools and community colleges, fees are minimal.

Obviously the amount and kind of financial support are major determinants of program content, of enrollee selection, of class size, of resources and physical facilities, and even of format or method. *Still, the interests and needs of women are surprisingly similar regardless of ability to pay.* When a program is partly subsidized by an educational institution or agency, a broader spectrum of women attend. Foundation-funded programs for women who presumably could not afford the costs of the educational offering are frequently approved with the understanding the institution will attempt to continue the program when the funds are depleted.

Subsidies are sometimes given for "pilot projects," thus making experimentation available while providing education for more women. For example, the Continuum Center of Oakland University (Michigan) developed a variety of services and courses with financial assistance from the Kellogg Foundation.

An interesting sidelight is the fact that a woman tends to find it more difficult to pay for her own education than for that of her children or her husband. Consequently, efforts are made to keep fees to a minimum.

Clientele and Promotion

Half the World's People, by G. Alison Raymond, refers to the fact that 50 percent of the world's population is female, and it is interesting to note that approximately 50 percent of the total participants in adult education are women. In special programs for women, enrollees come from every educational, occupational, socio-cultural and economic background. Most program developers are interested in reaching as widely as possible into the community and thus find the process of expanding their clientele a continuing operation. Once a woman is committed to the notion of continuing her education, she tends to continue wholeheartedly. She may have to make strenuous physical adjustments and rearrange her family life. Often the pattern of commitment starts with a general orientation ("women's-roles-in-contemporary-society") course and moves from that into credit or non-credit courses or into workshops and lecture series.

The number of women in educational programs is increasing constantly in all parts of the country. While the growth is due in part to the media that have brought the idea to women of continuing their education, satisfied customers are the best publicizers. Evaluative surveys reveal that women tend to enroll as the result of the recommendations of former participants. Experimentation with promotion from market profiles can be helpful, but the evidence indicates that growth is slow that way. If the goal is to reach a large number of women who have not previously been enrolled, it has been productive to present a rather special, carefully defined program aimed toward a particular interest. Once satisfied, participants enroll in other programs. Again, women's diverse interests and needs make program promoting and program development interdependent.

Typically, organizations and institutions depend upon direct mail promotion. It is difficult to assess the effectiveness of radio spot announcements and television interviews. Newspaper articles that are more than announcement (i.e., an interview that personalizes the program), also seem to be effective. Another aid in promotion is the co-sponsoring organization—a stamp of approval.

A pressing need is for procedures to promote the involvement of women in communities distant from what might be called the original accessible territory. The University of Missouri has established a network of coordinators responsible for the continuing education of women in various areas of the state. Essential administrative leadership is lodged in the home institution and utilizes the cooperative extension concept to broaden offerings. The University of Wisconsin has followed a similar pattern, while other universities are contemplating variations of this approach.

Resources

Many institutions have requested assistance from the Women's Bureau of the United States Department of Labor. This bureau is the major federal agency consistently interested in the needs and interests of women of all kinds—not just those who work or who are members of minority groups, but also those in voluntary associations and in continuing education. The Bureau has been helpful as a resource by providing:

> Printed materials, including special and continuing publications.
> Speakers or consultants for programs.
> Continuing information and assistance from regional directors located countrywide in major cities.
> Special projects concerning the education of women.

The references for this chapter list several publications of the Bureau. State Advisory Commissions on the Status of Women are resources in some states. Their activities have ranged from holding public hearings on women's views about legislation, employment and education to establishing a counseling center. Many have published yearly reports of their activities and recommendations.

Women's organizaztions, generally speaking, are involved in providing education on two bases: subject matter, not only for their own members, but for any woman who is interested; and activities to upgrade the skills, abilities and understanding of their own members to meet the organization's needs—a form of in-service training. A double purpose was served by a policewoman's association that planned a one-day seminar to alert women to the physical hazards of an increasingly crowded society and also presented information about the role of policewomen in our society.

Another resource is the growing numbers of self-help groups that combine insight, experience and theoretical knowledge, e.g., the women who come into a broad-based continuing education program need backup from organizations like Parents Without Partners, Alcoholics Anonymous and community mental health agencies.

For program developers, resources exist in all disciplines; and use is made of speakers, relevant research, and those innovators who link disciplines.

Local libraries and the American Library Association occasionally initiate or sponsor programs for women. Their facilities are used as meeting places. Libraries also prepare displays and exhibits to help in the promotion of continuing education for women. As noted elsewhere, ERIC, at Syracuse University—as the repository for adult education research—provides assistance in this field.

Researchers, in and out of adult education, are contributing to the understanding of women and the education of women. A doctoral dissertation by Betty Rosenstein in 1967 treated life styles of middle-class women in their middle years [11]. Anne Steinmann has spent the past fifteen years researching women's behavior as it is based on their predication of what men wish it to be. Dr. Steinmann's work will be reported in detail in a book soon to be published. Schools of Business Administration and governmental agencies like the Bureau of Standards and the Department of Labor continue to conduct research studies in employment. A new area of research concerns part-time work opportunities and the steps needed to accelerate the development and the acceptance of professional part-time employment. (It is worth noting that research relevant to women's education is carried on by sociologists and psychologists as well as adult educators.)

Further Needs

Despite the relatively recent development of continuing education for women, practitioners in the field have indentified many pressing needs:

1. Enough financial and administrative flexibility to permit employing of a counselor on the continuing education for women staff.
2. More extensive evaluation of ongoing programs.
3. Careful examination of the qualifications of the researchers in the field. For example, an eminent, well-intentioned sociologist researched the vocational aspirations of high school girls as contrasted with high school boys. The data indicated lower achievement aspirations for girls. However, the impact of the acculturation process on the behavior of American girls was not taken into account.
4. Maintenance by institutions and agencies of better records for women who participate in their activities. The records should include data concerning previous experience that can be evaluated for equivalency credit.
5. More certification-type programs in which combinations of experiences are provided or accepted in qualifying for helping occupations.
6. Local clearinghouses to provide information about community resources. Almost every project description ends with a statement of need for more information about the activities of others. Such listings should also include psychological and medical resources, and employment, placement or job referral opportunities. Such

a clearinghouse becomes a service center which links all resources with continuing education for women.
7. More educational opportunities for women who aspire to high occupational levels or positions of community leadership. For example, multiple educational experiences are needed for women who are interested in entering political life as elected officials. It was reported in the *Harvard Business Review* that a study concerning women managers in business and industry had to be discontinued because of the scarcity of qualified women. Special efforts are needed to place women in management education.
8. More information concerning the effectiveness of university extension programs, which are the least researched yet the most active.

The Outlook

The "why" of continuing education programs for women will continue to be answered differently on every campus and in every agency. Sympathetic administrators will be eager to provide such programming while others will schedule a token curriculum. The larger programs with experience to draw upon will reflect more than the abilities, interests and drives of an individual programmer. The concern that building a special field (continuing education for women) may imply lesser quality distresses women as well as men, and that possibility will be watched closely. As programs grow, they will reflect the methods, formats and financing typical of all adult education—including credit and non-credit workshops, institutes and seminars. Experimentation in method and focus will accelerate. Regardless of socioeconomic-educational level, women will seek new employment opportunities and higher levels of educational experience.

It has not been easy for some college administrators and faculty to accept the woman seeking a degree. Yet husbands and children frequently have encouraged women to continue their education. (Occasionally husbands literally have enrolled for their wives.) With the shortage of classroom space and staff on college campuses, future programming will explore new methods of degree-designation and credentialing.

Rebuilding self-confidence will continue as a vital aspect of continuing education for women. But, as the female participant's fresh self-image becomes integrated with newly acquired skills, she will be ready for additional educational experiences. And ramifications for other audiences can be envisioned, such as enabling men to benefit from what is learned about the rewarding, recreative use of leisure time.

References

1. American Association of University Women Educational Foundation. *Counseling Techniques for Mature Women.* Report of the Adult Counselor Program, June 14–August 6, 1965. Washington, D.C.: American Association of University Women Educational Foundation, 1966.
2. Bird, Caroline, and Briller, Sara Welles. *Born Female, the High Cost of Keeping Women Down.* New York: David McKay, 1968.
3. Bowman, G. W. "Are Women Executives People?" *Harvard Business Review* (July, 1965), pp. 14–16.
4. Ginzberg, Eli, and others. *Life Styles of Educated Women.* New York: Columbia University Press, 1966.
5. Goldman, Freda. "A Turning to Take Next: Alternative Goal in Education for Woman." In: *Notes and Essays.* Boston, Mass.: Center for the Study of Liberal Education for Adults, 1967.
6. Gordon, Morton. *Daytime School for Adults.* Boston, Mass.: Center for the Study of Liberal Education for Adults, 1967.
7. Gross, Irma H., ed. *Potentialities of Women in the Middle Years.* East Lansing, Mich.: Michigan State University Press, 1956.
8. Lewis, Edwin. *Developing Women's Potential.* Ames, Iowa: Iowa State University Press, 1968.
9. O'Neill, Barbara Powell. *Professional Careers for Women After Marriage and Children.* New York: The Macmillan Company, 1965.
10. Raymond, G. Alison. *Half the World's People.* New York: Appleton-Century-Crofts, 1965.
11. Rosenstein, Betty. *Activity Patterns of Middle-Class Women in Their Mid-Years—with Implications for Adult Education.* Unpublished doctoral dissertation. Los Angeles, Calif.: University of California, 1967.
12. Stenzel, Anne L., and Feeney, Helen M. *Volunteer Training and Development: A Manual for Community Groups.* New York: Seabury Press, 1968.
13. U.S. Department of Labor, Wage and Labor Standards Administration. *Continuing Education Programs and Services for Women.* Pamphlet No. 10. Washington, D.C.: Government Printing Office, 1968.
14. Weisl, Reyna, and others, eds. *Washington Opportunities for Women: A Guide to Part-Time Work and Study for the Educated Woman.* Washington, D.C.: Robert B. Luce, 1967.
15. Wells, Jean. "Special Courses and Services for Mature Women." *Employment* (October–November, 1968).
16. "Women in America." *Daedalus,* XCIII, No. 2 (Spring, 1964).

Chapter 31

Education for Self-Fulfillment

GLENN JENSEN

Some indications exist that adult or continuing education has progressed in the direction recommended ten years ago by Robert Blakely in the 1960 *Handbook of Adult Education:* "The purpose of American life and of American education is, in this light, seen to be the development of individuals who will fulfill themselves and freely serve the society which values individuals [13, p. 6]." Blakely indicated this was a far different kind of adult education from that which had been traditionally envisioned. Interestingly too, it was only Blakely, of the 50 contributing authors, who spoke directly of self-fulfillment. The fact the editors of the present Handbook have decided to devote a chapter to self-fulfillment may indicate a move toward more careful consideration of individual adult needs and the role of the adult educator in helping to meet these needs.

The idea that the purpose of adult education should be self-fulfillment is not new. It has been expressed by a number of writers, including Walt Whitman in his classic poem:

I swear I begin to see the meaning of these things!
It is not the earth, it is not America, who is so great,
It is I who am great, or to be great—it is you up there or anyone:
It is to walk rapidly through civilizations, governments, theories,
Through poems, pageants, shows, to form great individuals.
Underneath all individuals!
I swear nothing is good to me now that ignores individuals. [19, p. 57]

Paul Bergevin, in his thoughtful little book titled *A Philosophy of Adult Education,* points out that adult education goals differ with different people and different situations but in the education of adults toward a creative fulfillment of their lives in a free society, certain goals are most appropriate. He lists these as:

> To help the learner achieve a degree of happiness and meaning in life.
> To help the learner understand himself, his talents and limitations, and his relationships with others.
> To help adults recognize and understand the need for lifelong learning.
> To provide conditions and opportunities to help the adult advance in the maturation process spiritually, culturally, physically, politically and vocationally.
> To provide education for survival in literacy, vocational skills and health measures. [3, pp. 30–31]

Perhaps this is self-fulfillment.

John Gardner, in the report of the President's Commission on National Goals, says about the purposes of education:

> Modern life has pressed some urgent and sharply defined tasks on education, tasks of producing certain specially needed kinds of educated talent. For the sake of our future we had better succeed in these tasks—but they cannot and should not crowd out the great basic goals of our educational system: to foster individual fulfillment and to nurture the free, rational and responsible men and women without whom our kind of society cannot endure. [19, p. 100]

Most would agree that self-fulfillment is an important adult education objective; yet, few administrators and leaders have given real consideration to this purpose in designing adult programs. Most agree with the statement that every individual should have the opportunity to advance educationally to his fullest capacity, but not many are willing to exert effort to help bring the opportunity to pass. Many people believe that the school dropout is a dullard, that those on welfare are lazy and shiftless, that the unemployed don't want to work. Following the Detroit riots, officials of Chrysler Corporation decided to hire unskilled residents of the inner-city. In less than a year, approximately 12,000 persons were hired, but thousands were found who were not equipped for any kind of work. These were so-called "hard-core" unemployed. With federal assistance, Chrysler developed a program to train some 1700 of the hardest of the hard core and prepare them for employment. When they found that many of those who were to participate "didn't show" or "showed late," the employers began to look into the reasons. They found certain

Education for Self-Fulfillment

conditions adult educators had been aware of but had done little to change.

For example, many of these hard core had no social security number, had never been counted in a census, had never registered to vote, belonged to no organization, had never read a newspaper and truly were isolated in a veritable backwater of society. They were late because they did not own an alarm clock and didn't know what it meant to keep an appointment; they didn't show because they couldn't read the destination signs on buses; they suffered from fear, resentment, hostility and the likelihood of failure. So they were taught, fitted with glasses, taken into plants, treated kindly and encouraged. Within 12 weeks the first 44 hard-core unemployables were on the job. To date, their records are exceptional. Of the first 650 persons trained, 83 percent were still on the job after 11 months. Perhaps this is self-fulfillment.

It is much easier to give examples than to define self-fulfillment, but in this writer's opinion the closest thing to a satisfactory definition is found in a platform plank of the Democratic Party in 1964:

> Our task is to make the national purpose serve the human purpose: that every person shall have the opportunity to become all that he or she is capable of becoming. We believe that knowledge is essential to individual freedom and to the conduct of a free society. We believe that education is the surest and most profitable investment a nation can make.

If, for the moment, the proposal that the chief task of adult education is to help the individual become all that he or she is capable of becoming is accepted, then it will be more fruitful to talk about self-fulfillment.

Problems and Issues

One of the faulty crevices of belief into which many Americans have fallen is that all people in this country have more leisure time than formerly and hence should be more receptive to fulfilling themselves through attendance at concerts, art galleries, music halls, lectures and all of the cultural things that encourage the best in people. For example, administrators of the Extension Division at the University of Colorado more than a decade ago decided to inaugurate a cultural program for the thousands of tourists who swarmed into Estes Park each summer and apparently had time on their hands. To the dismay of the administrators very few showed up to look at the art exhibit, to listen to the university band or to participate in the many cultural activities prepared for them. Instead the tourists drank beer, climbed mountains, danced and caused traffic problems. They had no time for cultural affairs and so the university abandoned its program. It was clear these folks were seeking fulfillment in ways not recognizable by adult education administrators.

Much has been written about cybernation, a guaranteed annual wage and the possibility that a small percentage of Americans can produce all that is needed in the way of food and fiber. The implication is that the rest will idle away their time in useless endeavors. Such will not likely be the case: academic people complain of increased demands on their time for teaching, research and travel; business executives spend longer and longer hours on the job; government employees have less and less leisure time; store owners remain open for longer hours; the service agencies find more and more to do; and many housewives, with all the gadgets, now work outside the home. It may well be that each person is seeking self-fulfillment by crowding into an already busy day additional things to do.

Those in adult education could well be missing a vital point in the interpretation of these phenomena as they relate their programs to these "busy people." Instead of offering cultural activities thought good for them, educators should rather be investigating their interests, attitudes and motivations in an effort to help them acquire the kinds of culture which may, indeed, be self-fulfilling.

There are other groups, however, that do have increased leisure time. Farm laborers in some states work about half the year and then draw unemployment insurance. There are unskilled hourly laborers who are forced from time to time into part-time employment, the hard-core unemployed, housewives not employed outside whose children are no longer at home, those retired persons not pursuing other vocational interests, and the hourly skilled worker with only one job and a 32-hour week. Many seek fulfillment through the excitement of televised sports such as pro football and wrestling. Many race to their deaths in automobiles, while others find nothing more exciting than getting drunk. Not that all of these activities are illegal or immoral but there are likely other activities that could enrich leisure time, give greater pleasure or deepen understanding.

Two quite distinct groups of people have been described thus far. Those who seek fulfillment by accepting vocational challenges and getting more heavily involved in their jobs, and those who have additional time off from a boring job or who have no job, and who seek fulfillment through a variety of activities, none of which contributes greatly to an individual's potential.

There could well be, at some point, a mixture of these two classifications and perhaps even a third identifiable group, but for the sake of

Education for Self-Fulfillment

focusing upon self-fulfillment these two will receive primary consideration.

Program Success

If program success is to be determined in light of the proposed definition of self-fulfillment (i.e., programs that assist a person to become all that he is capable of becoming), then the first look might be at what it is that keeps one from becoming all that he can. Here sociologists generally agree the chief negating factor is one that prohibits a person from considering himself or being considered by others a worthwhile representative of the human race. In turn successful adult education programs should encourage or help a person to consider himself and to be considered by others a worthwhile and contributing citizen. It is very likely many in the first group who turn to greater job involvement are truly searching for recognition as contributing persons, and it is certainly true that millions in the second group are restricted to the bare necessities of survival and are simply going through the motions of existing.

The sound adult education program, then, should help the participant become all he can by providing the kinds of educational experiences that:

Encourage communication with others than those in the learner's own group.
Help the learner learn how to learn.
Provide knowledge and skills about social aspects of living.
Help the learner arrive at his own solutions to personal problems.

On the surface it may appear easy to categorize programs under these headings but in reality it is not so. It might be useful, therefore, to examine adult education programming, considering these four criteria to determine to some degree how successful adult educators may have been. It should be remembered, however, that only the participants in these programs could really say whether or not a particular educational experience had been self-fulfilling.

Communication

There seems to be enough evidence today to indicate clearly the importance of the individual in influencing groups such as the family, work and civic groups. In fact, the concepts a person has about himself have great effect upon the way he behaves. As pointed out earlier, if a person feels he is not a worthwhile representative of the human race, he is apt to act quite differently than the person who feels he is the master of his fate. There seems to be, in this scheme, a great need for the individual to understand him or herself. He needs to know who he is, what values and attitudes he holds, what his strengths may be and what his goals are.

It may happen the adult can achieve these understandings by himself. They are more likely to come through interaction with other people in the group process. Self-fulfilling experiences do not necessarily come about in organized adult education programs, but there is some indication programming is being done today with the thought of helping the individual understand himself and become sensitive, as well, to the needs of others.

In spite of any successful inroads adult education may have made, man is apparently still a stranger to himself. C. P. Snow maintains we live in a period marked by a fundamental breakdown in the ability to communicate. We have the technical means to talk to each other but seem to lack the ability. Not only is this true with the disadvantaged adult but it also holds for the educated and the intellectuals. Should this continue the task of the adult educator will indeed be a difficult one. Programs in group leadership, group dynamics, the group process and social psychology are being offered by colleges and universities as well as privately organized groups in an attempt to deal with these adult needs. The National Training Laboratory, many business and industrial training programs, and the federal adult basic education program have self-understanding and self-realization as primary goals.

Because most adults tend to associate with those who speak a common language, have comparable incomes, and enjoy the same social activities, adult educators have been slow in developing programs that encourage a mixing of groups. It is highly probable that better learning situations would result if classes were made up of individuals with a variety of backgrounds and interests, because then each could grow and profit from what the others brought to the learning situation.

In a recent series of interviews on the campus of the University of Wyoming, the majority of 200 adult interviewees described leadership as that quality which enables a person to get others to do what the leader thinks best. It could well be that if this concept holds nationally, adult educators should make a much more determined effort to build programs designed to help adults communicate with persons outside their own groups.

Learning How to Learn

One of the unfortunate stereotypes that persists today is that after age 35 adults steadily lose their ability to learn and gradually go down-

Education for Self-Fulfillment

hill to senility. In spite of lectures, research findings and preachings even students in graduate professional programs frequently fail to change opinions and attitudes about this phenomenon.

This should offer adult educators a clue—perhaps the most important program areas are those devoted to helping the learner learn how to learn. Once this skill is developed progress in other areas will follow.

Some serious efforts along these lines are being made through university, industrial, and governmental programs (e.g., neighborhood youth corps, community action programs, adult basic education and job corps). Results are emerging that indicate that strongly held adult attitudes and values concerning learning are changing, and that many adults are beginning to realize they can learn anything they wish if they really have the desire to do so.

Teaching adults how to learn is probably a skill that should be an objective of every teacher of adults. There are indications the adult may be truly learning how to learn in those cases where the learner is considered to be the most important part of the endeavor. Some universities are now giving special attention to this need by providing areas of study in adult learning and teaching for administrators and teachers of adults. A proposal has been submitted by several administrators in the Rocky Mountain region requesting assistance for the design and conduct of a course concerning learning how to learn. These efforts have not been widespread but show every indication of growing.

In a report from the Center for Cognitive Learning support is given to learning how to learn as an ideal goal for adult educators, but serious questions are posed as to the nature of the concept, the relationships between the instructional methods and techniques applied to self-learning and the effect of college education on this process [14]. More research is needed, but should this research not be forthcoming every indication is that the adult education program which gives top priority to the individual, actively involves him in the educational experience and provides him with useful feedback will be helping him learn how to learn. In Health, Education and Welfare Region VIII the state directors of adult education are now considering the proposal of curriculum to state universities and colleges which might help teachers and administrators of adult basic education programs to better understand this concept.

The Social Aspects of Living

It is perhaps true adult educators have been especially successful in providing knowledge and skills related to the social aspects of living. Yet, many adult educators continue to labor under some assumptions that appear quite untenable. When it was known with some certainty what training adults needed to succeed in their vocational endeavors, programs could be designed to help them. Today, however, with adults changing jobs five or six times in a lifetime and with the technologies changing even more rapidly, it is unrealistic to try to build curricula that teach particular skills. No one knows what knowledge or what skills may be needed.

What has been done, then, is to add courses and materials to the existing curricula without making serious efforts to cull or select the best of the old. As a result educators are trying to cope with changing adult needs by insisting on mastery of more and more knowledge rather than searching and experimenting with techniques and methods of encouraging creativity and flexibility. There is another assumption that is even less defensible—that the subject matter the adult is dealing with means the same to the learner as to the teacher. This leads to the mistaken notion the subject matter, taken on authority, is in fact adult education. It is surprising the high dropout rate in adult programs is not higher.

Programs in drawing, music, acting, painting, writing, hobby development and recreation sponsored by a variety of agencies and enrolling more than 7 million adults each year probably offer the best hope for the emergence of the individual as a person who can manage his own education. In these areas he can experiment, create his own solutions, cast his own hopes, succeed or fail and try again without fear of rebuff or castigation by the teacher. In a proposal for a national center for Higher Continuing Education, Robert Hudson gave major attention to a dynamic field program of regional workshops and seminars in these areas, to prepare teachers and administrators who could in turn relate closely to the adult community [9]. He proposed support for such a program should come in part from the National Endowment for the Humanities and the National Science Foundation.

This or a similar program might play a significant role in the development of people who are knowledgeable, growing, maturing, and who are able to go beyond the point where the teacher leaves them. Self-fulfillment would come then, because adult education had opened the doors for advancement in a vocation, escape from the routine of hand-helping, entry into a brighter and livelier world of conversation, freedom from strict reliance upon others and escape from boredom. James Jarrett suggests that these should be functions of adult education and also that the free man must find meaning in his life by having the opportunity for soul searching, exploring, and taking soundings [12]. Adult education is attempting this role by providing some opportunities,

Education for Self-Fulfillment

but if self-fulfillment is to become a major concern, the movement must somehow be imbued with new energy and enthusiasm.

The Learner's Own Solutions

One of the reasons, perhaps the principal one, there has not been greater participation in adult education is that too many programs are uninteresting. Adults can learn by rote as effectively as youngsters, but they often see little use in doing so. Yet many adult education classes are geared to provide answers to problems the adult doesn't recognize or anticipate. What he seeks, instead, are ways to arrive at his own answers to problems that he helps to recognize. The adult can get such help by participation in programs that permit him to explore and to understand the processes through which he must move in order to solve his problems. The skills and abilities dealing with adult problems are not inherited; they are acquired and the process doesn't happen in a vacuum. Adult educators seriously concerned with the feelings of their students, address themselves to the life situations and problems the learner brings to class.

Adults frequently put on a cloak of school behavior that fits the demands of the teacher while in reality they are being tossed back and forth by a cross current of anxieties, problems, pressures and feelings generated outside the classroom. In proportion to the complexities and tensions of life, the adult builds fears and angers that affect his personality structure. Increasingly adult educators are realizing that a vital function of programs must be to help adults understand their own life situations and develop adequate means for meeting their problems and relieving their tensions. Perhaps this is another way of saying the adult needs self-fulfillment.

In the area of adult basic education this need has taken on added importance. Every state in the union now receives federal funds to conduct educational programs for undereducated adults. Some states have begun experimentation with adult high school programs wherein the participant involves himself in a series of educational experiences designed to help him function effectively in the problem-solving process. Heavy emphasis is being given to new ways of thinking, acting and feeling. On the university level, programs such as the Bachelor of Liberal Studies at the University of Oklahoma and the Brooklyn College experiment are indications of a tendency to move in the direction of intellectual-skills development to enable the adult to better solve pressing personal and social problems. But no sweeping trend is in sight as higher education institutions cling tenaciously to the traditional.

There is, however, cause for optimism in that millions of adults have great potential for developing increased skills in problem-solving. And when adult educators fully recognize the differences among people in flexibility of viewing problems, in the importance of feedback, in the necessity of the adult's operating in a free, permissive and supportive atmosphere, only then will there be educational programs truly designed to serve basic human needs.

Research Implications

Although there are a limited number of studies and reports specifically related to self-fulfillment, there is an abundance of writings from psychological and sociological research dealing with the self-concept, self-image, self-knowing, self-functioning, self-actualization and self-consistency. All somehow relate to self-fulfillment although this concept has not been researched extensively on its own.

In 1959, Arthur Burman conducted a study on aspirational fulfillment among disadvantaged adults to determine implications for adult education [4]. He found that interest in intellectual development was virtually non-existent, that the major interest of his sample was attaining a better standard of living and that few had any concrete plans for fulfilling their aspirations. He concluded that the fundamental task confronting adult education agencies was to discover means for engaging adults in experiences by which they might develop new interests, recognize educational needs and accept continuing education as a means for personal achievement.

An excellent resource on self-fulfillment is the ASCD Yearbook for 1962, entitled *Perceiving, Behaving, Becoming* [1]. It has many implications for adult education, particularly the chapter by Earl C. Kelly in which he declares that in order for the fully functioning self to develop, the adult must have the opportunity to live the good life and have a reason to be. He listed several criteria as important for the fully functioning personality: thinks well of himself, thinks well of others, sees himself as a part of a world in movement, sees the value of mistakes, lives in keeping with his values and is a creative person.

Abraham Maslow proposed in 1962 that there exists a hierarchy of needs for human fulfillment and classified these as: physiological, safety, love and belonging, esteem, and self-actualization [17]. In this hierarchy, Maslow proposes that only as needs at a lower level are met does the individual attempt to satisfy higher needs. Of great implication for the adult educator is Maslow's contention that the adult clamors to use his capacities and if he doesn't have this opportunity his capacities are likely to atrophy.

Education for Self-Fulfillment

Ted Landsman takes a similar approach by maintaining that the fulfilled life requires deep feelings of relationship—of one's self to others and to the physical world about him [16]. The nonparticipant in adult education is likely to be the "closed self." This is a person who is fearful of new tasks, anticipates failure, and generally avoids new experiences. Landsman's concepts take on great meaning for the adult educator in dealing with adults of this type.

In the same vein Puder and Hand identify a number of adult characteristics that tend to inhibit adult learning [18]. Among these are: alienation, avoidance, hostility, fear of school, rejection of desire to learn and self-image of illiteracy.

Of importance to adult education is considerable evidence that as the adult grows older his self-image deteriorates. He becomes increasingly susceptible to threat and develops a stronger need for defense. Kuhlen maintains that in adult education these feelings of threat are expressed by failure of the adult to participate, dropping out, resisting examinations, refusing to take part in discussion and becoming dogmatic [15]. Scattered research indicates adult learning is enhanced when these feelings of threat are removed, when positive attitudes are developed toward education, and when the adult attains a sense of self-confidence. Conversely, learning is impaired when the adult retains membership in a socially deprived group, when classroom conditions create a threatening climate, and when unrealistic goals prevail [10].

In examining personality traits of humans, Taylor found a positive relationship between level of achievement and (1) value placed on own worth, (2) acceptance by peers, (3) ability to handle anxiety and (4) ability to conform to authority demands [21].

Self-fulfillment appears then to have a negative relationship to alienation. Sociologists tend to agree that when an adult loses his sense of pride and commitment he is robbed of self-fulfillment. The loss of pride and commitment occur when he feels his own efforts have little to do with the good or bad fortune that befalls him. Some writers use the term alienation in reference to the psychological discomfort suffered by the worker in an industrialized society when he is cut off from both the means and the ends of production. Adult educators must be sensitive to, and learn how to deal with, the problem of alienation, for only in education does real hope reside for meaningful and self-directed living. Kenneth Benne puts the charge directly to adult educators:

> Educators must concern themselves with the individual's quest of identity, the quest for community, the proper uses of fraternity, the assumptions which underlie problems created by bureaucratic behavior, and the re-education of persons in human relations. [2, p. 198]

There appears to be a great need for additional research in the area of self-fulfillment and its implications for adult education. Freda Goldman demonstrates the need for more research when making a case for reassessing continuing education for women as she points out that our present attempts at providing self-fulfillment are geared toward paid employment for women when in reality a new type of curriculum should be developed with the aim of preparing and re-educating women for their chosen leisure occupations [4]. Edward Dubois makes the same case for employee education by stressing the need, not for formal training programs, but for general education programs designed to satisfy the employee's needs for self-actualization [5].

It is evident similar cases can be made for every segment in our society, yet adult education has been slow to respond in spite of the research findings. For example, the results of a study initiated at Western Kentucky University to determine the cultural needs and interests of the area it serves may very well contain important implications for other universities [22].

Two recent events designed to probe the relation of the arts to the community and to understand the implications for adult education have been reported by Goldman [8]. Each has important connotations for the development of methods and resources for advancing the arts in the small towns of America. One was the conference on arts in the community sponsored by the University of Wisconsin and the other was the Music Educators National Conference held at Tanglewood, New Jersey.

In a study of community services performed by community colleges in New York State, Armond Festine found that discrepancies existed between stated commitments and actual practice and that community colleges have not fully accepted community service as a major educational objective [6]. It may be unfair to generalize from this study but other evidence indicates this conclusion might apply to most other community colleges. If so, an important agency equipped to help satisfy the adults' needs for self-fulfillment is not being effectively utilized.

On the public school level, J. R. Smith found that of the six major goals for adult education, general education for self-realization rated high [20]. If such an objective were applicable to all public school adult education programs and if it should become functional, self-fulfillment might be actualized.

Other significant studies related to self-fulfillment might be listed but growing out of each is a pretty clear indication adults have certain basic needs other than vocational achievement with which adult educators must concern themselves. These needs are motivating factors in adult learning and as such demand attention as well as action.

It is apparent from an investigation of available research in the

Education for Self-Fulfillment

area of self-fulfillment that much remains to be done. Adult educators must find ways to identify the individual as a unique person and to properly place him alongside his fellow man in ways which will not inhibit or destroy his individuality. To do this requires an understanding of what the most effective adult education techniques and methods may be in contributing to self-fulfillment, what the internal and external factors are that lead to or promote self-fulfillment, what sociocultural factors encourage or inhibit the growth of individuality, and how the resources of the instructional group might best be used to maximize the achievement of self-fulfillment.

References

1. Association for Supervision and Curriculum Development. *Perceiving, Behaving, Becoming.* Washington, D.C.: National Education Association, 1962.
2. Benne, Kenneth D. *Education for Tragedy: Essays in Disenchanted Hope for Modern Man.* Lexington, Ky.: University of Kentucky Press, 1967.
3. Bergevin, Paul. *A Philosophy for Adult Education.* New York: Seabury Press, 1967.
4. Burman, Arthur. *Aspirational Fulfillment Among Adults of Lower Socio-Economic Levels with Implications for Adult Education.* Unpublished doctoral dissertation. Bloomington, Ind.: Indiana University, 1959.
5. Dubois, Edward. *The Case for Employee Education.* Management Bulletin No. 100. New York: American Management Association, 1967.
6. Festine, Armond J. *A Study of Community Services in the Community Colleges of State University of New York.* Unpublished doctoral dissertation. Syracuse, N.Y.: Syracuse University, 1967.
7. Goldman, Freda. "A Turning to Take Next, Alternative Goal in Education for Women." In: *Notes and Essays.* Boston, Mass.: Center for the Study of Liberal Education for Adults, 1965.
8. Goldman, Freda. "Pattern and Innovation." *Arts and Society,* V (Spring–Summer, 1968), pp. 180–184.
9. Hudson, Robert B. *Toward a National Center for Higher Continuing Education.* Boston, Mass.: Center for the Study of Liberal Education for Adults, 1968.
10. Jackson, Philip W., and Strattner, Nina. "Meaningful Learning and Retention, Non-Cognitive Variables." *Review of Educational Research,* XXXIV (1964), pp. 513–527.
11. Jackson, Philip W. "Alienation in the Classroom." *Psychology in the Schools,* II (October, 1965), pp. 299–308.
12. Jarrett, James. "Adult Education and Freedom." *Adult Education,* X (Winter, 1960), pp. 67–72.

13. Knowles, Malcolm, S., ed. *Handbook of Adult Education in the United States.* Chicago, Ill.: Adult Education Association of the USA, 1960.
14. Kreitlow, Burton. *Educating the Adult Educator: Taxonomy of Needed Research.* Madison, Wis.: Center for Cognitive Learning, University of Wisconsin, 1968.
15. Kuhlen, Raymond. "Patterns of Adult Development." In: *Notes and Essays.* Chicago, Ill.: Center for the Study of Liberal Education for Adults, 1955.
16. Landsman, Ted. "The Role of the Self-Concept in Learning Situations." *High School Journal,* XIV (April, 1962), pp. 289–295.
17. Maslow, Abraham H. *Toward a Psychology of Being.* New York: Van Nostrand, 1962.
18. Puder, W. H., and Hand, S. E. "Personality Factors Which May Interfere with the Learning of Adult Basic Education Students." *Adult Education,* XVIII (Winter, 1968), pp. 81–93.
19. Report of the President's Commission on National Goals. *Goals for Americans.* Englewood Cliffs, N.J.: Prentice-Hall, 1960.
20. Smith, Joseph Richard. *Validation of the Objectives of Public School Adult Education.* Unpublished doctoral dissertation. Los Angeles, Calif.: University of California, 1966.
21. Taylor, Ronald G. "Personality Traits and Discrepant Achievement." *Journal of Counseling Psychology,* XI (January, 1964), pp. 76–81.
22. Wilson, O. J. "Cultural Enrichment Through Community Action Project." *Annual Report.* Bowling Green, Ky.: Western Kentucky University, 1967.

Appendix I

Directory of Participating Organizations of the Committee of Adult Education Organizations

Compiled by The Library of Continuing Education, Syracuse University

In earlier editions of the Handbook the attempt was made to include many or most of the significant national organizations having educational activity for adults. Now, with scores of thousands of organizations in the field, no possibility exists of being comprehensive. It was therefore decided to build the directory around those organizations, mainly national, that participate in the Committee of Adult Education Organizations. Five others have been added—the American Foundation for Continuing Education, the American Society for Training and Development, the Cooperative Extension Service, the Division of Adult Education Programs of the U.S. Office of Education, and the ERIC Clearinghouse on Adult Education—24 organizations in all. The work of many other significant organizations is discussed throughout the Handbook. Additional information can be obtained from the Council of National Organizations which is included in this directory.

Participating Organizations of the Committee of Adult Education Organizations

Adult Education Association of the USA
The Adult Services Division of the
    American Library Association
Adult Student Personnel Association, Inc.
American Association of Junior Colleges
Association for Field Services in Teacher Education
Association of University Evening Colleges
Commission of the Professors of Adult Education
Council of National Organizations for Adult Education
Division of Adult Education Service of the
    National Education Association
Extension Committee on Organization and
    Policy of the National Association of State
    Universities and Land-Grant Colleges
International Congress of University Adult Education
The Library of Continuing Education,
    Syracuse University
National Association for Public Continuing and
    Adult Education
National Association of Educational Broadcasters
National Community School Education Association
National Home Study Council
National University Extension Association
Society of Public Health Educators, Inc.
University Council on Education for
    Public Responsibility

Some Other Adult Education Agencies

American Foundation for Continuing Education
American Society for Training and Development
Cooperative Extension Service
Division of Adult Education Programs,
    U.S. Office of Education
ERIC Clearinghouse on Adult Education

Adult Education Association of the USA
Affiliated with the Council of National Organizations for Adult Education

Founded   Columbus, Ohio, 1951

Purpose   To further the acceptance of education as a process continuing throughout life; to afford opportunities to professional and non-professional adult educators to increase their competence; to receive and disseminate information about adult education; to promote a balanced development of educational services for adults; and to cooperate with adult education agencies nationally and internationally.

Membership General, Professional, Student Professional, Retired Professional, Contributing, Organizational—Institutional

Commissions and Councils
Commission on Planning Adult Education Facilities, Systems and Environments
Commission on Research in Adult Education
Commission of Professors of Adult Education
Commission on Adult Basic Education
Council of National Associations for Adult Education
Council of State Associations

Standing Committees
Committees, Commissions and Sections
Nominations and Elections
Membership and Field Services
Publications
Social Philosophy
Personnel Policies
Finance and Development
Inter-Association Relations
Legislative Policy
Joint AEA-NAPCE
Future Conferences

Sections
Armed Forces Education and Training
Community College Adult Education
Community Development
Continuing Education for the Professions
Continuing Education for Women
Correctional Institution Education
Education for the Aging
Home and Family Life
International Affairs
Liberal Adult Education
Labor Education
Mass Media in Education
Public Affairs
Religious Adult Education
Residential Adult Education
Training—Education and Industry
Training and Professional Development

Services Available to all members: periodicals, special publications, field service, conferences, consultation, reference services and membership directory.

Directory of Participating Organizations   531

Publications   JOURNALS: *Adult Education* (quarterly)
              Adult Leadership (monthly, except July and August)
              PAMPHLETS: Leadership Series
              Theory and Method Series
              MONOGRAPHS AND REPRINTS: Various
              BOOKS: Various
              ADDRESS: Executive Director
              Adult Education Association of the USA
              1225 19th Street, N.W.
              Washington, D.C. 20036

The Adult Services Division of the American Library Association

Founded   1957 as an outgrowth of the Adult Education Section of the Public Libraries Division.

Purpose   To provide continuing educational, recreational and cultural development for adults in all types of libraries. To identify and evaluate book and non-book materials which are useful in adult services and stimulate production of such materials. To be responsible for publication, study and review of professional material related to adult services.

Membership   Personal, Organization

Standing Committees   Common Concerns (with Reference Services Division—RSD)
Conference Program
Joint Committee on Library Service to Labor Groups (with AFL–CIO)
Legislation
Library Service to an Aging Population
National Library Week
Notable Books Council
Orientation (with RSD)
Program Policy
Publications Advisory
Publishers Liaison (includes representation from American Book Publishers Council)
Reading Improvement for Adults
Relations with State and Regional Library Associations
Special Projects

Services   Inquiries addressed to ALA which relate to adult education, library services to adults, services to community organizations, adult reading, and aging are referred to the ASD office for reply.

Publications   JOURNALS: *ASD Newsletter* (quarterly)
              Library Service to Labor Newsletter (semiannually)

MONOGRAPHS: *Handbook for Librarians: How to Use the Reading for an Age of Change Series*
Literacy Activities in Public Libraries by Bernice MacDonald
Study Discussion Programs: A Guide to Their Evaluation and Use

OTHER: *Guides to the Literature of Adult Services* (bibliography)
Reading for an Age of Change (pamphlets)

Address Executive Secretary
Adult Services Division
American Library Association
50 E. Huron Street
Chicago, Illinois 60611

Adult Student Personnel Association, Inc.

Founded 1961

Purpose To foster and implement student personnel programs in evening colleges through the exchange of ideas between member schools, and to strive for greater understanding of the evening student and his problems.

Membership Institutional, Professional

Standing Committees Elections
Membership
Program

Publications
Liaison Representatives to AUEC, IAESC and CAEO

Services Consulting services to colleges and universities

Publications JOURNALS: *Journal of Student Personnel Work in Adult and Evening Education* (semi-annually)
BOOKS: *Student Personnel Services for Adults in Higher Education* by Martha L. Farmer

Address Adult Student Personnel Association, Inc.
One Hanson Place (Room 1205)
Brooklyn, New York 11217

American Association of Junior Colleges

Founded 1920

Purpose To represent the interests, stimulate the professional development, and promote the sound growth of America's community and junior colleges.

Directory of Participating Organizations 533

Membership	Institutional, Institutional Associates, Individual Associates
Standing Committees and Commissions	Committee on Continuing Education Committee on International Education Commission on Administration Commission on Curriculum Commission on Instruction Commission on Legislation Commission on Student Personnel Council of State Directors Council of University and College Professors
Services	Consultant and information services to member colleges on administration, curriculum, faculty, facilities, instruction, occupational education, legislation, and student personnel; information services to any and all persons interested in junior and community colleges.
Publications	JOURNALS: *Junior College Journal* (monthly) SERIES: *Student Personnel* (three volumes) MONOGRAPHS: Various PAMPHLETS: Various BOOKS: Various NEWSLETTERS: In the fields of developing institutions, occupational education, community services, facilities planning, and public relations. OTHER: *Junior College Directory* (annually)
Address	American Association of Junior Colleges Number 1, Dupont Circle Washington, D.C. 20036

Association for Field Services in Teacher Education

Founded	Chicago, 1922
Purpose	The cooperative improvement of college extension and field services in teacher education.
Membership	Institutional, Individual, Honorary
Standing Committees	Membership Research Standards
Services	Consultative services in relation to establishing standards and developing programs in field and extension services.
Publications	*The New Campus* (annually) *Newsletter* (triannually)

Address Secretary–Treasurer
Association for Field Services in Teacher Education
Indiana State University
Terre Haute, Indiana 47801

Association of University Evening Colleges

Founded 1939

Purpose To provide a forum for administrators of university evening programs and to focus public attention on and encourage acceptance and understanding of the aims of collegiate adult education. International in scope.

The primary concern of the Association is with the collegiate education of adults as a basic function and a responsibility of institutions of higher learning.

Membership Institutional, Associate, Association, Personal

Standing Committees Evening Student Personnel
Legislative
Local Arrangements
Membership
Membership Promotion
Nominating
Program
Public Relations
Regions
Relationships with Other Associations
Research
Resolutions

Publications JOURNAL: *Newsletter* (quarterly)
MONOGRAPHS: *Proceedings* (annually)
"*From the Dean's Desk*" (irregularly)

Address Executive Secretary
Association of University Evening Colleges
University of Oklahoma
Norman, Oklahoma 73069

Commission of the Professors of Adult Education

A division of the Adult Education Association of the USA

Founded 1956

Purpose To provide opportunities for adult education faculty members to gain knowledge that will help in planning and operating a graduate professional education program in adult education.

To increase the relevance and quality of dissertations in adult and extension education and encourage and help the professors in their own research.

To secure the adult education practitioners' support for graduate programs in adult education.

To encourage and facilitate theory-building, research and dissemination in adult education.

To constructively influence the applied field of adult education.

Membership Full membership only

Standing Committees Executive Committee
Federal Program Review
Membership Committee

Services Consultative services to universities establishing graduate programs in adult education.

Publications MONOGRAPH: *Adult Education: A New Imperative for Our Times*, 1961.
BOOK: *Adult Education: Outlines of an Emerging Field of University Study*. Adult Education Association of the USA, Washington, D.C., 1964.

Address Chairman, Commission of Professors of Adult Education
Adult Education Association of the USA
1225 19th Street, N.W.
Washington, D.C. 20036

Council of National Organizations for Adult Education
Affiliated with the Adult Education Association of the USA

Founded 1952

Purpose The furthering of adult and continuing education through the cooperative efforts and educational activities of the national and international associations which compose the membership and through a close working relationship with the Adult Education Association of the USA.

To encourage exchange of information among voluntary national organizations concerning developments and improvements in methods of adult education and to further research into how such organizations can most effectively engage in programs of adult and continuing education.

To improve and increase the leadership and activities of national organizations in the field of adult and continuing education.

Membership	Organizational members only.
Standing Committees	Membership Nominating Public Relations Program Publications Volunteer Accreditation
Services	Available to members only.
Publications	*Probing Volunteer—Staff Relations* (self-inventory list) *Ten Checkpoints for Better Booklets* (pamphlet) *Leadership in Voluntary Enterprise* (monograph) *The Government of Associations* (anthology) *The Leadership of National Organizations on the U.S. Scene* (report)
Address	Council of National Organizations for Adult Education 1225 19th Street, N.W. Washington, D.C. 20036

Division of Adult Education Service of the National Education Association

A Division of the National Education Association

Founded	1945
Purpose	To serve the needs and interests of the members of the NEA which are concerned with adult education.
Membership	No separate membership from that of the NEA itself.
Services	Consultation Information Reference To any member of the NEA
Address	Associate Director Division of Adult Education Services National Education Association 1201 16th Street, N.W. Washington, D.C. 20036

Extension Committee on Organization and Policy of the National Association of State Universities and Land-Grant Colleges

Founded	1914 by American Agricultural Colleges and Experiment Stations.

Directory of Participating Organizations

Purpose	To act upon policy matters affecting the Cooperative Extension Services in the 50 States, Puerto Rico, the District of Columbia and the Virgin Islands.
Membership	Three Directors or Central Staff from each region.
Standing Committees	Agricultural Community Development and Public Affairs 4-H Youth Home Economics International Programs Legislative Marketing Staff Training and Development
Services	Leadership and guidance on policy matters for the development of a national extension program. Recommendations are made to the Cooperative Extension Services in the 50 states, Puerto Rico, the District of Columbia and the Virgin Islands.
Publication	*Journal of Cooperative Extension* (quarterly)
Address	Extension Committee on Organization and Policy of the National Association of State Universities and Land-Grant Colleges 1785 Massachusetts Avenue Washington, D.C. 20036

International Congress of University Adult Education
Affiliated with UNESCO

Founded	1960
Purpose	The Congress is concerned with all aspects of adult education carried on by universities in every part of the world. In pursuit of this objective, it seeks to improve communication among university adult educators by such activities as: the establishment and continual revision of a directory of universities involved in adult education and of persons engaged in such activities; the establishment of an International Journal and other publications; the stimulation or promotion of university adult education; the establishment of regional information and library centers and the encouragement of exchanges of university adult educators.
Membership	Individual, Institutional
Standing Committees	Editorial Research and Training

Services	Serves as an agency of liaison in the field of adult education at the international level and as a clearinghouse for information and ideas.
Publications	JOURNALS: *International Congress of University Adult Education Journal* (triannually)
	International Congress of University Adult Education Newsletter (semi-annually)
	MONOGRAPHS: *Occasional Papers* (occasionally)
	Roster (periodically)
Address	Secretary
	International Congress of University Adult Education
	Syracuse University
	109 Roney Lane
	Syracuse, New York 13210

The Library of Continuing Education of Syracuse University

Founded	Major collection acquired in 1960. Library of Continuing Education established in 1964. Collection numbers about a quarter of a million documents.
Purpose	To recommend comprehensive information services for field of adult education.
	To maintain national library and archives in adult education.
	To act as bibliographic and information center for adult education.
	Provides reference services to faculty and students of Syracuse University.
Services	Provides information and referral services to the field of adult education.
	Sponsors workshops and institutes for adult education information users, in cooperation with the ERIC Clearinghouse on Adult Education.
Publications	MONOGRAPHS: *Adult Education Information Services: Establishment of a Prototype System* (3 parts), 1967.
	Adult Education Procedures, Methods and Techniques, 1965.
	Directory of Adult Education Organizations, 1968.
Address	Director
	The Library of Continuing Education
	107 Roney Lane
	Syracuse, New York 13210

National Association for Public Continuing and Adult Education
A Department of the National Education Association and
Affiliated with the World Confederation of
Organizations of the Teaching Profession

Founded   1952

Purpose   To give leadership to the development of adult education in the public schools.

Membership   Active Members, Associate Members, Emeritus, Communications Service

Standing Committees
Adult Basic Education
Awards
Community and Junior Colleges
Conference Planning
Curriculum
International Relations
Legislative
Membership
NAPCAE-AEA Joint Committee
Nominations and Elections
Professional Development
Publications
Secondary School Education for Adults
State and Affiliated Organizations

Services   Consultant services both through correspondence and personal contact in setting up new programs of adult education and in expanding existing programs. Comprehensive Information Clearinghouse of information on elementary–secondary education for adults. Service to state associations in securing improved state legislation for adult education. Conducts annual conference.

Publications
JOURNALS: *Pulse of Public School Adult Education* (8 issues per year)
Swap Shop for Administrators (bimonthly)
Techniques for Teachers of Adults (8 issues per year)
BOOKS: *Administration of Continuing Education: A Guide for Administrators*
Public School Adult Education Almanac (annually)
HANDBOOKS: Various
FILMS AND FILMOGRAPH: Various
POSTERS AND FOLDERS: Various

Address
Executive Secretary
National Association for Public School Adult Education
1201 Sixteenth Street, N.W.
Washington, D.C. 20036

National Association of Educational Broadcasters
A Member of the European Broadcasting Union and of the Asian Broadcasting Union

Founded 1925 under the name The Association of College and University Broadcasting Stations. Name changed in 1934.

Purpose From the Preamble to the Constitution: "to advance, by united effort the dissemination of knowledge, information and education by and concerning radio and television broadcasting . . . to produce and distribute educational programs for non-profit educational purposes; to further research in the educational uses of radio and television and their employment for the improvement of instruction at all levels of public learning; and to coordinate efforts of educational institutions in all areas of broadcasting and TV."

Membership
Authority Associates
Council of State Educational Telecommunications
Educational Associates
Educational Television Stations
Individual Member Division
Industrial Associates
International Associates
Instructional and Professional Services
National Educational Radio
Military Associates
Sustaining Members

Standing Committees
Awards and Citations
Convention Exhibitors
Engineering
History and Archives
International Relations
Publications
Research

DIVISION COMMITTEES
ETS Copyright
ETS CATV
ETS Interconnection
ETS Instructional Television
ETS Labor
ETS Program Practices
ETS Program Selection
ETS/PS Policy Committee
Instructional Radio
NER Network Program Advisory

Services Generates and supervises research projects and has responsibility for the coordination of proposals to agencies and founda-

Directory of Participating Organizations

tions. Maintains a library of educational broadcasting and research. Provides an opportunity to discuss issues with others involved in educational broadcasting through conventions and seminars. Acts as liaison with government and professional organizations. Participates in technical assistance programs for developing nations.

Publications JOURNALS: *Educational Broadcasting Review* (6 issues per year)
NAEB Newsletter (monthly)
MONOGRAPHS: Various
RECORDINGS: Various

Address National Association of Educational Broadcasters
1346 Connecticut Avenue, N.W.
Washington, D.C. 20036

National Community School Education Association

Founded 1966

Purpose To promote and expand the community school concept, and to establish community schools as an integral and necessary part of the educational plan of every community.

Membership Active, Associate

Standing Committees Association Services
Evaluation
Legislation and Lobbying
Liaison
Membership
National Convention
Public Relations
Research
Think Committee

Services Consultation, Workshops, Research, Legislation Development, Regional Conferences, National Conventions, Leadership Training, Job Placement

Publications JOURNALS: *Community School and Its Administration* (monthly)
NEWSLETTER: Monthly
PAMPHLETS: Various

Address National Community School Education Association
923 East Kearsley Street
Flint, Michigan 48502

National Home Study Council

Founded 1926

Purpose To establish standards for the operation and conduct of home study schools and to provide accreditation for schools meeting these standards. To promote ethical business practice in the private home study field. To cooperate with local, state, regional and national agencies and associations, public and private, in the development and exchange of information helpful to the advancement of the field of home study education. To conduct and promote research. To cooperate with other educational agencies in adult and extension education.

Membership All members must be schools accredited by the Council's independent Accrediting Commission.

Standing Committees
Annual Conference
Awards and Recognition
Business Standards
National Affairs
Public Relations
Research and Educational Standards

Services Accreditation is available to qualified private home study schools making application and which meet the standards. The Council provides assistance and consultation in the field of correspondence education to member and non-member schools. Information on accredited schools and the courses they offer is available to all making inquiry.

Publications DIRECTORY: *Directory of Accredited Private Home Study Schools*
OTHER: *NHSC News* (monthly)
Various Brochures and Handbooks

Address Executive Director
National Home Study Council
1601 Eighteenth Street, N.W.
Washington, D.C. 20009

National University Extension Association

Founded 1915

Purpose An association of institutions of higher learning and certain related organizations dedicated to continuing education and extension.

Membership Institutional

Divisions	Audio–Visual Communication Community Development Conferences and Institutes Independent Study Evening Colleges and Class Extension
Services	Manages national education and training programs for institutions of higher education. Holds annual professional meetings. Conducts research studies and publishes in-service education manuals. Encourages high professional and academic standards. Represents general university extension in Washington, D.C. Cooperates with other adult education associations and organizations in seeking solutions to problems and issues pertinent to the interest and needs of adults.
Publications	ANNUAL AND PERIODICAL: *Guide to Correspondence Study in Colleges and Universities, 1968–69* (biennially) *NUEA Newsletter* (biweekly) *Proceedings of Annual Meetings* *Programs and Registrations* (annually, jointly with AEUC) *The Spectator* (bimonthly) OTHER: Various, including adult basic education materials
Address	Executive Director National University Extension Association 900 Silver Spring Avenue Silver Spring, Maryland 20910

Society of Public Health Educators, Inc.

Affiliated with the International Union for Health Education (IUHE) through organizational membership in the American National Council for Health Education of the Public, Inc. (ANCHEP)

Founded	1950. Incorporated in New York State, 1952.
Purpose	The Society of Public Health Educators is a professional organization whose purposes are to promote, encourage and contribute to the advancement of the health of all people by encouraging study, improving health practices and elevating standards of achievement in the field of public health education. It is the national professional society for public health educators.
Membership	Active Fellows, Honorary Fellows, Emeritus Fellows

544   Appendix I

Standing Committees	Continuing Education Membership Professional Preparation and Practice Recruitment Research and Studies
Services	The Society's primary concern is to serve the professional needs of public health educators, especially SOPHE members, in the following ways: assists them in keeping up to date with the expanding field of public health and public health education; provides for the development, promotion and continuous analysis of professional standards; studies the changing needs of the profession and recommends the academic preparation and experiences needed for public health educators; stimulates interest in careers in the profession; promotes research; serves as a spokesman for the profession and works with related organizations on matters of mutual concern; stimulates citizen support for health education and desirable legislation.
Publications	JOURNALS: *Board Meeting Highlights* (semiannually) MONOGRAPHS: *Health Education Monographs and Supplements* (occasionally) HEALTH EDUCATION ABSTRACTS: Occasionally
Address	Administrative Secretary Society of Public Health Educators, Inc. 104 East 25th Street New York, New York 10010

University Council on Education for Public Responsibility

Founded	1962
Purpose	To achieve more concerted action through organization in the ship. education for public responsibility and more responsible citizen-
Membership	Regular, Associates
Standing Committees	Executive Committee of Presidents Program Planning Committee
Services	An informational exchange for members of the council and other institutions that wish to participate in the program of the council.
Address	Chairman Program Committee (UCEPR) Dean of Continuing Education Southwestern at Memphis Memphis, Tennessee 38112

American Foundation for Continuing Education

Founded 1947

Purpose To develop study–discussion programs in the natural sciences, social sciences and humanities which form the basis of adult study–discussion groups.

Services The AFCE is available for consultation, assistance in training discussion leaders, and in organizing and promoting discussion programs.

Publications Study–discussion materials in the fields of public policy, the humanities and the sciences which are used by adult groups as well as in regular college and university courses. The Foundation contracts with institutions and individuals to develop study–discussion programs. Catalogue of publications available.

Address American Foundation for Continuing Education
Publications in Continuing Education
Syracuse University
105 Roney Lane
Syracuse, New York 13210

American Society for Training and Development

Founded 1943

Purpose To foster education, development and expansion of the skills and standards of persons responsible for training and management development in business and industry.

Membership Individual in local chapters and/or in the national society.

Divisions Sales Training
Organization Development

Services Conducts position referral service for members. Conducts annual national conference and institutes on training function, planning procedures, methods and management development.

Publications JOURNAL: *Training and Development Journal*
DIRECTORY: *Membership Directory*
OTHER: *Members Memo* (periodically)
Training and Development Handbook

Address Executive Secretary
American Society for Training and Development
P.O. Box 5307
Madison, Wisconsin 53705

Cooperative Extension Service

U.S. Department of Agriculture and the Land-Grant Universities

Founded 1914 through passage of the Smith-Lever Act.

Purpose Conduct out-of-school informal educational programs for the benefit of the people of the United States.

Organization Cooperative Extension Service is a three-way partnership with the federal, state and county governments sharing in financing, planning and conducting Extension programs.

Standing Committee Extension Committee on Organization and Policy (ECOP)

Address Helps farmers and ranchers apply new production and marketing technology to their operations; helps firms marketing and processing agricultural commodities and firms supplying farmers, including cooperatives, to give better service at minimum costs; provides programs for homemakers on nutrition, clothing, home management, child development, and consumer information; conducts 4-H programs for youth to help discover the importance of science to everyday living and in development of employable skills, career study and selection, and leadership development; helps local governments and community leaders analyze needs and resources and develop organizations to secure community facilities and programs for resource and human development; provides special programs for low-income families and assists other agencies and groups concerned with helping low-income people.

Publications *Extension Service Review* (monthly)

Address Federal Extension Service
U.S. Department of Agriculture
Washington, D.C. 20250
or
Cooperative Extension Service at the land-grant universities in each of the States, the District of Columbia, Puerto Rico and the Virgin Islands

Division of Adult Education Programs

A division of the U.S. Office of Education, Department of Health, Education and Welfare

Founded 1959

Purpose Collect statistics, disseminate information and improve adult education.

Directory of Participating Organizations 547

Membership	None
Regional Organization	Department of Health, Education and Welfare has nine regional offices. Division of Adult Education Programs has one field representative in adult education in each office.
Standing Committees	National Advisory Committee on Adult Education National Advisory Council on Extension and Continuing Information
Services	Depending on resources and time, consultant services, information and services related to adult education are given to individuals, organizations, and associations. Administers grants under laws for extension programs, adult basic education, teacher training for adult basic education, and civil defense, and other experimental and demonstration projects in adult education.
Publications	*A Need to Read and Write* *Community Service and Continuing Education Programs*
Address	Division of Adult Education Programs U.S. Office of Education Washington, D.C. 20202

ERIC Clearinghouse on Adult Education

Sponsored by the Educational Resources Information Center of the U.S. Office of Education and Syracuse University

Founded	1967
Purpose	To provide easy access to information useful in the education, training and retraining of adults and out-of-school youth.
Services	Acquires, indexes, abstracts and disseminates information about research and other information data in adult education. Resource to agencies and associations to improve library services and help establish specialized information services.
Publications	NEWSLETTER: Three or four times yearly SERIES: Annual Registered Research and Investigation Basic Information Sources Current Information Sources MONOGRAPHS: Literature Reviews State-of-the-Art Reports
Address	Director, ERIC Clearinghouse on Adult Education 107 Roney Lane Syracuse, New York 13210

Appendix II

General Information Sources in Adult Education

Compiled in 1968 by
ERIC Clearinghouse on
Adult Education

This Appendix lists major periodicals abstracting services, current and retrospective bibliographies and other information services that are *general* in nature and likely to be useful to everyone involved in the education and training of adults. Bibliographies in specialized subjects appear in the relevant chapters of the Handbook. This Appendix is a supplement to Chapter 5.

Handbook users should be aware that many of these documents and many in the Chapter bibliographies may be available through the ERIC Document Reproduction Service (EDRS). Consult any monthly issue of *Research in Education* for instructions on ordering inexpensive hard copy or microfiche reproduction. In general, there is a good chance that any document mentioned in the Handbook which is not a commercial publication and which is dated 1966 or later will be available through ERIC. Please check carefully in *Research in Education* or its cumulative indexes to obtain order numbers and prices.

For more information on ERIC, consult Chapter 5 or write to: ERIC Clearinghouse on Adult Education, 107 Roney Lane, Syracuse, N.Y. 13210.

Adult Education Journals

Adult Education

Articles on research and philosophical issues, theoretical studies and book reviews are presented each quarter. Each Summer issue from 1955 to 1967 contained an inventory with abstracts of research completed during the year. Each Spring issue from 1961 to 1968 contained a list of persons receiving doctoral degrees in adult education. Published by the Adult Education Association of the USA, 1225 19th Street, N.W., Washington, D.C., 20036. Annual subscription $10.00.

Adult Education (London)

Articles on all aspects of adult education, book reviews and notes, and news of adult education in Great Britain. A 34-year cumulative index was published in 1962. Published by the National Institute of Adult Education, 35 Queen Anne Street, London, W.1, England. Annual subscription £1-10-0.

Adult Education Periodical Holdings

A list (with addresses and publication data) of foreign and domestic periodicals and newsletters of interest or use in various aspects of the education and training of adults contained in the ERIC Clearinghouse on Adult Education of the Library of Continuing Education of Syracuse University. October, 1967, 19 pp. ED 014 022; EDRS price: $0.25, HC $0.76.

Adult Leadership

Articles on practical applications of adult education at all levels and in many agencies, news of the profession, book reviews, and other articles appear monthly except in July and August. Published by the Adult Education Association of the USA, 1225 19th Street, N.W., Washington, D.C. 20036. Annual subscription $10.00.

Continuing Education

A quarterly listing of conferences, short courses and other educational opportunities, giving subject, sponsor, date, location, and fee. More information can be obtained by mail or telephone. Also contains articles in the areas of continuing education in scientific and technical areas, management development and the professions. Data Bases, 101 North 33rd Street, Philadelphia, Pennsylvania 19104. Annual subscription $15.00.

Continuous Learning

Bimonthly issues present essays and brief reports of events and philosophical issues in Canadian adult education. Published by the Canadian Association for Adult Education, Corbett House, Sultan Street, 21–23, Toronto 5, Ontario, Canada. Annual subscription $3.50.

Convergence

An international journal of adult education with articles in one of four languages (English, French, Russian or Spanish) and notes on each article in the three other languages. A translation service makes the full text of major articles available in all four languages. Published quarterly by the Ontario Institute for Studies in Education. Mailing address: Convergence, P.O. Box 250, Station "F," Toronto 5, Ontario, Canada. Annual subscription $4.00.

Journal of the Community Development Society

A professional journal, devoted to improving knowledge and practice in the field of purposive community change, includes articles on research; evaluation of theory, techniques and methods; current community problems; and the profession itself. It includes book lists and reviews and announcements of interest to members of the society. It is published semiannually by the Community Development Society, 909 University Avenue, Columbia, Missouri 65201. Subscription rates: $12.00 per annum; single copies of back issues in print $3.00.

Journal of Extension (formerly Journal of Adult Education)

Quarterly journal of research, program development and policy in Cooperative Extension and related areas. Book reviews, abstracts of research studies and research briefs. A 5-year cumulative index, 1963–1968, was issued as Part 2 of Number 4, Volume VI, Winter, 1968. Extension Journal, Room 216, Agricultural Hall, University of Wisconsin, Madison, Wisconsin 53706. $5.00 per year, $6.00 foreign.

Learning Resources; A Directory for Engineers, Scientists and Managers

Learning Resources is a cross-indexed compilation of essential information about short courses, seminars, conferences, workshops and other educational activities through which engineers, educators, scientists and managers may enhance their professional competence. It is published thrice yearly by Engineers Joint Council, 345 East 47th St., New York, N.Y. 10017. Single copies $15.00; yearly subscriptions in United States and Canada $30.00; all other countries $31.00.

Studies in Adult Education

Studies in this journal focus on adult education in Great Britain, although articles on work in other countries are included whenever their experience seems relevant to British problems. The book and research review columns are also open to significant work from abroad. Universities Council for Adult Education (England). Biannually. Journal is available from David & Charles Publishers, South Devon House, Newton Abbot, Devon, England; annual subscription 30 shillings.

Training Development Journal

Articles, book reviews and program development reports dealing with education and training for better use of manpower at all levels in business, industry and a wide range of other agencies are presented monthly. A five-year cumulative index was prepared in 1968. Published by the American Society for Training and Development, 313 Price Place, P.O. Box 5307, Madison, Wisconsin 53705. Annual subscription $10.00 for members, $12.50 for others.

Trends

This journal for adult educators presents research abstracts and/or general critical reviews of selected subject areas within or pertinent to adult education. Each issue focuses on one area of concern to practitioners, administrators or researchers. The initial issue, on psychological research and sensitivity training, will be followed by others on creativity research, educational television, research on adult learning environments and psychological factors relevant to adult learning. Published quarterly, the periodical is available from the Canadian Association for Adult Education, Corbett House, 21–23 Sultan St., Toronto 181, Ontario. Subscription rates: $6.00 per year; $2.00 per issue.

Current Indexing and Abstracting Services

Abstracts of Papers Presented to the National Seminar on Adult Education Research

Abstracts of 34 papers presented to the 1969 Seminar. Available from EDRS. Order number ED 030 003; MF $0.25; HC $2.40.

Aim

Abstracts of Instructional Materials in Vocational and Technical Education (AIM) includes many items suited to adult education use. Many documents are available in microfiche and hardcopy reproductions. Quarterly. Publications Clerk, Center for Vocational and Technical Education, Ohio State University, 1900 Kenny Road, Columbus, Ohio 43212. $9.00 per year.

Arm

Abstracts of Research and Related Material in Vocational and Technical Education (ARM) includes many documents relevant to adult vocational education. Format is similar to *Research in Education* and many documents may be obtained in microfiche and hardcopy reproductions. Quarterly. Publications Clerk, Center for Vocational and Technical Education, Ohio State University, 1900 Kenny Road, Columbus, Ohio 43212. $9.00 per year.

CIRF Abstracts

Extensive abstracts of documents related to education and training in all fields of economic and work activities. About 400 abstracts per year in six issues, in English and French, from worldwide coverage. Twice a year, bibliographies in the training field are issued. CIRF Publications, International Labour Office, CH 1211, Geneva 22, Switzerland. $8.00 per year.

Current Index to Journals in Education

Annotations and indexes for 352 publications. Annual subscription $34.00; foreign subscriptions have postage added, single copy $3.50. Semiannual cumulative index $12.50, annual cumulative index $24.50. Available from Crowell-Collier-Macmillan Information Corporation, 909 Third Ave., New York, N.Y. 10022.

Current Information Sources

A series of subject bibliographies with abstracts produced by the ERIC Clearinghouse on Adult Education (ERIC/AE). Each contains abstracts and ordering information for all documents handled by ERIC/AE on that subject during the preceding year. These bibliographies are not available from ERIC/AE, but are announced in *Research in Education* with information on ordering microfiche and hardcopy reproductions from the ERIC Document Reproduction Service. A list of all ERIC/AE publications is available from ERIC/AE, 107 Roney Lane, Syracuse, New York 13210.

Dissertation Abstracts

Section A, Humanities and Social Sciences. Extensive abstracts of doctoral dissertations from most universities in the USA including adult education and related fields. Cumulative author and subject indexes. Information for ordering in 35mm microfilm or hardcopy reproductions. University Microfilms, Inc., 300 Zeeb Road, Ann Arbor, Michigan 48103. $45.00 per year, $70.00 foreign; second copies to the same institution: $35.00 per year, $50.00 foreign. The same publisher produces *Masters Abstracts*, a similar service for masters theses with much more limited institutional coverage. Four issues per year. $6.00 per year, $8.00 foreign.

Education Index

Cumulative citation index to a wide range of educational journals including *Adult Education* and *Adult Leadership*. Monthly except July and August. H. W. Wilson Company, 950 University Avenue, Bronx, New York 10452.

Educational Media Index

A 14-volume guide to all types of non-book instructional and curriculum materials. Commonly available in audio–visual centers. New York, McGraw Hill, 1964. $62.45.

Educators Guide to Free Films

Title, subject and source index to 4700 films available without rental fees. Educators Progress Service, Randolph, Wisconsin 53956.

Manpower Research

Compiled by ERIC for the Interagency Committee on Manpower Research, this inventory for the years 1966 and 1967 contains citations, abstracts and indexing in standard ERIC format, with author, subject and other indexes. Covers manpower development reports for OEO, Labor Department and other federal agencies. Documents may be obtained in microfiche or hardcopy reproductions, singly, or the entire set as a special collection. Collections will be up-dated annually. Catalog Number FS 5.212; 12036. Superintendent of Documents, Government Printing Office, Washington, D.C. 20402. $2.75.

National Center for School and College Television

A national, non-profit Center providing sale and rental of instructional television materials from many sources, including the backlog of NET educational productions. Newsletter and further information: NCSCT, Box A, Bloomington, Indiana 47401.

Poverty and Human Resources (formerly Poverty and Human Resources Abstracts)

Extensive abstracts and supplementary bibliographies of citations in poverty, manpower and human resource development. Focus is on research and action programs, legislative and community developments and policy trends. Annual index. Institute of Labor and Industrial Relations, University of Michigan–Wayne State University, P.O. Box 1567, Ann Arbor, Michigan 48106. Bimonthly. Annual subscription: $40.00, organizational rate, $8.50, student rate; $10.00, faculty rate.

Psychological Abstracts

Abstracts of journal literature and reports in psychology and social psychology, including educational psychology and adult development. Monthly with semi-annual cumulative author and subject indexes. Subscription Office,

American Psychological Association, 1200 17th Street, N.W., Washington, D.C. 20036. $30.00 per year (foreign issue available).

Research and Investigation in Adult Education: 1969 Annual Register

Inventory of research completed and reported in the past year, with abstracts and information on ordering the reports, many of which are available in microfiche and hard copy reproductions from EDRS. Previous inventories appeared in each Summer issue of *Adult Education*, 1955–1967. Adult Education Association of the USA, 1225 19th Street, N.W., Washington, D.C. 20036. $4.50.

Research in Education

This monthly abstract bulletin announces documents entering the ERIC system and includes for each document: citation, abstracts, indexing terms, price and information for ordering microfiche or hardcopy reproductions of documents available from the ERIC Document Reproduction Service. Also contains résumés of USOE Bureau of Research projects in progress. Author, subject and institutional indexes cumulate twice a year. Government Printing Office, Washington, D.C. 20402. $21.00 per year, $26.25 outside the USA.

Research Studies in Education; A Subject and Author Index of Doctoral Dissertations Reports, Field Studies and a Research-Methods Bibliography

This annual publication on research studies in education lists completed doctoral dissertations and those in progress, and contains author indexes and a research-methods bibliography. Entries are grouped by subject, ranging from educational philosophy to adult and professional education, and including specific fields of study and other such concerns as educational administration, team teaching, child psychology, educational psychology, finance, public relations, guidance and counseling, special education, higher and graduate education, evaluation and measurement, vocational and industrial arts education, teaching techniques, and the problems of teachers. Available from F. E. Peacock, Inc., 401 Irving Park Rd., Itasca, Illinois 60143. Single copies are $10.00 postpaid.

Sociological Abstracts

Abstracts of sociological literature including urban and rural sociology and community development. Eight issues per year, the last being a cumulated index. $100.00 per year. Information Files, i.e., partial subscriptions to any of 21 sections of the classification (e.g., 0700 Community development and rural sociology) are also available at $5.00 per year. Sociological Abstracts, 2315 Broadway, New York, New York 10024.

General Information Sources in Adult Education

Training Abstracts Service

Extensive abstracts on cards, classified for filing, with some cross-references. Comprehensive coverage of British literature in the industrial training field and extensive coverage of other English language material. British Ministry of Labour, Training Department, 162 Regent Street, London, W.1, England.

U.S. Government Research and Development Reports

Semi-monthly catalog of abstracts of non-restricted research and other reports from Federal agencies. Field Five, Behavioral and Social Science, includes reports of military training research and some coverage of OEO and Labor Department manpower training programs. Much of this is incorporated into the ERIC system and announced through *Research in Education*. Citations, abstracts, index terms, information for ordering microfiche or hardcopy reproductions. Clearinghouse for Federal and Scientific and Technical Information, Springfield, Virginia 22151. $30.00 per year, $37.50 foreign.

Major Retrospective, General Bibliographies, Literature Guides and Research Reviews

Aker, George F. *Adult Education Procedures, Methods and Techniques: A Classified and Annotated Bibliography, 1953–1963.* Library of Continuing Education, Syracuse, New York, and University College, Syracuse University. Available from Syracuse University Press, Box 8, University Station, Syracuse, New York 13210. $7.00. Covers all methods and techniques, with a special section of 41 references on residential education.

Beals, Ralph A., and Brody, Leon. *The Literature of Adult Education.* American Association for Adult Education, New York, 1941. 493 pp. Extensive essays reviewing various aspects of adult education with extensive bibliography. Valuable index of early journal literature. Long out of print, but often available in libraries.

Brunner, Edmund de S., and others. *An Overview of Adult Education Research.* Adult Education Association of the USA, 1225 19th St., N.W., Washington, D.C. 20036, 1959. 273 pp. Comprehensive (in 1958) state-of-the-art summary review of research findings on all aspects of non-vocational adult education. Extensive bibliography in footnotes.

Burke, Arvid T. and Mary A. *Documentation in Education.* Teachers College Press, Columbia University, New York, 1967. Extensive coverage of sources useful to educational researchers; reference books, dictionaries, almanacs, yearbooks, subject matter summaries, sources for statistical data and so on. Audio-visual materials, and techniques for their use are discussed as well as microfiche and other media.

Burrichter, Arthur, and Jensen, Glenn. *Research Studies with Implications for Adult Education, Mountain–Plains Region, 1945–1966.* University of Wyoming, Department of Adult Education, Laramie, Wyoming, 1967. 84 pp. Available from EDRS: Order number ED 012 413; MF $0.50; HC $3.36. Abstracts of research studies completed in universities of the Mountain–Plains region.

Canadian Association for Adult Education. Non-degree Research in Adult Education in Canada, 1968. Les Recherches en Education des Adultes au Canada, 1968. Ontario Institute for Studies in Education, Toronto, Department of Adult Education. EDRS Order number ED 034 146, price in microfiche $0.50, hard copy $5.25. Text in English and French. 103 pp. July 1969. A bilingual document summarizes 118 Canadian nondegree research studies (both completed and in progress in adult education in 1968). There are 35 completed studies on adult dropouts, adult educator training, rural extension, secondary education, university extension, apprenticeships, inservice teacher education, residential education, manpower development, Communist adult education in Czechoslovakia, higher education in Ethiopia and other topics. The remaining 83 reflect such areas as student characteristics, audio–visual aids and instruction, educational needs, professional training and continuing education, language instruction, program planning and evaluation, the role of community colleges, vocational education, and experimental project "Sesame" in the Province of Quebec. Respondents (including those with no research report) are listed by geographical areas and organizations. An author and title index and a bilingual subject index also are included.

Carpenter, William, and Kapoor, Sudarshan. *Graduate Research in Adult Education and Closely Related Fields at Florida State University, 1950–1966.* Florida State University, Tallahassee, Florida 32306, 1966. 86 pp. Available from EDRS: Order number ED 010 681; MF $0.50; HC $3.44.

ERIC. Selective retrospective bibliographies, literature guides and research reviews are routinely produced by the ERIC Clearinghouse on Adult Education. They are announced in *Research in Education* and available from the ERIC Document Reproduction Service in microfiche and hardcopy reproduction. A list of these may be obtained from ERIC/AE, 107 Roney Lane, Syracuse, New York 13210.

Jensen, Gale; Hallenbeck, Wilbur; and Liveright, A. A. *Adult Education: Outlines of an Emerging Field of University Study.* Adult Education Association of the USA, 1225 19th Street, N.W., Washington, D.C. 20036, 1964. 334 pp. Commission of the Professors of Adult Education produced this overview of adult education as a field of study and its relation to other disciplines. Bibliography and footnotes include references to some of the key works in other disciplines.

Kelly, Thomas. *Select Bibliography of Adult Education in Great Britain.* National Institute of Adult Education, 35 Queen Anne Street, London, W.1, England, 1962. Citations and brief annotations of adult education literature in Great Britain with some coverage of American and other English language works. Continued in an annual Handlist compiled by C. D. Legge and more recently in a section of the Yearbook of the National Institute of Adult Education.

Kidd, J. Roby. *How Adults Learn.* Association Press, New York, 1959. 324 pp.

Adult learning capacities and related topics, with bibliography and suggested readings by chapter.

Knowles, Malcolm S. *The Adult Education Movement in the United States.* Holt, Rinehart & Winston, New York, 1962. 335 pp. The standard introductory history with extensive bibliography.

Knowles, Malcolm S., ed. *Handbook of Adult Education in the United States.* Adult Education Association of the USA, 1225 19th St., N.W., Washington, D.C. 20036, 1960. Footnotes and chapter references together constitute a selected bibliography covering the adult education field at publication date. Also contains information on the organization, work and publications of about 150 adult education organizations.

Mezirow, J. D. and Berry, Dorothea. *The Literature of Liberal Adult Education, 1945–1957.* Scarecrow Press, Metuchen, New Jersey, 1960. Out of print. Very valuable reference because of the thoroughness of many of the annotations. Extensive section on philosophy and objectives, research, bibliographies, work of universities and other agencies. Subject and author index. Available from EDRS: Order number ED 030 791; MF $1.25; HC $15.95.

Quattlebaum, Charles A., *Federal Educational Policies: Programs and Proposals. A Survey and Handbook*, Library of Congress, Legislative Reference Service, Washington, D.C., December 1968. Microfiche available from EDRS; hard copies available from Superintendent of Documents, Government Printing Office, Washington, D.C. 20402. *Part I. Background, Issues, Relevant Considerations.* 177 pp. EDRS order number ED 031 656; MF $0.75; HC $0.75. A compilation, analysis and summary of certain basic information needed by Congress for legislative decision on educational issues. *Part II. Survey of Federal Educational Activities.* 525 pp. EDRS order number ED 031 657; MF $2.00; HC $2.25. A report surveying the educational activities administered by federal agencies, describing each program and summarizing the activities, including data on funds allocated to them. *Part III. Analysis and Classification of the Programs.* 375 pp. EDRS order number ED 032 460; MF $1.50; HC $1.50. An analysis and classification of the federal training and educational programs with regard to method of administration, levels of education concerned, geographic areas affected and number and types of persons affected.

Review of Educational Research. June issues of 1950, 1953, 1959, and 1965 are devoted to adult education research. Brief summary chapters by subject experts review research and development, with extensive bibliographies. American Educational Research Association, 1201 16th Street, N.W., Washington, D.C., 20036.

Review of Extension Research. An annual inventory with long, analytical summaries of agricultural extension research in the period 1947–1964. Produced by the Federal Extension Service. Wide coverage, length of span covered and excellence of the summaries make this the outstanding research review publication in the history of adult education. Unfortunately, it was never widely distributed and is no longer produced. Files may sometimes be found in agricultural libraries and in Cooperative Extension offices. Some similar materials are now distributed on an intermittent basis by the Division of Extension Research and Education, Federal Extension Service, Department of Agriculture, Washington, D.C.

Special Information Centers and Services in Adult Education

Adult Education Association. *Federal Support for Adult Education; 1969 Directory of Programs and Services.* A guide to adult education programs and services in agencies throughout the federal government with list of pertinent legislation and publications. Available from the Macmillan Company, 866 Third Avenue, New York, N.Y. 10022. HC $6.95.

Datrix. A service of University Microfilms, Inc. provides computer searches by subject of files and doctoral dissertations since 1928. For price and procedures for this service contact: University Microfilms, Inc., 300 North Zeeb Road, Ann Arbor, Michigan 48106.

ERIC Clearinghouse on Adult Education (ERIC/AE). ERIC/AE processes adult education and training documents for announcement in *Current Index to Journals in Education* and in *Research in Education,* which also contains information on ordering microfiche and hardcopy reproductions of many of the documents. ERIC/AE produces bibliographies, literature guides and reviews which are also announced in *Research in Education.* ERIC/AE is not able to make document searches or provide reference services. It can, however, advise and assist other agencies in developing information service centers which will make efficient use of resources of the ERIC system. A newsletter and publication list are available upon request. ERIC/AE, 107 Roney Lane, Syracuse, New York 13210.

Gates, Jesse L. and Altman, James W. *Handbook of Information Sources in Education and the Behavioral Sciences, 1968.* 183 pp. Guide to directories of information sources and to special information agencies and services in government and other agencies. Description of services and how to use them. Compiled under a U.S. Office of Education contract. Available from EDRS. Order number: ED 020 447; MF $0.75; HC $7.48.

Greenleigh Associates, Inc. *Inventory of Federally Supported Extension and Continuing Education Programs.* Part One: Report and Recommendations; Part Two: Program Abstracts and Indexes. 1967. 342 pp. Guide to services of agencies throughout the federal government. Available from EDRS: Order number ED 012 415; MF $2.25; HC $14.92.

How to Use ERIC. Revised edition. A guide to use of the ERIC system. Contains an explanation of indexing, list of Clearinghouses. Order number: FS 5,212–12037–A. Government Printing Office, Washington, D.C. 20402. $0.30.

Kruzas, Anthony T. *Directory of Special Libraries and Information Centers, 1968.* Location, collections, services and publications of information centers in the U.S. and Canada. Gale Research Company, The Book Tower, Detroit, Michigan 48226.

Library of Congress. National Referral Center. *A Directory of Information Re-*

sources in the United States Federal Government. 1967. 411 pp. Collections, services and publications of federally supported information centers. Subject and institutional indexes. Government Printing Office, Washington, D.C. 20402. $2.75.

Library of Continuing Education at Syracuse University (LCE). LCE maintains the archives of numerous adult education associations, collects manuscripts and personal papers of individual adult educators, serves as a comprehensive "library record" backstopping the collections of other agencies and performs bibliographic services, as resources permit. Library of Continuing Education, 107 Roney Lane, Syracuse, New York 13210.

National Education Association Adult Education Clearinghouse (NAEC). NAEC provides reference and advisory services, newsletters and other publications in the area of public school adult education with emphasis on adult basic and secondary education. It maintains a collection of materials on adult education in Latin America. NEA Adult Education Clearinghouse, 1201 16th Street, N.W., Washington, D.C. 20036.

National Referral Center (NRC). NRC, operated by the Library of Congress, maintains files of persons who are expert in various areas and are willing to serve as resource persons or consultants. Education, including adult education, is covered, as well as a wide range of scientific and technical fields. Service is without charge and all persons listed have indicated their availability. NCR, Library of Congress, Washington, D.C. 20540.

School Research Information Service (SRIS). SRIS, operated by Phi Delta Kappa, provides document search services from its collection of ERIC documents and other materials, with emphasis on innovative programs in public school systems. It sells microfiche and hardcopy reproductions of documents and publishes *SRIS Quarterly*. Phi Delta Kappa, Eighth and Union Streets, Bloomington, Indiana 47401.

Science Information Exchange (SIE). Provides a computer search system based on files of research in progress from most federal government agencies, major foundations and other research funding agencies. Operated by the Smithsonian Institution, SIE covers education, including the education and training of adults, as well as scientific and technical research. Information on cost and procedures for searches is available from SIE, 209 Madison Bank Building, 1730 M Street, N.W., Washington, D.C. 20036.

U.S. Department of Health, Education and Welfare, Health Services and Mental Health Administration, *Training Methodology*, Public Health Service Publication No. 1862, Washington, D.C., December 1968. Available in microfiche from EDRS; also available from Superintendent of Documents, Government Printing Office, Washington, D.C. 20402. *Part One. Background Theory and Research. An annotated Bibliography.* 98 pp. MF $0.50; 0–334–245 $1.00. This annotated bibliography, including 310 abstracts, pertains to research and theory on individual behavior, group behavior and educational and training philosophy selected from over 6000 items mostly published from January 1960 to March 1968. *Part Two. Planning and Administration. An Annotated Bibliography.* 128 pp. MF $0.75; 0–334–246 $1.00. These 447 items pertain to instructional design, course planning and training program administration of articles published between January 1960 and March 1968. *Part Three. Instructional Methods and Techniques. An Annotated Bibliography.* 109 pp. MF $0.50; Government publications available. This part contains abstracts of 345 documents published between January 1960 and March 1968 on specific instructional methods and techniques for groups and individuals. *Part Four. Audio-visual Theory, Aids, and Equipment. An Annotated Bibliography.* 89 pp. MF $0.50; 0–334–248 $0.75. This list of 332 documents with abstracts on training methodology contains selected references on the media aspects of training: audio-visual theory and methods, aids, facilities, and equipment. Most items were published from January 1960 to March 1968.

Information Services: Studies and Indexing Tools

Allen, Lawrence, A. *The Growth of Professionalism in the Adult Education Movement, 1928–1958.* Ph.D. dissertation, University of Chicago, 1961. 245 pp. Tested the hypothesis that adult education has grown more professional by content analysis of samples of the literature at different times in the period covered. Microfilm available from: University of Chicago Photoduplication Department, Swift Hall, Box 132, Chicago, Illinois 60637.

Barhydt, Gordon, and Schmidt, Charles T. *Information Retrieval Thesaurus of Education Terms.* 1968. 133 pp. Alphabetical, faceted (i.e., classified) and permutated (i.e., rotated) displays of indexing terminology developed largely through indexing educational media research. Introductory essay on vocabulary control problems in education. Available from The Press of Case Western Reserve University, Cleveland, Ohio 44106. $5.50.

Canadian Association for Adult Education. *The CAAE Research Library in Adult Education.* 1961. 20 pp. Outline and explanation of the classification scheme, based on the Universal Decimal Classification, formerly used in the CAAE Library.

Cotton, Webster. *On Behalf of Adult Education; a Historical Examination of the Supporting Literature.* Center for the Study of Liberal Education for Adults, Boston, Massachusetts, 1968. 82 pp.

Cotton, Webster. *The Rationale for Liberal Adult Education in a Free Society; A Survey, Analysis and Critique of the Literature from 1919 to 1961.* Ed.D. thesis, University of California, Los Angeles, 1963. 362 pp. Critical analysis of the themes salient in the literature underlying the movement for liberal education for adults. Available from University Microfilms, Ann Arbor, Michigan 48106. Order number 63–6587; MF $4.65; HC $16.45.

DeCrow, Roger. *A Model Information System for the Adult Education Profession.* ERIC Clearinghouse on Adult Education, 1968. 25 pp. Recommendations of the report above for an ERIC style information service, supplemented by information activities in adult education organizations. Available from EDRS: Order number ED 015 412; MF $0.25; HC $1.00.

DeCrow, Roger, and others. *Adult Education Information Services, Establishment of a Prototype System.* Syracuse University Library of Continuing

Education, 1967. 417 pp. Report of a three-year project to examine adult education information needs, to propose new services and recommend methods to make them operational. Available from EDRS: Order number ED 020 489; MF $1.75; HC $16.76.

Great Britain. Ministry of Labour. Training Department. *Classification of Training Information.* 1967. 42 pp. Decimal classification for organizing information in industrial training. Used with the Ministry of Labour Training Abstracts Service. Available from EDRS: Order number ED 015 374; MF $0.25, HC $1.68.

International Labour Office. Central Library and Documentation Branch. *List of Descriptors*, Edition 2, 1966. 171 pp. Indexing word list with terms lumped by subject group with scope notes and an alphabetical index. Terminology covers the broader interests of ILO including workers and labor education and industrial training. ILO, 1211, Geneva 22, Switzerland.

Thesaurus of ERIC Descriptors. 1967; Supplement, 1968. Structured indexing wordlist showing synonyms, broader and narrower term relationships, with rotated term index. Available from Government Printing Office, Washington, D.C. Thesaurus order number: OE-12031, $2.50; Supplement order number OE-12031-1; $2.00.

U.S. Department of Agriculture. Federal Extension Service. Division of Extension Research and Education. *Classification Outline for Extension Research Materials.* ER&E-10 (2–68). 4 pp. Classification used in the *Review of Extension Research* and other bibliographic listings of the Federal Extension Service.

Appendix III

The Changing Focus

Contents of Past Handbooks

This Handbook is the fifth in a series that goes back to 1934. Malcolm Knowles and Eugene DuBois point out in the Prologue that these works, taken collectively, trace the evolution of the modern field of adult education. The tables of contents from preceding editions are reproduced here in order to
   (1)   provide scholars and researchers with a résumé of the contents of the preceding volumes, and
   (2)   assist the interested reader to gain perspective on the field of adult education—its changing concerns through recent stages of development.

HANDBOOK OF ADULT EDUCATION IN THE UNITED STATES, 1934

DOROTHY ROWDEN (ed.). American Association for Adult Education, New York

Table of Contents

Agricultural Extension, *Benson Y. Landis*	1
Alumni Education	16
American Association for Adult Education, *Ralph A. Beals*	29
The Arts in Adult Education, *Erwin O. Christensen*	33
Community and State Organizations of Adult Education Agencies	44
Private Correspondence Schools, *J. S. Noffsinger*	52
Courses in Adult Education	54
Adult Education and the Foreign Born, *Read Lewis*	58
Open Forums	63
Libraries and Adult Education, *Carl H. Milam*	70
Lyceums and Chautauquas	98
Men's and Women's Clubs	101
Museums and Adult Education, *Laurence Vail Coleman*	105
Music in Adult Education, *Augustus D. Zanzig*	115
Adult Education for Negroes	124
Parent Education, *Ralph P. Bridgman*	131
Political Education, *Charles Ascher*	146
The Education of Adult Prisoners, *Austin H. MacCormick*	152
Adult Education Under Public School Auspices, *L. R. Alderman*	158
Puppets in Adult Education, *Catherine F. Reighard*	175
The Radio in Adult Education, *Levering Tyson*	178
The Place of Recreation in Adult Education, *Weaver Pangborn*	185
Programs of Social Education Conducted by Religious Groups	195
Adult Education in Settlements, *Lillie M. Peck*	203
Special Schools and Institutes for Adults	216
The Little Theater	225
Training by Corporations	231
Training Leaders for Adult Groups	233
Educational Opportunities for the Unemployed, *Mary Frank*	238
University Extension, *W. S. Bittner*	254
Visual Education	273
Vocational Education for Adults, *Franklin J. Keller*	280
Vocational Guidance of Adults, *Robert Hoppock*	288
Vocational Rehabilitation of Physically Handicapped Adults, *Edgar B. Porter*	294
Workers' Education, *Spencer Miller, Jr.*	299
Schools for Women Workers in Industry, *Hilda W. Smith*	306
National Organizations with Adult Education Programs	309

HANDBOOK OF ADULT EDUCATION IN THE UNITED STATES, 1936

DOROTHY ROWDEN (ed.). American Association for Adult Education, New York.

Table of Contents

PREFACE	v
Alumni Education, *Ralph A. Beals*	1
American Association for Adult Education, *Ralph A. Beals*	12
The Arts in Adult Education, *F. A. Whiting*	17
Private Correspondence Schools, *J. S. Noffsinger*	26
The Federal Emergency Adult Education Program, *Emily Miller Danton*	28
Adult Education and the Foreign Born, *Read Lewis*	54
Public Forums, *Fred Atkins Moore*	59
Health Education for Adults, *Philip P. Jacobs*	66
Adult Education in Sanatoria, *Beulah Weldon Burhoe*	69
Adult Education in International Relations, *Edgar J. Fisher*	72
Libraries and Adult Education, *John Chancellor*	77
Lyceums and Chautauquas	103
Men's and Women's Clubs	106
Museums and Adult Education, *Laurence Vail Coleman*	110
Adult Education in Music, *Eric T. Clarke*	119
Adult Education for Negroes, *Alain Locke*	126
Parent and Family Education, *Ralph P. Bridgman*	132
Political Education, *Robert Paige*	151
The Education of Adult Prisoners, *Austin H. MacCormick*	159
Adult Education Under Public School Auspices, *John W. Studebaker*	166
The Radio in Adult Education, *Levering Tyson*	181
The Place of Recreation in Adult Education, *Weaver W. Pangburn*	188
Regional Organizations of Adult Education Agencies, *Ralph A. Beals*	197
Adult Education in Religious Institutions and Agencies, *Wilbur C. Hallenbeck*	206
Rural Adult Education, *Edmund deS. Brunner*	216
Schools and Institutes for Adults	233
Adult Education in Settlements, *Lillie M. Peck*	245
The Regional Theater, *Rosamond Gilder*	257
Training by Corporations, *Byron F. Field*	264
Training of Leaders and Teachers of Adults, *Thomas Fansler*	269
University and College Extension Work, *W. S. Bittner*	279
Visual Education, *Philip Paul Wiener*	309
Vocational Education for Adults, *L. H. Dennis*	317
Vocational Guidance of Adults, *Robert Hoppock*	323
Vocational Rehabilitation of Physically Handicapped Adults, *John A. Kratz*	332

The Changing Focus	569
Workers' Education, *Spencer Miller, Jr.*	336
National Organizations Having Adult Education Programs	345
Index	391

ADULT EDUCATION IN ACTION, 1936
MARY L. ELY (ed.). American Association for Adult Education, New York.

Table of Contents

Foreword, *Charles A. Beard*	vii
Preface	xi

PART ONE—PROLOGUE

We Need Adult Education

To Educate the Whole Man, *L. P. Jacks*	3
To Keep Our Minds Open, *Nicholas Murray Butler*	6
To Base Our Judgments on Facts, *Newton D. Baker*	9
To Meet the Challenge of Free Choice, *Dorothy Canfield Fisher*	12
To Keep Abreast of New Knowledge, *William F. Ogburn*	16
To Be Wisely Destructive, *A. E. Heath*	19
To Return to Creative Endeavor, *John Erskine*	22
To Prepare for New Occupations, *Charles A. Beard*	24
To Restore Unity to Life, *Ernst Jonson*	27
To Insure Social Stability, *James E. Russell*	30
To Direct Social Change, *Harry Elmer Barnes*	33
To Better Our Social Order, *Glenn Frank*	36
To Open a New Frontier, *William F. Russell*	38
To Liberalize the College Curriculum, *Robert D. Leigh*	41
To Improve Teachers and Teaching, *H. A. Overstreet*	44
To Attain True Security, *Alvin Johnson*	46
To Enlarge Our Horizons, *Lucy Wilcox Adams*	49
To See the View, *William Bolitho*	51

We Pause to Consider

Can People Go On Learning?, *James Harvey Robinson*	54
How Shall We Conceive the Task of Adult Education?, *William Heard Kilpatrick*	57
What Are Our Hindrances?, *Charles H. Judd*	60
Can We Afford Adult Education?, *A. Caswell Ellis*	64

PART TWO—THE MAIN ACTION

The Vanguard

Introduction	69
The American Lyceum, *Louis J. Alber*	71

The Chautauqua Movement, *Arthur E. Bestor, Jr.*	74
The Free Lecture System of New York, *Bonaro Wilkinson Overstreet*	76

The General Staff
Introduction	79
The American Association for Adult Education, *Morse Adams Cartwright*	80

The Forces of Adult Education—Agencies
PUBLIC LIBRARIES
Readers' Advisory Service, *Jennie M. Flexner*	92
Students' Information Service, *Annie P. Dingman*	95
A Variety of Services, *Malcolm G. Wyer*	97

THE UNITED STATES GOVERNMENT
Education on the Farms, *Clyde William Warburton*	100
Education in the C.C.C. Camps, *Frank Ernest Hill*	103
Education in the National Parks, *Harold C. Bryant*	105

THE EMERGENCY PROGRAMS IN THE PUBLIC SCHOOLS
Federal Emergency Education, *Arthur E. Bestor*	107
An Emergency School in Operation, *Benjamin Fine*	110
Emergency Education for Industrial Workers, *Hilda W. Smith*	112
Emergency Classes in Drama, *Eve Chappell*	114
Hopes and Fears for Emergency Education, *Walter Dan Griffith*	117

PUBLIC AND SEMI-PUBLIC PROJECTS
The Denver Opportunity School, *Robert Tudor Hill*	120
South Carolina's Opportunities for the Underprivileged, *Edgar Wallace Knight*	122
Shorewood (Wisconsin) Opportunity School, *Harvey M. Genskow*	125
High School Institutes, *Eve Chappell*	127

UNIVERSITIES
University Correspondence Courses, *Walton S. Bittner*	130
Far-flung University Extension, *Harmon B. Stephens*	132

MUSEUMS
New Uses for Museum Exhibits, *Laurence Vail Coleman*	134
Circulating Art through Branch Museums, *Philip N. Youtz*	136
Classes in an Art Museum, *Roberta Murray Fansler*	139

THEATERS
Our Emerging Native Theater, *Edith J. R. Isaacs*	141
A Thousand Little Theaters, *Kenneth Macgowan*	144

CHURCHES
The Church an Educational Asset, *F. Ernest Johnson*	146
Education in a Metropolitan Church, *Elsie Gray Cambridge*	149
Church Nights in a Suburban Church, *R. E. Wolseley*	152
A Church That Has Always Been a School, *Louis Wolsey*	154

RELIGIOUS ORGANIZATIONS
The Y.M.C.A., *Ruth Kotinsky*	156
The Y.W.C.A., *Sarah E. D. Sturges*	159

INDUSTRY
Training on the Job, *Nathaniel Peffer*	161

The Changing Focus 571

MECHANICS INSTITUTES
    Training off the Job, *George Wilson Hoke*   164
SETTLEMENTS
    Hull House, *Jane Addams*   167
    Greenwich House Pottery, *Maude Robinson*   169
PENAL INSTITUTIONS
    Prisoners Are Candidates for Education, *Austin H. MacCormick*   172
    Prison Classes in Session, *Anne E. M. Jackson*   175
HOSPITALS
    Patient Students, *Margaret Fitzgerald*   178
SPECIAL SCHOOLS
    A School for Educating the Educated in New York City, *Alvin Johnson*   180
    A Folk School in the Southern Mountains, *Olive Dame Campbell*   183
    A Hobo School in a Western Railroad Yard, *Walter Dan Griffith*   186

The Forces of Adult Education—Specialized Programs
PARENTS
    My Grandmother as a Young Mother, *Dorothy Canfield Fisher*   190
    Child Study Groups for Parents, *Sidonie Matsner Gruenberg*   192
    Parents Share Their Children's Studies, *Seymour Barnard*   194
    Parents Enjoy Progressive School Opportunities, *J. H. Newlon*   196
    Parents Form an Orchestra, *Theodora Perrine*   198
    A Euthenics Grandmother of Today, *Fanny Moncure Marburg*   200
WORKERS
    The Problems and Purposes of Workers' Education, *Spencer Miller, Jr.*   202
    Workers' Education during the Depression Years, *Mollie Ray Carroll*   204
    Special Programs for Office Workers, *Jean Carter*   207
    Labor Institutes, *Eve Chappell*   210
RURAL PEOPLE
    The A B C of Rural Education, *Kenyon L. Butterfield*   212
    Rural Culture *vs.* Urban Culture, *John D. Willard*   215
    An Institute of Rural Economics, *Elsie Gray Cambridge*   217
CITY DWELLERS
    Metropolitan Provincialism, *Alvin Johnson*   219
    An Urban College, *A. Caswell Ellis*   222
NEGROES
    Lessons of Negro Adult Education, *Alain Locke*   224
    Learning in Harlem, New York, *Eve Chappell*   227
COLLEGE ALUMNI
    Introduction   230
    Reading List Service, *Wilfred B. Shaw*   231
    Emily Dickinson Memorial Conference, *Genevieve Taggard*   233
YOUTH
    A New Era School for Youth, *Elmer Scott*   235
    Youth Incorporates for Education, *Bonaro Wilkinson Overstreet*   238

The Forces of Adult Education—Instruments
  BOOKS
    What People Read, *Ruth Munroe* — 241
    What Makes a Book Readable, *William S. Gray* and
      Bernice E. Leary — 244
    How to Write a Readable Book, *Percy W. Bidwell* — 246
    Incentives to Good Reading, *Douglas Waples* — 249
    Books Important but Not Essential, *Harry Miller Lydenberg* — 252
    Types of Books That Are Needed, *A. E. Heath* — 254
  NEWSPAPERS
    The Raw Material of Education, *John Cotton Dana* — 257
    Primarily Commercial Enterprises, *Elsie McCormick* — 258
  EDUCATIONAL BROADCASTING
    The Deeper Significance of Radio, *James T. Shotwell* — 261
    Radio a Medium for Mass Education, *William A. Orton* — 264
    A Popular Program, *Curtis E. Lakeman* — 267
  EDUCATIONAL FILMS
    An Experiment in Visual Education, *Edward H. Dewey* — 269
  PUBLIC FORUMS
    Forums in a Western State, *Lucy Wilcox Adams* — 272
    Forums in a Midwestern City, *Carroll H. Wooddy* — 275
    A Forum in a Village, *R. E. Dooley* — 278
  ROUND-TABLE DISCUSSIONS
    A Reader's Round Table, *Philip N. Youtz* — 280
    Discussion Groups in Libraries, *Lucy Wilcox Adams* — 283
    A Waterfront Cross-Section Round Table, *William Forbes Adams* — 285

PART THREE—CLOSE-UPS

Teachers
  Teachers at a World Convention, *Mary L. Ely* — 291
  Tools and the Teacher, *Gustav Francis Beck* — 294
  Lay Readers Are Better Than Experts, *Jessie Allen Charters* — 296
  Experts Preferred, *Thomas Fansler* — 298
  Teacher Training by Apprenticeship, *David L. MacKaye* — 301
  Teacher Training by Study and Practice, *Thomas Fansler* — 304
  Teacher Training by Joyous Living and Learning,
    Bonaro Wilkinson Overstreet — 306
  A Teacher of the Renaissance, *Everett Dean Martin* — 310
  A Teacher of a Generation Ago, *Gaynell Hawkins* — 312
  Confessions of a Would-Be Educator, *Anonymous* — 315
  Andrew Carnegie, Educator, *Alvin Johnson* — 318
Students
  Who Shall Be Our Students?, *Edward L. Thorndike* — 322
  The Few or the Many?, *George Edgar Vincent* — 324
  What Education Have the Many?, *Lyman Bryson* — 327
  What of the Capacities of Common Men?, *Edward S. Robinson* — 330
  Why Do Adults Study?, *L. D. Coffman* — 333

The Changing Focus

How Well Do Adults Learn?, *Herbert Sorenson* and *Richard R. Price* — 335
A Study of Correspondence Students, *C. L. Robbins* and *Wendell Johnson* — 338
Bryn Mawr Summer School Students, *Hilda W. Smith* — 340
Labor Temple Students, *Gustav Francis Beck* — 344
Letters from an Isolated Student, *Mary Hesse Hartwick* — 347
A Self-taught Boy, *Anonymous* — 351
The Self-taught Hero of a Self-taught Boy, *John H. Finley* — 354

The Content of Adult Education
Facts Are Our Best Weapons, *Edward L. Thorndike* — 358
Facts Should Be Tested by Ideas, *Scott Buchanan* — 360
The Argument for Utility: Education for Work, *James E. Russell* — 363
The Argument for Beauty: Education for Enlightenment, *Everett Dean Martin* — 365
Summing Up the Case of Utility vs. Beauty, *Charles A. Beard* — 368
The Diffusion of Science, *Benjamin C. Gruenberg* — 370
Interpreters of Science Are Needed, *Walter M. Gilbert* — 372
Directive Social Science, *Charles A. Beard* — 374
Civic Education, *Lucy Wilcox Adams* — 377
Education in the Arts, *Frederick P. Keppel* — 380
Art as an Avocation, *Frank L. McVey* — 383

Method
The Test of Method, *Thomas Fansler* — 385
The Function of the Lecture, *Anne E. M. Jackson* — 387
Panel Discussions, *Morse Adams Cartwright* — 390
The Panel as a Problem-solving Device, *H. A. Overstreet* — 393
The Clinic Method, *John Mantle Clapp* — 396
Conference Method, *Eduard C. Lindeman* — 399
How to Teach Art, *Ernst Jonson* — 401
How to Teach Creative Writing, *Bonaro Wilkinson Overstreet* — 404
How to Teach Music Appreciation, *A. D. Zanzig* — 407
How to Teach International Politics, *Eric J. Patterson* — 410

Educational Service Stations
The Importance of Service Stations, *Frederick P. Keppel* — 414
National Advisory Council on Radio in Education, *Levering Tyson* — 415
National Occupational Conference, *Franklin J. Keller* — 418
Adjustment Service of New York, *Anne Evans* — 420
Functions Indicated for Adjustment Services, *Franklin J. Keller* — 423
Lecture Bureaus, *Nathaniel Peffer* — 425
What Can Adult Education Councils Do?, *Jacques Ozanne* — 428
Begin with an Information Service, *Bonaro Wilkinson Overstreet* — 431

PART FOUR—FROM THE CRITICS' CORNER

Questions Raised
Is Adult Education Overpopularizing?, *Gustav Francis Beck* — 437
Is Adult Education Overspecializing?, *Glenn Frank* — 440
How Much of It Is Education?, *Abraham Flexner* — 442

What's It All For?, *Thomas Fansler*	444
Three Reviews	
Retrospect without Regret, *Nathaniel Peffer*	449
Recantation, *Nathaniel Peffer*	452
Reaffirmation, *Alvin Johnson*	455
Suggested Supplementary Reading	459
Index of Subjects	465
Index of Authors	476

HANDBOOK OF ADULT EDUCATION IN THE UNITED STATES, 1948

MARY L. ELY (ed.). Institute of Adult Education, Teachers College, Columbia University, New York.

Table of Contents

Foreword, *Alain Locke*	ix
Preface, *Morse A. Cartwright*	xi
PART I · INTRODUCTION	
What We Mean by Adult Education, *Lyman Bryson*	3
PART II · AREAS OF INTEREST, ACTIVITY AND NEED	
Vocational Efficiency	
Vocational Guidance for Adults, *Helen R. Smith*	7
Vocational Education for Adults, *L. H. Dennis*	11
Educational Activities of Corporations, *Leon Brody*	13
Private Correspondence Schools, *J. S. Noffsinger*	15
Vocational Rehabilitation, *Michael J. Shortley*	17
Adult Education in Hospitals and Sanatoria, *Holland Hudson*	25
Economic Understanding	
Workers' Education, *Eleanor G. Coit*	30
Labor-Management Programs, *Abbott Kaplan*	37
Consumer Education, *James E. Mendenhall*	42
Civic Participation and Responsibility	
The New Civic Education, *Russell H. Ewing*	46
Education of the Adult Foreign Born for Citizenship, *Henry B. Hazard*	52
Adult Education in Settlements, *Frances H. Edwards*	60
Adult Education of American Indians, *R. H. McCurtain*	65
Correctional Education, *Austin H. MacCormick*	70
Housing as a Subject of Study for Adults	75
Safety Education for Adults, *Thomas Fansler*	80
Better Human Relations and Community Improvement	
Education for Family Living, *Muriel W. Brown*	83

The Cooperative Extension Service of the United States Department of Agriculture, *Edmund deS. Brunner*	96
Intercultural Education, *Ruth Kotinsky*	101
The Community Council Movement in New York State, *John W. Herring*	107
The Montana Study, *Baker Brownell*	113
Special Projects in Adult Education, *Jean* and *Jess Ogden*	118
Adult Education in World Affairs, *Thomas R. Adam*	126

Group Interests

The Education of Young Adults, *Howard Y. McClusky*	133
Adult Education and Later Maturity, *George Lawton, Ph.D.* and H. A. Overstreet	138
Autonomous Groups, *Maria Rogers*	143
Men's and Women's Clubs as Agencies of Adult Education	153

Personal Growth and Self-Realization

The Creative Arts in Adult Education, *Students' Symposium*	159
The Nonprofit Theatre, *Sawyer Falk*	164
Music as an Educational and Recreational Field for the Adult, *Gertrude Borchard*	167
The Place of Recreation in Adult Education, *Robert R. Gamble*	173
Adult Health Education, *Mayhew Derryberry*	176

PART III · INSTITUTIONAL RESOURCES

Religious Institutions and Organizations

Adult Jewish Education in America, *Rabbi Israel M. Goldman*	179
Catholic Adult Educational Activity, *The Very Rev. Msgr. Frederick G. Hochwalt*	187
Protestant Christian Adult Education, *Dr. T. T. Swearingen*	192

Public Schools

Public School Adult Education Programs, *Thomas A. Van Sant*	196
State Legislation and Adult Education, *Everett C. Preston*	201

Colleges and Universities

University and College Extension, *Walton S. Bittner*	214
University Teaching by Correspondence, *Walton S. Bittner*	222
Alumni Education, *Elizabeth W. Durham*	225

Libraries

The Public Library and Adult Education, *Mildred V. D. Mathews*	228

Museums

The Place of the Museum in Adult Education, *Theodore L. Low*	236

Schools for Adults

Adult Education on Its Own, *Dorothy Hewitt*	240

PART IV · COMMON CONCERNS

Preparation of Teachers and Leaders

Training Adult Educators, *Wilbur C. Hallenbeck*	243
Professional Preparation for Public Library Adult Education, *Miriam D. Tompkins*	250

Media and Methods of Instruction
    Materials in Adult Education, *Robertson Sillars*   253
    Radio and Education, *H. B. McCarty*   259
    The Motion Picture in Adult Education, *Robertson Sillars*   263
    The Discussion Group in Adult Education in America, *Paul L. Essert*   269
    An Unparalleled Experiment in Adult Education, *Cyril O. Houle*   276
Coordination and Collaboration
    Community Organization for Adult Education, *Glen Burch*   281
    American Association for Adult Education, *Morse A. Cartwright*   289
    The United States Educational, Scientific and Cultural Organization,
        Stephen P. Dorsey   297

PART V · AGENCIES
Notes on Representative Organizational Programs   304

PART VI
Suggested Supplementary Reading   529
Index

HANDBOOK OF ADULT EDUCATION IN THE UNITED STATES, 1960

MALCOLM S. KNOWLES (ed.). Adult Education Association of the USA, Chicago.

Table of Contents

Foreword, *Philip Klein*   ix
Editor's Preface, *Malcolm S. Knowles*   xi

PART I: BACKGROUND AND OVERVIEW

What Is Adult Education, *Robert J. Blakely*   3
Historical Development of the Adult Education Movement,
    Malcolm S. Knowles   7
The Function and Place of Adult Education in American Society,
    Wilbur C. Hallenbeck   29

PART II: SOME COMMON CONCERNS OF ADULT EDUCATORS

Philosophies of Adult Education, *John Walker Powell* and
    Kenneth D. Benne   41
Learning Theory in Adult Education, *Jack R. Gibb*   54
Program Development in Adult Education, *Jack London*   65

The Changing Focus

Methods in Adult Education, *Warren H. Schmidt* and *Elwin V. Svenson*	82
Materials for Adult Education, *Gladys A. Wiggin*	96
Research in Adult Education, *Burton W. Kreitlow*	106
The Education of Adult Educational Leaders, *Cyril O. Houle*	117
Public Understanding of Adult Education, *Thomas L. Cotton*	129
Finance, Legislation, and Public Policy for Adult Education, *Wilmer V. Bell*	138
Architecture for Adult Education, *John W. Becker*	156
The Literature of Adult Education, *Coolie Verner*	162

PART III: INSTITUTIONAL PROGRAMS AND RESOURCES

Adult Education Associations and Councils, *Glenn S. Jensen*	179
Adult Education in Business and Industry, *Robert F. Risley*	196
Adult Education in Colleges and Universities, *A. A. Liveright*	203
The Cooperative Extension Service, *Joseph L. Matthews*	218
Foundations and Adult Education, *Paul L. Essert*	230
Adult Education Activities in Government Agencies, *Ambrose Caliver*	238
Adult Education Through Voluntary Health Organizations, *Levitte Mendel*	255
Adult Education in Independent and Residential Schools, *Henry Klein* and *Robert H. Schacht*	263
International Organizations in Adult Education, *William C. Rogers*	274
Adult Education in Labor Unions, *Joseph Mire*	286
Adult Education in Libraries, *Grace T. Stevenson*	302
The Mass Media and Adult Education, *Eugene I. Johnson*	314
Museums and Art Institutes and Adult Education, *Clifford Gregg*	330
Adult Education Through Proprietary Schools, *H. D. Hopkins*	339
Public School Adult Education, *Robert A. Luke*	345
Adult Education in Religious Institutions, *Edward R. Miller*	356
Adult Education in Voluntary Social Welfare Organizations, *Joe R. Hoffer*	336
Adult Education in General Voluntary Organizations, *Max Birnbaum*	378

PART IV: PROGRAM AREAS IN ADULT EDUCATION

Academic Education for Adults, *Peter E. Siegle*	393
Education for Aging, *Herbert C. Hunsaker* and *Martin Tarcher*	404
Community Development, *Howard Y. McClusky*	416
Creative Arts in Adult Education, *Max Kaplan* and *Carol L. Pierson*	428
Economic Education for Adults, *Albert L. Ayars*	440
Fundamental and Literacy Education for Native and Foreign-born Adults, *Angelica W. Cass*	455
Health Education of the Public, *Beryl J. Roberts* and *William Griffiths*	467
Home and Family Life Education, *Mary S. Lyle*	479
Human Relations and Leadership Training, *Leland P. Bradford*	491
Liberal Adult Education, *Harry L. Miller*	497

Public Affairs Education, *Abbott Kaplan* 513
Adult Recreation Education, *Joseph Prendergast* 527
Science for Adults, *Thurman White* and *Harry C. Kelly* 534
Adult Occupational Education, *Herbert M. Hamlin* 542

PART V: THE FUTURE OF ADULT EDUCATION IN AMERICA

Present Trends and Future Strategies in Adult Education, *Paul H. Sheats* 553

PART VI: NATIONAL ORGANIZATIONS, ASSOCIATIONS, AND AGENCIES IN ADULT EDUCATION

Directory of Organizations 565
Index 605

Index

Compiled by
MARY M. FLAD
ERIC Clearinghouse of
Adult Education

Abraham Baldwin College (Ga.), 219, 223, 224
Abstracts of adult education literature, 82–83
Accreditation
  proprietary correspondence schools, 389
Ad Hoc Committee for the Study of Research in Adult Education, 140
Ad Hoc Committee of Adult Education Organizations, 33, 187
Adler, Mortimer, 126
Adult basic education, 29, 103, 407–424
  in armed forces, 288–290
  church sponsored classes, 365
  definition, 407
  dropouts, 420
  finances, 421–422ff
  instructional materials, 418–419, 420–421
  participants, 409–410
  research and experimental projects, 416, 418
  sponsoring agencies, 416
  summer institutes, 410, 415
  teacher training, 415–416
  use of computers, 95
Adult Education, 139
Adult education
  definition, 28–31, 39–40
  publications relating to, 197–198
Adult education councils, 179–180

Adult Education Act of 1966
  adult basic education, 410, 415
Adult Education Association of the USA, 32, 49–50, 83, 175, 325, 326
  Commission of Professors of Adult Education, 145, 146–147
  institutional program evaluation, 185–186
  labor educators in, 310–311
  leadership development, 139
  Mass Media Section, 99
  membership, 186
  philosophical discussions, 131–132
  Research Commission, 141
  women's continuing education, 503
Adult Education Research Conference, 32, 140–141
Adult educationists
  definition, 121
Adult educators, 109 ff.
  in armed forces, 296–297
  communication network, 79–80
  foreign travel, 50
  institutes for, 118
  library and museum staffs, 259–260
  libary school training, 260
  museum personnel, 253, 258
  perspectives on research, 142
  professional associations, 174–175, 186–187
  professionalism, 112–113, 185–188
  and publications, 76–77

579

Adult educators (*cont.*)
 training, 325–329
 training for religious programs, 366–367
 see also Personnel; Teachers; Trainers
Adult learning, 518–519, 521–522
 armed forces research, 297–298
 conferences and workshops on, 326
 research, 145–146, 522–525
Adult students, 39
 participants in learning process, 66
 see also Adult learning; Participants
Affective behavior, 63, 64
African Adult Education Association, 49
Aged *see* Older adults
Agencies
 external programing, 59–60
 types of, 36–38
Agricultural education, 34, 480
Agricultural extension, 275
 see also Cooperative Extension Service
Air Force *see* Armed forces
Aker, George F.
 research needs, 138
Alienation
 of youth, 19–20
Allen, Charles, 321
Allen, Lawrence
 professionalism in adult education, 186
American Association for Adult Education, 27
American Association for Jewish Education, 356
American Association of Junior Colleges (AAJC), 215
American Association of University Women, 502
American Baptist Churches, 365
American College Personnel Association, 503
American Education Research Association, 141
American Federation of Labor—Congress of Industrial Organizations, 301, 311
American Foreign Policy Association, 502
American Heritage Programs, 246, 250
American-Jewish Congress, 365
American Library Association
 Library-Community Project, 246
American Lyceum, 26
American Red Cross, 339
American Social Hygiene Association, 448
American Society for Training and Development (ASTD), 320, 325, 326–327
Americanization of the foreign born, 26
Andragogy, 118

Annual Register of Research and Investigation in Adult Education, 88
Antipoverty programs *see* Poverty programs
Apel, John
 program change, 184
Apprenticeship training, 316
Armed forces, 283–300
 available education programs, 293–296
 degree programs, 286, 290–291
 off-duty education programs, 286–287
Army *see* Armed forces
Art classes, 258
Art museums, 256–259
Arts
 federal programs, 103–104
Asian South Pacific Bureau of Adult Education, 49
Association of University Evening Colleges (AUEC), 33, 175, 210
 participation survey, 458, 461
Audiotape recorders, 100
Audiovisual aids, 35, 69, 85
Autonomy of adult education institutions, 178–179

Baker-Hunt Foundation, 390
Beals, Ralph A., 251
Behavior
 change objectives, 63–65
Bellow, Saul, 109
Benne, Kenneth D., 122, 128, 523
Bergevin, Paul, 132, 514
Berkeley Adult School (Calif.), 481
Birth control, 448–449
Blakely, Robert, 129
 definition of adult education, 30
 goals of adult education, 33
 self-fulfillment, 513
Bloom, Benjamin S.
 curriculum development, 145
Blue collar jobs *see* Labor force
Booth, Alan
 definition of adult education, 30
Boston Center for Adult Education, 390
Brainstorming, 322
British Broadcasting Corporation, 115–116
British Ministry of Reconstruction, 26
Broadcasting, 97–101
Brookings Institute
 labor education, 303
Brunner, Edmond deS., 138
Brunner and Associates, 140
Bryson, Lyman, 29
Buck, Pearl, 402
Bureau of Adult and Vocational Education, U.S. Office of Education, 31–32

Index

Burman, Arthur, 522
Business training, 315-333
  international, 53
  see also Training, business and industrial

Cabrillo College, Calif., 225
California
  community college surveys, 222
Calif., University of, Los Angeles
  Extension Service Community Seminars, 103
Cambridge Center for Adult Education (Mass.), 390
Canadian Association for Adult Education, 49
Careers for the poor, See New careers
Carey, James
  higher adult education, 198-199
Carnegie Corporation, 32, 85
  international programs, 52-53, 55
  library reading programs, 250
  museum study, 253
  public affairs education, 461
Catholic Adult Education Center (CAEC), 358
Catholic institutions
  labor education programs, 302, 307, 311
Center for Cognitive Learning, 519
Center for the Study of Liberal Education for Adults, 49, 468
  publications, 198
Cerritos College, Calif., 224, 225
Chamberlain, Martin N.
  perspectives on research, 142
Chautauqua, 391
Chicago City College, 224
Chronic disease hospitals, 384-385
Chrysler Corporation
  hard-core unemployed training, 514-515
Cincinnati
  evening high schools, 233-234
Cities
  ghettos, 13
Citizenship education, 154-156
Civil rights
  church discussion programs, 365
  and religious institutions, 354
Civil Service Commission, 329
Class method, 35
Cleveland Public Library, 248
Clientele see Adult students; Participants
Coalition of Adult Education Organizations, 33, 187
Coffee houses, 362, 363

Cognitive behavior, 63, 64
Cohen, Samuel I., 355
Cohen, Wilbur J., 10, 11
Coles, E. K. Townsend, 46-47, 51
Cold Spring Institute (N.Y.), 391
College Entrance Examination Board, 85, 291-292
College Level Examination Program, 291-292
Colleges and universities
  public affairs education, 466-467
Commission of Professors of Adult Education, 27, 31, 32
Communication, 125-126, 517-518
  program publicity, 403
Community Chests, 339
Community colleges, 213 ff.
  and community needs, 164-165
  community service perspective, 214-215
  community service programs, 215-228, 524
  educational facilities, 177
  federal and state support, 181-182
  growth of, 232
  legislative influence, 182-183
  program evaluation, 221 ff.
  program planning, 219-221
  public affairs education, 467
Community control
  health institutions, 347
Community development
  community college programs, 224
  Cooperative Service Extension, 275-276
  U.S.A.I.D., 53
Community education programs, 204-206
Community learning centers, 208
Community service programs, 155-156
  community colleges, 215-228
  health and welfare agencies, 337-338, 342
  university extension, 183-184
Commuters' seminars, 362
Comparative adult education courses, 51-52
Comparative education, 45 ff.
Computer-assisted instruction, 321; see also Educational technology
Computers, 95
Conferences
  national and international, 55
Consultation on Church Union (COCU), 364
Consumer education, 480, 481
Content of adult education, 34
Continuing Education, 492

Continuing education
  definition, 28
Continuing medical education, 99
Continuing professional education, 202–203
Continuing religious education, 366
Cooper Union, 26
Cooperative Area Manpower Planning System (CAMPS), 482, 484
Cooperative extension, 146
Cooperative Extension Service, 265–281
  family life education, 445–446, 450–451
  federal funding, 139
  founding, 193
  information dissemination, 142
  objectives, 268–270
  organization, 270–272
  personnel, 112, 279
  program evaluation, 275–277
  program planning, 184, 272–274
  program trends, 278–280
  public affairs education, 461
  publications, 77
  records, 84
  Smith-Lever Act, 181
  Urban Extension, 204
  volunteer workers, 111
Cooperative Research Act of 1954, 139
Cornell University
  labor education programs, 303, 304, 307, 309, 326
Corporation mergers, 94
Correctional institutions, 372–383
  evaluation of education programs, 378–380
  misdemeanants, 382
  participants in programs, 373–374
  public opinion, 383
  scope of educational programs, 372–373, 374–377
  teaching methodology, 377–378
  women's, 382
Correspondence study, 35, 473–474
  in correctional institutions, 376–377
  higher education, 193
  proprietary schools, 388–389
Cost effectiveness, 324
Cotton, Webster E., 27
Cottrell, Leonard S., Jr., 440, 444
Council for the Continuing Education of Women, 502
Counseling
  community college sponsored, 223
  family life education, 451–452
  women's continuing education, 505

County programs
  Cooperative Extension Service, 271
Credit programs
  higher adult education, 201
Crime rates
  in urban areas, 5
Current Index to Journals in Education (CIJE), 87
Curriculum, 38
  definition, 397–398
  development, 145
  see also Program areas
Curriculum materials, 85
Customer training, 317
Cuyahoga Community College, Ohio, 223
Cybernation, 516
Cybernetics, 162

Dana, John Cotton, 258
DATRIX, 90
David Ranken Trade School (St. Louis), 474
Day care programs, 444
Deaconness Hospital, Evansville, Ind., 384
Decision-making
  in Cooperative Extension Service, 271–272
DeCrow, Roger, 144
Definition of adult education, 39–40
Degree programs
  in armed forces, 286, 290–291
  business and industrial training, 326–327
  in correctional institutions, 376
  higher adult education, 201
  labor education, 303–304
  union sponsored, 312
  university extension, 194–195
Del Mar College, Texas, 223, 225
Demographic trends, 3, 4–7
Demonstration Cities and Metropolitan Development Act of 1966, 104
Denmark
  folk schools, 46
Detroit Industrial Mission, 365
Detroit Public Library, 251
Developing nations, 45–46
Devices, 35
  definition, 93
Dial access systems, 99–100
Diekhoff, John S., 122, 126
Directories
  of education opportunities, 85–86
Disadvantaged groups
  public library programs for, 247–249
Discrimination, racial, 13–15

Index

Discussion groups, 35, 246
  community college sponsored, 218
  in correctional institutions, 377
  family life education, 450–451
  see also Training, human relations
Display methods
  museums, 254–256
Dissertations, doctoral, 141
Doctoral programs in adult education, 31, 116–118, 143–144; *see also* Graduate programs
Documentation in adult education, 80–82
Draper Youth Center (Elmore, Ala.), 377–378
Dropouts
  adult basic education, 420
  in correctional institutions, 373–374
  employment opportunities, 10
  public library programing, 247–249
  and public school adult education, 233–234
Dubois, Edward, 524
Dunwoody Institute (Minneapolis), 474

Early childhood programs, 444, 447
Eastern Orthodox institutions, 358–359
Economic Opportunity Act of 1964, 29, 140, 206, 248, 331, 483
  adult basic education, 410, 415
Ecumenical movement, 363–364
Education industry, 330–331
Education permanente, 47, 123, 404–405
Educational attainment level, 10–12; *see also* Dropouts
Educational facilities, 35, 161–162
  business and industrial training, 322–323
  community colleges, 220–221, 222–223
  and program expansion, 176–177
  public school adult education, 237
  see also Learning environment
Educational institutions
  models of change, 146
  organization of, 160–163
  social pressures upon, 158–159
Educational needs, 60–63
Educational objectives, 60–63
Educational opportunities
  directories, 85–86
Educational Resources Information Center (ERIC), 87–89; *see also* ERIC Clearinghouses
Educational service agencies and community needs, 165–166
Educational technology, 93–95
  adult basic education, 415

business and industrial training, 320–321
in community college programs, 218–219
individualization of learning, 404
Educational television *see* Television, educational
Educationally disadvantaged, 410–415
El Centro College, Texas, 218
Elementary and Secondary Education Act of 1965, 140
England, 46
Enoch Pratt Free Library, 247, 248, 251
Enrollments *see* Participants
Environment *see* Learning environment
ERIC Clearinghouse on Adult Education, Syracuse University, 55, 76–78, 82–84, 87–89, 419
  publications, 198
ERIC Clearinghouse on the New Educational Media, 94
Esalen Institute, 366, 435–436
Essert, Paul
  definition of adult education, 40
Essex Community College, Md., 224
Esso-Humble Oil Company, 331
Ethnic patterns, U.S., 4
European Bureau of Adult Education, 49
Evaluation
  of armed forces education programs, 292–293
  of correctional education programs, 378–380
  institutional perspective, 185–186
  of programs, 70–73
  setting standards, 71–72
  of training programs, 323–324
Evening colleges, 192, 193
  program content, 194
Everywoman's Village (Calif.), 502

Faculty *see* Teachers; Adult educators
Family
  education within, 156–157
Family education
  mental patients' families, 386
Family education centers
  union sponsored, 312
Family Life Councils, 447
Family life education, 34, 439–455
  college courses, 448
  Cooperative Extension Service, 445–446
  counseling, 451–452
  definitions, 441–443
  group discussions, 450–451

Family life education (*cont.*)
    mass media, 449–450
    research, 440–441, 443–444
    state programs, 444–445
    see also Parent education
Family planning, 448–449
Farmers
    in labor force, 8
    see also Rural population
Federal aid
    health, education, and welfare, 339–340
    university extension, 183–184
    see also Financial needs and support
Federal Extension Service
    research priorities, 147
Federal legislation, 139–140
    adult basic education, 409–410
Federal Mediation and Conciliation Service
    shop steward courses, 307
Festine, Armond, 524
Film loops, 101
Financial needs and support
    adult basic education, 421–422
    business and industrial training, 318–319
    Cooperative Extension Service, 267–268
    health and welfare agencies, 339–340
    higher adult education, 209–210
    labor education, 307, 309
    professional continuing education, 493
    public school adult education, 240–241
    women's continuing education, 506
Flint Community Junior College, Mich., 225
Florida State Prison System, 481
FM radio, 98–99
Folley, John D., Jr., 321
Foothill College, Calif., 222, 224–225
Ford Foundation, 32
    adult basic education summer institutes, 410
    international programs, 55
    labor education, 309
    public affairs education, 461
    urban research and extension, 206
    see also Fund for Adult Education
Foreign travel by adult educators, 50
Foundations, 32
    public affairs education, 461–462
    research support, 144
4-H Clubs and projects, 276–277
Franklin, Benjamin, 26, 390

Functional literacy, 408
    see also Adult basic education
Fund for Adult Education
    labor education programs, 309
    public library programs, 250
Fund-raising
    voluntary agencies, 339–340

Games, 69
Gardner, John, 349
    goals, 514
General Educational Development (GED) tests and program, 289, 291, 419
"Generation gap", 465
George-Barden Act of 1946, 476, 477
George-Deen Act of 1937, 476
The George Washington University, 327
Ghettos, 13
Glaser, Daniel, 375, 380
Goals of adult education, 33–34
Goldman, Freda, 524
Government agencies, 31
    employee training, 328–329
Government Employees Training Act (GETA), 328
Government programs, 102–104
Government role
    financing adult education institutions, 180–181
    financing community colleges, 181–182
    in interinstitutional coordination, 171
    professional continuing education, 492–493
    relations with voluntary agencies, 340
    sponsoring neighborhood centers and adult education councils, 180–181
Graduate fellowships, 144
Graduate programs, 31, 112, 116–118, 128
    business and industrial training, 327
    comparative courses, 51–52
    growth, 142–143, 144–145
    in mental health adult education, 386–387
    research directions, 138–139
Graduate theses, 141
Great Books Discussions, 246, 250
Great Decisions programs, 246, 250, 469
Griffith, William, 140
Gross, Bertram M., 10
Group learning
    business and industrial training, 319–320
    public library programs, 250–252
Groups *see* Discussion groups; Training, human relations

Index

Hallenbeck, Wilbur, 34
Hand, S. E., 523
Harper, William Rainey
   correspondence instruction, 172
Harris, Chester W., 70
Hatch Act of 1887, 266
Head Start programs
   parent education, 446
   public library support programs, 247
Health and welfare agencies, 335–350
   nature of educational activities, 335
   organizational structure, 336–338
   program evaluation, 346
   program methods, 343–344
   program planning, 344–346
   sponsorship and approach, 340–343
   see also Hospitals
Health careers education, 480–481
Helping professions, 155–156
Hendrickson, Andrew
   research needs, 138
Hermanson, Tenho, 326
Hero, A. O.
   public affairs education, 460–461
High school equivalency certificates, 236, 419
Higher adult education, 191 ff.
   credit and degree programs, 201
   financing, 209–210
   non-credit programs, 202
   professional associations, 210
   program organization, 198–201
   see also University extension: Evening colleges
Higher Education Act of 1965, 32, 140, 183
Higher Education Act of 1965, Title I, 182–183, 206, 465
   community education programs, 103
   public affairs education, 461
Highlander Folk School (Tenn.), 391
Hobbies, 34
Holbrook, Josiah
   Lyceum, 172
Home Economics Association, 503
Home study see Correspondence study
Homemaking skills, 480, 481
Hospitals, 383–387
   see also Health and welfare agencies
Houle, Cyril O.
   adult education agencies, 37
   classification of institutional forms, 174
   definition of adult education, 30, 40
   educational trends, 192
   leadership in adult education, 36
   learning motivation, 400
   professional continuing education, 487–488
Housing Act of 1964, 104
Hudson, Robert, 520
Hudson Valley Community College, New York, 218
Human Investment Act, 330
Human relations training see Training, human relations
Human resource development, 315
Human service occupations, 17–19, 155–156
   higher adult education for, 204

Immigrant education, 26
Independent study programs, 208; see also Correspondence study
Indexes of adult education literature, 81
Indiana University, 366–367
   Bureau of Studies in Adult Education, 118
Indiana Plan Institutes, 366–367
Indigenous personnel
   public library programs, 247
Individual development
   family life education, 440
Individuality, loss of, 153–154
Individualization of learning, 404
Individualized instruction
   public school adult education, 238
Industrial trainers, 77
Industrial training, 315–333; see also Training, business and industrial
Information retrieval, 82–84
   dial access systems, 99–100
Information services, 79–84
   public libraries, 251
Information sources, 551–564
In-service training programs, community college sponsored, 218–219, 223
   mental hospitals, 385
Institutes
   for adult educators, 118
   business and industrial training, 326–327
Institutional change, 184–185
Institutions
   evaluation, 185–186
   higher adult education, 193
   participation estimates, 173
   size, 184
   types, 36–38, 171 ff., 193
Instructional materials
   adult basic education, 418–419, 420–421

Inter-American Committee on Adult Education, 49
Interdenominational programs, 360, 363–364
Interdisciplinary research, 140, 142, 145, 158
Interinstitutional coordination, 171, 177–179
  higher adult education, 210–211
  public school adult education, 237–238
International affairs education, 461–462
  see also Public affairs education
International communication and exchange
  training, 329–330
International Confederation of Free Trade Unions, 48
International Congress of Schools of Social Work, 343
International Congress of University Adult Education, 49, 54
International Cooperative Alliance, 48
International Council on Social Welfare, 343
International Ladies Garment Workers Union (ILGWU), 303, 304
International organizations
  regional, 49–50
  specialized, 48–49
International understanding, 404–405
International Workers' Education Association, 48
Interpersonal competence, 434, 517–518
  family life education, 440
  see also Training, human relations
Iowa, University of
  Institute of Public Affairs, 104

Jarrett, James, 520
Jensen, Gale, 29
  interdisciplinary research, 145
Jessup, Frank W., 46–47, 51, 173
Jewish institutions, 355–357
Job rotation, 320
John C. Campbell Folk School (North Carolina), 391
Johnson, Eugene, 51
Johnstone, John W. C.
  adult education agencies, 36
  adult students, 39
  methodology of adult education, 35
  participation, 179
  public affairs education, 460
The Journal of Cooperative Extension, 278

Junior colleges
  definition, 213–214
  publications, 77
  see also Community colleges
Junto, Philadelphia, 390

Kallen, Horace M., 131
  goals of adult education, 33
Kawin, Ethel, 451
Keisler, Evan R., 141
Kellogg Foundation, 32, 144
  residential conferences, 207
Kelly, Earl C., 522
Kerner Report, 365
Keys, V. O.
  public affairs education, 460
Kidd, J. Roby, 48
Knapp, Seaman Asahel
  Cooperative Extension Service, 172
Knowles, Malcolm S.
  adult education agencies, 37
  adult education in Europe, 46
  andragogy, 118
  classification of institutional forms, 174
  definition of adult education, 30
  religious institution programs, 353
Kreitlow, Burton, 140
  interdisciplinary research, 145
  research needs, 138
Kuhlen, Raymond, 523

Labor education, 301 ff.
  degree programs, 303–304
  financing, 309
  personnel, 308–309, 310–311
  union staff training, 303–304
Labor force, 7–8
  new careers, 17–19
  racial discrimination, 14, 15
  women in, 8–10
Labor unions
  publications, 77; see also Labor education
Land grant universities, 265, 266–267
Landsman, Ted, 523
Laubach, Frank C., 408
Laubach literacy programs, 53, 365
Law enforcement officials
  programs for, 204
Leadership, 131, 517–518
  among adult educators, 31–33, 111–116
  in developing nations, 50
  for discussion groups, 250
  individual, 36
  institutional forms, 172
  labor unions, 311

Index

public school adult education, 239
training, 115–116
universities, 197
League for Parent Education, 447
League of Women Voters, 502
Learning Center, North Carolina State University, 95
Learning environment, 65–66
business and industrial training, 319–320
see also Educational facilities
Learning experiences, 65–67
Learning processes, 518–519
participant role, 66
see also Adult learning
Lectures, 35
Lee, Robert Ellis
library community study, 246, 250
Leisure time activities, 515–516
Liberal education programs, 202
Librarians
public, 111
Libraries
of adult education literature, 83
public affairs education, 263
women's continuing education, 508
see also Public libraries
Library of Continuing Education, Syracuse University, 84
Library schools
training for adult education, 260
Library Services and Construction Act, 248
Life expectancy, 6
Lilly Foundation, 367
Lindeman, Edward C., 137
Literacy education
in armed forces, 289
church sponsored classes, 365
international programs, 53
Literacy education programs, 408–409
Literature reviews of adult education, 81–82
Liveright, A. A.
adult education in foreign countries, 46
goals of adult education, 33
graduate programs, 128
research developments, 140–141
university adult education, 191
Living Room Dialogues, 363–364
Long Beach City College, Calif., 224
Los Angeles Public Library, 247
Los Angeles public school system, 502
Los Rios Junior College, California, 218
Low income families
parent education, 446–447

Lowe, John, 45–46, 47
Lowell, James Russell, 398
Lowell Institute, 26
Luke, Robert, 49
Lutheran Church—Missouri Synod, 361

McCall Industrial School (Cincinnati, Ohio), 390
MacCormick, Austin, 374–375
McLuhan, Marshall, 403–404
Management
international training programs, 53
Management development, 317
Mannheim, Karl, 464, 465
Manpower Development and Training Act of 1962, 139, 248, 330, 482–484
adult basic education, 410
Manpower development programs, 315, 481–482, 483–484
Manpower Development Training centers, 231–232
Marines *see* Armed forces
Marital statistics, 6
Maslow, Abraham H., 61, 522
Mass media, 193
Cooperative Extension Service, 274–275
education within the family, 157
family life education, 449–450
Massachusetts, University of
labor education programs, 303
Mead, Margaret, 465
Media developments, 93–95
Media technology, 162–163
Medical education *see* Continuing medical education
Mental hospitals, 385–387
Methodology of adult education
Cooperative Extension Service, 274–275
Miami-Dade Junior College, Fla., 223
Michigan State Prison, 380
Microform publications, 83–84, 87
Migratory workers, 5
Military services
information and education officers, 111
training, 95
see also Armed forces
Miller, Harry, 140
Milwaukee Institute of Technology, 223, 224
Minnesota, University of, 501
Minority groups, 4, 5, 13–15
recruiting trainers from, 331–332: *see also* Race relations
Missionary activities, 54
Missouri, University of, 507

Mobility, 5–6
Model of Educational Improvement, 146
Models
  of adult education institutions, 176–177
  of change in educational institutions, 146
  human relations training, 430
  training program planning, 321
Montgomery Junior College, Md., 222–223
Morrill Act of 1862, 266
Mortality rate, 6
Motivation, 399, 400–401
  correctional education, 381
  research, 140
Mott Foundation (Flint, Mich.), 476
Mount San Antonio College, Calif., 223
Multimedia programs, 101–102
Museum curators, 111
Museums
  art, 256–259
  display methods, 254–256
  history, 252–254
  personnel, 111, 253, 258, 259–260

National Advisory Commission on Civil Disorders, 13
National Advisory Council on Extension and Continuing Education, 32
National Agricultural Extension Center for Advanced Study, 144
National Alliance of Businessmen, 331
National Association of Educational Broadcasters, 175
National Association of Manufacturers, MIND, 102
National Association for Public Continuing and Adult Education (NAPCAE), 33, 83, 146, 175, 236–237
  adult basic education, 410
  membership, 186–187
National Association for Public School Adult Education (NAPSAE), 234
National Association of Trade and Technical Schools, 474
National Association of Women's Deans and Counselors, 503
National Catholic Welfare Conference (NCWC), 342
National Community School Educational Association, 175
National Congress of Parents and Teachers, 447–448, 450
National Council of Churches, 342, 359, 360, 469
National Defense Education Act, 139, 476
  graduate fellowships, 144

National Education Association
  Adult Education Clearinghouse (NAEC), 84, 89, 419–420
  Department of Immigrant Education, 26
  Division of Adult Education, 49
National Educational Television (NET), 97, 466
  programing, 464
National Home Study Council, 85, 175, 473–474
National Institute of Labor Education
  early programs, 309
  resident schools, 303
National Jewish Welfare Board, 342
National Opinion Research Center, 140
  participation survey, 258
National organizations see Health and welfare agencies
National Referral Center, 90
National Training Laboratories, 435
National Training School for Boys, 377–378
National Seminar of Adult Education Research, 27
National Society for Programmed Instruction (NSPI), 326
National University Extension Association, 33, 175, 210
  Correspondence Study Division, 85
  and federal legislation, 183
  participation survey, 458, 461
National Vocational Guidance Association, 503
Navy see Armed forces
Neff, Frederick C., 129
Neighborhood centers, 179–180
New careers, 17–19, 155–156, 331–332
  library programs, 248
New Jersey State Museum, 253
New media, 93–95
New Orleans Parish Family Planning Demonstration Program, 449
New School for Social Research program organization, 200
New York City Community College, Brooklyn, 223, 224
New York Public Library
  discussion groups, 250
New York State Guidance Center for Women, 223
Newark (N.J.) Museum, 253, 258
Non-credit programs, 202
North Carolina State University
  adult basic education, 103
  Learning Center, 95
North Florida Junior College, 223

Index

Oakland Community College, Mich., 218, 224
Objectives of adult education, 33–34
Occupational skills, 154
Office of Economic Opportunity, 410, 465
Office education, 480
Ohliger, John
   adult education in foreign countries, 46
Older adults, 15–16
   Cold Spring Institute, 391
On-the-job training, 35, 316, 320
   community college sponsored, 218
   hospitals, 383–384
Operation analysis of adult education, 39–40
Operation Mainstream, 482–483
Orange County, Calif., 435
Organic Act of 1862, 266
Overstreet, Harry A., 137

Paraprofessionals, 17–19
   in business and industry, 332
   higher adult education for, 204
Parent education, 6, 441–442
   hospital-sponsored, 384
   mass media, 449–450
   see also Family life education
Parent-teacher organizations, 447–448
Participants
   adult basic education programs, 409–410, 417
   armed forces educational programs, 284–285
   business and industrial training, 316–317
   health and welfare agency programs, 338–339
   higher adult education, 198
   labor education programs, 303
   in learning process, 66
   in major development programs, 484
   motivation, 399, 400–401
   museum programs, 259
   program evaluation, 221
   proprietary school programs, 387–388
   public affairs education, 458–461
   public library programs, 252
   women's continuing education, 506–507
Participation, 179
   by institutional type, 173
Participation research, 140
Participation training, 433–434
Participatory democracy see Community control

Paterson, R. W. K., 129–131
Peace Corps, 53
Penland School of Handicrafts (North Carolina), 391
Peralta College, Calif., 224
Personality development, 34
Personnel
   business and industrial training, 318–319
   Cooperative Extension Service, 272–273, 277–278, 279
   correctional education, 381
   hospital training programs, 383–384
   labor education, 308–309, 310–311
   mental hospitals, 385
   women's continuing education, 503–504
   see also Adult educators; Teachers; Trainers
Petersen, Renee and William, 196
Phi Delta Kappa
   School Research Information System, 89–90
Philosophers
   and educational practice, 133
Policy formation
   in Cooperative Extension Service, 271–272
Population, increase, 4
Population, U.S.
   characteristics, 4–7
Population control, 448–449
Poverty, 16–17
Poverty programs, 462–463
   Cooperative Extension Service, 276
   family life education, 446–447
Powell, John Walker, 122, 123, 125–126
Pre-school children see Early childhood programs
Prisons see Correctional institutions
Private teachers see Tutors
Processes of adult education, 34–36
Professional associations, 32–33, 171, 186–187
   of adult educators, 174–175
   higher adult education, 210
   labor educators, 310–311
   and professional continuing education, 493–494
   public school adult education, 240
Professional continuing education, 202–203, 487–498
Professionalism
   among adult educators, 185–188
   armed forces adult educators, 296–297

Professionalism (*cont.*)
  business and industrial training, 327, 330
  in Cooperative Extension Service, 277–278
Program
  definition, 59, 397–398
  growth of, 143
Program areas, 38
Program content, 401–403
Program evaluation, 70–73, 398
  community colleges, 221 ff.
  Cooperative Extension Service, 275–277
  health and welfare agencies, 346
  labor education, 310
Program location, 399–400
Program materials, 85
Program planning and development, 59 ff.
  adult educators' responsibilities, 114–115
  community colleges, 219–221
  community service programs, 217–219
  Cooperative Extension Service, 272–274
  government agencies, 31–32
  health and welfare agencies, 338, 344–346
  innovation, 184
  legislative influence, 182–183
  professional continuing education, 490–492
  women's continuing education, 501–506
Program publicity, 403
Programed instruction
  in correctional institutions, 377–378
Programed texts, 69
Project, 100,000, 288–289
Proprietary schools, 387–389
Protestant institutions, 359–363
Psychomotor behavior, 63, 64
Public affairs education, 34, 154–156, 457–471
  churches, 469
  higher educational institutions, 466–467
  libraries, 263
  participants, 458–461
  public schools, 467–468
  race relations, 463, 465
  television, 463–464
Public libraries
  community study and services, 246
  history, 245–246
  outreach programs, 247–249
  personnel, 259–260
  services to individuals, 249–250

Public officials
  training, 104
Public school adult education, 231–242
  public affairs education, 467–468
Public school adult educators, 77
Public school personnel
  human relations training, 435
Public schools
  and community needs, 165
Publications, 76–78
  international, 55
Publicity, 403
  women's continuing education, 506–507
Puder, W. H., 523
Purdue University
  industrial education, 327

Race
  and university extension programs, 206
Race relations
  public affairs education, 463, 465
Racial differences
  educational attainment, 7, 14
  employment, 14, 15
  income, 14
Racial discrimination, 13–15
Racial subcultures, 5
Racial patterns, U.S., 4
Racism, 13
Radio, FM
  programing, 98–99
Radio and television stations, campus run, 224
Reading improvement programs, 102
Reading skills *see* Adult basic education
Recidivism
  and correctional education, 379
Recreational adult education, 34
Regional associations, 175
Religion, 34
Religious institutions, 353–367
  public affairs education, 469
Religious organizations
  publications, 77
Religious voluntary agencies, 341–343
Residential centers, 390–391
  business and industrial training, 323
Residential continuing education, 193
Residential programs, 207
  labor education, 303, 304, 312
Retention
  human relations training, 436–437
Retired persons *see* Older adults
Research
  adult basic education, 420–421
  adult learning, 522–525

Index

family life education, 440–441, 443–444
  on training, 324–325
  women's continuing education, 508–509
Research developments
  current projects, 140–141
Research in Education (RIE), 87, 89
Research needs, 138–139
Research priorities, 147
Review of Educational Research, 138
Rice Institute (Houston), 474
Ringer, Wayne
  program planning, 184
Rivera, Ramon J.
  adult education agencies, 36
  adult students, 39
  methodology of adult education, 35
  public affairs education, 460
Rockland Community College, N.Y., 223
Roman Catholic institutions, 354, 357–358
  labor education programs, 302, 307, 311
Rosenstein, Betty, 509
Rural population, U.S., 4

Saden, S. J., 380
St. Petersburg Junior College, Fla., 218
San Bernardino Valley College, Calif., 218
San Francisco Public Library, 247
Sarah Lawrence College, 501
Scheduling
  women's continuing education, 504–505
Science Information Exchange (SIE), 90, 144
Science museums, 254
School Research Information System (SRIS), 89–90
Schutz, William C., 435–436
Seattle Public Library, 251
Sectarian voluntary agencies, 341–343
Seminars, commuters', 362
Sensitivity groups
  religious institutional programs, 360
Sensitivity training *see* Training, human relations
Sex education, 443
  see also Family life education
Short courses
  community college sponsored, 218, 223
Simulation, 69
Skill development, 520
  techniques, 35
  vocational and technical education, 485

Sloan, Alfred P., Foundation, 215
Smith, Helen Lyman
  library community study, 246
Smith, J. R., 524
Smith-Hughes Act, 476, 477
Smith-Lever Act, 181, 265, 266–267, 268, 269
Social change, 152–154
  health and welfare agency programs, 347–350
  religious institutions, 354
  strategies, 157
Social issues, 459–460
  see also Public affairs education
Social patterns, 3
Social problems, 12 ff.
  and helping professions, 155–156
  in urban areas, 5
Social Science Research Council, 141
Society for International Development, 50
Southern Baptist Convention, 365
Southwest Educational Laboratory, Albuquerque, 95
Southwest Human Relations Training Laboratories, 431
Special interest groups
  higher adult education for, 203–204
Speeches *see* Lectures
Standards
  public school adult education, 240
State Boards of Vocational Education, 478
State programs
  Cooperative Extension Service, 271
  family life education, 444–445
  leadership, 32
  vocational and technical education, 477–478
  women's continuing education, 508
State surveys
  community college programs, 222
State University of New York, Farmingdale Center for Community Educational Services, 218–219, 223
Statistics *see also* Participants
Steinmann, Anne, 509
Subject matter of adult education, 34
Summer institutes
  adult basic education, 410, 415
Summer schools, 192
Supervisory training, 317
Syracuse University
  Library of Continuing Education, 84
Systems approach
  to education, 163–166
  human relations training, 431–432
Sweden, 46

Index

T-groups, 428; *see also* Training, human relations
Talks *see* Lectures
Tape recorders, 100
Tax support of adult education programs, 178
Taxonomies of educational objectives, 64, 66–67
Taylor, Ronald G., 523
Teacher needs
 adult education, 239
Teacher salaries
 public school adult education, 236
Teacher training
 adult basic education, 415–416
Teachers, 131
 evening school and extension, 111
 higher adult education, 200–201
 instructional behavior, 67–68
 see also Adult educators; Trainers
Teaching machines, 69, 331
Teaching methodology, 67–68
 in correctional institutions, 377–378
 professional continuing education, 492
Technical education *see* Vocational and technical education
Technical personnel *see* Labor force
Techniques, 35
 definition, 92–93
Technology *see* Educational technology
Television
 commercial, 464–465
 educational, 35, 461, 463, 464
 public, 463–464
 slow scan, 99
Television programing, 97–98
Television stations
 campus run, 224
Therapy for Normals, 432–433
Theses, 141
Title I *see* Higher Education Act of 1965
Tocqueville, Alexis de, 172
Trailers for training programs, 323
Trainers, 315, 318–319
 human relations training, 429–430
 recruiting minority group members, 331–332
Training, business and industrial
 adult illiteracy, 331
 definition, 315
 education industry, 330–331
 evaluation, 323
 facilities and resources, 322–323
 international exchange concerning, 329–330
 international programs, 53
 methods and techniques, 319–321

multimedia programs, 102
organization and finance, 318–319
program planning, 321–322
research on, 324–325
Training, human relations
 definition, 425–427
 Esalen Institute, 435–436
 participation training, 433–434
 program design and characteristics, 427–428
 for public school personnel, 435
 systems approach, 431–432
 Therapy for Normals, 432–433
 trainer role, 429–430
 transfer of training, 436–437
 and urban problems, 435
Training and Development Journal, 325
Training institutes, 326–327
Training laboratories, 428; *see also* Training, human relations
Transfer of training, 436–437
Travers, R. M. W.
 instructional behavior, 67
Tulane University
 family planning, 449
Tutors, 35
Tyler, Ralph W., 67
 curriculum development, 145
 educational objectives, 62

Unemployed
 hard-core training programs, 414–415
 leisure time, 516
 training programs for, 317, 331–332
Unesco
 definition of adult education, 47
 literacy programs, 408
 museum techniques, 255
 programs and conferences, 48
 publications, 84
 World Conference on Adult Education (Montreal, 1960), 49
Union education, 304–306; *see also* Labor education
U.S.S.R., 46
United Auto Workers (UAW), 303, 304, 308, 309, 311, 312
United Church of Christ, 361
United Funds, 339
United Methodist Church, 361
United Presbyterian Church, USA, 361, 364
United States
 history of adult education, 25–27
 population characteristics, 4–7
U.S. Agency for International Development, 53–54, 343
U.S. Armed Forces Institute, 287–292

Index

U.S. Bureau of the Census, 3
U.S. Department of Agriculture, 54
U.S. Department of Defense
 training programs and expenditures, 283–284
U.S. Department of Health, 54
U.S. Department of Housing and Urban Development, 465–466
U.S. Department of Labor
 union safety programs, 307
 Women's Bureau, 507–508
U.S. National Archives, 84
U.S. Office of Education
 adult basic education, 410
 research support, 139, 141, 147
 see also Bureau of Adult and Vocational Education
U.S. Peace Corps, 53
U.S. Public Health Service
 health manpower training, 102
Universities, 76–77
 adult education leadership, 197
 and community needs, 163–164
University Center for Adult Education, Detroit, 435
University City Science Center, Philadelphia, 104
University extension, 146
 community service programs, 195–196
 degree programs, 194–195
 development of concept, 192–193
 program content, 194
 and race, 206
 see also Higher adult education; National University Extension association
University Microfilm system, 83
University programs
 labor education, 302, 306–307
Urban areas
 social change strategies, 157–158
Urban Extension, 204–206
Urban Job Corps Centers, 317
Urban migration, 241
Urban population growth, 4–5
Urban problems
 and human relations training, 435
 school dropouts, 233
Urbanization, U.S., 4, 5

Van Hise, Charles E.
 University extension, 172
Vatican Council II, 354, 357
Verner, Coolie
 adult education agencies, 37
 definition of adult education, 30, 39–40
 processes of adult education, 34–35
 program evaluation, 398
Veterans Readjustment Benefits Act of 1966, 287
Video tape recorders, 100
Vincent, John Heyl
 Chautauqua, 172
Vocational Education Act of 1963, 140, 410, 476–477, 478
Vocational Rehabilitation Act of 1954, 139
Vocational and technical education, 34, 473 ff.
 in correctional institutions, 375–376
 federal and state support, 181, 476–477
 state programs, 477–478
Voluntary organizations and agencies, 51, 468
 family life education, 448
 publications, 77
 relations with government, 340
 sectarian, 341–343
 sponsorship and approach, 340–343
 see also Health and welfare agencies
Volunteers, 111, 113

Wallace, Henry, 7
Wallen, N. W.
 instructional behavior, 67
Watkins Institute (Nashville, Tenn.), 390
Wedemeyer, Charles, 54
Welfare agencies *see* Health and welfare agencies
Wentworth Institute (Mass.), 474
West Virginia University
 labor education programs, 303
Western Kentucky University, 524
White collar jobs *see* Labor force
William Hood Dunwoody Industrial Institute (Minneapolis), 474
Wisconsin, University of, 507
 Articulated Instructional Media (AIM), 102
 continuing medical education, 99
 graduate fellowships, 144
 research priorities, 147
Wisconsin Historical Society, 84
Women
 correctional institutions, 382
 counseling programs for, 223
 educational attainment, 6–7
 in labor force, 8–10
 life expectancy, 6
 sociocultural factors, 499–500

Women's continuing education, 9–10, 499–511, 524
  counseling, 505
  finances, 506
  goals, 500–501
  participants, 506–507
  personnel, 503–504
  program development, 503–506
  program sponsorship, 501–503
  publicity, 506–507
  research, 508–509
  scheduling, 504–505
  supportive services, 505–506
Workers' education *see* Labor education
Works Progress Administration
  art classes, 258
World Affairs Councils, 469

World Association for Adult Education, 48
World Confederation of Organizations of the Teaching Profession (WCOTP), 53
  Adult Education Committee, 49–54
World Literacy Incorporated, 53

YMCA Organizational Development Project, 434, 435
Youth
  alienation of, 19–20
Youth programs
  Cooperative Extension Service, 276–277

Ziegler, Jerome
  definition of adult education, 30–31